How Organizations Learn

How Organizations Learn

Managing the search for knowledge

Ken Starkey, Sue Tempest and Alan McKinlay

THOMSON

Australia · Canada · Mexico · Singapore · Spain · United Kingdom · United States

How Organizations Learn – 2nd edition

Copyright © Ken Starkey, Sue Tempest and Alan McKinlay 2004

The Thomson logo is a registered trademark used herein under licence.

For more information, contact Thomson Learning, High Holborn House, 50-51 Bedford Row, London WC1R 4LR or visit us on the World Wide Web at:
http://www.thomsonlearning.co.uk

British Library Cataloguing-in-Publication Data
A catalogue record for this book is available from the British Library

ISBN 978-1-86152-746-2

First edition published by Routledge in 1996
Reprinted 2002 by Thomson Learning
This edition 2004 by Thomson Learning
Reprinted 2005 and 2007 by Thomson Learning

Typeset by Laserscript Limited, Mitcham, Surrey
Printed in the UK by TJ Digital, Padstow, Cornwall

Contents

List of figures

List of tables

Acknowledgements

We would like to thank the following journals for granting permissions to enable us to realise this revised edition of *How Organizations Learn*:

Academy of Management Executive for 'GE's Crotonville: a staging ground for Corporate revolution' (1989) by Noel M. Tichy.

Academy of Management Review for 'Organizational identity and learning: A psychodynamic perspective' (2000) by Andrew D. Brown and Ken Starkey.

California Management Review for 'Communities of creation: Managing distributed innovation in turbulent markets' (2000) by Mohanbir Sawhney and Emanuela Prandelli and 'Strategic dissonance' (1996) by Robert A. Burgelman and Andrew S. Grove.

Human Relations for 'Knowledge work: Ambiguity image and identity' (2001) by Mats Alvesson.

Information, Communication and Society for 'Trusting strangers: Work relationships in four high-tech communities' (2002) by J.A. Enlish-Lueck, Charles N. Darrah and Andrew Saveri.

Journal of Management Inquiry for 'Making sense of managerial wisdom' (1998) by Leon C. Malan and Mark. P Kriger.

Journal of Management Studies for 'What is organizational knowledge?' (2001) by Haridimos Tsoukas and Efi Vladimirou.

Management Education and Development for 'Second thoughts on teambuilding' (1984) by Bill Critchley and David Casey.

Management Learning for 'The concept of learning in the strategy field' (1998) by Brian Leavy.

MIT Sloan Management Review for 'The link between individual and organizational learning' (1993) by Daniel H. Kim and 'The leader's new work: Building learning organizations' (1990) by Peter M. Senge.

Organization for 'Communities of practice and social learning systems' (2000) by Etienne Wenger.

Organizational Dynamics for 'A conversation with Chris Argyris: The father of organizational learning' (1998) by Robert M. Fulmer and J. Bernard Keys, 'Designing the innovating organization' (1982) by Jay R. Galbraith and 'To avoid organizational crises, unlearn' (1984) by Paul C. Nystrom and William H. Starbuck.

Organization Science for 'Market, hierarchy and trust: The knowledge economy and the future of capitalism' (2001) by Paul S. Adler, 'A dynamic theory of organizational knowledge creation' (1994) by Ikujiro Nonaka and 'Beyond networks and hierarchies: Latent organizations in the UK television industry' (2000) by Ken Starkey, Christopher Barnatt and Sue Tempest.

Organization Studies for 'Knowledge, knowledge work and organizations: An overview and interpretation' (1995) by Frank Blackler.

Regional Studies for 'Cool projects, boring institutions: temporary collaboration in social context' (2002) by Gernot Grabher.

Strategic Management Review for 'Transformative capacity: Continual Structuring by intertemporal technology transfer' (1994) by Raghu Garud and Praveen R. Nayyar, 'Top management teams and organizational renewal' (1989) by David K. Hurst, James, C. Rush and Roderick E. White and 'The dominant logic: a new linkage between diversity and performance' (1986) by C.K. Prahalad and Richard Bettis.

We would also like to thank Emma Foster, Susan Stocken, Jane Aston, and Stephanie Gorst of the Nottingham University Business School for their help in preparing this manuscript.

Introduction

The end of the previous millennium witnessed a 'desperate quest' for new approaches to management (Eccles and Nohria, 1992: 2). Driving this quest was a growing sense of unease with existing ways of thinking about management and organization and out of the unease has arisen a search for new paradigms (Hamel and Prahalad, 1994). The new millennium finds us still preoccupied with this search. One of its latest outcomes is the theory and practice of the learning organization. This book sets out to explore the concept and practice of the learning organization in a collection of key contributions that examine the theories and practices of learning, organization and strategic management.

The aim of the book is to illustrate that the concept of the learning organization is a powerful one for understanding the nature of contemporary organizations and the key strategic tasks they face. In particular, an emphasis upon learning focuses our attention upon a critical analysis of an organization's past and how this affects its present. Learning also raises important issues concerning the future and how we are to deal with the future is a focus of much debate in strategy. Building upon the resource-based view of the firm, the book argues that learning and knowledge are major strategic resources, crucial to competitive advantage. The book also considers psychodynamic perspectives on management as an antidote to overly rational views of organization.

Until recently, the Western view of management has been based upon a top-down view that has bred conservatism. Management was seen as a science. Frederick Taylor's 'scientific management' provided a dominant image of organization as a kind of machine (Morgan, 1986). Information was 'out there', to be gathered and processed rationally in search of the 'one best' answer to problems. This view was challenged, but not demolished, by writers such as Mintzberg (1973) who showed that successful managerial work was based upon skills that it was hard to codify and upon intuitions that were hard to make explicit. The 1980s saw a plethora of studies extolling the virtues of leadership, most notably Peters and Waterman's (1982) best-selling *In Search of Excellence*. The lure of the powerful charismatic leader was strong at a time when new competition from Japan had demonstrated the vulnerability of Western firms.

Hubris was at hand and new models of world class manufacturing arrived from the Far East to change our view of the world. To the champions of leadership, it was the heroic efforts of charismatic supermen (and some superwomen) that were crucial to any hope of change. Japan gave us another image of organizational effectiveness built upon the collective effort of many 'little brains' (Womack *et al.*, 1991). The focus here was on learning to promote continuous improvement. Gradually, the issue of learning emerged as a key organizational concern.

The learning organization is a metaphor with its roots in the vision of and the search for a strategy to promote individual self-development within a continuously self-transforming organization. Historically, the subject of individual learning has been a central concern of psychology. How to apply the insights from individual and social psychology to the understanding of organizations has been a major concern of those who have studied and practised organizational learning. In this book we argue that learning is a strategic necessity for organizations. The competitive context for contemporary management is one where success depends upon the leveraging of competence for cost and/or innovation advantage. The demands of competition require that the human resource is utilized to its fullest capability. Strategy formation is quintessentially a learning process. The learning company is 'design-led', 'as befits an "information age" in which ideas provide the engines of the new industrial order' (Pedler *et al.*, 1989: 7).

Rethinking the future

Many of the ideas upon which the concept of the learning organization is based are prefigured in earlier work, for example, in the writings of Mary Parker Follett of more than half a century ago. Another echo in recent work on the learning organization recalls the organization development movement of the 1960s as exemplified in the writings of Schein, Beckhard, Bennis, Argyris and Schon, and Blake and Mouton. One should also mention the pioneering work of Peter Drucker who has long argued that knowledge is the only lasting resource of competitive advantage (see, for example, Drucker, 1988), and that, in a 'knowledge society', the 'knowledge worker' is crucial to organizational survival and success. What we find in these authors is a critical reflection upon the nature of existing management paradigms.

The context for current debates about these paradigms is a sense of increasing turbulence and uncertainty about the future. Toffler and Toffler (1997) argue that we need a shift in our thinking about the epistemology and ontology of management theory and practice and compare 'Second Wave' with 'Third Wave' management thinking. Second wave, orthodox management thinking, encapsulated in the MBA curriculum of leading US and European business schools, is based upon assumptions of linearity and equilibrium and aims at quantification. This dominant management paradigm replicates the mechanistic assumptions of Western economics which, themselves, attempt to replicate the 'certainties' of Newtonian physics, thus spawning faith in such things as vertical integration, economies of scale and command-and-control organization.

Third Wave management is more postmodern in its concerns with heterarchy, networks, empowerment and challenging accepted knowledge.

Indeed, knowledge is a key concern of new age management – how to assess and manage knowledge assets, how to promote individual and organizational learning as forms of critical self-analysis – issues that Second Wave disciplines, such as economics, find hard to deal with.

Even the old-style strategy gurus, of whom Michael Porter is the most eminent, now see learning as an integral feature of the successful companies of the future. 'The companies that are going to be able to become successful, or remain successful, will be the ones that can learn fast, can assimilate this learning and develop new insights. ... companies are going to have to become much more like universities than they have been in the past. Companies tended to think that they knew a lot, and therefore tried to be efficient in doing what they thought they knew. But now it's a matter of learning' (Porter, 1997: 59).

The new strategy gurus emphasize learning and competence as the fundamental building blocks in the creation of a strategic architecture that links the present and the future. Competitive advantage will, they argue, accrue to those firms that succeed in building new competences in new opportunity areas. Underpinning this conclusion is the argument that we need new ways of thinking about the future.

In the words of Gary Hamel (1997: 81), perhaps the major strategy thinker of the current moment: 'We had a wrong focus for many years when we used to think about the future. The primary focus was on forecasting and trying to identify [one] particular future, rather than developing a deep-down sense of 'discontinuities' – the things that are driving change, or that potentially could be harnessed to drive change. And then, out of that understanding trying to imagine or construct a point of view about the unique opportunities we might create' (Hamel, 1997: 81). What is also required is a new way of thinking about strategy because 'you cannot create the future using the old strategy tools' (Hamel, 1997: 88). Prahalad (1997: 71) emphasizes unlearning: 'Companies are going to have to unlearn a lot of their past – and also to forget it! The future will not be an extrapolation of the past.'

Prahalad and Hamel differ on potential sources of new learning in organizations. Prahalad sees corporate restructuring/downsizing as a form of lost opportunity, the loss arising because so much of older employees' knowledge disappears in the process. Prahalad thus equates knowledge with age and experience. 'Think what might have happened if companies had used all the "redundant" brainpower that they got rid of to imagine new markets for tomorrow, or to build new core competencies that would give them an advantage in those markets' (Prahalad, 1997: 65).

Hamel, however, is critical of existing hierarchies of age and experience and their effect upon learning. 'If you want to create a point of view about the future, if you want to craft a meaningful strategy, you have to create in your company a hierarchy of imagination. And that means giving a disproportionate share of voice to the people who have until now been disenfranchised from the strategy-making process. It means giving a disproportionate share of voice to the young people. It means giving a disproportionate share of voice to the geographic periphery of your organization – because, typically, the farther away you are from headquarters, the more creative people are: they don't have the dead hand of bureaucracy and orthodoxy on them. And it means giving a disproportionate share of voice to newcomers' (Hamel, 1997: 91).

Unlearning the past is particularly difficult for the senior managers who have a great emotional investment in old ways of working. The essence of leadership is senior executives' ability to distinguish between knowing what they still have to contribute and recognizing what they need to learn from others (Sonnenfeld, 1988). Senge (1997) makes the crucial point that we need to be more reflexive in our thinking, analysing how we think because if we do not change our mindsets the future will see us stuck in the present.

Senge argues for two levels of change. The first is at the personal level of new skills and capabilities, both individual and collective. In particular, he argues, we have to learn how to improve our ability to 'think together'. The second level of change, he argues, concerns the ways in which we organize ourselves to support learning. Here Senge presents the vision of the learning organization that has grown out of his work and that of his colleagues at MIT, the development of learning capabilities in more fexible, responsive, adaptive, and less bureaucratic organizations.

New learning capabilities, according to Senge, are best articulated in terms of the five 'disciplines' that have been the cornerstone of his work. These include: 'the capacity of people to have a sense of purpose and to build genuinely shared visions (based on people, individually, knowing what they care deeply about); the ability of people to see larger patterns and understand interdependency – by developing what we call 'systems thinking'; and people having increased reflective capabilities, so that they can be more and more aware or their own assumptions – particularly assumptions that they would not normally question' (Senge, 1997: 130–1).

A key issue for Senge is how to design new forms of organization so that learning is not merely a residue of other processes in the organization. The 'command and control' organization is the antithesis of the learning organization as it stifles imagination and intelligence. 'The trouble is that most business relationships work like dysfunctional families. Everybody is basically concentrating on just pleasing the boss and avoiding getting their ass kicked, rather than on building real relationships' (Senge, 1997: 138).

Top-down control-dominated organizations cannot cope with the new business. 'Hence, we have massive institutional breakdown and massive failure of the centralized nervous systems of hierarchial institutions in the face of growing interdependence and accelerating change' (Senge, 1997: 126). The learning organization, therefore, poses significant challenges to existing ways of thinking about leadership. Learning is predicated upon the willingness to challenge and change existing mental models.

> This is much easier said than done. In practice, it is disorienting and deeply humbling, because our old mental models were the keys to our confidence and our competence. *To be a real learner is to be ignorant and incompetent. Not many executives may be up to that.* (Senge, 1997: 139)

A key task in understanding the learning organization is to integrate frameworks of individual and organizational learning, management development and organizational culture so as to cope with change. Its starting point is expressed as follows: 'Learning is at a premium because we are not so much masters of change as beset by it. ... Multiple possible futures, the need for discontinuity almost for the sake of it, means that we must be able to think imaginatively, to be able to develop ourselves and, in generative relationships with others, to continually organize and reorganize ourselves' (Dixon, 1994: xi). This captures some of the key elements of debate in this area – the inexorability of change, the unpredictability of the future, the importance of imagination, and, by implication, innovation, a new quality of relationship in organizations that cling to bureaucratic principles at their peril.

The emphasis in the learning organization is upon using collective reasoning and the intelligence of the whole organization in making learning rather than intimidation (control based upon fear) the major tool of management. Learning is seen as the key to making organizations more democratic, more responsive to change and to creating organizations in which individuals can grow and develop. Here conversation and dialogue is crucial. 'Organizational dialogue is interaction in a collective setting that results in mutual learning upon which the organization can act. [It is] a specific kind of organizational talk; talk that reveals our meaning structures to each other' (Dixon, 1997: 83).

Reality and truth are, according to this perspective, socially constructed and learning is about the collective creation of meaning rather than the insights of experts.

The psychodynamics of learning

Bennis (1993) argues for a rethinking of the role of the leader in the learning organization. Senge (1990: 168) develops the idea of a new kind of leadership based upon the integration of intuition and rationality. If we are to develop a more holistic philosophy of management then we do need to pay more attention to the non-rational aspects of management. As we have seen above, the quality of leadership is seen as a crucial feature of the learning organization with the emphasis upon intimacy, reciprocity and a sense of belonging, precisely the kind of qualities proponents of the learning organization set out to develop. All too often the relationship between leaders and followers is the antithesis of this desired state.

Organization is about connecting. Kets de Vries (1995) examines the issue of human connectedness: the ease or difficulty with which individuals establish relationships and have empathic feelings for others; the capacity for intimacy and reciprocity and the ability to establish and maintain long-term relationships; the extent to which we experience a sense of belonging, of being part of a group and being satisfied in a social context.

A psychodynamic perspective, with its emphasis upon surfacing that which is unconscious, provides useful insight into how organizations function and how they do or do not learn. Such a perspective also provides a useful antidote to the myth of rationality. 'The crucial issue is whether the typical corporate executive really is a logical, dependable being. Is management in reality a rational task performed by rational people according to sensible organizational objectives? We all know better, yet the myth of rationality persists' (Kets de Vries, 1995: x).

Much of what 'really goes on in organizations' takes place in an intrapsychic world below the surface of day-to-day behaviours and needs to be understood in terms of conflicts, defensive behaviour, tensions, anxiety, the real heart of organizations according to Kets de Vries (1995: xv). Organizations, like relationships, get stuck. 'In my clinical work. I am often struck by the number of people who fail to realize the extent to which there is continuity between our past, our present, and our future. These people make the same mistakes over and over again because they are unable to recognize the repetitive patterns in their behavior that have become dysfunctional. They are stuck in a vicious circle and do not know how to get out.'

The widening of choice involves more than optimizing rational decision-making. 'There [is] a need to balance rational, analytical approaches with intuitive thinking processes. Executives will have to become better at picking up the weak signals. They will have to become more attuned to what psychotherapists describe as counter-transference reactions. They will have to cultivate the ability to interpret the kind of feelings that can be stirred up in interpersonal situations. The emotional agenda in professional encounters is often glossed over. ... executives have a notoriously underdeveloped capacity for self-reflection. Many are inclined to act first and think later. They seem reluctant to ask themselves why they act the way they do' (Kets de Vries, 1995: 96).

Learning is important in the psychodynamic perspective upon organizations. First of all, it is important to understand how present patterns are shaped by past experience. Without understanding of the past we are condemned to relive it. Organizations, too, need to understand their past or they too will relive it and grow increasingly out of touch with the changing environment. 'In this new, dynamic, and turbulent world, there will be increased emphasis on planned change and organizational renewal. Change will have to become a permanent phenomenon in the new corporation, and the executive of the future had better learn how to live with it. To facilitate change, a corporate culture that fosters a continuous learning process should be created' (Kets de Vries, 1995: 97).

Successful companies are 'great believers in institutional learning, in creating an environment where some form of continuity is established between the generation in power and the next group of executives' (Kets de Vries, 1995: 91). A psychodynamic perspective highlights the importance of identity: 'one very important criterion of mental health and normality is whether we possess a stable identity, a secure sense of self-esteem' (Kets de Vries, 1995: 232). A psychodynamic perspective is also useful in broadening our thinking about leadership and its role in learning in the development of cognitive structures that minimize un-ease in dealing with uncertainty.

Leaders are responsible for creating a learning architecture. 'Leaders have to be organizational architects. They have to create the kind of designs and structures that facilitate the envisioning, empowering, and energizing processes of leadership. ... The way people go about creating this kind of holding environment distinguishes effective from ineffective leaders. ... the derailment of a CEO is seldom caused by a lack of information about the latest techniques in marketing, finance, or production; rather, it comes about because of a lack of interpersonal skills – a failure to get the best out of the people who possess necessary information' (Kets de Vries, 1995: 12).

But leadership is frequently dysfunctional: 'when I ask CEOs to describe their management style, I am given a description of a reborn philosopher-king – only to find out quickly, by watching them interact with their subordinates, that an Attila-the-Hum style is much closer to the truth' (Kets de Vries, 1995: 44). Excellent companies take great trouble to avoid destructive conflict and politicization and to build a climate of trust into the organization. In this context the good leader is akin to a philosopher king, or a psychotherapist, skilled in the building of trusting relationships in which individuals can learn about themselves and their potential, 'a container' of the emotions of subordinates, who guides individual and organizational development through the quality of dialogue.

A major potential outcome of learning is an ability to act more creatively. Kets de Vries compares creative thinkers to Prometheus whose name means 'wise before the events'. 'It is as if creative people had some form of power to look into the future' (Kets de Vries, 1995: 140). Creative thinking takes the organization into a 'transitional space'. The term is adapted from D.W. Winnicott's notion of the 'transitional object', one form of which is the plaything that helps the child in play to come to terms with the relationship between outer and inner realities and to arrive at a mature sense of self. In organizations a more playful less pre-determined form of engagement with the issues facing the company is necessary if organizations really want to change. Playfulness is a defining characteristic of healthy organizations and a necessary antidote to stress: 'a key value of [a healthy] corporate culture is openness to change. Executives have to create a protean organization – one that has the capacity to learn and change. Where there is no change, there can be no creativity' (Kets de Vries, 1995: 150–1).

Strategy as learning

A learning perspective suggests that we pay more explicit attention to the conditions of ambiguity and uncertainty concerning the future that more traditional approaches to strategy ignore. As a result it introduces learning into the very heart of strategic planning. Strategy is about preparing for an essentially unknowable future. 'The most fundamental aspect of introducing uncertainty in the strategic equation is that it turns planning for the future from a one-off episodic activity into an ongoing learning proposition' (van der Heijden, 1996: 7).

Scenario planning is the most advanced variant of this approach. Its aim is to create a management process that envisages new ways of thinking the future. Using the work of David Kolb, who himself synthesized the idea from the theories of John Dewey, Jean Piaget, Kurt Lewin and others, the idea of the learning loop is central to the scenario approach. 'The processualist hold that we need to get into a loop linking action, perception and thinking towards continual learning. An effective strategy is one which triggers our entry into that learning loop' (van der Heijden, 1996: 37). At the centre of this approach, recalling Dixon's (1994) emphasis upon dialogue in the organizational learning cycle, is conversation.

The essence of scenario planning is the creation of a range of alternative scenarios about the future. The aim is to be prepared to deal with a variety of possible futures rather than *one* most likely future. Scenario planning was developed by Royal Dutch/Shell in the oil industry. If Shell's experience of the oil industry in the last quarter of a century has taught them anything it is that there are no guarantees that the most probable future will actually occur. Scenarios are derived 'from shared and agreed upon mental models of the external world. They are created as internally consistent and challenging descriptions of possible futures. They are intended to be representative of the ranges of possible future developments and outcomes in the external world' (van der Heijden, 1996: 5).

A key aim of the scenario approach is to develop processes that 'enhance the capability of the organisation to mobilise resources towards greater inventiveness and innovation' (van de Heijden, 1996: 41). Crucial here is the development of shared concepts and a shared language for discussing the future. It is through 'dialectic' conversation in which diverse views confront each other that scenario planning identifies uncertainties and structures events and identifies patterns in the environment. 'Only through a process of conversation can elements of observation and thought be structured and embedded in the accepted and shared organisational theories in use. ... An effective strategic conversation must incorporate a wide range of initially unstructured thoughts and views, and out of this create shared interpretations of the world' (van der Heijden, 1996: 41–2).

In strategic conversation we move from perception to theory building to joint action. Scenarios are 'stories describing the current and future states of the business environment' (van der Heijden, 1996: 7). Shared stories are the outcome of far-ranging strategic conversations both within and without the organization. 'Sharing multiple stories about the future makes the organisation more perceptive about its environment, and forces reflection on experience and adjustment of mental theories' (van der Heijden, 1996: 54; Denning, 2001). Story-making has the power to liberate creativity. Rutenberg (1985), incidentally, describes the use of scenarios as 'playful planning'.

An organizational learning perspective on strategy cautions scepticism about existing business ideas. The business idea is the organization's existing mental model of its current and future success. A crucial first stage in the scenario planning process is to articulate this idea so that it can be studied, discussed, modified and improved. The process provides the (new) language through which key issues relating the future of the organization and its environment can be discussed and managed. By critically reflecting upon existing mental models of decision makers as a starting point, issues can be reframed, new theories of action developed and shared and mental models can be aligned as a prelude to effective joint action.

An important part of the scenario process is to facilitate the articulation of the organizational self. This concept can be linked to notions of core competence, as reflected in current discussions of the resource-based view of the firm, and Selznick's (1957) concept of 'distinctive competence'. Notions of self and competence are, in turn, linked to the concept of strategic vision, most notably in the work of Wack (for example, 1985), one of the key exponents of the scenario approach. Wack sees strategic vision as the counterpart of scenarios and as a important complexity reducer which can be used as a way of coping with turbulence and uncertainty by providing a common frame of reference within which information and knowledge can be organised.

The structure of the book

We develop these themes in the readings chosen for this book and in the chapters written specifically for this purpose. The book is divided into four parts. Part I, 'Organizational learning and strategy', examines the sources of learning and knowledge creation, linking learning to new models of organization, managerial work and to the strategic management of resources and competence. Part II, 'Learning, structure and process', presents studies of organization structures and management processes that create learning. In particular, it focuses upon innovation as a crucial aspect of organizational effectiveness and analyses how new ways of thinking about organization can open up new potential for corporate transformation in a context where old models of organization are giving way to complex, dispersed network forms. Part III, 'Knowledge management' examines the latest variant of the learning organization debate. Knowledge has been increasingly heralded as the only durable source of competitive advantage. Knowledge is the outcome of the learning process and the basis for the effective exercise of competence. Part IV, 'Leadership and the learning process', makes explicit the link between leadership and learning. Learning, it suggests, is the key to management innovation. The quality of leadership, embedded in the top management team process, and embodied in wisdom and identity, determines the organization's ability to learn, but we should seek to develop a deeper, more psychodynamically oriented perspective to help us understand why change is so difficult.

References

Bennis, W. (1993) *An Invented Life: Reflections on Leadership and Change*, Reading MA: Addison-Wesley.

Denning, S. (2001) *The Springboard. How Storytelling Ignites Action in Knowledge-Era Organizations*, Boston: Butterworth-Heinemann.

Dixon, N.M. (1994) *The Organizational Learning Cycle. How We Can Learn Collectively*, London/New York: McGraw Hill.

Drucker, P. (1988) 'The coming of the new organization', *Harvard Business Review*, 66, January–February, 45–53.

Eccles, R.G. and Nohria, N. (1992) *Beyond the Hype. Rediscovering the Essence of Management*, Boston, MA: Harvard Business School Press.

Gibson, R. (ed.) (1997) *Rethinking the Future*, London: Nicholas Brealey Publishing.

Hamel, G. (1997) 'Reinventing the basis for competition', in Gibson, R. (ed.) *Rethinking the Future*, London: Nicholas Brealey Publishing, 76–91.

Hamel, G. and Prahalad, C.K. (1994) 'Strategy as a field of study: Why search for a new paradigm?', *Strategic Management Journal*, 15, Special Issue, Summer, 5–16.

Kets de Vries, M. (1995) *Life and Death in the Executive Fast Lane. Essays on Irrational Organizations and their Leaders*, San Francisco: Jossey-Bass.

Mintzberg, H. (1973) *The Nature of Managerial Work*, New York: Harper & Row.

Morgan, G. (1986) *Images of Organization,* Beverly Hills: Sage.

Pedler, M., Boydell, T. and Burgoyne, J. (1989) 'Towards the learning company', *Management Education and Development*, 20, 1, 1–8.

Peters, T. and Waterman Jr, R.H. (1982) *In Search of Excellence,* New York, Harper & Row.

Porter, M. (1997) 'Creating tomorrow's advantages', in Gibson, R. (ed.) *Rethinking the Future*, London: Nicholas Brealey Publishing, 48–60.

Prahalad, C.K. (1997) 'Strategies for growth', in Gibson, R. (ed.) *Rethinking the Future*, London: Nicholas Brealey Publishing, 62–74.

Rutenberg, D. (1985) 'Playful planning', Working Paper, School of Business, Queen's University, Kingston, Ontario.

Selznick, P. (1957) *Leadership in Administration*, Harper & Row, reissued in 1984 by University of California Press, Berkeley, CA.

Senge, P. (1990) *The Fifth Discipline. The Art and Practice of the Learning Organization*, New York: Doubleday/Currency.

Senge, P. (1997) 'Through the eye of the needle', in Gibson, R. (ed.) *Rethinking the Future*, London: Nicholas Brealey Publishing, 122–45.

Sonnenfeld, J. (1988) *The Hero's Farewell,* New York and Oxford: Oxford University Press.

Toffler, A. and Toffler, H. (1997) 'Foreword', in Gibson, R. (ed.) *Rethinking the Future.* London: Nicholas Brealey Publishing, vii–x.

van der Heijden, K. (1996) *Scenarios. The Art of Strategic Conversation*, Chichester/New York: John Wiley & Sons.

Wack, P. (1985) 'Scenarios, shooting the rapids', *Harvard Business Review*, November–December, 73–90.

Womack, J.P., Jones, D.T. and Roos, D. (1991) *The Machine that Changed the World*, London and New York: Rawson Associates/Macmillan.

Organizational learning and strategy

Introduction

Part I starts with an interview with one of the founding fathers of the theory and practice of organizational learning, Chris Argyris. His books on organization development and organizational learning have become classics in the field. He has focused especially on barriers to learning, for example, the perhaps paradoxical problems smart people have in learning to think and act differently, and the defensive routines that individuals and organizations use to defend themselves from the need to learn. He links learning to issues of justice and sees 'honest inquiry', balancing trust and risk-taking, as the basis for more effective organizations of the future. Argyris emphasizes practice in learning and 'actionability'. One of his major contributions has been to show how 'truth' is an acceptable idea until it poses a threat to existing sense-making and how, to promote learning, we need to reduce defensive organizational routines. His distinctions between theory-in-use and theory-in-action, between Model 1 and Model 2 organizations and between single- and double-loop learning remain as relevant today as they have ever been. His design principles for organizational learning also remain current – design situations or environments where participants can be original and can experience high personal causation (psychological success, confirmation and essentiality).

Chapter 2 explores the link between individual and organizational learning, and, in particular, the role of mental models and organizational memory in supporting shared meaning. Mental models can be powerful barriers to learning. Organizations are both behavioural systems and interpretive systems which can combine to support world-views and operating procedures that are resistant to change. The process of organizational learning makes these systems visible and promotes change by challenging mental models, existing world-views and standard operating procedures. The chapter also builds on the notion of double-loop learning, surfacing and challenging deep-rooted assumptions and norms that have previously not been accessible, either because they were unknown or because they were considered undiscussable. It examines the use of systems archetypes to elicit and capture management understanding that is frequently intuitive or tacit. There needs to be a way to go beyond fragmented individual learnings and to diffuse learning throughout an organization so that it becomes a common good.

Chapter 3 takes as its focus the link between learning and competitiveness. The interest in learning has intensified in the strategy field with the growing focus upon competence as a key source of competitive advantage. The chapter examines the role of learning in diversification and vertical integration decisions and in the link between strategy and structure. Learning is seen as crucial to the strategy of innovation and is embedded in the concept of 'absorptive capacity', an organization's ability to acquire and exploit new knowledge. The concept of learning in the strategy field is a major theme running through work on innovation right through the value chain. Learning as 'creative absorption' underpins reverse engineering, competitive bench-marking and continuous improvement programmes in many organizations and industries. Leading firms conceive of day-to-day operations as mini-laboratories for testing and learning from experiments with new ideas. New debates in strategy adopt a learning perspective as an alternative to the traditional planning model of strategy. New approaches see successful strategy as emergent, flexible and responsive to changing environmental conditions. The view is that effective strategic management is akin to craft skills and that strategies are moulded through a process that combines technology, imagination, analysis and a tacit sense of the products or services that customers want that comes from experience. Learning has a major role to play in strategy in promoting creative tension and in 'stretching' corporate aspiration.

Chapter 4 addresses the issue of the link between managerial knowledge and strategic action. This is analysed from the perspective of strategy content and also in terms of the conditions that create logics of managerial thought. The dominant logic of an organization consists of managers' mental maps developed through years of experience of a firm's core business. These mental maps dictate what managers expect and cause them to process events through existing knowledge systems or schemas, beliefs, theories and propositions based upon previous learning. Interpretation is based upon expectations of the patterning of events by the dynamics of particular industries. Existing and entrenched logics may resist efforts of new managers to change them. Unlearning must take place to open up psychic space for the drawing of new mental maps but, ironically, the greater past success the more difficult the unlearning process! Most important to strategy are the mental maps of top management, the dominant coalition in organizations. The Japanese gained competitive advantage in a range of industries by pioneering new strategies while incumbent Western management remained trapped by their existing mental models. Changes in business variety in the direction of greater complexity, through industry change or through internal change brought about, for example, by acquisition, present major challenges. In times of change top management must learn how to discard or revise dominant logics. Unlearning must take place to open up new psychic space for the drawing of new mental maps and, too often, this process is only begun when crisis strikes. Ironically, the greater past success the more difficult the unlearning process.

Chapter 5 examines the limits of the competence concept, arguing that we need to consider competence in the context of debates about knowledge and 'dynamic capability'. It traces the long history of competence-based approaches in strategy. From the resource-based perspective that informs competence thinking, competitive advantage is likely to be most durable when it is based upon tacit knowledge which is hard to surface and, therefore, very difficult for competitors to understand or imitate. The chapter examines the link between competence and knowledge, examining how knowledge can act as the basis for competence building, and how competence is best understood as a relational process. A focus on competence and knowledge leads us naturally to a consideration of human resource management (HRM) and the recent growing convergence between the fields of HRM and strategic management. The chapter poses the question: how will recent changes in HR practices, along with the restructuring and frequent downsizing of organizations impact upon the ability of firms to leverage the learning and knowledge of its employees. It is suggested that one way of understanding these changes is through the lens of social capital, a construct that is receiving increasing attention in the management literature and in the social sciences in general.

Chapter 6 looks at the role of learning in crisis situations. Learning can generate inertia and a complacent view that change is unnecessary. To prepare an organization for change requires 'unlearning'. To avoid crisis organizations have to challenge their existing beliefs and values and to foster a culture of constructive dissent and of active experimentation with new ways of thinking and acting. The chapter argues that the best alternative to 'harsh' unlearning is to put in place learning processes that focus upon 'unlearning continuously'. To stay in control of the future, top managers need to accept their own fallibility. This demands both objectivity and humility as well as self-confidence. To stimulate unlearning, top management can adopt three strategies – listen to dissent, convert events into learning opportunities and adopt experimental frames of reference.

The final chapter in Part I, Chapter 7, examines periods of change in high-tech industries. Positive change is associated with the ability of managers to learn how to take advantage of 'strategic dissonance', those periods when the existing strategic intent seems at odds with a changing external reality. These periods are described as 'strategic inflection points'. Skilful managers negotiate such transition periods by building up repertoires of adaptive behaviours and rethinking strategic intent. The particular focus of the chapter is Intel and the computer industry and one of its authors was CEO of Intel. A crucial lesson here is that an organization cannot rely on its old competencies when times change and, therefore, that the search for new knowledge to act as the basis for new forms of competitive advantage is crucial to strategic effectiveness. Over time, an organization's competence and the basis for competition will inexorably diverge. Top management needs to learn the skills of 'strategic recognition' to enable it to pick out from the plethora of conflicting information the signals that can form the foundation for a new strategic direction.

A conversation with Chris Argyris:
the father of organizational learning
Robert M. Fulmer and J. Bernard Keys

Chris Argyris is James B. Conant Professor Emeritus and holds positions in both the Harvard University School of Business and School of Education. His books on organizational development and organizational learning have become classics in the field.

Argyris has received eight honorary degrees from universities in the USA and abroad. He spent 20 years at Yale University where a Chair in Social Psychology of Organization and Intervention is named after him. He was the 1997 recipient of the Kurt Lewin Award.

Publications by Argyris include a book reviewing much of his work entitled *On Organizational Learning* (Blackwell Publishers, Inc.), published in 1994, and *Organizational Learning II* with Donald Schon, 1996 (Addison Wesley). His most recent book is titled *Knowledge for Action: A Guide to Overcoming Barriers to Organizational Change*, published by Jossey-Bass.

This interview was conducted by Robert M. Fulmer, W. Brooks George Professor at William and Mary, and J. Bernard Keys, Callaway Professor of Business, Center for Managerial Learning, Georgia Southern University.

F/K: Of all of the contributions you have made to the management discipline, which do you reflect on with greatest satisfaction?

ARGYRIS: As I look back on my academic research, I think it's fair to say that my first fundamental interest has been the notion of justice and then, after that, the notion of truth. I put it that way because I know good research that has been done under dictators who were unjust. My feeling is that scholars ought to work first on justice because, if you have that, you can have free research. If you have that in an organization, there can also be free inquiry. So justice, truth, competence, effectiveness, learning – these are my keys.

What gives me the greatest satisfaction is what I call the "theory of action perspective" that I developed with Donald Schon. And I'm able to connect my research with the latest findings on the way the human mind/brain works. Now the reason I think that is important is, first, individuals are the key when they are acting in order to learn, or when they are acting to produce a result. Second, it's not possible to act without using your mind/brain. Three, if this is so, then all of our knowledge somehow has to be generalized and crafted in ways in which the mind and brain can use it in order to make it actionable.

Unfortunately too many social scientists don't worry about that criterion. They're from the mental notion that if we can describe the world as accurately or as honestly as we can, then we can predict, and that's enough. But they don't ask about the applications that can be made, or how these can be implemented enough or used by the human mind. To me, the ability to increase learning, to change behavior, or to improve performance is essential.

F/K: One of the major complaints about business academia today is the issue of "relevance." Your work is unique in that it has had major impact on a variety of academic disciplines, but also is widely used in the business community. How do you compare the impact of your work in the business and academic worlds?

ARGYRIS: I'm interested in producing knowledge that is actionable. In order to be actionable, it must be actionable by practitioners. I think practitioners have found my work useful because of my interest in actionability. In the last 10 to 15 years, I have especially focused on the defensive routines of organizations that prevent actionability. And what I get from executives is a continual awareness of how important it is to overcome these defensive routines, especially if you're interested in changing organizations.

There is no course that I'm aware of that teaches how to be good at creating defensive routines in order to avoid discomfort or to maintain the status quo, but everyone manages to learn them. The point is, too often these defensive routines have been bypassed or ignored. Now, if you go to the academic community, I think my impact has been as a person trying to describe what he sees as accurately as he can. And there is, if I can judge from the citations, a lot of interest in things like the defensive routines, the research that Don and I did on organizational learning, and so on. There is another part of my work which is just beginning to gain overt acceptance, and that is my claim that most good social science research is not actionable. (By good, I mean it follows the rules of rigorous methodology.) Calling attention to this has irritated colleagues of mine, but I think they're beginning to see there's some validity to this, and my younger colleagues do see this concern as valid.

When I received the 1997 Kurt Lewin Award, the audience, especially the younger people, seemed really quite interested in this tension, but felt helpless. They don't have the skills to deal with the issue. They're not taught these skills. So even if those little bits of data are valid, there's an increasing number who say, "Yes, these concepts are important, let's keep them in mind." So I think that recognizing the importance of actionability has been appreciated by the business community and is beginning to have an impact on the academic world.

F/K: It's a little like the member of the British Parliament who said of Darwin's theory, "It may be true, but if it's true, it's a damnable truth and it shouldn't be admitted."

ARGYRIS: Yes. I wrote an article in 1968 in the *Psychological Bulletin,* and I got letters back from the reviewers, which inadvertently included a note to the editor that was not intended for me to see. The reviewer said, "You should not consider him as a traitor or as an enemy in social psychology. He raises important questions." The other reviewer said, "He is a traitor!"

Apparently the editor decided to publish anyway, but that gives you an idea of the initial reaction.

F/K: Since your retirement in 1995, your work has grown in a couple of ways. First, you've been incredibly productive, but there's also a wider recognition and respect for your work. Is this just the new generation or does something else account for this growing appreciation and recognition?

ARGYRIS: I'm really not sure, but here are some possibilities. One is that by luck or whatever, I've been studying issues that are controversial and it takes a while for those who think they are worth supporting to be able to support them. I just suggested that the notion of rigorous methodology being consistent with Model I is not something that was easily accepted by most social scientists. But people like Donald Campbell [the father of quasi-experimental methodology – ed.], in a public dialogue we had, said, "No, we have to listen to this." And then he said the problem would be that none of us is educated on how to overcome this and "maybe quite a few of us aren't motivated." So I think people are beginning to see that you cannot deny the validity of things like defensive routines.

F/K: Perhaps people haven't denied the impact, but failed to recognize how pervasive it is. It's easy to think about defensive routines in the abstract or to agree that they exist with other people, but the degree to which we are all hemmed in is really astounding.

ARGYRIS: Yes, but in my experience, managers see the pervasiveness immediately and say, "You mean you can do something about this? Where? How?" And I think the work that Don and I did was increasingly seen as a way of really beginning to do something. However, their problem became "Does it have to be this difficult?"

It's as difficult to learn as it is to learn a poor game of tennis. The concepts aren't that complicated, but practice is what's needed. So I think increasingly we're finding business executives who realize that it is going to be difficult, but that it has to be done. Now the fundamental message of Model I organizations is that truth is a good idea when it isn't threatening. If it's threatening, massage it, hide it, distort it, but don't deal with it. Information science technology has become increasingly sophisticated and it's making things transparent that years ago could be hidden. And transparency requires a reduction of defensive routines. Years ago I remember somebody saying, "Boy, you're right Chris, but there's nothing you can do about it." But today they're beginning to see there is something you can do about it.

One of the failures, I believe, in the organizational development movement is that in order to do something about this problem, we've got to find ways of integrating the functional disciplines such as finance, accounting or operations with the OB stuff.

F/K: Your work has been cited in so many different disciplines. My question may be naive, but was this a planned strategy in your early career development or was this a pleasant surprise that your work has been so widely received?

ARGYRIS: It wasn't planned in the sense of "I've got to be relevant to the various disciplines." I put it the other way. It goes back to the notions of justice and actionability. I was very much interested wherever actionability occurred, be it public or private organizations. I believe that the attraction to other disciplines was partly due to my studying governmental as well as private organizations. More importantly, I was interested in seeing how we could do research that helps managers.

My interest in justice and actionability was driven by seeking an answer to the question, "What the hell is really going on?" So I went from social psychology to sociology to anthropology to public administration. In fact the chair that I've held until recently allowed me to teach at the Harvard Business School, in the School of Education, at the Kennedy School of Government and in the law school. And I was getting ready to see if they might consider me at the Divinity School.

F/K: Where did this come from, Chris? Was this a cultural thing or was it part of your academic training to develop this commitment to actionability?

ARGYRIS: Oh, no, it wasn't part of my academic training. I remember there were four or five of us, I'm told, who were funded by the National Institute for Mental Health, in a sort of preferred basis because someone had identified us as doing the "outlier things that might well be important." There was a committee that met once a year to review our grants. When I wrote a book entitled *Interpersonal Competence and Organizational Effectiveness*, in which I became much more normative, the panel had trouble. They said he's gone too far. This is not something that NIH traditionally funded. Fortunately, the NIH administrators disagreed. They said that that's exactly what we want. The panel gave me another two years or so of funding.

The only support in my training came from Bill Whyte [William F.] at Cornell, Roger Barker, and Kurt Lewin. I remember Bill Whyte putting us in a station wagon and saying "go and get data." With Roger Barker, we were studying a town in Kansas. Kurt Lewin, whom I met just before he died, was always interested in taking a look at what was really going on. What impressed me is that we weren't going to help the world out there unless we could get to actionable knowledge. It took me a while to realize that not only was it a good idea to help practitioners, but the toughest test of rigorous methodology is not to see if you can predict, but if you can create what you're talking about. So I like to ask, "How do you know when you know something?" My answer is when you can create what you say you know.

F/K: When I review your work, the ideas that I think of first, maybe because I studied them first, are the concepts of single and double loop learning. I suspect people would mention those more than any of your other contributions. Would you mind repeating these basic concepts for our readers?

ARGYRIS: Our fundamental notion is that human beings have theories of action in their heads as to how to behave. There are two kinds: One is the one they espouse, and the other the one they actually use. The "theory in use" we found is the same all over the world. We couldn't believe this – for two years, we couldn't believe that something we called Model I wouldn't be different in any culture, between men and women, blacks and whites, young and old, poor and wealthy, well-educated and so on. We thought that if you had no variance, you were doing lousy research or you had a terrible theory or both. We began to realize that there is one way to better understand it, which is that the theory in use is like a master program that doesn't vary. But the behavior that people use to implement it may vary. So bypassing defensiveness in Britain is called being civilized, in Japan it may be called "saving face." And their words about being civilized or diplomatic may vary, but the theory in use is always the same. "If you sense an embarrassment or threat, bypass the embarrassment or threat and act as if you're not bypassing." That rule holds across all cultures, but the way they implement it doesn't. This master design is called Model I. Single loop learning is when you detect and correct an error and don't monkey with Model I. You leave that alone.

Figure 1.1   Theory-in-use models

Model one theory-in-use	*Model two theory-in-use*
Governing values held by users	**Governing values held by users**
1. Be in unilateral control of situations.	1. Utilize valid information.
2. Strive to win and not to lose.	2. Promote free and informed choice.
3. Suppress negative feelings in sell and others.	3. Assume personal responsibility to monitor one's effectiveness.
4. Be as rational as possible.	
	Action strategies
Action strategies	1. Design situations or environments where participants can be original and can experience high personal causation (psychological success, confirmation, essentiality).
1. Advocate your position	
2. Evaluate the thoughts and actions of others (and your own thoughts and actions).	2. Protection of self is a joint enterprise and oriented toward growth (speak in directly observable categories, seek to reduce blindness about own inconsistency and incongruity).
3. Attribute causes for whatever you are trying to understand.	3. Protection of others is promoted bilaterally.
Learning outcomes	
1. Limited or inhibited.	**Outcomes**
2. Consequences that encourage misunderstanding.	1. Learning is facilitated.
3. Self-fueling error processes.	2. Persistent reduction of defensive organizational routines is facilitated.
4. Single-loop learning.	3. Double-loop learning is generated.

In Model II learning, double-loop learning, you detect and correct an error by first reexamining the underlying values. In Model I you just say, "Oh, something's wrong. Well I'll change my words or I'll change the subject."

F/K: It may be an oversimplification, but I've made the comparison that single loop learning is maintenance learning or getting better at what we already know how to do, and double-loop learning is basically asking if we are doing the right thing.

ARGYRIS: That's exactly right. But what's happening in the world today is that the executives who have spent millions on all sorts of cultural changes and seen little payoff have begun to conclude that the single-loop learning stuff is inadequate for cultural changes. It may be adequate to teach people how to manipulate a punch press function more effectively or, as you put it, how to do the routine more effectively.

F/K: In my opinion, the best title of all the things you've written was "Teaching Smart People How to Learn." Why do smart people find it difficult to learn?

ARGYRIS: There are two reasons. I interviewed about 800 people who were MBAs and had gone to work in business, most of them in consulting. They were bright, had very good academic records, and, compared to other human beings, they had few academic failures. They may have had other kinds of failures, but not academic. Therefore, their muscles, if you will, for dealing with failure were not very strong. And since they were bright, they had developed all sorts of fancy footwork to prevent themselves from experiencing failure. Some of that footwork included out-talking other people, outgunning them, and so on.

F/K: So they have more sophisticated defensive routines?

ARGYRIS: Much more so. These people did not only fear failure, they feared even thinking of fearing failure. So they became very brittle. And if they made an error, it seemed to me they overreacted. So what happens when I try to help them do some double-loop learning? At Harvard, in one instance, students were trying to learn something in any way they could. Finally one student said, "Look I do it this way, I see it's wrong, I do it that way, I see it's wrong, hell, I'm stuck." And I said, "Yes, this is the moment for learning. What I'm asking you to leave is your 'program.' It's almost wired in – this Model I." Most of the students almost panicked, but a few, and it's interesting – as I recollect the women were in the lead on this – were willing to say, "Wait a minute, why can't we learn this other model?" So they gave themselves permission to stumble in the process of learning. Many of them were Baker scholars and great at one kind of learning. But this was not something they had expected to be asked to do in a course on organization and individual learning.

F/K: There's a wonderful scene in "Dead Poet's Society" where you can see the class valedictorian taking notes on an essay entitled "How to Appreciate Poetry." After the essay has been completed, Robin Williams tells the class to tear it out of the book because the idea of directions on how to appreciate poetry was terrible. As less successful students get into tearing up part of the text, this "good student" goes to pieces because the new approach is not how he got to be valedictorian.

ARGYRIS: And in a world where they're paid highly because they're bright, especially in the consulting world, they rarely face up to their own defensive routines. I remember one young man who made an interesting presentation and the CEO said, "I don't know what you're talking about." The consultant became flustered. In order to increase the level of proof he brought in more slides and more regression analysis and consequently frustrated the client even more. The senior officer of the consulting firm said to the young man, "I don't hear him [the CEO] telling you that you need more of this kind of information. Why don't we ask him what it is that he's seeking, what kind of knowledge could we give him to prompt him to say, 'Now that's my company'." The senior person was willing to be sensitive to the fears and frustrations of the CEO. I don't think the younger person was willing or capable of doing so at that time. But he learned to become more capable through coaching and experience.

F/K: In our interview with Peter Senge, he made reference to something you said 20 years or so ago about organizational learning. Do you remember where that was and what the context was?

ARGYRIS: Oh yes, we refer back to that in *Organizational Learning II*. In fact, we have a section on "What is an organization that it might learn?" The gist of the argument is that when organizational learning is being created, it is done by individuals. Organizations can create contexts in which they enable these individuals to do single- or double-loop learning. And organizations have an important responsibility to create these enabling contexts. But it's the individual who has the skill or the competence to be enabled to do something – to create actionability.

F/K: This was 20 years before anyone else was using the term "organizational learning." To your knowledge, was this the first reference to this concept?

ARGYRIS: Yes. Our first book was published in the mid-70s, and the comments of every publisher we approached were, "We know you and we know Don and respect both of you, but do you think this topic will ever be of interest to the business community?" So, as you can see, they were kind of perplexed. But I think we were a bit lucky in two ways. One, we said yes and turned out to be right. And two, they were willing to take the chance. And so I would say that, to the best of my knowledge, ours is the first book that focused on organizational learning.

F/K: You laid the foundation very early for some concepts in organizational learning that Arie de Geus and Peter Senge focus on. Peter particularly has extended the audience. You two seem to possess mutual respect and friendship, and he gives you a lot of credit in his own work. What did Peter provide that had been missing before?

ARGYRIS: I remember writing a review of his book and beginning with the sentence: "Read this book!" There are two important things that Peter did. He included concepts like systems dynamics and experimental methods of learning that I had omitted. He widened the context, and he connected our work with that extension. He also wrote an extremely well-written book that was well organized and that communicated to the practitioner at just the right time.

With regards to single- and double-loop learning, given the obvious trends of global competitiveness and the impact of information technology, it's likely that boards are going to require companies to be more adaptive and to turn around problems and be more flexible. If it works, single-loop learning becomes a routine and often becomes intractable, so you need double-loop learning to promote adaptability and flexibility. That's another reason why I think the executives are finding this of interest. They deal with skilled incompetence all of the time.

F/K: Skilled incompetence. What is that?

ARGYRIS: First of all, something is incompetent when the behavior doesn't produce what is intended. There's a mismatch. Model I, if you use it skillfully, will lead to escalating error, self-protectiveness, and self-fulfilling prophecies that are anti-learning.

F/K: A "vicious cycle" to use the terminology of systems dynamics.

ARGYRIS: Yes, but the people we are describing and the routines they use are highly skilled. Model I tells the person, "If you get in trouble, blame someone else. And keep in mind 'win, don't lose.'" This doesn't encourage the kind of reflection where you become aware of what you are unaware of. So when Model I-type negative consequences are being produced, they are often unaware that they're doing it, and the unawareness is skilled. If you ask yourself the question "What is skillful behavior?" I would answer, (1) it works; (2) it appears effortless; and (3) you take it for granted. Indeed you could lose your skill if you start focusing on it. If you're playing a good game of tennis and someone says, "Bend your wrist just a bit," you may say "Aw, come on, let me alone." If you then start hitting the ball out of the court, it is probably because you have become conscious of how you hold your wrist.

The dilemma is that once you're skillful at Model I (or indeed skillful at anything), you no longer pay attention to what creates the skill because you've now internalized it. You are unaware of the impact, but the unawareness is due to the skills you have. It's not an empty hole in your head. The brain is not at all unaware of how to help you be unaware.

Years ago there was a major accounting firm where I met with 17 members of the top management team. We started Sunday night working through cases. Tuesday the CEO said to his group, "I know we're supposed to meet at 8:30 tomorrow, but can we meet at 8:00? I've looked at my case and other cases we will deal with, and there is a pattern to the problems. These are the problems that I thought we'd solved with this cultural change that we spent $3 million on and now, two years later, we are doing exactly what we thought we had changed." The partner in charge of human resources said, "Yes, but you attended the program, and rated it very highly." And the CEO replied: "That's my big dilemma. I honestly felt I had learned something. So I'm asking us to consider what we did learn."

F/K: And that kind of "honest inquiry" laid the foundation you needed to help make that program successful.

ARGYRIS: Yes. First, you've got to get a program that gets at the theories people actually use. That means we have to focus on their actual behavior because with skilled incompetence and skilled unawareness, people may not give us the data we should get, not because they're hiding it – they're just unaware. Often we find that people are skillfully unaware of their own negative impact and skillfully aware of everybody else's negative impact and skillfully incompetent to help do anything about it. The best source of the data we need are actual physical transcripts of meetings where they're trying to solve a problem. We either take copious notes or tape the meetings.

F/K: May I ask you about the use of personal cases? Isn't this essentially the use of the "two column exercise" where people describe a dialogue where they had (or might have) attempted to deal with a problem in their organization? They write two or three double-spaced pages about their conversations, thoughts or feelings about overcoming barriers; each page is divided into two columns. In the right-hand column, they describe what actually was (or might have been) said. In the left-hand column, they describe any thoughts or feelings that they experience while having this kind of conversation. Do you agree that the left-hand column helps reveal "the theory in practice?"

ARGYRIS: Exactly. We use personal cases quite often. First, it's economical from their point of view and ours. Second, with all the observations we make with a group, we still don't know much about what's on the left hand side of the problem – the thoughts and feelings that they are censoring. And if they are skillful at censoring, we wouldn't be able to detect it. Therefore these cases become critical. With the cases and with the tape recordings, we can make an analysis of what's going on. We develop a prognosis of the defensive routines, and then give them the left hand/right hand contrasts, and develop a diagnosis of how they create these defensive routines. I remember Mark Fuller [CEO of Monitor] saying, "This is fascinating, but Monday morning I'm not going to be able to change my Model I patterns." I said, "No, what you need is practice." "So are we gonna get some booster shots?" he responded. "No, I'm going to be available to work with the directors individually or in small groups, when you're trying to deal with discipline problems. Call me, I'm available, we'll record it, analyze it and so on." In *Knowledge for Action,* there are a lot of transcripts that show that is exactly what we do.

So the theory is really simple. First, help them become aware of their Model I. Next, help them become aware of skilled unawareness and skilled incompetence. Third, mix that with the organizational consequences like the organizational defensive routines. Fourth, let them connect those kinds of knowledge with the business decisions they're making. Fifth – practice, but practice must focus on problems they consider to be important. Finally, our notion was we don't go to the next layer of an organization until we can see evidence through tape recordings that the top people are beginning to behave consistently with Model II. By the way, this doesn't mean we throw out Model I – Model I is very good for incremental improvements or single-loop learning.

Eventually the top level got pretty good, but the people at the next level were frustrated and wanted to know what we were talking about with terms like "skilled unawareness," etc. So, on a voluntary basis, the top executives explained the concepts to the next level of management. Interestingly, that turned out not to be a good idea. It's not that they didn't learn, it's simply that they did not possess the skills to teach other people the model. What we did was to prepare a two-day seminar for groups of lower-level people who wanted to learn.

F/K: You have made numerous contributions to many different disciplines, but how did you come to be a co-author of accounting articles? This would appear to be a long way from social psychology.

ARGYRIS: As you know, Activity-Based Costing (ABC) is a technical theory that emerged in the mid-1980s to provide more accurate information to managers about the cost and productivity of business processes, products, services, and customers. Bob Kaplan, who was one of the principal originators of this concept, intended to provide assistance to managers in making better decisions about the use and deployment of their resources. Frequently, after an activity-based cost study revealed new insights about the relative cost and profitability of certain activities, operating managers were reluctant to act on this information. (R. Cooper 1985, Schrader Bellows, HBS case #9-186-051.) In the Schrader/Bellows case, they made a cost analysis using ABC, and to make a long story short, everyone thought it was great, but almost no one did anything about it. That's why Bob Kaplan decided to contact me to see if maybe the lack of action might be due to defensive routines.

F/K: Is it fair to say that Bob Kaplan developed the concepts of Activity-Based Costing and then worked with you on implementation issues?

ARGYRIS: Yes. ABC is a great concept but the principles weren't being implemented. I had two interests in this. One was to develop a way in which organizational behavior could help functional leaders become more effective in Activity-Based Costing and other technical issues. The other objective was to see if I could help them implement this stuff – help change the underlying technical theories that people had.

F/K: In "Today's Problems with Tomorrow's Organizations," you cited the requirements for the organization of the future. We'd like to summarize those. Has your thinking changed in regard to these recommendations since it was written?

ARGYRIS: My ideas have not changed but they may have been somewhat abstract. We've learned how to make the challenges more actionable. In order to implement, you need a much better integration of the technical and behavioral. And I believe you can see examples of how we've done that in *Organization Learning II.*

F/K: You made the point that the real test of an organization was its ability to produce valid knowledge. I assume there is a step beyond that, which says that valid knowledge results in productive, profitable action.

ARGYRIS: Yes, you produce valid knowledge in the service of choice – action that makes choice. Non-action prevents choice.

This relates to what is being called "Knowledge Management" today. The goal which is usually recommended is to simply pull knowledge together and make it available. Unfortunately, I found places where that's been done, but what is assembled is not used with any great enthusiasm by the people who should be using it. A different way of looking at knowledge management is to ask: "How do we manage knowledge while we are interacting with each other?"

If you asked me the ultimate requirement for leadership, I would say it is the everyday, face-to-face relationships to create ways that knowledge is managed so that it is valid and actionable.

F/K: Since retirement from Harvard, you haven't slowed down. Do you still find surprises when you're analyzing data, talking to executives or conducting research? What's a recent surprise?

ARGYRIS: Yes. In fact, that's why I'm so involved and have lots of energy. If I weren't learning, I'd lose a lot of the energy. A current surprise: I'm working with a top management group of a multibillion-dollar organization, and the CEO is a person who understands Model II and also rigorous reasoning. He moved into this firm a couple of years ago and was helping vp's learn these things. We've been observing that group as it has developed, and I would say the majority of people believe that CEO is tough-minded but is convertible and impressionable.

F/K: Is there any assumption that a Model II manager would not be tough-minded?

Figure 1.2 Requirements of tomorrow's organizations

Modern organizations need (1) much more creative planning, (2) valid and useful knowledge about new products and new processes, (3) increased concerted and cooperative action with internalized long-range commitment, and (4) increased understanding to meet the challenges of complexity.

These requirements in turn depend upon (1) continuous and open success between individuals and groups, (2) free, reliable communication, where (3) interdependence is the foundation of cohesiveness, (4) trust, risk-taking, and helping each other is prevalent, so that (5) conflict is identified and managed.

These conditions, in turn, require individuals who (1) do not fear stating their complete views, (2) value and seek to integrate their contributions into a creative total (3) rather than needing to be individually rewarded, thus (4) finding the search for valid knowledge and the development of the best possible solutions.

ARGYRIS: The traditional assumption in whatever was the equivalent of Model I was that the boss would be tough but stay away from pressing people's reasoning and confronting them on issues that might be embarrassing. As I read the recent books on leadership, they talk about being tough. Model II says be tough, you don't back down – you do it constructively. Most of the executives will espouse that, but they often opt for Model I because it has social virtues.

F/K: Have you learned about any of your own defenses through doing this work?

ARGYRIS: Yes, I believe I have learned to make sure that in the interest of being an effective and successful human being, I didn't push people beyond the pace at which they were capable of learning. In fact, my life's work was partially determined by a personal experience with my defensive routines. Toward the end of World War II, I was a young lieutenant with fairly significant responsibilities for an operation in Chicago. As the war effort wound down, I was making plans for my discharge and turning the operation over to a civilian employee. On my last day in the office, I noticed one of the informal leaders in the office, a large, rotund woman, coming towards my office with most of the staff trailing behind her. She proceeded to present me with two nice gifts to tell me how much they had enjoyed working with me and to wish me well in my civilian endeavors. After the brief ceremony ended, she gave me a big hug and kissed me on the cheek. It was a very pleasant, flattering experience.

After I had returned home to New Jersey, I found the people there didn't seem to appreciate me as much as they had back in Chicago. I had a couple of job offers in the Chicago area because the results we had achieved had attracted some attention in the civilian sector. So I returned to Chicago and visited with my successor. During our conversation I asked him, "What was it really like to work for me?" He responded, "Do you really want to know?" Of course what I really wanted was to hear about what a wonderful job I had done, but I do have a commitment to truthfulness, so I asked him to proceed. He began to talk about how demanding and autocratic I had been, and how difficult it was to work for me.

As I was shrinking from this unexpected information, I saw the office leader, so I waved her into the office and explained what had been taking place. I turned to her and said, "What do you think about what he's saying?" With just a moment's hesitation, she responded, "Well, that's pretty much how you were." "But," I responded, "you hugged and kissed me and said that you had enjoyed working for me."

She said "Well, the war was over and we were happy that things had turned out well. But the truth is, we were really glad to see you move back into the civilian world."

That experience was somewhat painful to me, but it was a tremendous opportunity to learn. I suppose that had something to do with my decision to spend my professional career trying to find out what it is that causes people to believe that they can't be truthful in organizational settings.

References

For coverage of many of the points reviewed in this interview, see Chris Argyris, *On Organizational Learning*, Cambridge, MA, Blackwell Publishers, Inc., 1994, and *On Organizational Learning II*, with Donald Schon, Addison Wesley, 1996.

Another recent reference helpful in phrasing our questions was Chris Argyris, "Tacit Knowledge and Management," a working paper, dated November 4, 1996.

Selected bibliography

Organizational Dynamics has published a collection of distinguished articles on this subject, including pieces by Fred Kofman and Peter Senge, Chris Argyris, William Isaacs, Edgar Schein, Dave Ulrich, Todd Jick and Mary Ann Von Glinow, Michael McGill, John Slocum, and David Lei. See *The Learning Organization in Action: A Special Report From Organizational Dynamics,* American Management Association, 1994. To view the work that spurred worldwide discussion and development of learning in organization, see Peter Senge's *Fifth Discipline: The Art and Practice of the Learning Organization,* Doubleday, 1990. The work and contributions of Arie de Geus are summarized in Arie de Gues' *The Living Company,* Harvard Business School Press, Boston, 1997. See Sue Canney Davison in *Executive Development and Organizational Learning for Global Business* (J. Bernard Keys and Robert Fulmer, International Business Press, 1998). For a splendid rationale for learning as competitive advantage, see John W. Slocum, Jr., Michael McGill and David T. Lei, "The New Learning Strategy: Anytime, Anything, Anywhere," *Organizational Dynamics,* 23 (2), 33–47. The concept of dialogue is based on David Bohm's essay, "On Dialogue," and based on a meeting that took place, November 6, 1989 in Ojai, California. Our understanding of "The Tragedy of the Commons" is based on the article by that title that appeared in *Science* (162:1243–8, 1968).

For more rationale on the need for learning in organizations, see R. W. Revans, "What Is Action Learning?" *The Journal of Management Development,* 15, 3, 1982, 64–75; M. Pedler, J. Burgoyne, and T. Boydell, *The Learning Company,* McGraw-Hill, Maidenhead, 1991; P. Hawlins, "Organizational Learning: Taking Stock and Facing the Challenge," *Management Learning,* 25, 1, 1994, PP. 71–82.

For new and emerging practices in organizational learning and leadership development, see Robert M. Fulmer, "The Emerging Paradigm of Leadership Development," *Organizational Dynamics,* Summer, 1997; Albert A. Vicere and Robert M. Fulmer, *Leadership by Design,* Harvard Business School Press, 1998; Robert M. Fulmer and Albert A. Vicere, "Executive Development: An Analysis of Competitive Forces," *Planning Review,* January, 1996; Robert M. Fulmer and Solange Perret, "The Merlin Experience: Future by Forecast or Future by Invention?" *The Journal of Management Development,* Volume 12, No. 6, 1993; Robert M. Fulmer, "The Tools of Anticipatory Learning," The Journal of Management Development, Volume 12, No. 6, 1993; "Tools for the Global Learning Organization" (with Marshall Sashkin), *American Journal of Management Development,* Volume 1, No. 3, 1995; Robert M. Fulmer and Albert A. Vicere, "The Changing Nature of Executive Development and Leadership Development," *The American Journal of Management Development,* Volume 1, No. 2, 1995, Robert M. Fulmer and Jack Goodwin, "The System Dynamics of Executive Education," *Executive Development,* Volume 8, No. 4, 1995; and Robert M. Fulmer, "A New Model For How Organizations Learn," *Planning Review,* (June, 1994). For more information on the development of scenarios for organizational learning, see John A. Gutman, "Creating Scenarios and Cases for Global Anticipatory Learning," *American Journal of Management Development,* Vol. 1, No 3, 1995. Also see, Robert M. Fulmer (SME), *Leadership Development: Building Executive Talent,* APQC International Benchmarking Clearinghouse, Houston, TX, 1998.

2 The link between individual and organizational learning

Daniel H. Kim

All organizations learn, whether they consciously choose to or not – it is a fundamental requirement for their sustained existence. Some firms deliberately advance organizational learning, developing capabilities that are consistent with their objectives; others make no focused effort and, therefore, acquire habits that are counterproductive. Nonetheless, all organizations learn.

But what does it mean that an organization learns? We can think of organizational learning as a metaphor derived from our understanding of individual learning. In fact, organizations ultimately learn via their individual members. Hence, theories of individual learning are crucial for understanding organizational learning. Psychologists have studied individual learning for decades, but they are still far from fully understanding the workings of the human mind. Likewise, the theory of organizational learning is still in its embryonic stage.[1]

The purpose of this chapter is to build a theory about the process through which individual learning advances organizational learning. To do this, we must address the role of individual learning and memory, differentiate between levels of learning, take into account different organizational types, and specify the transfer mechanism between individual and organizational learning. This transfer is at the heart of organizational learning: the process through which individual learning becomes embedded in an organization's memory and structure. Until now, it has received little attention and is not well understood, although a promising interaction between organization theory and psychology has begun.[2] To contribute to our understanding of the nature of the learning organization, I present a framework that focuses on the crucial link between individual learning and organizational learning. Once we have a clear understanding of this transfer process, we can actively manage the learning process to make it consistent with an organization's goals, vision, and values.

Individual learning

The importance of individual learning for organizational learning is at once obvious and subtle – obvious because all organizations are composed of individuals; subtle because organizations can learn independent of any specific individual but not independent of all individuals. Psychologists, linguists, educators, and others have heavily researched the topic of learning at the individual level. They have made discoveries about cognitive limitations as well as the seemingly infinite capacity of the human mind to learn new things.[3] Piaget's focus on the cognitive-development processes of children and Lewin's work on action research and laboratory training have provided much insight into how we learn as individuals and in groups.[4] Some of these theories are based on stimulus-response behaviorism. Some focus on cognitive capabilities, and others on psychodynamic theory. Numerous other theories have been proposed, debated, and tested, such as Pavlov's classical conditioning, Skinner's operant conditioning, Tolman's sign learning, Gestalt theory, and Freud's psychodynamics.[5]

Despite all the research done to date, we still know relatively little about the human mind and the learning process. It seems that the more knowledge we gain, the more we realize how little we know. But let's start at the beginning – we need a common definition of the word "learning" on which to build.

A working definition of learning

Jacques has noted that most words in the field of organizational development – even "manager, ... plan," and "work" – are ill defined. Such words have "so many meanings that they have value only as vague slogans."[6] Such is the case with the word "learning," a term whose meaning varies widely by context.

Levels of Learning: Operational and Conceptual

The dictionary definition states that learning is "the acquiring of knowledge or skill." Thus learning encompasses two meanings: (1) the acquisition of skill or know-how, which implies the physical ability to produce some action, and (2) the acquisition of know-why, which implies the ability to articulate a conceptual understanding of an experience. A number of theorists make this connection between thought and action.[7] Argyris and Schon argue that learning takes place only when new knowledge is translated into different behavior that is replicable.[8] For Piaget, the key to learning lies in the mutual interaction of accommodation (adapting our mental concepts based on our experience in the world) and assimilation (integrating our experience into existing mental concepts).[9] As Kolb states: "Learning is the process whereby knowledge is created through the transformation of experience."[10] Thus both parts of the definition are important: what people learn (know-how) and how they understand and apply that learning (know-why).

For example, a carpenter who has mastered the skills of woodworking without understanding the concept of building coherent structures like tables and houses can't utilize those skills effectively. Similarly, a carpenter who possesses vast knowledge about architecture and design but who has no complementary skills to produce designs can't put that know-why to effective use. Learning can thus be defined as increasing one's capacity to take effective action.

Another way to think about the two facets is as operational and conceptual learning. This distinction is an important part of the model developed here.

Experiential learning model

Experiential learning theory is the school of thought that best accommodates these two aspects of learning.[11] One of the theorists associated with this school is Lewin, whose learning cycle is represented in Figure 2.1.[12]

As Lewin describes it, a person continually cycles through a process of having a concrete experience, making observations and reflections on that experience, forming abstract concepts and generalizations based on those reflections, and testing those ideas in a new situation, which leads to another concrete experience. This basic cycle has appeared in a variety of settings. In the total quality management (TQM) literature, it shows up as the Deming cycle of plan-do-check-act.[13] Deming himself refers to it as the Shewhart cycle of plan-do-study-act.[14] In organizational development, Schein calls his version the observation-emotional reaction-judgment-intervention cycle.[15] Argyris and Schon refer to a discovery-invention-production-generalization cycle of learning.[16]

At the risk of added confusion, I have based my model of individual learning on Kofman's version of the learning cycle, as shown in Figure 2.2.[17] The observe-assess-design-implement (OADI) cycle preserves the salient features of the versions mentioned above, but the terms have clearer connections to activities conducted in an organizational context. In the OADI cycle, people experience concrete events and actively observe what is happening. They assess (consciously or subconsciously) their experience by reflecting on their observations and then design or construct an abstract concept that seems to be an appropriate response to the assessment. They test the design by implementing it in the concrete world, which leads to a new concrete experience, commencing another cycle.

Figure 2.1 The Lewinian experiential learning model

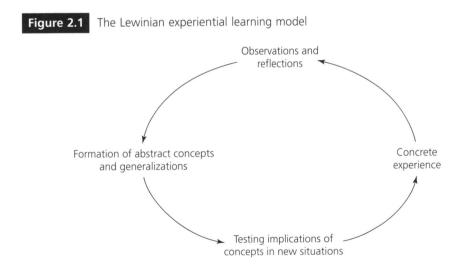

Source: D.A. Kolb, *Experiential Learning: Experience as the Source of Learning and Development* (Englewood Cliffs, New Jersey: Prentice-Hall, 1984), p.21.

| Figure 2.2 | The observe-access-design-implement cycle |

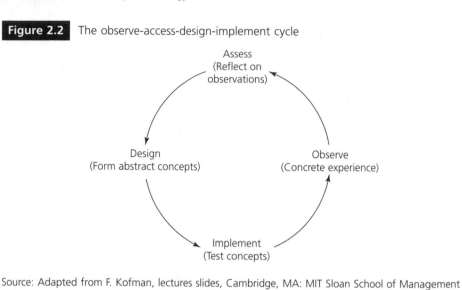

Source: Adapted from F. Kofman, lectures slides, Cambridge, MA: MIT Sloan School of Management

The role of memory

Although the OADI cycle helps us understand learning, for our purposes it is incomplete. It does not explicitly address the role of memory, which plays a critical role in linking individual to organizational learning. Integrating the role of memory will require us to make a more explicit distinction between conceptual and operational learning.

Psychological research makes a distinction between learning and memory.[18] Learning has more to do with acquisition, whereas memory has more to do with retention of whatever is acquired. In reality, however, separating the two processes is difficult because they are tightly interconnected – what we already have in our memory affects what we learn and what we learn affects our memory. The concept of memory is commonly understood to be analogous to a storage device where everything we perceive and experience is filed away. However, we need to differentiate between stored memory like baseball trivia and active structures that affect our thinking process and the actions we take. That is, we need to understand the role of memory in the learning process itself. A good way to understand these active structures is the concept of mental models.

Individual mental models

In Figure 2.3, mental models are added to the OADI learning cycle. Senge describes mental models as deeply held internal images of how the world works, which have a powerful influence on what we do because they also affect what we see.[19] Troubles can arise when we take actions on the basis of our mental models as if they were reality. The concept of mental models differs from the traditional notion of memory as static storage because mental models play an active role in what an individual sees and does.

Simple model of individual learning: OADI-individual mental models (IMM) cycle

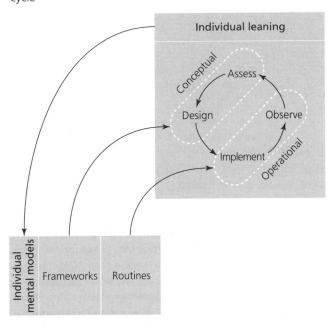

Mental models represent a person's view of the world, including explicit and implicit understandings. Mental models provide the context in which to view and interpret new material, and they determine how stored information is relevant to a given situation. They represent more than a collection of ideas, memories, and experiences – they are like the source code of a computer's operating system, the manager and arbiter of acquiring, retaining, using, and deleting new information. But they are much more than that because they are also like the programmer of that source code with the know-how to design a different source code as well as the know-why to choose one over the other.

Mental models not only help us make sense of the world we see, they can also restrict our understanding to that which makes sense within the mental model. Senge gives this example:

> Have you ever heard a statement such as, "Laura doesn't care about people," and wondered about its validity? Imagine that Laura is a superior or colleague who has some particular habits that others have noted. She rarely offers generous praise. She often stares off into space when people talk to her and then asks, "What did you say?" She sometimes cuts people off when they speak. She never comes to office parties ... From these particular behaviors, Laura's colleagues have concluded that she doesn't care much about people. It's been common knowledge – except, of course, for Laura, who feels that she cares very much about people ... Once Laura's colleagues accept as fact that she doesn't care about people, no one questions her behavior when she does

things that are "non-caring," and no one notices when she does something that doesn't fit the [mental model]. The general view that she doesn't care leads people to treat her with greater indifference, which takes away any opportunity she might have had to exhibit more caring.[20]

People's untested assumptions about Laura play an active role in creating the set of interactions that make their mental model of her a self-fulfilling prophecy. Whenever we take actions on the basis of stereotypes, we risk committing the same error as Laura's colleagues.

Frameworks and routines

The two levels of learning – operational and conceptual – can be related to two parts of mental models. Operational learning represents learning at the procedural level, where one learns the steps in order to complete a particular task. This know-how is captured as routines, such as filling out entry forms, operating a piece of machinery, handling a switchboard, and retooling a machine. Not only does operational learning accumulate and change routines, but routines affect the operational learning process as well. The arrows going in both directions in the diagram represent this mutual influence.

Conceptual learning has do with the thinking about why things are done in the first place, sometimes challenging the very nature or existence of prevailing conditions, procedures, or conceptions and leading to new frameworks in the mental model. The new frameworks, in turn, can open up opportunities for discontinuous steps of improvement by reframing a problem in radically different ways.

To make the dynamics of the link between learning and mental models clearer, let's consider a simple example of driving a car home from work. Most of us probably know several ways to get home. The route we use most often has been chosen based on our beliefs about what makes a "good" route home from work. These belief systems are our frameworks that guide our choice between a route with the fewest stoplights and the one with the most scenic views. Once we have settled on a route, it becomes a routine that we execute whenever we want to go home. Now we can drive home on automatic pilot. If we encounter road construction that blocks our normal route or if our route becomes consistently congested, however, we rethink our criteria of what the best route home means and select a new route. This is our model, then, of individual learning – a cycle of conceptual and operational learning that informs and is informed by mental models.

Organizational learning

Organizational learning is more complex and dynamic than a mere magnification of individual learning. The level of complexity increases tremendously when we go from a single individual to a large collection of diverse individuals. Issues of motivation and reward, for instance, which are an integral part of human learning, become doubly complicated within organizations. Although the meaning of the term "learning" remains essentially the same as in the individual case, the learning process is fundamentally different at the organizational level. A model of organizational learning has to resolve the dilemma of imparting intelligence and learning capabilities to a nonhuman entity without anthropomorphizing it.

The individual-organization learning dilemma

What do we mean by organizational learning? In the early stages of an organization's existence, organizational learning is often synonymous with individual learning because the organization consists of a small group of people and has minimal structure. As an organization grows, however, a distinction between individual and organizational learning emerges, and a system for capturing the learning of its individual members evolves. Argyris and Schon posed one of the main dilemmas shared by all who tackle this issue:

> There is something paradoxical here. Organizations are not merely collections of individuals, yet there are no organizations without such collections. Similarly, organizational learning is not merely individual learning, yet organizations learn only through the experience and actions of individuals. What, then, are we to make of organizational learning? What is an organization that it may learn?[21]

Clearly, an organization learns through its individual members and, therefore, is affected either directly or indirectly by individual learning. Argyris and Schon present a theory whereby organizational learning takes place through individual actors whose actions are based on a set of shared models.[22] They argue that most organizations have shared assumptions that protect the status quo, preclude people from challenging others' troublesome or difficult qualities and characteristics, and provide silent assent to those attributions; hence, very little learning is possible. For example, when confronted with a leader's tendency to steamroll over any opposition, people tend to accept it with resignation as "the way X is," rather than to point out the occasions when the steamrolling occurs. Furthermore, we assume that the person is aware and doing it on purpose, or we assume that the person doesn't want to talk about it. We don't make our own mental models explicit. We don't test our assumptions with that person. Whenever we interact with such people, we "know" they will steamroll, so we act in ways that make it easy for them to do it.

There is little agreement on what constitutes "appropriate" learning, those actions or lessons that should be incorporated into an organization's memory. Organizational routines, such as standard operating procedures (SOPs), are generally viewed as an important part of an organization's memory and a repository of its past learning. However, some argue that SOPs are dangerous because they become so institutionalized that they delay the search for new procedures when the environment changes radically.[23] These theorists advocate minimal levels of consensus, contentment, affluence, faith, consistency, and rationality. Levitt and March, on the other hand, caution that such a situation can lead people to make mistakes faster by, for example, specializing prematurely in inferior technologies.[24]

In reality, both views are correct to a degree; the crux of the matter is knowing when organizational routines such as SOPs are appropriate and when they are not. As Winter argues:

> Routinized competence clearly does not dictate inattention to considerations that fall outside of the scope of the routines; in fact, it should make possible higher levels of attention to such considerations. But the wider the range of situations subsumed by the routines and the better the routinized performance, the fewer reminders there are that something besides routinized competence might on occasion be useful or even essential to survival.[25]

But how does an organization decide when once-appropriate routines are no longer the correct actions to take? Can an organization anticipate obsolescence of their SOPs, or must it always learn by first making inappropriate decisions in the face of changing conditions? Are organizational SOPs different from individual routines? These are the types of issues that a model of organizational learning must address.

Organizations as behavioral systems

Simon proposed the following hypothesis:

> A man, viewed as a behaving system, is quite simple. The apparent complexity of his behavior over time is a reflection of the complexity of the environment in which he finds himself.[26]

This behavioral perspective can be extended to organizations. For example, Cyert and March see the organization as an adaptively rational system that basically learns from experience.[27] A firm changes its behavior in response to short-term feedback from the environment according to some fairly well-defined rules and adapts to longer-term feedback on the basis of more general rules. At some level in this hierarchy, they suggest, lie "learning rules."

March and Olsen make a distinction between individual and organizational action in their model of organizational learning (see Figure 2.4).[28] In this model, individual actions are based on certain individual beliefs. These actions, in turn, lead to organizational action, which produces some environmental response. The cycle is completed when the environmental response affects individual beliefs. Tracing this loop, we see that if the environmental response is static and unchanging, individual beliefs, actions, and therefore organizational actions will also remain unchanged. If there are changes in the

Figure 2.4 Model of organizational learning

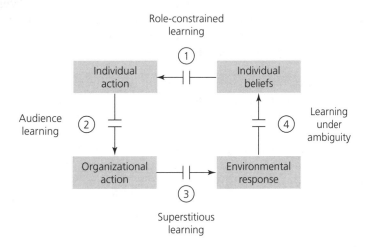

Source: Modified from J.G. March and J.P. Olsen, "The uncertainty of the past: organizational learning under ambiguity," *European Journal of Political Research* 3 (1975): 147–71

environment, however, individual beliefs about the nature of the environment could change, thus precipitating a different set of individual and organizational actions. This will, in turn, set off a new cycle of learning.

March and Olsen's model also addresses the issue of incomplete learning cycles, where learning in the face of changing environmental conditions is impaired because one or more of the links is either weak or broken. They identify four cases where the learning cycle is incomplete and leads to dysfunctional learning. Role-constrained learning can occur when individual learning has no effect on individual action because the circle is broken by the constraints of the individual's role. Audience learning occurs when the individual affects organizational action in an ambiguous way. In superstitious learning, the link between organizational action and environmental response is severed. Thus, actions are taken, responses are observed, inferences are drawn, and learning takes place, but there is no real basis for the connections made between organizational action and environmental response. With learning under ambiguity, the individual affects organizational action, which affects the environment, but the causal connections among the events are not clear. That is, operational learning occurs but conceptual learning does not. Effective organizational learning requires a balance of conceptual and operational learning.

Organizations as interpretation systems

The behavioral view above is consistent with the view of organizations as interpretation systems. Daft and Weick propose a model that represents the overall learning process of an organization: scanning, interpretation, and learning (see Figure 2.5).[29] Scanning involves monitoring and obtaining data about the environment. Interpretation is the process of translating events and developing concepts consistent with prior understanding of the environment. Learning is knowledge about the interrelationship between the organization's actions and the environment as well as the actions that are taken on the basis of such knowledge.

Although Daft and Weick likened interpretation to an individual learning a new skill, I would again separate know-how from know-why and say that interpretation occurs more at the conceptual than the operational level. Their typology of four different interpretation types – undirected viewing, conditioned viewing, discovering, and enacting – is shown in Figure 2.6. The horizontal axis, organizational intrusiveness, is a measure of an organization's willingness to look outside its own boundaries. For example, a technology-focused company's efforts may be inwardly directed (intensive research in core technologies) whereas a marketing-focused company's efforts are outwardly

Figure 2.5 Relationships among organizational scanning, interpretation, and learning

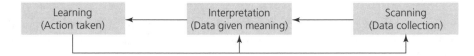

Source: R.L. Daft and K.E. Weick "Toward a model of organization as interpretation systems," *Academy of Management Review* 9 (1984): 286

Figure 2.6 Types of organizational interpretation systems

Assumptions about environment		
Unanalyzable	**Undirected viewing** Constrained interpretations. Nonroutine, informal data. Hunch, rumor, chance opportunities.	**Enacting** Experimentation, testing, coercion, invent environment. Learn by doing.
Analyzable	**Conditioned viewing** Interprets within traditional boundaries. Passive detection. Routines, formal data.	**Discovering** Formal search. Questioning, surveys, data gathering. Active detection.
	Passive	Active

Organizational intrusiveness

Source: R.L. Daft and K.E. Weick "Toward a model of organization as interpretation systems," *Academy of Management Review* 9 (1984): 286

focused (customer focus groups and market surveys). The two axes represent an organization's assumptions about the world and its role in it, the combination of which captures an organization's worldview or *weltanschauung*. An organization's *weltanschauung* determines how it interprets environmental responses, whether it will act on them, and what specific means it will employ if it chooses to act.

The missing link: from individual to organizational learning

Various theories of organizational learning have been based on theories of individual learning.[30] However, if a distinction between organization and individual is not made explicit, a model of organizational learning will either obscure the actual learning process by ignoring the role of the individual (and anthropomorphizing organizations) or become a simplistic extension of individual learning by glossing over organizational complexities.

Daft and Weick's model of organizations as interpretation systems does not explicitly deal with individual actors at all. March and Olsen's model also largely ignores the interactions between individual learning and learning at the organizational level. In their model, individual learning is driven primarily by environmental responses, and organizational learning occurs when the whole cycle is completed. It implies that all organizational learning must be driven in some measure by what is happening in the environment and does not explain what learning occurs within a firm, independent of the outside environment. Other theorists equate organizational learning with the actions of a group of individuals, such as a top management group.[31] They do not identify an explicit transfer process through which individual learning is retained by the organization. Hence, if individuals should leave, the organization is likely to suffer a tremendous loss in its learning capacity. In the next section, I will attempt to build an integrated model that will address some of these shortcomings.

An integrated model of organizational learning

An integrated model of organizational learning organizes all of the elements discussed thus far into a cohesive framework (see Figure 2.7). I call it the OADI-SMM model: observe, assess, design, implement–shared mental models.[32] It addresses the issue of the transfer of learning through the exchange of individual and shared mental models. Analogous to individual learning, organizational learning is defined as increasing an organization's capacity to take effective action.

The role of individuals in organizational learning

In the OADI-SMM model, I have substituted "individual beliefs" in March and Olsen's model with the OADI-IMM model of individual learning. The individual learning cycle is the process through which those beliefs change and those changes are then codified in the individual mental models. The cycles of individual learning affect learning at the organizational level through their influence on the organization's shared mental models. An organization can learn only through its members, but it is not dependent on any specific member, as denoted in Figure 2.7 by the multiple boxes representing individual learning. Individuals, however, can learn without the organization.

Individuals are constantly taking actions and observing their experience, but not all individual learning has organizational consequences. A person may enroll in a dance class and learn a new dance step, but we would not expect such actions to be relevant to organizational learning.

Although such influences as the development and enforcement of group norms, group polarization, and other factors have an effect on individuals, group effects are not explicitly included in the model.[33] However, if we view a group as a mini-organization whose members contribute to the group's shared

Figure 2.7 An integrated model of organizational learning

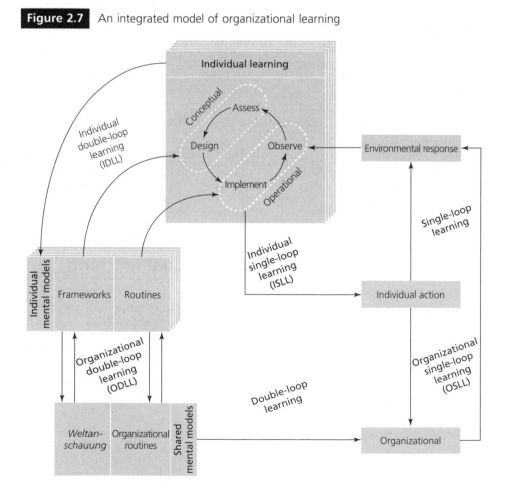

mental models, then the model can represent group learning as well as organizational learning. A group can then be viewed as a collective individual, with its own set of mental models, that contributes to the organization's shared mental models and learning. This is consistent with the notion that groups themselves are influenced by organizational structure and type of management style and, therefore, can be treated as if they were "extended individuals."[34]

The transfer mechanism: shared mental models

Organizational memory, broadly defined, includes everything that is contained in an organization that is somehow retrievable. Thus storage files of old invoices are part of that memory. So are copies of letters, spreadsheet data stored in computers, and the latest strategic plan, as well as what is in the minds of all organizational members. However, as with individual learning, such a static definition of memory is not very useful in the context of organizational learning.

The parts of an organization's memory that are relevant for organizational learning are those that constitute active memory – those that define what an organization pays attention to, how it chooses to act, and what it chooses to remember from its experience – that is, individual and shared mental models. They may be explicit or implicit, tacit or widely recognized, but they have the capacity to affect the way an individual or organization views the world and takes action. Organizational learning is dependent on individuals improving their mental models; making those mental models explicit is crucial to developing new shared mental models. This process allows organizational learning to be independent of any specific individual.

Why put so much emphasis on mental models? Because the mental models in individuals' heads are where a vast majority of an organization's knowledge (both know-how and know-why) lies. Imagine an organization in which all the physical records disintegrate overnight. Suddenly, there are no reports, no computer files, no employee record sheets, no operating manuals, no calendars – all that remain are the people, buildings, capital equipment, raw materials, and inventory. Now imagine an organization where all the people simply quit showing up for work. New people, who are similar in many ways to the former workers but who have no familiarity with that particular organization, come to work instead. Which of these two organizations will be easier to rebuild to its former status?

Most likely, retaining all the people will make it easier to rebuild than retaining only the systems and records. In the first scenario, the organizational static memory is eliminated, but not the shared mental models of the people. In the second scenario, individual mental models and their linkages to the shared mental models are obliterated. Thus when new individuals come in, they have their own mental models that have no connection to the remaining organizational memory.

Even in the most bureaucratic of organizations, despite the preponderance of written SOPs and established protocols, there is much more about the firm that is unsaid and unwritten; its essence is embodied more in the people than in the systems. Comparatively little is put down on paper or stored in computer memories.[35] The intangible and often invisible assets of an organization reside in individual mental models that collectively contribute to the shared mental models. The shared mental models are what make the rest of the organizational memory usable. Without these mental models, which include all the subtle interconnections that have been developed among the various members, an organization will be incapacitated in both learning and action.

This assertion is not as radical as it may sound. There is some empirical support for it in the form of turnover data. As everyone knows, high turnover is costly in terms of time and money because new recruits have to 'learn the ropes' while being paid and consuming an experienced person's time. In fact, the second scenario described above is precisely the case of high turnover taken to an extreme. Companies with a 40 percent to 50 percent annual turnover rate have a hard time accumulating learning because their experience base is continually being eroded.

Radical changes brought about by a new CEO or by a hostile takeover are examples of the first scenario. In many such cases, the organization is completely gutted of its previous **management** style, procedures, and structures and replaced with a different one altogether. Although transitions are times of great upheaval, the organization as a whole usually remains intact.

Weltanschauung and SOPs

As stated earlier, mental models are not merely a repository of sensory data; they are active in that they build theories about sensory experience. Each mental model is a clustering or an aggregation of data that prescribes a viewpoint or a course of action. Conceptual learning creates changes in frameworks, which lead to new ways of looking at the world. Operational learning produces new or revised routines that are executed in lieu of old ones. The revised mental models contain not only the new frameworks and routines but also knowledge about how the routines fit within the new frameworks.

Individual frameworks become embedded in the organization's weltanschauung. The organization's view of the world slowly evolves to encompass the current thinking of the individuals within. In similar fashion, individual routines that are proved to be sound over time become standard operating procedures. Like an individual driving a car, the routines become the organization's autopilot reflexes. The strength of the link between individual mental models and shared mental models is a function of the amount of influence exerted by a particular individual or group of individuals. CEOs and upper management groups are influential because of the power inherent in their positions. A united group of hourly workers can have a high degree of influence due to its size.

For example, Procter & Gamble's *weltanschauung* can be characterized as one in which the company has a sense of community responsibility and believes in the importance of corporate and product brand image. Its *weltanschauung* is also a reflection of its culture, deep-rooted assumptions, artifacts, and overt behavior rules. All of these things moderate its decision making as it encounters unpredictable, nonroutine events. Its SOPs, on the other hand, may include things like a marketing plan to launch a new product, procedures for paying suppliers, employee performance reviews, and hiring criteria. These SOPs allow the organization to respond to routine needs in predictable ways.

Double-loop learning

The OADI-SMM model also incorporates Argyris and Schon's concept of single-loop and double-loop learning on both the individual and organizational levels. Double-loop learning involves surfacing and challenging deep-rooted assumptions and norms of an organization that have previously been inaccessible, either because they were unknown or known but undiscussable. Individual double-loop learning (IDLL) is traced out in Figure 2.7 as the process through which individual learning affects individual mental models, which in turn affect future learning.

Organizational double-loop learning (ODLL) occurs when individual mental models become incorporated into the organization through shared mental models, which can then affect organizational action. In both cases, double-loop learning provides opportunities for discontinuous steps of improvement where reframing a problem can bring about radically different potential solutions. The distinction between conceptual and operational learning and between *weltanschauung* and organizational routines are also integrated throughout the different stages. There is a box around the diagram to emphasize that the whole model is required to represent organizational learning.

Incomplete learning cycles

March and Olsen identified four possible disconnects whereby organizational learning would be incomplete. I have identified three additional types of incomplete learning cycles that affect organizational learning: situational, fragmented, and opportunistic (see Figure 2.8).

Situational learning

An individual encounters a problem, improvises on the spot, solves the problem, and moves on to the next task. Situational learning occurs when the individual forgets or does not codify the learning for later use; the link between individual learning and individual mental models is severed. Regardless of whether the learning occurs at the conceptual or operational level, it does not change the person's mental models and therefore has no long-term impact – the learning is situation specific. Because the individual's mental model is not changed, the organization does not have a way of absorbing the learning either.

   Crisis management is an example of situational learning. Each problem is solved, but no learning is carried over to the next case. Quality improvement is a counter-example; it focuses on minimizing situational learning through systematic data gathering, analysis, and standardization.

Fragmented learning

There are many instances in which individuals learn, but the organization as a whole does not. When the link between individual mental models and shared mental models is broken, fragmented learning occurs. In such a case, loss of individuals means loss of the learning as well. Universities are a classic example of fragmented learning. Professors within each department may be the world's leading experts on management, finance, operations, and marketing, but the university as an institution cannot apply that expertise to the running of its own affairs. Very decentralized organizations that do not have

Figure 2.8   Incomplete learning cycles

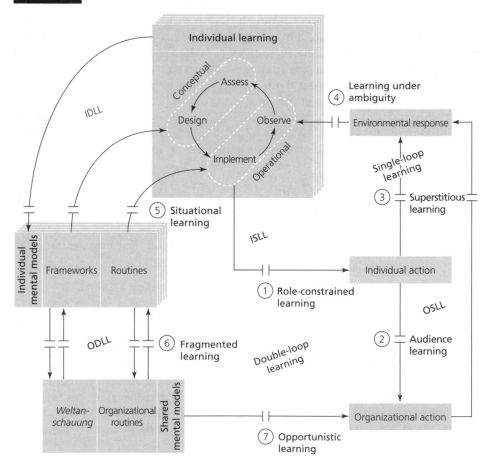

the networking capabilities to keep the parts connected are also susceptible to fragmented learning.

Opportunistic learning

There are times when organizations purposely try to bypass the standard procedures because their established ways of doing business are seen as an impediment to a particular task. They want to sever the link between shared mental models and organizational action in order to seize an opportunity that cannot wait for the whole organization to change (or it may not be desirable for the whole organization to change). Opportunistic learning occurs when organizational actions are taken based on an individual's (or small group of individuals') actions and not on the organization's widely shared mental models (values, culture, myths, or SOPs).

The use of skunk works to develop the IBM personal computer is a good example. The company bypassed its normal bureaucratic structure and created an entirely separate, dedicated team to develop the PC, which it was able to do in record time. General Motors' Saturn is an example on a grander scale, as are joint ventures when appropriately structured.

Implications for research

In the OADI-SMM model, individual mental models play a pivotal role, yet that is precisely an area where we know little and there is little to observe. One challenge is to find ways to make these mental models explicit; another is to manage the way these mental models are transferred into the organizational memory. Clearly, this involves creating new devices and tools for capturing a wide range of knowledge.

Making mental models explicit

If what matters is not reality but perceptions of reality, then fundamental to learning is a shared mental model. However, mental models are a mixture of what is learned explicitly and absorbed implicitly. That's why it's so difficult to articulate them and share them with others. Making mental models explicit requires a language or tool with which to capture and communicate them.

Some progress is being made in this area.[36] However, most efforts at mapping mental models result in static representations of what are usually highly dynamic and nonlinear phenomena. New tools, such as causal loop diagrams and system dynamics computer models, are proving more effective. They allow us to address the problem of incomplete learning cycles.

Beyond situational learning

To close the loop on situational learning, individuals must learn to transfer specific insights into more general maps that can guide them in future situations.

This requires having the appropriate tools for the type of knowledge that is being mapped. Although the English language is useful for communicating on many different levels, imprecise words can lead to ambiguous meanings or inadequate descriptions of complex, dynamic phenomena. Thus English may be perfectly adequate for making one's mental model of a Shakespearean play explicit but be grossly ineffective in explicating a mental model of how the wage-price spiral affects capital investment decisions.

The analysis of dynamic systems, in particular, requires a new set of tools. Senge makes an important distinction between *dynamic* complexity and *detail* complexity.[37] A system can have hundreds, perhaps thousands, of parts that have to be managed, but the dynamics of the whole system may be relatively simple. On the other hand, a system with only a dozen or so pieces can be extremely complex and difficult to manage.[38] The complexity lies in the nature of the interrelationships among the parts whose cause–effect relationships are highly nonlinear and distant in space and time.

Some of the new tools for mapping such phenomena are systems archetypes, a collection of systemic structures that recur repeatedly in diverse settings.[39] Archetypes can help to elicit and capture the intuitive under-standing of experienced managers about complex dynamic issues. They are particularly powerful for advancing conceptual learning because they help explicate know-why and offer guidelines for operationalizing those insights into know-how.

To illustrate, let's look at an archetype called "tragedy of the commons" and how it was used in a car product development team at Ford.[40] In a tragedy-of-the-commons structure, each individual pursues actions that are individually beneficial but that, over time, deplete a common resource and result in a worse situation for everyone. At Ford, component design teams were competing for a limited amount of alternator power output. It made sense for each component team to draw as much power as it required to maximize the functionality of its part. The collective result was an impasse in the design process, as no team could concede what it saw as in the best interest of its own component.

What typically happens in situations like this is that the teams will continue to struggle among themselves until the program timing is jeopardized and someone has to make a decision. This usually means that the program manager has to step in and dictate what each team can have. This makes the teams unhappy because they don't make the decision themselves and some of them don't get what they want. The manager is not happy about having to intervene. The teams think the problem is a heavy-handed manager; the manager thinks the problem is poorly aligned teams. There is no general framework for them to learn from.

The tragedy-of-the-commons structure provides a framework for solving the issue and for transferring learning to the next problem. When the teams saw their situation in this structure, they realized that the problem could not be solved at the individual level; only a collective governing body or an individual with the authority to impose constraints on all the teams could resolve the situation. The course of action was obvious. The program manager would consider all the component designs and decide how much power to allocate to each of them. Those who had to give up some functionality did not like it, but they understood why. Subsequent teams looked at other common resources, such as available torque, and realized that they too fell into the tragedy-of-the-commons structure. A systemic understanding is emerging among the teams that a heavyweight program manager with wide authority over the entire car program makes sense (most Japanese car programs are structured that way).

Mapping the teams' interrelationships allowed them to make explicit the underlying dynamic structure. Once there was a shared understanding of that structure, they could prescribe a course of action. The archetype provides a way of mapping the individual instance to a general framework to guide future learning.

From fragmented to organizational learning

Capturing individual mental models alone is not sufficient to achieve organizational learning. There needs to be a way to get beyond the fragmented learning of individuals and spread the learning throughout the organization. One way is through the design and implementation of microworlds or learning laboratories.[41] Senge describes them as the equivalent of fields where teams of managers can practice and learn together.[42]

The spirit of the learning lab is one of active experimentation and inquiry where everyone participates in surfacing and testing each other's mental models. Through this process, a shared understanding of the organization's key assumptions and interrelationships emerges. The use of an interactive computer "flight simulator" offers the participants an opportunity to test their assumptions and to viscerally experience the consequences of their actions. Management flight simulators represent mental models that have been translated into a more formalized and explicit computer model.

The Ford product development team described above has been running a learning lab codeveloped with MIT's Center for Organizational Learning. The learning lab is now spreading the Ford/MIT core learning team's insights among the rest of the car program members. The learning lab participants worked in pairs with a computer simulator to manage a product development project to meet cost, timing, and quality objectives. Encouraged to make the reasoning behind their decisions explicit, they surfaced the mental models that drove their decision making. They discovered, for example, how their assumptions about the right pace of staffing and the coordination between product and process engineering led to missing all three targets.

At Hanover Insurance, a property and casualty insurance company, groups of claims managers went through a three-day learning lab on claims management. Through the use of the simulator, managers surfaced tacit assumptions about what constituted "right" performance numbers and learned how those mental models directly affected the strategies and decisions they made. In short, they began to see how their actions created their own reality.

Wide use and successive iterations of a learning lab are expected to affect the organization's shared mental models through changes in its *weltanschauung* and SOPs. People leave a learning lab with tools they can use in their work settings; these advance operational learning. The principles embodied in such tools help advance conceptual learning as individuals use them. In terms of the OADI-SMM model, systems archetypes and computer simulators make mental models explicit, thus improving the transfer mechanism and reducing situational and fragmented learning.

Building shared meaning

I believe that the process of surfacing individual mental models and making them explicit can accelerate individual learning. As mental models are made explicit and actively shared, the base of shared meaning in an organization expands, and the organization's capacity for effective coordinated action increases. Johnson & Johnson's handling of the Tylenol poisoning incident is a vivid example of how a deeply shared belief (or *weltanschauung*) on the value of a human life can have a powerful effect on an organization's ability to mount a coordinated response quickly.

On a less grand scale, systems archetypes provide a glimpse of the possibility of developing a similar capability for enhancing coordinated action. As more people understand the meaning behind the tragedy-of-the-commons archetype, for example, the use of the term itself will conjure up the whole story line behind it as well as its implications for action.

At this point, my discussion is more a set of assertions based on anecdotal evidence and preliminary research than a set of facts that has been supported by extensive longitudinal studies and rigorous research. Little empirical work has been done on the construct of organizational memory and shared mental models. Further work is needed for a better understanding of the role of mental models in individual and organizational learning, the types of mental models that are appropriate for representing dynamic complexity, the methods with which to capture the understanding of such complexity, and the means through which new learning can be transferred to the whole organization. I propose the model developed in this chapter as a guide for pursuing these goals.

Notes

1. H.P. Sims *et al.*, *The Thinking Organization* (San Francisco: Jossey-Bass, 1986); and G.P. Huber, "Organizational Learning: The Contributing Processes and the Literature," *Organization Science* 2 (1991): 88–115.
2. See B. Hedberg, "How Organizations Learn and Unlearn," in *Handbook of Organizational Design*, ed. P.C. Nystrom and W.H. Starbuck (London: Oxford University Press, 1981), pp. 3–27; and M.D. Cohen, "Individual Learning and Organizational Routine: Emerging Connections," *Organization Science* 2 (1991): 135–9.
3. On limitations, see: H.A. Simon, *Models of Man* (New York: John Wiley, 1957). On capacity to learn, see: P.M. Restak, *The Mind* (New York: Bantam, 1988).

4. D.A. Kolb, *Experiential Learning: Experience as the Source of Learning and Development* (Englewood Cliffs, New Jersey: Prentice-Hall, 1984).

5. E.R. Hilgard and G.H. Bower, *Theories of Learning* (New York: Appleton-Century-Crofts, 1966). See also: G.A. Miller, "The Magic Number Seven, Plus or Minus Two: Some Limits on Our Capacity for Processing Information," *The Psychology Review* 63 (1956): 81–97; Simon (1957); and A. Tversky and D. Kahneman, "Rational Choice and the Framing of Derisions," in *Rational Choice: The Contrast between Economics and Psychology,* ed. P.M. Hogarth and M.W. Reder (Chicago: University of Chicago Press, 1987).

6. E. Jacques, *Requisite Organization* (Arlington, Virginia: Cason-Hall Associates, 1989).

7. E.H. Schein adds a third dimension – emotional conditioning and learned anxiety – that can have a powerful effect on the first two types of learning. See: E.H. Schein, "How Can Organizations Learn Faster? The Challenge of Entering the Green Room," *Sloan Management Review,* Winter 1993, pp. 85–92.

8. C. Argyris and D. Schon, *Organizational Learning' A Theory of Action Perspective* (Reading, Massachusetts: Addison-Wesley, 1978).

9. J. Piaget, *Structuralism* (New York: Basic Books, 1970).

10. Kolb (1984), p. 38.

11. Other schools include behavioral and rationalist learning theory. See: Kolb (1984), p. 38.

12. *Ibid.,* p. 21.

13. K. Ishikawa, *What Is Total Quality Control?* (Englewood Cliffs, New Jersey: Prentice-Hall, 1985), p. 59.

14. W.E. Deming, *Quality, Productivity, and Competitive Position: Dr. W. Edwards Deming's Seminar Notes* (Ford Quality Education and Training Center, 1992).

15. E.H. Schein, *Process Consultation, Volume II: Lessons for Managers and Consultants* (Reading, Massachusetts: Addison-Wesley, 1987), p. 64.

16. Argyris and Schon (1978), p. 141.

17. F. Kofman, lecture slides (Cambridge, Massachusetts: MIT Sloan School of Management, 1992).

18. L. Postman, "Methodology of Human Learning," in Handbook of Learning and Cognitive Processes, Vol. 3., ed. W.K. Estes (New York: John Wiley, 1976), pp. 11–69.

19. P.M. Senge, *The Fifth Discipline* (New York: Doubleday, 1990a). See also: J.W. Forrester, *Worm Dynamics* (Cambridge, Massachusetts: Productivity Press, 1971).

20. Senge (1990a), pp. 192–3.

21. Argyris and Schon (1978), p. 9.

22. *Ibid.,* p. 17.

23. *Ibid.*; S.G. Winter, "The Case for 'Mechanistic' Decision Making," in *Organizational Strategy and Change,* ed. H. Pennings (San Francisco: Jossey-Bass, 1985), pp. 99–113; C. Perrow, *Complex Organizations* (New York: Random House, 1986); and B.L.T. Hedberg, P.C. Nystrom, and W.H. Starbuck, "Camping on Seesaws: Prescriptions for a Self-Designing Organization," *Administrative Science Quarterly* 21 (1976): 41–65.

24. B. Levitt and J.G. March, "Organizational Learning," *Annual Review of Sociology* 14 (1988), pp. 319–40.

25. Winter (1985), p. 111.

26. H.A. Simon, *Sciences of the Artificial* (Cambridge, Massachusetts: MIT Press, 1981), p. 65.

27. R.M. Cyert and J.G. March, *A Behavioral Theory of the Firm* (Englewood Cliffs, New Jersey: Prentice-Hall, 1963).

28. J.G. March and J.P. Olsen, "The Uncertainty of the Past: Organizational Learning under Ambiguity," *European Journal of Political Research* 3 (1975): 147–71.

29. P.L. Daft and K.E. Weick, "Toward a Model of Organizations as Interpretation Systems," *Academy of Management Review* 9 (1984): 284–95.

30. For example, adaptation theories can be viewed as analogs of individual stimulus-response theories and strategic choice models having similarities with psychodynamic theories.

31. R.E. Miles et al., "Organizational Strategy, Structure, and Process," *Academy of Management Review* 3 (1978): 546–63.

32. For a fuller treatment of this model, see: D. Kim, "A Framework and Methodology for Linking Individual and Organizational Learning: Application in TQM and Product Development" (Cambridge, Massachusetts: MIT Sloan School of Management, Ph.D. Diss., 1993).

33. See D.C. Feldman, "The Development and Enforcement of Group Norms," *Academy of Management Review* 9 (1984): 47–53; D.J. Isenberg, "Group Polarization: A Critical Review and Meta-analysis," *Journal of Personality and Social Psychology* 50 (1986): 1141–51; and J.R. Hackman, "Group Influences on Individuals in Organizations," in *Handbook of Industrial and Organizational Psychology*, ed. M.D. Dunnette (Chicago: Rand-McNally, 1976).

34. R.E. Walton and J.R. Hackman, "Groups under Contrasting Management Strategies," in *Designing Effective Work Groups*, ed. P.S. Goodman (San Francisco: Jossey-Bass, 1986).

35. H.A. Simon, "Bounded Rationality and Organizational Learning," *Organization Science* 2 (1991): 125–34; and J.W. Forrester, "System Dynamics and the Lessons of Thirty-Five Years," *Systems-Based Approach to Policy Making*; ed. K.B. DeGreene (Norwell, Massachusetts: Kluwer Academic Publishers, 1993).

36. See, for example: A. Bostrom, B. Fischhoff, and G.M. Granger, "Characterizing Mental Models of Hazardous Processes: A Methodology and an Application to Radon," *Journal of Social Issues* 48 (1992): 85–100.

37. Senge (1990a).

38. J.D. Sterman, "Modeling Managerial Behavior: Misperceptions of Feedback in a Dynamic Decision-Making Experiment," *Management Science* 35 (1989): 321–39.

39. Senge (1990a); and D.H. Kim, *Toolbox Reprint Series: Systems Archetypes* (Cambridge, Massachusetts: Pegasus Communications, 1992).

40. N. Zeniuk, "Learning to Learn: A New Look at Product Development," *The Systems Thinker* 4 (1993): 1.

41. P.M. Senge, "The Leader's New Work: Building Learning Organizations," *Sloan Management Review*, Fall 1990b, pp. 7–23; and D.H. Kim, *Toward Learning Organizations: Integrating Total Quality Control and Systems Thinking* (Cambridge, Massachusetts: Pegasus Communications, 1990).

42. Senge (1990b).

The concept of learning in the strategy field

Brian Leavy

Competitive analysis-from experience curve to core competencies

The 'experience curve' concept represents the most enduring link between learning and competitiveness in the strategy field to date. During the 1960s the Boston Consulting Group (BCG) under the leadership of Bruce Henderson demonstrated that costs tended to decrease with experience in a predictable and exponential way. In the then emerging semiconductor industry, for example, unit costs were seen to decrease by 30 percent for every doubling of cumulative volume. For Henderson and his group the experience effect was the main justification for strategies designed to build share and win the race to market leadership in developing industries. Superior economies of experience offered a market leader potentially more control over pricing and margins than any of its competitors, and could be used to sustain its competitive advantage. For example, in the early years of the ball-point pen industry, BIC Corporation used experience-based pricing aggressively to accelerate its rise to market dominance and deter late entrants. Lincoln Electric in arc-welding, Bosch and Lomb in contact lenses and Texas Instruments in calculators are among the many examples of companies that have successfully pursued experience-based strategies at various stages in their development.

Experience-based strategies have not always been successful (Ghemawat, 1985). The effect tends to vary from industry to industry, being very strong in semiconductors but weak in many retailing applications. Du Pont in titanium and Monsanto in acrylonitrile are among the many examples where experience-based strategies failed to live up to expectations. In Monsanto's case the strength of the effect was overestimated and the anticipated cost advantages were never fully realized. Even in semiconductors where the effect has been traditionally strong, short product life cycles have tended to undermine its impact. Perhaps the most serious limitation with traditional experience-curve thinking is the implicit assumption that all companies learn at the same rate (i.e. that the effect is related to the cumulative volume produced, independent of time). This assumption has been recently challenged. 'How else can we explain the success of the Japanese automobile industry which learned faster than the U.S. industry with substantially less cumulative volume', as Stata (1989: 64) has argued. A more current view of competitiveness based on learning is that the experience effect is related to both learning opportunity (cumulative volume) and to learning efficiency (time).

Interest in the link between learning and competitiveness has intensified since the late 1980s. This development reflects the recent rise to prominence of the resource-based view of the firm (Wernerfelt, 1984; Barney, 1991; Conner, 1991; Grant, 1991; Peteraf, 1993), to challenge the traditional dominance of the industry organization perspective (Caves, 1980; Porter, 1980, 1981) in strategic analysis. In today's environment, where product life cycles are shortening, technologies are converging, and industry structures are becoming more diffuse, there is a growing belief that the key focus for building competitiveness no longer begins with market selection and positioning but with the development and nurturing of widely applicable distinctive internal capabilities that are relatively enduring (Rumelt *et al.*, 1991).

The notion of building strategy on core competencies (Prahalad and Hamel, 1990) reflects the shift in emphasis towards the resource-based view of strategy, with implications for our traditional way of thinking about the link between learning and competitiveness. First, it changes our perspective on the link between market share and competitive advantage implied in the traditional representation of the experience curve. The core competency perspective draws attention to the reality that in products of any complexity and sophistication 80 percent of the learning advantages that really matter are to be found in only 20 percent of the key components or subsystems. World manufacturing share of such core products is often a more reliable indicator of where the most important economies of experience are to be found than the market share of end products. Canon laser engines and Honda powertrains are among the most cited examples. Second, it elaborates on the nature of the learning advantage and why it can be difficult to imitate. According to Prahalad and Hamel (1990) core products, like Honda powertrains, embody the more fundamental drivers of competitiveness, a company's core competencies. The most significant feature of core competencies, as Prahalad and Hamel conceive of them, is that they reflect collective learning in how to coordinate diverse operating skills and integrate multiple streams of technologies. It is their deep embeddedness within the social fabric of an organization that makes such competencies difficult to isolate and imitate. Reverse-engineering Honda powertrains will reveal the company's key technologies but not its most strategically significant know-how, which is usually rooted in myriads of shared tacit knowledge sets and intuitive understandings, that are not so easy to identify and replicate.

This firm-specific view of organizational learning, and its potential as a source of enduring competitiveness, contrasts sharply with that implicit in traditional experience-curve thinking, where not only are all companies assumed to learn at the same rate, but the nature of the learning is largely taken to be generic. It focuses attention on to the creation of an appropriate and effective learning culture within the organization as the key to competitiveness, as much if not more so than the obsessive pursuit of market leadership. However, the question of how to create the effective learning organization is still a very challenging one. Furthermore, the deeply-embedded nature of the learning in question is not unproblematic, and may eventually become a barrier to further learning, turning today's advantage into tomorrow's liability, as we will see later on.

Core competencies and corporate strategy

Diversification

The corporate strategy literature, since the beginning, has been concerned with two major issues; diversification and vertical integration. The concept of learning is helping to generate some fresh perspective in both of these areas.

For most of the 1960s and 1970s the concept of strategy was seen as almost synonymous with diversification. The classic Chandler (1962); Wrigley (1970); Rumelt (1974) series of studies on strategy and structure were all concerned with how the match between diversification strategy (related or unrelated) and structure (centralized or decentralized) was linked to economic performance. This was the period when the decentralized, multi-divisional form of organization seemed to offer a structural innovation capable of accommodating almost unlimited growth across a wide array of disparate business activities within a single corporate entity. At the time, the spectacular success of conglomerates like Textron, with interests in activities as diverse as military helicopters, gold bracelets, chain saws, writing paper, and fine china, seemed to confirm this view (Bettis and Hall, 1983). The dominant strategy paradigm of the time, the Boston Consulting Group's growth-share matrix (Henderson, 1973), was developed to help diversifying companies with two major strategic issues; what businesses to be in, and how to allocate scarce corporate resources among them. The diversifying corporation was seen as a portfolio of businesses or strategic business units, each with its own distinct markets, products and dedicated resources and skills. The goal of corporate strategy was to develop a balanced portfolio of growing ('stars'-net cash users) and mature businesses ('cash cows'-net cash generators) to maintain the rate of expansion that shareholders had come to expect, while being able to fund it primarily from internal sources.

In spite of the early successes of companies like Textron, the history of extensive diversification over the longer term has been anything but spectacular. In the 1980s, Nathanson and Cassano (1982), in a study of over two hundred companies, found that returns had actually declined with increasing product diversity. Likewise, Porter's (1987: 43) research demonstrated that the longer run track record of diversification strategies in even the most prestigious companies was 'dismal' and the overall impact on shareholder value was disappointing.

Prahalad and Bettis (1986), Porter (1987), and Prahalad and Hamel (1990) have all offered explanations for the relatively poor track records of diversification strategies that have the concept of learning as a central element.

According to Prahalad and Bettis (1986) any corporate management team, at any given point in time, has an inbuilt limit to the extent of diversity that it can successfully manage. This limit may have less to do with product/market variety than with strategic diversity. Coherence can often be achieved by following a similar strategic emphasis or 'dominant logic' across a diverse range of businesses, as companies like Emerson Electric have been able to do. Any corporate management team may have only a limited range of dominant logics or shared cognitive schemata through which it can manage diverse activities effectively. For example, the 'mental maps' that guided the diverse manufacturing activities of the British conglomerate BTR did not extend successfully to its diversification into distribution (Campbell *et al.*, 1995: 127). According to Prahalad and Bettis (1986: 499) the capacity to add or change dominant logics, in order to extend the amount of strategic variety that can be managed, may 'revolve around the ability of the firm or its dominant coalition to learn'.

For Porter (1987) the main reason for the poor track record of diversification strategies has been the failure to address the question of how a corporation adds value to its individual businesses. The business portfolio approach, represented in the BCG growth share matrix, tended to concentrate primarily on the role of the corporation as 'banker' or supplier of capital (Besanko *et al.*, 1996) . However, where efficient capital markets exist, this role alone adds little value. For Porter (1987) one of the keys to successful diversification is to find opportunities to transfer skills and share learning among the different businesses. Marriot and Banc One are among the many examples of companies that have successfully diversified based on the transfer of expertise and the sharing of learning.

While Porter (1987) and Prahalad and Hamel (1990) both emphasize the significance of learning in successful diversification, their perspectives are different. According to Porter (1987) successful corporate strategies must grow out of and reinforce competitive strategy at the business unit level. This is the traditional view of corporate strategy which starts with the question of what businesses to be in and then considers how the opportunity to transfer learning should influence the selection of additions to the overall portfolio. Prahalad and Hamel (1990) argue for the opposite starting point. For them the central question in corporate strategy should begin with the selection of the deeply layered learning sets or enduring and enhanceable core competencies on which the future of the corporation is to be built, and only then to consider to what attractive business opportunities such competencies should be applied. Where Porter (1987: 46) argues that 'diversified corporations do not compete, only their business units do', Prahalad and Hamel (1990: 81) suggest that competitiveness derives from 'management's ability to consolidate corporate-wide technologies and production skills' into core competencies that can 'spawn unanticipated products'.

For Prahalad and Hamel, the distinguishing feature of those companies with long track records of successful diversification, like Honda and Canon, is their tendency to conceive of their companies as portfolios of competencies and not just businesses. The major problem with the traditional business portfolio approach is that it tends to fragment key resources and skills and lock them in at the individual strategic business unit level. This inhibits the development of the critical corporate-wide competencies on which successful diversification strategies are based. Such strategies are built upon depth of firm-specific learning in a limited number of critical areas combined with breadth of imagination in their application, since few companies are likely to excel in more than five or six of these fundamental competencies. It is Honda's learning in small engines and powertrains, applied successfully to product markets as diverse as motorcycles, automobiles, lawnmowers and snow blowers. It is Canon's depth of expertise in fine optics, precision mechanics, fine chemicals and semiconductors, applied to such diverse businesses as calculators, cameras, office copiers and laser printers. Successful diversification, based on depth of learning and breadth of application is not confined to manufacturing. Wal-Mart, in the services area, has been very successful in leveraging its depth of learning in core logistical capabilities across a diverse range of imaginative retailing and wholesaling formats.

Vertical integration

Corporate strategy has always been concerned with the question of vertical as well as horizontal scope. Until quite recently a notable characteristic of the process of economic development had been the rise of the vertically integrated corporation and the increase in the volume of economic activity transacted within large corporate hierarchies. For a long time this trend seemed inexorable (Galbraith, 1956; Chandler, 1977). However, since the early 1980s, the trend towards vertical integration has been stemmed and even reversed (Peters, 1992b; Carroll, 1994). The economic rules of the game in many industries have since changed to favour more focused players and more extensive outsourcing, with the emergence of more sophisticated intermediate markets for key components, subsystems and services, and the growing influence of the non-traditional partnership approach to relationships with suppliers (Verity, 1992).

The core competency approach to corporate strategy, when combined with the partnership approach to supplier relations, is providing a new perspective on the strategic analysis of vertical integration. Traditionally, companies were advised to avoid close dependency on a limited number of suppliers, and the development of any substantial specialized investments or switching costs in supplier relations because of the risk of opportunism (Williamson, 1975; Porter, 1980). However, this central tenet of the transaction cost economics perspective on vertical integration and outsourcing has since been challenged by the widespread empirical evidence of the substantial economies of cooperation enjoyed by many firms, like Toyota and Marks and Spencer, based on close partnerships with suppliers. Such economies typically include closer coordination of schedules, cooperation on product and process improvements and joint efforts on reductions in cost and inventory investment (Leavy, 1994). For authors like Quinn and Hilmer (1994: 43) the core competency and supplier-partnership perspectives combine to provide a strong argument for companies to concentrate their resources on those activities in which they can achieve 'definable preeminence and provide unique value for customers' and to outsource as much of the rest as possible, particularly where suitable intermediate markets exist. Strategic outsourcing can offer a company 'the full utilization of external suppliers' investments, innovations and specialized professional capabilities that would be prohibitively expensive or even impossible to duplicate internally' (Quinn and Hilmer, 1994: 43). Such an approach allows a network of focused partners with complementary core competencies to produce 'more overall learning and innovation than would occur in highly integrated, bureaucratic firms' (Dyer and Ouchi, 1993: 58). Partnering companies are thus able to harness each other's cumulative learning and still further deepen their own through the wider access to new ideas that such relationships can provide.

However, there are dangers with strategic outsourcing that are also learning related. Critics of extensive outsourcing point out that activities like engineering and manufacturing are not so much discrete as related sets of skills and know-how. Outsourcing the one can impoverish the other. Core competencies, as Prahalad and Hamel (1990) emphasize, are synonymous with neither discrete functions nor technologies but are deeply rooted in the collective know-how that is reflected in their integration. The most proprietary elements are rooted in tacit knowledge and intuitive understanding, like the 'combustion recipe' at Cummins Engineering, which cannot be simply replicated even by competitors using identical components (Venkatesan, 1992: 99). That is why some companies that are extensive users of outsourcing often retain some manufacturing capability or on-site engineering presence in their suppliers' plants in order to protect and develop the underlying cross-functional competencies that are the key to their future success. Even in the most traditional industries, companies that seek to consciously build their competitiveness on deeply-layered learning see the integration of engineering and manufacturing as key to this process. The chief executive of Chaparral Steel, Gordon Forward, has recently described his company as a learning organization in which 'everybody is in research and development' and the 'plant is our laboratory' (Leonard-Barton, 1992a: 29).

Outsourcing strategies can run the risk not only of fragmenting current competencies but also of mortgaging the company's future. As Lei and Slocum (1992: 81) pointed out, many firms relying on outsourcing to improve their competitiveness 'may find their skill sets deteriorating as they become "locked out" from learning new skills and technologies critical to participating in industry evolution'. Increasingly in many industries, from consumer electronics to personal computers, the key technologies are moving further upstream from final products to critical subsystems and components (Kumpe and Bolwijn, 1988), and outsourcing for present advantage can result in the unintended transfer of the most significant part of an industry's experience curve from a company to its suppliers. For example, future developments in the television industry will take place in integrated circuits, surface mount devices and picture tubes, and any manufacturer not deepening its own internal competencies in these critical areas will be in a weak competitive position. Competing for the future increasingly involves a commitment to winning the 'race to learn' in the present and to 'capture investment initiative from firms that are either unwilling or unable to invest in core competency leadership' (Hamel and Prahalad, 1994: 167). Locking in key learning opportunities is the logic that influences companies with proprietary component technologies, like Canon in laser printer engines, to supply their competitors at the expense of short term advantage.

How to use outsourcing to complement and enhance critical competencies rather than to undermine them remains a formidable strategic challenge. For companies like Canon, itself an extensive user of outsourcing, the key is to recognize which combination of learning sets will be most vital to the market opportunities of tomorrow. For example, the company continues to manufacture semiconductors in house, although it readily recognizes that it cannot compete with the leaders in that industry in terms of either technology or efficiency. However, it retains this capability and learning opportunity in the belief that the key to its own future, in the office products industry and beyond, lies in the anticipated technological convergence of optics and electronics, and in the optoelectronic competencies that it can develop.

Learning and innovation

One of the most fundamental ways in which the concept of learning is influencing current perspectives on strategy is in its links with innovation.

During the expansionary 1960s and 1970s the main preoccupation of the strategy field was with the question of what businesses to be in, and much of strategic management theory and practice was focused on helping companies to target appropriate markets to enter, often by acquisition, to sustain growth beyond the limits of the core business. In the 1980s the emphasis shifted dramatically. The combination of low growth, intensifying international competition, and poor diversification records, forced many companies to concentrate on the revitalization of their core businesses and on the need to become more innovative (Peters and Waterman, 1982; Kanter, 1983; Drucker, 1985; Quinn, 1985). In the volatile and dynamic environment of the 1990s this need has, if anything, become even more pressing. 'To innovate is to survive', according to the Canadian expert on the new economy, Nuala Beck (1992), while Tom Peters (1990, 1991) warns companies even more imperatively to 'get innovative or get dead'.

The concept of learning in the strategy field is associated with innovation at a number of levels. We see it involved in an organization's research and development efforts, through which it tries to develop the core scientific and technological competencies from which its future product streams will flow. We also see learning impact innovative capability at the business process level, as organizations seek to improve their ability to bring technologies to market in the most timely fashion. Finally we see learning impact innovation at the institutional level as companies try to harness the creative potential of all of their people and the cumulative power of myriads of small ideas, or what Kanter (1988) and others have referred to as the 'thousand flowers' approach to innovation, through systematic programmes for continuous improvement.

Technological trajectories and competency development

The technological trajectories of many industries appear to follow a cyclical pattern, with long periods of evolutionary development punctuated by sharp discontinuities of a frame-breaking or disruptive nature (Tushman and Anderson, 1986; Utterback, 1994; Bower and Christensen, 1995). When any radically new technology appears on the scene, it typically heralds a period of ferment where a number of competing designs vie to win the race for widespread market acceptance. Sooner or later the underlying economics of commercialization will favour the emergence of a dominant design as industry standard (Tushman and Anderson, 1986; Utterback, 1994). It is only after its emergence that the technological trajectory becomes predictable enough to encourage the industry as a whole to concentrate on generating the kind of economies of experience and standardization that are typically needed to bring the cost down to the level required to create a mass market.

The first period after the emergence of the dominant design is, therefore, usually one of continuous development, characterized by incremental, competency-enhancing innovations to improve the product and the production process. These industry-wide improvements happen through the interaction of many organizations, as experience with the new technology becomes more widely dispersed. These improvements tend to 'extend the underlying technology and reinforce the established technological order' (Tushman and Anderson, 1986: 441). This situation can change radically following a technological breakthrough that offers a sharp price-performance improvement.

The overall effect on the industry's future evolution and each individual company's competitive position depends on whether the discontinuity is competency-enhancing or competency-destroying (Abernathy and Clark, 1985; Tushman and Anderson, 1986). Competency-enhancing innovations, like the turbofan advance in jet engines, are rooted in the know-how of the technology that they are replacing. Competency-destroying innovations, on the other hand, threaten to make this know-how obsolete and destabilize the industry structure, as happened in the case of the electronic watch. Learning capability, at both the technological and business process levels, is clearly an important determinant of how any company will fare during these rare but future-defining periods.

Absorptive capacity and technological leadership

According to economic commentators like Robert Reich (1987), the technological trajectories of many industries, from automobiles to electronics, will continue to be evolutionary, and to favour continuous, incremental innovation over frame-breaking invention. Often the key to being competitive in such industries rests less on inventive capability than on the ability to push an existing technology in new directions, continuously refining it into a growing stream of new products, which in turn can spawn even further technological evolution. Western thinking on innovation has tended to concentrate excessively on the activities of the upstream inventor at the expense of the downstream engineer (Reich, 1987), and to be 'overly Schumpeterian in its preoccupation with discontinuities and creative destruction and its neglect of the cumulative power of numerous small, incremental changes' (Rosenberg and Steinmueller, 1988: 230). The success of many Japanese companies in propelling themselves to market leadership in industries founded on western invention, like Matsushita in electrical appliances, has helped to redirect attention in the West to the importance of elements in the innovation process, other than invention.

In industries with evolutionary trajectories, the capacity to creatively extend an existing technology, using externally-generated knowledge, is often the key to market leadership and sustained competitiveness. Cohen and Levinthal (1990: 131) refer to an organization's ability to innovate through the acquisition and exploitation of new knowledge, as its 'absorptive capacity'. The deeper and more diverse a company's pre-existing knowledge structure, the greater is its absorptive capacity. Furthermore, absorptive capacity is a potentially difficult-to-imitate source of competitive advantage because of its firm-specific and cumulative nature, and it can be enhanced as a by-product of the firm's research and development, and other knowledge-gathering activities. Absorption alone, or just learning-by-watching, does not confer competitive advantage. It is the ability to creatively use the externally generated knowledge that is the key. Creative absorption requires the active adaptation of technology through the company-wide development of learning processes, external linkages, and strategic information systems that can be quite proprietary because they can only be grown effectively from within (Bolton, 1993).

At the institutional level the ability to integrate the know-how and activities of the major functions like marketing, engineering and manufacturing is also important in speeding up the product development cycle to new competitive standards. As Hamel and Prahalad (1994) have stressed, absorption and integration are just as central to successful innovation in commercial contexts as invention, and are often ultimately more decisive processes in industries with fairly stable underlying technological orders.

At the institutional level the increasing interest in such practices as reverse engineering, competitive benchmarking and continuous improvement programmes in leading western companies is testimony to the widening recognition of the potency of creative absorption in innovation. In all cases the approach is at its most successful when the learning mind-set is institutionalized so that the knowledge absorbed and created is efficiently transferred across the organization. As Prahalad and Hamel (1990) point out, the overall impact depends not only on the stock of knowledge generated but also on the velocity of its circulation, somewhat analogous to money. There are few if any businesses in which the institutionalization of such processes, and the leveraging of the cumulative impact of myriads of small ideas, will not make an impact. This is particularly true of many service industries like mass retailing, where competency-destroying frame-breaking innovations are rare. Leading service companies, like Wal-Mart Stores and Banc One, operate their hundreds of branch outlets as a network of mini-laboratories, where thousands of small, independent experiments are happening every day in diverse locations, as part of the relentless search for further improvements in marketing and operations. The independence and scope of this experimentation provides the requisite variety that improves the odds for success in the idea generating process. The ability of these companies to circulate the knowledge so generated with speed throughout the entire network, greatly amplifies the overall impact.

In this way, organizations like Wal-Mart and Banc One manage to combine successfully the advantages of a vibrant internal market mechanism with a strong sense of corporate purpose; an apparent paradox that would be difficult to live with, let alone turn to advantage, without effective institutional learning processes, and a company culture that supports them. Furthermore, such learning processes are typically unique, firm-specific creations that are 'comprehensible only as an organic whole' and must be grown from within (Leonard-Barton, 1992a: 24). Since such processes are themselves capable of continuous improvement, the difficult-to-imitate competitive advantage that they offer can be sustainable over the longer term (Schroeder and Robinson, 1991).

Learning as a model of the strategy process

The concept of learning is not just becoming more central to many of the traditional content areas of strategy such as competitive analysis, diversification and innovation, but also as a model for the strategy process itself.

When the field first emerged in the 1960s, the development of strategy was primarily conceptualized as a planning process. The early love affair of western business with the notion of strategic planning reached its zenith in the 1970s. However, as the 1970s progressed, developments like the two oil 'shocks', exchange rate volatility and rampant inflation conspired to undermine the credibility of strategic planning as an effective practice in an increasingly unpredictable and turbulent business environment. During the early 1980s further doubts were raised as many leading western companies with sophisticated planning systems saw their markets increasingly eroded by international competitors with less detached and more hands-on approaches to managing their businesses (Peters and Waterman, 1982). Critics now argue that strategic planning has risen and fallen over its 30-year history (Mintzberg, 1994), while even its more ardent defenders at least acknowledge that it has mutated into the more responsive and flexible notion of strategic management (Ansoff, 1994). Most agree that our overall perspective on the strategy process has now moved well beyond the early planning models to encompass a more dynamic and complex view of how effective strategies are developed in organizational settings in which the concept of strategy-as-learning is becoming a recurring theme (Mintzberg, 1987; de Geus, 1988; Stata, 1989; Senge,1990a).

While the debate over the value of strategic planning continues unabated, the notion of strategy as learning continues to gain currency as a more interesting, accurate and useful model of the strategy process. The early roots of the learning model of the strategy process can be traced back to Quinn (1978) and Mintzberg (1978). Mintzberg (1978) found that strategies are formed as much as formulated, with emergent as well as deliberate features, while Quinn's (1978) research indicated that the cohesive strategies of many companies seemed to come from somewhere other than the formal planning process, and were developed in an incremental way as they proceeded flexibly and experimentally from broad concepts to specific commitments. In both cases the strategy-as-learning notion is central. More recently, Mintzberg (1987) has developed the concept of emergent strategy into the notion that strategies are crafted rather than planned, and are moulded through a process that combines technology with imagination, and self-conscious analytical processes with a more tacit experiential sense of things. 'All strategy making walks on two feet, one deliberate and one emergent'; the emergent dimension fosters learning while the deliberate dimension fosters control (Mintzberg, 1987: 69). The crafting/emergent model of strategy making also shifts the unit of analysis from the decision maker (s) to the organization, and from strategy as a blueprint to strategy as a process 'that bubbles up through the system', as Mintzberg has described it (Lloyd, 1992: 103).

This view of strategy as a process of innovation and learning more accurately reflects the way in which strategies are developed today in many companies, like Intel Corporation and General Electric. According to chief executive, Andy Grove, the people at Intel tend to make strategy 'with their fingertips' as happened when the core business shifted from memories to microprocessors in the mid-1980s (Bartlett and Ghoshal, 1994: 81), and his company encourages 'constructive confrontation' between competing technologies and their internal champions as it learns its way into the future in a high risk, winner-take-all business environment (Burgleman and Grove, 1996: 23). In General Electric, once the epitome of the strategy-as-planning approach and the source of the PIMS (Profit Impact of Marketing Strategy) programme and the directional matrix for portfolio planning, the emphasis under Jack Welch's leadership since the early 1980s has shifted in a very pronounced way towards a bubble-up learning approach to strategy generation, designed to release and harness the energies of people throughout the organization (Tichy and Charan, 1989).

The concept of strategy as learning rather than simply planning or decision making has proved to be particularly useful for thinking about organizational transformation, where the process of renewal can often be best understood as a paradigm shift that requires both unlearning and relearning (Sheldon, 1980; Johnson 1988, 1990). This was certainly true in the well documented cases of ICI, Cadbury's and Ford, as well as many others (Pettigrew, 1985; Child and Smith, 1987; Schlesinger *et al.*, 1990). As Nonaka (1988: 57) put it, the 'self-renewal of an organisation can been seen as a process of dissolving an existing order and creating a new one'. The learning involved often seems to require the catalyst of a crisis because top managers and their organizations tend to 'live in worlds circumscribed by their cognitive structures' (Nystrom and Starbuck, 1984: 57). At AT&T, for example, the traditional engineering mindset had to be replaced with a more market-oriented ideology, while the transformation at Ford required the weakening of the finance-dominated mindset before significant renewal was possible (Kennedy, 1989; Schlesinger *et al.*, 1990).

A growing number of proponents of the strategy-as-learning view of process now argue that well-developed learning processes based on principles like 'creative tension' (Senge, 1990a) and 'stretch' (Hamel and Prahalad, 1993) can help to institutionalize the process of organizational self-renewal without waiting for the trauma of crisis to catalyse the process. In today's dynamic environment the process of continual organizational self-renewal has never been more critical. As Ari de Geus of Shell (1988: 71) put it, the real purpose of effective strategic planning today 'is not to make plans but to change the microcosm, the mental models that [the] decision makers carry in their heads', and the critical question in corporate planning is 'can we accelerate institutional learning?'

In sum, the concept of strategy as learning is now attracting increasing attention within the strategy field because of its conceptual and practical potential. As Dodgson (1993: 376) has pointed out, the concept is attractive because (1) it has broad analytical value, which is reflected in the ever widening range of disciplines using it, from industrial economics and strategic management to organizational theory and psychology; (2) it is essentially dynamic in nature and as such its use in theory generation emphasizes the continually changing nature of organizations, and (3) it is inherently 'integrative' and capable of unifying individual, organizational and sectoral levels of analysis. All of these characteristics make the notion of learning particularly attractive in the strategy area because the field of strategic management is itself inherently interdisciplinary (Meyer, 1991; Rumelt *et al.*, 1991; Prahalad and Hamel, 1994), and is concerned with multiple levels of analysis, from the individual and organization right through to the industry and international economy. The dynamic nature of learning, with its emphasis on change and continual renewal, is particularly apt in today's new economy, in which strategies must be continually developed in conditions of transition and non-equilibrium at industry level, where the static notions of strategy as decision making, positioning and fit are becoming less useful and appealing (Stalk *et al.*, 1992; Hamel and Prahalad, 1993).

Issues and challenges

In spite of the growing appeal of the concept of learning in the strategy field, many challenges remain for both theory and practice. We would do well to heed the caution of Hawkins (1994: 71) that the field of organizational learning is still in its infancy, and rigorous, patient research is in danger of being all too quickly overtaken by 'evangelism and commercialization'.

To begin with, the concept of learning at the level of the individual lacks precision because of the complexity of the process, and there are many theories and interpretations that have been advanced to explain it, from Skinner's operant conditioning to Freud's psychodynamics. Do we learn primarily by experimentation or through more cognitive means? Such questions go right to the heart of the current debate between Mintzberg (1990, 1991) and Ansoff (1991), which has recently energized the strategy field. What Mintzberg characterized as a debate between the strategy-as-planning and strategy-as-learning models of strategy formation, Ansoff saw as in fact two competing views of strategy-as-learning, the inductive 'existential model' which he ascribes to Mintzberg, and his own more deductive cognitive model which he further develops into the notion of 'strategic learning' or the 'cognition-trial-cognition-trial' approach. The debate can be likened to the 'grand tension' between theoretical physics ('think-then-do') and experimental physics ('do-then-think') or between strategy as a process of learning through hypothesis generation and revision, and strategy as a process of learning through exploration and discovery.

The debate over how individuals learn is not the only conceptual and practical challenge facing the further development of the strategy-as-learning perspective. Extending the concept of learning to organizations poses its own difficulties. While interest in organizational learning is almost as old as organization theory itself (March and Simon, 1958; Cyert and March, 1963), it is only more recently that the concept of the learning organization has really moved to centre stage in strategic management and organizational analysis. However, according to Kim (1993: 37) there is still 'little agreement on what organisational learning means and even less on how to create the learning organisation', while to Peters (1992a: 385) the notion remains 'maddeningly abstract' and 'perpetually falls short on the specifics'. Most theorists recognize that organizations ultimately learn through individuals (Senge, 1990b; Kim, 1993; Dodgson, 1993). Nevertherless it is also now commonly recognized that the concept of organizational learning means more than the aggregate learning of the individual members, and while such entities may not have brains, they do appear to have the capacity to store and mobilize knowledge and preserve certain behaviours in the face of leadership changes and personnel turnover (Hedberg, 1981; Levitt and March, 1988).

The question of how to build organizational learning capability is further complicated by the widening recognition that learning is a multi-level process. Recently, for example, Quinn *et al.* (1996: 72) argued that the 'professional intellect' of an organization operates at four levels: cognitive knowledge (know-what), advanced skills (know-how), systems understanding (know-why), and self-motivated creativity (care-why). More traditionally the distinctions made between single-loop and double-loop learning (Argyris and Schon, 1978), adaptive and generative learning (Senge, 1990a), higher and lower level learning (Fiol and Lyles, 1985) or first-order and second-order learning (Levinthal and March, 1993) differ somewhat in emphasis but broadly converge around the recognition that the learning processes that foster efficiency are not the same as those that foster strategic renewal and transformation. Adaptive or lower-level learning is the type best understood in today's organizations and most associated with the continuous improvement programmes of total quality management and the like. This type of learning is capable of being preserved in databases and standard operating procedures, and is the level at which modern developments in information and communications technologies are likely to have the most immediate impact on an organization's learning capacity. It is also the type of learning that is focused on improving the competitiveness of existing strategies and exploiting existing capabilities in stable and predictable environments rather than on the development of new ones for more dynamic and uncertain conditions (Ansoff, 1991; March, 1991).

Learning of the higher-level, generative or double-loop variety appears to be required for the crafting of new strategies or for strategic renewal, and relates to fundamental readjustments to the organization as a whole. For such learning to occur a firm must have some institutionalized capacity for 'rethinking' the nature of its business and its current strategic posture in the most fundamental way. The shared cognitive structures implied in such a capacity have been variously represented as organizational ideologies (Brunnson, 1982; Meyer, 1982), paradigms (Sheldon, 1980; Johnson, 1988, 1990) and shared mental models (Fiol and Lyles, 1985; de Geus, 1988; Stata, 1989; McGill and Slocum, 1993; Kim, 1993; Day, 1994; Campbell *et al.*, 1995) in the strategic management and organizational analysis literature. Senge's (1990b: 8) characterization is typical: 'Mental models are deeply ingrained assumptions, generalisations, or even pictures or images that influence how we understand the world and how we take action'. Such mental models are often difficult to surface and change because of their deeply ingrained nature, and finding ways to accelerate this process is one of the major priorities facing those who most strongly espouse the strategy-as-learning perspective (de Geus, 1988). Part of the difficulty in unearthing these models is a reflection of their deep-rooted and often tacit character. Finding new ways to 'express the inexpressible' through the 'store of figurative language and symbolism that managers draw on to articulate their intuitions and insights', remains a major challenge for those who see the process of organizational learning as involving the generation, absorption and sharing of intuitive and tacit knowledge as well as that which is more formal and explicit (Nonaka, 1991: 99–100). Organizational learning of the more tacit and intuitive kind presents a formidable but exciting opportunity for further research, since it is mainly on this type of learning that the most difficult-to-imitate competitive advantages can be developed and the most imaginative strategies created (Mintzberg, 1987; Nonaka, 1991).

The debate on what the learning organization is and how to create it is further fuelled by some fundamental differences in perspective among those most active in the field. Many, like Huber (1991) and Day (1994), still view the concept of the learning organization in information-processing terms. Others, like Nonaka (1991) and Kofman and Senge (1993), see it in a more transcendent way. According to Nonaka (1991: 97) the 'knowledge creating company is as much about ideals as it is about ideas', and about building a 'truly "humanistic" knowledge society beyond the limitations of mere "economic rationality"' (Nonaka, 1994: 34). In a similar vein, Kofman and Senge (1993: 7) see the true learning organization as characterized by a 'commitment to changes needed in the larger world and to seeing our organisations as vehicles for bringing these changes about'. Pragmatists like Garvin (1993: 78) are impatient with the 'reverential and utopian' tones of the transcendents and their tendency to focus on 'high philosophy' rather than on the 'gritty details of practice'. For such pragmatists the acid test for any approach to building the learning organization is that 'if you can't measure it you can't manage it'. Nonaka (1994: 14) would counter with the argument that the pragmatists tend to overemphasize the role of explicit knowledge and problem-solving, 'which centres on what is given to the organisation – without due attention to what is created by it through more tacit, experiential knowledge, rooted in the value systems of individuals'.

These tensions have their roots in the deeper differences between western and eastern philosophies on the processes of learning, experience and knowledge creation (see Capra, 1982), and will continue to energize the debate on how to build the learning organization for many years to come. The pragmatists, with their Cartesian perspective, believe that the learning organization can be designed and finessed, once we understand the basic elements and how they can be made to fit together. The transcendents, with a more organic and holistic view (de Geus, 1997), believe that the basic elements are more active, and interact in a more dynamic, nonlinear (self-amplifying) and loosely-coupled way than that portrayed in the pragmatist approach. As such they believe that the recently emergent theories of chaos and complexity (Lovelock, 1988; Gleick, 1993; Coveney and Highfield, 1995) may offer a much more promising route to understanding how to develop the learning organization than conventional analysis of the structural-functionalist variety. Their model is not so much the machine as the garden, and they view the process of leading the development of the learning organization as more analogous to horticulture than it is to engineering. Where the transcendents and pragmatists do agree is that the development of organizational learning capability requires a 'systems perspective' and the encouragement of greater real-time interaction among people from diverse functions and operations, conditions that are likely to be greatly enhanced by the rapid and exciting developments in modern information and communications technologies.

Finally, there is the danger that the high level of interest in the notion of learning in the strategy field will lead to the uncritical perspective that all learning is virtuous, and inherently linked to values that rise above the level of sectional interests. As Levitt and March (1988: 335) have warned, it is important to recognize that 'learning does not always lead to intelligent behaviour', and that 'the same processes that yield experiential wisdom' in organizations 'also produce superstitious learning, competency traps, and erroneous inferences'. The core capabilities of today can become the 'core rigidities' of tomorrow (Leonard-Barton, 1992b). Furthermore, the recognition that organizational renewal almost always requires some degree of unlearning as well as learning (Nystrom and Starbuck, 1984; McGill and Slocum, 1993) highlights the political character of many organizational learning processes. Strategic renewal, and by implication the higher-order learning intrinsically involved, 'does not occur in a vacuum' but 'takes place in a system in which a certain distribution of power is already entrenched', as Hardy (1996: S9) has argued. Lower-order learning that incrementally refines and finesses an existing strategic paradigm, can also lead to the increasing sedimentation of the existing power structure and its dominance over the company's official ideology or world view (Brunsson, 1982; Starbuck, 1982). Indeed, according to Pascale (1991: 239), lower-level learning systems that tend to reinforce the political status quo can 'take shape in forms that are unseen and undiscussable'. Higher-order learning can therefore rarely take place without political action, and our understanding of the political nature of such organizational learning processes and its implications remains limited and requires much further study.

Furthermore, most organizations find it difficult to achieve the appropriate balance in their learning processes between exploitation and exploration that is essential to long run success (March, 1991). Moreover, many companies seem to face a learning dilemma, where learning is seen primarily as a process of trial and error, with error or failure being the main source of the lessons learned. Successful companies and leaders, with the least experience of failure, usually find it the hardest to learn, and often succumb eventually to hubris (Miller, 1990, 1991). They are frequently very good at single-loop learning of the continuous improvement kind, but ironically this also explains why they are often so bad at double-loop learning of the more strategic kind. Must most organizations face impending failure before they will challenge and change their mental models in any fundamental way, as the literature on strategic transformation and renewal has shown to have been too often the case in the past (Starbuck *et al.*, 1978; Kanter, 1983; Child and Smith, 1987; Pettigrew, 1987; Nonaka, 1988; Johnson, 1988; Stopford and Baden-Fuller, 1990)? Or can other ways be found to encourage this kind of fundamental higher-level learning in successful organizations, through the imaginative use of games, simulations, scenarios and metaphors to generate 'creative tension', or through the early detection of 'strategic dissonance', as some theorists and practitioners are currently trying to explore (de Geus, 1988; Stata, 1989; Senge, 1990a; Nonaka, 1991; Burgleman and Grove, 1996)?

In sum, the concept of learning has never been more central to our future understanding of competitiveness and even more fundamentally to our understanding of the strategy processs itself. In spite of this, however, many interesting questions and challenges remain. Now, more than ever, it presents the basis for a research agenda in the strategy field that is likely to grow in significance for some time to come.

References

Abernathy, W.J. and Clark, K.B. (1985) 'Innovation: mapping the winds of creative destruction', *Research Polity* 14: 3–22.

Ansoff, H.I. (1991) 'Critique of Henry Mintzberg's "The Design School: reconsidering the basic premises of strategic management"', *Strategic Management Journal* 12: 449–61.

Ansoff, H.I. (1994) 'Comment on Henry Mintzberg's rethinking strategic planning', *Long Range Planning* 27(3): 31–2.

Argyris, C. and Schon, D.A. (1978) *Organizational Learning: A Theory of Action Perspective*, Reading, MA: Addison-Wesley.

Barney, J.B. (1991) 'Firm resources and sustained competitive advantage', *Journal of Management* 17(1): 99–120.

Bartlett, C.A. and Ghoshal, S. (1994) 'Changing the role of top management: beyond strategy to purpose', *Harvard Business Review* 72 (Nov–Dec): 79–88.

Beck, N. (1992) *Shifting Gears: Thriving in the New Economy*, Toronto: HarperCollins.

Besanko, D., Dranove, D. and Shanley, M. (1996) *Economics of Strategy*, New York: John Wiley.

Bettis, R.A. and Hall, W.K. (1983) 'The business portfolio approach – where it falls down in practice', *Long Range Planning* 16(2): 95–104.

Bolton, M.K. (1993) 'Imitation versus innovation: lessons to be learned from the Japanese', *Organizational Dynamics* 22 (Winter): 30–45.

Bower, J.L. and Christensen, C.M. (1995) 'Disruptive technologies: catching the Wave', *Harvard Business Review* 73 (Jan–Feb): 43–53.

Bower, J.L., Bartlett, C.A., Uyterhoeven, H.E.R. and Walton, R.E. (1996) *Business Policy: Managing Strategic Processes*, Homewood, IL; Irwin.

Brunnson, N. (1982) 'The irrationality of action and action rationality: decisions, ideologies and organizational action', *Journal of Management Studies* 19(1): 29–44.

Burgleman, R.A. and Grove, A.S. (1996) 'Strategic dissonance', *California Management Review* 38(1): 8–28.

Campbell, A., Goold, M. and Alexander, M. (1995) 'Corporate strategy: the quest for parenting advantage', *Harvard Business Review* 73 (Mar–Apr): 120–32.

Capra, F. (1982) *The Turning Point*, New York: Simon & Schuster.

Carroll, G.R. (1994) 'Organizations: the smaller they get', *California Management Review* 37(1): 28–41.

Caves, R.E. (1980) 'Industrial organization, corporate strategy and structure', *Journal of Economic Literature* XVIII: 64–92.

Chandler, A.D. (1962) *Strategy and Structure: Chapters in the History of the American Industrial Enterprise*, Cambridge, MA: MIT Press.

Chandler, A.D. (1977) *The Visible Hand: The Managerial Revolution in American Business*, Cambridge, MA: Harvard University Press.

Child, J. and Smith, C. (1987) 'The context and process of organizational transformation Cadbury Limited in its sector', *Journal of Management Studies* 24(6): 565–93.

Cohen, W.M. and Levinthal, D.A. (1990) 'Absorptive capacity: a new perspective on learning and innovation', *Administrative Science Quarterly* 35: 128–52.

Conner, K.R. (1991) 'A historical comparison of resource-based theory and five schools of thought within industrial organization economics: do we have a new theory of the firm', *Journal of Management* 17(1): 121–54.

Coveney, P. and Highfield, R. (1995) *Frontiers of Complexity: The Search for Order in a Chaotic World*, New York: Ballantine Books.

Cyert, R.M. and March, J.G. (1963) *A Behavioral Theory of the Firm*, Englewood Cliffs, NJ: Prentice-Hall.

Day, G.S. (1994) 'Continuous learning about markets', *California Management Review* (Summer): 9–31.

de Geus, A.P. (1988) 'Planning as learning', *Harvard Business Review* 66 (March–April): 70–4.

de Geus, A.P. (1997) 'The living company', *Harvard Business Review* 75 (March–April): 51–9.

Dodgson, M. (1993) 'Organizational learning: a review of some literature', *Organization Studies* 14(3): 375–94.

Drucker, P.F. (1985) *Innovation and Entrepreneurship*, London: William Heinemann.

Dyer, J.H. and Ouchi, W.G. (1993) 'Japanese-style partnerships: giving companies a competitive edge', *Sloan Management Review* (Fall): 51–63.

Fiol, C.M. and Lyles, M.A. (1985) 'Organizational learning', *Academy of Management Review* 10(4): 803–13.

Galbraith, J.K. (1956) *American Capitalism: The Concept of Countervailing Power*, 2nd edn, Boston: Houghton Miffin.

Garvin, D.A. (1993) 'Building a learning organization', *Harvard Business Review* 71 (July–August): 78–91.

Ghemawat, P. (1985) 'Building strategy on the experience curve', *Harvard Business Review* 63 (March–April): 143–9.

Gleick, J. (1993) *Chaos: Making A New Science*, London: Abacus.

Grant, R.M. (1991) 'The resource-based theory of competitive advantage: implications for strategy formulation', *California Management Review* (Spring): 114–35.

Hamel, G. and Prahalad, C.K. (1993) 'Strategy as Stretch and Leverage', *Harvard Business Review* 71 (March–April): 75–84.

Hamel, G. and Prahalad, C.K. (1994) *Competing for the Future*, Boston: Harvard Business School Press.

Hardy, C. (1996) 'Understanding power: bringing about strategic change', *British Journal of Management* 7 (Special Issue): S1–S16.

Hawkins, P. (1994) 'Organizational learning: taking stock and facing the challenge', *Management Learning* 25(1): 71–82.

Hedberg, B. (1981) 'How organizations learn and unlearn', in P.C. Nystrom and W.H. Starbuck (eds) *Handbook of Organizational Design*, Volume 1, New York: Oxford University Press.

Henderson, B. (1973) 'The experience curve revisited: the growth share matrix of the product portfolio', *Perspectives*, Boston Consulting Group.

Huber, G.P. (1991) 'Organizational learning: the contributing processes and the literatures', *Organization Science* 2(1): 88–115.

Johnson, G. (1988) 'Rethinking incrementalism, *Strategic Management Journal* 9: 75–91.

Johnson, G. (1990) 'Managing strategic change: the role of symbolic action', *British Journal of Management* 1: 183–200.

Kanter, R.M. (1983) *The Change Masters*, New York: Simon & Schuster.

Kanter, R.M. (1988) 'When a thousand flowers bloom: structural, collective and social conditions for innovation in organizations', *Research in Organization Behavior* 10: 169–211.

Kennedy, C. (1989) 'The transformation of AT & T', *Long Range Planning* 22(3): 10–17.

Kim, D.H. (1993) 'The link between individual and organizational learning', *Sloan Management Review* (Fall): 37–50.

Kofman, F. and Senge, P.M. (1993) 'Communities of commitment: the heart of learning organizations', *Organizational Dynamics* 22 (Autumn): 5–23.

Kumpe, T. and Bolwijn, P.T. (1988) 'Manufacturing: the new case for vertical integration', *Havard Business Review* 66 (March–April): 75–81.

Leavy, B. (1994) 'Two strategic perspectives on the buyer-supplier relationship', *Production and Inventory Management Journal* 35(2): 47–51.

Lei, D. and Slocum, J.W. (1992) 'Global strategy, competence-building and strategic alliances', *California Management Review* (Fall): 81–97.

Leonard-Barton, D. (1992a) 'The factory as a learning laboratory', *Sloan Management Review* (Fall): 23–38.

Leonard-Barton, D. (1992b) 'Core capabilities and core rigidities: a paradox in managing new product development', *Strategic Management Journal* 13: 111–25.

Levinthal, D.A. and March, J.G. (1993) 'The myopia of learning', *Strategic Management Journal* 14: 95–112.

Levitt, B. and March, J.G. (1988) 'Organizational learning', *Annual Review of Sociology* 14: 319–40.

Lloyd, B. (1992) 'Mintzberg on the rise and fall of strategic planning', *Long Range Planning* 25(4): 99–104.

Lovelock, J. (1988) *The Ages of Gaia: A Biography of our Living Earth*, Oxford: Oxford University Press.

McGill, M.E. and Slocum, J.W. (1993) 'Unlearning the organization', *Organizational Dynamics* 22 (Autumn): 67–79.

March, J.G. (1991) 'Exploration and exploitation in organizational learning', *Organization Science* 2(1): 71–87.

March, J.G. and Simon, H.A. (1958) *Organizations*, New York: John Wiley.

Meyer, A.D. (1982) 'How ideologies supplant formal structures and shape responses to environments', *Journal of Management Studies* 19(1): 45–61.

Meyer, A.D. (1991) 'What is strategy's distinctive competence?', *Journal of Management* 17(4): 821–33.

Miller, D. (1990) *The Icarus Paradox*, New York: Harper Business.

Miller, D. (1991) 'Stale in the saddle: CEO tenure and the match between organization and environment', *Management Science* 37(1): 34–52.

Mintzberg, H. (1978) 'Patterns in strategy formation', *Management Science* 24(9): 934–48.

Mintzberg, H. (1987) 'Crafting strategy', *Harvard Business Review* 65 (July–August): 66–75.

Mintzberg, H. (1990) 'The design school: reconsidering the basic premises of strategic management', *Strategic Management Journal* 11: 171–95.

Mintzberg, H. (1991) 'Learning 1, planning 0: reply to Igor Ansoff', *Strategic Management Journal* 12: 463–6.

Mintzberg, H. (1994) *The Rise and Fall of Strategic Planning*, Englewood Cliffs, NJ: Prentice-Hall.

Nathanson, D. and Cassano, J. (1982) 'Organization, diversity, and performance', *Wharton Magazine* (Summer): 19–26.

Nonaka, I. (1988) 'Creating organizational order out of chaos: self-renewal in Japanese firms', *California Management Review* (Spring): 57–73.

Nonaka, I. (1991) 'The knowledge-creating Company', *Harvard Business Review* 69 (November–December): 96–104.

Nonaka, I. (1994) 'A dynamic theory of organizational knowledge creation', *Organization Science* 5(1): 14–37.

Nystrom, P.C. and Starbuck, W.H. (1984) 'To avoid organizational crises, unlearn', *Organizational Dynamics* 12: 53–65.

Pascale, R.T. (1991) *Managing on the Edge*, Harmondsworth: Penguin.

Peteraf, M.A. (1993) 'The cornerstones of competitive advantage: a resource-based view', *Strategic Management Journal* 14: 179–91.

Peters, T. (1990) 'Get innovative or get dead' (part one), *California Management Review* 33 (Fall): 9–26.

Peters, T. (1991) 'Get innovative or get dead' (part two), *California Management Review* 33 (Winter): 9–23.

Peters, T. (1992a) *Liberation Management*, London: Macmillan.

Peters, T. (1992b) 'Rethinking scale', *California Management Review* (Fall): 7–29.

Peters, T.J. and Waterman, R.H. (1982) *In Search of Excellence*, New York: Harper & Row.

Pettigrew, A.M. (1985) *The Awakening Giant*, Oxford: Basil Blackwell.

Pettigrew, A.M. (1987) 'Context and action in the transformation of the firm', *Journal of Management Studies* 24(6): 649–70.

Porter, M.E. (1980) *Competitive Strategy*, New York: Free Press.

Porter, M.E. (1981) 'The contributions of industrial organization to strategic management', *Academy of Management Review* 6: 609–20.

Porter, M.E. (1987) 'From competitive advantage to corporate strategy', *Harvard Business Review* 65 (May–June): 43–59.

Prahalad, C.K. and Bettis, R.A. (1986) 'The dominant logic: a new linkage between diversity and performance', *Strategic Management Journal* 7(6): 485–501.

Prahalad, C.K. and Hamel, G. (1990) 'The core competence of the corporation', *Harvard Business Review* 68 (May–June): 79–91.

Prahalad, C.K and Hamel, G. (1994) 'Strategy as a field of study: why search for a new paradigm?', *Strategic Management Journal* 15: 5–16.

Quinn, J.B. (1978) 'Strategic change: logical incrementalism', *Sloan Management Review* (Fall): 7–21.

Quinn, J.B. (1985) 'Managing innovation: controlled chaos', *Harvard Business Review* (May–June): 73–84.

Quinn, J.B. and Hilmer, F.G. (1994) 'Strategic outsourcing', *Sloan Management Review* (Summer): 43–55.

Quinn, J.B., Anderson, P. and Finkelstein, S. (1996) 'Managing professional intellect: making the most of the best', *Harvard Business Review* 74 (March–April): 71–80.

Reich, R.B. (1987) 'Entrepreneurship reconsidered: the team as hero', *Harvard Business Review* (May–June): 77–83.

Rosenberg, N. and Steinmueller, W.E. (1988) 'Why Americans are such poor imitators', *American Economic Review* 78: 229–34.

Rumelt, R.P. (1974) *Strategy, Structure and Economic Performance*, Boston: Division of Research, Graduate School of Business Administration, Harvard University.

Rumelt, R.P., Schendel, D. and Teece, D.J. (1991) 'Strategic management and economics', *Strategic Management Journal* 12 (S): 5–29.

Schlesinger, L.A., Pelofsky, M., Pascale, R.T. and Ehrlich, S.P. (1990) 'The transformation at Ford', *Case No.* 9–390–083, Harvard Business School.

Schroeder, D.M. and Robinson, A.G. (1991) 'America's most successful export to Japan: continuous improvement programs', *Sloan Management Review* (Spring): 67–81.

Senge, P.M. (1990a) 'The leader's new work: building learning organizations', *Sloan Management Review* (Fall): 7–23.

Senge, P.M. (1990b) *The Fifth Discipline: The Art and Practice of the Learning Organization*, New York: Doubleday.

Sheldon, A. (1980) 'Organizational paradigms: a theory of organizational change', *Organizational Dynamics* (Winter): 61–80.

Stalk, G., Evans, P. and Shulman, L.E. (1992) 'Competing on capabilities: the new rules of corporate strategy', *Harvard Business Review* 70 (March–April): 57–69.

Starbuck, W.H. (1982) 'Congealing oil: inventing ideologies to justify acting ideologies out', *Journal of Management Studies* 19(1): 3–27.

Starbuck, W.H., Greve, A. and Hedberg, B.L.T. (1978) 'Responding to crises', *Journal of Business Administration* 9(2): 111–37.

Stata, R. (1989) 'Organizational learning: the key to management innovation', *Sloan Management Review* (Spring): 63–74.

Stopford, J.M. and Baden-Fuller, C. (1990) 'Corporate rejuvenation', *Journal of Management Studies* 27(4): 399–415.

Tichy, N. and Charan, R. (1989) 'Speed, simplicity, self-confidence: an interview with Jack Welch', *Harvard Business Review* 67 (September–October): 112–20.

Tushman, M.L. and Anderson, P. (1986) 'Technological discontinuities and organizational environments', *Administrative Science Quarterly* 31: 439–65.

Utterback, J.M. (1994) *Mastering the Dynamics of Innovation*, Boston: Harvard Business School Press.

Venkatesan, R. (1992) 'Strategic sourcing: to make or not to make', *Harvard Business Review* 70 (November–December): 98–107.

Verity, J. (1992) 'Deconstructing the computer industry', *Business Week* (23 November): 44–52.

Wernerfelt, B. (1984) 'A resource-based view of the firm', *Strategic Management Journal* 5: 171–80.

Williamson, O.E. (1975) *Markets and Hierarchies: Analysis and Antitrust Implications*, New York: Free Press.

Wrigley, L. (1970) 'Divisional autonomy and diversification', unpublished DBA dissertation, Harvard Business School.

The dominant logic:
a new linkage between
diversity and performance

C.K. Prahalad and Richard Bettis

For the past 35 years product-market diversification of large firms has continued at a rapid pace. Today, over two-thirds of the firms in the USA Fortune 500 are highly diversified and similar patterns of diversification exist in Western Europe and Japan (Rumelt, 1974; Pavan, 1972; Thanheiser, 1972; Pooley, 1972; Channon, 1973; Suzuki, 1980). As a consequence, interest in the relationship between corporate diversification and financial performance has grown among practitioners, academics, and public policy makers.

Accompanying this interest has been a spate of research on the patterns of diversification and the determinants of performance in diversified firms by the academic community. Concurrently, consulting firms have been actively promoting a variety of approaches for managing diversified firms. The results of these efforts have been mixed, at best. There is, as yet, no overall theory that links diversification with performance and the linkage, if any, remains elusive.

The purpose of this chapter is to propose a crucial linkage, which has largely been ignored in the literature on the relationship between diversification and performance; and to show how this approach can add significantly to our managerial understanding of performance in the diversified firms.

This linkage is referred to as the 'dominant general management logic' (or dominant logic) and consists of the mental maps developed through experience in the core business and sometimes applied inappropriately in other business.

A brief review of research on diversity and performance

The purpose of this section is to review briefly the major academic research streams and consulting framework relevant to the relationship between diversity and performance. These represent alternative approaches to research in this area. While significant literature exists in support of each of the streams of research outlined below, we will reference and discuss only the seminal works in each area.

The strategy of diversification

Pioneering work by Chandler (1962) and Ansoff (1965) established the motivations for diversification and the general nature of the diversified firm. Wrigley (1970) refined and extended Chandler's study by investigating the various options open to a diversifying firm. Building on the work of Chandler, Wrigley and others, Rumelt (1974, 1977) investigated the relationships among diversification strategy, organizational structure, and economic performance. Rumelt used four major and nine minor categories to characterize the diversification strategy of firms. The major categories were single business, dominant business, related business and unrelated business. These categories provide a spectrum of diversification strategies – from firms that remained essentially undiversified to firms that diversified significantly into unrelated areas. Using statistical methods, Rumelt was able to relate diversification strategy to performance. The related diversification strategies – related-constrained and related-linked (e.g. General Foods and General Electric) – were found to outperform the other diversification strategies on the average (relatedness was defined in terms of products, markets, and technology). The related-constrained was found to be the highest performing on the average. (In related-constrained firms most component businesses are related to each other, whereas in related-linked firms only one-to-one relationships are required.) By contrast, the unrelated conglomerate strategy was found to be one of the lowest performing on the average.

In 1982 Natharison and Cassano conducted a statistical study of diversity and performance using a sample of 206 firms over the years 1973–8. They developed a two-dimensional typology (market diversity and product diversity) for capturing diversification strategy that refines Rumelt's categories. They found returns remained relatively steady as market diversity increased. However, they also found that size plays an important moderating role on the relationships. For both the market and product diversity, smaller firms did well relative to larger firms in categories marked by no diversification and in categories of extremely high diversification. Larger firms did significantly better than smaller firms in the in-between categories – those characterized by intermediate levels of diversification.

In both these studies linking diversification and performance (Rumelt and Nathanson/Cassano) the key point to note is that *choosing the generic strategy of diversification (how much and what kind of relatedness)* is the key to achieving performance.

Economic characteristics of individual businesses

Porter (1980), among others, established that the characteristics of the various industries in which a firm participates, and the position of the firm's businesses in these industries, impacts overall on firm performance.

Two studies have in fact empirically validated these influences for diversified firms. The widely discussed PIMS program of the Marketing Science Institute (see Scholeffler *et al.*, 1974, for an introduction) has shown that variables such as market share and relative product quality directly influence the profitability of constituent businesses in large diversified firms. More recently, Montgomery (1979) has examined the performance differences in diversified firms using the market structure variables of industrial organization economics. Montgomery found that diversified firms with higher levels of performance tended to have well-positioned businesses in industries with 'favourable' market structures.

In summary, for both studies (PIMS and Montgomery) *the structure of the industries in which the firm completes and the competitive position of the firm's businesses within these industries are the key determinants of performance.*

Portfolio concepts

What are here called 'portfolio concepts' go by various names such as portfolio grids, SBU concepts, and SBU matrices. Although there are numerous slight variations among the approaches used by various consultant groups and firms, they all rely on a matrix or grid with two axes. The matrix classifies businesses by product-market attractiveness, or some variant of it, along one axis and by competitive position or some variant of it along the other axis. Typically these matrices are divided into either four or nine boxes. (For a thorough discussion see Hofer and Schendel, 1978.) The position (box) that each business occupies represents its strategic position and determines the role that the business should play in the corporate portfolio. This role involves varying degrees of cash generation or cash usage. Studies by Bettis (1979) and Haspeslagh (1982) suggest that managers use these concepts to varying degrees – as a tool or as dogma – in managing a diversified portfolio of businesses.

For each variant of the portfolio concept the key points are: (1) the strategic position of each business determines its cash flow characteristics; and (2) it is the 'balance' of these cash flow characteristics of the collection of businesses that determines the overall performance of the diversified firm.

Et cetera

In addition to the streams of research discussed above, a number of studies focusing on performance in large firms, by researchers concerned with organizational theory and human motivation, have appeared recently. Representative of this line of research are Peters and Waterman (1982), Deal and Kennedy (1982), Pascale and Athos (1981), and Ouchi (1981). While these studies do not consider the problems of managing diversity explicitly, they often do make some implicit recommendations on the issue, but the nature of the recommendations varies widely. (For example, Peters and Waterman suggest that 'excellent firms' confine their operations to businesses they know or 'they stick to the knitting'.)

The three streams of research lead to somewhat different conclusions. To summarize, the linkage between diversity and performance would appear to be a function of:

1. the generic diversification strategy (how much and what kind of relatedness), or
2. the profit potential of the industries in which the individual businesses are positioned and the actual competitive position of the businesses in each industry, or
3. the cash flow characteristics of the various businesses and the internal cash flow balance for the total firm.

Undoubtedly all three perspectives provide partial answers to the question. Just how partial these answers are becomes more obvious when you consider that Rumelt (1974) was able to explain less than 20 percent of the variance in performance, while Montgomery could explain only about 38 percent of the variance in performance. These results suggest that further conceptual development could enhance our understanding of diversity and performance.

The importance of 'quality of management'

Bettis *et al.* (1978) have argued that, if we move away from the traditional research preoccupation with central tendencies, but focus on outliers –the very high and very poor performers – we may learn more about the elusive linkage between diversity and performance. By studying just 12 firms, six of which were high performers and six low performers, across the three generic categories of dominant, related, and unrelated diversifiers (with a sample of four firms each, two in high- and two in low-performance categories), they concluded that the quality of management was as critical in explaining performance as any other factor. (It should be noted that their definition of quality was somewhat ambiguous.) The study was not based on the large sample (and it could not be by design, as their concern was with outliers), and the conclusions were tentative. (In a much larger study, Bettis and Mahajan were able to show that the high-performance attributes usually attributed to related diversification were not recognized in the overwhelming majority of related diversifiers.)

The real departure in the academic perspective on diversity and performance indicated by the study was the concern with very good and very poor performances in the same generic diversification category – or a desire to study outliers – and the inclusion of the concept of the 'quality of management' as a major variable linking diversity and performance.

Top management in a diversified firm a distinct skill?

Two in-depth clinical studies suggest that the skills that constitute the 'quality of management' in a single-business firm are distinct from a diversified firm; and that as firms diversify, top managers have to acquire those skills. Rajan Das (1981) studied one firm's attempt to diversify out of the core business (tobacco) and how it had to learn the process of general management in the new businesses into which it ventured. The conclusion was that it was not the quality of the business – its competitive structure – or the pattern of diversification *per se* that determined early failures and successes later, but the evolution of the top management and its ability to acquire new skills and recognize that its approach to managing a diversified firm must be different from the way it had managed the single-business firm. The study by Miles (1982) of tobacco companies in the USA and their attempts to diversify away from tobacco, also leads to a similar conclusion. The firms had to learn as much about general management in the diversified firm, as a distinct process and skill, as about the characteristics of the new businesses. Both these studies indicate that the work of top management in diversified firms is a distinct skill and can contribute to the success or failure of any one of the businesses within the firm or the firm as a whole.

The management of a diversified firm

Studies of the work of top management and the process by which they manage a diversified firm are not numerous. Bower (1972a) demonstrated that top managers influence the strategic choices made by unit-level managers by orchestrating the organizational context – the formal structure and systems. In other words, the tools of top management were administrative in character. He labelled the term 'metamanagement' (Bower, 1972b) to describe the job of top managers in diversified firms. Hamermesh (1977) outlined the process by which top managers intervene in a divisional profit crisis. Prahalad and Doz (1981) outlined, in detail, how top managers can use administrative tools to shift the strategic direction of a business. This line of research established the broad scope of the work of top management, but more importantly how that influences the strategic choices made by lower-level managers at the business-unit level, thereby impacting on the overall performance. There exists a logical, though only partially empirically verified, link between the quality of management – or the quality of the processes by which top managers influence the business-level managers in their work – and the performance of the firm.

The two questions that we posed ourselves based on the literature were:

1. If top managers in single-business firms had to learn the process of managing a diversified portfolio, should top managers in diversified firms go through a similar learning process when they add new businesses? Is the task of top management in the diversified firm dependent on, or at least partially influenced by, the underlying strategic characteristics of the businesses?

2. If the tools available to top managers in diversified firms to influence the strategic direction of businesses are essentially administrative as regards the organizational context, does it follow that the substance of businesses is irrelevant? In other words, can the same conceptual organizational context management capabilities suffice if the mix of businesses changes?

The elusive linkage

It is important before proceeding to differentiate at least two distinct levels of general management in a diversified firm – that at the SBU (strategic business unit) or business level and the corporate management team. Often, in diversified firms, there tends to be an intermediate level of general management, called group or sector executives, between business level and corporate management. Our focus will be on the corporate management team, and its relationships with business- and group-level managers, as it pertains to managing the totality of the firm.

Given this focus on corporate management, the conceptual framework linking diversity and performance proposed in this chapter is based on the following premises:

1. Top management of a (diversified) firm should not be viewed 'as a faceless abstraction', but as a 'collection of key individuals' (i.e. a dominant coalition) who have significant influence on the way the firm is managed. This collection of individuals, to a large extent, influences the style and process of top management, and as a result the key resource allocation choices (Donaldson and Lorsch, 1983).

Few organizational events are approached by these managers (or any managers) as being totally unique and requiring systematic study. Instead, they are processed through pre-existing knowledge systems. Known as schemas (see Norman, 1976, for a discussion of schemas), these systems represent beliefs, theories and propositions that have developed over time based on the manager's personal experiences. At a broader unit of analysis, Huff (1982) implied the possibility that organizations' actions can be characterized as schemas. An organizational schema is primarily a product of managers' interpretations of experiences while operating within certain firms and industries.

Schemas permit managers to categorize an event, assess its consequences, and consider appropriate actions (including doing nothing), and to do so rapidly and often efficiently. Without schemas a manager, and ultimately the organizations with which he/she is associated, would become paralysed by the need to analyse 'scientifically' an enormous number of ambiguous and uncertain situations. In other words, managers must be able to scan environments selectively so that timely decisions can be made (Hambrick, 1982). The selection of environmental elements to be scanned is likely to be affected by a manager's schema.

Unfortunately, schemas are not infallible guides to the organization and its environments. In fact, some are relatively inaccurate representations of the world, particularly as conditions change. Furthermore, events often are not labelled accurately, and sometimes are processed through inaccurate and/or incomplete knowledge structures.

For the purpose of this research it is important to understand what managers' schemas actually represent. Kiesler and Sproul (1982) offer the following concise description: 'Managers operate on mental representations of the world and those representations are likely to be of historical environments rather than of current ones' (p. 557). (Furthermore, as Weick, 1979, discusses, it is the schema concept that provides the vehicle for his concept of the social construction (or enactment) of a firm's environment.)

For the present purposes the schema concept is introduced as a general mental structure that can store a shared dominant general management logic. (The specific nature and content of this 'logic' is discussed below.)

2. The strategic characteristics of businesses in a diversified firm, determined by the underlying competitive structure, technologies, and customers of specific businesses, vary. The differences in strategic characteristics of the businesses in the portfolio of the firm, a measure of *strategic variety*, impact the ability of a top management group to manage. This premise implies that complexity of the top management process is a function of the strategic variety, not just the number of distinct businesses or the size of those businesses. For example, the management of a very large, primarily one-industry firm (e.g. General Motors), or the management of a diversified firm in strategically similar businesses (e.g. Procter and Gamble), is a lot simpler than managing a diversified firm in strategically dissimilar industries (e.g. General Electric).

3. Strategically similar businesses can be managed using a single dominant general management logic. A dominant general management logic is defined as the way in which managers conceptualize the business and make critical resource allocation decisions – be it in technologies, product development, distribution, advertising, or in human resource management. These tasks are performed by managing the infrastructure of administrative compensation, career management, and organization structure. If the businesses in a diversified firm are strategically similar, one dominant general management logic would suffice. However, diversified firms with strategic variety impose the need for multiple dominant logic.

The dominant logic is stored via schemas and hence can be thought of as a structure. However, some of what is stored is process knowledge (e.g. what kind of process should be used in a particular kind of resource alleviation decision or how new technologies should be evaluated). Hence, more broadly the dominant logic can be considered as both a knowledge structure and a set of elicited management processes. (The actual content of this knowledge structure and how this context is established is discussed below.)

4. The ability of the top management group (a group of key individuals) to manage a diversified firm is limited by the dominant general management logic(s) that they are used to. In other words, the repertoire of tools that top managers use to identify, define, and make strategic

decisions, and their view of the world (mind sets), is determined by their experiences. Typically, the dominant top management logic in a diversified firm tends to be influenced by the largest business or the 'core business' which was the historical basis for the firm's growth (e.g. semiconductors at Texas Instruments, public switching and telephones at GTE). The characteristics of the core business, often the source of top managers in diversified firms, tend to cause managers to define problems in certain ways and develop familiarity with, and facility in the use of, those administrative tools that are particularly useful in accomplishing the critical tasks of the core business (Figure 4.1).

The sources of dominant logic

Dominant logic, as we have defined it here, is a mind set or a world view or conceptualization of the business and the administrative tools to accomplish goals and make decisions in that business. It is stored as a shared cognitive map (or set of schemas) among the dominant coalition. It is expressed as a learned, problem-solving behaviour. As such, in order to understand dominant logic, we first need to examine the research streams that deal with the development of cognitive maps and the associated problem-solving behaviour. We identified four streams of research – operant conditioning, paradigms, cognitive biases, and artificial intelligence – to highlight the process by which a dominant logic evolves (i.e. how the cognitive map originates and changes) and the difficulties in changing it or adding new logic to one's repertoire. The relationships of these four streams to problem-solving behaviour are shown in Figure 4.2.

Figure 4.1 Dominant general management logic evolves due to . . .

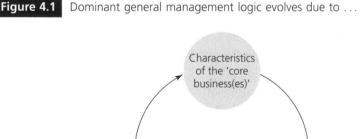
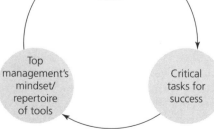

Figure 4.2 Conceptual foundations of dominant logic

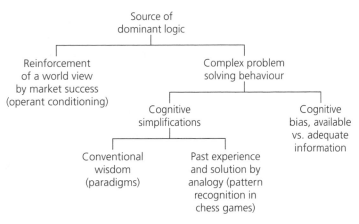

Operant conditioning

Skinner (1953), in his seminal work on operant conditioning, argued that behaviour was a function of its consequences. Behaviour could be understood by considering the contingencies that were administered by the environment in response to certain behaviour. Behaviour was administered by the environment in response to certain behaviours. Behaviour that was reinforced was emitted more frequently in the future. By contrast, behaviour that was ignored or punished (negative reinforcement) was likely to diminish over time. A dominant logic can be seen as resulting from the reinforcement that results from doing the 'right things' with respect to a set of businesses. In other words, when top managers effectively perform the tasks that are critical for success in the core business they are positively reinforced by economic success. This reinforcement results in their focusing effort on the behaviours that led to success. Hence they develop a particular mind set and repertoire of tools and preferred processes. This in turn determines the approaches that they are likely to use in resource allocation, control over operations, and the approach to intervention in a crisis. If the firm acquires or develops a business for which the critical tasks for success are substantially different from those in the core business, because of operant conditioning the behaviour of top managers and the approaches they use to manage the new business are likely to remain those that were appropriate for the core business even though they may be inappropriate in the new business. In other words it is difficult for a top management group to be effective in managing a new business by learning and using a new dominant logic in a short time. The problems faced by American Can (e.g. Pickwick International), and Exxon (e.g. office systems), in managing acquisitions of businesses totally different from their core businesses, in the early stages, are an illustration of the power of operant conditioning on the dominant logic used by top management.

The power of paradigms

The concept of dominant logic also derives direct support from Kuhn's (1970) work on scientific paradigms and Allison's (1971) work on the importance of alternate paradigms in the context of analysing government actions during the Cuban missile crisis.

Kuhn, a historian of science, argued that a particular science at any point in time can be characterized by a set of 'shared beliefs' or 'conventional wisdom' about the world that constitutes what he called the 'dominant paradigm'. What Kuhn calls 'normal science' is carried out efficiently under this set of shared beliefs. In a sense, Kuhn's 'paradigm' is simply a way of defining and managing the world and a basis for action in that world. Kuhn points out how difficult it is to shift dominant paradigms, and illustrates this with several examples such as the shift from the Ptolemaic view of the universe (earth-centred) to the Coperican view of the universe (sun-centred) in astronomy. The analogy from science to a business firm is simple and direct. The dominant paradigm and the dominant logic are conceptually similar but employed in different fields. Allison used paradigmatic analysis to show how the adoption of a particular paradigm powerfully affects our evaluation of events. He characterized a paradigm as 'a systematic statement of the basic assumptions, concepts and propositions employed by a school of analysis'. Different paradigms resulted in dramatically different analyses of his chosen example: the Cuban missile crisis. The parallel between Allison's use of the word paradigm and our use of dominant logic is obvious.

The pattern-recognition process

As part of the development of 'intelligent' computer programs there have been numerous efforts to develop chess-playing programs (see Newell and Simon, 1972, for a review). Inevitably such research has required intense studies of how chess experts make decisions in a chess game. In particular, the decision-making and problem-solving process used by grand masters and masters has been compared to that of lesser players (de Groot, 1965). These studies have shown that the better players could remember more 'patterns' of previous games than the lesser players. Simon (1979) estimated that class A players could remember about 1,300 familiar patterns while masters or grand masters remember about 50,000. This 'vocabulary' of previous games lets players make effective decisions by comparison with earlier games. In other words, chess players decide on the basis of experience or 'what worked before', not on the basis of some best strategy or optimizing procedure. Now consider a situation where the design of the gameboard or rules of chess are changed. The stored 'vocabulary' of games is no longer as useful in this new game. Similarly, when the economic gameboard or rules are changed either by structural changes in existing businesses or by a diversification move, the vocabulary of economic moves stored through experience in the core business may no longer be as useful. In other words, solutions based on 'past experience' or solution by 'analogy' may be inappropriate.

Cognitive biases

A final area from which research results are suggestive of the concept of a dominant top management logic is cognitive psychology. The psychology of cognitive biases is the study of how people in making decisions sometimes make systematic (and often severe) errors (see Tversky and Kahneman, 1974, for an introduction and survey). When dealing with uncertain and complex tasks people often rely on a limited number of heuristic principles which greatly simplify the decision process. In general these heuristics are useful, but on some occasions they can result in significant errors.

For present purposes the most interesting of these heuristic principles is what is called the availability heuristic (see Tversky and Kahneman, 1974, for a thorough discussion). Basically, the availability heuristic leads people to make decisions by using information that can easily be brought to mind (i.e. information that is 'available'). This often leads to severe and systematic errors. This field of research also suggests that decision-makers do not necessarily use analytical approaches to evaluate the information content of available data or search for 'adequate information' (Nisbett and Ross, 1980). For example, Tversky and Kahneman (1974) point out that one may assess the risk of heart attack among middle-aged people by recalling such occurrences among one's acquaintances even if it can be shown that it is an inappropriate basis for drawing such a conclusion. Obviously, for top managers, knowledge of the core business and the business they are most familiar with will be a significant source of available information. They tend to apply it to other businesses where it may or may not be appropriate (Das, 1981). Research on cognitive processes suggests that the mind set and repertoire of tools that constitute the dominant logic are likely to be inappropriately applied by managers confronted with a 'different' business, and that there is significant 'learning' that precedes change in those biases. The difficulty of operating in diverse businesses which require multiple dominant logics is obvious.

Strategic variety and the dominant logic

The premises outlined above help us develop a framework for assessing the linkage between diversity and performance. Essentially they relate strategic variety amongst businesses in the firm, and changes in it, with the appropriateness of the dominant general management logic(s) that top managers in that firm use. We will examine in the rest of the chapter the problems that diversified firms face in relating strategic variety and the dominant general management logic(s).

Strategic variety

Strategic variety in a diversified firm depends on the characteristics of the mix of business the firm is engaged in. During the past decade top managers have tended to reduce the strategic variety (not necessarily the number of district businesses) in the portfolio of the firm. This is accomplished, often, by divesting businesses that do not 'fit' – those that increase strategic variety. Many of the businesses divested are profitable (e.g. Sperry's sale of Vickers to concentrate on information technology, ITT's sale of its bakery division). Divesting businesses to get more 'focus' to the portfolio results from an implicit recognition that the demands on top management of strategic variety can be significant. Not all diversified firms have been proactive in reducing strategic variety. Some have been forced to divest businesses, after years of poor profit performance and an inability on their part to turn around the 'sick businesses'.

An alternative to the approach outlined above – reducing strategic variety by restricting the mix of businesses in the firm to those whose strategic characteristics are similar – is followed by firms like General Electric, Textron, or 3M. Typically, businesses with similar strategic characteristics tend to be grouped together into 'sectors' for management purposes. As a result there is little strategic variety within a sector, but across sectors there can be significant differences. This approach reduces the strategic variety that top managers have to deal with by creating an intermediate level of general management. These group- or sector-level executives tend to manage the strategic direction of specific businesses within the sector. Conceptually, this arrangement explicitly recognizes the need to contain strategic variety for effective management. However, in practice, the role of sector executives and their relationship both with business-level managers and with the top management of the firm can become unclear if top management of the firm attempts to directly influence the conduct of any one business or a group of businesses.

Changing strategic variety

So far we have considered how firms can contain strategic variety in a diversified firm, at a given point in time. But over time, even with an unchanging mix of businesses, the strategic variety can change. For example, the strategic characteristics of businesses can change due to changes in the structure of industries. The toy industry was changed, in a relatively short period of time, by the availability of inexpensive microprocessors. The combination of telecommunication and computers and deregulation is changing the financial services industry. Globalization has changed the nature of competition in several industries such as TV, hi-fl, autos, steel, machine tools, etc. As a result, even firms which do not ostensibly change the mix of businesses will have to cope with increasing strategic variety, as the underlying structural characteristics of businesses change. Top managers, as a result, must possess the ability to revise the dominant logic they used to manage those businesses. The inability of top managers both to identify changing structural characteristics of businesses and to accept the need for change in dominant logic(s), may provide at least a partial explanation for the difficulties traditional businesses like steel, machine tools, and autos have faced during the past five years in the US.

An addition of a new business, either through internal development or acquisition, can also change the strategic variety within the firm. If the new business is distinctly different (e.g. General Motors' acquisition of EDS, or General Electric's acquisition of Utah International) the strategic variety it adds is easily recognized. In such acquisitions, top managers also recognize that hasty attempts to impose the dominant logic of the firm on the acquired business may be dysfunctional. Often the acquired firm is 'left alone', at least for a time.

When a new business is created through internal development it is harder to recognize the different structural characteristics of that business compared to those in the current mix of businesses; more so if the new business is technologically not dissimilar to existing businesses. For example, the experience of the calculator, digital watch, and personal computer businesses at Texas Instruments illustrates the point. The dominant logic which worked so well for TI in the semiconductor business, when applied to the new business, led to failure. A dramatic contrast is the early recognition at IBM that the personal computer business was structurally quite distinct. This recognition resulted in the creation of an independent business unit for managing that business. It was not subject to the dominant logic of the mainframe business. As the PC business evolves, and as it takes on the characteristics of the mainframe business, at least in some applications and with some customer segments, IBM may reimpose the dominant logic of mainframes on that business. To summarize, strategic variety in a diversified firm can change due to:

- changes in the structural characteristics of the existing mix of businesses, or
- changes in the mix of businesses caused by acquisitions or internal development.

In either case, top managers must explicitly examine the implications of changes in strategic variety. In other words, major structural changes in an industry have the same effect on the strategic variety of a firm as acquiring a new business.

The task of top management is to constantly re-examine its portfolio to ascertain if there are perceptible changes in the strategic variety as well as explicitly to assess the impact of new businesses on dominant logic(s) in the firm. The task of top management under various combinations of 'sources of strategic variety' and 'top management orientation' give us six possible combinations, as shown in Table 4.1. In a firm with a single dominant logic, if the nature of the core business changes significantly, then top managers will have to revise the dominant logic (A). If a new business is added, and is strategically similar (B), no change in dominant logic is needed. If, however, the new business is dissimilar, top managers have to create the capacity within the firm to cope with multiple dominant logics (C). In a firm operating with multiple dominant logic, if the nature of a significant business changes, then top managers may have to revise the dominant logic applied to that business or regroup it under a different 'sector' or 'group' (D). If the new business is strategically similar to one of the 'groups' or 'sectors' within the firm, then top

Table 4.1 Nature of top management tasks in diversified firms

	Sources of strategic variety		
		Addition of a new business	
Top management orientation	Significant structural changes in core business	Similar to existing business	Dissimilar from existing business
Single dominant logic	(A) Revise the dominant logic	(B) No change required	(C) Create the capacity for multiple dominant logic(s)
	(D) Revise the dominant logic applied to that business or regroup it under another sector	(E) Assign business to appropriate 'sector'	(F) Add to the variety of dominant logic(s)

managers may assign it to the appropriate sector (E). If the new business is dissimilar to the existing businesses, then top managers have to add variety to the dominant logic within the firm (F).

Conclusions

The concept of dominant general management logic and the role of top managers in understanding and managing the logic(s) are important aspects to be considered in the research on diversity and performance. There are several implications of including these concepts in the study of diversity and performance. Some are dealt with in the following sections.

Limits to diversity

We have argued that the 'real diversity' in a managerial sense in a firm does not arise from the variety in technologies or markets or by the number of distinct businesses *per se*, but from the strategic variety among businesses requiring a variety in the dominant logic used by top management. Further, the variety of dominant logic that top management can handle depends on the composition of the team, and their experiences, as well as their attitude toward learning. These factors suggest that we ought to recognize that the limit to the diversity of businesses within a firm is determined by the strategic variety, and that the strategic variety that a firm can cope with is dependent on the composition of a top management team.

Undoubtedly, organization structure can help cope with increased strategic variety. One basic aspect of decentralization is to make decisions at the level where the proper expertise is available. In other words, the cognitive map is more likely to fit the strategic imperatives of the business. However, not all decision making can be decentralized. For example, resource allocation decisions among a firm's portfolio of businesses must be made. Furthermore, plans, strategies, and budgets must be reviewed at the corporate level and managerial performance must be assessed. Hence organizational structure, although useful, is limited. It can attenuate the intensity of strategic variety that corporate level management must deal with, but it cannot substitute for the need to handle strategic variety at the corporate level.

An alternative or supplementary approach is to reduce the strategic variety in the businesses of the firm – what has come to be known as 'focus' in the portfolio. An interesting variant on this is to impose a single strategic approach on each business. For example, as Porter *et al.* (1983) discuss, Emerson Electric has a uniform goal across businesses of being the low-cost producer in each of its markets. Such an approach reduces strategic variety but may impose an inappropriate logic on a particular business. Interestingly, Emerson usually seeks to divest businesses that cannot meet this goal.

Ultimately many firms exceed the limits of organizational structure in attenuating the intensity of strategic variety and / or cannot reduce or limit strategic variety adequately. These firms face the reality of having to deal intensively with strategic variety at the corporate level and the necessity of developing multiple dominant logic if performance is to be sustained.

The bottom line is that each top management team at a given point in time has an inbuilt limit to the extent of diversity it can manage. Organizational structure and focus in the portfolio can help extend this limit but they cannot eliminate it.

Diversity and performance: the hidden costs

A high level of performance in a diversified firm requires the ability to 'respond fast' to competitor moves, as well as 'respond appropriately'. One of the implications of our thesis, so far, is that top managers are less likely to 'respond appropriately' to situations where the dominant logic is different, as well as not respond quickly enough, as they may be unable to interpret the meaning of information regarding unfamiliar businesses. The 'hidden costs' associated with diversifying into non-familiar businesses are shown schematically in Figure 4.3. These 'hidden costs' are not explicitly recognized when the overall business climate is very favourable. Problems surface when the newly acquired businesses (which are strategically dissimilar) encounter competitive problems or are faced with a profit crisis. Top managers find themselves unable to respond to the crisis under those circumstances (Hamermesh, 1977).

Changing or adding dominant logic

The process of adding dominant logic is, given the previous discussion, obviously an important aspect in the management of diversified firms. Also, as the argument so far suggests, the process of changing dominant logic is important to any firm that encounters rapid change in the structure of the industries in which it competes. These issues revolve around the ability of the firm or its dominant coalition to learn. Fortunately, there is a small but growing literature on organizational learning (see Hedberg, 1981, for an introduction and survey). This literature suggests ways in which organizations can change or add dominant logic.

First, let us consider the situation involved in changing the dominant logic of a (single-logic) firm. The explicit assumption here is that the structure of the core industry the firm competes in is or has changed significantly.

In general it appears that changes in the ways organizations solve significant new problems (i.e. change dominant logics) are triggered by substantial problems or crises (see March and Simon, 1958; Downs, 1967; Terreberrey, 1968; Cyert and March, 1963; Starbuck, 1976; Hedberg, 1973; Hedberg *et al.*, 1976). Hedberg (1981) also suggests that opportunities or changes in key executives may also trigger learning, but here the evidence is small by comparison. (Key executive changes are often made in response to crises.) It would appear that in

Figure 4.3 Diversity and performance

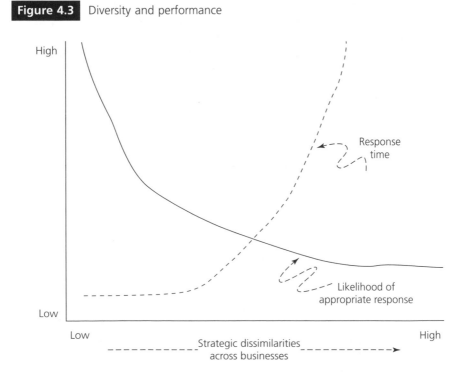

the overwhelming number of instances a crisis is needed to precipitate change (e.g. 'Why fix it if it is not broke?'). Not only must there be a crisis but as Nystrom *et al.* (1976) propose and illustrate, the initial response to the crisis is likely to be inappropriate. In other words the initial response is likely to draw on the now inappropriate but still current dominant logic. This, of course, provokes a deepening of the crisis and a search for other solutions. Survival is likely to become dependent on finding a new logic.

Given that the opportunity for learning has been elicited by a crisis (or other event) the organizational learning literature (e.g. Hedberg, 1981) suggests that unlearning must occur to make way for new mental maps. Unlearning is simply the process by which firms eliminate old logics and behaviours and make room for new ones. Interestingly, the more successful organizations have been, the more difficult unlearning becomes (Argyris and Schon, 1978; Starbuck and Hedberg, 1977).

Given that these two preconditions, a precipitating crisis and a start of unlearning, have occurred, the stage is set for the kind of learning that can result in a new dominant logic. However, as Michael (1973) and Hedberg (1981) have observed, little is known about how organizations' cognitive structures are changed. Hence, the discussion here must be largely speculative. Hedberg (1981) makes four general suggestions: (1) making organizations more experimental; (2) regulating organizations' sensitivity to environmental changes to an optimal level (neither too low nor too high); (3) redesigning organizations' inner and outer environments; and (4) achieving a dynamic balance between stabilizing and destabilizing influences. Beyond these general areas the current authors suggest: (1) structuring the top management team to include individuals with significantly different experience bases; (2) encouraging top managers to enrich their experience bases through sabbaticals and educational experiences; (3) rehearsing as a management team for a broad range of future industry scenarios; (4) separating economic evaluation from manager evaluation so that executives can be rewarded for experimenting even when projects fail; and (5) legitimizing dissent. Furthermore, in an interesting article about managerial responses to changing environments, Kiesler and Sproul (1982) suggest developing schemas that incorporate the expectation of change as a fundamental component. Unfortunately, again the 'how to' remains largely undefined.

The discussion in this section so far has considered changing dominant logics, not adding new ones. Adding new logics implies retaining the old one and not unlearning it, but developing the ability to deal simultaneously with other logics. This generally falls beyond what has been studied in the organizational learning literature. Diversification is often not triggered by a crisis, and unlearning as described above is not desirable. It appears that what must occur is some kind of meta-learning in which the dominant coalition learns to simultaneously conceptualize different types of businesses. Perhaps some sort of meta-logic evolves that specifies the necessity of, and rules for, picking between partially contradictory mental maps. Further research here is obviously needed.

The meaning of 'relatedness'

The concept of related or conglomerate diversification was typically based on an analysis of the technological and market characteristics. The view presented here suggests that we may have to develop a concept of relatedness based on the 'strategic similarities' of businesses and the cognitive composition of the top management team. Relatedness may be as much a cognitive concept as it is an economic and technical concept.

Future research

The concept of a dominant logic presents opportunities to deepen our understanding of the management of diversification and the relationships between diversity and performance. A first necessary step is to move beyond the purely conceptual stage to measurement of the construct, or, in other words, to being able to specify just what a particular dominant logic actually is. The authors have had experience in trying to construct the dominant logic of a firm by in-depth interviewing of the top management team, and believe that useful results and insights can be achieved. However, such an approach, though useful as a consulting framework, lacks the rigour necessary to establishing general results. Furthermore, quantification is complicated by the cognitive nature of the dominant logic.

Decision-makers' descriptions of their own policies are often inaccurate (Hoffman, 1960; Slovic, 1969; Balke *et al.*, 1973). Similarly, stated policies and intentions often vary from what is actually used. Argyris and Schon (1974) describe this as the difference between 'espoused theories' and 'theories in use' that actually govern behaviour. These researchers suggest that a person's theory in use cannot be obtained simply by asking for it. Creative questionnaires and analysis procedures, however, can be developed that elicit the true nature of the dominant logic. For example, the policy-capturing methodology (Slovic and Liechtenstein, 1971; Slovic *et al.*, 1977) would seem to be a powerful approach to measuring a firm's dominant logic.

Another approach to establishing a firm's dominant logic could be through the use of historical analysis. As previous arguments have discussed, the dominant logic is developed as a result of the experiences of the key executives. Hence, delving into the industry and firm experience of these key individuals would seem to be a fruitful approach, especially when coupled with in-depth interviews of the individuals and their immediate subordinates.

A second important area for future research is the previously mentioned process of learning to use multiple dominant logics. The organizational learning literature deals primarily with changing cognitive maps. It does not deal with the process of learning to use multiple, partially contradictory maps. Some firms have obviously been able to solve this problem. Longitudinal clinical investigation is necessary to determine how.

References

Allison, Graham J. (1971) *Essence of Decision: Explaining the Cuban Missile Crisis*, Boston, MA: Little, Brown.

Ansoff, H. Igor (1965) *Corporate Strategy*, New York: McGraw-Hill.

Argyris, C. and Schon, D.A. (1974) *Theory in Practice: Increasing Professional Effectiveness*, San Francisco, CA: Jossey-Bass.

Argyris, C. and Schon, D. (1978) *Organizational Learning*, Reading, MA: Addison-Wesley.

Balke, W.M., Hammond, K.R. and Meyer, C.D. (1973) 'An alternative approach to labor–management negotiations', *Administrative Science Quarterly* 18: 311–27.

Bettis, R.A. (1979) 'Strategic portfolio management in the multibusiness firm: implementing the portfolio concept'. Unpublished doctoral dissertation, University of Michigan.

Bettis, R.A. and Mahajan, V. (1985) 'Risk/return performance of diversified firms', *Management Science*, 31: 785–99.

Bettis, R.A., Hall, W.K. and Prahalad, C.K. (1978) 'Diversity and performance in the multibusiness firm', *National Proceedings of the American Institutefor Decision Sciences*, pp. 210–12.

Bower, J.L. (1972a) *Managing the Resource Allocation Process*, Homewood, IL: Irwin.

Bower, J.L. (1972b) 'Metamanagement: a technology and a philosophy'. Paper presented at the Winter meeting of AAAS, 20 November.

Chandler, Alfred D. (1962) *Strategy and Structure*, Cambridge, MA: MIT Press.

Channon, Derek (1973) *The Strategy and Structure of British Enterprise*, Graduate School of Business Administration, Harvard University, Boston.

Cyert, R. and March, J. (1963) *A Behavioral Theory of the Firm*, Englewood Cliffs, NJ: Prentice-Hall.

Das, Rajan (1981) *Managing Diversification: The General Management Perspective*, New Delhi: Macmillan India.

Deal, Terrence E. and Kennedy, Allan A. (1982) *Corporate Cultures*, Reading, MA: Addison-Wesley.

de Groot, A.D. (1965) *Thought and Choice in Chess*, The Hague: Mouton.

Donaldson, G. and Lorsch, Jay (1983) *Decision Making at the Top*, New York: Basic Books.

Downs, A. (1967) *Inside Bureaucracy*, Boston, MA: Little, Brown.

Hambrick, D.C. (1982) 'Environmental scanning and organizational strategy', *Strategic Management Journal*, 3: 159–74.

Hamermesh, R.G. (1977) 'Responding to the divisional profit crisis'. Unpublished doctoral dissertation, Harvard Business School.

Haspeslagh, P. (1982) 'Portfolio planning: uses and limits', *Harvard Business Review*, January–February: 58–73.

Hedberg, B. (1973) 'Organizational stagnation and choice of strategy'. Working paper, International Institute of Management, Berlin.

Hedberg, B. (1981) 'How organizations learn and unlearn', in Nystron, P. and Starbuck, W. (eds) *Handbook of Organizational Design*, Oxford: Oxford University Press.

Hedberg, B., Nystrom, P. and Starbuck, W. (1976) 'Camping on seesaws: prescriptions for a self-designing organization', *Administrative Science Quarterly* 21: 41–65.

Hofer, Charles W. and Schendel, Dan (1978) *Strategy Formulation: Analytical Concepts*, St Paul, MN: West.

Hoffman, P. (1960) 'The paramorphic representation of clinical judgment', *Psychological Bulletin* 47: 116–31.

Huff, A.S. (1982) 'Industry influence on strategy reformulation', *Strategic Management Journal*, 3: 119–31.

Kiesler, S. and Sproul, L. (1982) 'Managerial response to changing environments: perspectives and problem sensing from social cognition', *Administrative Science Quarterly* 37: 548–70.

Kuhn, Thomas S. (1970) *The Structure of Scientific Revolutions*, 2nd edn, Chicago, IL: University of Chicago Press.

March, J. and Simon, H. (1958) *Organizations*, New York: Wiley.

Michael, Donald N. (1973) *On Learning to Plan and Planning to Learn*, San Francisco, CA: Jossey-Bass.

Miles, R.H. (1982) *Coffin Nails and Corporate Strategies*, Englewood Cliffs, NJ: Prentice-Hall.

Montgomery, Cynthia (1979) 'Diversification, market structure and firm performance: an extension of Rumelt's model', PhD dissertation, Purdue University.

Nathanson, Daniel and James Cassano (1982) 'Organization, diversity, and performance', *Wharton Magazine*, Summer, pp. 19–26.

Newell, A. and Simon, Herbert (1972) *Human Problem Solving*, Englewood Cliffs, NJ: Prentice-Hall.

Nisbett, R. and Ross, L. (1980) *Human Inference: Strategies and Shortcomings of Social Judgement*, Englewood Cliffs, NJ: Prentice-Hall.

Norman, D. (1976) *Memory and Attention*, 2nd edn, New York: Wiley.

Nystrom, P., Hedberg, B. and Starbuck, W. (1976) 'Interacting processes as organizational designs', in Kilman, R., Pondy, L. and Slevin, D. (eds) *The Management of Organization Design*, New York: Elsevier.

Ouchi, William C. (1981) *Theory Z*, Reading, MA: Addison-Wesley.

Pascale, Richard J. and Athos, Anthony C. (1981) *The Art of Japanese Management*, New York: Simon & Schuster.

Pavan, R.J. (1972) 'Strategy and structure of Italian enterprise'. Unpublished doctoral dissertation, Harvard Business School.

Peters, Thomas J. and Waterman, Jr, Robert H. (1982) *In Search of Excellence*, New York: Harper & Row.

Pooley, C. (1972) 'Strategy and structure of French enterprise', Unpublished doctoral dissertation, Harvard Business School.

Porter, M. (1980) *Competitive Strategy*, New York: The Free Press.

Porter, M., Collis, D., DeBelina, J., Elsasser, J., Hornthal, J. and Shearer, R. (1983) 'The chain saw industry in 1974', in Porter, M. (ed.) *Cases in Competitive Strategy*, New York: The Free Press.

Prahalad, C.K. and Doz, Y. (1981) 'An approach to strategic control in MNCs', *Sloan Management Review*, Summer: 5–13.

Rumelt, Richard (1974) 'Strategy, structure, and economic performance', Division of Research, Graduate School of Business Administration, Harvard University.

Rumelt, Richard P. (1977) 'Diversity and profitability', Paper NGL–51, Managerial Studies Center, Graduate School of Management, University of California, Los Angeles.

Scholeffler, Sidney, Buzzell, Robert D. and Heany, Donald F. (1974) 'Impact of strategic planning on profit performance', *Harvard Business Review*, March–April: 137–45.

Simon, Herbert A. (1979) 'Information processing models of cognition', *Annual Review of Psychology* 30: 363–96

Skinner, B.F. (1953) *Science and Human Behaviour*, New York: Macmillan.

Slovic, P. (1969) 'Analysing the expert judge: a descriptive study of stockbrokers' decision processes', *Journal of Applied Psychology* 53: 255–63.

Slovic, P. and Liechtenstein, S. (1971) 'Comparison of Bayesian and regression approaches to the study of information processing in judgement', *Organisational Behaviour and Human Performance* 6: 649–744.

Slovic, P., Fishcoff, B. and Liechtenstein, S. (1977) 'Behavioural decision theory', in Rosenzweig, R. and Porter, L.W. (eds) *Annual Review of Psychology*, Annual Review, Palo Alto, CA, pp. 1–39.

Starbuck, W. (1976) 'Organisations and their environments', in Dunnette, M. (ed.) *Handbook of Industrial and Organisational Psychology*, Chicago, IL: Rand McNally.

Starbuck, W. and Hedberg, B. (1977) 'Saving an organization from a stagnating environment', in Thorelli, H. (ed.) *Strategy + Structure = Performance*, Bloomington, IN: Indiana University Press.

Suzuki, Y. (1980) 'The strategy and structure of top 100 Japanese industrial enterprises 1950–1970', *Strategic Management Journal* 3: 265–91.

Terreberrey, S. (1968) 'The evolution of organizational environments', *Administrative Science Quarterly* 12: 590–613.

Thanheiser, H. (1972) 'Strategy and structure of German enterprise', unpublished doctoral dissertation, Harvard Business School.

Tversky, Amos and Kahneman, Daniel (1974) 'Judgement under uncertainty: heuristics and biases', *Science* 185: 1124–31.

Weick, K. (1979) *The Social Psychology of Organizing*, 2nd edn, Reading, MA: Addison-Wesley.

Wrigley, Leonard (1970) 'Divisional autonomy and diversification', DBA dissertation, Harvard University.

5 The management of competence and its limits

Ken Starkey and Sue Tempest

The concept of competence and its origins

It was Prahalad and Hamel (1990) who popularized the concept of competence within the field of strategic management although the term does have a long history. Strategic management is quintessentially concerned with sources of firm competitive advantage. Prahalad and Hamel argue that one of the most powerful sources of competitive advantage is core competence.[1] They defined core competencies as 'the collective learning in the organization, especially how to coordinate diverse production skills and integrate multiple streams and technologies' (Prahalad and Hamel, 1990: 64).

The interest in competence in strategy refocused attention on sources of competitive advantage internal to the organization rather than the external focus on product markets and competitive environments. This marked a gradual sea-change in thinking about strategy.

> In an environment where product life cycles are shortening, technologies are converging, and industry structures are becoming more diffuse, there is a growing belief that the key focus for building competitiveness no longer belongs with market selection and positioning but with the development and nurturing of widely applicable distinctive internal capabilities that are relatively enduring.
> (Leavy, 1998: 448; Rumelt et al., 1991)

The interest in competence has a long history in strategy which has led to what is now called the resource-based view of the firm. The resource-based view argues that competitive advantage arises from firm-specific resources. This view has its origins in the pioneering work of the economist Edith Penrose (1959: 24–5) who viewed the firm as 'an administrative organization and a collection of productive resources', 'a bundle of potential services'. The key bridge from micro-economics to strategy theory was in the seminal article published in *Strategic Management Journal* by Wernerfelt (1984).

The resource-based view of the firm recognizes resources in their widest sense to include assets, processes, attributes, knowledge,[2] and information. To confer competitive advantage resources must: be rare/scarce, difficult or, better, impossible to imitate, non-substitutable and appropriable by the firm (Barney, 1991). Barriers to replication of resource advantage are higher if the resources are tacit or diffused through the systems, processes or psyche of an organization (Godfrey and Hill, 1995). From the resource-based perspective advantage can best be derived from tacit knowledge because such knowledge has rarity value, imperfect mobility, imperfect imitation, and imperfect substitutability making it hard for outsiders to imitate or copy (Ambrosini and Bowman, 1998).

In order for a firm to profit from resources it must have advantageous access to the resources. This does not necessitate ownership of resources but does imply, in the absence of ownership, effective relationships being key to resource access[3] (Nanda, 1996).

From resource base to knowledge base

The resource-based, competence view is increasingly seen as a knowledge-based view of the firm, with knowledge emerging as the most valuable of resources, and how to access, manage and apply knowledge a major research issue (Grant, 1996). A knowledge-based view conceptualizes the firm as a self-regulating system that optimizes the interactions of individuals and groups to create, circulate, and apply knowledge to the strategies of the firm (Spender, 1996: 57). Knowledge presents particular management challenges because of its unique nature as a resource, in particular, the 'absence of commodity-like markets for knowledge assets, a condition that arises in part from the nature of knowledge itself and, in particular, the difficult to articulate and codify tacit dimension' (Teece, 2000: 36). Much knowledge remains tacit 'because it cannot be articulated fast enough, because it is impossible to articulate all that is necessary to a successful performance, and because language cannot simultaneously serve to describe relationships and characterize the things related' (Nelson and Winter, 1982).

Knowledge works in mysterious ways. For example, 'Toyota's knowledge of how to make cars lies embedded in highly specialized social and organizational relationships that have evolved through decades of common effort. It rests in routines, information flows, ways of making decisions, shared attitudes, and expectations, and specialized knowledge that Toyota managers, workers, suppliers and purchasing agents, and others have about different aspects of their business, about each other, and about how they can all work together. None of these parties knows what Toyota as a whole "knows" about making cars' (Badaracco, 1991: 87). The overall sum is greater than the sum of the parts.

Knowledge raises important issues of learning as the basis of competence acquisition and development. Prahalad and Hamel (1990: 82) define core competence as 'the collective learning of the organization'. The advantage of a learning organization built on distinctive core competencies is that it generates new knowledge through experience, is adaptive at coping with changing circumstances and generative in creating new solutions and it thus combines both refinement and renewal capabilities. A learning organization also enables its members to let go of competencies that are no longer relevant and to embrace new skills and techniques offering flexibility to its knowledge base.

Business history contains many rich examples of how knowledge can act as the basis for competence building. Sony learnt to excel in miniaturization, Honda in engines, Federal Express in logistics management. There are also some telling examples of how management failed to develop knowledge and competence into a strategic advantage. One of the most powerful examples of this was Xerox. Just as firms do not always know what they are good at so firms do not always know what they know. In the mid-1970s Xerox's Palo Alto Research Center (PARC) invented the first personal computer and much of the technology, such as the mouse, that we now take for granted. Xerox was in advance of firms such as Apple and possessed a huge potential innovation advantage. However, Xerox never capitalized upon this knowledge and remained committed to photocopying.

Xerox's top management, based in the East of the US, and not where the future of computing was taking shape in Silicon Valley, did not understand the nature of the knowledge it had created. The company remained complacent after years of prosperity. Xerox's dominant culture, numbers-oriented, non-technical and risk-averse, threw away the future, inventing then ignoring the new technology, the first personal computer, that would drive the growth of one of the fastest growing markets of all time (Smith and Alexander, 1988). The rest is history.

Learning, capability and capacity

Learning, innovation and competence come together in the concept of 'dynamic capabilities' defined as 'the firm's ability to integrate, build and reconfigure internal and external competences to address rapidly changing environments' (Teece *et al.*, 1997: 530). 'A dynamic capability is a learned pattern of collective activity through which the organization systematically generates and modifies its operational routines in pursuit of improved effectiveness' (Zollo and Winter, 2002: 13).

Dynamic capability links competence to the actions embedded in routines which are themselves the outcome of previous learning. 'Dynamic capabilities … are the organizational and strategic routines by which firms achieve new resource reconfigurations as markets emerge, collide, split, evolve, and die' (Eisenhardt and Martin, 2000). To survive and change the firm needs to develop processes that integrate, reconfigure, gain, and then apply to respond to or, perhaps the most powerful strategic move, to create market change.

Capabilities are embedded in routines for action. Nelson and Winter (1982) see organizational routines as the skills of the organization that are path-dependent, idiosyncratic and experience-based. Capabilities are the enactment of core competencies. Roos and Von Krogh (1996: 425) contend that competence is not an asset which can be stock-piled rather it is a relational process because 'competence simply means the intersection between a particular task and the knowledge (and skill) of the person or the team doing it'. In other words, competence can be thought of as a capability realized through the effective interaction of individuals and the environment surrounding a particular project.

Competence and the limits of organization

The competence perspective provides an alternative to transaction cost economics arguments about how to manage vertical integration and relationships external to the firm (Leavy, 1998: 451). Thinking in terms of the strategic importance of a limited number of core competences has led firms to question their thinking about the very nature of what they do and what their organizations should comprise. Here the issue is one of the limits of organization.

If the strategic imperative is to limit investment to what you do best then the competence perspective suggests the outsourcing of non-core activities. As firms unbundle, downsize, refocus and reconfigure, one begins to recognize strategy as residing in a network of cooperative relationships. Outsourcing becomes strategic, offering a new level of 'utilization of external suppliers' investments, innovations and specialized professional capabilities that would be prohibitively expensive or even impossible to duplicate internally' (Quinn and Hilmer, 1994: 43).

The focus on competence implies a different way of thinking about both strategy and organization that challenges much previously accepted wisdom, for example, how to think about portfolio management. Prahalad and Hamel (1990: 81) argue that competitive advantage comes from 'management's ability to consolidate corporate-wide technologies and production skills'. Portfolios of competence rather than of separate business units imply a different dominant logic in thinking about strategy. You start with what the firm is good at and use this to unite and focus the organization rather than basing one's corporate decisions on a hands-off financial logic that manages the separate units only according to the numbers and as separate entities.

Competence and organization interact in other ways internal to the organization. Organization embodies important aspects of a firm's unique character and, to the extent that the resource-based view emphasizes unique competences as primary sources of competitive advantage, the organization itself is likely to be an important factor in strategy. Firms vary in their social architecture of values, cultures and relationships which cannot be readily replicated. It is the nature of the organization that will determine the commitment of individuals and groups to the creation and sharing of knowledge and to the best expression of their competence (Starkey and Tempest, 2001; Eisenhardt, 2002).

Competence and human resource management

The focus on competence and resources leads naturally to issues of human resource management (HRM) and one is seeing a degree of convergence between the fields of strategy and strategic HRM (Wright *et al.*, 2001). If to confer competitive advantage resources must: be rare/scarce, difficult, impossible to imitate, non-substitutable and appropriable (Barney, 1991), then we can consider HRM from this perspective. Firms regularly state that 'our people are our most important resource'. A strategic perspective on HRM (Kamoche, 2001) conceptualizes scarcity in terms of human resources, knowledge and skills. Crucial to a competence strategy is the firm's 'capacity to secure, nurture, retain and deploy human resources through HR policies and practices' and HR practices that 'seek to ensure that people are utilizing their skills towards the achievement of the organization's strategies' (Kamoche, 2001: 89).

The developing human and social capital perspective argues that the firm's ability to attract and retain a stock of human talent is central to learning and innovatory activity and, thus, to effective strategy (Starkey and Tempest, 2001). Human capital brings knowledge, skill and ability (Wright *et al.*, 2001). Acquisition and retention of human assets are crucial as more and more firms see themselves as competitors in a 'knowledge economy': 'if control over scarce resources is the source of economic profit, then it follows that such issues as skill acquisition, the management of knowledge and know how and learning become fundamental strategic issues' (Teece *et al.*: 1997: 514–15). But to make it useful, firms have to appropriate knowledge and translate it into useful action. Firms can acquire new talent, individual or groups of individuals, but unlocking the capacity for action is a more difficult challenge: 'even if the resources that constitute the team are transferred, the nature of organizational routines – in particular, the role of tacit knowledge and unconscious coordination – makes the recreation of capabilities within a new corporate environment uncertain' (Grant, 1991: 127).

The ways in which we think about organization and human resource management in the developing 'new economy' raise important issues about managing competence. The resource-based view of the firm has informed our understanding of recent developments in corporate refocusing as firms de-diversify to concentrate on areas where they possess a critical competence. New modes of organization – downsizing, restructuring, making our organizations more flexible and more responsive to evermore dynamic markets – challenge our ability to manage. Knowledge builds over time; competence is embedded and embodied in complex routines which are themselves embedded in modes of organizing that have a history and a heritage. We dismantle this heritage at our peril.

'[R]esources like knowledge, trust, commitment and so forth are by definition intangible and tacit and have to be built up over time. The tradability of such resources appears rather limited: can one buy trust, or commitment? ... The stock of skills, talents and competencies is tied in with a complex web of other tacit resources in the social context of organizations, including such nebulous constructs as trust and loyalty' (Kamoche, 2001: 48–9). The new economy and the dictates of short-term responses to short-term (including financial) market needs runs the risk of undermining what takes a long time to develop. 'How can we decide what is of lasting value in ourselves ... How can long-term goals be pursued in an economy devoted to the short-term? How can mutual loyalties and commitments be sustained in institutions which are constantly breaking apart or continually being redesigned. These are the questions ... posed by the new flexible capitalism' (Sennett, 1998: 10).

Conclusion

The resource-based view remains the most important recent development in strategic management thinking. It helps us understand the sources of competitive advantage in scarce resources, competence, and uniqueness. An approach to strategy that is informed by an awareness of critical competences makes a firm more sensitive to issues of innovation, building upon competence and searching for new sources of competitive advantage, than a financial control-based view of strategy, and thus more likely to develop the skills necessary to promote the long-term development of core businesses (Lockett and Thompson, 2001).

The competence-based view also helps us to understand strategy as an activity that is permeated by time. The dynamic capability addition to the debate about the sources of competitive advantage is based on the premise that, in successful firms, the firm's 'bundle' of resources is evolving along its own unique trajectory as a consequence of the firm's unique history (Lockett and Thompson, 2001: 744). We thus need to be far more sensitive to a company's history, as both an enabling resource and as a constraint.

Significant questions, though, remain unanswered. The resource-based view is poor at discriminating between resources that managers can manage and those beyond managerial control. There are, in particular, many questions about how to turn the knowledge that tacit knowledge is a powerful source of competitive advantage into actual competitive advantage. We understand only imperfectly how resources are built and leveraged for superior returns (Priem and Butler, 2001).

How is the possession of knowledge translated into successful practice (Evans, 2002)? We suggest that the translation of knowledge into competence and then into action is one of the most important questions for future research. Also, how are firms to become better at knowing what they are good at? One major telecommunications firm of our acquaintance was very surprised, when it performed a competence audit, to find that what it considered its core competences was different from what those external to the firm judged as core. The firm was not sure of what it was best at!

The focus on competence can go too far and even make us myopic. An organization that focuses purely on refining existing competences may become strategically vulnerable as these become too specific to a particular context. If change occurs an organization can find it hard to respond. This is captured by Leonard-Barton's (1992) notion of 'core rigidities' whereby over time core competences can become dysfunctional to performance. Renewal competency is the ability of an organization to discover a new production function leading to new market/product opportunities (Nanda, 1996). Renewal builds on Schumpeter's (1950) notion of creative destruction that involves depreciating existing resources by redefining what is relevant and useful to success. Intel's shift to microprocessor technology or IBM's redefinition of computers with its 360 system are examples of renewal. The process of creative destruction symbolizes the radical shift in relevant knowledge during periods of discontinuous change. The dynamic capability necessary to chart this kind of change is linked to the concept of 'absorptive capacity' (Cohen and Levinthal, 1990), the capacity of the firm to absorb new knowledge, competencies and to develop out of these new routines and actions.

The notion of competence now extends beyond the limits of the firm. We need to think of competence as a firm-specific attribute and also as an attribute of a network of relationships. Here, the need is to think of competence as a clustering phenomenon in which the firm is only one player. Porter (1990) links firm competitive advantage to developments at the regional and national level whereby firms cluster in specific regions and jointly develop robust new business models for particular industries. Examples here include information technologies in Silicon Valley, film and media around Hollywood, fashion clusters around Milan and motor racing clusters around the Thames Valley in the United Kingdom. In these clusters, firm competence is developed in intense competition with competitors, in collaboration with key suppliers with their own unique competences, and in response to demanding customers.

However, the focus on networks of competence has its limits too. The importance of concentrating on core competence has led, in many cases, to corporate refocusing and back to basics, with more outsourcing. However, this does have its dangers as it can distance the firm from key developments in an industry and in those parts of the value-chain from which it has distanced itself. Over-reliance on outsourcing can lead to 'skill sets deteriorating as [firms] become "locked out" from learning new skills and technologies critical to participating in industry evolution' (Lei and Slocum, 1992: 81).

The legacy of the competence-based view in strategy continues to develop. The future, in our opinion, should see further integration with the growing body of work on organizational learning, knowledge, dynamic change, and the challenge of deepening our understanding of the link between competence/ knowledge and different organizational contexts. Can we assume that core competences are at the heart of competitive advantage as suggested by the resource-based view of the firm? The answer is – yes and no. Yes, in that the notion of competence and the view of the firm as a collection and collectivity of resources gives us an important way of thinking about strategy. No, in that the notion of dynamic capabilities sensitizes us to the realization that the competences that give advantage at one point in time can cease to be the most useful in a changing environment. Ironically, core competences can become impediments, core rigidities.

At the core of companies that do last is a sense of direction and a small number of core values (Collins and Porras, 1994). Competences that work are developed and re-developed around this value core. The importance of the competence approach is that it raises interesting questions rather than providing us with durable answers. In a time of extraordinary change that is the best we can expect from a theory. To paraphrase Taylor (1990: 34) by substituting the word 'competence' for 'identity', 'What I am, my competence, is essentially defined by the way things have significance for me ... and the issue of my competence is worked out, only through a language of interpretation which I have come to accept as a valid articulation of these issues ... we are only selves insofar as we move in a certain space of questions' (Taylor, 1989: 34). The question of what we are good at and what we want to be good at is central to how we define ourselves in organizations and as human beings.

Notes

1. The term 'competence' is sometimes used synonymously with the terms 'competency' and 'capability'. It is difficult to distinguish these terms so we tend to use them synonymously, although we do talk about 'capabilities' specifically later in the chapter.
2. See below.
3. See below.

References

Ambrosini, V. and Bowman, C. (1998) 'The dilemma of tacit knowledge: tacit routines as a source of sustainable competitive advantage', paper presented to British Academy of Management Conference, at the University of Nottingham, September.

Badaracco, J.L. (1991) *The Knowledge Link*, Boston: Harvard Business School Press.

Barney, J.B. (1991) 'Firm resources and sustained competitive advantage' , *Journal of Management* 17 (1): 99–120.

Cohen, W.M. and Levinthal, D.A. (1990) 'Absorptive capacity: a new perspective on learning and innovation', *Administrative Science Quarterly* 35: 128–52.

Collins, J.C. and Porras, J.I. (1994) *Built to Last: Successful Habits of Visionary Companies*, New York: Harper Business.

Eisenhardt, K.M. (2002) 'Has strategy changed?' *MIT Sloan Management Review* Winter, 88–91.

Eisenhardt, K.M. and Martin, J.A. (2000) 'Dynamic capabilities: what are they?' *Strategic Management Journal* 21: 1105–21.

Evans, N. (2002) 'Through the looking glass: reflections on organizational integration, knowledge and the transfer of knowledge between firms, Ph.d. Dissertation, Lancaster University, UK.

Godfrey, P.C. and Hill, C.W.L. (1995) 'The problem of unobservables in strategic management research', *Strategic Management Journal* 16: 519–33.

Grant, R.M. (1991) 'The resource-based theory of competitive advantage: implications for strategy formulation', *California Management Review* 33, Spring, 114–35.

Grant, R.M. (1996) 'Toward a knowledge-based theory of the firm', *Strategic Management Journal* 17 (Winter Special Issue): 108–22.

Hamel, G. and Prahalad, C.K. (1994) *Competing for the Future*, Boston: Harvard Business School Press.

Kamoche, K. (2001) *Understanding Human Resource Management*, Buckingham: Open University Press.

Leavy, B. (1998) 'Learning in the strategy field', *Management Learning* 29: 447–66.

Lei, D. and Slocum, J.W. (1992) 'Global strategy, competence-building and strategic alliances', *California Management Review* Fall: 81–97.

Leonard-Barton, D. (1992) 'Core capabilities and core rigidities: a paradox in managing new product development', *Strategic Management Journal* 13: 111–25.

Lockett, A. and Thompson, S. (2001) 'The resource-based view and economics', *Journal of Management* 27: 723–54.

Nanda, A. (1996) 'Resources, capabilities, and competencies', in Moingeon, B. and Edmondson, A. (eds) *Organizational Learning and Competitive Advantage*, London: Sage.

Nelson, R.R. and Winter, S.G. (1982) *An Evolutionary Theory of Economic Change*, Cambridge, MA: Harvard University Press.

Penrose, E. (1959) *The Theory of the Growth of the Firm*, New York: John Wiley and Sons.

Porter, M. (1990) *The Competitive Advantage of Nations*, New York: Free Press.

Prahalad, C.K. and Hamel, G. (1990) The core competence of the corporation, *Harvard Business Review* May–June: 79–91.

Priem, R. and Butler, J.E. (2001) 'Is the resource-based view a useful perspective?' *Academy of Management Review* 26: 22–40.

Quinn, J.B. and Hilmer, F.G. (1994) 'Strategic outsourcing', *Sloan Management Review* Summer: 43–55.

Roos, J. and Von Krogh, G. (1996) 'The epistemological challenge: managing knowledge and intellectual capital, *European Management Journal* 14(4): 333–7.

Rumelt, R.P., Schendel, D. and Teece, D.J. (1991) 'Strategic management and economics', *Strategic Management Journal* 12(S): 5–29.

Schumpeter, J.A. (1950) *Capitalism, Socialism and Democracy*, 3rd edn, New York, Harper & Row.

Sennett, R. (1998) *The Corrosion of Character*, New York: W.W. Norton.

Smith, D. and Alexander, R. (1988) *Fumbling the Future: How Xeros Invented then Ignored the First Personal Computer*, New York: William Morrow & Co.

Spender, J.C. (1996) 'Making knowledge the basis of a dynamic theory of the firm', *Strategic Management Journal* 17 (winter special issue): 45–62.

Starkey, K. (1998) *How Organizations Learn*. London: Thomson International Business.

Starkey, K. and Tempest, S. (2001) *'Connectivity and empathy: future sources of competitive advantage in financial services'*. University of Nottingham, Financial Services Research Forum Report.

Taylor, C. (1989) *Sources of Self: The Making of Modern Identity*, Cambridge: Cambridge University Press.

Teece, D.J. (2000) 'Strategies for managing knowledge assets: the role of firm structure and industrial context', *Long Range Planning* 33: 35–54.

Teece, D.J., Pisano, G. and Schuen, A. (1997) 'Dynamic capabilities and strategic management', *Strategic Management Journal* 18: 509–37.

von Krogh, G., Roos, J. and Slocum, K. (1994) 'An essay on corporate epistemology', *Strategic Management Journal* 15: 53–71.

Wernerfelt, B. (1984) 'A resource-based view of the firm,' *Strategic Management Journal* 5(2) 171–80.

Wright, P.M., Dunford, B.B. and Snell, S.A. (2001) 'Human resources and the resource based view of the firm', *Journal of Management* 27: 701–21.

Zollo, M. and Grinter, S.G. (2002) 'Deliberate learning and the evolution of dynamic capabilities', *Organization Science* 13(3): 339–51.

6 To avoid organizational crises, unlearn

Paul C. Nystrom and William H. Starbuck

Organizations learn. Then they encase their learning in programs and standard operating procedures that members execute routinely. These programs and procedures generate inertia, and the inertia increases when organizations socialize new members and reward conformity to prescribed roles. As their successes accumulate, organizations emphasize efficiency, grow complacent, and learn too little. To survive, organizations must also unlearn.

Top managers' ideas dominate organizational learning, but they also prevent unlearning. Encased learning produces blindness and rigidity that may breed full-blown crisis. Our studies of organizations facing crises show that past learning inhibits new learning: Before organizations will try new ideas, they must unlearn old ones by discovering their inadequacies and then discarding them. Organizations in serious crisis often remove their top managers as a way to erase the dominating ideas, to disconfirm past programs, to become receptive to new ideas, and to symbolize change.

This chapter begins by describing some organizational crises and the ways in which top managers' past learning only made the crises worse. The following section shows how clever managers have executed remarkable turnarounds by changing their organizations' beliefs and values. After considering why organizations unlearn by the drastic step of replacing top managers en masse, this chapter urges top managers to accept dissents, to interpret events as learning opportunities, and to characterize actions as experiments.

Learning from crises

Many managers and scholars think that organizational survival indicates effectiveness. Survival is an insufficient measure of effectiveness, but the organizational survival rates are so low that there is clearly much room for improvement. Table 6.1 gives some approximate statistics for American corporations: Only 10 percent survive 20 years. Moreover, of those that do survive 20 years, more than a fourth disappear during the ensuing five years. The statistics for U.S. federal agencies look much like those for corporations.

A crisis is a situation that seriously threatens an organization's survival. We have spent several years studying organizations in crises – why crises arise, and

Table 6.1 Survival by US corporations

Ages in years	Percentages surviving to various ages	Percentages surviving at least five years after various ages
5	38	55
10	21	65
15	14	70
20	10	73
25	7	76
50	2	83
75	1	86
100	0.5	88

how organizations react. Our studies suggest that most organizational failures are quite unnecessary. The following two cases illustrate typical patterns.

Company H successfully published a prestigious daily newspaper for more than 100 years. Circulation reached a new peak in 1966, and the managers invested in modern printing equipment. The following year, circulation leveled off and advertising income dropped, while costs increased. Despite altered accounting procedures, the next year brought losses and a severe cash shortage. The board reacted by focusing even more intensely on cost control; a proposal to change the product a bit was rejected with laughter. Another bad year led the managers to raise prices radically and to form a task force to study corrective actions. Of five alternatives proposed by the task force, the board chose the only one that avoided all strategic reorientation. That is, the board decided to concentrate on those things the organization had always done best and to cut peripheral activities. Many key staff departed. Financial losses escalated. In 1972, the managers sold the printing equipment to pay operating costs, and Company H disappeared altogether a year later.

In the late 1960s, Company F made and sold mechanical calculators as well as typewriters and office furnishings. The company had succeeded consistently for nearly 50 years, and its top managers believed that no other company in the world could produce such good mechanical calculators at such low costs. These beliefs may have been accurate, but they soon proved irrelevant, for an electronic revolution had begun. Although some of the company's engineers had designed electronic calculators and computers, the board decided against their production and sale. The board understood how to succeed with mechanical calculators, the company had invested heavily in new plants designed specifically to manufacture mechanical calculators, this industry had always evolved slowly, and the board believed that customers would switch to electronic calculators only gradually. However, sales began a dramatic decline in 1970, and profits turned into losses. The board retrenched by closing the factories that manufactured typewriters and office furnishings in order to concentrate on the company's key product line: mechanical calculators. After three years of losses, bankruptcy loomed and the board sold Company F to a larger company. What happened next is reported later in this chapter.

These cases illustrate that top managers may fail to perceive that crises are developing. Other people see the looming problems, but either their warnings do not reach the top, or the top managers discount the warnings as erroneous. When top managers eventually do notice trouble, they initially attribute the problems to temporary environmental disturbances, and they adopt weathering-the-storm strategies: postpone investments, reduce maintenance, halt training, centralize decision making, liquidate assets, deny credit to customers, raise prices, leave positions vacant, and so forth. During this initial phase of crises, top managers rely on and respond to routine formal reports, particularly accounting statements, that present only superficial symptoms of the real problems. A major activity becomes changing the accounting procedures in order to conceal the symptoms.

In real crises, weathering-the-storm strategies work only briefly. Then the symptoms of trouble reappear; only this time, the organizations start with fewer resources and less time in which to act. The second phase in organizations' reactions to crisis involves unlearning yesterday's ideas. People in organizations rarely abandon their current beliefs and procedures merely because alternatives might offer better results: They know that their current beliefs and procedures have arisen from rational analyses and successful experiences, so they have to see evidence that these beliefs and procedures are seriously deficient before they will even think about major changes. Continuing crises provide this evidence. People start to question the conceptual foundations of their organizations, and they lose confidence in the leaders who advocated and perpetuated these concepts. Conflicts escalate as dissenters, voicing new ideas, challenge the ideas of top managers.

Reorienting by changing cognitive structures

Some people see potential crises arising and others do not; some understand technological and social changes and others do not. What people can see, predict, and understand depends on their cognitive structures – by which we mean logically integrated and mutually reinforcing systems of beliefs and values. Cognitive structures manifest themselves in perceptual frameworks, expectations, world views, plans, goals, sagas, stories, myths, rituals, symbols, jokes, and jargon.

Not only do top managers' cognitive structures shape their own actions, they strongly influence their organizations' actions. Albert King conducted a field experiment that reveals the power of a top manager's expectations. A top manager of Company J told the managers of plants 1 and 2 that he expected job redesigns would raise productivity, and he told the managers of plants 3 and 4 that he expected job redesigns would improve industrial relations but would not change productivity. What actually happened matched the top manager's initial statements. In plants 3 and 4, productivity remained about the same, and absenteeism declined. In plants 1 and 2, productivity increased significantly, while absenteeism remained the same. What makes the experiment even more interesting is that different types of job redesign were used in plants 1 and 3 than in plants 2 and 4. Plants 1 and 3 implemented job enlargement whereas plants 2 and 4 implemented job rotation, yet both types of job redesign produced the same levels of productivity and absenteeism. Thus, differences in actual job activities produced no differences in productivity and absenteeism, whereas different expectations did produce different outcomes.

Expectations and other manifestations of cognitive structures play powerful roles in organizational crises, both as causes and as possible cures. The Chinese exhibited great wisdom when they formed the symbol for crisis by combining the symbols for danger and opportunity: top managers' ideas strongly influence whether they and their organizations see opportunities as well as dangers. For example, Company F, one of the companies described earlier in this chapter, surmounted its crisis primarily because a change in its top managers introduced different beliefs and perceptions.

Its top managers and board saw Company F as being designed to adapt to slow, predictable changes in technologies and markets. They initially predicted that electronic calculators would have slow, predictable effects, and the sudden electronic revolution both bewildered and terrified them. They decided that, for their company, the electronic revolution posed an insurmountable challenge. As it floundered at the brink of disaster, Company F was acquired by Company E, which promptly fired all of F's former top managers.

The top managers of Company E soon discovered opportunities that seemed obvious to them: demands for typewriters and office furnishings were two to three times production capacities; sales staff had been turning down orders because the plants could not fill them! Also, the company's engineers had designed good electronic calculators and computers that the previous board had refused to put into production. The new top managers talked optimistically about opportunities rather than dangers, challenges rather than threats. They borrowed a small amount of money from the parent company with which to experiment, they converted plants producing mechanical calculators into ones making typewriters and office furnishings, and they authorized production and energetic marketing of electronic products. Within a year of acquisition, losses converted into profits, production and employment began rising, and optimism prevailed again.

Top managers' cognitive structures also block recoveries from crises. In Company H, the newspaper described earlier, the top managers' beliefs intensified their commitment to a faulty strategy, generating actions and inactions that sealed the company's fate.

Top managers who clung steadfastly to incorrect ideas also undermined the success of Company T, which made and sold consumer electronics equipment such as television receivers, tape recorders, loudspeakers, and radios. Sales had doubled about every three years over its 40 years' existence. The top managers invested in two new plants in order to replace labor with capital because they thought that labor costs were rising too rapidly relative to sales revenues. Sales growth slowed substantially while these new plants were being constructed. The top managers attributed this deceleration to various environmental factors even though available evidence contradicted each of their attributions. The top managers asserted that these problems would be solved by the new plants with low labor costs that would enable lower prices. In the fourth year of this crisis, the national government lent Company T many millions of dollars to save it from collapse.

But the loan only postponed the collapse for two years ... and increased its cost.

A harsh way to unlearn

Organizations succumb to crises largely because their top managers, bolstered by recollections of past successes, live in worlds circumscribed by their cognitive structures. Top managers misperceive events and rationalize their organizations' failures. Some top managers, like those in Company F, admit privately that they do not understand what is happening and do not know what to do, while publicly they maintain facades of self assurance and conviction. Other top managers, like those in Company T, never doubt that their beliefs and perceptions have more validity than anyone else's.

Because top managers adamantly cling to their beliefs and perceptions, few turnaround options exist. And because organizations first respond to crises with superficial remedies and delays, they later must take severe actions to escape demise. They must replace constricting, hopeless cognitive structures. But if only one or a few new managers join an ongoing group, either they adopt the prevailing cognitive structure or the other managers regard them as deviants with foolish ideas. Crises intensify these social processes by creating a wagon-train-surrounded-by-Indians atmosphere. So the top managers must be removed as a group, except for the rare individuals who dissented from the prevailing beliefs and perceptions. Moreover, revitalizing a crisis-ridden organization requires enthusiasm and energy ... these from people who have grown cynical after hearing their top managers make failed promises and hollow excuses for several years. Before they will replace their cynicism with effort and vision, the people have to be convinced that this time, at last, someone is serious about making real changes. One way to do this, usually the only way, is to turn the former top managers into scapegoats.

Cognitive reorientations spark corporate turnarounds. Some enterprising people take over ailing corporations and successfully convert losses into profits by seeing opportunities that the former managers overlooked. Conversely, William Hall reported that turnaround efforts generally fail when firms in stagnating industries get subsidies from their parent corporations or from governments. The difference in outcomes seems to spring from infusions of new ideas, not solely infusions of financial resources. Indeed, the financial infusions are usually small in successful turnarounds. Strategic reorientations are rooted in cognitive shifts, and turnarounds almost always involve both significant changes in top management and changes in overall strategies.

Company S, which made ferrous screws, lapsed into persistent losses caused by aging machinery and brisk competition. A new president and vice-president for marketing embarked on a strategic reorientation: shifting from large orders of ferrous screws to small orders of nonferrous screws. But two years of persuasion failed to loosen the other top managers' adherence to old modes of acting and thinking. Because the two new managers could not afford to waste more time, they replaced their colleagues. Company S subsequently achieved substantial success.

Removing people is a quick, effective way of erasing memories. Our colleague, Bo Hedberg, reviewed the psychological literature and concluded that unlearning must precede the learning of new behaviors. But top managers show a quite understandable lack of enthusiasm for the idea that organizations have to replace their top managers en masse in order to escape from serious crises. This reluctance partially explains why so few organizations survive crises.

Unlearning continuously

Top managers might try to keep emerging crises from becoming serious, by reacting promptly to early symptoms of trouble and by avoiding weathering-the-storm strategies and superficial cover-ups. But not all symptoms warrant prompt reactions, and weathering-the-storm strategies can be useful. The top managers we studied all believed that they were acting wisely (at least when they took the actions), but they were misled by their faulty beliefs and perceptions. Faulty cognitive structures do not always plunge organizations into crises, but they do always keep managers from controlling their organizations' destinies.

To stay in control of their futures, top managers have to combat the inevitable errors in their own beliefs and perceptions. This is, of course, very difficult. It demands exceptional objectivity and humility as well as enough self-confidence to face errors within oneself. But it is easier to keep managers' cognitive structures continuously realistic and up-to-date than to try abruptly to correct errors that have added up and reinforced each other. And it is easier to correct cognitive structures while things are going well than to do so after troubles develop.

Top managers can stimulate their own unlearning and new learning in at least three ways: they can listen to dissents, convert events into learning opportunities, and adopt experimental frames of reference. The next three sections give examples of ways in which top managers can use these methods to benefit themselves and their organizations. However, we intentionally stop short of offering how-to-do-it prescriptions. Managers often get into trouble by trying to follow prescriptions that have been formulated by someone else in a different situation. For one thing, obeying someone else's prescriptions requires a partial substitution for one's best judgment. The simpler and more practical prescriptions sound, the more trust one puts in them, and so the more danger they pose. For another thing, effective methods of getting things done respect the constraints and exploit the opportunities that distinguish specific situations. We also question the view that "if managers knew how to do it, they would already be doing it." Many managers exhibit great skill at creating pragmatic techniques and procedures to achieve the goals they are pursuing. Top managers who want to unlearn will likely find ways to do it, ways that mesh with the other aspects of their jobs. But the top managers we studied never looked upon their past learning as impediments and they never tried to unlearn.

Listening to dissents

Complaints, warnings, and policy disagreements should cause reflection that sometimes leads to unlearning. Because such messages assert that something is wrong, top managers ought to respond by reconsidering their beliefs and practices. However, well-meaning colleagues and subordinates normally distort or silence warnings and dissents. So top managers receive only some of the messages sent, and even these messages arrive in watered-down forms, often accompanied by defensive rationalizations.

Moreover, research shows that people (including top managers) tend to ignore warnings of trouble and interpret nearly all messages as confirming the rightness of their beliefs. They blame dissents on ignorance or bad intentions – the dissenting subordinates or outsiders lack a top manager's perspective, or they're just promoting their self-interests, or they're the kind of people who would bellyache about almost anything. Quite often, dissenters and bearers of ill tidings are forced to leave organizations or they quit in disgust, thus ending the dissonance. For example, after Company F had struggled with its crisis for two years, the head of the typewriter division quit in protest over his colleagues' decisions to sell typewriter plants in order to get funds to subsidize the production of mechanical calculators. His division was the only division earning a profit.

Lyman Porter and Karlene Roberts reviewed research showing that top managers do not listen carefully to their subordinates. People in hierarchies talk upward and listen upward: they send more messages upward than downward, they pay more attention to messages from their superiors than to ones from their subordinates, and they try harder to establish rapport with superiors than with subordinates. People also bias their upward messages to enhance good news and to suppress bad news, yet they overestimate how much real information they transmit upward. Although these communication patterns are understandable, they are also harmful. In every crisis we studied, the top managers received accurate warnings and diagnoses from some of their subordinates, but they paid no attention to them. Indeed, they sometimes laughed at them.

After studying 20 corporations enmeshed in crises, Roger Dunbar and Walter Goldberg concluded that the chief executives generally surrounded themselves with yes-sayers who voiced no criticisms. Worse yet, the yes-sayers deliberately filtered out warnings from middle managers who saw correctly that their corporations were out of touch with market realities. Many of these middle managers resigned and others were fired for disloyalty.

Top managers might maintain more realistic cognitive structures if they would personally interview some of the people leaving their organizations. But why wait until people exhaust their loyalty and decide to leave? Top managers should listen to and learn from dissenters, doubters, and bearers of warnings. Not all dissents are valid, and warnings are often wrong, but dissents and warnings should remind one that diverse world views exist, that one's own beliefs and perceptions may well be wrong. Indeed, top managers should worry if they hear no such messages: long silences signal distortion, not consensus. Although consensus sometimes occurs within top-management groups, we have found no organizations in which strong consensus pervaded the managerial ranks. Furthermore, Peter Grinyer and David Norburn conducted careful research that found no benefits from strategic consensus: firms in which managers disagree about goals, policies, and strategies earn just as much profit as firms in which managers agree.

How are top managers to know which dissents and warnings to consider seriously? They certainly dare not rely on their own judgments about ideas' validity because everyone's beliefs and perceptions contain errors. Messages that sound obviously correct add little to knowledge. On the other hand, messages that sound fanciful can highlight defects in one's knowledge, because they arise from premises quite different from one's own.

We recommend this screening procedure: first, assume that all dissents and warnings are at least partially valid. Second, evaluate the costs or benefits that would accrue if messages turn out to be correct: fanciful messages typically entail high costs or benefits; realistic messages likely entail low costs or benefits. Third, try to find some evidence, other than the messages' content, about the probabilities that messages might prove to be correct. For instance, have the messages' sources acted as if they truly believe what they are saying? Are the sources speaking about their areas of special expertise? Fourth, find ways to test in practice those dissents and warnings that might yield significant costs or benefits. Launch experimental probes that will confirm, disconfirm, or modify the ideas.

Exploiting opportunities

Changes induce people to question their world views. One very successful organization, Company G, actually appointed a vice-president for revolutions, who stepped in approximately every four years and shook up operations by transferring managers and reorganizing responsibilities. When asked how he decided what changes to make, he answered that it made little difference so long as the changes were large enough to introduce new perceptions. Statistics show that productivity rose for about two years after each shake-up, then declined for the next two years, until another shake-up initiated another productivity increase.

Company G's practice should be imitated widely. The vice-president for revolutions injected unexpected and somewhat random question marks into operations that, otherwise, would have grown smug and complacent through success and would have lost opportunities and alertness through planning. Indeed, Company G itself might have benefited from more frequent doses of its own medicine: shouldn't the shake-ups have happened every two years, when productivity had peaked and before it began to decline?

However, managers would not have to generate so many question marks if they turned spontaneous events into question marks. Managers can create unlearning opportunities by analyzing the consequences of such events as new laws, technological innovations, natural disasters, disrupted supplies, fluctuating demands for outputs, and recessions. Our colleague, Alan Meyer, learned a lot about the dynamics of hospital organizations because he happened to be studying some hospitals when they were jolted by a doctors' strike. To his surprise, he found that ideologies were more powerful than structures as forces guiding organizational responses. The hospitals that took best advantage of the strike were ones with ideologies that cherish dispersed influence in decision making, frequent strategic reorientations, and responsiveness to environmental events. Such hospitals both anticipated the effects of the strike and used the strike as a stimulus for long-run improvements.

One of the most successful adaptations to the doctors' strike was made by Hospital C. This hospital's culture values innovation, professional autonomy, and pluralism; its administrator urges the subunits to act entrepreneurially and to maintain bonds with the community. The administrator himself devotes 70 percent of his time to outside relationships, and he predicted the strike two months before it began – well before other hospitals anticipated it. Because he purposely avoids codifying procedures and formalizing relationships, he subtly encouraged the (overtly spontaneous) coalescing of an informal group to consider the strike's impacts. This group sent all supervisors a scenario of what might happen and asked them to write up plans for response. When the strike occurred, Hospital C cut costs and reallocated resources so quickly that it continued to earn a profit; and after the strike ended, the hospital easily adapted back. The administrator said, "We learned that we could adapt to almost anything – including a drastic drop in our patient load – and, in the process, we discovered some new techniques for cutting our operating costs."

Experimenting

Experimentation offers many benefits as a central frame of reference for top managers. People who see themselves as experimenting are willing to deviate temporarily from practices they consider optimal in order to test the validity of their assumptions. When they try out other people's ideas that they themselves expect to be suboptimal or foolish, they create opportunities to surprise themselves. They also manage experiments in ways that cut down the losses that failures would produce; for instance, they attend carefully to feedback. Because they place fewer personal stakes on outcomes looking successful, they evaluate outcomes more objectively. They find it easier to modify their beliefs to accommodate new observations. And they keep on trying for improvements because they know experiments never turn out perfectly.

A team from McKinsey & Company studied ten companies that executives think are unusually well run. Experimenting tops the list of characteristics they have in common. To quote Thomas Peters' conclusion from *Business Week* (July 21, 1980):

> Controlled experiments abound in these companies. The attitude of management is to "get some data, do it, then adjust it", rather than wait for a perfect overall plan.

Managers can program some searches for better ideas. For example, evolutionary operation (EVOP) is a well thought-out method for continual experimentation. The basic idea is to run experiments that entail little risk because they deviate only incrementally from what the experimenters believe to be optimal operation. The experiments should be planned and interpreted by committees that are carefully designed to meld technical expertise and political clout. Although Gorge Box and Norman Draper created EVOP as a way to improve manufacturing processes, the basic ideas generalize to repetitive activities in finance, marketing, personnel management, and office procedures.

Experiments need not be carefully designed in order to be revealing, and they need not be revealing in order to stimulate unlearning, but it is better to use experiments fruitfully. Company K's experience suggests some of the differences between fruitful and unfruitful experiments.

Company K had successfully made and repaired railroad rolling stock for almost 90 years; then, in 1963, the nation's major railroad announced that it would buy no more new rolling stock from anyone for the foreseeable future. Company K's managers saw the railroad industry collapsing about them, so they studied several possibilities and chose three new product lines for development. After two years, however, the company had achieved no sales whatever in two of these lines. The managers launched two more experimental product lines, but they concentrated their efforts on the one new product line that looked most promising: a small automobile. Sales multiplied two and a half times over the next five years, but profits were only 0.8 percent of sales! Despite frequently repeated dire predictions, railroad rolling stock was accounting for 95 percent of sales; and despite frequent hopeful predictions, the automobile had not yet gotten into production and was generating high costs. When the automobile finally did come into production in 1970 the result was horrendous losses in both 1970 and 1971 – so horrendous that the directors decided to close the company.

Why did Company K's experiments turn out so badly? One reason was too many eggs in one basket. The managers poured all their energies and most of their company's money into the automobile; their experiments with other new product lines were half-hearted and ritualistic. A second reason was an absence of feedback. The managers ignored evidence that the automobile project was developing badly and evidence that the rolling-stock business was doing well. Nor did they learn from their failures. Recall that two of their experimental product lines yielded zero sales: might this have occurred because Company K had no sales personnel, not even a sales manager? Might it have forewarned what would happen when the automobile came into production? Company K did add a sales department to promote the automobile: a sales manager and one salesman!

Shortly after the directors decided to close Company K, five of the six top managers and half of the lower-level employees departed voluntarily. The board appointed the remaining senior manager president, with orders to continue shutting the company down. Instead, the new president (who had nothing to lose) launched some new experiments. These disclosed substantial foreign demand for railroad rolling stock – the previous managers had ignored foreign markets. The experiments also showed that the blue-collar workers could run the factory themselves with very little assistance from managers – the previous managers had created a competitive game in which managers and workers were trying to outsmart each other. In fact, after they took charge, the bluecollar workers doubled productivity: by 1974, production was 36 percent higher than in 1963 even though employment was only 69 percent of the earlier figure. Two new product lines were tried, and one of these became as important as rolling stock. By then, the directors had decided to keep the company in business. Profits in 1975 were six times the highest profits the company had ever earned previously, and they have continued upward since.

Why did the second wave of experiments turn out so differently? The directors' decision to close Company K initiated unlearning: The people who departed took with them their convictions about how the company should operate and what opportunities the environment offered; the people who remained became ready to abandon their past beliefs. No longer sure they knew what to do, people tried some experiments that they would previously have rejected as outrageous or silly. The company had no resources to squander on experiments that were turning out badly, so everyone paid close attention to how the experiments were turning out: feedback quickly had real effects. Not least, the new president was an unusually wise man who knew how to engender enthusiasm, entrepreneurship, and a team spirit.

Conclusion

Our studies underline top managers' dominance of their organizations' survival and success. Top managers are the villains who get blamed for steering organizations into crises, and they are the heroes who get the credit for rescuing organizations from crises. Such blaming and crediting are partly ritualistic, but also partly earned. Top managers do in fact guide organizations into crises and intensify crises; they also halt crises by disclosing opportunities, arousing courage, and stirring up enthusiasm.

The top managers who instigate dramatic turnarounds deserve admiration, for they have accomplished very difficult tasks of emotional and conceptual leadership. Even greater heroes, however, are the top managers who keep their organizations from blundering into trouble in the first place. To do this, they have had to meet the still more difficult challenge of conquering the errors of their own beliefs and perceptions.

Selected bibliography

For more detailed descriptions of our studies about organizational crises, see Paul Nystrom, Bo Hedberg, and William Starbuck's "Interacting Processes as Organization Designs" in Ralph Kilmann, Louis Pondy, and Dennis Slevin's (eds.) *The Management of Organization Design*, Vol. 1 (Elsevier North-Holland, 1976); William Starbuck and Bo Hedberg's "Saving an Organization from a Stagnating Environment" in Hans Thorelli's (ed.) *Strategy + Structure = Performance* (Indiana University Press, 1977); William Starbuck, Arent Greve, and Bo Hedberg's "Responding to Crises" (*Journal of Business Administration*, Spring 1978); William Starbuck and Paul Nystrorn's "Designing and Understanding Organizations" in Paul Nystrom and William Starbuck's (eds.) *Handbook of Organizational Design*, Vol. 1 (Oxford University Press, 1981); and in Bo Hedberg's "How Organizations Learn and Unlearn" in Paul Nystrom and William Starbuck's (eds.) *Handbook of Organizational Design*, Vol. 1 (Oxford University Press, 1981).

Related studies of organizational crises appear in Roger Dunbar and Walter Goldberg's "Crisis Development and Strategic Response in European Corporations" in Carolyne Smart and William Stanbury's (eds.) *Studies on Crisis Management* (Toronto's Institute for Research on Public Policy, 1978); also see William Hall's "Survival Strategies in a Hostile Environment" (*Harvard Business Review*, September–October 1980).

More information on Albert King's study of job redesigns appears in "Expectation Effects in Organizational Change" (*Administrative Science Quarterly*, June 1974).

Research concerning communications between people in superior and subordinate roles is reviewed in Lyman Porter and Karlene Roberts' "Communication in Organizations" in Marvin Dunnette's (ed.) *Handbook of Industrial and Organizational Psychology* (Rand McNally, 1976).

Alan Meyer's study of hospitals' reactions to the physicians' strike are reported in his article, "How Ideologies Supplant Formal Structures and Shape Responses to Environments" (*Journal of Management Studies*, January 1982).

A detailed study of 21 companies' planning systems appears in Peter Grinyer and David Norburn's "Planning for Existing Markets: Perceptions of Executives and Financial Performance" (*Journal of the Royal Statistical Society*, Series A, Vol. 138, Part 1, 1975).

Readers interested in EVOP philosophy and procedures should refer to George Box and Norman Draper's *Evolutionary Operation* (Wiley, 1969).

7 Strategic dissonance

Robert A. Burgelman and Andrew S. Grove

Aligning corporate strategy and strategic action is a key top management responsibility. Such alignment is viewed by some as driven by the strategic intent of the CEO who sets ambitious targets within a 10 to 20 year time horizon, relentlessly develops the firm's capabilities, and transforms the basis of competition in the industry to the firm's advantage.[1] This is an inspiring view, to which many CEOs no doubt aspire. But it is a view premised on top managers having extraordinary foresight. Extraordinary foresight can, of course, always be assumed to explain successful strategies after the fact. But there is convincing evidence that it is very improbable in high-technology industries.[2]

If extraordinary foresight is unavailable, how can top management make strategic decisions in high-technology industries? Our answer to this central question is based on research concerning Intel Corporation's strategic evolution[3] as well as our analysis of more than a dozen case studies of major players in the information processing and telecommunications industries.[4]

Strategic dissonance

Our key premise is that in extremely dynamic industries[5] alignment between a firm's strategic intent and strategic action is not likely to last. Inevitably, strategic actions will begin to lead or lag strategic intent. Such divergences between intent and action cause "strategic dissonance" in the organization. While new strategic intent is necessary to lead the company out of strategic dissonance, our key proposition is that new strategic intent must be based on top management's capacity to take advantage of the conflicting information generated by strategic dissonance.

Not all dissonance, of course, is strategic. Companies continuously experience some level of dissonance as a result of routine disagreements and conflicts because no division of labor is ever perfect and no project ever unfolds exactly as planned. Companies need managers precisely to mediate and resolve these sorts of frictions. Dissonance, however, is strategic when it signals impending industry or corporate transformation. Here are three examples from Intel.

In 1970, newly-founded Intel Corporation introduced dynamic random access memory (DRAM) products in the market. DRAMs replaced magnetic core memory as the standard technology used by computers to store instructions and data as they executed programs, and Intel became the first successful semiconductor memory company in the world. Throughout the 1970s and early 1980s, DRAMs continued to be viewed as Intel's core business. While the DRAM industry grew tremendously during that period, the onslaught of Japanese entrants caused Intel's DRAM business to be hurt by the late 1970s. By the end of 1984, there was serious disagreement within the company regarding the importance of DRAMs in Intel's future. The disagreement had been latent for several years. It was resolved when, during 1984–85, Intel's top management completed the drawn out process of exiting from the DRAM business and realized that Intel had transformed itself from a memory company into a microprocessor company.

In 1990–91, Intel top management faced a strategic decision about what to do about the company's RISC architecture efforts. During the 1980s, a middle-level technical manager had developed the i860 RISC chip within Intel and had convinced several higher-level managers of its commercial potential. The technical development had been somewhat surreptitious because it was sold to top management as the development of a co-processor for the i486 chip but did in fact involve a stand-alone processor. The managers involved in the i860 project launched a successful marketing effort and top management had little real choice but to adopt the i860 as a new strategic product. Commercial success subsequently slowed down in the face of the competition of a plethora of other RISC chips. But large amounts of Intel's development resources had begun to flow to RISC architecture efforts and there had developed two camps within the company with different views about the future of RISC versus CISC. After a protracted debate, top management, in 1991, decided to reaffirm its commitment to the x86CISC architecture and to scale down the RISC effort.

In November 1994, a flaw in the first release of the Pentium microprocessor – a routine event associated with most first releases of new microprocessors to OEMs – triggered a discussion among technical users on the Internet which was picked up quickly by CNN and other news media. Intel's initial reluctance to replace the flawed chips, except for those highly technical users that were likely to engage in mathematical operations that could be affected by the flaw, created an uproar and escalated the event into a full blown "Pentium processor crisis."

While the national press hammered Intel for not being forthcoming enough in replacing the flawed products with no questions asked, Intel's OEM and distribution channel sales data indicated that demand for Pentium processors continued unabated. After several difficult weeks of internal debate, Intel top management decided to exchange all flawed Pentium processors for new ones simply upon request. By that time, Intel's top management had come to grips with the fact that Intel's prominence in end-user space, in part as the result of the Intel Inside campaign started in April 1991, had dramatically changed the rules of the game for Intel, and probably for all high-technology companies marketing to end-users.

Strategic dissonance signals a strategic inflection point

A common thread running through these vignettes of strategic dissonance is that they signaled that Intel had reached (DRAM exit, Pentium processor crisis), or was about to reach (i860 RISC chip), what we call a "strategic inflection point" (SIP) in its development. Inflection point has a rigorous mathematical meaning[6] but here we use it more loosely – metaphorically – to describe the giving way of one type of industry dynamics to another; the change of one winning strategy into another; the replacement of an existing technological regime by a new one. These changes-witness the computer industry-create a "valley of death"[7] for the incumbents because they materially affect their profitable growth trajectories. If an incumbent's top management is able to come up with new strategic intent that takes advantage of the new industry conditions, it can traverse the valley of death and enter a new era of profitable growth. Otherwise, it continues to survive with severely reduced performance prospects, or dies (see Figure 7.1).

Unfortunately, it is very difficult for anyone in an extremely dynamic industry, including top management, to clearly perceive the new industry equilibrium, winning strategy, or new technological regime, that loom beyond a SIP. Think about a computer-generated image being morphed from one state to another – you cannot tell when one ends and the other starts; only the beginning (old image) and the end (new image) are clear. In-between is a dizzying succession of intertwined, overlapping, blurred, fuzzy images.

So, how can top management know when dissonance is strategic-signaling a SIP – as opposed to a minor and/or transitory change in competitive dynamics, strategy, or technology? How to tell signal from noise? Sometimes the telling signs are quite obvious. For instance, in 1984, every clear-minded senior manager in the telecommunications industry had to realize that Judge Green's

Figure 7.1   Strategic inflection point

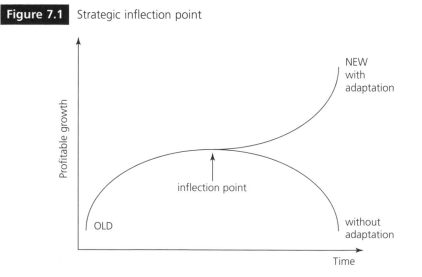

"Modified Final Judgement" inaugurated a period of momentous change that would transform the competitive dynamics in the industry in major ways.[8] In other instances, however, the telling signs may be subtle and intangible. For example, after the Japanese had become powerful players in DRAMs, Intel managers visiting Japan would come back with the feeling that they were viewed with newly found derision – "Something changed; it was different now," they would say upon return. It took Intel's top management several more years to realize that the competitive dynamics, the winning strategy, and the key technological competencies in the DRAM industry had fundamentally changed.

In the face of a SIP, voices sounding danger ahead will emerge. These voices usually rise form the middle-management ranks or from the sales organization: From people that know more because they spend time outdoors where the storm clouds of creative destruction gather force and – unaffected by company beliefs, dogmas, and rhetoric-start blowing into their face. Some will flag their concern to top management – and it's wise to pay heed as it would have been very wise to give serious weight to the troubled comments of the Intel travelers. Other middle managers will just quietly adjust their own work to respond to the strategic change. For instance, in the early 1980s Intel got down to 1 factory out of 8 manufacturing DRAMs because the finance and production planning people (middle-level managers) month-by-month allocated scarce capacity from where it seemed unprofitable to where it seemed to be more fruitful. Often, these words and actions don't seem strategic at first glance: they seem peripheral. But it is wise to keep in mind that when spring comes, snow melts first at the periphery: That's where it is most exposed.

The need for strategic recognition

Managing strategic dissonance requires "strategic recognition" – the capacity of top managers to appreciate the strategic importance of managerial initiatives after they have come about but before unequivocal environmental feedback is available. Top management's strategic recognition that the set of changing circumstances is a SIP happens in three key stages:

- recognizing the growing divergence between what the company currently puts forth as its strategy and the actions taken by its managers – what we call here strategic dissonance,

- asking the (anxiety provoking) question "is it one – a SIP?" and

- trying to discern the newly emerging strategic picture and providing a framework in which the divergence can be combated and new strategic intent formulated.

The method of resolution is broad debate, involving different technical, marketing, and strategic points of view, and representatives of different levels in the organization. This takes time. Dealing with the strategic dissonance associated with a SIP is a fundamental test of the resilience of a company's culture and its leadership.

Strategic dissonance, strategic inflection point, and strategic recognition are the three interrelated key concepts that answer the question of how top management can decide on strategic intent in high-technology industries.

A framework for analysis

We propose a theoretical framework of five dynamic forces[9] that shape a company's evolution and the emergence of strategic dissonance (see Figure 7.2). This framework can help top managers determine whether manifestations of dissonance are strategic and/or ask questions that help surface latent signs of strategic dissonance.

The first of these forces – the basis of competitive advantage in the industry is determined by the industry factors identified by Michael Porter[10] as key determinants of the attractiveness of an industry: bargaining power of customers and suppliers, the nature of the rivalry among incumbents, and the threat of new entrants and of substitution. Technological change, legislation, or government regulation can affect each of these elements and their relative importance. The second force concerns the company's distinctive competence: the competencies that have made it possible to develop a competitive advantage and to survive.[11] The third force is the company's official corporate strategy which reflects top management's beliefs about the basis of the firm's current success and anticipated changes in the familiar environment.[12] The fourth force – strategic action – is what the company actually does. Finally, the fifth force concerns the company's internal selection environment which mediates the link between corporate strategy and strategic action and the link between distinctive competence and the basis of competitive advantage. The internal selection environment comprises admin-

Figure 7.2 Dynamic forces in firm evolution

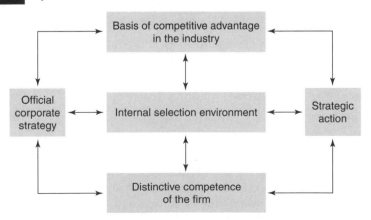

Source: R.A. Burgelman, "Fading memories: a process theory of strategic business exit in dynamic environments," *Administrative Science Quarterly* 39, 1994

istrative elements (e.g., resource allocation rules) and cultural elements (e.g., norms governing internal communication).[13]

During some periods in a company's history, these five forces are in harmony: The company's distinctive competence is consistent with the basis of competition in the industry; its official strategy and the strategic actions of its managers are co-aligned; and its internal selection environment is relatively peaceful with no signs of strategic dissonance.

This was the case at Intel in the early 1970s. Intel had established itself as a leader in semiconductor memories by pioneering a new semiconductor process called metal-oxide-silicon (MOS) technology. This process technology allowed Intel to increase the number of transistors on a chip while simultaneously reducing its production cost. This, in turn, allowed Intel to successfully introduce the world's first DRAM into the market in 1970. While other companies, notably Advanced Memory Systems, had been able to design a working DRAM, they had failed to develop a process technology to manufacture the new device successfully in volume. Process technology became Intel's distinctive competence. During the next half a dozen years these competencies served Intel to remain the dominant competitor in the DRAM business. During that period, Intel's corporate strategy was to offer semiconductor memory chips as alternatives for mainframe computer memories, and this strategy guided Intel's strategic actions. The internal selection environment routinely allocated resources to semiconductor memories.

Over time, however, the dynamic forces shown in Figure 7.1 tend to diverge and their harmonious relationships are broken, thereby creating strategic dissonance in the organization.

Sources of strategic dissonance

Divergence of the basis of competition and distinctive competence

The most fundamental and often least readily visible source of strategic dissonance derives from a divergence between the changing basis of competition in the industry and the firm's distinctive competencies; the latter becoming less relevant for competitive advantage. This happened in Intel's DRAM business. In the late 1970s, Japanese entrants used their large-scale precision manufacturing skills to obtain high yields early on in new DRAM generations, thereby outcompeting Intel, which had much weaker manufacturing skills. High yields had great impact on unit cost, and this was a crucial advantage as DRAMs became a commodity product.

Companies often experience an inertial aftermath of success: They have become sharply aware of the competencies that made them successful against the initial competition and they continue to rely on these distinctive competencies even when the competition changes. Also, companies usually organize themselves in such a way that the employees representing these competencies are likely to have the greatest influence in the strategic decision-making process. Changes in the basis of competition thus often evoke inertial responses by incumbents.[14] Intel's DRAM business, again, provides an example. Falling behind the Japanese, Intel tried to compete by creating advanced products based on the company's strong process technology skills. Process technology had been the technological competency that had given Intel its initial competitive advantage. Process technologists continued to play the dominant role in Intel's DRAM product development for the 16K (kilobit), 64K, 256K, and 1 Meg (megabit) generations, in spite of the industry-wide shift in the basis of competition toward manufacturing competence.

On the other hand, strong technological competencies may also evolve in new, sometimes unanticipated, directions and provide the basis for generating new business opportunities. Important examples at Intel are the invention of erasable programmable read only memories (EPROMs) and, even more so, the invention of the microprocessor. These developments have strategic repercussions for the company's existing core business and require difficult top management decisions. The successful EPROM and microprocessor businesses soon began to compete with Intel's relatively weak core DRAM business for scarce manufacturing resources. Later on, the increasingly strong microprocessor business also competed with the weakening EPROM business. This internal competition turned out to be advantageous for the company, transforming Intel gradually from a lagging "memory company" into a leading "microprocessor company." Evolving technological competence, however, may also create fundamental strategic dilemmas. The development of the i860 RISC processor at Intel, for instance, threatened to undermine the company's strong core microprocessor business based on the x86 architecture.

In sum, firm-level competencies and the basis of competition in the industry often evolve along independent paths. Our framework suggests that dynamically matching firm-level distinctive competencies and the basis of competition in the industry is a tough top management challenge. It requires top management to closely watch the evolution of the industry structure as well as to be alert to the strategic implications of unanticipated new developments in the company's competencies.

Divergence between stated strategy and strategic action

A second major source of strategic dissonance, one that is usually more readily visible, originates in the divergence between corporate strategy and strategic action. One driver of this divergence is inertia in corporate strategy.[15] Corporate strategy reflects top management's beliefs about the basis of success of the firm. Top managers usually rise through the ranks and are deeply influenced by their perception of what made the company successful. Intel's exit from the DRAM business, for instance, was delayed by the fact that top management was still holding on to Intel's identity as a memory company, even though the company had become a non-factor in DRAMs with 2–3 percent market share by 1985. IBM's slowness in taking advantage of the RISC microprocessor architecture (which it had invented in the mid-1970s)[16] was, no doubt, attributable, at least in part, to top management's perception of IBM as the leading "mainframe computer" company in the world. Similarly, Microsoft's relatively weak past strategy in networking operating systems probably was, in part, due to their corporate identity throughout the 1980s as the "desktop operating system" company. Intertwined with these inertial self-perceptions is emotional attachment on the part of top management to the business that made the company successful. As one middle-level manager put it in relation to Intel's exit from the DRAM business: "It was kind of like Ford getting out of cars."[17] Last, but not least, top management often hesitates to change the strategy because the consequences are not completely clear. For instance, Intel's slowness in moving away from defining itself as a memory company were, in part, due to the fact that DRAMs were viewed as the company's technology driver having been the largest volume product (in units) historically.

If inertia in corporate strategy leads to change that is too slow, top managers can also change the corporate strategy too fast – in ways that stretch beyond what the company is capable of doing and the market is ready to accept. In the early 1990s, Apple Computer's CEO John Sculley was clearly in front of his organization when he pushed the strategy of developing personal digital assistants (PDA) and personally championed the Newton operating system. Sculley's strategic intent stretched beyond Apple's available innovative capabilities and the market's readiness. At the same time, Apple was facing a major battle in its core personal computer business after the barriers that separated the Macintosh's niche from the rest of the PC industry weakened in the face of the success of Windows 3.0. Sculley's ambitious strategy for PDAs required the development of new innovative capabilities while at the same time the demands of the PC business required major cultural change to achieve greater cost consciousness and discipline in product development. Apple could not do both, and Sculley's strategic goals thus created enormous, top-driven dissonance within the organization.[18]

The other driver of this divergence are the independent strategic actions taken by middle-level managers. During the late 1970s and into the early 1980s, Intel's new EPROM and microprocessor businesses began to compete with the DRAM business for scarce manufacturing capacity. As noted earlier, middle-level managers in manufacturing planning allocated scarce manufacturing to the new, higher margin EPROM and microprocessor businesses, thereby gradually diminishing the role of DRAMs as Intel's core business. In 1984, another middle-level manager responsible for process technology development for static random access memory (SRAM) and microprocessors made the crucial choice to support a new process technology that favored micro-processors and speciality memory products over commodity memories.[19] This decision effectively de-coupled the commodity memory business from the rest of Intel's business. Ironically, this move turned out to be beneficial after the new strategic intent (Intel the "micro-processor company") was formulated.

While some actions may turn out to be helpful, there is also potential danger associated with strategic actions of middle-level managers that diverge from the official strategy. The technical and initial commercial success of the i860 RISC chip as an unplanned stand-alone processor created a strategic dilemma for Intel's top management and extremely strong, eventually divisive, tensions within the organization.

Role of the internal selection environment

If the basis of competition in the industry, the company's distinctive competencies, the firm's official strategy, and the strategic actions of middle-level managers all start diverging from each other, how can a company possibly survive? Research suggests that in the face of a SIP, a company's internal selection environment may be more important for survival than its stated strategy.[20] The role of the internal selection environment is to regulate the allocation of the company's scarce resources – cash, competencies and capabilities, and senior management attention – to strategic action while the official strategy is in flux and new strategic intent has not yet been formulated and articulated.

A company can continue to be successful for some time if its internal selection environment selects actions that are consistent with competitive reality even while becoming decoupled from the official (stated or implicit) corporate strategy. The continued success provides then a time cushion for bringing corporate strategy back in line with strategic action. At Intel, for instance, the capacity allocation decisions favoring EPROMs and micropro-cessors over DRAMs were initially not driven by official corporate strategy. Rather, they were driven by the internal resource allocation rule – maximize margin per-wafer-start – that favored products with greater profitability and hence greater competitive advantage in the external environment. The deteriorating competitive position of DRAMs required top management to make a fundamental strategic choice in 1984: Stay in DRAMs and invest several hundred million dollars to get on a par with the market share leader in a commodity market, or exit from DRAMs and concentrate key resources to become a leading microcprocessor company. This strategic choice was facilitated by the results of the internal selection processes which had already shifted the "mainstream" away from memories toward microprocessors.

The internal selection processes leading up to the formulation of new strategic goals critically depends on top management's strategic recognition capacity. One type of strategic recognition involves top management's ability to recognize the strategic importance of actions by middle-level managers who try to tie a new business initiative to the corporate strategy-providing legitimacy for the new business. For instance, the internal and external success of microprocessors eventually made top management realize that Intel's future lay with becoming a microprocessor company. A second type of strategic recognition involves top management's ability to recognize the strategic importance of actions of middle-level managers that diminish the legitimacy of an existing business and decouple it from the corporate strategy. As an example, the allocation of manufacturing capacity away from DRAMs and the decision by a middle-level manager to give up a process technology that was important for commodity memory products eventually helped top management recognize that DRAMs were no longer a core business for Intel.[21]

Managing strategic dissonance

Strategic dissonance, strategic inflection points, and strategic recognition are tools for managing the major transformations that companies must bring about in the face of discontinuous change. As the company moves through the valley of death, the old and the new basis of competition, the old and the new distinctive competence, the old and the new strategy, and the old and new strategic action are all in play together. Figure 7.3 shows a picture of the transformation process.[22]

So, what are the characteristics of the internal selection environment and what are the top management behaviors that help a company take advantage of strategic dissonance and survive the turbulence of a SIP?

Help internal selection reflect external reality; allow dissent

Top management must help ensure that the firm's internal selection environment continues to reflect the real competitive pressures in the external environment. A necessary condition is that the company has a management information system that reflects how its businesses are really doing in the competitive environment. This allows top management to ask sharp questions, on a regular basis, about why the company's businesses are performing the way they are. Intel's rule to allocate scarce manufacturing capacity based on margin-per-wafer-start, for instance, forced the DRAM middle-level managers to come up with their best strategic arguments for why the company should forego profits by allocating scarce capacity to DRAMs. Constantly watching competitors – old and new – is mandatory behavior for top management. Why are they strong competitors? What do they do that we cannot do better? This is one set of questions senior managers should ask. In the DRAM case, for instance, Intel top management should have asked why the Japanese new entrants into the DRAM industry seemed to be getting much higher yields in manufacturing from the start.

It is also important that the firm's internal selection environment values dissent and controversy surrounding the interpretation of the data. This is difficult, because organizations are uncomfortable with internal dissent. Debating tough issues is only possible where people will speak their minds without fear of punishment. The debate between CISC and RISC at Intel during 1990–1 strained this ideal at Intel. The debate became acrimonious at times; different factions were beginning to engage in a civil war. People were voicing concerns: "How will I work for so and so when this is all over?" The DRAM crisis did likewise. A key role of top management is to provide an umbrella against such fears. Top management may not be competent to personally judge the issues but it is up to them to create a fear-free internal selection

Figure 7.3 The transformation process

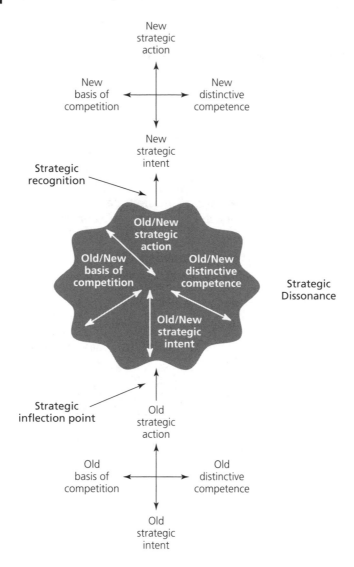

environment. So, our advice to top managers is: First, don't shut people up; and, second, if they disagreed and were right, congratulate them!

Don't dismiss strategic dissonance

A company's capacity for getting through a SIP depends predominantly on a very human issue: How the top management reacts, emotionally, to strategic dissonance. This is no surprise. Business people, like all people, have emotions, and a lot of emotions are tied up in the status and well-being of their business.

In spite of the best attempts at business and engineering schools to inculcate rational analysis, when the business gets into serious difficulties or key managerial assumptions are challenged, objective analysis takes second seat to personal/emotional reactions.

In fact, the top managers in charge are likely to go through some variation of the stages of dealing with a catastrophe:

DENIAL → ESCAPE or DIVERSION → ACCEPTANCE → PERTINENT ACTION

Denial is prevalent in the early stages of almost every instance. To appreciate this, read the annual report management letters of companies that, in retrospect, we know were facing a SIP. Escape refers to the personal actions of top managers. For instance, frequent public speeches on vague subjects given by CEOs of companies facing difficult times or the move of corporate headquarters away from the center of business action are signs of attempted escape. Diversion, by contrast, refers to the worst kind of escape, often involving major acquisitions unrelated to the core business that faces a SIP.

Effective top managers go through these first two stages as well, but they are able to move on to the acceptance and pertinent action stages before it is too late. Ineffective top managers are unable to do so and have to be removed. Those that replace them are not necessarily more capable, but usually do not have the emotional investment in the current strategy. In our view, replacement of corporate leaders in the face of a SIP is far more motivated by the need to put distance between the present and the past than by getting someone "better." Intel's DRAM crisis became resolved when Grove went to see CEO Gordon Moore and asked him what a new top management would do if he and Moore were replaced. The answer was clear: Get out of DRAMs. Grove then suggested that Moore and he go through the revolving door, come back in, and do it themselves – a forced way to put distance between present and past.

Formulate new strategic intent based on strategic recognition

Top management must try to surmise how the new equilibrium of forces in the industry will look like and what the new winning strategy will be, knowing that they cannot get it completely right. Getting out of the valley of death associated with a SIP requires top management to develop a mental image of what the industry will look like and the company should look like when it climbs out on the other side. Top management must use the information that is generated by strategic dissonance when trying to discern the true new shape of the company on the other side of the valley. It must be a realistic picture grounded in the company's distinctive competencies – existing ones or new ones that are already being developed. For instance, when Intel finally got out of the DRAM business it had also become clear that the company had to be reconceptualized as a microprocessor rather than a memory company. By that time, Intel had moved from a silicon-based distinctive competence in memory products to a distinctive competence in implementing computer architectures in silicon chips.

Coming out of a difficult period, top management is more likely to have a sense of what they *don't* want the company to become before they know what they *do* want it to become. For instance, as middle-level managers in the DRAM business experienced difficulties in obtaining capacity allocations, they proposed, several times, that Intel restructure itself and give DRAMs their own manufacturing capability instead of sharing with other products. These requests helped top management decide that they did not want Intel principally to become a supplier of commodity type products. This decision was made before it was clear to top management that Intel would become a leading microprocessor company. Management writers use the word "vision" for this. But that is too lofty for our purpose. Leadership here implies changing with the environment and the organization. Reality must lead top management rather than the other way around. This is difficult because top management is expected to have vision.

Getting through the period of immense change requires reinventing – or perhaps rediscovering – the company's identity. Since companies and their leaders are shaped by their past, this is truly hard. If top management got its experience running a hardware company, how can they and their key staff imagine what it is to run a software company? Steve Jobs, for instance, must have struggled with that at NeXT. It is not surprising that it took many years before he was able to redefine NeXT as a software company and got rid of the desire to produce esthetically pleasing, well-designed "computers." Today, Intel is outgrowing its identity as a leading microprocessor company and faces the challenge of redefining itself as a company that wants to be a supplier of building blocks for the computing and communications industries.

Move from strategic intent to strategic action

Seeing, imagining, sensing the new shape of the company is only one step. Getting there requires more wrenching actions. These moves we have called strategic actions and they involve (re)assigning resources in order to pursue the new strategic intent. The fact is, corporate strategy is realized by performing a series of such strategic actions, and not via strategic planning. Strategic plans are abstract, far away, and give managers a lot of chances to reconsider as they go along – so, they don't command the true attention their action-oriented counterparts do.

Clearly, the wisdom necessary to guide a company through transformational changes cannot, as a practical matter, reside only in the head of the CEO. If it did, he or she would have guided the company through those changes in the first place. If, on the other hand, the CEO comes from the outside, chances are he or she does not really understand the evolving subtleties in such situations. Middle managers have the hands-on exposure, but, by necessity their experience is specialized, not company wide.

What is needed is real-time mining of the middle managers' insights, exposing all that information to searing intellectual debate, and letting this ferment take place until the shape of the other side of the valley is sufficiently clear that a dedicated march in its direction is feasible. Once that starts, the ferment needs to stop, and all hands need to be committed to this new direction. We think, therefore, that there is an inverted-U type of relationship between the intensity and duration of constructive intellectual debate in a company and its long-term ability to manage through SIPs (see Figure 7.4).

At one extreme, too little intellectual debate means that middle managers do not challenge one another as long as the favor is reciprocated. The result: A lack of strategic dissonance and a hard fall off the curve. At the other extreme, too much intellectual debate paralyzes the company because most energy is used up seeking to win the debate for the sake of winning rather than for the sake of the company. Strategic action is delayed indefinitely and, again, a hard fall off the curve. So, during strategic dissonance, top management must let go some while they are not sure. (This is not easy: top management is paid for being sure!) But then they must pull strategic action and strategy back in line and direct the march. Strategic leadership means encouraging debate and bringing debate to a conclusion.[23]

Take advantage of the "bubble"

Top management must deliberately use the company's uncommitted resources that accumulate in good times – what we call the "bubble" – by responding to early signs of strategic dissonance and by supporting new initiatives before strategic dissonance emerges. This too is difficult, particularly so when the prospects of the mainstream business in the foreseeable future continue to be favorable (abundant profits and growth expected) and everybody is very busy exploiting the existing opportunities. Senior and top management, under such

Figure 7.4 Relationship between adaptability and internal debate

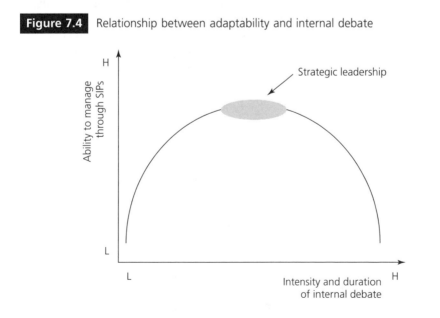

circumstances, are likely to pay only lip service to supporting new initiatives; it is easy to delay action to "tomorrow." When the prospects are not so good, it is easier to take action. In the early 1990s, Apple Computer had about $1 billion in free cash, but the prospects of the mainstream PC business looked less good because Apple's niche was not growing and was threatened by Microsoft's Windows 3.0.[24] While the choice of strategic intent can be questioned, John Sculley deserves credit for anticipating the need for change in Apple's strategy and starting the change process.

Manage unanticipated invention

While senior management should constantly look for ways to harvest the benefits of unanticipated invention generated by the company's technological competencies, the first, and foremost, question should be: is this invention useful to our core business? If not, where could we use it? Is the new area suggested by this invention of interest to us? Does it make use of other competencies we have? Implicit in these actions of senior management is the will to terminate investment in areas that, after careful examination, do not fit the firm. This may sound cold, but the willingness to terminate experiments has to be viewed as an integral part of the process of creating such experiments. If such will is lacking, eventually the weight of accumulated and undisposed of experimentation will dissipate the bubble and inhibit the start of new ones.[25]

Culture is the key

The internal selection environment that we are describing is one in which there are both strong bottom-up and top-down forces. If the company is dominated by the top-down force, chances are that it will efficiently march in lockstep toward an important strategic intent, but the strategic intent better continue to be the right one. If the bottom-up force dominates, chances are that the company will drift aimlessly from one limited strategic intent to another and dissipate its resources. Obviously, if there is neither top-down nor bottom-up force, the company will experience something like "Brownian motion."

But how can these forces both be strong at the same time? They can, if the company has the rugged, confrontational/collegial culture that is desirable in high-technology industries. Such a culture has two attributes: First, it tolerates even encourages – debate (at Intel, the name for it is "constructive confrontation"). These debates are vigorous, devoted to exploring issues, and indifferent of rank.[26] They are focused on finding what is best for the company (as opposed to the individual or group). Second, it is capable of making – and accepting clear decisions; with the entire organization capable of supporting the decision.

An organization that has a culture that approximates these two requirements is a powerful adaptive (learning) organization. This is the culture that works best when top management has to navigate between letting chaos reign and reining in chaos. For instance, there was enormous contention in the CISC versus RISC debate. There was rebellion within the Microprocessor Group against its management. After a period of exhausting debate, everybody was ready for a clear new direction. While a few people decided to leave, the adoption and execution of the new direction unified everyone.

Other companies that have survived in extremely dynamic industries by transforming themselves probably have a similar set of characteristics, even though they shape them in their own way. Hewlett-Packard, for instance, has such a culture (judging by the results), perhaps more so than any other large company. Their history has been and continues to be a series of transformations, all achieved by "peaceful means" in the hands of internal management. To see this, compare their ability to move from instruments to computers (and their growth spurt) with that of their major competitors in instruments. When computers moved from minicomputer-based technology to microprocessor-based technology, compare their performance with that of other minicomputer manufacturers. HP made the transformation with hardly working up a sweat. In recent years, HP has transformed itself again, becoming the world leader in desktop printing[27] and gradually working itself into a strong position in desktop computers. HP's culture is more "SIP-ready" than any we can think of.

Conclusion

We started this article by asking: How can top management in extremely dynamic environments decide on the right strategic intent? We have offered a conceptual framework and three interrelated key concepts – strategic dissonance, strategic inflection point, and strategic recognition – for answering that central question. Our conceptual framework helps examine the evolving linkages between a company's distinctive ("core") competencies and the basis of competition in the industry, and its official corporate strategy and strategic action. The research underlying our framework has revealed that, over time, there will unavoidably emerge divergences between competence and basis of competition, and between strategy and action. We view these divergences as natural outcomes of the internal and external dynamic forces that move and shake companies and industries. We also view the strategic dissonance that these divergences create as an opportunity for top management to learn about the changing reality of the competitive world that the company faces and the new opportunities generated by its own competencies. Strategic dissonance signals a strategic inflection point in the firm's development trajectory and alerts top management to the fact that the familiar picture of the industry is being morphed into a completely new one – involving a fundamental change in the basis of competition, requiring fundamentally different competencies, or both. Strategic recognition is top management's major tool for dealing with strategic dissonance and a SIP. Strategic recognition picks out of the mass of conflicting information the elements that can form the foundation for new, viable strategic goals. Top management's capacity for strategic recognition is enabled in major ways by the ability of the company's internal selection environment to distinguish signal from noise. This, in turn, depends on the comprehensiveness, depth, and rigor of intellectual debate among middle and top managers, which is the cultural feature most telling of a company's long-term ability to manage through SIPs.

Notes

1. Gary Hamel and C.K. Prahalad, *Competing for the Future* (Boston, MA: Harvard Business School Press, 1994). These authors introduced the idea of "strategic intent." See Gary Hamel and C.K. Prahalad, "Strategic Intent," *Harvard Business Review* (May/June 1989).
2. A current example concerns the impact of the Internet on the computer and telecommunications industries. Few of the key players in these industries foresaw the speed and force with which the Internet has evolved during the last 18 months. For a general discussion of the difficulty of foreseeing the implications of new technologies, see Nathan Rosenberg, "Uncertainty and Technological Change," paper prepared for the Conference on Growth and Development: The Economics of the 21st Century, organized by the Center for Economic Policy research of Stanford University, June 3–4, 1994.
3. This research is reported in: Robert A. Burgelman, "Intraorganizational Ecology of Strategy Making and Organizational Adaptation: Theory and Field Research," *Organization Science* (August 1991); Robert A. Burgelman, "Fading Memories: A Process Theory of Strategic Business Exit in Dynamic Environments," *Administrative Science Quarterly* (March 1994); Robert A. Burgelman, "A Process Model of Strategic Business Exit: Implications for an Evolutionary Perspective on Strategy," *Strategic Management Journal* (Special Issue, Summer 1996, forthcoming).
4. These case studies are used in our MBA elective course "Strategy and Action in the Information Processing Industry" at the Stanford Business School. Some of these cases were written at the Stanford Business School: George W. Cogan and Robert A. Burgelman, "Intel Corporation (A): The DRAM Decision," 1990; Bruce K. Graham and Robert A. Burgelman, "Intel Corporation (B): Implementing the DRAM Decision," 1991; George W. Cogan and Robert A. Burgelman, "Intel Corporation (C): Strategy for the 1990s," 1991; Dan Steere and Robert A. Burgelman, "Intel Corporation (D): Microprocessors at the Crossroads", 1993; Dan Steere and Robert A. Burgelman, "Intel Corporation (E): New Directions for the 1990s," 1993; Alva H. Taylor, Robert A. Burgelman, and Andrew S. Grove, "A Note on the Telecommunications Industry in 1993," 1994; Alva H. Taylor, Robert A. Burgelman, and Andrew S. Grove, "The Wireless Communications Industry: After AT&T-McCaw," 1994; Thomas Kurian and Robert A. Burgelman, "The Operating Systems Industry in 1994," 1994; Jeffrey Skoll, David Zinman, and Robert A. Burgelman, "The Consumer On-Line Services Industry in 1995," 1995. Other cases, written at the Harvard Business School, include: "The Global Semiconductor Industry in 1987"; "The Global Computer Industry; Note on the PC Network Software Industry, 1990"; "Microsoft's Networking Strategy; Mips Computer Systems (A)"; "Motorola and Japan (A); The Transformation of IBM"; "Apple Computer 1992, and Reshaping Apple Computer's Destiny," 1992. These are all published in David B. Yoffie, *Strategic Management in Information Technology* (Englewood Cliffs, NJ: Prentice-Hall, 1994).
5. For a discussion of different types of dynamic environments, see Jeffrey Williams, "How Sustainable is Your Competitive Advantage?" *California Management Review*, 34/3 (Spring 1992): 29–51. For a discussion of the managerial challenges of operating in "high-velocity" environments, see Kathleen Eisenhardt, "Speed and Strategic Choice: How Managers Accelerate Decision Making," *California Management Review*, 32/3 (Spring 1990): 39–54.
6. Mathematically, an inflection point is reached when the first derivative (the slope of the trajectory) becomes zero and the second derivative (the rate of change) changes sign (positive to negative or vice versa).

7. Andrew S. Grove, "PCs Trudge out of the Valley of Death," *The Wall Street Journal*, January 18, 1993; "Invest or Die," *Fortune*, February 22, 1993 (cover story).

8. Nevertheless, even in 1995 it is by no means obvious what the new competitive equilibrium in the telecommunications industry will look like; what the winning strategies and the dominant technologies will be. For instance, Bell Atlantic, one of the most aggressive regional Bell operating companies (RBOCs) planning to diversify into delivering video and television services, abruptly called a halt to its plans in April 1995. See "Bell Atlantic Halts Plan for Video Services,' *The New York Times*, April 26, 1995. Recently, AT&T decided to split itself up into three parts – telecommunications services, telecommunications equipment, and computers – in order to be able to compete in a more focused way in each of these dynamic industries. One reason for the split-up was that AT&T experienced enormous strategic dissonance as the RBOCs, in anticipation of the deregulation of the local exchange business, were increasingly reluctant to buy telecommunications equipment from a potential major rival.

9. Burgelman (March 1994), op. cit.

10. Michael E. Porter, *Competitive Strategy* (New York, NY: Free Press, 1980).

11. The concept of distinctive competence was first proposed by Philip Selznick, *Leadership in Administration: A Sociological Interpretation* (New York, NY: Harper & Row, 1957). Distinctive competence is similar to core competence, but emphasizes the relative uniqueness of the competencies that the company initially assembles and the evolutionary processes through which they evolve. As a result of these evolutionary processes, distinctive competencies have inertia and may become "competence traps." See Barbara Levitt and James March, "Organizational Learning," in W. Richard Scott, ed., *Annual Review of Sociology*, 14 (1988): 319–40. For a discussion of core competence see C.K. Prahalad and Gary Hamel, "The Core Competence of the Corporation," *Harvard Business Review* (May/June 1990).

12. See Robert A. Burgelman, "SA Model of the Interaction of Strategic Behavior, Corporate Context, and the Concept of Strategy," *Academy of Management Review* (1983); Gordon Donaldson and Jay W. Lorsch, *Decision Making at the Top: The Shaping of Strategic Direction* (New York, NY: Basic Books, 1983); Karl E. Weick, "Substitutes for Corporate Strategy," in David J. Teece, ed., *The Competitive Challenge* (Boston, MA: Ballinger, 1987).

13. Burgelman (March 1994), op. cit.

14. Arnold C. Cooper and Dan E. Schendel, "Strategic Responses to Technological Threats," *Business Horizons* (1976); William J. Abernathy, Kim B. Clark, and Alan M. Kantrow, *Industrial Renaissance: Producing a Competitive Future for America* (New York, NY: Basic Books, 1983); Michael E. Tushman and Philip Anderson, "Technological Discontinuities and Organizational Environments," *Administrative Science Quarterly* (1986); Barbara Levitt and James March, "Organizational Learning," *Annual Review of Sociology*, 14 (1988); Rebecca M. Henderson and Kim B. Clark, "Architectural Innovation: The Reconfiguration of Existing Product Technologies and the Failure of Established Firms," *Administrative Science Quarterly* (1990); Dorothy Leonard-Barton, "Core Capabilities and Core Rigidities: A Paradox in Managing New Product Development," *Strategic Management Journal* (1992).

15. Michael T. Hannan and John H. Freeman, "Structural Inertia and Organizational Change," *American Sociological Review* (1984); Henry Mintzberg and James A.Waters, "Tracking Strategy in an Entrepreneurial Firm," *Academy of Management Journal* (1982); Danny Miller and Peter H. Friesen with the collaboration of Henry Mintzberg, Organizations: *A Quantum View* (Englewood Cliffs, NJ: Prentice-Hall, 1984).

16. See for instance "Mips Computer Systems," in Yoffie (1994), op. cit.

17. Burgelman (March 1994), op. cit., p. 41.

18. See "Reshaping Apple Computer's Destiny 1992," in Yoffie (1994), op. cit.

19. See "Intel Corporation (A): The DRAM Decision," Stanford Business School case PS-BP–256, p. 10.

20. See Burgelman (August 1991) and (March 1994), op. cit.

21. Theses two processes are called "strategic context determination" and "strategic context dissolution," respectively. See Burgelman (1996, forthcoming), op. cit.

22. A vivid example from the late 19th century concerns the transition from wind to steam as the dominant means for powering ships. For a while, some ship builders produced hybrids featuring both sails and steam engines. See R.N. Foster, Innovation: The Attacker's Advantage

(New York, NY: Summit, 1986). Today, in the face of uncertainty as to whether TDMA or CDMA will become the dominant technology in cellular telephony, some telecommunications companies are planning to bring out cellular phones that embody both technologies.

23. We think that strategic recognition and strategic leadership must meet the tests for "statesmanship," put forth by Henry A. Kissinger. Kissinger writes: "The ultimate test of statesmanship ... is a combination of *insight and courage* [emphasis provided]. Insight leads to assessments that define a society's freedom of action, while courage enables the statesman to act on his convictions before they are generally understood. Great statesmen operate on the outer margin of their society's capabilities; weak statesmen tend to be overwhelmed by events." See Henry A. Kissinger, Review of "Churchill: The Unruly Giant" by Norman Rose, *The New York Times Book Review*, July 16, 1995, p. 7.

24. See "Reshaping Apple Computer's Destiny 1992," in Yoffie (1994), op. cit.

25. For an assessment framework, see Robert A. Burgelman, "Designs for Corporate Entrepreneurship in Established Firms, *California Management Review*, 26/3 (Spring 1984).

26. Andrew S. Grove, *High Output Management* (New York, NY: Random House, 1983); Andrew S. Grove, "Breaking the Chain of Command, *Newsweek*, October 3, 1983. There is some useful social science literature on the quality of decision making in teams with dissent. One line of inquiry concerns the role of minority views in increasing group performance. There is evidence that distinct minority points of view help generate novel solutions that lead to improved group performance. See, for instance, Charlan Nemeth, "Style without Status Expectations: The Special Contributions of Minorities", in Murray Webster and Martha Foschi, eds., *Status Generalization: New Theory and Research* (Stanford, CA: Stanford University Press, 1988). Another line of inquiry concerns the use of conflict as a means for improving decision effectiveness. Two techniques for introducing conflict in decision processes are Devil's Advocate and "Dialectical Inquiry. Devil's Advocate involves assigning an individual or group the task of criticizing a particular course of action. Dialectical Inquiry involves creating a debate between opposing views. See, for instance, Richard A. Cosier and Charles R. Schwenk, "Agreement and Thinking Alike: Ingredients for Poor Decisions," *Academy of Management Executive* (February 1990). Much of this research, however, is based on experiments involving students in contrived settings. A study of how Lyndon Johnson used George Ball as "devil's advocate" in top-level government decision making during the Vietnam war to isolate and defuse, rather than to integrate, a different point of view suggests the potential pitfalls of some of these techniques. See Irving L. Janis, *Victims of Group Think* (Boston, MA: Houghton Mifflin, 1972) and Irving L. Janis and Leon Mann, *Decision Making: A Psychological Analysis of Conflict, Choice, and Commitment* (New York, NY: Free Press, 1977).

27. "How H-P Used Tactics of the Japanese to Beat Them at Their Game, " *The Wall Street Journal*, September 8, 1994.

Learning, structure and process

Introduction

A key theme of several chapters in Part I was the analysis of how organizations change their cognitive structures, the thought and thinking structures that underpin behaviour, and develop new mental models to drive new strategies. Part II addresses issues of organization structure and process and, in particular, how structure and process can be managed to encourage organizational learning.

Hierarchical organization structure might be appropriate in stable and simple environments but not when competitive advantage is dependent upon innovatory capacity, the ability to respond to and shape fast-changing and varied consumer demand. In conditions of rapid technological change, organizational learning is crucial. Chapter 8 addresses the issue of the design of innovating organizations. The building blocks of any organization – structures, processes, rewards and people – need a special configuration if innovation is to result and the chapter compares structure, processes, reward systems and people management in operating and innovating organizations. In the latter, people self-select for key roles that focus upon the getting and blending of ideas rather than upon the implementation of plans that are realized through rules handed down from the top. Programmes are more important than a precise division of labour. The opportunity and autonomy to pursue self-realization motivates as much as the compensation package. Top management must orchestrate a process (innovation) that is 'destructive' of previous investments and career plans. It must also find a means of legitimizing the challenge to the status quo. Creative destruction requires innovative approaches to integration across functional and divisional divides. Innovation depends upon the simultaneous coupling of knowledge from a variety of sources rather than its linear sequential processing.

Chapter 9 focuses upon learning processes and links organizational innovation to knowledge creation. Innovation is understood as a process in which an organization creates and defines problems and then actively develops new knowledge to solve them. The chapter examines the relationship between tacit and explicit knowledge and how these different forms of knowledge relate to alternative modes of knowledge creation. The process of organizational knowledge creation is conceptualized as a spiral, tapping into the explicit and the tacit and into individual, group, organizational and inter-organizational levels of learning. The prime mover in the process is, finally, the individual and a key source of learning is the contact with customers. Self-organizing teams are crucial to the learning process because it is in this environment that individual perspectives are articulated and conflicts resolved for the common good. The chapter also links teams to communities of practice and learning to stories as a means of sharing understanding. Reference is made to the Japanese adoption of 'rugby-style' product development to speed up this process by swift exchange/passing of information and sharing of knowledge. Organizational factors that enable knowledge creation include 'creative chaos', 'redundancy' and 'requisite variety' and the chapter concludes by suggesting two new management models – 'middle-up-down management' (as opposed to top-down or bottom-up) and 'hypertext' organization – as means of maximizing learning.

Chapter 10 offers another angle on learning through the analysis of the ways in which organizations build 'transformative capacity', a phrase which captures the ability to develop and store knowledge over time and to activate this knowledge at the appropriate time to develop competitive advantage. The chapter builds on the resource-based view of the firm to discuss how firms can create this capacity. Existing resources can entrap firms into modes of operation that cease to be effective when the environment changes. In effect, firms get stuck in 'competency traps'. The way to escape this danger is to create new competencies out of re-combination of existing resources, i.e. a process of new knowledge creation by combining old knowledge. This is analysed as a process of pollination. Pollination permits the creation of hybrid varieties by crossing one species with another and is path-dependent and cumulative. Underlying transformative capacity is the ability to create knowledge in the first place, then the ability to maintain this knowledge through time and to reactivate and synthesize learning at appropriate moments.

Innovation and change can be construed as radically altering the 'genetic code' of the corporation. The next chapter (Chapter 11) examines General Electric's efforts to break its old genetic code under the leadership of CEO Jack Welch. A corporate 'revolution' requires a new breed of leader to redesign the 'social architecture' of the organization. At GE the redesign process was spearheaded by Crotonville, GE's Management Development Institute. Under Welch, Crotonville reported direct to executive management and not to employee relations staff. The old textbooks were 'symbolically burned'. Management development initiatives were carefully constructed to link closely to new thinking about career development and succession planning. Course membership was devised to cut through the old chain of command and to forge a direct link to top management. The learning process itself was validated by top managerial commitment and participation in courses. Such commitment is a measure of leadership in the learning organization. The focus is on learning from experience and from reflection upon that experience. Crucial here is that the company develop a framework that provides guidelines that integrate on-the-job development with the development that takes place during formal learning periods.

Chapter 12 focuses on the idea of community, a concept that is increasingly central to debates about organizational learning. The 'community of practice' has emerged as a major design theme in thinking about organizational learning systems. The chapter examines modes of participation in social learning systems and how these span firms, industries, regions and beyond, distinguishing between three modes of belonging to such systems – engagement, imagination and alignment. Communities of practice are crucial to learning because they are the embodiment of learning and the context for the exercise of competence. They possess shared repertoires of communal resources – language, routines, tools stories, etc. Members are connected by common knowledge, jointly created, and by relationships of mutuality. Crucially, out of their membership of such communities individuals develop a sense of identity. Identity is crucial to learning because it is fashioned out of experiences and a sense of competence that profoundly affects our way of knowing. It also sets boundaries to our learning – 'our identities are the living vessels in which communities and boundaries become realized as an experience of the world'.

Chapter 13 explores the fluid world of new network forms of organization and develops the concept of 'latent organization', an approach to organization which has emerged as a way of managing in project-based industries. The chapter examines the shift from hierarchy to network in the television industry and the development of project-based organizations periodically drawn together by 'network brokers'. It is the network broker who functions as primary knowledge broker in this new environment and as a key source of knowledge about how the different parts of a network can be made to function together effectively. However, the chapter raises questions about the continuing viability of this system from a learning perspective. Skills that support the network have, ironically, been learned in the traditional vertically integrated organization with the resources to support such development in-house. And there is a danger that the perpetual reconfiguration of such networks might compromise production effectiveness in the long term due to the continual learning curves that newly configured project teams have to constantly negotiate.

The final chapter of Part II (Chapter 14) also develops the theme of the network economy and of community in a context where firms are narrowing their knowledge and competence bases in the search for cost-effectiveness and focus, while, at the same time, markets are becoming more diverse and turbulent. In such an environment the premium is upon distributed learning that spans organizational and industrial divides. The chapter proposes a new model of community, the 'community of creation', designed for this context and lying somewhere between the closed hierarchical system and an open market-based model, thus offering an alternative to either too much structure or to chaos. Learning and knowledge creation are conceived as collaborative activity that spans divides. The community of creation model is grounded in the concept of *ba*, a Japanese term for a shared space for emerging relationships, which is compared with the Greek notion of *agora*, the meeting place below the

Acropolis in Athens where the great philosophers developed their teaching on knowledge and the citizens met to discuss. The chapter develops a mode of community creation drawing upon a broad range of perspectives, economic, sociological, scientific, and examines the role of the Internet in sustaining knowledge networks. The chapter envisages a new open and democratic regime of knowledge creation and ideas sharing.

Transformative capacity:
continual structuring by intertemporal technology transfer

Raghu Garud and Praveen R. Nayyar

If U.S. giants started making better use of their vast storehouse of technology, "we would not be able to compete with them." (Hiroshi Kashiwaga, Director General, Electrotechnical Laboratory, Ministry of International Trade & Industry, Japan (quoted in O. Port, *Business Week*, 1992))

Periodic scrutiny of previously shelved projects will often reveal ones that are now ripe for "unshelving" and subsequent commercial success. (From Wilson and Hlavacek, *Research Management*, 1984)

Corporate restructuring is an attempt to regain lost competitive advantages by making substantial changes in a firm's business portfolio, internal organization, or financial structure. These changes result in a realignment of a firm's key resources. However, the resource-based view of the firm suggests that it might be difficult to regain lost competitive advantages through restructuring (Barney, 1986; Conner, 1991; Dierickx and Cool, 1989; Penrose, 1959; Rumelt, 1984; Wernerfelt, 1984). The resource-based view considers firms as unique bundles of resources yielding sustainable above normal profits. Some of these key resources accumulate in a path dependent manner. Therefore, they are difficult to replace or acquire quickly when needed. Consequently, substantial changes in resource bundles that corporate restructuring entails destroy key resources and do not allow acquisition of other resources that could provide sustainable competitive advantages.

For instance, corporate restructuring may result in divesting resources that could prove useful later. Similarly, greatly changing internal organizational arrangements could destroy knowledge stocks. Moreover, starting afresh to gather new resources during corporate restructuring implies a time lag before a firm accumulates a critical mass to become competitive. In competitive and changing environments, firms may never catch-up with their competitors and their environments. Thus, for firms competing with path-dependent resources, restructuring may be an option of last resort.

An alternative course of action to maintain corporate vitality is to continually create and exploit new business opportunities. *Continual structuring* avoids the detrimental consequences of *restructuring*. This is consistent with Schumpeter's (1975) view on institutionalizing technological innovation to create new business opportunities (see also Quinn, 1969).

New business opportunities can emerge from either internal or external technologies. Although both are important, a firm's ability to exploit external technologies is not sufficient to maintain a sustainable competitive advantage (Barney, 1991; Ghemawat, 1986). This is because external technologies are also accessible to other firms (Mansfield, 1988). In contrast, internal technologies are not widely accessible, thereby forming the basis for sustainable competitive advantage. This is illustrated by 3M's ability to generate a return on assets about 50 percent higher from its 'historic' businesses – adhesives, coating, abrasives, and non-woven technologies – than from its 'added' businesses – those that were based on acquired technologies beyond its origins such as imaging and instrumentation (Quinn, 1992).

Pavitt (1984) also demonstrated the relative importance of internal technologies compared to external ones. Nearly 59 percent of 3013 significant innovations in the United Kingdom from 1945 to 1979 were based on knowledge from *within* innovating firms. In some industries such as dyestuffs, aluminum, motor vehicles and textiles, internal sources accounted for nearly 70 percent of all innovations.[1] Thus, internal technologies are important for corporate vitality and we focus on them in this chapter.

Creating new technological opportunities entails significant risk because only a few efforts succeed (see, for example, Burgelman, 1991 and Van de Ven, 1986); most languish, due to a lack of markets or complementary technologies. Lacking markets or complementary technologies, technological knowledge (hereafter knowledge) created by start-up firms may be irrevocably lost if a venture fails. In contrast, established firms can choose to retain knowledge created, although it is not immediately used, because they may have the necessary organizational resources to do so. For example, Corning spent millions on special glass for lasers and on methods to make high-quality car windshields. However, neither project yielded products right away. Many years later, the laser research led to pure optical fibers, and the windshield technology led to glass for flat-panel displays (Carey, 1992).[2]

Thus, maintaining knowledge for later use can contribute to corporate vitality. This facet of corporate vitality has received surprisingly little attention. A recent article in *Business Week* suggested that U.S. firms have not adequately capitalized on their storehouse of technology (Port, 1992). It is reported that in the U.S. pharmaceutical industry alone "thousands of drugs have been shelved ... (although their) death is premature" (Hamilton and Weber, 1988: 90). The value of this storehouse is indicated by the finding that 8 of 10 projects unshelved were successful (Wilson and Hlavacek, 1984), a success rate far greater than for new venture development projects. Hence, a firm can significantly increase returns from technological investments by exploiting its storehouse of technology (Foster, 1982).

Exploiting a storehouse of technology requires firms to transfer technology across time. This ability is termed *transformative capacity*. We offer the concept of transformative capacity as a complement to Cohen and Levinthal's (1990) notion of absorptive capacity. Absorptive capacity is the ability to recognize and exploit technological opportunities from *outside* a firm. In contrast, transformative capacity is the ability to continually redefine a product portfolio based on technological opportunities created *within* a firm.[3]

Both absorptive capacity and transformative capacity are important. However, absorptive capacity is not sufficient for creating a sustainable competitive advantage when: (1) path-dependent, cumulative knowledge is involved;[4] (2) entry timing is important, or (3) a firm operates in a continually changing environment in which it does not just react to external changes, but instead, creates them by its own actions.[5]

Relying solely on absorptive capacity may result in the loss of competitive advantage as illustrated by the plight of IBM. IBM absorbed external technology for its line of personal computers during the past decade while failing to utilize technologies it created such as its RISC chip. As competitors too absorbed the same technology, IBM lost its competitive advantage (Ferguson and Morris, 1993). Its recent attempts to restructure have so far been unsuccessful because: (1) massive internal change affecting the type of technological resources in question requires considerable time to initiate and implement – time within which the industry has moved far ahead, (2) first mover advantages preclude external technologies as viable means of regaining competitive advantage, and (3) IBM operates in a rapidly changing environment in which a forfeited competitive position cannot be regained.

In contrast, the power of transformative capacity in building and sustaining competitive advantages is illustrated by Honda's approach emphasizing in-house development of all product and process technologies it uses (Shook, 1988). These technologies have helped Honda establish a formidable competitive advantage over its rivals. Recognizing the future importance of internal technologies, "Hitachi never backs off or lets go of a division (because) ... the company is thinking years down the road" (Gross, 1992: 100). In addition, Hitachi continues to invest in biotechnology, a pursuit unlikely to benefit Hitachi's main businesses for years (Gross, 1992).

In this chapter, we suggest that firms can maintain their corporate vitality by developing transformative capacity. First, we show that time lags in the development of knowledge and markets create the need for storehouses of technology. Second, we examine three dimensions of knowledge affecting its maintenance and transfer across time. Third, we discuss the resource-based-view of the firm to understand tasks involved in intertemporal knowledge transfer. Fourth, we use concepts from literature on organizational memory, decision making, and the information processing view of organization design to explore mechanisms affecting transformative capacity. In conclusion, we discuss some implications of transformative capacity for theory and practice. Figure 8.1 presents a summary of the key elements of our analysis.

Note that there are some bounds to the theory developed in this chapter. It applies to firms seeking competitive advantages from certain types of technologies. The theory also assumes that firms are able to create new technologies because, without innovation, there will be nothing to transfer over time. In addition, the theory assumes that firms have the general ability to commercialize innovations.

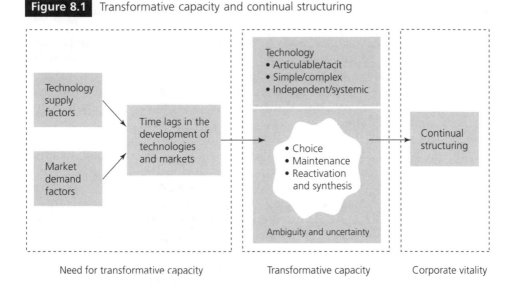

Figure 8.1 Transformative capacity and continual structuring

Time lags in the development of knowledge and markets

New technological fields emerge through researchers' problem solving activities. These efforts result in ideas and techniques representing knowledge (Allen, 1966; Laudan, 1984; Layton, 1974; Rosenberg, 1982). Since technology is a form of knowledge, technological change can be understood by examining knowledge development.

Knowledge development proceeds through a cumulative progression of ideas and techniques (Crane, 1972). Antecedent ideas and techniques influence the choice of future problems, thereby making knowledge development path-dependent (David, 1985; Dosi, 1982). The acquisition of relevant experience determines success in solving these problems. This experience translates into 'rules of thumb' (Sahel, 1981) or search 'heuristics' (Nelson and Winter, 1982) that researchers employ. In this way, knowledge development is a cumulative process with only infrequent major disruptions (Rosenberg, 1982).

Levenhagen, Thomas, and Porac (1990) represented the cumulative process of knowledge development with the concept of "knowledge vectors." While knowledge within these vectors develops cumulatively, Levenhagen *et al.* suggested that new knowledge is created when vectors intersect. The intersection of vectors represents a moment of cumulative synthesis as once unrelated fields converge (Usher, 1954). Therefore, there is not only knowledge accumulation within vectors, but also occasional knowledge synthesis across different vectors to create new knowledge.

The development of the video tape-recorder vividly illustrates this process. Figure 8.2, which is taken from Irvine and Martin (1984), highlights the long

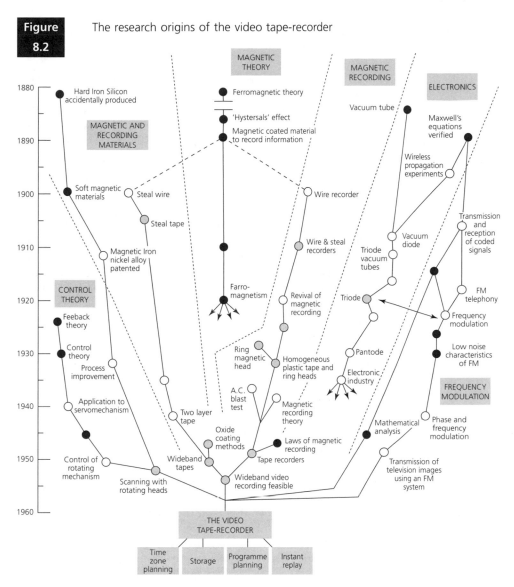

Figure 8.2 The research origins of the video tape-recorder

Source: Adapted from Irvine, J. and Martin, B. *Foresight in Science: Picking the Winners*, Dover, NH: Francis Pinter, 1984. (●, Nonmission research; ◐, mission-oriented research; ○, development and application. Note: BTL = Bell Telephone Laboratories; NRL = Naval Research Laboratory; AEG = Allgemeine Elektrizitats Gesellschaft.

time of 80 years over which the video tape-recorder slowly evolved. During this time several intermediary products were also developed from the confluence of knowledge vectors from many seemingly unrelated areas such as magnetic and recording materials, electronics, and frequency modulation. Some of these vectors were found useful although a specific purpose had not been envisioned when they were initiated. As the chronology of events suggests, these knowledge vectors developed at different rates at different points in time ultimately culminating in products and technologies by the synthesis of old and new knowledge.

This depiction is consistent with Rosenberg's (1982) observation that knowledge vectors progress at different rates. Some vectors lag others thereby becoming bottlenecks in knowledge development. Researchers then direct their attention to these bottleneck vectors. Advances along these vectors in turn create other bottlenecks. In this way knowledge development is a 'compulsive process' with vectors leading and lagging each other at different points in time. As a result vectors that are ahead must be maintained and later reactivated to be synthesized with other vectors. Thus, knowledge development lags are a supply side reason for maintaining knowledge.

In addition, market lags are a demand side reason for maintaining knowledge. Many innovations flounder because of inadequate product demand (Wilson and Hlavacek, 1984). Demand for a product may emerge at a future date because of institutional changes or because other scientific and technological advances render products more attractive to customers. For example, there is recent renewed interest in video-telephones, the synthetic material Kevlar that DuPont developed, and energy-saving fluorescent lamps. Also, a firm may choose to shelve a product superior to the one it currently markets until a competing firm challenges its market position (Conner, 1988). For example, Intel decided to delay introduction of its new-generation Pentium microprocessor.

Thus, time lags in the development of knowledge and markets create the need for intertemporal knowledge transfer. To understand how this transfer can be affected within firms, it is useful to examine dimensions of knowledge affecting its intertemporal transfer.

Dimensions of knowledge affecting its intertemporal transfer

One dimension of knowledge is whether it is tacit or articulable (Polanyi, 1962; Winter, 1987). Tacit knowledge cannot be described fully. In contrast, articulable knowledge can be codified. A second dimension of knowledge is whether it is simple or complex. It is possible to describe simple knowledge with little information. In contrast, a larger amount of information is required to describe complex knowledge. A third dimension of knowledge is whether it is embedded in a larger system (systemic), or whether it is independent. Systemic knowledge has to be described in relation to other knowledge vectors. In contrast, independent knowledge can be described by itself.[6]

Winter (1987) treated each dimension as a continuum along which any knowledge could be located. As each dimension becomes salient, the ease with which knowledge can be transferred decreases. Winter considered the impact of these dimensions on transferability as being simply additive without any interactive effects. In addition, each dimension evokes different issues in the transfer process. For these reasons, it is useful to separately consider the transfer issues that each dimension raises.

The position of knowledge along each continuous dimension affects the amount and nature of information required to describe it. Therefore, it also affects the relative ease of intertemporal knowledge transfer. Greater knowledge complexity requires greater information for knowledge transfer; and greater knowledge tacitness requires richer media for knowledge transfer (Teece, 1981). Further, systemic knowledge requires the transfer of several interrelated knowledge vectors over time. Knowledge positioned towards the left on each dimension in Figure 8.3 is relatively easier to transfer across time compared to knowledge positioned towards the right.

It could be argued that ease of knowledge transfer across time also implies ease of its transfer across space to other firms, which reduces its strategic value. This argument alone may suggest that easy-to-transfer knowledge must not be maintained. However, a decision to maintain easy-to-transfer knowledge for a firm's own use also depends on two other factors. First, it depends on a firm's ability to prevent others from accessing this preserved knowledge. Thus, proprietary, yet easy-to-transfer knowledge must be maintained. Second, a decision to maintain easy-to-transfer knowledge also depends on the extent to which knowledge is firm-specific. Firm-specific knowledge is valuable because of a firm's complementary resources (Teece, 1981). Such knowledge may be of little value to other firms who do not possess similar complementary resources. Thus, firm-specific knowledge must also be maintained by a firm possessing it.

In summary, time lags in knowledge and market development create the need for intertemporal knowledge transfer. In addition, three dimensions of knowledge affect its intertemporal transfer. Knowledge transferred across time can form the basis for new businesses. Thus, appropriately managed knowledge is a key resource that can maintain corporate vitality.

Intertemporal knowledge transfer and the resource-based view of the firm

Dierickx and Cool (1989) employed the resource-based view to describe how a firm's assets, or resources, can provide a sustainable competitive advantage. To establish their argument, they drew an analogy between a firm as a bundle of resources and a firm as a bath-tub. In this analogy, inputs are compared with

Figure 8.3 Dimensions affecting intemporal knowledge transfer

ARTICULABLE	_____	TACIT
SIMPLE	_____	COMPLEX
INDEPENDENT	_____	SYSTEMIC

Source: Adapted from Winter (1987)

flows of water into a tub, while asset stocks, or resource bundles, are compared with the stock of water in a tub. Dierickx and Cool argued that a sustainable competitive advantage cannot be obtained from resource flows, but instead, it can only be obtained from the resource stock in a tub.

A resource stock provides a sustainable competitive advantage because imitating it is difficult. One reason for this is the existence of time-compression diseconomies (Dierickx and Cool, 1989).[7] Resources characterized by time compression diseconomies are expensive to create under crash conditions. This is illustrated by Mansfield's (1988) data on the mean elasticity of cost with respect to time to develop and commercialize an innovation. He found that the cost increase for a 1 percent reduction in time ranged from 2.5 to 15.7 percent. Further, he found that the cost to accomplish each additional percent time reduction increased at an increasing rate, indicating the presence of time-compression diseconomies. In addition, it may not even be possible to once again create resources abandoned earlier. Firms possessing such *difficult-to-create* anew resources must maintain existing stocks and not rely on creating them again as and when needed.

However, relying only on existing resource stocks can harm corporate vitality. Existing resource stocks can entrap firms into particular modes of operation while the environment changes (Russo, 1992). This creates a need for restructuring. This adverse aspect of resources, which may otherwise be considered as assets, has been called 'competency traps' (Levitt and March, 1988). To avoid competency traps, it is necessary to create new resources from combinations of existing resources.

The bath-tub analogy that Dierickx and Cool proposed does not suggest how new resources can be created. This is because the bath-tub analogy is largely static in nature evoking a vision of stagnant water. One way of making this analogy dynamic is by adding 'leaks' and 'swirls' to the tub.[8] Leaks reduce resources over time. Swirls help mix existing resources to create new ones. Thus, combined with flows of fresh resources, leaks and swirls may evoke insights on how the bath-tub is continually rejuvenated.

We believe, however, that these additions extend the bath-tub analogy beyond its usefulness in understanding knowledge creation. Lacking are fine details of new knowledge creation by combining old knowledge. The bath-tub analogy does not help identify specific tasks affecting intertemporal knowledge transfer and reuse. Hence, it is necessary to replace the bath-tub analogy with another capturing evolutionary facets of resource creation.

Our analogy is the *process of pollination*. Pollination transfers pollen from one flower's stamen to another's stigma. Similar to any evolutionary process, pollination is a probabilistic process. Moreover, it is path-dependent and cumulative, both essential elements of the resource-based perspective. Pollination permits creation of hybrid varieties by crossing one species with another. The success of such cross-pollination depends upon many factors such as wind and rain. Not all hybrids survive. Some are selected out as they cannot survive environmental demands. Other, better adapted ones, propagate their species through self-pollination.

This evolutionary process of survival of the fittest represents 'first-order' learning. In contrast, 'second-order' learning represents artificial interventions in pollination to affect hybrid types created.[9] Artificial-pollination entails the following three tasks: *choice* of pollen, maintaining it *over time and space,* and its *reactivation and synthesis* to produce a hybrid. In this way, artificial-pollination allows pollinators to overcome myopic selection pressures of natural environments by transferring desired pollen across time and space.

Elster (1983) noted that technological change too is a second-order learning process that can overcome myopic selection pressures of natural environments. Elster pointed out that this requires the ability to 'wait.' In particular, a firm's technological knowledge, just like a flower's pollen, must be preserved until conditions favor its use and synthesis. That is, using the pollination analogy, pollen and stigma represent a firm's technological knowledge with the potential (though, as yet unrealized) to create new business opportunities.

Transformative capacity

Knowledge is like pollen; it creates new knowledge by interacting with other knowledge vectors acting as stamen. As with the creation of hybrid plant varieties, creating new businesses is a probabilistic and path-dependent process. Therefore, consistent with the pollination analogy, time lags in knowledge and market development create the need to: (1) choose technologies, (2) maintain them over time, and (3) reactivate and synthesize them with ongoing technology development efforts. Transformative capacity is the ability to accomplish these three tasks. Table 8.1 contains illustrations of key elements determining the need for transformative capacity and the mechanisms required to create it. Table 8.2 presents a summary of information processing demands of the three tasks underlying transformative capacity. These demands vary across the three knowledge dimensions discussed earlier.

Maintaining knowledge for future use is costly because resources must be assigned to keep knowledge "alive" (Levitt and March, 1988; Wilson and Hlavacek, 1984). Consequently, it is necessary to determine whether to maintain knowledge for future use or to generate it again when needed.[10] As discussed earlier, easy-to-create knowledge need not be maintained for future use. In contrast, difficult-to-create knowledge must be maintained. In addition, consistent with the pollination analogy, firms must choose *which* difficult-to-create knowledge to maintain given limited organizational resources.

One facet of choice is ambiguity due to multiple and conflicting views about the future strategic value of knowledge (Daft and Lengel, 1986), and decision makers' divergent preferences (March, 1978). The extent of ambiguity varies across knowledge vectors. There is a lower potential for ambiguity as the ability to articulate knowledge increases. In contrast, as knowledge tacitness increases, the likelihood of it being misunderstood also increases. Therefore, ambiguity increases with knowledge tacitness.

| Table 8.1 | Illustrative quotations pertaining to transformative capacity |

Quotations	Key elements
• A study of how successful unshelvings occur revealed that the incremental returns from unshelved projects were most attractive indeed. Nearly every research person interviewed could cite one successful unshelving, and many identified prospective unshelvings in their organizations. *The unrealized potential from the shelved projects is thus of great importance to any research manager.* (Wilson and Hlavacek, 1984: 27)	• Increasing returns from R&D • Retrieval
• *Seeing an opportunity to make money from compounds collecting dust on their shelves,* drug-makers such as Bristol-Myers, Squibb, Upjohn, American Home Products, and Eli Lilly are aggressively licensing compounds to small players. (Hamilton and Weber, 1988: 90)	• Technology supply factors • Technology maintenance
• *We have thousands of compounds and hundreds of projects that go in and out of favor, often because of perceived marketing issues* says Robert A. Dougan, manager of corporate development for American Cyanamid (Hamilton and Weber, 1988: 90)	• Market demand factors
• Nearly *three decades* after they burst on the scene, why are massmarket video-phones finally at hand? Because of cheap but powerful computer chips, small but reliable cameras and breakthroughs in simultaneously sending video and audio signals over phone lines . . . *Everything is coming together in 1993.* (Bulkeley, 1992)	• Time lags in the development of markets and technologies • Synthesis of knowledge vectors
• *Companies can improve the profit per dollar of R&D investment by 200 300 percent* if they learn how to select the "best" technology to pursue and the best time to pursue it. (Foster, 1982: 22)	• Technology choice • Maintenance and retrieval and synthesis
• American Cyanamid is *taking an* inventory *of its drug library for resurrection candidates.* (Hamilton and Weber, 1988: 90)	• Maintenance of technology
• Object oriented programming is analogous to ordering entire rooms as units and joining them together with far less effort and expense. *Once written, these self-contained, re-usable chunks of software code – the objects – can be mixed and matched by programmers to create new applications without having to start from scratch each time.* (Fisher, 1992: 51)	• Technology maintenance • Retrieval and synthesis

Note: Emphasis added in quotations

Table 8.2 Information processing demands placed by transformative capacity

Dimensions of technological knowledge	Tasks underlying transformative capacity		
	Choice	Maintenance	Reactivation and synthesis
Articulable/tacit	The more tacit the knowledge, the greater the ambiguity and therefore greater the need for richer media to make choices.	The more tacit the knowledge, the greater the need for rich media to preserve knowledge over time.	Both articulable and tacit knowledge have to be internalized when received.
Simple/complex	The greater the complexity of knowledge, the greater the uncertainty and therefore the need to collect more information to make choices.	The greater the complexity of knowledge, the greater the amount of information that must be maintained over time.	The more complex the knowledge, the greater the amount of information that must be retrieved.
Independent/ systemic	The more systemic the knowledge, the greater the need for configurational choices.	The more systemic the knowledge, the greater the need for maintaining information about different knowledge vectors.	The more systemic the knowledge, the greater the need to integrate information pertaining to different knowledge vectors.

Firms deal with ambiguity by using rich media to exchange views and opinions among managers about the future of technologies. They might use a combination of formal planning mechanisms, face-to-face meetings and boundary spanning roles to elicit, discuss and exchange interpretations about the future of technologies before choosing to maintain some of them. Under conditions of ambiguity, decision makers employ their judgments and consensus among themselves about a course of action even as they proceed to implement it (Daft and Lengel, 1986).

A second facet of choice is uncertainty due to incomplete information about future demand and supply conditions, competitors' actions, and other externalities (Daft, Sormunen and Parks, 1988; Wernerfelt and Karnani, 1987). Incomplete information arises from a gap between information needed and available. This gap creates difficulties in determining the future strategic value of knowledge. The information gap decreases as knowledge becomes simple.

In contrast, as knowledge becomes complex, the information gap increases. Therefore, uncertainty increases with knowledge complexity.

Firms deal with uncertainty by collecting more data. They use organizational practices yielding additional data required to make decisions about which knowledge vectors to focus on, which to abandon, and which to maintain. They might use one or a combination of rules and procedures, formal information systems, special studies, and formal planning mechanisms to gather and process data about the future strategic value of knowledge vectors before choosing to maintain some of them (Daft and Lengel, 1986: Galbraith, 1973).

Additional data reduce uncertainty. In many instances, this will permit assigning probabilities to outcomes and making choices considering risk. These choices are based on decision makers' risk preferences and expected pay-offs of choices including opportunity costs of not maintaining particular knowledge vectors. Thus, decision makers focus on defining their risk preferences and the pay-off matrix (Hogarth, 1980; March and Shapira, 1987).

However, there remain some knowledge vectors for which probabilities cannot be assigned to alternative outcomes despite collecting additional data. Under these conditions, decision makers use their judgment to estimate future strategic values of knowledge vectors. This results in categorizing knowledge vectors into three categories: (1) clearly worth maintaining, (2) clearly not worth maintaining, and (3) requiring more information (Janis and Mann, 1977; Lippman and McCardle, 1991). Decision makers consider the last category more carefully when reviewing knowledge stocks. For example, they may use criteria such as maximization of minimum gain to make a choice (Luce and Raiffa, 1957).

A third facet of choice is the systemic nature of some knowledge vectors. To the extent that knowledge is independent, information about other knowledge vectors is not required to make choice decisions. In contrast, the more systemic the knowledge, the greater the need for information about several inter-dependent vectors to make choice decisions. Therefore, the need for configurational choices increases as knowledge becomes more systemic.

Under these conditions, decisions are driven by heuristics using information most familiar to decision makers (March, 1991, Nelson and Winter, 1982). That is, a decision about whether to maintain or to terminate projects is based on local knowledge (Baba, 1988). However, as knowledge becomes more systemic, its future strategic value can only be determined in relationship with other knowledge not in the local knowledge set. Therefore, the more systemic the knowledge, the greater the need to consider a diversity of perspectives to make a better informed choice decision (Milliken, 1990), resulting in more desirable outcomes (Gupta and Govindarajan, 1986; Kahneman and Lovallo, 1993).

We illustrate challenges associated with choice within the context of a technology development program we tracked over its 10-year history. Beginning with an idea to develop a biomedical implant, the program quickly proliferated with spin-off projects. Given limited resources, program members decided they would need to focus on certain projects, maintain some for future development, and abandon others.

To prepare for this decision, program members first gathered information about each potential project. Information gathered pertained to issues such as potential markets, developmental time frame, resource deployment, and competition. This information formed the basis for organizing a 2-day retreat to evaluate opportunities.

Recognizing the systemic nature of knowledge required to evaluate each project, managers from several different functional departments attended the retreat. These managers had to first reach a consensus on the criteria against which each project should be evaluated. These included criteria such as technical performance, market penetration, and production cost. The multiplicity of perspectives and associated criteria created ambiguity, especially when knowledge could not be articulated.

To deal with this ambiguity, considerable discussions and negotiations occurred in the group. Recognizing trade-offs, group members allocated weights to criteria. Next, they estimated the extent to which project ratings would drop as performance declined on each criterion. For instance, a project might score 80 points for a 30 percent market penetration and only 40 points for a 10 percent penetration. Since higher performance on any criterion required greater resources, which were limited, this led to a discussion of trade-offs among criteria.

Following this, the group determined a desired level of performance on each criterion. For each project, information collected earlier was shared with the group by respective functional managers. Based on this information, the group estimated the probability of achieving the desired performance level for each project on each criterion.

The group then assessed their risk preferences – whether they were risk seeking, risk averse or neutral. An external consultant encouraged the group to adopt a risk neutral stance. These steps set the stage for a final session to score projects and to prioritize them according to cumulative scores. Based on cumulative scores, the group reached a consensus on which projects they should focus on and which ones they should maintain. A decision to discontinue the development of remaining projects was not taken immediately. Instead, laboratories not associated with the program were informed about projects identified for possible termination to determine whether they would be interested in pursuing them.

Maintenance

Just as it is necessary to maintain pollen for cross-pollination to succeed, it is necessary to maintain knowledge to facilitate its retrieval and use later. If not maintained, knowledge decays as skills, routines and assets fall into disuse, knowledge is lost when personnel leave a firm, or knowledge becomes obsolete (Epple, Argote and Devadas, 1991; Huber, 1991; Kanter, 1988; Levitt and March, 1988).

The notion of 'organizational memory' is relevant to study how firms retain knowledge (Duncan and Weiss, 1979; Levitt and March, 1988; Walsh and

Ungson, 1991; Weick, 1979). We suggest that the process of creating memory for technological knowledge varies with the dimensions of knowledge. For instance, as knowledge becomes more articulable, it need only be codified to be available for later use. This can be accomplished by preserving documents and blueprints (Foster, 1971). In contrast, the more tacit the knowledge, the richer the media required to maintain it. As Wilson and Hlavacek (1984) found, firms that benefited from technologies created in the past kept knowledge alive by the active presence of a core group of people. One manager quoted in their study stated: "In some of our cases, work was never completely terminated, although at times, efforts were minimal" (1984: 28).

Knowledge complexity affects the amount of information needed to maintain it. Two considerations determine how much information about a knowledge vector must be maintained. First, it is important to know how much information will be required to successfully reconstruct an entire knowledge vector. It might be impossible to reactivate a knowledge vector if the information gap (i.e., difference between information needed and available) is greater than a certain threshold level. To safeguard against this contingency, it is necessary to maintain at least the threshold level of information about a knowledge vector so that it can be reactivated later. Greater knowledge complexity requires more information to describe it. Therefore, the more complex the knowledge, the higher this threshold level.

The case of Xerox and personal computers illustrates the existence of a threshold level and it underscores the difficulties associated with attempts to reactivate a technology development effort. Although Xerox developed the first personal computer (Smith and Alexander, 1988), it has been unsuccessful in reentering the computer industry because it discontinued developmental efforts thereby creating gaps in knowledge. Moreover, time compression diseconomies prevent Xerox from catching up.

Thus, a second consideration determining how much information about a knowledge vector must be maintained is the speed at which it must be reactivated. At any level of complexity, time required to generate additional information needed for knowledge reactivation increases with the information gap. This is especially important in fast-moving environments where knowledge must be reactivated quickly. Under these conditions, greater information about a knowledge vector must be maintained than in environments allowing slower reactivation.

The extent of interdependence between knowledge vectors affects the number of vectors that must be maintained simultaneously. As another manager quoted in Wilson and Hlavacek's (1984) study commented: "Totally shelved projects seem not to occur here. A small core of people, or one person, remained active even if it was part time" (1984: 28). Independent knowledge can be maintained by one or more experts in that knowledge area. For example, venture capitalists retained only Mr. Chen, who had a doctorate in image coding, a critical technology, and a dream of a picture telephone when initial efforts at developing a video-telephone failed (Bulkeley, 1992). Similarly, when Hitachi factories were not interested in hard-to-fabricate semiconductor lasers, a lone researcher, Yasutsugu Takeda, wrote up a catalog of semiconductor lasers he could custom-produce at his workbench and mailed it to customers such as IBM, Bell Telephone, Xerox, and Canon. Once he received orders, he gave the list to a Hitachi plant. That was the beginning of Hitachi's flourishing optoelectronics business. Today, Hitachi has a 60 percent market share for devices using this technology (Gross, 1992).

In contrast, as knowledge becomes more systemic, the greater the need to keep entire teams active even if on a part time basis. For example, in the early 1980s, a Hitachi CEO ordered research on hydroelectric power stopped. However, "the research team went underground, taking advantage of the ample allotment of unmonitored research time to pursue the project. Several years later, they surfaced with a new system that scored big with power companies facing environmental restrictions" (Gross, 1992: 98).

Maintenance is costly. Therefore, firms must continually evaluate maintained knowledge vectors to determine whether any should be discarded, maintained further, or used in some ongoing project. To do this, firms must catalog maintained knowledge vectors and create organizational mechanisms to review the catalog periodically. Otherwise, maintained knowledge vectors may be "lost" for all practical purposes. The importance of a catalog of shelved, and even ongoing projects, is highlighted by the observation that "some companies have no idea what projects they have in their inventory" (Gupta, 1989: B2). It should not be assumed, however, that a catalog is enough to ensure the use of shelved technologies. For example, although Sony has many avenues for researchers to share information, the Sony PalmTop "came out of an engineer's imagination (who) ... discovered by *chance* that Sony's research labs had devised handwriting recognition software" (Schlender, 1992: 79).

Reactivation and synthesis

The promise of the pollination analogy we have proposed lies in a firm's ability to couple knowledge vectors at appropriate points in time. This involves several interrelated tasks: recognizing a business opportunity, reactivating maintained knowledge, and coupling reactivated knowledge with other knowledge vectors to exploit new business opportunities.

Technology supply and market demand triggers lead to recognition of new business opportunities. Supply triggers arise from apparently serendipitous intersections of knowledge vectors such as those that occurred in video tape-recorder development (Graham, 1986; Irvine and Martin, 1984). Demand triggers arise when market conditions become more conducive for using maintained knowledge. For example, this is now occurring for certain contraceptive and abortion methods and pharmaceutical products (Hamilton and Weber, 1988; Newman, 1993).

Firms must recognize technology supply and market demand triggers. As El Sawy and Pauchant (1988) summarized, firms may adopt either reactive or proactive modes to recognize triggers. In a reactive mode, the occurrence of a problem serves as a trigger. In contrast, in a proactive mode, firms engage in exploratory surveillance activities. Suggesting the importance of the proactive approach, Daft et al. (1988) found that high performing firms scanned more frequently and more broadly under conditions of strategic uncertainty than low performing firms.

Lenz and Engledow (1986) described several scanning mechanisms to enhance firms' ability to generate and recognize opportunities. These mechanisms include corporate monitors, brainstorming exercises, seminars, reliance on information services, participation in business issues committees, and scanning units. The effectiveness of scanning units in recognizing technological opportunities is illustrated by the experience of a manager we interviewed at a large diversified firm. Recently, this manager was assigned the responsibility for developing new business opportunities from ideas within the firm. Assisted by two other employees, this New Business Opportunities (NBO) manager systematically scanned the firm to identify currently unused technologies thereby generating over 50 new business ideas. These new ideas were created as the firm's other employees became aware of the NBO team's activities and they offered ideas they were pursuing outside their main activities. Of four ideas ultimately chosen for commercialization, one was created from the synthesis of two different knowledge vectors residing dormant within the firm. The remaining three ideas were based on unused single knowledge vectors resident in the firm and were developed further to exploit emerging market opportunities.

Another way to recognize triggers is illustrated by a practice at Sony Corporation. "Sony thinks the best technicians are those who are willing to move around among product groups and try their hand at technologies they haven't studied ... To encourage employees to move around, Sony has a policy it calls 'self-promotion,' which allows enterprising engineers to seek out projects elsewhere in the company without notifying their supervisors" (Schlender, 1992: 78). The Sony PalmTop is the brainchild of one such "self-promoted" engineer, Tomoshi Hirayama.

Sony's corporate research group also organizes an annual exposition as a way to recognize triggers for knowledge retrieval. This exposition, open only to employees, provides a forum to display what Sony's engineers and scientists have been tinkering with. According to Schlender, this 3-day event helps to "cross-pollinate ideas among various business groups" (1992: 84) and it "keeps the magic going" as Sony introduces a constant stream of innovative products. At NEC Research Institute, Inc. in Princetown, New Jersey, "curiosity is flourishing at the institute as posters in the corridors highlight topics that NEC investigators are probing" (Weber, 1992: 137). Researchers at Hitachi "fraternize at technical conferences, swap ideas, and informally advise Hitachi's board on important technology developments" (Gross, 1992: 98).

Once the potential for exploiting a maintained knowledge vector is recognized, the next task is to retrieve the required knowledge. This retrieval is different from the task of picking up a book from a library. This is because firms have difficulty in retrieving old, unused knowledge or skills (Argote, Beckman and Eppel, 1987). As Levitt and March pointed out "even with a consistent and accepted set of routines, only part of a firm's memory is likely to be evoked at a particular time, or in a particular part of the firm. Some parts of organizational memory are more available for retrieval than others. Availability is associated with the frequency of use of a routine, the recency of its use and its organizational proximity" (1988: 328). Therefore, as discussed earlier, ensuring availability via a catalog of knowledge is important for knowledge retrieval.

Retrieval requires adapting maintained knowledge to changed circumstances. Technology transferred across space and cultures must be modified to complement prevailing social, political and economic conditions (Teece, 1981; Rogers, 1983). Similarly, useful knowledge retrieval requires its modification to suit current needs. This might imply reinvention as new individuals interpret maintained knowledge in different ways (Rogers, 1983). This process of reinvention can reduce the reliability of retrieved knowledge (Levitt and March, 1988). Since reinvention is inevitable, it is necessary to assess reliability of retrieved knowledge before it can be used. In addition, it is necessary to assess the validity of retrieved knowledge in changed circumstances. For example, infrequently used testing equipment is often recalibrated to previous standards to establish its reliability. Moreover such equipment is also occasionally updated to meet new testing standards to establish its validity.

Retrieval entails several interdependent tasks varying with knowledge characteristics. Maintained knowledge, whether tacit or articulable, must be converted into a usable form (Lindblom and Cohen, 1979). To successfully use maintained knowledge, it must be internalized once again through experience (Nonaka, 1988). For example, knowing physics does not result in expert tool designers. Instead, this knowledge must be internalized by designing tools and by using them in manufacturing settings. In other words, knowledge reactivation requires learning-by-doing (Arrow, 1962) and learning-by-using (Rosenberg, 1982).[11]

As knowledge becomes more complex, the greater the information needed to reactivate a maintained knowledge vector. This task takes time because reactivation entails accessing and bringing into use all of the necessary facets of knowledge, so that information gaps do not remain in a knowledge vector. The more complex the knowledge the greater the information gaps simply because more information is needed to describe more complex knowledge compared to the information needed for relatively simple knowledge. Therefore, the more complex the knowledge, the greater the time needed to reactivate it.

Retrieved systemic knowledge must be integrated with other knowledge vectors. This presents both technological and organizational challenges. From a technological perspective, integration requires establishing common interfaces among knowledge vectors. For example, Honeywell's electronic controls group ensures that future generations of products are backward and forward compatible. It does this by careful attention to interface specifications between the various technologies used in its products.

From an organizational design perspective, knowledge integration requires information processing among diverse groups within a firm. This suggests the need for lateral information processing mechanisms (Galbraith, 1973). For example, at Hitachi's Central Research Laboratory in Tokyo, synergy and integration are explicitly stressed to focus the entire company on electronic systems for the 21st century. Hitachi intends to draw together its far-flung laboratories and factories to "reinvent the world out of its own toy box of machines and mad science" (Gross, 1992: 94).

Discussion and conclusions

A recent issue of *Business Week* noted "In the global economy, knowledge is king" (Farrell and Mandel, 1992: 70). Later in the same issue the editor noted "In such an environment, knowledge counts for more than capital or labor. The nations that will prosper will be those that create new knowledge best" *(Business Week,* April 6, 1992: 104). Several suggestions for a "growth Policy for the 90s" are offered (Farrell and Mandel, 1992: 74) but none focus on how to better utilize the existing vast "storehouse of technology" that U.S. firms possess.

In this chapter, we offer the concept of transformative capacity to help understand not only how firms can utilize their existing storehouse of technological knowledge through reactivation and synthesis of technologies, but also how they can actively create and maintain such a storehouse for future use. To explore the concept of transformative capacity, we built upon the resource-based perspective of the firm to offer the process of pollination as an analogy to gain insights on how firms can create new knowledge from existing knowledge. This analogy led to the identification of three tasks constituting transformative capacity. These tasks are choice, maintenance, and reactivation and synthesis of knowledge vectors. Organizational information processing demands of these three tasks were then explored. In conclusion, we explore some implications of transformative capacity for theory and practice.

Implications for theory

Continuity and change appear to be antithetical to one another. Emphasizing continuity while ignoring the need for change can entrap firms in the past. Therefore, when change becomes imperative, restructuring is required. In contrast, emphasizing change while ignoring continuity denies the past. Therefore, many innovations fail because they are inconsistent with existing resources. The challenge is to promote change while building upon past resources. This chapter offers ideas and concepts on how firms can manage this process to continually structure their portfolios by investing in transformative capacity.

IBM's current plight illustrates the importance of maintaining a fine balance between continuity and change. IBM's adherence to the main-frame technology even as it became obsolete exemplifies how a firm can get locked-in to a technology. In IBM's case, lock-in occurred for cognitive, economic and behavioral reasons. Cognitive forces pertain to technological myopia (Dosi,

1982) that crept in as executives at IBM were caught up in a "main-frame logic" (C. K. Prahalad quoted in Markoff, 1993). Economic forces pertain to reluctance on IBM's part to cannibalize their main-frame business with systems capable of distributed and parallel processing (Ferguson and Morris, 1993). Behavioral forces (David, 1985) pertain to organizational routines that led to persistence with the main-frame business.

These forces have created a situation where it is now difficult for IBM to revitalize itself with its existing resources. IBM has to undertake a significant break from the past to regain its competitive position in the computer industry. Present managers are ill equipped to accomplish this risky restructuring because of their historical association with the corporation. According to Kotter, an outsider is required to carry out this change, underscoring its disruptiveness (Hayes, 1993).

Restructuring, as the IBM example suggests, is disruptive. This disruption can be avoided if a firm is geared to continually innovate. Continual innovation is more likely if a firm institutes an organizational system to better use internal technologies and not be solely dependent on external technologies. As Mr. Welch of GE stated: "Control your destiny or someone else will" (Tichy and Sherman, 1993). According to industry analysts, GE's transformation under Mr. Welch is perhaps the classic contemporary case of successful revolution led from within an aging corporate giant" (Hayes, 1993).

Transformative capacity is an important element of this institutionalized process to develop technologies within firms. The asynchronous nature with which technologies and markets develop requires firms to keep their technologies alive for an appropriate time. Failure to keep technologies alive increases burdens on the chancy and expensive R&D process.

The extent to which a firm may want to undertake such activities is moderated by its size. Size confers on a firm the ability to deploy resources to develop and maintain knowledge vectors in different areas, only some of which may be useful later. The 3M Corporation is one such example. Following a dictum of generating at least 25 percent of its revenues from products introduced in the previous 3 years, this $13 billion company is able to generate above $1 billion in net profits while spending nearly $1 billion in R&D activities annually. Indeed, 3M's early history of the creation of "Post-it" notes from a failed abrasive technology epitomizes how a firm can create and sustain corporate vitality from intertemporal technology transfer (Nayak and Ketteringham, 1986).

Nelson (1959) pointed out that smaller firms may not have the necessary resources to create diverse knowledge vectors without immediate commercial applications. This may suggest that the usefulness of transformative capacity is moderated by firm size. Specifically, active creation and maintenance of knowledge vectors, without any immediate pay-offs but with the potential for creating future opportunities, may be appropriate only in large firms.

However, a different facet of transformative capacity may be essential for smaller firms. Smaller firms, especially venture start-ups, will have to pursue a technological opportunity on which they were initially based because a decision to discontinue or delay technology development may often imply the demise of a venture. Therefore, smaller firms also have to transfer technologies across time. Consequently, knowledge maintenance, reactivation and synthesis is necessary in small firms as well.

Implications for practice

Cohen and Levinthal (1990) noted that absorptive capacity is an intangible asset. Similarly, transformative capacity is also an intangible asset. Moreover, both these capacities lead to long-term pay-offs that are difficult to measure. Firms may, therefore, be reluctant to invest scarce resources in activities that build these capacities but yield uncertain benefits sometime in the future. Instead, there might be a tendency to focus on other more immediate and tangible actions such as acquisitions, divestitures and other components of corporate restructuring.

However, transformative capacity is a way by which firms may reduce the likelihood that corporate restructuring will be needed. Based on the information processing tasks discussed above and the several examples that illustrated how some firms were dealing with these tasks, Table 8.3 summarizes some practical implications of the concept of transformative capacity. Additional practical issues are discussed below.

Choice

Transformative capacity creates future options by placing technologies on-the-shelf. From this perspective, the problem of choice is one of valuing the "option." This requires determining whether it is worth maintaining a technology for future use considering the maintenance cost given an uncertain and ambiguous future. Managers can exercise the option at any point in time when technological and market conditions are appropriate. Otherwise they can either decide to maintain the technology for future use, or else, to discontinue its maintenance. Thus, managers have the right but not the obligation of exercising such options.

We draw upon the stock options pricing literature (Copeland, Koller, and Mirvin, 1990) to suggest a heuristic managers can employ while making choice decisions about whether to maintain a technology vector for possible future use. A stock option, just like maintained knowledge, provides the owner an opportunity to purchase stock at a specified price (exercise price) at any time prior to an agreed-upon date. Whether or not an option is purchased (cost of keeping the technology alive) depends upon an estimate of future investments needed to capitalize on the R&D program when an investment is made (exercise price) and on an estimate of returns from the investment. This permits an estimation of the value of the stock option. If the estimated value of the stock option is greater than its cost, then it is worthwhile to purchase it. In other words, it is worthwhile to maintain a technology if its value as an option is estimated to be greater than the cost of keeping it alive.

| **Table 8.3** | Some practical implications of transformative capacity |

Choice

Gather information.
Choose difficult-to-create knowledge to maintain.
Adopt rich media when making choice decisions concerning tacit knowledge.
Coordinate efforts across businesses and research laboratories to identify technologies for shelving.
Develop criteria for evaluating technological options.
Brainstorm on which technological paths to follow and which ones to abandon.
Consider the impact on other businesses and technologies when making technology maintenance decisions.

Maintenance

Catalog shelved technologies.
Periodically review the catalog of shelved technologies.
Develop avenues for researchers to share information.
Permit "underground" research and development activity.
Conduct internal scanning for shelved technologies.
Provide incentives for maintaining currently unwanted technologies.
Retain key personnel who possess tacit knowledge.
Maintain a minimum threshold of knowledge.
In fast-moving environments, retain more knowledge.
Retain entire teams when knowledge is systemic.

Reactivation and synthesis

Encourage scientists, technologists, and engineers to move around among product groups and research laboratories.
Coordinate the work of businesses and research laboratories through sharing information.
Organize symposia and expositions to share information.
Install lateral information processing mechanisms to encourage cooperation among researchers and businesses.
Internally publicize topics being researched.
Periodically review the catalog of shelved technologies.
Formalize the task of recognizing demand and supply triggers.
Minimize any negatives associated with the not-invented-here-and-now syndromes.
Reward reactivation.
Assess reliability and validity of retrieved knowledge.
Allow enough time for successful reactivation and synthesis.
Encourage the development of interface standards to allow synthesis later.

There are several practical benefits of viewing R&D activities from an options perspective. First, by maintaining a technology, major investment decisions can be deferred to a time when uncertainty is lower and the market is ready. This reduces the downside risk of major investments. When subject to traditional capital budgeting analyses, some technological investments may appear very unattractive. Yet time lags in the development of technological knowledge and markets preclude a short-term perspective. Therefore, transformative capacity suggests that top managers in firms must adopt a long-term perspective as embodied in the options approach.

Second, the options approach also helps understand parameters affecting choice decisions over time. With use, many models and their parameters have been identified to value stock options. Similarly, by adopting an options perspective, managers can develop over time an intuitive understanding of factors determining the value of a technology option and when and whether it should be exercised.

Mitchell and Hamilton (1988) illustrated the usefulness of this approach with technology development in the telecommunications industry. They pointed out that relentless progress in microelectronics has had and will continue to have a powerful influence on design, performance, reliability, and cost. Thus, research programs directed towards understanding and developing microelectronics will be critical, not simply for the immediate next generation of products, but for many others not yet identified. Given the considerable uncertainty and ambiguity associated with future developments in this industry, firms would be well advised to consider their investment as options.

Viewing R&D programs as options has implications for the common debate on whether or not firms should invest in basic research with little immediate commercial application. This debate extends to investments in developing technologies with few links to current technologies in use. If made public, such investments might even appear misguided. Our concept of transformative capacity suggests that investing in basic research and technology may be justifiable if it helps to keep knowledge alive for later use. Moreover, firms with greater transformative capacity are more likely to invest in basic research and technology development because they can utilize knowledge developed in-house later.

Maintenance

Perhaps the most important practical maintenance issue is the status of maintenance as a legitimate activity for researchers. Difficulties associated with legitimizing maintenance activity are illustrated by the case of AT&T in videophone technology. No one at AT&T wanted to be associated with a technology regarded as a failure (Bulkeley, 1992).

Viewing technological "setbacks" as mistakes will discourage researchers from maintaining technologies. In contrast, viewing technological setbacks as latent opportunities might encourage researchers to maintain a technology. Therefore, fostering a culture that views technological development as a means to create and use knowledge over time is essential to build transformative capacity.

Incentive systems are a powerful determinant of organizational culture. Providing incentives only for entirely new knowledge as measured by patents and publications will discourage researchers from being associated with maintenance activities. Therefore, appropriate incentive systems must be designed to encourage researchers to undertake tasks that build transformative capacity.

Another essential maintenance activity is to catalog shelved technologies. An example of the importance and use of cataloging is provided by the increasing reuse of computer software in the software programming industry (Fisher, 1992). Software is often idiosyncratic because it is written to accomplish a particular task. Often, only the programmer who wrote the software fully understands it. Further, different programmers, and even the original writer, will often accomplish the same task later by using different lines of code. When similar tasks have to be accomplished in another software application, considerable resources can be saved if existing software codes can be used. Such software reuse was relatively uncommon until the recent advent of object-oriented-programming. This system of programming permits software to be written in modules (or objects) with standardized interfaces between modules. Proper cataloging of these modules facilitates easy access when required to build other software applications.

It is also necessary to periodically review the catalog of maintained knowledge. Reviewing maintained knowledge may be considered as an internal scanning process similar to the often discussed external environmental scanning undertaken by most firms (Daft *et al.*, 1988). Arguing that all firms can obtain the same information about competitive opportunities from external scanning and then act on it similarly, Barney suggested that firms may obtain significant competitive advantages by "turning inwardly and analyzing information about the assets a firm already controls" (1986: 1239). Such internal information is more likely to be firm-specific, proprietary and rare. Therefore, it offers opportunities that other firms may not have. For example, a few years ago, several pharmaceutical firms were reportedly scanning their shelves looking for unique drugs and compounds that could be introduced (Hamilton and Weber, 1988).

Reactivation and synthesis

Many firms may have inadvertently encouraged the maintenance of technologies that were not immediately used. These technologies may be put to good use now, or in the future. Thus, even in firms that may not have proactively thought about maintaining technologies in the past, searching for shelved technologies may increase returns from technological investments (Hamilton and Weber, 1988; Wilson and Hlavacek, 1984).

A case in point is the apparently "surreptitious" development and introduction of RISC based chips at Intel Corporation (Burgelman, 1991). Another case is the firm discussed earlier that found four new business opportunities by assigning a team of managers to search among technologies lying "dormant" within the firm. The concept of transformative capacity suggests that firms can increase the likelihood of such events. One way to do this is to catalog shelved technologies as discussed above and to circulate the catalog widely within a firm, although with appropriate safeguards to prevent the dissemination of proprietary technological knowledge outside a firm.

Our discussion of the tasks underlying transformative capacity suggests that the reactivation and synthesis of maintained technologies is neither easy nor automatic. This is because the retrieval process is potentially fraught with the possibility of failure arising from a "not-invented *here-and-now*" syndrome. The difficulties associated with a not-invented-here syndrome are well known. The not-invented-now syndrome may introduce other difficulties. Not only do new technologies evoke greater excitement, but also old and unused technologies may have the stigma of failure attached to them (Wilson and Hlavacek, 1984).

Therefore, firms must guard against biases toward new technologies in comparison to old ones. In the current "throw-away" society it is easy to overlook significant opportunities firms can seize if only they would explore their storehouses of technology. It is here that we can see the full benefits of developing transformative capacity. Creation, choice, and maintenance activities would be useful only if reactivation and synthesis occur when needed. Firms that recognize the worth of past efforts will be best able to maintain their corporate vitality.

Acknowledgments

We have benefited from discussions with our colleague Zur Shapira and with several technology managers who requested that they remain anonymous. We thank the two anonymous reviewers for Strategic Management Journal for their thoughtful and constructive comments and suggestions. This research was partially funded by a grant from the Center for Entrepreneurial Studies, New York University.

Notes

1. Emphasizing internal technology, Masaru Ibuka Sony Corporation Founder, stated the "key to success for Sony ... is never to follow others ... We bet the company on that basic technology (the Trinitron TV), and in 23 years nobody has been able to match it" (Schlender, 1992: 77–82). Hitachi can build a nationwide (in Japan) high-speed maglev train system relying only on its own technology (Gross, 1992). Using internal technology only, Hitachi has perfected the world's highest-performance disk drive (Gross, 1992).
2. Kevlar, a synthetic fiber developed by DuPont, was a failure. Nearly 20 years later it is being used in bulletproof vests and Army helmets (McMurray, 1992). An antinoise technology developed in the 1930s has now become practical with the advent of advanced electronics (Naj, 1991). Sony's successful PalmTop was delayed because it required hardware, software, and manufacturing innovations (Schlender, 1992).
3. Cohen and Levinthal (1990) used annual spending on research and development as an indicator of a firm's absorptive capacity. Our concept of transformative capacity refers to adoption of organizational mechanisms enabling a firm to transfer technology through time.
4. Absorptive capacity may be of greater relevance at nascent stages of technological development when ideas still have to be translated into specific technologies and products. This is because

once technologies have become firm-specific, it becomes progressively more difficult for others to absorb them even if they have absorptive capacities (Ghemawat, 1991). In contrast, transformative capacity is relevant for technological resources at all stages of their development.

5. Change creates uncertainty and ambiguity. This creates considerable obstacles for firms using absorptive capacity to identify and evaluate external technologies. In contrast, it is relatively easier to evaluate internal technologies. Thus, when firms face uncertainty and ambiguity, relying on transformative capacity rather than absorptive capacity should result in better informed decisions about which technologies to pursue.

6. As Winter (1987) pointed out, locating knowledge on the simple/complex and independent/ systemic dimensions must be based on a consideration of the relevant context. Winter (1987) illustrated this point by the ceramic material used in spark plugs. In the context of spark plugs, the ceramic material is relatively complex. However, in the context of an automobile engine in which such spark plugs are used, the ceramic material is relatively simple. Similarly, the microprocessor used in personal computers is on the one hand a part of a larger system, the computer. On the other hand, it could also be considered as a relatively independent knowledge vector because its development can occur independently of other components of a computer.

7. Other reasons for inimitability are asset mass efficiencies, interconnectedness of asset stocks, asset erosion and causal ambiguity. Asset mass efficiencies arise if an existing resource stock facilitates accumulation of additional resource stocks. Interconnectedness implies that additions to existing resource stocks are linked to the level of other resource stocks. Asset erosion occurs when resource stocks decay if not maintained. Causal ambiguity arises when it is impossible to specify how resource stocks are accumulated (Dierickx and Cool, 1989).

8. We thank an anonymous reviewer for suggesting this way to extend the bath-tub analogy.

9. We thank an anonymous reviewer for suggesting we consider this distinction between first-order and second-order learning in this context.

10. Maintaining knowledge should not be construed to mean innovation is not necessary. Innovation is required to create new knowledge vectors that can be combined with others maintained over time.

11. If firms reuse employees who maintained a technology, then they need not go through with the internalization process with them but with others whose participation is required. In contrast, firms could reuse persons once associated with the development of a technology but who were not associated with its maintenance. In this case, whether an internalization process is required depends on the time elapsed since a technology was shelved. This is because knowledge decays and the context changes over time.

References

Allen, T.J. (1966) "Studies of the problem-solving process in engineering design," *IEEE Transactions on Engineering Management* EM–18, 13(2): 72–83.

Argote, L., Beckman, S. and Epple, D. 1987 "The persistence and transfer of learning in industrial settings", paper presented at the TIMS/ORSA Joint National Meetings, St. Louis, MO.

Arrow, K.J. (1962) "The economics of learning by doing", *Review of Economic Studies* 29: 166–73.

Baba, M.L. (1988) "The local knowledge content of technology-based firms: rethinking informal organization," *Proceedings of the Conference on Managing the High-Technology Firm,* Graduate School of Business, University of Colorado, pp. 66–70.

Barney, J.B. (1986) "Strategic factor markets: Expectations, luck and business strategy," *Management Science* 33(10): 1231–41.

Barney, J.B. (1991). "Firm resources and sustained competitive advantage," *Journal of Management* 17(1): 99–120.

Bulkeley, W.M. (March 10, 1992) "The videophone era may finally be near, bringing big changes," *Wall Street Journal*, p. Al.

Burgelman, R.A. (1991) "Intraorganizational ecology of strategy making and organizational adaptation: theory and field research," *Organization Science* 2(3): 239–62.

Business Week (April 6, 1992) "Forging a growth policy for America," p. 104.

Carey, J. (1992) "Moving the lab closer to the marketplace," *Business Week*, Special Issue on Reinventing America, pp. 164–71.

Cohen, W.M. and Levinthal, D.A. (1990) "Absorptive capacity: a new perspective on learning and innovation," *Administrative Science Quarterly* 35(1): 128–52.

Conner, K.R. (1988) "Strategies for product cannibalization," *Strategic Management Journal*, 9, Summer Special Issue, pp. 9–26.

Conner, K.R. (1991) "A historical comparison of resource-based theory and five schools of thought within industrial organization economics: do we have a new theory of the firm?," *Journal of Management* 17(1): 121–54.

Copeland, T., Koller, T. and Mirvin, J. (1990) *Valuation: Measuring and Managing the Value of Companies*, New York: John Wiley.

Crane, D. (1972) *Invisible Colleges: Diffusion of Knowledge in Scientific Communities*, Chicago, IL: The University of Chicago Press, Chicago.

Daft, R.L. and Lengel, R.H. (1986). "Organizational information requirements, media richness and structural design," *Management Science* 32(5): 554–71.

Daft, R., Sormunen, J. and Parks, D. (1988) "Chief executive scanning, environmental characteristics, and company performance: an empirical study", *Strategic Management Journal* 9(1): 123–39.

David, P. (1985) "Clio and the economics of QWERTY," *American Economic Review* 75(2): 332–7.

Dierickx, I. and Cool, K. (1989) "Asset stock accumulation and sustainability of competitive advantage," *Management Science* 35(12): 1504–11.

Dosi, G. (1982) "Technological paradigms and technological trajectories," *Research Policy* 11(3): 147–62.

Duncan, R. and Weiss, A. (1979) "Organizational learning: Implications for organizational design," in Staw, B. and Cummings, L. (eds) *Research in Organizational Behavior*, Greenwich, CT: *JAI Press* pp. 75–123.

El Sawy, O.A. and Pauchant, T.C. (1988) "Triggers templates and twitches in the tracking of emerging strategic issues," *Strategic Management Journal* 9(5): 455–73.

Elster, 1. (1983) *Explaining Technical Change: A Case Study in the Philosophy of Science*, New York: Cambridge University Press.

Epple, D., Argote, L. and Devadas, R. (1991) "Organizational learning curves: a method for investigating intra-plant transfer of knowledge acquired through learning by doing," *Organization Science* 2(1): 58–70.

Farrell, C. and Mandel, M.J. (April 6, 1992) "Industrial policy," *Business Week*: 70–6.

Ferguson, C.H. and Morris, C.R. (1993) *Computer Wars: How the West Can Win in a Post-IBM World*, New York: Times Books.

Fisher, L.M. (March 14, 1992) "Paint-by-the-numbers programming," *New York Times*, pp. 39 and 51.

Foster, R.N. (1971) "Organize for technology transfer," *Harvard Business Review* 49(6): 110–20.

Foster, R.N. (1982) "Boosting the pay-off from R&D," *Research Management* 25(1): 22–7.

Galbraith, J.R. (1973) *Designing Complex Organizations*, Reading, MA: Addison-Wesley.

Ghemawat, P. (1986) "Sustainable competitive advantage," *Harvard Business Review* 61(5): 53–8.

Ghemawat, P. (1991) *Commitment: The Dynamic of Strategy*, New York: The Free Press.

Graham, M.B.W. (1986) *RCA and the VideoDisc: The Business of Research*. Cambridge: Cambridge University Press.

Gross, N. (September 29, 1992). "Inside Hitachi," *Business Week*, pp. 92–100.

Gupta, A.K. and Govindarajan, V. (1986) "Resource sharing among SBUs: strategic antecedents and administrative implications," *Academy of Management Journal* 29(4): 695–714.

Gupta, U. (April 15, 1989) "M.B.A. students try to revive dead ideas," *Wall Street Journal*, p. B2.

Hamilton, J.O. and Weber, J. (December 19, 1988) "The rewards in raising drugs from the dead," *Business Week*, pp. 90–1.

Hayes, T.C. (January 18, 1993) "Faltering companies seek outsiders," *New York Times*, p. D1.

Hogarth, R. (1980) *Judgement and Choice: A Psychology of Decision*, New York: John Wiley & Sons.

Huber, G. (1991) "Organizational learning: the contributing processes and the literatures," *Organization Science* 2(1): 88–15.

Irvine, J. and Martin, B.R. (1984). *Foresights in Science: Picking the Winners*. Frances Printer Dover, NH.

Janis, I.L. and Mann, L. (1977) *Decision Making: A Psychological Analysis of Conflict, Choice, and Commitment*, New York: The Free Press.

Kahneman, D. and Lovallo, D. (1993) "Timid choices and bold forecasts: A cognitive perspective on risk taking," *Management Science* 39(1), 17–31.

Kanter, R.M.K. (1988) "When a thousand flowers bloom," in Staw, B. and Cummings, L.L. (eds) *Research in Organizational Behavior*, Greenwich, CT: JAI Press pp. 169–211.

Laudan, R. (1984) *The Nature of Knowledge*, Dordrecht: Reidel.

Layton, E. (1974) "Technology as knowledge," *Technology and Culture*, 15(1): 31–41.

Lenz, R.T. and Engledow, J.L. (1986). "Environmental analysis units and strategic decision-making: a field study of selected 'leading-edge' corporations," *Strategic Management Journal* 7(1): 69–89.

Levenhagen M., Thomas, H. and Porac, J.F. (1990) 'A model of market formation', paper presented at the Strategic Management Society–Cranfeld Workshop on Leadership and Strategic Change, Robinson College, Cambridge.

Levitt, B. and March, J.G. (1988) "Organizational learning," *Annual Review of Sociology* 14: 319–40.

Lindblom, C.E. and Cohen, D.K. (1979) *Usable Knowledge: Social Science and Social Problem Solving*, New Haven, CT: Yale University Press.

Lippman, S.A. and McCardle, K.F. (1991) "Uncertain search: a model of search among technologies of uncertain values," *Management Science* 37(11): 1474–90.

Luce, R.D. and Raiffa, H. (1957) *Games and Decisions*, New York: John Wiley and Sons.

Mansfield, E. (1988) "Speed and cost of industrial innovation in Japan and the United States," *Management Science* 34(10): 1157–68.

March, J.G. (1978) "Bounded rationality, ambiguity, and the engineering of choice," *Bell Journal of Economics* 9(2): 587–608.

March, J.G. (1991) "Exploration and exploitation in organizational learning," *Organization Science* 2(1): 71–87.

March, J.G. and Shapira, Z. (1987) "Managerial perspectives on risk and risk-taking," *Management Science* 33(11): 1404–18.

Markoff, J. (January 27, 1993) "Help wanted: Computer skills a must," *New York Times*, p. D1.

McMurray, S. (March 27, 1992) "Changing a culture: DuPont tries to make its research wizardry serve the bottom line," *Wall Street Journal*, p. A1.

Milliken, F. J. (1990) "Perceiving and interpreting environmental change: An examination of college administrators" interpretation of changing demographics', *Academy of Management Journal*, 33(1): 42–63.

Mitchell, G.R. and Hamilton, W.F., (1988) "Managing R&D as a strategic option," *Research and Technology Management* 31(3): 15–22.

Naj, A.K. (February 6, 1991) "Anti-noise system may exhaust need for car mufflers," *Wall Street Journal*, p. Bl.

Nayak, P.R. and Ketteringham, J.M. (1986). *Breakthroughs!* New York: Rawson Associates.

Nelson, R.R. (1959) "The simple economics of basic scientific research," *Journal of Political Economy* 67(3): 297–306.

Nelson, R.R. and Winter, S.G. (1982) *An Evolutionary Theory of Economic Change*, Cambridge, MA: Harvard University Press.

Newman, B. (February 22, 1993) "Among those wary of abortion pill is maker's parent firm," *Wall Street Journal*, p. A1.

Nonaka I. (1988) "Toward middle-up-down management: accelerating information creation," *Sloan Management Review* 29(3): 9–18.

Pavitt, K. (1984) "Sectoral patterns of technical change: towards a taxonomy and a theory," *Research Policy* 13(6): 343–73.

Penrose, E.T. (1959) *The Theory of the Growth of the Firm*, New York, John Wiley & Sons.

Polanyi, M. (1962) *Personal Knowledge: Toward a Post-critical Philosophy*, New York: Harper Torchbooks.

Port, O. (January 27, 1992) "Learning from Japan," *Business Week*, pp. 52–60.

Quinn, J.B. (1969) "Technology transfer by multinational companies," *Harvard Business Review* 47(6): pp. 147–61.

Quinn, J.B. (1992) "The intelligent enterprise: a new paradigm," *Academy of Management Executive* 6(4): 48–63.

Rogers E.M. (1983) *Diffusion of Innovation*, New York: Free Press.

Rosenberg, N. (1982) *Inside the Black Box*, Cambridge: Cambridge University Press.

Rumelt, R.P. (1984) "Toward a strategic theory of the firm," in Lamb, R.B. (ed.) *Competitive Strategic Management*, Englewood Cliffs, Prentice Hall: pp. 557–70.

Russo, M.V. (1992) "Power plays: Regulation, diversification, and backward integration in the electric utility industry," *Strategic Management Journal* 13(1): 13–27.

Sahal, D. (1981) *Patterns of Technological Innovation*, Reading, MA: Addison-Wesley.

Schlender, B.R. (February 24, 1992) "How Sony keeps the magic going," *Fortune*, pp. 76–84.

Schumpeter, J.A. (1975) *Capitalism' Socialism and Democracy*, Reading, MA: Addison-Wesley.

Shook, R.L. (1988) *Honda: An American Success Story*, Englewood Cliffs, NJ: Prentice-Hall.

Smith, D. and Alexander, R. (1988) *Fumbling the Future: How Xerox Invented, Then Ignored, the First Personal Computer*, New York: William Morrow & Co..

Teece, D.J. (1981) "The market for know-how and the efficient international transfer of technology," *Annals of the American Academy of Political and Social Science*, pp. 81–96.

Tichy, N. and Sherman, S. (1993) *Control Your Own Destiny or Someone Else Will: How Jack Welch Is Making General Electric the World's Most Competitive Company*, New York: Currency/Doubieday.

Usher, A.P. (1954) *A History of Mechanical Inventions*, Cambridge, MA: Harvard University Press.

Van de Ven, A.H. (1986) "Central problems in the management of innovation," *Management Science* 32(5): 590–607.

Walsh, J.P. and Ungson, G.R. (1991) "Organizational memory," *Academy of Management Review* 16(1): 57–91.

Weber, J. (July 13, 1992) "Pure research, compliments of Japan," *Business Week*, pp. 136–7.

Weick, K. (1979) *The Social Psychology of Organizing*, Reading, MA: Addison-Wesley.

Wernfelt, B. (1984) "A resource-based view of the firm," *Strategic Management Journal* 5(2): 171–80.

Wernerfelt, B. and Karnarni, A. (1987) "Competitive strategy under uncertainty," *Strategic Management Journal* 8(2): 187–94.

Wilson, T.L. and Hlavacek, J.D. (1984) "Don't let good ideas sit on the shelf," *Research Management* 27(3): 27–34.

Winter, S.G. (1987) "Knowledge and competence as strategic assets," in Teece, D.J. (ed.) *The competitive challenge: Strategies for Industrial Innovation and Renewal*, Cambridge, MA: Ballinger Publishing Company, pp. 159–84.

9

A dynamic theory of organizational knowledge creation

Ikujiro Nonaka

1 Introduction

It is widely observed that the society we live in has been gradually turning into a "knowledge society" (Drucker, 1968; Bell, 1973; Toffler, 1990). The ever increasing importance of knowledge in contemporary society calls for a shift in our thinking concerning innovation in large business organizations – be it technical innovation, product innovation, or strategic or organizational innovation.[1] It raises questions about how organizations process knowledge and, more importantly, how they create new knowledge. Such a shift in general orientation will involve, among other things, a reconceptualization of the organizational knowledge creation processes.

The theory of organization has long been dominated by a paradigm that conceptualizes the organization as a system that "processes" information or "solves" problems. Central to this paradigm is the assumption that a fundamental task from the organization is how efficiently it can deal with information and decisions in an uncertain environment. This paradigm suggests that the solution lies in the "input-process-output" sequence of hierarchical information processing. Yet a critical problem with this paradigm follows from its passive and static view of the organization. Information processing is viewed as a problem-solving activity which centers on what is given to the organization – without due consideration of what is created by it.

Any organization that dynamically deals with a changing environment ought not only to process information efficiently but also create information and knowledge. Analyzing the organization in terms of its design and capability to process information imposed by the environment no doubt constitutes an important approach to interpreting certain aspects of organizational activities. However, it can be argued that the organization's interaction with its environment, together with the means by which it creates and distributes information and knowledge, are more important when it comes to building an active and dynamic understanding of the organization. For example, innovation, which is a key form of organizational knowledge creation, cannot be explained sufficiently in terms of information processing or problem solving. Innovation can be better understood as a process in which the organization creates and defines problems and then actively develops new knowledge to solve them. Also, innovation produced by one part of the

165

organization in turn creates a stream of related information and knowledge, which might then trigger changes in the organization's wider knowledge systems. Such a sequence of innovation suggests that the organization should be studied from the viewpoint of how it creates information and knowledge, rather than with regard to how it processes these entities.

The goal of this chapter is to develop the essential elements of a theory of organizational knowledge creation. In the sections which follow, the basic concepts and models of the theory of organizational knowledge creation are presented. Based on this foundation, the dynamics of the organizational knowledge creation process are examined and practical models are advanced for managing the process more effectively.

2 Basic concepts and models of organization knowledge creation

The following subsections explore some basic constructs of the theory of organization knowledge creation. They begin by discussing the nature of information and knowledge and then draw a distinction between "tacit" and "explicit" knowledge. This distinction represents what could be described as the epistemological dimension to organizational knowledge creation. It embraces a continual dialogue between explicit and tacit knowledge which drives the creation of new ideas and concepts.

Although ideas are formed in the minds of individuals, interaction between individuals typically plays a critical role in developing these ideas. That is to say, "communities of interaction" contribute to the amplification and development of new knowledge. While these communities might span departmental or indeed organizational boundaries, the point to note is that they define a further dimension to organizational knowledge creation, which is associated with the extent of social interaction between individuals that share and develop knowledge. This is referred to as the "ontological" dimension of knowledge creation.

Following a consideration of the two dimensions of knowledge creation, some attention is given to the role of individuals and, more specifically, to their "commitment" to the knowledge creating process. This covers aspects of their "intention," the role of autonomy, and the effects of fluctuations or discontinuities in the organization and its environment.

Next, a "spiral" model of knowledge creation is proposed which shows the relationship between the epistemological and ontological dimensions of knowledge creation. This spiral illustrates the creation of a new concept in terms of a continual dialogue between tacit and explicit knowledge. As the concept resonates around an expanding community of individuals, it is developed and clarified. Gradually, concepts which are thought to be of value obtain a wider currency and become crystalized. This description of the spiral model is followed by some observations about how to support the practical management of organizational knowledge creation.

2.1 Knowledge and information

Knowledge is a multifaceted concept with multilayered meanings. The history of philosophy since the classical Greek period can be regarded as a never-ending search for the meaning of knowledge.[2] This chapter follows traditional epistemology and adopts a definition of knowledge as "justified true belief." It should be noted, however, that while the arguments of traditional epistemology focus on "truthfulness" as the essential attribute of knowledge, for present purposes it is important to consider knowledge as a personal "belief," and emphasize the importance of the "justification" of knowledge. This difference introduces another critical distinction between the view of knowledge of traditional epistemology and that of the theory of knowledge creation. While the former naturally emphasizes the absolute, static, and nonhuman nature of knowledge, typically expressed in propositional forms in formal logic, the latter sees knowledge as a dynamic human process of justifying personal beliefs as part of an aspiration for the "truth."

Although the terms "information" and "knowledge" are often used interchangeably, there is a clear distinction between information and knowledge. According to Machlup (1983), information is a flow of messages or meanings which might add to, restructure or change knowledge. Dretske (1981) offers some useful definitions. In his words:

> Information is that commodity capable of yielding knowledge, and what information a signal carries is what we can learn from it (Dretske, 1981: 44). Knowledge is identified with information-produced (or sustained) belief, but the information a person receives is relative to what he or she already knows about the possibilities at the source (ibid.: 86).

In short, information is a flow of messages, while knowledge is created and organized by the very flow of information, anchored on the commitment and beliefs of its holder. This understanding emphasizes an essential aspect of knowledge that relates to human action.

The importance of knowledge related to action has been recognized in the area of artificial intelligence. For example, Gruber (1989) addresses the subject of an expert's "strategic knowledge" as that which directly guides his action, and attempts to develop the tools to acquire it. Since the 1980s, the development of cognitive science has been based on a serious reflection on behavioralist psychology's neglect of such traditional questions as, "Why do human beings act in a certain way?," which was a central issue for so-called "folk psychology" (Stich 1986). Searle's discussion on the "speech act" also points out a close relationship between language and human action in terms of the "intention" and "commitment" of speakers (Searle 1969). In sum, as a fundamental basis for the theory of organizational creation of knowledge, it can be argued that attention should be focused on the active, subjective nature of knowledge represented by such terms as "belief" and "commitment" that are deeply rooted in the value systems of individuals.

The analysis of knowledge and information does not stop at this point. Information is a necessary medium or material for initiating and formalizing knowledge and can be viewed from "syntactic" and "semantic" perspectives. The syntactic aspect of information is illustrated by Shannon's analysis of the volume of information which is measured without regard to its meaning or value. A telephone bill, for example, is not calculated on the basis of the content of a conversation but according to the duration of time and the distance involved. Shannon said that the semantic aspects of communication, which center on the meaning of information, are irrelevant to the engineering problem (Shannon and Weaver, 1949). A genuine theory of information would be a theory about the content of our messages, not a theory about the form in which this content is embodied (Dretske, 1981).

In terms of creating knowledge, the semantic aspect of information is more relevant as it focuses on conveyed meaning. The syntactic aspect does not capture the importance of information in the knowledge creation process. Therefore, any preoccupation with the formal definition will tend to lead to a disproportionate emphasis on the role of information processing, which is insensitive to the creation of organizational knowledge out of the chaotic, equivocal state of information. Information, seen from the semantic standpoint, literally means that it contains new meaning. As Bateson (1979: 5) put it, "information consists of differences that make a difference." This insight provides a new point of view for interpreting events that make previously invisible connections or ideas obvious or shed light on unexpected connections (Miyazaki and Ueno, 1985). For the purposes of building a theory of knowledge creation, it is important to concentrate on the semantic aspects of information.

2.2 Two dimensions of knowledge creation

Although a great deal has been written about the importance of knowledge in management, relatively little attention has been paid to how knowledge is created and how the knowledge creation process can be managed. One dimension of this knowledge creation process can be drawn from a distinction between two types of knowledge – *"tacit knowledge"* and *"explicit knowledge."* As Michael Polanyi (1966: 4) put it. "We can know more than we can tell."[3] Knowledge that can be expressed in words and numbers only represents the tip of the iceberg of the entire body of possible knowledge. Polanyi classified human knowledge into two categories. "Explicit" or codified knowledge refers to knowledge that is transmittable in formal, systematic language. On the other hand, "tacit" knowledge has a personal quality, which makes it hard to formalize and communicate. Tacit knowledge is deeply rooted in action, commitment, and involvement in a specific context. In Polanyi's words, it "indwells" in a comprehensive cognizance of the human mind and body.

While Polanyi articulates the contents of tacit knowledge in a philosophical context, it is also possible to expand his idea in a more practical direction. Tacit knowledge involves both cognitive and technical elements. The cognitive elements center on what Johnson-Laird (1983) called "mental models" in which human beings form working models of the world by creating and manipulating analogies in their minds. These working models include schemata, paradigms, beliefs, and viewpoints that provide "perspectives" that help individuals to perceive and define their world. By contrast, the technical element of tacit knowledge covers concrete know-how, crafts, and skills that apply to specific contexts. It is important to note here that the cognitive element of tacit knowledge refers to an individual's images of reality and visions for the future, that is to say, what is and what ought to be. As will be discussed later, the articulation of tacit perspectives-in a kind of "mobilization" process – is a key factor in the creation of new knowledge.

Tacit knowledge is a continuous activity of knowing and embodies what Bateson (1973) has referred to as an "analogue" quality. In this context, communication between individuals may be seen as an analogue process that aims to share tacit knowledge to build mutual understanding. This understanding involves a kind of "parallel processing" of the complexities of current issues, as the different dimensions of a problem are processed simultaneously. By contrast, explicit knowledge is discrete or "digital." It is captured in records of the past such as libraries, archives, and databases and is assessed on a sequential basis.

The ontological dimension: the level of social interaction. At a fundamental level, knowledge is created by individuals. An organization cannot create knowledge without individuals. The organization supports creative individuals or provides a context for such individuals to create knowledge. Organizational knowledge creation, therefore, should be understood in terms of a process that "organizationally" amplifies the knowledge created by individuals, and crystallizes it as a part of the knowledge network of organization.

In this line, it is possible to distinguish several levels of social interaction at which the knowledge created by an individual is transformed and legitimized. In the first instance, an informal community of social interaction provides an immediate forum for nuturing the emergent property of knowledge at each level and developing new ideas. Since this informal community might span organizational boundaries – for example, to include suppliers or customers – it is important that the organization is able to integrate appropriate aspects of emerging knowledge into its strategic development. Thus, the potential contribution of informal groups to organizational knowledge creation should be related to more formal notions of a hierarchical structure. If this is done effectively, new knowledge associated with more advantageous organizational processes or technologies will be able to gain a broader currency within the organization.

In addition to the creation of knowledge within an organization, it is also possible that there will be formal provisions to build knowledge at an interorganizational level. This might occur if informal communities of interaction, that span the link between customers, suppliers, distributors, and even competitors, are put on a more formal basis, for example, through the formation of alliances or outsourcing.

2.3 Commitment on the part of the knowledge subject: intention, autonomy, and fluctuation

The prime movers in the process of organizational knowledge creation are the individual members of an organization. Individuals are continuously committed to recreating the world in accordance with their own perspectives. As Polanyi noted, "commitment" underlies human knowledge creating activities. Thus, commitment is one of the most important components for promoting the formation of new knowledge within an organization. There are three basic factors that induce individual commitment in an organizational setting: "intention," and "autonomy," and a certain level of environmental "fluctuation."

Intention. Intention is concerned with how individuals form their approach to the world and try to make sense of their environment. It is not simply a state of mind, but rather what might be called an action-oriented concept. Edmund Husserl (1968) called this attitude on the part of the subject "intentionality." He denied the existence of "consciousness" per se, which was generally assumed by psychologists in 19th century, and argued that consciousness arises when a subject pays attention to an object. In other words, any consciousness is a "consciousness of something." It arises, endures, and disappears with a subject's commitment to an object.

Eigen (1971) argued, in his evolutionary theory, that evolution involves the process of acquiring environmental information for better adaptation. Eigen insisted that the degree of meaningfulness of information, or a value parameter, needs to be introduced to explain this system. Human beings, as organic systems, derive meaning from the environment which is based on their ultimate pursuit of survival (Shimizu, 1978). Man cannot grasp the meaning of information about his environment without some frame of value judgment.

The meaning of information differs according to what a particular system aims to do (manifest purpose or problem consciousness) and the broader environment in which that system exits (context). It is more concerned with the system's future aspirations than its current state. Weick (1979) explains this "self-fulfilling prophecy" of a system as the "enactment" of the environment, which may be a projection of its strong will for self-actualization. While mechanistic information-processing models treat the mind as a fixed capacity device for converting meaningless information into conscious perception, in reality cognition is the activity of knowing and understanding as it occurs in the context of purposeful activity (Neisser 1976). Intention becomes apparent against this background. Without intention, it would be impossible to judge the value of the information or knowledge perceived or created. "The intentionality of the mind not only creates the possibility of meaning, but also limits its form" (Searle, 1983: 166).

Autonomy. The principle of autonomy can be applied at the individual, group, and organizational levels – either separately or all together. However, the individual is a convenient starting point for analysis. Individuals within the organization may have different intentions. Every individual has his or her own personality. By allowing people to act autonomously, the organization may increase the possibility of introducing unexpected opportunities of the type that are sometimes associated with the so-called "garbage can" metaphor (Cohen *et al.*, 1972). From the standpoint of creating knowledge, such an organization is more likely to maintain greater flexibility in acquiring, relating, and interpreting information. In a system where the autonomy of individuals is assured, or where only "minimum critical specification" (Morgan, 1986) is intended, it is possible to establish a basis for self-organization.

Individual autonomy widens the possibility that individuals will motivate themselves to form new knowledge. Self-motivation based on deep emotions, for example, in the poet's creation of new expressions, serves as a driving force for the creation of metaphors. A sense of purpose and autonomy becomes important as an organizational context. Purpose serves as the basis of conceptualization. Autonomy gives individuals freedom to absorb knowledge.

Fluctuation. Even though intention is internal to the individual, knowledge creation at the individual level involves continuous interaction with the external world. In this connection, chaos or discontinuity can generate new patterns of interaction between individuals and their environment. Individuals recreate their own systems of knowledge to take account of ambiguity, redundancy, noise, or randomness generated from the organization and its environment. These fluctuations differ from complete disorder and are characterized by "order without recursiveness" – which represents an order where the pattern is hard to predict in the beginning (Gleick, 1987).

Winograd and Flores (1986) emphasize the role of periodic "breakdowns" in human perception. Breakdown refers to the interruption of an individual's habitual, comfortable "state-of-being." When breakdowns occur, individuals question the value of habits and routine tools, which might lead to a realignment of commitments. Environmental fluctuation often triggers this breakdown. When people face such a breakdown or contradiction, they have an opportunity to reconsider their fundamental thinking and perspectives. In other words, they begin to question the validity of basic attitudes toward the world. This process necessarily involves deep personal commitment by the individual and is similar in context to Piaget's (1974) observations about the importance of the role of contradiction in the interaction between the subject and its environment in such a way that the subject forms perceptions through behavior.

2.4 Knowledge conversion and the spiral of knowledge

It is now possible to bring together the epistemological and ontological dimensions of knowledge creation to form a "spiral" model for the processes involved. This involves identifying four different patterns of interaction between tacit and explicit knowledge. These patterns represent ways in which existing knowledge can be "converted" into new knowledge. Social interaction between individuals then provides an ontological dimension to the expansion of knowledge.

The idea of "knowledge conversion" may be traced from Anderson's ACT model (Anderson, 1983) developed in cognitive psychology. In the ACT model, knowledge is divided into "declarative knowledge" (actual knowledge) that is expressed in the form of propositions and "procedural knowledge" (methodological knowledge) which is used in such activities as remembering how to ride a bicycle or play the piano. In the context of the present discussion, the former might approximate to explicit knowledge and the latter to tacit knowledge. Anderson's model hypothesizes that declarative knowledge has to be transformed into procedural knowledge in order for cognitive skills to develop. This hypothesis is consistent with Ryle's classification (1949) of knowledge into categories of knowing that something "exists" and knowing "how" it operates. Anderson's categorization can be regarded as a more sophisticated version of Ryle's classification. One limitation of the ACT model is the hypothesis that transformation of knowledge is unidirectional and only involves transformations from declarative to procedural knowledge, while it can be argued that transformation is bidirectional. This may be because the ACT model is more concerned with maturation than with the creation of knowledge.

Four Modes of Knowledge Conversion. The assumption that knowledge is created through conversion between tacit and explicit knowledge allows us to postulate four different "modes" of knowledge conversion: (1) from tacit knowledge to tacit knowledge, (2) from explicit knowledge to explicit knowledge, (3) from tacit knowledge to explicit knowledge, and (4) from explicit knowledge to tacit knowledge.

First, there is a mode of knowledge conversion that enables us to convert tacit knowledge through interaction between individuals. One important point to note here is that an individual can acquire tacit knowledge without language. Apprentices work with their mentors and learn craftsmanship not through language but by observation, imitation, and practice. In a business setting, on-the-job training (OJT) uses the same principle. The key to acquiring tacit knowledge is experience. Without some form of shared experience, it is extremely difficult for people to share each others' thinking processes. The mere transfer of information will often make little sense if it is abstracted from embedded emotions and nuanced contexts that are associated with shared experiences. This process of creating tacit knowledge through shared experience will be called "socialization."

The second mode of knowledge conversion involves the use of social processes to combine different bodies of explicit knowledge held by individuals. Individuals exchange and combine knowledge through such exchange mechanisms as meetings and telephone conversations. The reconfiguring of existing information through the sorting, adding, recategorizing, and recontextualizing of explicit knowledge can lead to new knowledge. Modern computer systems provide a graphic example. This process of creating explicit knowledge from explicit knowledge is referred to as "combination."

The third and fourth modes of knowledge conversion relate to patterns of conversion involving both tacit and explicit knowledge. These conversion modes capture the idea that tacit and explicit knowledge are complementary and can expand over time through a process of mutual interaction. This interaction involves two different operations. One is the conversion of tacit knowledge into explicit knowledge, which will be called "externalization." The other is the conversion of explicit knowledge into tacit knowledge, which bears some similarity to the traditional notion of "learning" and will be referred to here as "internalization." As will be discussed later, "metaphor" plays an important role in the externalization process, and "action" is deeply related to the internalization process. Figure 9.1 illustrates the four modes of knowledge conversion.

Three of the four types of knowledge conversion – socialization, combination, and internalization, have partial analogs with aspects of organizational theory. For example, socialization is connected with theories of organizational culture, while combination is rooted in information processing and internalization has associations with organizational learning. By contrast, the concept of externalization is not well developed. The limited analysis that does exist is from the point of view of information creation (see Nonaka, 1987).

Theories of organizational learning do not address the critical notion of externalization, and have paid little attention to the importance of socialization even though there has been an accumulation of research on "modeling" behavior in learning psychology. Another difficulty relates to the concepts of "double-loop learning" (Argyris and Schön 1978) or "unlearning" (Hedberg, 1981), which arises from a strong orientation toward organization development (OD). Since the first integrated theory of organizational learning presented by Argyris and Schön, it has been widely assumed, implicitly or explicitly, that double-loop learning, i.e., the questioning and reconstruction of existing perspectives, interpretation frameworks, or decision premises, can be very difficult for organizations to implement by themselves. In order to overcome this difficulty, they argue that some kind of artificial intervention such as the use of organizational development programs is required. The limitation of this

Figure 9.1 Modes of the knowledge creation

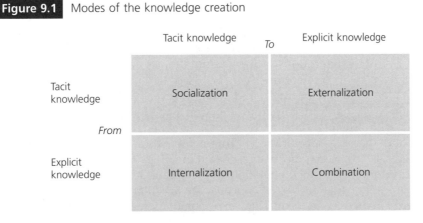

argument is that it assumes implicitly that someone inside or outside an organization knows "objectively" the right time and method for putting double-loop learning into practice. A mechanistic view of the organization lies behind this assumption. Seen from the vantage point of organizational knowledge creation, on the contrary, double-loop learning is not a special, difficult task but a daily activity for the organization. Organizations continuously create new knowledge by reconstructing existing perspectives, frameworks, or premises on a day-to-day basis. In other words, double-loop learning ability is "built into" the knowledge creating model, thereby circumventing the need to make unrealistic assumptions about the existence of a "right" answer.

Modal Shift and Spiral of Knowledge. While each of the four modes of knowledge conversion can create new knowledge independently, the central theme of the model of organizational knowledge creation proposed here hinges on a dynamic interaction between the different modes of knowledge conversion. That is to say, knowledge creation centers on the building of both tacit and explicit knowledge and, more importantly, on the interchange between these two aspects of knowledge through internalization and externalization.

A failure to build a dialogue between tacit and explicit knowledge can cause problems. For example, both pure combination and socialization have demerits. A lack of commitment and neglect of the personal meaning of knowledge might mean that pure combination becomes a superficial interpretation of existing knowledge, which has little to do with here-and-now reality. It may also fail to crystallize or embody knowledge in a form that is concrete enough to facilitate further knowledge creation in a wider social context. The "sharability" of knowledge created by pure socialization may be limited and, as a result, difficult to apply in fields beyond the specific context in which it was created.

Organizational knowledge creation, as distinct from individual knowledge creation, takes place when all four modes of knowledge creation are "organizationally" managed to form a continual cycle. This cycle is shaped by a series of shifts between different modes of knowledge conversion. There are various "triggers" that induce these shifts between different modes of knowledge conversion. First, the socialization mode usually starts with the building of a "team" or "field" of interaction. This field facilitates the sharing of members' experiences and perspectives. Second, the externalization mode is triggered by successive rounds of meaningful "dialogue." In this dialogue, the sophisticated use of "metaphors" can be used to enable team members to articulate their own perspectives, and thereby reveal hidden tacit knowledge that is otherwise hard to communicate. Concepts formed by teams can be combined with existing data and external knowledge in a search of more concrete and sharable specifications. This combination mode is facilitated by such triggers as "coordination" between team members and other sections of the organization and the "documentation" of existing knowledge. Through an iterative process of trial and error, concepts are articulated and developed until they emerge in a concrete form. This "experimentation" can trigger internalization through a process of "learning by doing." Participants in a "field" of action share explicit knowledge that is gradually translated, through interaction and a process of trial-and-error, into different aspects of tacit knowledge.

While tacit knowledge held by individuals may lie at the heart of the knowledge creating process, realizing the practical benefits of that knowledge centers on its externalization and amplification through dynamic interactions between all four modes of knowledge conversion. Tacit knowledge is thus mobilized through a dynamic "entangling" of the different modes of knowledge conversion in a process which will be referred to as a "spiral" model of knowledge creation, illustrated in Figure 9.2. The interactions between tacit knowledge and explicit knowledge will tend to become larger in scale and faster in speed as more actors in and around the organization become involved. Thus, organizational knowledge creation can be viewed as an upward spiral process, starting at the individual level moving up to the collective (group) level, and then to the organizational level, sometimes reaching out to the interorganizational level.

2.5 From metaphor to model: methodology of knowledge creation

Before concluding this presentation of the basic constructs of the theory, it is helpful to consider some general principles for facilitating the management of knowledge conversion. One effective method of converting tacit knowledge

Figure 9.2 Spiral of organizational knowledge creation

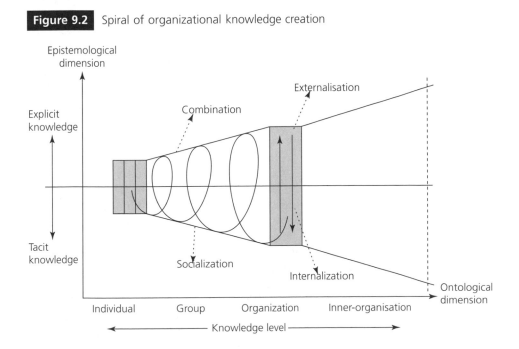

into explicit knowledge is the use of metaphor. As Nisbet (1969: 5) noted, "(m)uch of what Michael Polanyi has called 'tacit knowledge' is expressible – in so far as it is expressible at all-in metaphor." "The essence of metaphor is understanding and experiencing one kind of thing in terms of another (Lakoff and Johnson, 1980: 5)." Even though the metaphor is not in itself a thinking process, it enables us to experience a new behavior by making inferences from the model of another behavior. The use of metaphor is broader than the traditional, lexical definition of the term (meta = change; phor = move). According to Lakoff and Johnson: "metaphor is pervasive in everyday life, not just in language but in thought and action. Our ordinary conceptual system, in terms of which we both think and act, is fundamentally metaphorical in nature" (Lakoff and Johnson 1980: 3).

As a method of perception, metaphor depends on imagination and intuitive learning through symbols, rather than on the analysis or synthesis of common attributes shared by associated things. Rosch (1973) suggested that man describes the world, not in the formal attributes of concepts, but in terms of prototypes. For example, the robin could be seen as a better prototype than the turkey for a small bird. Prototypes provide a mechanism for recognizing the maximum level of information with a minimum of energy.

Metaphor is not merely the first step in transforming tacit knowledge into explicit knowledge; it constitutes an important method of creating a network of concepts which can help to generate knowledge about the future by using existing knowledge. Metaphor may be defined as being "two contradicting concepts incorporated in one word." It is a creative, cognitive process which relates concepts that are far apart in an individual's memory. While perception through prototype is in many cases limited to concrete, mundane concepts, metaphor plays an important role in associating abstract, imaginary concepts. When two concepts are presented in a metaphor, it is possible not only to think of their similarity, but also to make comparisons that discern the degree of imbalance, contradiction or inconsistency involved in their association. The latter process becomes the basis for creating new meaning.[4] According to Bateson (1973) metaphors cut across different contexts and thus allow imaginative perceptions to combine with literal levels of cognitive activities. This experience, he further argues, will promote the type of "presupposition-negation" learning that is closely related with the formation of new paradigms.

Contradictions incorporated in metaphor may be harmonized through the use of analogies. Analogy reduces ambiguity by highlighting the commonness of two different things. Metaphor and analogy are often confused. The association of meanings by metaphor is mostly driven by intuition, and involves images. On the other hand, the association of meanings through analogy is more structural/functional and is carried out through rational thinking. As such, metaphors provide much room for free association (discontinuity). Analogy allows the functional operation of new concepts or systems to be explored by reference to things that are already understood. In this sense, an analogy – that enables us to know the future through the present – assumes an intermediate role in bridging the gap between image and logic.

It follows from the preceding discussion that tacit knowledge may be transformed into explicit knowledge by (1) recognizing contradictions through metaphor, and (2) resolving them through analogy. Explicit knowledge represents a model within which contradictions are resolved and concepts become transferable through consistent and systematic logic. In the business organization, a typical model is the prototype that represents the product concept. The prototype's specification is then explicit knowledge. It has been pointed out that metaphor, analogy, and model are all part of the process of scientific discovery.[5] Whether the metaphoranalogy-model sequence is indispensable in all such processes will depend upon the nature of the question under study; yet in creating new concepts, the model is usually generated from a metaphor.

3 The process of organizational knowledge creation

The theoretical constructs and models described in §2 may now be related to organizational knowledge creation in a corporate organizational setting. This will be approached by assessing the processes that enable individual knowledge to be enlarged, amplified, and justified within an organization.

3.1 The enlargement of an individual's knowledge

The prime mover in the process of organizational knowledge creation is the individual. Individuals accumulate tacit knowledge through direct "hands-on" experience. The quality of that tacit knowledge is influenced by two important factors. One factor is the "variety" of an individual's experience. If this experience is limited to routine operations, the amount of tacit knowledge obtained from monotonous and repetitive tasks will tend to decrease over time. Routine tasks mitigate against creative thinking and the formation of new knowledge. However, increasing the variety of experience is not sufficient by itself to raise the quality of tacit knowledge. If the individual finds various experiences to be completely unrelated, there will be little chance that they can be integrated to create a new perspective. What matters is "high quality" experience which might, on occasion, involve the complete redefinition of the nature of a "job."

A second factor that determines the quality of tacit knowledge is "knowledge of experience." The essence of "knowledge of experience" is an embodiment of knowledge through a deep personal commitment into bodily experience. Varela *et al.* (1991) have pointed out that the embodied nature of human knowledge has long been neglected in Western epistemological traditions that have followed from Descartes. They define embodiment as: "a reflection in which body and mind have been brought together" (1991: 27). Yuasa (1987) describes this "oneness of body-mind" as the free state of minimal distance between movement of the mind and of the body, as for example in the dynamic performance of a master actor on a stage (1987: 28). As Merleau-Ponty

(1964) pointed out, bodily experience plays a critical role in the process of crystallization. Commitment to bodily experience means an intentional self-involvement in the object and situation which transcends the subject-object distinction, thereby providing access to "pure experience" (Nishida, 1960). This notion is prevalent in oriental culture. As Yuasa mentions:

> One revealing characteristic of the philosophical uniqueness of Eastern thought is presupposed in the philosophical foundation of the Eastern theories. To put it simply, true knowledge cannot be obtained simply by means of theoretical thinking, but only through "bodily recognition or realization" (*tainin* or *taitoku*), that is, through the utilization of one's total mind and body. Simply stated, this is to "learn with the body" not the brain. Cultivation is a practice that attempts, so to speak, to achieve true knowledge by means of one's total mind and body (1987: 25–6).

A good case in point is "on-the-spot-ism" in Japanese management. In developing the products and identifying the markets, Japanese firms encourage the use of judgment and knowledge formed through interaction with customers – and by personal bodily experience rather than by "objective," scientific conceptualization. Social interaction between individuals, groups and organizations are fundamental to organizational knowledge creation in Japan. Nevertheless, since this approach uses hands-on experience and action, it sometimes falls in the category of "experiencism" which neglects the importance of reflection and logical thinking. It tends to overemphasize action and efficiency at the expense of a search for higher level concepts which have universal application.

While the concepts of "high-quality experience" and "knowledge of experience" may be used to raise the quality of tacit knowledge, they have to be counterbalanced by a further approach to knowledge creation that raises the quality of explicit knowledge. Such an approach may be called a "knowledge of rationality," which describes a rational ability to reflect on experience. Knowledge of rationality is an explicit-knowledge-oriented approach that is dominant in Western culture. It centers on the "combination" mode of knowledge conversion, and is effective in creating digital, discrete declarative knowledge. Knowledge of rationality tends to ignore the importance of commitment, and instead centers a reinterpretation of existing explicit knowledge.

In order to raise the total quality of an individual's knowledge, the enhancement of tacit knowledge has to be subjected to continual interplay with the evolution of relevant aspects of explicit knowledge. In this connection, Schön (1983) pointed out the importance of "reflection in action," i.e., reflecting while experiencing. Individual knowledge is enlarged through this interaction between experience and rationality, and crystallized into a unique perspective original to an individual. These original perspectives are based on individual belief and value systems, and will be a source of varied interpretations of shared experience with others in the next stage of conceptualization.

3.2 Sharing tacit knowledge and conceptualization

As we saw in the previous section, the process of organizational knowledge creation is initiated by the enlargement of an individual's knowledge within an organization. The interaction between knowledge of experience and rationality enables individuals to build their own perspectives on the world. Yet these perspectives remain personal unless they are articulated and amplified through social interaction. One way to implement the management of organizational knowledge creation is to create a "field" or "self-organizing team" in which individual members collaborate to create a new concept.

In this connection, it is helpful to draw on the concept of an organization's "mental outlook" as articulated in Sandelands and Stablein's (1987) pioneering work on "organizational mind." While making caveats about the dangers of reification and anthropomorphism, these authors use the analogy of "mind" to identify the process by which organizations form ideas. Mind is distinct from the brain in the same way that computer software is distinct from hardware. Against this background, intelligence may be seen as the ability to maintain a working similarity between mind and nature.

The development of ideas associated with organizational mind requires some form of physical substrate (i.e. hardware) which Sandelands and Stablein (1987) argue might be derived from "patterns of behavior traced by people and machines" (p. 139). Organizational behaviors can convey ideas and, like the firing of neurons in the brain, may trigger other behaviors and so form a trace of activation.

In the brain, whether or not one neuron influences another depends on a complex set of factors having primarily to do with physical proximity, availability of pathways, intensity of the electrochemical signal, and whether or not the target neuron is inhibited by other neurons. Similarly, whether one behavior influences another in social organizations depends on a complex of factors primarily concerned with physical access, lines of communication, power, and competition from other behaviors. At an abstract formal level, at least, the politics of the social organization and the physiology of the brain share much in common. (Sandelands and Stablein, 1987: 140)

It is human activity that creates organizational mind as individuals interact and trigger behavior patterns in others. Managing a self-organizing team involves building an appropriate degree of flexibility into the system which can accommodate a diversity of imaginative thinking in the pursuit of new problems and solutions.

Constructing a Field: Building a Self-organizing Team. To bring personal knowledge into a social context within which it can be amplified, it is necessary to have a "field" that provides a place in which individual perspectives are articulated, and conflicts are resolved in the formation of higher-level concepts. Berger and Luchman (1966) say that reality in everyday life is socially constructed. Individual behavior ought to be relativized through an interactive process to construct "social reality."

In the business organization, the field for interaction is often provided in the form of an autonomous, self-organizing "team" made of several members coming from a variety of functional departments. It is a critical matter for an organization to decide when and how to establish such a "field" of interaction in which individuals can meet and interact. It defines "true" members of knowledge creation and thus clarifies the domain in which perspectives are interacted.

The team needs to be established with regard to the principles of self-organization. In Lewin's (1951) development of the field theory in social psychology, a group is defined as "a dynamic whole based on interdependence rather on similarity." Some indication of the number of members and the composition of their background can be achieved using the principle of "requisite variety" (Ashby, 1956). According to our observation of successful project teams in Japanese firms, the appropriate team size may be in the region between 10 and 30 individuals, with an upper limit arising because direct interaction between all the group members tends to decrease as group size increases. Within the team, there are usually 4 to 5 "core" members who have career histories that include multiple job functions. These core members form focal points in the team and could be seen as the organizational equivalent of the central element in a series of nested Russian dolls.[6] That is to say there is a radial pattern of interaction with other members, with closer links being associated with key individuals. Core members play a critical role in assuring appropriate "redundancy" of information within the cross-functional team. Other attributes of members such as formal position, age, gender, etc. might be determined with regard to Morgan's (1986) four principles of "learning to learn, requisite variety, minimum critical specification, and redundancy of functions."

The span of team activities need not be confined to the narrow boundary of the organization. Rather, it is a process that frequently makes extensive use of knowledge in environment, especially that of customers and suppliers. As Norman (1988) argues, the mental outlook of an organization is shaped by a complex pattern of factors within and outside the organization.[7] In some Japanese firms, for example, suppliers of parts and components are sometimes involved in the early stages of the product development. The relationship between manufacturers and suppliers is less hierarchial and arm's length than in Western countries. Some other Japanese companies involve customers in the field of new product planning. In both cases, sharing tacit knowledge with suppliers or customers through coexperience and creative dialogue play a critical role in creating relevant knowledge.

The significance of links between individuals that span boundaries, both within and outside the organization, has been highlighted by Brown and Duguid's (1991) revealing insight into the operation of "evolving communities of practice." These communities reflect the way in which people actually work as opposed to the formal job descriptions or task-related procedures that are specified by the organization. Attempts to solve practical problems often generate links between individuals who can provide useful information. The exchange and development of information within these evolving communities facilitate knowledge creation by linking the routine dimensions of day-to-day work to active learning and innovation. Collaboration to exchange ideas through shared narratives and "war stories" can provide an important platform on which to construct shared understanding out of conflicting and confused data.

By contrast with conceptions of groups as bounded entities within an organization, evolving communities of practice are "more fluid and interpenetrative than bounded, often crossing the restrictive boundaries of the organization to incorporate people from outside" (Brown and Duguid, 1991: 49). Moreover, these communities can provide important contributions to visions for future development. Thus these communities represent a key dimension to socialization and its input to the overall knowledge creation process.

The self-organizing team triggers organizational knowledge creation through two processes. First, it facilitates the building of mutual trust among members, and accelerates creation of an implicit perspective shared by members as tacit knowledge. The key factor for this process is sharing experience among members. Second, the shared implicit perspective is conceptualized through continuous dialogue among members. This creative dialogue is realized only when redundancy of information exists within the team. The two processes appear simultaneously or alternatively in the actual process of knowledge creation within a team.

Before discussing these two processes further, it is necessary to mention another dimension of the knowledge creating process that can be associated with the self-organizing team. Scheflen (1982) proposed an idea of "interaction rhythms," in which social interactions were viewed as being both simultaneous and sequential. The management of interaction rhythms among team members, i.e., that of divergence and convergence of various interaction rhythms, plays a critical role in accelerating the knowledge creation process. Within the team, rhythms of different speed are first generated and amplified up to certain point of time and level, and then are given momentum for convergence towards a concept. Therefore, the crucial role of team leader concerns how to balance the rhythm of divergence and convergence in the process of dialogues and shared experience.

In sum, the cross-functional team in which experience sharing and continuous dialogue are facilitated by the management of interaction rhythms serves as the basic building block for structuring the organization knowledge creation process. The team is different from a mere group in that it induces self-organizing process of the entire organization through which the knowledge at the group level is elevated to the organizational level.

Sharing Experience. In order for the self-organizing team to start the process of concept creation, it first needs to build mutual trust among members. As we shall see later, concept creation involves a difficult process of externalization, i.e., converting tacit knowledge (which by nature is hard to articulate) into an explicit concept. This challenging task involves repeated, time-consuming dialogue among members. Mutual trust is an indispensable base for facilitating this type of constructive "collaboration" (Schrage, 1990). A key way to build mutual trust is to share one's original experience – the fundamental source of tacit knowledge. Direct understanding of other individuals relies on shared experience that enables team members to "indwell" into others and to grasp their world from "inside."

Shared experience also facilitates the creation of "common perspectives" which can be shared by team members as a part of their respective bodies of tacit knowledge. The dominant mode of knowledge conversion involved here is socialization. Various forms of tacit knowledge that are brought into the field by individual members are converted through coexperience among them to form a common base for understanding.

As was mentioned earlier, tacit knowledge is a distinctly personal concept. Varela *et al.* (1991) point out the limitation of the cognitivist view of human experience in comparison with the non-Western philosophical view, and suggest that cognitive experience is "embodied action" rather than a mere representation of a world that exists independent of our cognitive system. The mutual conversion of such embodied, tacit knowledge is accelerated by synchronizing both body and mind in the face of the same experience. Coexperience with others enables us to transcend the ordinary "I-Thou" distinction, and opens up the world of common understanding, which Scheflen (1982) called "Field Epistemology." Condon (1976) shared this view that communication is a simultaneous and contextual phenomenon in which people feel a change occurring, share the same sense of change, and are moved to take action. In other words, communication is like a wave that passes through people's bodies and culminates when everyone synchronizes himself with the wave. Thus, the sharing of mental and physical rhythm among participants of a field may serve as the driving force of socialization.

Conceptualization. Once mutual trust and a common implicit perspective have been formed through shared experience, the team needs to articulate the perspective through continuous dialogues. The dominant mode of knowledge conversion here is externalization. Theories of organizational learning have not given much attention to this process. Tacit "field-specific" perspectives are converted into explicit concepts that can be shared beyond the boundary of the team. Dialogue directly facilitates this process by activating externalization of individual levels.

Dialogue, in the form of face-to-face communication between persons, is a process in which one builds concepts in cooperation with others. It also provides the opportunity for one's hypothesis or assumption to be tested. As Markova and Foppa (1990) argue, social intercourse is one of the most powerful media for verifying one's own ideas. As such, dialogue has a congenetic quality, and thus the participants in the dialogue can engage in the mutual codevelopment of ideas. As Graumann (1990) points out, dialogue involves "perspective-setting, perspective-taking, and multiperspectivity of cognition." According to the theory of language action suggested by Austin

(1962) and Searle (1969), illocutionary speech does not only involve a description of things and facts but the taking of action itself. The expression "language is behavior," therefore, implies that language is a socially creative activity and accordingly reveals the importance of the connection between language and reality created through dialogue.

For these purposes, dialectic is a good way of raising the quality of dialogue. Dialectic allows scope for the articulation and development of personal theories and beliefs. Through the use of contradiction and paradox, dialectic can serve to stimulate creative thinking in the organization. If the creative function of dialectic is to be exploited to the full, it is helpful to pay regard to certain preconditions or "field rules." First, the dialogue should not be single-faceted and deterministic but temporary and multifaceted so that there is always room for revision or negation. Second, the participants in the dialogue should be able to express their own ideas freely and candidly. Third, negation for the sake of negation should be discouraged. Constructive criticism substantiated by reasoned arguments should be used to build a consensus. Fourth, there should be temporal continuity. Dialectic thinking is a repetitive, spiral process in which affirmation and negation are synthesized to form knowledge. Strict and noncontinuous separation of affirmation and negation will only result in logical contradictions and thus hamper the creation of knowledge. Team leaders, therefore, should not discourage the dramatic and volatile dimensions of dialogue. If these conditions are met, dialogue will add much to the potential of the group in knowledge creation.

The process of creating a new perspective through interpersonal interaction is assisted by the existence of a degree of redundant information. Making and solving new problems are made possible when its members share information by obtaining extra, redundant information which enables them to enter another person's area and give advice. Instances of "learning by intrusion" (Nonaka, 1990) are particularly widespread in Japanese firms.[8] In the meantime, redundancy of information also functions to determine the degree to which created perspectives are diffused. It may sound paradoxical; yet the degree of information redundancy will limit the degree of diffusion. In this sense, information redundancy can serve to regulate the creation of perspectives.

It is now possible to turn to the question of how to conceptualize new perspectives created from shared tacit knowledge. According to Bateson (1979), concepts are created through deduction, induction, and abduction. Abduction has a particular importance in the conceptualization process. While deduction and induction are vertically-oriented reasoning processes, abduction is a lateral extension of the reasoning process which centers on the use of metaphors. Deduction and induction are generally used when a thought or image involves the revision of a preexisting concept or the assigning of a new meaning to a concept. When there is no adequate expression of an image it is necessary to use abductive methods to create completely new concepts. While analytical methods can be used to generate new concepts via inductive or deductive reasoning, they may not be sufficient to create more meaningful – or radical – concepts. At the early stages of information creation, it is very useful to pursue creative dialogues and to share images through the metaphorical process by merging perspectives, i.e., tacit knowledge.

3.3 Crystallization

The knowledge created in an interactive field by members of a self-organizing team has to be crystallized into some concrete "form" such as a product or a system. The central mode of knowledge conversion at this stage is internalization. Crystallization may then be seen as the process through which various departments within the organization test the reality and applicability of the concept created by the self-organizing team. These internalization processes are facilitated by encouraging experimentation. It should be noted that because the instrumental skill, a part of tacit knowledge, is exploited in this process, a new process of knowledge creation is triggered by crystallization. While this usually leads to refinement of the concept, sometimes the concept itself is abandoned and fundamentally recreated.

The process of crystallization is a social process which occurs at a collective level. It is realized through what Haken (1978) called "dynamic cooperation relations" or "synergetics" among various functions and organizational departments. This relationship tends to be achieved most effectively when redundancy of information creates scope for critical knowledge conversion processes to take place. In an organization where there is redundancy of information, the initiative for action can be taken by the experts who have more information and knowledge. This characteristic is what McCulloch (1965) called the "principle of redundancy of potential command." In this principle, all parts of a system carry the same degree of importance, and each part's impact upon the system is determined by the importance of information it contains in each specified context. In sum, each part has the potential of becoming the leader of the entire system when there exists redundancy of information.

The speed at which Japanese firms develop new products seems to be assisted by information redundancy. In the product development process of Japanese firms, different phases of the process are loosely linked, overlapping in part, and the creation and realization of information is carried out flexibly. The loosely linked phases, while simultaneously maintaining mutual independence, have redundant information that activates their interactive inquiry thereby facilitating cyclical generation and solution of problems (Imai et al., 1985). This "rugby-style" product development is equipped with the flexible capacity of knowledge conversion. Clark and Fujimoto (1991) showed that Japanese firms take relatively less time for product development than American and European firms.

The specific characteristics of the product development in Japanese firms is its lateral breadth covering the whole organization. In other words it is overlapping and synthetic rather than analytic or linear. In this system, development staff can traverse overlapping phases and, to a certain extent, share each other's functions. This is far different from the usual product development process of U.S. firms, which have definite partitions between phases over which a baton is relayed. In the Japanese "rugby-style" product development (Takeuchi and Nonaka, 1986), staff involved in one phase also may be in the next phase. Thus, some development staff can be involved in all phases of development. Sometimes this process also involves those outside the organization such as suppliers and customers in order to mobilize and explicit environment knowledge.

One problem with this development style is the potential risk of confusion if, for example, the design changes or other alterations take place. Participants might have to exert more effort to organize the process due to the lack of strict specifications at each phase and definite boundaries between them. However, these risks are counterbalanced by a tendency to create and realize concepts quickly and flexibly in an integral fashion. In this context, redundant information can play a major role in facilitating the process.

3.4 The justification and quality of knowledge

While organizational knowledge creation is a continuous process with no ultimate end, an organization needs to converge this process at some point in order to accelerate the sharing of created knowledge beyond the boundary of the organization for further knowledge creation. As knowledge is conventionally defined as "justified true belief," this convergence needs to be based on the "justification" or truthfulness of concepts. Justification is the process of final convergence and screening, which determines the extent to which the knowledge created within the organization is truly worthwhile for the organization and society. In this sense, justification determines the "quality" of the created knowledge and involves criteria or "standards" for judging truthfulness.

What matters here are the evaluation "standards" for judging truthfulness. In the business organizations, the standards generally include cost, profit margin, and the degree to which a product can contribute to the firm's development. There are also value premises that transcend factual or pragmatic considerations. These might be opinions about such things as the extent to which the knowledge created is consistent with the organization's vision and perceptions relating to adventure, romanticism, and aesthetics. The inducements to initiate a convergence of knowledge may be multiple and qualitative rather than simple and quantitative standards such as efficiency, cost, and return on investment (ROI).

In knowledge-creating organizations, it is the role of top or middle management to determine the evaluation standard. Determining the turning point from dissipation to convergence in the creation process is a highly strategic task which is influenced by the *"aspiration"* of the leaders of the organization. Justification standards have to be evaluated in terms of their consistency with higher-order value systems. The ability of leaders to maintain continuous self-reflection in a wider perspective is indispensable when it comes to increasing the quality of knowledge created.

3.5 Networking knowledge

The realization of new concepts, described above, represents a visible emergence of the organization's knowledge network. During this stage of organizational knowledge creation, the concept that has been created, crystallized and justified in the organization is integrated into the organizational knowledge-base which comprises a whole network of organizational knowledge. The organizational knowledge base is then reorganized through a mutually-inducing process of interaction between the established organizational vision and the newly-created concept.

Speaking in sociological terms, this mutually-inducing relationship corresponds to the relationship between a grand concept and a middle-range concept. A middle-range concept is induced from an equivocal knowledge base as a grand concept and then is condensed into concrete form. The grand concept is not fully understood at the organizational level unless these middle-range concepts are verified on site. This verification also induces the creation or reconstruction of a grand concept, causing the interactive proliferation of grand concepts presented by top management, and middle-range concepts created by middle management. This interaction, mediated by the concrete form as condensed information, is another dynamic self-organizing activity of knowledge network that continuously creates new information and meaning.

It should be noted that the process of organizational knowledge creation is a never-ending, circular process that is not confined to the organization but includes many interfaces with the environment. At the same time, the environment is a continual source of stimulation to knowledge creation within the organization. For example, Hayek (1945) pointed out that the essential function of market competition is to discover and mobilize knowledge "on-the-spot," i.e, the implicit, context-specific knowledge held by market participants.

In the case of business organizations, one aspect of the relationship between knowledge creation and the environment is illustrated by reactions to the product by customers, competitors, and suppliers. For example, many dimensions of customer needs take the form of tacit knowledge that an individual customer or other market participants cannot articulate by themselves. A product works as a trigger to articulate the tacit knowledge. Customers and other market participants give meaning to the product by their bodily actions of purchasing, adapting, using, or not purchasing. This mobilization of tacit knowledge of customers and market will be reflected to the organization, and a new process of organizational knowledge creation is again initiated.

The total process of organizational knowledge creation is summarized in Figure 9.3. Even though the figure is illustrated as a sequential model, the actual process progresses forming multilayered loops. Respective stages can take place simultaneously, or sometimes jump forward or backward.

Figure 9.3 Organizational knowledge creation process

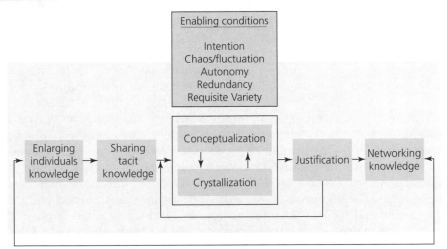

Process of generating information/knowledge in the market

4 Managing the process of organizational knowledge creation: creative chaos, redundancy, and requisite variety

This section draws on preceding arguments in order to develop a practical perspective on the management of organizational knowledge creation. Its main purpose is to complement the aspects of "individual commitment" to the knowledge creating process (i.e., intention, autonomy, and fluxation, discussed in 2.2) with, what could be seen as, "organization-wide" enabling conditions that promote a more favorable climate for effective knowledge creation[9] (see Figure 9.3). An analysis of these enabling conditions – creative chaos, redundancy of information, and requisite variety – is developed below, prior to making specific proposals for two management models: "middle-up-down management" and a "hypertext" organization. The former model relates to management style, while the latter centers on organizational design.

As was mentioned earlier, environmental fluctuation is one of the three factors that induce individual commitment. At an organizational level environmental fluctuation can generate "creative chaos" which triggers the process of organizational knowledge creation. When the organization faces nonrecursiveness that cannot be dealt with by existing knowledge, it might try to create a new order of knowledge by making use of the fluctuating itself. According to the principle of "order out of noise" proposed by von Foerster (1984) the self-organizing system can increase its ability to survive by purposefully introducing its own noise. In the context of evolutionary theory, Jantsch (1980) argues:

> In contrast to a widely held belief, planning in an evolutionary spirit therefore does not result in the reduction of uncertainty and complexity, but in their increase. Uncertainty increases because the spectrum of options is deliberately widened; imagination comes into play (1980: 267).

This represents a circular process in which chaos is perceived in its interaction with cosmos and then becomes a cosmos, which in turn produces another chaos.

Creative chaos is generated naturally when the organization faces a real "crisis" such as rapid decline of performance due to changes in technologies or market needs, or the realization of a significant competitive advantage on the part of a rival firm. It can also be generated intentionally when leaders of an organization try to evoke a "sense of crisis" among organizational members by proposing challenging goals. This creative chaos increases tension within the organization and focuses attention on forming and solving new problems. In the information processing paradigm, a problem is simply given and a solution is reached through a process of combining relevant information based on a preset algorithm. But this process ignores the importance of problem setting – defining the problem to be solved. In reality, problems do not present themselves as given but instead have to be constructed from the knowledge available at a certain point in time and context.

It should be noted, however, that this process takes place only when organizational members reflect on their actions. Without reflection, the introduction of fluctuation tends to produce "destructive" chaos. As Schön (1983) observed, "When someone reflects while in action, he becomes a researcher. He is not dependent on the categories of established theory and technique, but constructs a new theory of the unique case" (1983: 68). The knowledge-creating organization is required to institutionalize this reflection-in-action in its process as well as in its structure to make the chaos truly "creative."

A second principle for managing organizational knowledge creation is redundancy. In business organizations, this means the conscious overlapping of company information, business activities, and management responsibilities. To Western managers, the term "redundancy" with its connotations of unnecessary duplication and waste, may sound unappealing. Nevertheless, redundancy (Landau, 1969 and Nonaka, 1990) plays a key role, especially in the process of knowledge creation at the level of the organization. Redundant information can be instrumental in speeding up concept creation. A concept that was created by an individual or a group often needs to be shared by other individuals who may need the concept immediately. The redundancy of information refers to the existence of information more than the specific information required immediately by each individual. The sharing of extra information between individuals promotes the sharing of individual tactic knowledge. Since members share overlapping information, they can sense what others are trying to articulate. Especially in the concept development stage, it is critical to articulate images rooted in tacit knowledge. In this situation, individuals can enter each others' area of operation and can provide advice. This allows people to provide new information from new and different perspectives. In short, redundancy of information brings about "learning by intrusion" into an individual's sphere of perception.

Redundant information can be an instrument factor in reducing the impact of managerial hierarchy. That is to say, redundant information provides a vehicle for problem generation and knowledge creation which follows procedures that are different from those specified by the "official" organizational structure. This concept of "nonhierarchy" has been described by Hedlund (1986) as "heterarchy." The important point to note is that redundancy of information makes the interchange between hierarchy and nonhierarchy more effective in problem solving and knowledge creation. It enables all members of the organization to participate in the process on the basis of consensus and equal preparation. In this sense, redundancy of information is an indispensable element in inducing the "synergetics" and to realize the "principle of redundancy of potential command."

Deep, mutual trust between the members of the organization – the creators of knowledge – can be promoted through information redundancy and, in this way, the organization can control its knowledge creation. If an organization contains enough redundancy of information to deal with as many contingencies as possible, it can generate various combinations of information flexibility. This redundancy also facilitates interaction among organizational members and consequently makes it easier to transfer tacit knowledge among them. Redundancy can eliminate cheating among organizational members and facilitates establishment of mutual trust. Williamson (1975) argues convincingly that opportunism tends to appear less frequently in internally organized activities than in market transactions. Close interaction and trust based upon sharing of redundant information minimizes the possibility of cheating. Since "trust is a critical lubricant in social systems" (Arrow, 1974), it would be impossible to form "synergetics" needed for knowledge creation without trust.

Sharing of extra information also helps individuals to recognize their location in the organization, which in turn increases the sense of control and direction of individual thought and behavior. This state is different from the one in which all members are scattered with no relationship to each other. Redundancy of information connects individuals and the organization through information, which converges rather than diffuses.

There are several ways to build redundancy into the organization. One is to adopt an overlapping approach and internal competition in product development. As was stressed in the section on crystallization, Japanese companies manage product development as an overlapping, "rugby-style" process where different functional divisions work together in a shared division of labor. Some of them also divide the product-development team into competing groups that develop different approaches to the same project and then argue over the advantages and disadvantages of their proposals. Internal rivalry encourages the team to look at a project from a variety of perspectives. Under the guidance of a team leader, the team eventually develops a common understanding of the "best" approach. In one sense, such internal competition is wasteful. But when responsibilities are shared, information proliferates, and the organization's ability to create and implement concepts is accelerated.

Another way to build redundancy into an organization is through strategic rotation, especially between different areas of technology and between functions such as R&D and marketing. Rotation helps members of an organization understand the business from a multiplicity of perspectives. This makes organizational knowledge more fluid and easier to put into practice. Wide access to company information also helps build redundancy. When information differentials exist members of an organization can no longer interact on equal terms, which hinders the search for different interpretations of new knowledge.

Since redundancy of information increases the amount of information to be processed, it is important to strike a balance between the creation and processing of information. One way of dealing with this issue is to determine the appropriate location of information and knowledge storage within an organization. Ashby (1956) has suggested the concept of "requisite variety" which refers to the constructing of information process channels that match the information load imposed by the environment. According to the principle of requisite variety, an organization can maximize efficiently by creating within itself the same degree of diversity as the diversity it must process. Following Ashby, requisite variety may be seen as the third principle of organizing knowledge creating activities.

Efficient knowledge creation requires quick inquiry and preprocessing of existing knowledge and information. Therefore, it is a practical requirement here that everyone is given access to necessary information with the minimum number of steps (Numangami et al., 1989). For this purpose, (1) organizational members should know who owns what information, and (2) they should be related to the least number of colleagues so that they are not loaded with information in the excess of each one's cognitive capacity.

4.1 middle-up-down management: leadership for parallel process

In earlier work, a new model of management called "middle-up-down management" was proposed and contrasted with typical "top-down" management or "bottom-up" management (Nonaka, 1988b). This middle-up-down management model is suitable for promoting the efficient creation of knowledge in business organizations. The model is based on the principle of creative chaos, redundancy, and requisite variety mentioned above; much emphasis is placed on the role of top and middle management for knowledge creation, which has been almost neglected in traditional accounts of managerial structure.

The essence of a traditional bureaucratic machine is top-down information processing using division of labor and hierarchy. Top managers create basic managerial concepts (the premises of decision making) and break them down hierarchically – in terms of objectives and means – so that they can be implemented by subordinates. Top managers' concepts become operational conditions for middle managers who then decide how to realize the concepts. Again, middle managers' decisions constitute operational conditions for lower managers who implement their decisions. In consequence, the organization as a whole executes a huge amount of work that can never be done by individuals.

If we visualize the dyadic relations between top vs. middle managers, the middle vs. lower members, an organization assumes a tree-shaped or pyramidal structure. In this "top-down" model, it is desirable to organize the whole structure in the way it will conform to the above relations. To clearly break down the end-means relations, it is necessary to get rid of any ambiguity or equivocality in the concepts held by top managers. In sum, the concepts anchor on the premise that they only have one meaning. By corollary, the concepts are also strictly functional and pragmatic. An implicit assumption behind this traditional model of organization is that information and knowledge are processed most efficiently in a tree structure. The division of labor taking place within such a bureaucratic organization is associated with a hierarchial pattern of information processing. Moving from the bottom to the top of the organization, information is processed selectively so that people at the peak would get simple, processed information only. Moving in the reverse direction, on the other hand, information is processed and transformed from the general to the particular. It is this deductive transformation that enables human beings with limited information processing capacity to deal with a mass of information.

It should be noted that information processing by middle and lower members in this model is of minor relevance to knowledge creation. Only top managers are able and allowed to create information. Moreover, information created by these top managers exists for the sole purpose of implementation; therefore it is a tool rather than a product. On the contrary, in the bottom-up model, those who create information are not top managers, but middle and lower managers. In a typical bottom-up managed company, intracompany entrepreneurs or "intrapreneurs" (Pinchot, 1985) are fostered and developed by the system. In reality there are not many larger firms that have bottom-up management style. In this model, top managers remain sponsors for individual employees who function as intracompany entrepreneurs – including knowledge creation. However, this model is also anchored on the critical role of the individual as independent, separate actor as in the top-down model.

Unlike the above two models, the middle-up-down model takes all members as important actors who work together horizontally and vertically. A major characteristic of the model regarding knowledge creation is the wide scope of cooperative relationships between top, middle, and lower managers. No one major department or group of experts has the exclusive responsibility for creating new knowledge.

But this is not to say that there is no differentiation among roles and responsibilities in this style of management. In the middle-up-down model, top management provides "visions for direction" and also the deadline by which the visions should be realized. Middle management translates these visions into middle range visions, which are to be realized in the fields – the groups. Middle managers create their visions out to those from top and lower managers and materialize then vis-à-vis the two levels. In other words, while top management articulates the dreams of the firm, lower managers look at the reality. The gap between these two forms of perspectives is narrowed by and through middle management. In this sense, it is a leadership style that facilitates the parallel knowledge creation process taking place simultaneously at top, middle, and lower management respectively.

Table 9.1 summarizes the comparison of the three models, top-down, bottom-up, and middle-up-down management, in terms of knowledge creator, resource allocation, structural characteristics, process characteristics, knowledge accumulation, and inherent limitation. The roles and tasks of lower, top, and middle managers in the middle-up-down management will now be discussed in detail.

Frontline employees and lower managers are immersed in the day-to-day details of particular technologies, products, and markets. No one is more expert in the realities of a company's business than they are. But, while these employees and lower managers are deluged with highly specific information,

Table 9.1 A comparison of three management models

	Top-down	*Middle-up-down*	*Bottom-up*
Agent of knowledge creation	top management	Self-organizing team (with middle managers as team leaders)	Entrepreneurial individual (intrapreneur)
Resource allocation	hierarchically	from diverse viewpoints	self-organizing principle
Pursued synergy	"synergy of money"	"synergy of knowledge"	"synergy of people"
Organization	*big* and powerful headquarters staff use manuals	team-oriented affiliated firms by intrapreneurs	*small* headquarters self-organizing suborganizations
Management processes	leaders as commanders emphasis on information processing chaos not allowed	leaders as catalysts create organizational knowledge create/amplify chaos/noise	leaders as sponsors create personal information chaos/noise premised
Accumulated	explicit computerized/ documented	explicit and tacit shared in diverse forms	tacit incarnated in individuals
Weakness	high dependency on top management	human exhaustion lack of overall control of the organization	time consuming difficult to coordinate individuals

they often find it extremely difficult to turn that information into useful knowledge. For one thing, signals from the marketplace can be vague and ambiguous. For another, employees and lower managers can become so caught up in their own narrow perspective, that they lose sight of the broader context. Moveover, even when they try to develop meaningful ideas and insights, it can still be difficult to communicate the importance of that information to others. People do not just passively receive new knowledge; they actively interpret it to fit their own situation and perspectives. Thus, what makes sense in one context can change or even lose its meaning when communicated to people in a different context.

The main job of top and middle managers in the model of middle-up-down management is to orient this chaotic situation toward purposeful knowledge creation. These managers do this by providing their subordinates with a conceptual framework that helps them make sense of their own experience.

In both top-down management and bottom-up management, a high degree of emphasis is given to charismatic leadership. By contrast, middle-up-down management views managers as catalysts. In this role as a "catalyst," top management sets the direction, provides the field of interaction, selects the participants in the field, establishes the guidelines and deadlines for project, and supports the innovation process.

Top management gives voice to a company's future by articulating metaphors, symbols, and concepts that orient the knowledge-creating activities of employees. In other words, they give form to "organizational intention" that is beyond the personal intention of top management as an individual. This is achieved by asking questions on behalf of the entire organization: What are we trying to learn? What do we need to know? Where should we be going? Who are we? If the job of frontline employees and lower managers is to know "what is," then the job of management is to know "what ought to be." In other words, the responsibility of top management in middle-up-down management is to articulate the company's "conceptual umbrella": the grand concepts expressed in highly universal and abstract terms identify the common features linking seemingly disparate activities or businesses into a coherent whole. Quinn (1992) called this conceptual umbrella a "future vision" that gives intellectual members of organizations some challenges for intellectual growth and develops their capacity for continuous change.

Another way in which top management provides employees with a sense of direction is by setting the standards for justifying the value of knowledge that is constantly being developed by the organization's members. As earlier comments on the "justifications" of knowledge indicated, deciding which efforts to support and develop is a highly strategic task. In order to facilitate organizational knowledge creation, qualitative factors such as truthfulness, beauty, or goodness are equally important to such qualitative, economic factors as efficiency, cost or ROI.

In addition to the umbrella concepts and qualitative criteria for justification, top management articulates concepts in the form of committed, equivocal visions, which are open-ended and susceptible to a variety of, and even conflicting, interpretations. If a vision is too sharply focused, it becomes more akin to an order or instruction, which will not foster the high degree of personal commitment. A more equivocal vision gives employees and self-organizing teams the freedom and autonomy to set their own goals. The final role of top management in middle-up-down management is to clear away any obstacles and prepare the ground for self-organizing teams headed by middle management. Knowledge creation, in this type of management, takes place intensively at the group level, at which middle managers embody top managers' vision. Middle managers are selected by top management, and therefore staffing is an important strategic consideration. Top managers should be able to provide middle managers with a sense of challenge or crisis and trust them.

As we have seen before, teams play a central role in the process of organizational knowledge creation. The main role of middle managers in middle-up-down management is to serve as a team leader who are at the intersection of the vertical and horizontal flows of information in the company. The most important knowledge creating individuals in this model are neither charismatic top managers nor the entrepreneur-like lower managers, but every employee who works in association with middle managers. It is the middle manager that takes a strategic position at which he or she combines strategic, macro, universal information and hands-on, micro, specific information. They work as a bridge between the visionary ideals of the top and the often chaotic reality on the frontline of business. By creating middle-level business and product concepts, middle managers mediate between "what is" and "what ought to be." They even remake reality according to the company's vision.

In addition, middle management forms the strategic knot that binds the top-down and bottom-up models. As the self-organizing team, headed by middle management moves up and down the organization, much redundancy and fluctuation can be created. As such, the organization with middle-up-down management naturally has a strong driver of self-reorganization. The middle management sometimes plays the role of "change-agent" for the self-revolution of the organization.

In sum, middle managers synthesize the tacit knowledge of both frontline employees and top management, make it explicit, and incorporate it into new technologies and product. They are the true "knowledge engineers" of the knowledge creating organizations.

4.2 Hypertext organization: a design prototype of a knowledge creating organization

Finally, an image can be presented of organizational design that provides a structural base for the process of organizational knowledge creation. Middle-up-down management becomes most efficient if supported by this infrastructure. The central requirement for the design of the knowledge-creating organization is to provide the organization with a strategic ability to acquire, create, exploit, and accumulate new knowledge continuously and repeatedly in a circular process. Earlier work has described an image of organizational design equipped with such a dynamic cycle of knowledge under the concept of a "hypertext organization," (Nonaka *et al*: 1992). This term is borrowed from a concept of computer software where "hypertext" allows users to search large quantities of text, data, and graphics by means of a friendly interface. It links related concepts and areas of knowledge to allow a problem to be viewed from many angles. In many ways, this is analogous to the ability of individuals to relate stories in different ways according to the nature of the audience. The same knowledge might be used but in different formats, making it easier to draw relationships between different sets of information.

The core feature of the hypertext organization is the ability to switch between the various "contexts" of knowledge creation to accommodate changing requirements from situations both inside and outside the organization. Within the process of organizational knowledge creation, it is possible to distinguish several "contexts" of knowledge creation such as the acquisition, generation, exploitation, and accumulation of knowledge. Each context has a distinctive way of organizing its knowledge creation activities. Nonhierarchical, or "heterarchical" self-organizing activities of teams are indispensable to generate new knowledge as well as to acquire "deep" knowledge through intensive, focused search. On the other hand, a hierarchial division of labor is more efficient and effective for implementations, exploitation, and accumulation of new knowledge as well as acquisition of various information through extensive, unfocused search.

Hypertext organization design first distinguishes the normal routine operation conducted by a hierarchical formal organization from the knowledge creating activities carried out by self-organizing teams. But it does not mean that the two activities need to operate separately and independently. Rather, it stresses the need for the careful design of the two activities which takes account of their distinctive contributions to knowledge creation. The important point to note is that the design of the hierarchy and self-organizing teams should enable the organization to shift efficiently and effectively between these two forms of knowledge creation. In terms of the theory of organizational knowledge creation, while hierarchical formal organization mainly carries out the task of combination and internalization, self-organize teams perform the task of socialization and externalization. This also improves the ability of an organization to survive. By establishing the most appropriate organizational setting for the two activities, an organization can maximize the efficiency of its routine operations, which is determined by bureaucratic principles of division of labor and specialization, and also the effectiveness of its knowledge creation activities. In this type of organization, the knowledge creating activities of self-organizing teams work as a measure which serves to prevent the so-called "reverse function of bureaucracy" (Merton, 1957).

Thus the hypertext organization combines the efficiency and stability of a hierarchical bureaucratic organization with the dynamism of the flat, cross-functional task-force organization. Nevertheless, it should be noted that a critical factor for the design of the hypertext organization lies in the coordination of time, space, and resources to realize the "requisite variety." Jacques (1979) pointed out that positions in the hierarchial organization have responsibility of different time-span. This implies that the hierarchical organization is a coordination device for these works of diverse time-span, and generates a "natural frequency" by "orchestrating" various rhythms. As the previous section indicated, each self-organizing team also creates its own "natural frequency" by synchronizing various rhythms brought into the field by members from diverse positions in hierarchical organizations. The hypertext organization is an organizational structure that enables orchestration of different rhythms or "natural frequency" generated by various project teams and the hierarchical organization. It coordinates the allocation of time, space, and resource within the organization so as to compose an "organizational" rhythm that makes organizational knowledge creation more effective and efficient. In this sense, the hypertext organization is a structural device to build "requiste variety," which cannot be secured solely by middle-up-down management.

The image of the hypertext organization is illustrated in Figure 9.4. It can be visualized as a multilayered organization comprised of three layers; knowledge-based, business-system, and project team. At the bottom is the "knowledge-base" layer which embraces tacit knowledge, associated with organizational culture and procedures, as well as explicit knowledge in the form of documents, filing systems, computerized databases, etc. The function

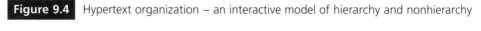

Figure 9.4 Hypertext organization – an interactive model of hierarchy and nonhierarchy

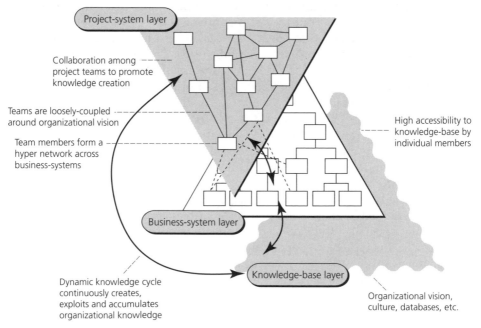

Source: Nonaka, Konno, Tokuoka and Kawamura (1992).

of this archival layer may be seen in terms of a "corporate university." The second layer is the "business-system" layer where normal routine operation is carried out by a formal, hierarchical, bureaucratic organization. The top layer relates to the area where multiple self-organization project teams create knowledge. These teams are loosely linked to each other and share in the "joint creation of knowledge" using "corporate vision." Thus the hypertext organization takes different "forms," depending on the perspective from which it is observed.

The process of organizational knowledge creation is conceptualized as a dynamic cycle of knowledge and information traversing the three layers. Members of project teams on the top layer are selected from diverse functions and departments across the business-system layer. Based on the corporate vision presented by top management, they engage in knowledge creating activities interacting with other project teams. Once the task of a team is completed, members move "down" to the knowledge-based layer at the bottom and make an "inventory" of the knowledge acquired and created in the project. After categorizing, documenting, and indexing the new knowledge, they come back to upper business-system layer and engage in routine operation until they are called again for another project. A key design requirement in the hypertext organization is to form such a circular movement of organization members, who are the fundamental source and subject of organizational knowledge creation. From the vantage point of strategic management, the true "core competence" (Prahalad and Hamel, 1990) of the organization, which produces sustainable competitive advantage, lies in its management capability to create relevant organizational knowledge (Nonaka, 1989, 1991). This is a continuous process and the ability to switch swiftly and flexibly between the three layers in the hypertext organization is critical to its success.

5 Conclusion

The theory of organizational knowledge creation proposed here has been constructed mainly on the basis of hands-on research and practical experience of Japanese firms. Nevertheless, it should be stressed that the principles described have a more general application to any organization, either economic or social, private or public, manufacturing or service, in the coming age despite their field of activities as well as geographical and cultural location. The theory explains how knowledge held by individuals, organizations, and societies can be simultaneously enlarged and enriched through the spiral, interactive amplification of tacit and explicit knowledge held by individuals, organizations, and societies. The key for this synergetic expansion of knowledge is joint creation of knowledge by individuals and organizations. In this sense, the theory of organizational knowledge creation is at the same time a basic theory for building a truly "humanistic" knowledge society beyond the limitations of mere "economic rationality."

Organizations play a critical role in mobilizing tacit knowledge held by individuals and provide the forum for a "spiral of knowledge" creation through socialization, combination, externalization, and internalization. All of these conversion modes interact in a dynamic and continuous "entanglement" to drive the knowledge creation process. These modes operate in the context of an organization and, while acknowledging the role of individuals as essential actors in creating new knowledge, the central theme of this chapter has been to address the processes involved at an organizational level.

By concentrating on the concept of organizational knowledge creation, it has been possible to develop a perspective which goes beyond straightforward notions of "organizational learning." In the language of the present discussion, learning can be related to "internalization" which is but one of the four modes of conversion required to create new organizational knowledge. Taken by itself, learning has rather limited static connotations wheras organizational knowledge creation is a more wide-ranging and dynamic concept.

Finally, hypertext and middle-up-down management have been offered as practical proposals for implementing more effective knowledge creation. As knowledge emerges as an ever more important feature of advanced industrial development, it is necessary to pay increased attention to the processes by which it is created and the assessment of its quality and value both to the organization and society.

Acknowledgments

The author would like to thank Arie Y. Lewin, John Seely Brown, Takaya Kawamura, doctoral student at Hitotsubashi University, and Tim Ray for their insightful comments and assistance.

Notes

1. See Lewin and Stephens (1992) for arguments on challenges to and opportunities for organizational design in the post industrial society.
2. Discussion on epistemology here is based on such classical accounts as Plato's *Theaetetus* and *Phaedo*, Descartes's *Discourse on Method*, Locke's *An Essay Concerning Human Understanding*, Hume's *An Enquiry Concerning Human Understanding*, and Kant's *Critique of Pure Reason*. For interpretation of these works, see Hospers, (1967) Dancy, (1985) Hallis, (1985) Moser and Nat (1987), and Winograd and Flores (1986).
3. See also Polanyi (1958) and Gelwick (1977).
4. Metaphor should not be understood as mere rhetoric or an issue of expression; it is deeply connected with knowledge creation. For this point, see Black (1962) and McCormac (1985).
5. For comprehensive discussion on metaphor, analogy, and model, see Leatherdale (1974) and Tsoukas (1991).
6. The self-organizing team may be depicted by Maturana and Varela's (1980) concept of an "autopoietic system." Living organic systems are composed of various organs, which are again composed of numerous cells. Each unit, like an autonomous cell, is self-regulating. Moreover, each unit determines its boundary through self-reproduction, and is separate from the environment. This self-referential or self-reflecting nature is a quintessential feature of autopoietic systems.

7. Gibson (1979) suggested an interesting hypothesis that knowledge lies in the environment itself, contrary to the traditional epistemological view that it exists inside the human brain. According to him, man perceives information ("affordance") which natural objects afford to human cognitive activity, i.e., according to the degree of affordance of the environment. Information on chair, knife, and cliff are revealed when the actions of sitting, cutting, and falling are made, in other words, in the course of interactions between the subject and the object of perception.

8. Jaikumar and Born (1986) pointed to this as the characteristics of Japanese firms' production methods. According to them, the production method for most American firms is clearly defined as the function of the basic manufacturing technology, assigned works, organizational goals, and environment. In this mode of production, then, workers are well aware of their work and thus simply follow the routine procedure. On the other hand, Japanese workers do not get prior knowledge and thus become part of the given work, rather than being separate from the work itself. Therefore, anomaly, or nonroutine nature, of the work itself becomes an important opportunity for learning.

9. The development of these concepts are based on a series of theoretical and empirical research studies (Kagono *et al.*, 1985, Takeuchi *et al.*, 1986, and Nonaka, 1988a).

References

Anderson, J.R. (1983) *The Architecture of Cognition*, Cambridge, MA: Harvard University Press.

Argyris, C. and Schon, D.A. (1978) *Organizational Learning*, Reading, MA: Addison-Wesley.

Arrow, K.J. (1974) *The Limits of Organization*, New York: John Brockman Associates.

Ashby, W.R. (1956) *An Introduction to Cybernetics*, London: Chapman & Hall.

Austin, J.L. (1962) *How to Do Things with Words*, Oxford; Oxford University Press.

Bateson, G. (1973) *Steps to an Ecology of Mind*, London: Paladin.

Bateson, D. (1979) *Mind and Nature: A Necessary Unit*, New York: Bantam Books.

Bell, D. (1973) *The Coming of Post-industrial Society: A Venture in Social Fostering*, New York: Basic Books.

Berger, P.L. and Luchman, T. (1966) *Social Construction of Reality*, New York: Doubleday.

Black, M. (1962) *Models and Metaphors*, Ithaca, NY: Cornell University Press.

Brown, J.S. and Duguid, P. (1991) "Organizational Learning and Communities of Practice: Towards a unified view of working, learning and organization," *Organization Science* 21: 40–57.

Clark, K.B. and Fujimoto, T. (1991) *Product Development Performance*, Boston, MA: Harvard Business School Press.

Cohen, M.D., March, J.G. and Olsen, J.P. (1972) "A garbage can model of organizational choice," *Administrative Science Quarterly* 17: 1–25.

Condon, W.S. (1976) "An analysis of behavioral organization," *Sign Language Studies* 13.

Dancy, J. (1985) *Introduction to Contempory Epistemology*, New York: Basil Blackwell.

Dretske, F. (1981) *Knowledge and the Flow of Information*, Cambridge, MA: MIT Press.

Drucker, P. (1968) *The Age of Discontinuity: Guidelines to Our Changing Society*, New York: Harper & Row.

Eigen, M. (1971) "Self-organization of matter and the evolution of biological macro-molecules," *Naturwissenshaften* 58.

Gelwick, R. (1977) *The Way of Discovery: An Introduction to the Thought of Michael Polanyi* Oxford: Oxford University Press.

Gibson, J.J. (1979) *The Ecological Approach to Visual Perception*, Boston, MA: Houghton-Mifflin.

Gleick, J. (1987) *Chaos*, New York: Viking.

Graumann, C.F. (1990) "Perspective Structure and Dynamics in Dialogues," in Markova, I. and Foppa, K. (eds) *The Dynamics of Dialogue*, New York: Harvester Wheatsheaf.

Gruber, T.R. (1989) *The Acquisition of Strategic Knowledge*, San Diego, CA: Academic Press.

Hallis, M. (1985) *Invitation to Philosophy*, Oxford: Basil Blackwell.

Haken, H. (1978) *Synergetics: Nonequilibrium Phase Transitions and Self-Organization in Physics, Chemistry and Biology*, 2nd edn, Berlin: Springer.

Hayek, F.A. (1945) "The use of knowledge in society," *American Economic Review*, 35(4): 519–30.

Hedberg, B.L.T. (1981) "How organizations learn and unlearn," in Nystrom, P.C. and Starbuck, W.H. (eds) *Handbook of Organizational Design*, Oxford: Oxford University Press.

Hedlund, G. (1986) "The Hypermodern MNC – a Heterarchy?," *Human Resource Management* 25: 1.

Hospers, J. (1967) *An Introduction to Philosophical Analysis*, 2nd edn, London: Routledge & Kegan Paul.

Husserl, E. (1968) *The Ideas of Phenomenology*, The Hague: Nijhoff.

Imai, K., Nonaka, I. and Takeuchi, H. (1985) "Managing the new product development process: how Japanese companies learn and unlearn," in Clark, K.B., Hayes, R.H. and Lorenz, C. (eds.), *The Uneasy Alliance: Managing the Productivity-Technology Dilemma*, Boston, MA: Harvard Business School Press.

Jacques, E. (1979) "Taking time seriously in evaluating jobs," *Harvard Business Review*, September–October, 124–32.

Jaikumar, R. and Born, R.E. (1986) "The development of intelligent system for industrial use: a conceptual framework," *Research on Technological Innovation, Management and Policy*, 3, JAI Press.

Jantsch, E. (1980) *The Self-Organizing Universe*, Oxford: Pergamon Press.

Johnson-Laird (1983) *Mental Models*, Cambridge: Cambridge University Press.

Kagono, T., Nonaka, I., Sakakibara, K. and Okumura, A. (1985) *Strategic vs. Evolutionary Management*, Amsterdam: North-Holland.

Lakoff, G. and Johnson, M. (1980) *Metaphors We Live By*, Chicago, IL: University of Chicago Press.

Landau, M. (1969) "Redundancy, rationality, and the problem of duplication and overlap," *Public Administration Review* 14(4).

Leatherdale, W.H. (1974) *The Role of Analogy, Model and Metaphor in Science*, Amsterdam: North Holland.

Lewin, A.Y. and Stephens, C.V. (1992) "Designing post-industrial organization: theory and practice," in Huber, G.P. and Glick, W.H. (eds.) *Organization Change and Redesign: Ideas and Insights for Improving Managerial Performance*, New York: Oxford University Press.

Lewin, K. (1951) *Field Theory in Social Science*, New York: Harper.

Machlup, F. (1983) "Semantic quirks in studies of information," in Machlup, F. and Mansfield, U. (eds.) *The Study of Information*, New York: John Wiley.

Markova, I. and Foppa, K. (eds) (1990) *The Dynamics of Dialogue*, New York: Harvester Wheatsheaf.

Maturana, H.R. and Varela, F.J. (1980) *Autopoiesis and Cognition: The Realization of the Living*, Dordrecht, Holland: Reidel.

McCormac, E.R. (1985) *A Cognitive Theory of Metaphor*, Cambridge, MA: MIT Press.

McCulloch, W. (1965) *Embodiments of Mind*, Cambridge, MA: MIT Press.

Merleau-Ponty, M. (1964) *The Structure of Behavior*, Boston, MA: Beacon Press.

Merton, R.K. (1957) *Social Theory and Social Structure*, New York: Free Press.

Miyazaki, K. and Ueno, N. (1985) *Shiten* (The view point), Tokyo: Tokyo Daigaku Shuuppankai (in Japanese).

Morgan, G. (1986) *Images of Organization*, Beverly Hills, CA: Sage Publications.

Moser, P.K. and Nat, A.V. (1987) *Human Knowledge*, Oxford: Oxford University Press.

Neisser, U. (1976) *Cognition and Reality*, New York: W. H Freeman.

Nisbet, R.A. (1969) *Social Change and History: Aspects of the Western Theory of Development*, London: Oxford University Press.

Nishida, K. (1960) *A Study of Good* (Zen no kenkyu), Tokyo: Printing Bureau, Japanese Government.

Nonaka, I. (1987) "Managing the firms as information creation process," Working Paper, January published in Meindl, J. (ed.) (1991) *Advances in Information Processing in Organizations* 4, JAI Press.

—— (1988a) "Creating organizational order out of chaos: self-renewal in Japanese firms," *California Management Review* 15(3): 57–73.

—— (1988b) "Towards middle-up-down management: accelerating information creation," *Sloan Management Review* 29(3): 9–18.

—— (1989) "Organizing innovation as a knowledge-creation process: a suggestive paradigm for self-renewing organization," Working Paper, University of California at Berkeley, Berkeley, CA, No. OBIR-41.

—— (1990) "Redundant, overlapping organizations: a Japanese approach to managing the innovation process," *California Management Review* 32(3): 27–38.

—— (1991) "The knowledge-creating company," *Harvard Business Review*, November–December, 96–104.

—— Konno, N., Tokuoka, K. and Kawamura, T. (1992) "Hypertext organization for accelerating organizational knowledge creation," *Diamond Harvard Business*, August–September (in Japanese).

Norman, D.A. (1988) *The Psychology of Everyday Things*, New York; Basic Books.

Numagami, T., Ohta, T. and Nonaka, I. (1989) "Self-renewal of corporate organizations: equilibrium, self-sustaining, and self-renewing models," Working Paper, University of California at Berkeley, Berkeley, CA, No OBIR-43.

Piaget, J. (1974) *Recherches sur la contradiction*, Paris: Presses Universitaires de France.

Pinchot, G. III (1985) *Intrapreneuring*, New York: Harper & Row.

Polanyi, M. (1958) *Personal Knowledge*, Chicago, IL: The University of Chicago Press.

—— (1966) *The Tacit Dimension*, London: Routledge & Kegan Paul.

Prahalad, C.K. and Hamel, G. (1990) "The core competition of the corportation," *Harvard Business Review*, May–June, 79–91.

Quinn, J.B. (1992) *Intelligent Enterprise*, New York: Free Press.

Rosch, E.H. (1973) "Natural categories," *Cognitive Psychology* 4, 328–50.

Ryle, G. (1949) *The Concept of Mind*, London: Huchinson.

Sakakibara, K., Kagono, T., Okumura, A. and Nonaka, I. (1986) *Kigyo no jiko kakushin* (Corporate self-renewal), Tokyo: Chuo koronsha (in Japanese).

Sandelands, Lloyd E. and Stablein, R.E. (1987) "The concept of organization mind," *Research in the Sociology of Organizations* 5.

Scheflen, A.E. (1982) "Comments on the significance of interaction rhythms," in Davis, M. (ed.) *Interaction Rhythms*, New York: Free Press.

Schön, D.A. (1983) *The Reflective Practitioner*, New York: Basic Books.

Schrage, M. (1990) *Shared Minds: The New Technologies of Collaboration*, New York: John Brockman.

Searle, J.R. (1969) *Speech Acts: An Essay in the Philosophy of Language*, Cambridge: Cambridge University Press.

—— (1983) *Intentionality: An Essay in the Philosophy of Mind*, Cambridge: Cambridge University Press.

Shannon, C.E. and Weaver, W. (1949) *The Mathematical Theory of Communication*, Urbana, IL: University of Illinois Press.

Shimizu, H. (1978) *Seimei o toraennaosu* (Capturing the nature of life), Tokyo: Chuo koronsha (in Japanese).

Stich, S. (1986) *From Folk Psychology to Cognitive Science: The Case Against Belief*, Cambridge, MA: MIT Press.

Takeuchi, H. and Nonaka, I. (1986) "The new new product development game," *Harvard Business Review*, January–February, 137–46.

Toffler, A. (1990) *Powershift: Knowledge, Wealth and Violence at the Edge of 21st Century*, New York: Bantam Books.

Tsoukas, H. (1991) "The missing link: a transformation view of metaphor in organizational science," *Academy of Management Review* 16(3): 566–85.

Varela, F.J., Thompson, E. and Rosch, E. (1991) *Embodied Mind: Cognitive Science and Human Experience*, Cambridge, MA: MIT Press.

Von Foerster, H. (1984) "Principles of self-organization in a socio-managerial context," in Ulrich, H. and Probs, G.J.B. (eds) *Self-organization and Management of Social Systems*, Berlin: Springer-Verlag.

Weick, K.E. (1979) *The Social Psychology of Organizing*, 2nd edn, Reading, MA: Addison-Wesley.

Williamson, O.E. (1975) *Market and Hierarchies: Antitrust Implications*, New York: The Free Press.

Winograd, T. and Flores, (1986), *Understanding Computer and Cognition*, Reading, MA: Addison-Wesley.

Yuasa, Y. (1987) *The Body: Toward an Eastern Mind-Body Theory*, Kasulis, T.P. (ed.), translated by Nagatomi, S. and Kasulis, T.P., New York; State University of New York Press.

10 Designing the innovating organization

Jay R. Galbraith

Innovation is in. New workable, marketable ideas are being sought and promoted these days as never before in the effort to restore US leadership in technology, in productivity growth, and in the ability to compete in the world marketplace. Innovative methods for conserving energy and adapting to new energy sources are also in demand.

The popular press uses words like revitalization to capture the essence of the issue. The primary culprit of our undoing, up until now, has been management's short-run earnings focus. However, even some patient managers with long-term views are finding that they cannot buy innovation. They cannot exhort their operating organizations to be more innovative and creative. Patience, money, and a supportive leadership are not enough. It takes more than these things to achieve innovation.

It is my contention that innovation requires an organization specifically designed for that purpose – that is, such an organization's structure, processes, rewards, and people must be combined in a special way to create an innovating organization, one that is designed to do something for the first time. The point to be emphasized here is that the innovating organization's components are completely different from and often contrary to those of existing organizations, which are generally operating organizations. The latter are designed to efficiently process the millionth loan, produce the millionth automobile, or serve the millionth client. An organization that is designed to do something well for the millionth time is not good at doing something for the first time. Therefore, organizations that want to innovate or revitalize themselves need two organizations, an operating organization and an innovating organization. In addition, if the ideas produced by the innovating organization are to be implemented by the operating organization, they need a transition process to transfer ideas from the innovating organization to the operating organization.

This chapter will describe the components of an organization geared to producing innovative ideas. Specifically, in the next section I describe a case history that illustrates the components required for successful innovation. Then I will explore the lessons to be learned from this case history by describing the role structure, the key processes, the reward systems, and the people practices that characterize an innovating organization.

The innovating process

Before I describe the typical process by which innovations occur in organizations, we must understand what we are discussing. What is innovation? How do we distinguish between invention and innovation? Invention is the creation of a new idea. Innovation is the process of applying a new idea to create a new process or product. Invention occurs more frequently than innovation. In addition, the kind of innovation in which we are interested here is the kind that becomes necessary to implement a new idea that is not consistent with the current concept of the organization's business. Many new ideas that are consistent with an organization's current business concept are routinely generated in some companies. Those are not our current concern; here we are concerned with implementing inventions that are good ideas but do not quite fit into the organization's current mold. Industry has a poor track record with this type of innovation. Most major technological changes come from outside an industry. The mechanical typewriter people did not invent the electronic typewriter; vacuum tube companies did not introduce the transistor, and so on. Our objective is to describe an organization that will increase the odds that such non-routine innovations can be made. The following case history of a non-routine innovation presents a number of lessons that illustrate how we can design an innovating organization.

The case history

The organization in question is a venture that was started in the early 1970s. While working for one of our fairly innovative electronics firms, a group of engineers developed a new electronics product. However, they were in a division that did not have the charter for their product. The ensuing political battle caused the engineers to leave and form their own company. They successfully found venture capital and introduced their new product. Initial acceptance was good, and within several years their company was growing rapidly and had become the industry leader.

However, in the early 1970s Intel invented the microprocessor, and by the mid-to-late 1970s, this innovation had spread through the electronics industries. Manufacturers of previously "dumb" products now had the capability of incorporating intelligence into their product lines. A competitor who understood computers and software introduced just such a product into our new venture firm's market, and it met with high acceptance. The firm's president responded by hiring someone who knew something about microcomputers and some software people and instructing the engineering department to respond to the need for a competing product.

The president spent most of his time raising capital to finance the venture's growth. But when he suddenly realized that the engineers had not made much progress, he instructed them to get a product out quickly. They did, but it was a half-hearted effort. The new product incorporated a microprocessor but was less than the second-generation product that was called for.

Even though the president developed markets in Europe and Singapore, he noticed that the competitor continued to grow faster than his company and had started to steal a share of his company's market. When the competitor became the industry leader, the president decided to take charge of the product development effort. However, he found that the hardware proponents and software proponents in the engineering department were locked in a political battle. Each group felt that its "magic" was the more powerful. Unfortunately, the lead engineer (who was a co-founder of the firm) was a hardware proponent, and the hardware establishment prevailed. However, they then clashed head-on with the marketing department, which agreed with the software proponents. The conflict resulted in studies and presentations, but no new product. So here was a young, small (1,200 people) entrepreneurial firm that could not innovate even though the president wanted innovation and provided resources to produce it. The lesson is that more was needed.

As the president became more deeply involved in the problem, he received a call from his New England sales manager, who wanted him to meet a field engineer who had modified the company's product and programmed it in a way that met customer demands. The sales manager suggested, "We may have something here."

Indeed, the president was impressed with what he saw. When the engineer had wanted to use the company's product to track his own inventory, he wrote to company headquarters for programming instructions. The response had been: It's against company policy to send instructional materials to field engineers. Undaunted, the engineer bought a home computer and taught himself to program. He then modified the product in the field and programmed it to solve his problem. When the sales manager happened to see what had been done, he recognized its significance and immediately called the president.

The field engineer accompanied the president back to headquarters and presented his work to the engineers who had been working on the second generation product for so long. They brushed off his efforts as idiosyncratic, and the field engineer was thanked and returned to the field.

A couple of weeks later the sales manager called the president again. He said that the company would lose this talented guy if something wasn't done. Besides, he thought that the field engineer, not engineering, was right. While he was considering what to do with this ingenious engineer, who on his own had produced more than the entire engineering department, the president received a request from the European sales manager to have the engineer assigned to him.

The European sales manager had heard about the field engineer when he visited headquarters, and had sought him out and listened to his story. The sales manager knew that a French bank wanted the type of application that the field engineer had created for himself; a successful application would be worth an order for several hundred machines. The president gave the go-ahead and sent the field engineer to Europe. The engineering department persisted in their view that the program wouldn't work. Three months later, the field engineer successfully developed the application, and the bank signed the order.

When the field engineer returned, the president assigned him to a trusted marketing manager who was told to protect him and get a product out. The engineers were told to support the manager and reluctantly did so. Soon they created some applications software and a printed circuit board that could easily be installed in all existing machines in the field. The addition of this board and the software temporarily saved the company and made its current product slightly superior to that of the competitor.

Elated, the president congratulated the young field engineer and gave him a good staff position working on special assignments to develop software. Then problems arose. When the president tried to get the personnel department to give the engineer a special cash award, they were reluctant. "After all," they said, "other people worked on the effort, too. It will set a precedent." And so it went. The finance department wanted to withhold $500 from the engineer's pay because he had received a $1,000 advance for his European trip, but had turned in vouchers for only $500.

The engineer didn't help himself very much either; he was hard to get along with and refused to accept supervision from anyone except the European sales manager. When the president arranged to have him permanently transferred to Europe on three occasions, the engineer changed his mind about going at the last minute. The president is still wondering what to do with him.

There are a number of lessons about the needs of an innovative organization in this not uncommon story. The next section elaborates on these lessons.

The innovating organization

Before we can draw upon the case history's lessons, it is important to note that the basic components of the innovating organization are no different from those of an operating organization. That is, both include a task, a structure, processes, reward systems, and people as shown in Figure 10.1.

Figure 10.2 compares the design parameters of the operating organization's components with those of the innovating organization's components.

This figure shows that each component must fit with each of the other components and with the task. A basic premise of this chapter is that the task of the innovating organization is fundamentally different from that of the operating organization. The innovating task is more uncertain and risky, takes place over longer time periods, assumes that failure in the early stages may be desirable, and so on. Therefore, the organization that performs the innovative task should also be different. Obviously, a firm that wishes to innovate needs both an operating organization and an innovating organization. Let's look at the latter.

Figure 10.1 Organization design components

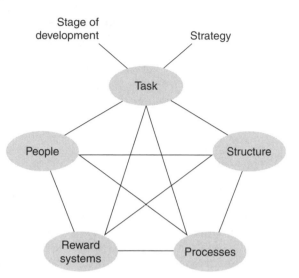

Figure 10.2 Comparison of components of operating and innovating organizations

	Operating organizations	Innovating organizations

Structure	Division of labor
	Departmentalization
	Span and control
	Distribution of power
		Roles:
		   Orchestrator
		   Sponsor
		   Ideas generator (champion)
		Differentiation
		Reservations

Process	Providing information and communication Planning and budgeting Measuring performance Linking departments	Planning/funding Getting ideas Blending ideas Transitioning Managing programs
Reward systems	Compensation Promotion Leader style Job design	Opportunity/autonomy Promotion/recognition Special compensation
People	Selection/recruitment Promotion/transfer Training/development	Selection/self-selection Training/development

Structure of the innovating organization

The structure of the innovating organization encompasses these elements: (1) people to fill three vital roles – idea generators, sponsors, and orchestrators; (2) differentiation, a process that differentiates or separates the innovating organization; and (3) 'reservations,' the means by which the separation occurs – and this may be accomplished physically, financially, or organizationally.

The part that each of these elements plays in the commercialization of a new idea can be illustrated by referring to the case history.

Roles

Like any organized phenomenon, innovation is brought about through the efforts of people who interact in a combination of roles. Innovation is not an individual phenomenon. People who must interact to produce a commercial product – that is, to innovate in the sense we are discussing – play their roles as follows:

Every innovation starts with an idea generator or idea champion. In the above example, the field engineer was the person who generated the new idea – that is, the inventor, the entrepreneur, or risk taker on whom much of our attention has been focused. The case history showed that an idea champion is needed at each stage of an idea's or an invention's development into an innovation. That is, at each stage there must be a dedicated, full-time individual whose success or failure depends on developing the idea. The idea generator is usually a low-level person who experiences a problem and develops a new response to it. The lesson here is that many ideas originate down where "the rubber meets the road." The low status and authority level of the idea generator creates a need for someone to play the next role.

Every idea needs at least one sponsor to promote it. To carry an idea through to implementation, someone has to discover it and fund the increasingly disruptive and expensive development and testing efforts that shape it. Thus idea generators need to find sponsors for their ideas so they can perfect them. In our example, the New England sales manager, the European sales manager, and finally the marketing manager all sponsored the field engineer's idea. Thus one of the sponsor's functions is to lend his or her authority and resources to an idea to carry the idea closer to commercialization.

The sponsor must also recognize the business significance of an idea. In any organization, there are hundreds of ideas being promoted at any one time. The sponsor must select from among these ideas those that might become marketable. Thus it is best that sponsors be generalists. (However, that is not always the case, as our case history illustrates.)

Sponsors are usually middle managers who may be anywhere in the organization and who usually work for both the operating and the innovating organization. Some sponsors run divisions or departments. They must be able to balance the operating and innovating needs of their business or function. On the other hand, when the firm can afford the creation of venture groups, new product development departments, and the like, sponsors may work full time for the innovating organization. In the case history, the two sales managers spontaneously became sponsors and the marketing manager was formally designated as a sponsor by the president. The point here is that by formally designating the role or recognizing it, funding it with monies earmarked for innovation, creating innovating incentives, and developing and selecting sponsorship skills, the organization can improve its odds of coming up with successful innovations. Not much attention has been given to sponsors, but they need equal attention because innovation will not occur unless there are people in the company who will fill all three roles.

The third role illustrated in the case history is that of the *orchestrator*. The president played this role. An orchestrator is necessary because new ideas are never neutral. Innovative ideas are destructive; they destroy investments in capital equipment and people's careers. The management of ideas is a political process. The problem is that the political struggle is biased toward those in the establishment who have authority and control of resources. The orchestrator must balance the power to give the new idea a chance to be tested in the face of a negative establishment. The orchestrator must protect idea people, promote the opportunity to try out new ideas, and back those whose ideas prove effective. This person must legitimize the whole process. That is what the president did with the field engineer; before he became involved, the hardware establishment had prevailed. Without an orchestrator, there can be no innovation.

To play their roles successfully, orchestrators use the processes and rewards to be described in the following sections. That is, a person orchestrates by funding innovating activities and creating incentives for middle managers to sponsor innovating ideas. Orchestrators are the organization's top managers, and they must design the innovating organization.

The typical operating role structure of a divisionalized firm is shown in Figure 10.3. The hierarchy is one of the operating functions reporting to division general managers who are, in turn, grouped under group executives. The group executives report to the chief executive officer (CEO). Some of these people play roles in both the operating and the innovating organization.

The innovating organization's role structure is shown in Figure 10.4. The chief executive and a group executive function as orchestrators. Division managers are the sponsors who work in both the operating and the innovating organizations. In addition, several reservations are created in which managers of research and development (R&D), corporate development, product development, market development, and new process technology function as full-time sponsors. These reservations allow the separation of innovating activity from the operating activity. This separation is an organizing choice called differentiation. It is described next.

Differentiation

In the case history we saw that the innovative idea perfected at a remote site was relatively advanced before it was discovered by management. The lesson

Figure 10.3 Typical operating structure of divisionalized firm

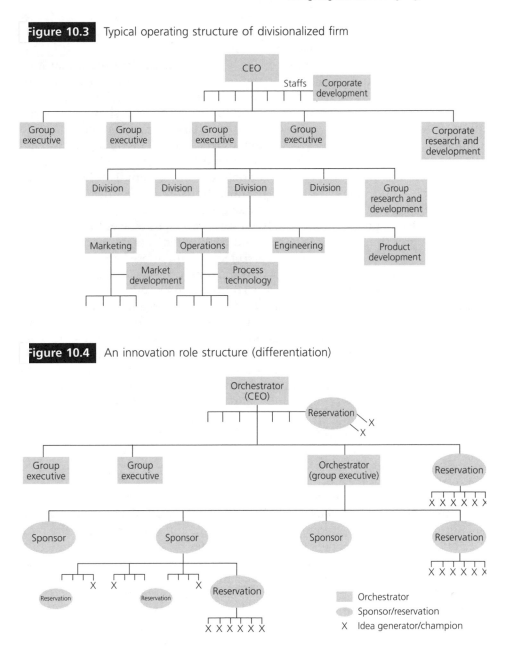

Figure 10.4 An innovation role structure (differentiation)

to be learned from this is that if one wants to stimulate new ideas, the odds are better if early efforts to perfect and test new "crazy" ideas are differentiated – that is, separated – from the functions of the operating organization. Such differentiation occurs when an effort is separated physically, financially, and/or organizationally from the day-to-day activities that are likely to disrupt it. If the field engineer had worked within the engineering department or at company headquarters, his idea probably would have been snuffed out prematurely.

Another kind of differentiation can be accomplished by freeing initial idea tests from staff controls designed for the operating organization. The effect of too much control is illustrated by one company in which a decision on whether to buy an oscilloscope took about 15 to 30 minutes (with a shout across the room) before the company was acquired by a larger organization. After the acquisition, that same type of decision took 12 to 18 months because the purchase required a capital appropriation request. Controls based on operating logic reduce the innovating organization's ability to rapidly, cheaply, and frequently test and modify new ideas. Thus, the more differentiated an initial effort is, the greater the likelihood of innovation.

The problem with differentiation, however, is that it decreases the likelihood that a new proven idea will be transferred back to the operating organization. Herein lies the differentiation/transfer dilemma: the more differentiated the effort, the greater the likelihood of producing a new business idea, but the less likelihood of transferring the new idea into the operation organization for implementation. The dilemma occurs only when the organization needs both invention and transfer. That is, some organizations may not need to transfer new ideas to the operating organization. For example, when Exxon started its information systems business, there was no intention to have the petroleum company run this area of business. Exxon innovators had to grow their own operating organizations; therefore, they could maximize differentiation in the early phases. Alternatively, when Intel started work on the 64K RAM (the next generation of semiconductor memories, this random access memory holds roughly 64,000 bits of information), the effort was consistent with their current business and the transfer into manufacture and sales was critical. Therefore, the development effort was only minimally separated from the operating division that was producing the 16K RAM. The problem becomes particularly difficult when a new product or process differs from current ones but must be implemented through the current manufacturing and sales organizations. The greater the need for invention and the greater the difference between the new idea and the existing business concept, the greater the degree of differentiation required to perfect the idea. The only way to accomplish both invention and transfer is to proceed stagewise. That is, differentiate in the early phases and then start the transition process before development is completed so that only a little differentiation is left when the product is ready for implementation. The transition process is described in the section on key processes (p. 212).

In summary, invention occurs best when initial efforts are separated from the operating organization and its controls – because innovating and operating are fundamentally opposing logics. This kind of separation allows both to be performed simultaneously and prevents the establishment from prematurely snuffing out a new idea. The less the dominant culture of the organization supports innovation, the greater is the need for separation. Often this separation occurs naturally as in the case history, or clandestinely, as in "bootlegging." If a firm wants to foster innovation, it can create reservations where innovating activity can occur as a matter of course. Let us now turn to this last structural parameter.

Reservations

Reservations are organizational units, such as R&D groups, that are totally devoted to creating new ideas for future business. The intention is to reproduce a garage-like atmosphere where people can rapidly and frequently test their ideas. Reservations are havens for "safe learning." When innovating, one wants to maximize early failure to promote learning. On reservations that are separated from operations, this cheap, rapid screening can take place.

Reservations permit differentiation to occur by housing people who work solely for the innovating organization and by having a reservation manager who works full time as a sponsor. They may be located within division and/or at corporate headquarters to permit various degrees of differentiation.

Reservations can be internal or external. Internal reservations may include some staff and research groups, product and process development labs, and groups that are devoted to market development, new ventures, and/or corporate development. They are organizational homes where idea generators can contribute without becoming managers. Originally, this was the purpose of staff groups, but staff groups now frequently assume control responsibilities or are narrow specialists who contribute to the current business idea. Because such internal groups can be expensive, outside reservations like universities, consulting firms, and advertising agencies are often used to tap non-managerial idea generators.

Reservations can be permanent or temporary. The internal reservations described above, such as R&D units, are reasonably permanent entities. But members of the operating organization may be relieved of operating duties to develop a new program, a new process, or a new product on a temporary basis. When these are developed, they take the idea into the operating organization and resume their operating responsibilities. But for a period of time they are differentiated from operating functions to varying degrees in order to innovate, fail, learn, and ultimately perfect a new idea.

Collectively the roles of orchestrators, sponsors, and idea generators working with and on reservations constitute the structure of the innovating organization. Some of the people, such as sponsors and orchestrators, play roles in both organizations; reservation managers and idea generators work only for the innovating organization. Virtually everyone in the organization can be an idea generator, and all middle managers are potential sponsors. However, not all choose to play these roles. People vary considerably in their innovating skills. By recognizing the need for these roles, developing people to fill them, giving them opportunity to use their skills in key processes, and rewarding innovating accomplishments, the organization can do considerably better than just allowing a spontaneous process to work. Several key processes are part and parcel of this innovating organizational structure. These are described in the next section.

Key processes

In our case history, the idea generator and the first two sponsors found each other through happenstance. The odds of such propitious match-ups can be significantly improved through the explicit design of processes that help sponsors and idea generators find each other. The chances of successful match-ups can be improved by such funding, getting ideas, and blending ideas. In addition, the processes of transitioning and program management move ideas from reservations into operations. Each of these is described below.

Funding

A key process that increases our ability to innovate is a funding process that is explicitly earmarked for the innovating organization. A leader in this field is Texas Instruments (TI), a company that budgets and allocates funds for both operating and innovating. In essence the orchestrators make the short-run/long-run tradeoff at this point. They then orchestrate by choosing where to place the innovating funds – with division sponsors or corporate reservations. The funding process is a key tool for orchestration.

Another lesson to be learned from the case history is that it frequently takes more than one sponsor to launch a new idea. The field engineer's idea would never have been brought to management's attention without the New England sales manager. It would never have been tested in the market without the European sales manager. Multiple sponsors keep fragile ideas alive. If engineering had been the only available sponsor for technical ideas, there would have been no innovation.

Some organizations purposely create a multiple sponsoring system and make it legitimate for an idea generator to go to any sponsor who has funding for new ideas. Multiple sponsors duplicate the market system of multiple bankers for entrepreneurs. At Minnesota Mining and Manufacturing (3M), for example, an idea generator can go to his or her division sponsor for funding. If refused, the idea generator can then go to any other division sponsor or even to corporate R&D. If the idea is outside current business lines, the idea generator can go to the new ventures group for support. If the idea is rejected by all possible sponsors, it probably isn't a very good idea. However, the idea is kept alive and given several opportunities to be tested. Multiple sponsors keep fragile young ideas alive.

Getting ideas

The process of getting ideas occurs by happenstance as it did in the case history. The premise of this section is that the odds of match-ups between idea generators and sponsors can be improved by organization design. First, the natural process can be improved by network-building actions such as multidivision or multireservation careers or company-wide seminars and conferences. All of these practices plus a common physical location facilitate matching at 3M.

The matching process is formalized at TI, where there is an elaborate planning process called the objectives, strategies, and tactics or OST system, which is an annual harvest of new ideas. Innovating funds are distributed to managers of objectives (sponsors) who fund projects based on ideas formulated by idea generators, and these then become tactical action programs. Ideas that are not funded go into a creative backlog to be tapped throughout the year. Whether formal, as at TI, or informal, as at 3M, it is noteworthy that these are known systems for matching ideas with sponsors.

Ideas can also be acquired by aggressive sponsors. Sponsors sit at the crossroads of many ideas and often arrive at a better idea by putting two or more together. They can then pursue an idea generator to champion it. Good sponsors know where the proven idea people are located and how to attract such people to come to perfect an idea on their reservation. Sponsors can go inside or outside the organization to pursue these idea people.

And finally, formal events for matching purposes can be scheduled. At 3M, for example, there's an annual fair at which idea generators can set up booths to be viewed by shopping sponsors. Exxon Enterprises held a "shake the tree event" at which idea people could throw out ideas to be pursued by attending sponsors. The variations of such events are endless. The point is that by devoting time to ideas and making innovation legitimate, the odds that sponsors will find new ideas are increased.

Blending ideas

An important lesson to be derived from our scenario is that it is no accident that a field engineer produced the new product idea. Why? Because the field engineer spent all day working on customer problems and also knew the technology. Therefore, one person knew the need and the means by which to satisfy the need. (An added plus: the field engineer had a personal need to design the appropriate technology.) The premise here is that innovation is more likely to occur when knowledge of technologies and user requirements are combined in the minds of as few people as possible – preferably in that of one person.

The question of whether innovations are need-stimulated or means-stimulated is debatable. Do you start with the disease and look for a cure, or start with a cure and find a disease for it? Research indicates that two-thirds of innovations are need-stimulated. But this argument misses the point. As shown in Figure 10.5a, the debate is over whether use or means drives the downstream efforts. This thinking is linear and sequential. Instead, the model suggested here is shown in Figure 10.5b. That is, for innovation to occur, knowledge of all key components is simultaneously coupled. And the best way to maximize communication among the components is to have the communication occur intrapersonally – that is, within one person's mind. If this is impossible, then as few people as possible should have to communicate or interact. The point is that innovative ideas occur when knowledge of the essential specialties is coupled in as few heads as possible. To encourage such coupling, the

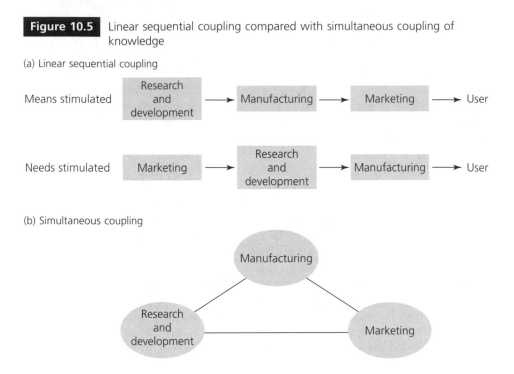

Figure 10.5 Linear sequential coupling compared with simultaneous coupling of knowledge

(a) Linear sequential coupling

Means stimulated — Research and development → Manufacturing → Marketing → User

Needs stimulated — Marketing → Research and development → Manufacturing → User

(b) Simultaneous coupling

Manufacturing

Research and development

Marketing

organization can grow or select individuals with the essential skills or it can encourage interaction between those with meshing skills. These practices will be discussed on p. 219ff.

A variety of processes are employed by organizations to match knowledge of need and of means. At IBM marketing people are placed directly in the R&D labs where they can readily interpret the market requirement documents for researchers. People are rotated through this unit, and a network is created. Wang holds an annual users' conference at which customers and product designers interact and discuss the use of Wang products. Lanier insists that all top managers, including R&D management, spend one day a month selling in the field. It is reported that British scientists made remarkable progress on developing radar after actually flying missions with the Royal Air Force. In all these cases there is an explicit matching of the use and the user with knowledge of a technology to meet the use. Again these processes are explicitly designed to get a user orientation among the idea generators and sponsors. They increase the likelihood that inventions will be innovations. The more complete a new idea or invention is at its inception, the greater the likelihood of its being transferred into the operating organization.

Transitioning

Perhaps the most crucial process in getting an innovative product to market is the transitioning of an idea from a reservation to an operating organization for implementation. This process occurs in stages, as illustrated in the case history. First, the idea was formulated in the field before management knew about it. Then it was tested with a customer, the French bank. And finally, at the third stage, development and fullscale implementation took place. In other cases, several additional stages of testing and scale-up may be necessary. In any case, transitioning should be planned in such stages. At each stage the orchestrator has several choices that balance the need for further invention with the need for transfer. The choices and typical stages of idea development are shown in Table 10.1.

At each stage these choices face the orchestrator: Who will be the sponsor? Who will be the champion? Where can staff be secured for the effort? At what physical location will work be performed? Who will fund the effort? How much autonomy should the effort have, or how differentiated should it be? For example, at the initial new idea formulation stage the sponsor could be the corporate ventures group with the champion working on the corporate reservation. The effort could be staffed with other corporate reservation types and funded at the corporate level. The activity would be fully separate and autonomous. If the results were positive, the process could proceed to the next stage. If the idea needed further development, some division people could be brought in to round out the needed specialties. If the data were still positive after the second stage, then the effort could be transferred physically to the division, but the champion, sponsor, and funding might remain at the corporate level. In this manner, by orchestrating through choices of sponsor, champion, staff, location, funding, and autonomy, the orchestrator balances the need for innovation and protection with the need for testing against reality and transfer.

The above is an all-too-brief outline of the transition process; entire books have been written on the subject of technology transfer. The goal here is to highlight the stagewise nature of the process and the decisions to be made by the orchestrator at each stage. The process is crucial because it is the link between the two organizations. Thus to consistently innovate, the firm needs an innovating organization, an operating organization, and a process for transitioning ideas from the former to the latter.

Table 10.1 Transitioning ideas by stages

	Stages			
Choices	I	II	Nth	Implementation
Sponsor	Corporate	Corporate	. . .	Division
Champion	Corporate	Corporate	. . .	Division
Staffing	Corporate	Corporate-division	. . .	Division
Location	Corporate	Corporate	. . .	Division
Funding	Corporate	Corporate	. . .	Division
Autonomy	Corporate	Corporate	. . .	Division

Managing programs

Program management is necessary to implement new products and processes within divisions. At the stage of the process, the idea generator usually hands the idea over to a product/project/program manager. The product or process is then implemented across the functional organization within the division. The systems and organizational processes for managing projects have been discussed elsewhere and will not be discussed here. The point is that a program management process and skill is needed.

In summary, several key processes – that is, funding, getting ideas, blending ideas, transitioning and managing programs – are basic components of the innovating structure. Even though many of these occur naturally in all organizations, our implicit hypothesis is that the odds for successful innovation can be increased by explicitly designing these processes and by earmarking corporate resources for them. Hundreds of people in organizations choose to innovate voluntarily, as did the field engineer in the case history. However, if there were a reward system for people like these, more would choose to innovate, and more would choose to stay in the organization to do their innovating.

Reward system

The innovating organization, like the operating organization, needs an incentive system to motivate innovating behavior. Because the task of innovating is different from that of operating, the innovating organization needs a different reward system. The innovating task is riskier, more difficult, and takes place over longer time frames. These factors call for some adjustment of the operating organization's reward system, the amount of adjustment depending on how innovative the operating organization is and how attractive outside alternatives are.

The functions of the reward system are threefold: First, the rewards must attract idea people to the company and the reservations and retain them. Because various firms have different attraction and retention problems, their reward systems must vary. Second, the rewards provide motivation for the extra effort needed to innovate. After 19 failures, for example, something has to motivate the idea generator to make the 20th attempt. And, finally, successful performance deserves a reward. These rewards are primarily for idea generators. However, a reward measurement system for sponsors is equally important. Various reward systems will be discussed in the next sections.

Rewards for idea generators

Reward systems mix several types of internal motivators, such as the opportunity to pursue one's ideas, promotions, recognition, systems and special compensation. First, people can be attracted and motivated intrinsically by simply giving them the opportunity and autonomy to pursue their own ideas. A reservation can provide such opportunity and autonomy. Idea people – who are internally driven – such as the field engineer in our story can come in a reservation, pursue their own ideas, and be guided and evaluated by a reservation manager. This is a reward in itself, albeit a minimal reward. If that minimal level attracts and motivates idea people, the innovating organization need go no further in creating a separate reward system.

However, if necessary, motivational leverage can be obtained by promotion and recognition for innovating performance. The dual ladder – that is, a system whereby an individual contributor can be promoted and given increased salary without taking managerial responsibilities – is the best example of such a system. At 3M a contributor can rise in both status and salary to the equivalent of a group executive without becoming a manager. The dual ladder has always existed in R&D, but it is now being extended to some other functions as well.

Some firms grant special recognition for high career performance. IBM has its IBM fellows program in which the person selected as a fellow can work on projects of his or her own choosing for five years. At 3M, there is the Canton Award, which is described as an internal Nobel Prize. Such promotion and recognition systems reward innovation and help create an innovating culture.

When greater motivation is needed, and/or the organization wants to signal the importance of innovation, special compensation is added to the aforementioned systems. Different special compensation systems will be discussed in the order of increasing motivational impact and of increasing dysfunctional ripple effects. The implication is that the firm should use special compensation only to the degree that the need for attraction and for motivation dictate.

Some companies reward successful idea generators with one-time cash awards. For example, International Harvester's share of the combine market jumped from 12 percent to 17 percent because of the introduction of the axial flow combine. The scientist whose six patents contributed to the product development was given $10,000. If the product continues to succeed, he may be given another award. IBM uses the "Chairman's Outstanding Contribution Award." The current program manager on the 4300 series was given a $5,000 award for her breakthrough in coding. These awards are made after the idea is successful and primarily serve to reward achievement rather than to attract innovators and provide incentive for future efforts.

Programs that give a 'percentage of the take' to the idea generator and early team members provide even stronger motivation. Toy and game companies give a royalty to inventors – both internal and external – of toys and games they produce. Apple Computer claims to give royalties to employees who write software programs that will run on Apple equipment. A chemical company created a pool by putting aside 4 percent of the first five years' earnings from a new business venture, which was to be distributed to the initial venture team. Other companies create pools from percentages that range from 2 to 20 percent of cost savings created by process innovations, in any case, a predetermined contract is created to motivate the idea generator and those who join a risky effort at an early stage.

The most controversial efforts to date are attempts to duplicate free-market rewards within the firm. For example, a couple of years ago, ITT bought a small company named Qume that made high-speed printers. The founder became a millionaire from the sale; he had to quit his previous employer to found the venture capital effort to start Qume. If ITT can make an outsider a millionaire, why not give the same change to entrepreneurial insiders? Many people advocate such a system but have not found an appropriate formula to implement the idea. For example, one firm created five-year milestones for a venture, the accomplishment of which would result in a cash award of $6 million to the idea generator. However, the business climate changed after two years, and the idea generator, not surprisingly, tried to make the plan work rather than adapt to the new, unforeseen reality.

Another scheme is to give the idea generator and the initial team some phantom stock, which gets evaluated at sale time in the same way that any acquisition would be evaluated. This process duplicates the free-market process and gives internal people the same venture capital opportunities and risk as they would have on the outside.

The special compensation programs produce motivation and dysfunctions. People who contribute at later stages frequently feel like second-class citizens. Also, any program that discriminates will create perceptions of unfair treatment and possible fallout in the operating organization. If the benefits are judged to be worth the effort, however, care should be taken to manage the fallout.

Rewards for sponsors

The case history also demonstrates that sponsors need incentives, too. In the example, because they were being beaten in the market, the sales people had an incentive to adopt a new product. The point is that sponsors will sponsor ideas, but these may not be innovating ideas unless there's something in it for them. The orchestrator's task is to create and communicate those incentives.

Sponsor incentives take many forms. At 3M, division managers have a bonus goal that is reached if 25 percent of their revenue comes from products introduced within the previous five years. When the percentage falls below the goal, and the bonus is threatened, these sponsors become amazingly receptive to new product ideas. The transfer process becomes much easier as a result. Sales growth, revenue increase, numbers of new products, and so on, may be the bases for incentives that motivate sponsors.

Another company can arise if the idea generators receive phantom stock. Should the sponsors who supervise these idea people receive phantom stock, too? Some banks have created separate subsidiaries so that sponsors can receive stock in the new venture. To the degree that sponsors contribute to idea development, they will need to be given such stock options, too.

Thus, the innovating organization needs reward systems for both idea generators and sponsors. It should start with a simple reward system and move to more motivating, more complex and possibly more upsetting types of rewards only if and when attraction and motivation problems call for them.

People

The final policy area to be considered involves people practices. The assumption is that some people who are better at innovating are not necessarily good at operating. Therefore, the ability of the innovating organization to generate new business ideas can be increased by systematically developing and selecting those people who are better at innovating than others. But first the desirable attributes must be identified. These characteristics that identify likely idea generators and sponsors are spelled out in the following sections.

Attributes of idea generators

The field engineer in our case history is the stereotype of the inventor. He is not mainstream. He's hard to get along with, and he wasn't afraid to break company policy to perfect his idea. Such people have strong egos that allow them to persist and swim up-stream. They generally are not the type of people who get along well in an organization. However, if an organization has reservations, innovating funds, and dual ladders, these people can be attracted and retained.

The psychological attributes of successful entrepreneurs include great need to achieve and to take risks. But, to translate that need into innovation, several other attributes are needed. First, prospective innovators have an irreverence for the status quo. They often come from outcast groups or are newcomers to the company; they are less satisfied with the way things are and have less to lose if there's a change. Successful innovators also need "previous programming in the industry" – that is, an in-depth knowledge of the industry gained through either experience or formal education. Hence, the innovator needs industry knowledge, but not the religion.

Previous startup experience is also associated with successful business ventures, as are people who come from incubator firms (for example high-technology companies) and areas (such as Boston and the Silicon Valley) that are noted for creativity.

The amount of organizational effort needed to select these people varies with the ability to attract them to the organization in the first place. If idea people are attracted through reputation, then by funding reservations and employing idea-getting processes, idea people will, in effect, select themselves – they will want to work with the organization – and over time their presence will reinforce the organization's reputation for idea generation. If the firm has no reputation for innovation, then idea people must be sought out or external reservations established to encourage initial idea generation. One firm made extensive use of outside recruiting to accomplish such a goal. A sponsor would develop an idea and then attend annual conferences of key specialists to determine who was most skilled in the area of interest; he or she would then interview appropriate candidates and offer the opportunity to develop the venture to those with entrepreneurial interests.

Another key attribute of successful business innovators is varied experience, which creates the coupling of a knowledge of means and of use in a single individual's mind. It is the generalist, not the specialist, who creates an idea that differs from the firm's current business line. Specialists are inventors; generalists are innovators. One ceramics engineering firm selects the best and the brightest graduates from the ceramics engineering schools and places them in central engineering to learn the firm's overall system. They are then assigned to field engineering where they spend three to five years with customers and their problems and then they return to central engineering product design. Only then do they design products for those customers. This type of internal coupling can be created by role rotation. Some aerospace firms rotate engineers through manufacturing liaison.

People who have the characteristics that make them successful innovators can be retained, however, only if there are reservations for them and sponsors to guide them.

Attributes of sponsors and reservation managers

The innovating organization must also attract, develop, train and retain people to manage the idea development process. Because certain types of people and management skills are better suited to managing ideas than others, likely prospects for such positions should have a management style that enables them to handle idea people, as well as early experience in innovating, the capability to generate ideas of their own, the skills to put deals together, and generalist business skills.

One of the key skills necessary for operating an innovating organization is the skill to manage and supervise the kind of person who is likely to be an idea generator and champion – that is, people who, among other characteristics, do not take very well to being supervised. Idea generators and champions have a great deal of ownership in their ideas. They gain their satisfaction by having "done it their way." The intrinsic satisfaction comes from the ownership and autonomy. However, idea people also need help, advice, and sounding boards. The successful sponsor learns how to manage these people in the same way that a producer or publisher learns to handle the egos of their stars and writers. This style was best described by a successful sponsor:

> It's a lot like teaching your kids to ride a bike. You're there. You walk along behind. If the kid takes off, he or she never knows that they could have been helped. If they stagger a little, you lend a helping hand, undetected preferably. If they fall, you catch them. If they do something stupid, you take the bike away until they're ready.

This style is quite different from the hands-on, directive style of managers in an operating organization. Of course, the best way to learn this style is to have been managed by it and seen it practiced in an innovating organization. Therefore, experience in an innovating organization is essential.

More than the idea generators, the sponsors need to understand the logic of innovation and to have experienced the management of innovation. Its managers need to have an intuitive feel for the task and its nuances. Managers whose only experience is in operations will not have developed the managerial style, understanding, and intuitive feel that is necessary to manage innovations because the logic of operations is counterintuitive in comparison with the logic of innovations. This means that some idea generators and champions who have experienced innovation should become managers as well as individual contributors. For example, the president in our case history was the inventor of the first-generation product and therefore understood the long, agonizing process of developing a business idea. It is also rare to find an R&D manager who hasn't come through the R&D ranks.

The best idea sponsors and idea reservation managers, therefore, are people who have experienced innovation early in their careers and are comfortable with it. They will have been exposed to risk, uncertainty, parallel experiments, repeated failures that lead to learning, coupling rather than assembly-line thinking, long time frames, and personal control systems based on people and ideas, not numbers and budget variances. Sponsors and reservation managers can be developed or recruited from the outside.

Sponsors and reservation managers need to be idea generators themselves. Ideas tend to come from two sources. The first is at low levels of the organization where the problem gap is experienced. The idea generator who offers a solution is the one who experienced the problem and goes to a sponsor for testing and development. One problem with these ideas is that they may offer only partial solutions because they come from specialists whose views can be parochial and local. But sponsors are at the crossroads of many ideas. They may get a broader vision of the emerging situation as a result. These idea sponsors can themselves generate an idea that is suitable for the organization's business, or they can blend several partial ideas into a business-adaptable idea. Sponsors and reservation managers who are at the crossroads of idea flow are an important secondary source of new ideas. Therefore, they should be selected and trained for their ability to generate new ideas.

Another skill that sponsors and reservation managers need is the ability to make deals and broker ideas. Once an idea has emerged, a reservation manager may have to argue for the release of key people, space, resources, charters, for production time, or a customer contact. These deals all require someone who is adept at persuasion. In that sense, handling them is no different than project or product management roles. People do vary in their ability to make deals and to bargain and those who are particularly adept should be selected for these roles. However, those who have other idea management skills may well be able to be trained in negotiating and bargaining.

And, finally, sponsors and reservation managers should be generalists with general business skills. Again, the ability to recognize a business idea and to shape partial ideas into business ideals are needed. Sponsors and reservation managers must coach idea generators in specialisms in which the idea generator is not schooled. Most successful research managers are those with business skills who can see the business significance in the good ideas that come from scientists.

In summary, the sponsors and reservation managers who manage the idea-development process must be recruited, selected, and developed. The skills that these people need relate to their style, experience, idea generating ability, deal-making ability, and generalist business acumen. People with these skills can either be selected or developed.

Thus some of the attributes of successful idea generators and idea sponsors can be identified. In creating the innovating organization, people with these attributes can be recruited, selected, and/or developed. In so doing, the organization improves its odds at generating and developing new business ideas.

Summary

The innovating organization described is one that recognizes and formalizes the roles, processes, rewards, and people practices that naturally lead to innovations. The point we have emphasized throughout this chapter is that the organization that purposely designs these roles and processes is more likely to generate innovations than is an organization that doesn't plan for this function. Such a purposely designed organization is needed to overcome the obstacles to innovation. Because innovation is destructive to many established groups, it will be resisted. Innovation is contrary in operations and will be ignored. These and other obstacles are more likely to be overcome if the organization is designed specifically to innovate.

Managers have tried to overcome these obstacles by creating venture groups, by hiring some entrepreneurs, by creating "breakthrough funds," or by offering special incentives. These are good policies but by themselves will not accomplish the goal. Figure 10.1 conveyed the message that a consistent set of policies concerning structure, process, rewards, and people is needed. The innovating organization is illustrated in Figure 10.6. It is the combination of idea people, reservations in which they can operate, sponsors to supervise them, funding for their ideas, and rewards for their success that increase the odds in favor of innovation. Simply implementing one or two of these practices will result in failure and will only give people the impression that such practices do not work. A consistent combination of such practices will create an innovating organization that will work.

Figure 10.6 An innovating organization's design components

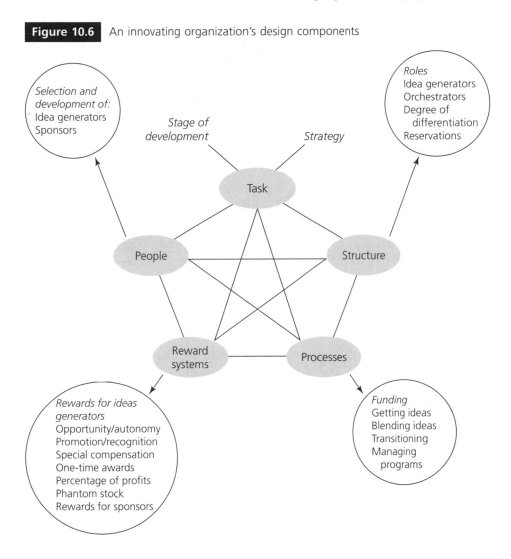

Selected bibliography

The basic ideas of organization design and of blending structure, processes, rewards and people practices are described in my earlier book, *Organization Design* (Addison-Wesley, 1978). The idea of differentiation comes from Paul Lawrence and Jay Lorsch's *Organization and Environment* (Harvard Business School, 1967). One can also find there the basic ideas of contingency theory.

The structure of the innovative organization and the three roles involved are similar to those identified in the investment idea and capital budgeting process. These have been identified by Joseph Bower in *The Resource Allocation Process* (Division of Research at Harvard University, 1968).

Innovation itself has been treated in various ways by many people. Some good ideas about technological innovation can be found in Lowell Steele's *Innovation in Big Business* (Elsevier, 1975).

GE's Crotonville:
a staging ground for corporate revolution
Noel M. Tichy

Radically altering the genetic code of a large, successful corporation requires revolutionary action. Since 1981 John F. Welch, CEO of General Electric, has been struggling to break the company's old genetic code. This code was built around a core set of principles based on growth in sales greater than GNP, with many SBUs (strategic business units), relying on financial savvy, meticulous staff work, and a domestically focused company. The new genetic code is to build shareholder value in a slow-growth environment through operating competitive advantage with transformational level leadership at all levels of the organization.

After five years of this effort – which included downsizing GE by over 100,000 employees, divesting $6 billion and acquiring $13 billion in businesses (RCA being the largest), doubling investment in plant equipment and R&D, and at the same time increasing earnings and shareholder value (GE moved up to no. 3 in the United States in market value from no. 10) – Welch was asked, "What was your biggest mistake?" He answered, "I was too timid and cautious. I did not move fast enough ... bureaucracies need quantum change, not incremental change." Three years later, in 1989, Welch was still accelerating change at GE.

To accomplish the quantum change in GE, a new breed of leader is required. These are leaders who can:

1 **Transform the organization**; that is, creatively destroy and remake an organization around new visions, supported by revamping the social architecture of the organization. This is needed at all levels of GE and is a continuous process.

2 **Develop global product and service strategies**. As GE more aggressively looks to world markets, it is faced with developing world-class products and services at world-class cost. This means changes in product and service design, production, distribution, and marketing. Leaders must be able to:

   create new forms of design teams;
   make strategic use of sourcing;
   drive world-class standards for design, service, and performance.

3 **Develop strategic alliances**. To deliver on global strategies, more and varied alliances are emerging. These alliances are partnerships that are needed to gain market entry, achieve price competitiveness, gain technology, learn more about management, and so on. The success of these alliances will be determined by a set of leadership factors: skill and pre-screening of potential partners, proper negotiation, the right condition for partnering, and good coordination and integration mechanisms.

4 **Develop global coordination and integration**. As the boundaries of GE span wider geopolitical and cultural diversities, it becomes increasingly difficult to integrate the organization. Better communication and cultural integration will be required since all human resource systems will be impacted by this development.

5 **Develop global staffing and development**. Growing world-class leaders will be the key to competitiveness. Staffing and development systems at GE are outmoded and are undergoing total revamping to develop a new brand of leader.

This chapter chronicles the evolution of a revolutionary agenda at GE. Crotonville, GE's Management Development Institute, is increasingly being used by Welch as a key lever in the radical transformation of the company's culture. The overall Crotonville strategy and particular developmental stagecraft will be discussed. Finally, lessons for other CEOs are articulated. This chapter is based on my two years as leader of the last phase of Crotonville's transformation. I was the manager of GE's Management Development Operation from 1985 through 1987.

The crotonville heritage as a lever of change

In 1956, when Crotonville launched its first 13-week advanced management program, Ralph Cordiner, who became CEO in 1950, was using development as a direct lever for change. Cordiner believed that decentralization by product line would best position GE to capitalize on the post-World War II market opportunities. He hired Harold Smiddy, a former Booz-Allen consultant, to engineer a massive restructuring. Cordiner and Smiddy quickly saw that GE did not have managerial talent – that is, multi-functional general managers – to run a decentralized company. A major effort was launched to design an advanced management curriculum and build Crotonville, a campus-like-setting in Ossining, New York. The design of the curriculum drew on the expertise of academicians from around the country and resulted in the creation of a multi-volume set of books on how to be a multi-functional general manager in GE. These books were referred to as the "GE blue books," which became Crotonville's "catechism." The critical point here is that Crotonville's birth was as a CEO-driven lever for change. This continued under the next

CEO, Fred Borth, as Crotonville was used to introduce strategic planning to GE. Borch's successor, Reginald Jones, used Crotonville to round out the strategic planning effort and improve cash management and inflationary accounting practices. In the Welch era, Crotonville again became a centerpiece for the CEO's efforts to make change happen at GE, but on a scale unheard of since Cordiner's days.

The early Welch effort

The first act of a transformation is creating a sense of urgency for change and dealing with the inevitable resistance to a new order.[1] From 1981 to 1985 Welch worked closely with Crotonville and its leader, James Baughman, to delayer, downsize, and change GE's portfolio. Baughman revitalized the curriculum, faculty, staff, and the facility to get the message across to thousands of managers, to try to impact their hearts and minds. Baughman joined GE after a year on the Harvard Business School faculty. He had taught at Crotonville since 1968 and was aware of its shortcomings as well as its potential. As eager as Baughman was to revitalize Crotonville, he was not prepared for the passion of Welch's challenge to him when they met for the first time in January 1981: "I want a revolution to start at Crotonville. I want it to be part of the glue that holds GE together."

Under Baughman's leadership, the first moves were to do a program-by-program upgrade of the faculty, curriculum, and staff, and set the stage for a total revamping of the Crotonville strategy. This resulted in the top-level executive programs being tied directly to the GE succession planning process; thus, there was much more selectivity, with business heads accountable to the CEO for seeing to it that Crotonville development experiences were carefully planned and carried through for their managers. New programs were targeted for populations previously unserved by Crotonville. The first of these was a New Manager Program, targeted to those managers who hire, train, and supervise the vast majority of GE employees. If Welch was to "drive a stake in the ground" for the new GE culture, this was a critical population to win over.

Another very significant, substantive, and symbolic event was the change in the physical facilities at Crotonville. As GE was going through a very dramatic set of changes, including downsizing, delayering, and divesting, Welch was investing in the future in terms not only of business but also of leadership. The facilities would provide living and development space in the 21st century. This development was Welch's second stake in the ground.

The New Manager Program began the process of shifting Crotonville's focus back toward the new college hire. In addition, during this period horizontal integration began with Crotonville's acquisition of the functional development responsibilities in marketing, finance, computer information systems, and human resources.

By 1985, the Crotonville transformation was well on its way. Two significant changes occurred that year. First, the reporting relationship of Crotonville was shifted from the employee relations organization to the executive management staff. This enabled Crotonville to be better integrated with the succession planning process and the CEO's office. Second, Baughman was promoted to broader responsibilities on GE's Executive Management Staff, and it was his suggestion that his successor be brought in from the outside to keep up the momentum for change and new perspectives. Furthermore, it was proposed that this individual would take on the assignment as a two-year leave of absence from the academic world. Baughman would retain GE oversight of Crotonville, but the person hired would be in full charge of all educational and development programs. Thus, when my two-year assignment began, the revolution had progressed and a vision was emerging for Crotonville. This was a vision that embodied much more than a development agenda; it was a centerpiece in the transformation agendas for GE and its culture. The challenge of leading Crotonville during this historic period was what led me to take a two-year leave of absence from the University of Michigan and join GE.

Welch's second act: crystallizing the vision

By 1985, Crotonville was well on its way to becoming once again a lever for change at GE. Ironically, a series of evolutionary experiments and changes led to a revolutionary agenda. Although the following premises were never made explicit by Welch or senior executives in GE, they were clearly implicit, based on the behavior and actions taken regarding the role of Crotonville.

Premise 1: Revolutionaries do not rely solely on the chain of command to bring about quantum change; they carefully develop multichannel, two-way interactive networks throughout the organization. So did Jack Welch.

(a) The chain of command, with its vested interests, is where much of the resistance to change resides. Therefore, there is a need to stir up the populace of the organization and begin developing new leaders for the new regime.

(b) There is a need for a new set of values and templates in the organization.

(c) There is a need for mechanisms to implement all of these changes. Therefore, new socialization and new development processes are required.

Premise 2: Revolutionary change occurs by blending the hard and the soft issues.

(a) Welch understood this blending of hard and soft issues quite well, since it was the hallmark of his experience in building the plastics business in GE. On the one hand, he was a tough person, while on the other he invested a great deal of time and energy in coaching and developing team players and team building. He insisted that those who had to depart were treated compassionately; that is, "a soft landing." Thus, the cornerstone of Welch's strategy for building an organization and a winning team is this blending of the hard issues (budget, manufacturing, marketing, distribution, head-count, finance, etc.) and the soft issues (values, culture, vision, leadership, style, innovative behavior, etc.).

(b) Welch felt that US leadership in general and GE leadership in particular were weak on both the hard and the soft issues from World War II through the late 1970s, until increased competition from Japan and elsewhere led to a rude awakening.

(c) Since the early 1980s, GE has been very aggressive about getting strong leadership on the hard issues, such as downsizing, reducing levels of management, and driving productivity. However ...

(d) Driving solely on the hard issues will only work so long as the primary focus is on bottom-line improvement – and you can only squeeze so far. The long-term need is for top-line growth via new markets, products, innovations, and so on. Driving on the hard issues also takes the excitement out of the organization and can suck the psychological reserve out of people. Thus, the challenge for GE by the mid-1980s was to be strong on the soft issues as well as the hard.

(e) Welch uses Crotonville as a lever for blending the hard and soft, for getting at the hearts and minds of thousands of high-leverage middle managers to test, revise, and inculcate new GE values. It enables him to cut through the chain of command and get at the grass roots, from new college hires up to officers.

Premise 3: Revolutionaries rewrite the textbooks and revamp the education systems. Welch did the same.

The GE "blue books" – the 25-year-old Crotonville bible – were symbolically burned. Welch has said repeatedly that there are no more textbook answers; leaders must write their own textbooks.

The new Crotonville – GE's giant workshop for staging revolution

Starting in the early 1980s under the leadership of Jim Baughman, the focus at Crotonville moved from the ivory tower end of the training spectrum toward the practical; thus, it became a workshop for wrestling with real organizational and people issues. During this period, more and more live cases from GE were brought into the curriculum; Outward Bound-type activities were introduced for team building; and there was increased personal involvement on the part of the CEO and officers in teaching the programs.

In 1985 this trend was explicitly recognized. A new mission statement and a new management and OD [organization development] strategy were articulated for Crotonville, followed by the aforementioned rapid shift toward the workshop end of the development spectrum.

The mission for Crotonville was spelled out thus:

To leverage GE's global competitiveness, as an instrument of cultural change, by improving the business acumen, leadership abilities and organizational effectiveness of General Electric professionals.

The management and OD strategy built on a new set of concepts concerning the depth and impact of management and organization development. Out of this effort came a framework, later known as the 'Tichy Development Model,' which provided the concept and rationale for shifting much of the curriculum and emphasis at Crotonville.

Figure 11.1 lays out the strategic framework used to transform Crotonville. This framework conceptualizes development along two dimensions. Along the top of the matrix the focus is on depth of development experience. This ranges from one end of the spectrum, which entails developing awareness, to the opposite end, which entails developing fundamental change. The other dimension refers to the target of the development experience. Here it ranges from change targeted at individuals to change targeted at the organizational level. Historically, at Crotonville, as is true of most university schools of business, the primary focus was on the cognitive understanding of the individual. Managers from all over GE attended Crotonville programs as individuals and participated in classrooms where they learned finance, marketing, accounting, and organizational behavior largely through case studies, reading, discussions, simulations, and so on. The major impact was cognitive understanding with some skill development. The problem with this approach, as with executive education in business schools, is that when the individuals return to their organization, they have difficulty translating their classroom experiences into the work situation because they haven't fundamentally changed and, just as importantly, their organizations often resist individuals with new ideas. These people do not have a support system – a group of co-workers – that has gone through the experience with them. This was the challenge facing Crotonville: how to move development toward the upper left-hand part of the matrix to help deal with the revolutionary agenda of transforming GE. The challenge was to take a large number of participants a year – approximately 8,000 – in a 53-acre, 145-bed residential educational center and move the development experience as far as possible toward the workshop end, while at the same time dealing with the economies-of-scale issue – which meant that customized workshops were not the answer.

The shift in the Crotonville mindset from a training to a workshop mentality has led to a totally new program design. An increasing number of teams attend sessions whenever possible. Participants bring with them real business problems and leave with action plans, and representatives from various GE businesses bring unresolved live cases to Crotonville for participants to help

Figure 11.1 The Tichy development model

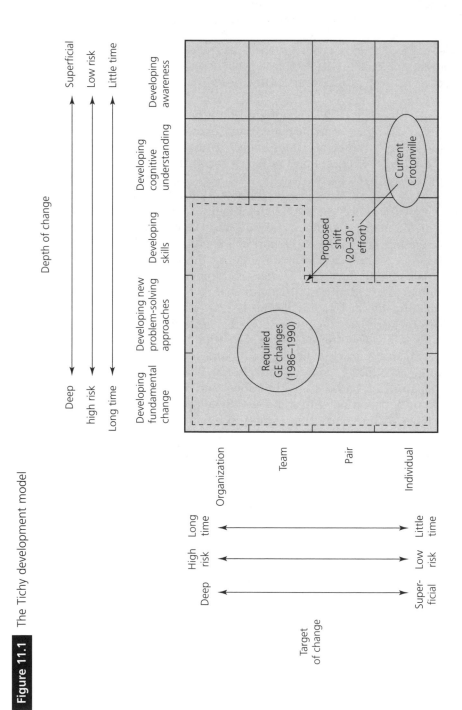

solve. Leadership behaviors are rated by participants' direct reports, peers, and boss before the program so the change can be linked back to the work setting. Executives consult to real GE businesses on unresolved strategic issues; teams also spend up to a week in the field consulting with these businesses on these issues. As mentioned above, members such as the CEO and officers come to Crotonville to conduct workshops on key GE strategic challenges.

Along the way, participants find the development experiences increasingly unsettling and emotionally charged. They feel uncomfortable with feedback from their back-home organization; they wrestle with very difficult, unresolved, real-life problems, not case studies; and they make presentations to senior executives, argue among themselves, and work through intensive team-building experiences. The measure of program success shifts from participants' evaluation of how good they felt about the learning experience to how the experience impacted on their organization and their leadership behavior over time.

Who gets developed?

The other key strategic issue was deciding what populations are to participate in the Crotonville experiences. At GE, the assumption is that over 80 per cent of development is through experience, i.e. on-the-job learning. The remaining 20 per cent of formal development occurs out in the various businesses. Therefore, Crotonville represents only a small percentage of the formal development resources. The critical question thus is, "Who gets to come to Crotonville and at what point in their career?"

This challenge resulted in a reevaluation of leadership development in the 1990s and beyond, from new campus recruits up through to the CEO. The CEO and others worked on the career model of leadership development to identify key transition points in people's careers – that is, "moments of opportunity" (joining GE as a new recruit, becoming a manager for the first time, and so on) – where they could and should be impacted by a set of shared values and leadership characteristics. The result: by 1986, a core development sequence was implemented. This sequence extends from new college hires up through the officer population.

A result of rethinking the strategy was the new, core Crotonville curriculum, shown in Figure 11.2.

Stage I: corporate entry leadership conferences I and II

Close to 2,000 new off-campus hires come to Crotonville within three months of joining GE to learn about global competition, what it takes to win on that global playing field, GE's strategy for winning, and the changing GE values, as well as to undergo a personal examination of their core values *vis-à-vis* GE values. They come in groups of 100. Officers, senior human resource executives, and young managers teach and lead these programs, At the end of each year, 200

Figure 11.2 Core development sequence

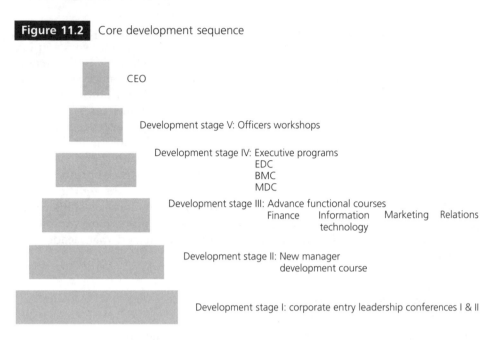

CEO

Development stage V: Officers workshops

Development stage IV: Executive programs
EDC
BMC
MDC

Development stage III: Advance functional courses
Finance   Information   Marketing   Relations
technology

Development stage II: New manager
development course

Development stage I: corporate entry leadership conferences I & II

facilitators, 30 officers, and 30 human resource executives have taught in this program. All of them are the target of change. As many senior officers comment, "There is nothing like teaching Sunday School to force you to confront your own values."

Three years later this group of new hires returns for a program on total business competitiveness. They have real projects to work on, are taught by GE executives, and have to return to their organization with change agendas. These young professionals are again inculcated with a total GE strategy and value mindset. In 1989, the CELC–II program moved out to the businesses as a joint venture with Crotonville.

Stage II: new manager development program

Over 1,000 new managers a year come to Crotonville to learn how to manage and lead in GE. Through a leadership survey they get feedback from their direct reports to help them plan ways of improving their leadership skills. The focus at this stage is making sure that these managers have the right "soft" people skills for hiring, appraising, developing, motivating, and building the high-performing teams that are needed by this critical group.

Stage III: senior functional programs

Senior functional managers come for several weeks of leadership development in their specific areas – marketing, finance, information systems, human resources, engineering and manufacturing, among others. All the programs involve change projects and some actually require the participants to invite senior line managers (their bosses or major clients) to spend several days at Crotonville to tackle these change projects. Obviously, making real change happen and leadership are the agendas.

Stage IV: executive programs

There are three four-week executive programs for GE managers, which are taken over a five-to-eight-year period. These programs integrate outdoor leadership challenge experiences, consulting team projects, and CEO projects.

One program, the BMC (Business Manager Course), is organized around consulting projects. The head of a GE business presents a difficult, unresolved strategic business problem that is carefully packaged prior to the start of the program; market and industry analysis, financial, and other data are pulled together along with a clear project statement and set of deliverables specified by the head of the business. Teams of BMC managers spend the third week of the program in the field interviewing customers, managers, and competitors, and collecting background information to make recommendations. During the fourth week of the program the heads of the businesses involved with projects come to Crotonville for the presentations. The sessions are electric; the teams, the heads of the businesses, make hard-hitting business recommendations as well as advise on how to implement the recommendations, and they specially emphasize the soft, human side of change.

The participants are also given feedback on both the hard and the soft issues. They debrief their own team members, providing each member with concrete behavioral feedback based on the intense four weeks of teamwork, on how to be a more effective GE leader. The participants and business clients reconvene six months later to follow up on the progress of the implementation, recommendations, and each participant's leadership agenda.

Stage V: officer workshops

Officer workshops, which are held periodically, consist of groups of 20 to 30 officers who wrestle for several days on unresolved, company-wide issues. The CEO actively participates in these sessions.

Elective programs

In addition to the core sequence described above, Crotonville provides a portfolio of elective programs ranging from courses on leading change – similar to the experienced manager program – to functionally specific courses on information systems, marketing, and human resources. This portfolio is constantly changing as the needs of the corporation change.

The continued transformation of Crotonville

Since 1987 Crotonville has played a key role in both transforming GE and developing a new pipeline for human resources for the future. When I left in 1987, Crotonville's portfolio was enlarged again. All the technical education at GE was brought under Jim Baughman's direction, along with the campus recruiting and early corporate training programs for targeted new college hires. Crotonville thus became GE's integrating device for coordinating developing from off-campus up through the office level.

Figure 11.3 summarizes the agenda for Crotonville as it enters the 1990s. The agenda has three primary development objectives: (1) help develop "global" maturity and sophistication, (2) help develop technical and business know-how, and (3) help develop leadership abilities. These objectives are worked on differently at each stage of development, from entry-level college hire up through the head of a business.

In 1989 Crotonville is being used by Welch to spearhead an effort to liberate middle management at GE. The "old way," hierarchical bureaucracy, needs to be radically altered to create the "new way," non-hierarchical, fast-paced, flexible organizations of the future. The transformation must be led from the middle. A series of workshops will provide the catalyst for mobilizing 30,000 to 40,000 middle managers, removing unnecessary carryovers from the past bureaucracy – processes, reports, approvals, measures, and meetings. These workshops will be run in every business and involve the business heads and all their middle-level managers. The process is called "work out."

Figure 11.3 The development challenge – who and what?

	Developing 'global' maturity and sophistication	Developing technical and business know-how	Developing leadership abilities
For business leaders			
For functional leaders			
For experienced managers			
For new managers			
For functional contributors			
At entry-level			

Lessons for other CEOs

Crotonville is not unique. It does not require a large campus and bricks and mortar investment to use development as a tool for both bringing about quantum change in an organization and developing future generations of leaders. For this to happen, the leadership challenge for a CEO must entail the following.

Vision

For the CEO to leverage change via development, he or she must have a reasonably clearly articulated future vision for the company. This vision must include the organization culture and shared values that will likely be needed in the future. Such a vision must go well beyond the faddish articulation of values triggered by the "excellence" fad of the early 1980s, when everyone had a list of company values that read like the Boy Scout handbook. The values must be closely integrated with the imperatives of winning in the marketplace.

Leadership characteristics

The CEO must be able to articulate the appropriate characteristics of leaders; that is, the characteristics that will fit with the culture and shared values of the future organization. All too often, companies undertake competency studies focusing on who are the successful managers and leaders of today. This will only ensure that development is focused backward on yesterday's successes, not on the harder task of thinking through what is the new template for leadership in the future. This is not a task to be delegated to human resource staff people, who often have little idea of where the industry, the business, and the company are headed. Only the CEO can lead this effort, albeit with strong staff support.

Career transition points

To maximize the impact of any formal development experience, timing is critical. The challenge here is to have clearly articulated "theory of the case." This enables the organization to deal with the 80/20 dilemma; that is, the 80 per cent of development that really takes place as a result of life experiences and on-the-job development; and the 20 per cent that takes place via formal development programs. Again, this is a responsibility of the CEO, with strong human resource support. The company must have a framework that provides guidelines in blending on-the-job development and other developmental tools, such as secondary assignment activities and coaching and counseling emphases, with formal development experiences. At each career phase, what tools are to be used for what purposes must be identified.

CEO involvement

For development to leverage the kind of change and impact discussed in this chapter, the CEO must visibly lead the development process by participating in the overall design and architecture, delivery, and integration of the development process as it gets tied to succession planning and rewards. This is not a voluntary, open university-type approach to development. It is a very personal tool of the top leadership of the organization as well as a very central part of organization effectiveness.

CEO role model

No CEO should undertake the challenge of using development as a lever for change and as a creator of the new shared values in leadership without also understanding that such a process will put more pressure on the senior leadership to demonstrate personal adherence to those values. An open-dialogue, interactive development process also means that top management must be able to take criticism. Hypocrisy will be uncovered and a great deal of subtle pressure placed on leaders to overcome the schizophrenia often found in changing cultures; that is, where people in the middle rightfully point out that top management gives a great deal of lip service to change but in reality their practice is "Do as I say, and not as I do." The CEO must lead a critical group of senior executives to undergo the same kind of rigorous self-examination as do participants in the development process. For example, if middle managers are being asked to have subordinates fill out surveys of their management practices, the CEO and the top team must do the same.

Organizational resistance

Perhaps the final and real test of the CEO is how he or she deals with resistance to change, as well as how he or she handles the transition from the more comfortable awareness and cognitive learning portion of the matrix in Figure 11.1 to the area of fundamental change, in which a great deal of emotion and turmoil are stirred up. This means that the development and human resource staff will have to deal with the fact that the daily "smile sheet" – that is, evaluation of how happy participants are with each day of the program – tends to go up and down during a real transformation experience. Not everyone is always happy; officers have to wrestle with business problems with participants and are made to feel uncomfortable (and sometimes accused of hypocrisy), and there is a tendency for some people to think that things are getting out of hand. It is here that the CEO must stay the course. At times such as this it might serve well to remember that no one ever gave a high rating to his drill sergeant during the middle of boot camp.

Conclusion

In this chapter I have laid out a challenge to those CEOS who are wrestling with the transformation of their organizations for global competitiveness. It is my contention that one of the most underutilized levers for change is the rather elaborate investment in development that most large corporations make. One reason why it is so underutilized is that there is little or no personal commitment or involvement by the CEO. Obviously, the challenges laid out here are not for everyone. Once the CEO decides to use development as a lever of change, he or she must make the commitment and follow through on the size principles outlined above. Doing so will be a real test of leadership for all involved.

Note

1. *The Transformational Leader,* Noel Tichy and Mary Anne Devanna, Wiley, 1986.

12 Communities of practice and social learning systems

Etienne Wenger

You probably know that the earth is round and that it is in orbit around the sun. But how do you know this? What does it take? Obviously, it takes a brain in a living body, but it also takes a very complex social, cultural, and historical system, which has accumulated learning over time. People have been studying the skies for centuries to understand our place in the universe. More recently, scientific communities have developed a whole vocabulary, observation methods, concepts, and models, which have been adopted by other communities and have become part of popular thinking in various ways. You have your own relationships to all these communities, and these relationships are what enable you to "know" about the earth's position in the universe. In this sense, knowing is an act of participation in complex "social learning systems."

This chapter assumes this view of knowing to consider how organizations depend on social learning systems. First, I outline two aspects of a conceptual framework for understanding social learning systems: a social definition of learning in terms of social *competence* and personal *experience,* and three distinct *modes of belonging* through which we participate in social learning systems: *engagement, imagination,* and *alignment.* Then I look at three structuring elements of social learning systems: *communities of practice, boundary* processes among these communities, and *identities* as shaped by our participation in these systems. About each of these elements I use my conceptual framework to ask three questions. Why focus on it? Which way is up, that is, how to construe progress in this area? And, third, what is doable, that is, what are elements of design that one can hope to influence? Finally, I argue that organizations both are constituted by and participate in such social learning systems. Their success depends on their ability to design themselves as social learning systems and also to participate in broader learning systems such as an industry, a region, or a consortium.

The conceptual framework I introduce here is intended for organizational design as well as analysis. The questions I ask are meant to guide the inquiry of the researcher as well as the actions of the practitioner: what to pay attention to, how to give direction to our initiatives, and where to focus our efforts. As Kurt Lewin used to say, there is nothing as practical as a good theory.

Aspects of a conceptual framework

A framework for understanding social learning systems must make it possible to understand learning as a social process. What is learning from a social perspective? And what are the processes by which our learning constitutes social systems and social identities?

A social definition of learning

In a social learning system, competence is historically and socially defined. How to be a physicist or how to understand the position of the earth in the universe is something that scientific communities have established over time. Knowing, therefore, is a matter of displaying competences defined in social communities. The picture is more complex and dynamic than that, however. Our experience of life and the social standards of competence of our communities are not necessarily, or even usually, congruent. We each experience knowing in our own ways. Socially defined competence is always in interplay with our experience. It is in this interplay that learning takes place.

Consider two extreme cases. Sometimes, we are a newcomer. We join a new community. We are a child who cannot speak yet. Or we are a new employee. We feel like a bumbling idiot among the sages. We want to learn. We want to apprentice ourselves. We want to become one of them. We feel an urgent need to align our experience with the competence "they" define. Their competence pulls our experience.

Sometimes, it is the other way round. We have been with a community for a long time. We know the ropes. We are thoroughly competent, in our own eyes and in the eyes of our peers. But something happens. We are sent overseas. We go to a conference. We visit another department. We meet a "stranger" with a completely different perspective. Or we just take a long walk or engage in a deep conversation with a friend. Whatever the case may be, we have an experience that opens our eyes to a new way of looking at the world. This experience does not fully fit in the current practice of our home communities. We now see limitations we were not aware of before. We come back to our peers, try to communicate our experience, attempt to explain what we have discovered, so they too can expand their horizon. In the process, we are trying to change how our community defines competence (and we are actually deepening our own experience). We are using our experience to pull our community's competence along.

Whether we are apprentices or pioneers, newcomers or oldtimers, knowing always involves these two components: the *competence* that our communities have established over time (i.e. what it takes to act and be recognized as a competent member), and our ongoing *experience* of the world as a member (in the context of a given community and beyond). Competence and experience can be in various relations to each other – from very congruent to very divergent. As my two examples show, either can shape the other, although usually the process is not completely one-way. But, whenever the two are in close tension and either starts pulling the other, learning takes place. Learning so defined is an interplay between social competence and personal experience. It is a dynamic, two-way relationship between people and the social learning systems in which they participate. It combines personal transformation with the evolution of social structures.

Modes of belonging

Our belonging to social learning systems can take various forms at various levels between local interactions and global participation. To capture these different forms of participation, I will distinguish between three modes of belonging.

- *Engagement:* doing things together, talking, producing artifacts (e.g. helping a colleague with a problem or participating in a meeting). The ways in which we engage with each other and with the world profoundly shape our experience of who we are. We learn what we can do and how the world responds to our actions.

- *Imagination:* constructing an image of ourselves, of our communities, and of the world, in order to orient ourselves, to reflect on our situation, and to explore possibilities (e.g. drawing maps, telling a story, or building a set of possible scenarios to understand one's options). I use imagination here in the sense proposed by Benedict Anderson (1983) to describe nations as communities: it does not connote fantasy as opposed to factuality. Knowing that the earth is round and in orbit around the sun, for instance, is not a fantasy. Yet it does require a serious act of imagination. It requires constructing an image of the universe in which it makes sense to think of our standing on the ground as being these little stick figures on a ball flying through the skies. Similarly, thinking of ourselves as a member of a community such as a nation requires an act of imagination because we cannot engage with all our fellow citizens. These images of the world are essential to our sense of self and to our interpretation of our participation in the social world.

- *Alignment* making sure that our local activities are sufficiently aligned with other processes so that they can be effective beyond our own engagement (e.g. doing a scientific experiment by the book, convincing a colleague to join a cause, or negotiating a division of labor and a work plan for a project). The concept of alignment as used here does not connote a one-way process of submitting to external authority, but a mutual process of coordinating perspectives, interpretations, and actions so they realize higher goals. Following the scientific method, abiding by a moral code, or discussing important decisions with our spouse can all become very deep aspects of our identities.

Distinguishing between these modes of belonging is useful for two reasons. First, analytically, each mode contributes a different aspect to the formation of social learning systems and personal identities. Engagement, imagination, and alignment usually coexist and every social learning system involves each to some degree and in some combination. Still, one can dominate and thus give a different quality to a social structure. For instance, a community based mostly on imagination such as a nation has a very different quality from a community of practice at work, which is based primarily on engagement. I would in fact argue that these modes of belonging provide a foundation for a typology of communities.

Second, practically, each mode requires a different kind of work. The work of engagement, which requires opportunities for joint activities, is different from the work of imagination, which often requires opportunities for taking some distance from our situation. The demands and effects of these three modes of belonging can be conflicting. Spending time reflecting can detract from engagement, for example. The modes can also be complementary, however. For instance, using imagination to gain a good picture of the context of one's actions can help in fine-tuning alignment because one understands the reasons behind a procedure or an agreement. It is therefore useful to strive to develop these modes of belonging in combination, balancing the limitations of one with the work of another. For instance, reflective periods that activate imagination or boundary interactions that require alignment with other practices around a shared goal could be used to counteract the possible narrowness of engagement (Wenger, 1998).

Communities of practice

Since the beginning of history, human beings have formed communities that share cultural practices reflecting their collective learning: from a tribe around a cave fire, to a medieval guild, to a group of nurses in a ward, to a street gang, to a community of engineers interested in brake design. Participating in these "communities of practice" is essential to our learning. It is at the very core of what makes us human beings capable of meaningful knowing.

Why focus on communities?

Communities of practice are the basic building blocks of a social learning system because they are the social "containers" of the competences that make up such a system. By participating in these communities, we define with each other what constitutes competence in a given context: being a reliable doctor, a gifted photographer, a popular student, or an astute poker player. Your company may define your job as processing 33 medical claims a day according to certain standards, but the competence required to do this in practice is something you determine with your colleagues as you interact day after day.

Communities of practice define competence by combining three elements (Wenger, 1998). First, members are bound together by their collectively developed understanding of what their community is about and they hold each other accountable to this sense of *joint enterprise*. To be competent is to understand the enterprise well enough to be able to contribute to it. Second, members build their community through mutual engagement. They interact with one another, establishing norms and relationships of *mutuality* that reflect these interactions. To be competent is to be able to engage with the community and be trusted as a partner in these interactions. Third, communities of practice have produced a *shared repertoire* of communal resources – language, routines, sensibilities, artifacts, tools, stories, styles, etc. To be competent is to have access to this repertoire and be able to use it appropriately.

Communities of practice grow out of a convergent interplay of competence and experience that involves mutual engagement. They offer an opportunity to negotiate competence through an experience of direct participation. As a consequence, they remain important social units of learning even in the context of much larger systems. These larger systems are constellations of interrelated communities of practice.

Which way is up?

Communities of practice cannot be romanticized. They are born of learning, but they can also learn not to learn. They are the cradles of the human spirit, but they can also be its cages. After all, witch-hunts were also community practices. It is useful, therefore, to articulate some dimensions of progress.

- *Enterprise: the level of learning energy.* How much initiative does the community take in keeping learning at the center of its enterprise? A community must show leadership in pushing its development along and maintaining a spirit of inquiry. It must recognize and address gaps in its knowledge as well as remain open to emergent directions and opportunities.
- *Mutuality: the depth of social capital.* How deep is the sense of community generated by mutual engagement over time? People must know each other well enough to know how to interact productively and who to call for help or advice. They must trust each other, not just personally, but also in their ability to contribute to the enterprise of the community, so they feel comfortable addressing real problems together and speaking truthfully. Through receiving and giving help, they must gain enough awareness of the richness of the community to expect that their contribution will be reciprocated in some way.
- *Repertoire: the degree of self-awareness.* How self-conscious is the community about the repertoire that it is developing and its effects on its practice? The concepts, language, and tools of a community of practice embody its history and its perspective on the world. Being reflective on its repertoire enables a community to understand its own state of development from multiple perspectives, reconsider assumptions and patterns, uncover hidden possibilities, and use this self-awareness to move forward.

The three dimensions work together. Without the learning energy of those who take the initiative, the community becomes stagnant. Without strong relationships of belonging, it is torn apart. And without the ability to reflect, it becomes hostage to its own history. The work associated with each mode of belonging can contribute to these criteria. Table 12.1 illustrates how the modes of belonging interact with community elements.

What is doable?

When designing itself, a community should look at the following elements: events, leadership, connectivity, membership, projects, and artifacts.

Table 12.1 Community dimensions

	Enterprise: learning energy	Mutuality: social capital	Repertoire: self-awareness
Engagement	What are the opportunities to negotiate a joint inquiry and important questions? Do members identify gaps in their knowledge and work together to address them?	What events and interactions weave the community and develop trust? Does this result in an ability to raise troubling issues during discussions?	To what extent have shared experience, language, artifacts, histories, and methods accumulated over time, and with what potential for further interactions and new meanings?
Imagination	What visions of the potential of the community are guiding the thought leaders, inspiring participation, and defining a learning agenda? And what picture of the world serves as a context for such visions?	What do people know about each other and about the meanings that participation in the community takes in their lives more broadly?	Are there self-representations that would allow the community to see itself in new ways? Is there a language to talk about the community in a reflective mode?
Alignment	Have members articulated a shared purpose? How widely do they subscribe to it? How accountable do they feel to it? And how distributed is leadership?	What definitions of roles, norms, codes of behavior, shared principles, and negotiated commitments and expectations hold the community together?	What traditions, methods, standards, routines, and frameworks define the practice? Who upholds them? To what extent are they codified? How are they transmitted to new generations?

Events

You can organize public events that bring the community together. Obviously, these may or may not be attended, but if they are well tuned to the community's sense of its purpose, they will help it develop an identity. A community will have to decide the *type* of activities it needs: formal or informal meetings, problem-solving sessions, or guest speakers. It will also have to consider the *rhythm* of these events given other responsibilities members have: too often and people just stop coming, too rare and the community does not gain momentum. This rhythm may also have to change over time or go through cycles.

Leadership

Communities of practice depend on internal leadership, and enabling the leaders to play their role is a way to help the community develop. The role of "community coordinator" who takes care of the day-to-day work is crucial, but a community needs multiple forms of leadership: thought leaders, networkers, people who document the practice, pioneers, etc. These forms of leadership may be concentrated on one or two members or widely distributed, and this will change over time.

Connectivity

Building a community is not just a matter of organizing community events but also of enabling a rich fabric of connectivity among people. This could involve brokering relationships between people who need to talk or between people who need help and people who can offer help. It is also important to make it possible for people to communicate and interact in multiple media.

Membership

A community's members must have critical mass so that there is interest, but it should not become so wide that the focus of the community is diffuse and participation does not grab people's identities. Including those who are missing can be very helpful in consolidating the legitimacy of the community to itself and in the wider organization. Conversely, realizing that the membership is overextended allows the community to split up into subgroups. Finally, devising processes by which newcomers can become full members helps ensure access for newcomers without diluting the community's focus.

Learning projects

Communities of practice deepen their mutual commitment when they take responsibility for a learning agenda, which pushes their practice further. Activities toward this goal include exploring the knowledge domain, finding gaps in the community practice, and defining projects to close these gaps. Such learning projects could involve, for instance, assessing some tools, building a generic design, doing a literature search, creating a connection with a university doing research in the area, or simply interviewing some experts to create a beginner's guide.

Artifacts

All communities of practice produce their own set of artifacts: documents, tools, stories, symbols, websites, etc. A community has to consider what artifacts it needs and who has the energy to produce and maintain them so they will remain useful as the community evolves.

Boundaries

The term boundary often has negative connotations because it conveys limitation and lack of access. But the very notion of community of practice implies the existence of boundary. Unlike the boundaries of organizational units, which are usually well defined because affiliation is officially sanctioned, the boundaries of communities of practice are usually rather fluid. They arise from different enterprises; different ways of engaging with one another; different histories, repertoires, ways of communicating, and capabilities. That these boundaries are often unspoken does not make them less significant. Sit for lunch by a group of high-energy particle physicists and you know about boundary, not because they intend to exclude you, but because you cannot figure out what they are talking about. Shared practice by its very nature creates boundaries.

Yet, if you are like me, you will actually enjoy this experience of boundary. There is something disquieting, humbling at times, yet exciting and attractive about such close encounters with the unknown, with the mystery of 'otherness': a chance to explore the edge of your competence, learn something entirely new, revisit your little truths, and perhaps expand your horizon.

Why focus on boundaries?

Boundaries are important to learning systems for two reasons. They connect communities and they offer learning opportunities in their own right. These learning opportunities are of a different kind from the ones offered by communities. Inside a community, learning takes place because competence and experience need to converge for a community to exist. At the boundaries, competence and experience tend to diverge: a boundary interaction is usually an experience of being exposed to a foreign competence. Such reconfigurations of the relation between competence and experience are an important aspect of learning. If competence and experience are too close, if they always match, not much learning is likely to take place. There are no challenges; the community is losing its dynamism and the practice is in danger of becoming stale. Conversely, if experience and competence are too disconnected, if the distance is too great, not much learning is likely to take place either. Sitting by that group of high-energy particle physicists, you might not learn much because the distance between your own experience and the competence you are confronting is just too great. Mostly what you are learning is that you do not belong.

Learning at boundaries is likely to be maximized for individuals and for communities when experience and competence are in close tension. Achieving a generative tension between them requires:

- something to interact about, some intersection of interest, some activity;
- open engagement with real differences as well as common ground;
- commitment to suspend judgment in order to see the competence of a community in its terms;
- ways to translate between repertoires so that experience and competence actually interact.

Boundaries are sources of new opportunities as well as potential difficulties. In a learning system, communities and boundaries can be learning assets (and liabilities) in complementary ways.

- Communities of practice can steward a critical competence, but they can also become hostage to their history, insular, defensive, closed in, and oriented to their own focus.
- Boundaries can create divisions and be a source of separation, fragmentation, disconnection, and misunderstanding. Yet, they can also be areas of unusual learning, places where perspectives meet and new possibilities arise. Radically new insights often arise at the boundaries between communities. Think of a specialization like psychoneuroimmunology: its very name reflects its birth at the intersection of multiple practices.

In social learning systems, the value of communities and their boundaries are complementary. Deep expertise depends on a convergence between experience and competence, but innovative learning requires their divergence. In either case, you need strong competences to anchor the process. But these competences also need to interact. The learning and innovation potential of a social learning system lies in its configuration of strong core practices and active boundary processes (Wenger, 1998).

Which way is up?

Not all boundary processes create bridges that actually connect practices in deep ways. The actual boundary effects of these processes can be assessed along the following dimensions.

- *Coordination.* Can boundary processes and objects be interpreted in different practices in a way that enables coordinated action? For instance, an elegant design may delight designers but say little to those concerned with manufacturability. Across boundaries, effective actions and use of objects require new levels of coordination. They must accommodate the practices involved without burdening others with the details of one practice and provide enough standardization for people to know how to deal with them locally.

- *Transparency.* Do boundary processes give access to the meanings they have in various practices? Coordination does not imply that boundary processes provide an understanding of the practices involved. For instance, forms like US tax returns enable coordination across boundaries (you know how to fill them out by following instructions line by line), but often afford no windows into the logic they are meant to enforce (following instructions often tells you little about why these calculations are "fair").

- *Negotiability.* Do boundary processes provide a one-way or a two-way connection? For instance, a business process reengineering plan may be very detailed about implementation (coordination) and explicit about its intentions (transparency), but reflect or allow little negotiation between the perspectives involved. Boundary processes can merely reflect relations of power among practices, in which case they are likely to reinforce the boundary rather than bridge it. They will bridge practices to the extent that they make room for multiple voices.

What is doable?

Boundary processes are crucial to the coherent functioning of social learning systems. A number of elements can be intentionally promoted in an effort to weave these systems more tightly together. Here, I will talk about three types of bridges across boundaries: *people* who act as "brokers" between communities, *artifacts* (things, tools, terms, representations, etc.) that serve as what Star and Griesemer (1989) call "boundary objects," and a variety of forms of *interactions* among people from different communities of practice.

Brokering

Some people act as brokers between communities. They can introduce elements of one practice into another. Although we all do some brokering, my experience is that certain individuals seem to thrive on being brokers: they love to create connections and engage in "import – export," and so would rather stay at the boundaries of many practices than move to the core of any one practice. Brokering can take various forms, including:

- *boundary spanners:* taking care of one specific boundary over time;
- *roamers:* going from place to place, creating connections, moving knowledge;
- *outposts:* bringing back news from the forefront, exploring new territories;
- *pairs:* often brokering is done through a personal relationship between two people from different communities and it is really the relationship that acts as a brokering device.

Brokering knowledge is delicate. It requires enough legitimacy to be listened to and enough distance to bring something really new. Because brokers often do not fully belong anywhere and may not contribute directly to any specific outcome, the value they bring can easily be overlooked. Uprootedness, homelessness, marginalization, and organizational invisibility are all occupational hazards of brokering. Developing the boundary infrastructure of a social learning system means paying attention to people who act as brokers. Are they falling through the cracks? Is the value they bring understood? Is there even a language to talk about it? Are there people who are potential brokers but who for some reason do not provide cross-boundary connections?

Boundary objects

Some objects find their value, not just as artifacts of one practice, but mostly to the extent that they support connections between different practices. Such boundary objects can take multiple forms.

Table 12.2 Boundary dimensions

	Coordination	Transparency	Negotiability
Engagement	What opportunities exist for joint activities, problem-solving, and discussions to both surface and resolve differences through action?	Do people provide explanations, coaching, and demonstrations in the context of joint activities to open windows on to each other's practices?	Are joint activities structured in such a way that multiple perspectives can meet and participants can come to appreciate each other's competences?
Imagination	Do people have enough understanding of their respective perspectives to present issues effectively and anticipate misunderstandings?	What stories, documents, and models are available to build a picture of another practice? What experience will allow people to walk in the other's shoes? Do they listen deeply enough?	Can both sides see themselves as members of an overarching community in which they have common interests and needs?
Alignment	Are instructions, goals, and methods interpretable into action across boundaries?	Are intentions, commitments, norms, and traditions made clear enough to reveal common ground and differences in perspectives and expectations?	Who has a say in negotiating contracts and devising compromises?

- *Artifacts,* such as tools, documents, or models. For instance, medical records and architectural blueprints play a crucial role in connecting multiple practices (doctors/nurses/insurers/architects/contractors/city planners).
- *Discourses.* A critical boundary object is the existence of a common language that allows people to communicate and negotiate meanings across boundaries. This was an important thrust behind the quality movement, and it was typified by the six sigma discourse at Motorola.
- *Processes.* Shared processes, including explicit routines and procedures, allow people to coordinate their actions across boundaries. Business processes, for instance, are not just fixed prescriptive definitions. At their best, they act as boundary objects that allow multiple practices to coordinate their contributions.

Boundary objects do not necessarily bridge across boundaries because they may be misinterpreted or interpreted blindly. Rethinking artifacts and designs in terms of their function as boundary objects often illuminates how they contribute to or hinder the functioning of learning systems. An organizational structure, for instance, is often considered as an overarching umbrella that incorporates multiple parts by specifying their relationships. But, in fact, it is more usefully designed as a boundary object intended to enable multiple practices to negotiate their relationships and connect their perspectives.

Boundary interactions

- *Boundary encounters.* These encounters – visits, discussions, sabbaticals – provide direct exposure to a practice. They can take different forms for different purposes. When one person visits, as in a sabbatical, it is easier to get fully immersed in the practice, but more difficult to bring the implications home because the very immersion into a "foreign" practice tends to isolate you from your peers. GM, for instance, has had difficulty learning from people sent on sabbatical at its more experimental units such as NUMMI and Saturn because their transformed perspectives could not find a place back home. When a delegation of two or more people visit, as in a benchmarking expedition, they may not get as fully immersed, but they can negotiate among themselves the meaning of the boundary interaction for their own practice, and therefore find it easier to bring their learning back home.
- *Boundary practices.* In some cases, a boundary requires so much sustained work that it becomes the topic of a practice of its own. At Xerox, as in many companies, some people are charged with the task of maintaining connections between the R&D lab and the rest of the corporation. They are developing a practice of crossing these boundaries effectively. Of course, the risk of these boundary practices is that they create their own boundaries, which can prevent them from functioning as brokers. It is

necessary, therefore, to keep asking how the elements of the boundary practice – its enterprise, its relationships, its repertoire – contribute to creating a bridge and how the community deals with its own boundaries. And, sometimes, a new practice in its own right does develop at these boundaries, which is worth paying attention to in its own terms.

- *Peripheries.* Communities often have to take steps to manage their boundaries to serve people who need some service, are curious, or intend to become members. Many communities have found it useful to create some facilities by which outsiders can connect with their practice in peripheral ways. Examples of such facilities include lists of "frequently asked questions," visitors' rooms on websites, open houses and fairs. Some communities have even established "help desks" to provide access to their expertise in a more efficient way. The idea behind many of these facilities is to provide for some boundary activities without overwhelming the community itself with the task of accommodating outsiders' demands. For newcomers, some communities organize introductory events, mentoring relationships, or even formal apprenticeship systems.

Cross-disciplinary projects

In most organizations, members of communities of practice contribute their competence by participating in cross-functional projects and teams that combine the knowledge of multiple practices to get something done. Simultaneous participation in communities of practice and project teams creates learning loops that combine application with capability development. In these double-knit organizations, as Richard McDermott (1999) calls them, the learning and innovation that is inherent in projects is synthesized and disseminated through the home communities of practice of team members. The new knowledge can then be applied and expanded in new projects, and the cycle goes on.

Such a perspective brings up a different way of thinking about these projects. From the standpoint of the task to be accomplished, these projects are cross-disciplinary because they require the contribution of multiple disciplines. But, from the perspective of the development of practices, they are boundary projects. Indeed, participating in these kinds of projects exposes practitioners to others in the context of specific tasks that go beyond the purview of any practice. People confront problems that are outside the realm of their competence but that force them to negotiate their own competence with the competences of others. Such projects provide a great way to sustain a creative tension between experience and competence when our participation in a project leverages and nourishes our participation in a community of practice.

Identities

As I said, you probably know that the earth is round and in orbit around the sun. Of course, it is not a flat plate in the way it appears to be at first glance. You actually want to make sure you know this. It is part of your identity as the kind of well-educated adult you probably are if you are reading this chapter. You may even know that the orbit is not an exact circle, but a slight ellipse. Chances are, however, you do not know the exact distance between the earth and the sun or the precise difference between the apogee and the perigee. This kind of ignorance, your identity can accept without existential angst because your relationship to the communities where such knowledge matters is very peripheral at best.

I am not trying to make you feel self-conscious about your knowledge of astrophysics. There will be no test at the end of this chapter. (Did I hear a sigh of relief? No, no, you are perfectly OK just knowing the earth is round, and many of our fellow human beings have lived very good lives not even knowing that.) My point is that, if knowing is an act of belonging, then our identities are a key structuring element of how we know.

Why focus on identity?

Knowing, learning, and sharing knowledge are not abstract things we do for their own sake. They are part of belonging (Eckert, 1989). When I was working with claims processors in an insurance company, I noticed that their knowing was interwoven in profound ways with their identities as participants in their community of practice. Their job did not have a high status in the company (and in their own eyes, for that matter), so they were careful not to be interested in it more than was absolutely necessary. What they knew about their job, what they tried to understand and what they accepted not to understand about the forms they had to fill out, what they shared with each other, all that was not merely a matter of necessity to get the job done, but it was also a matter of identity. Knowing too much or failing to share a crucial piece of knowledge would be a betrayal of their sense of self and of their community (Wenger, 1998).

In the landscape of communities and boundaries in which we live, we identify with some communities strongly and not at all with others. We define who we are by what is familiar and what is foreign, by what we need to know and what we can safely ignore. You are a cello player, but not the conductor who signals your entry, or the dancer who dances the ballet you are playing, or the lawyer whom you saw this afternoon about your uncle's estate. We define ourselves by what we are not as well as by what we are, by the communities we do not belong to as well as by the ones we do. These relationships change. We move from community to community. In doing so, we carry a bit of each as we go around. Our identities are not something we can turn on and off. You don't cease to be a parent because you go to work. You don't cease to be a nurse because you step out of the hospital. Multimembership is an inherent aspect of our identities.

Identity is crucial to social learning systems for three reasons. First, our identities combine competence and experience into a way of knowing. They are the key to deciding what matters and what does not, with whom we identify and whom we trust, and with whom we must share what we understand. Second, our ability to deal productively with boundaries depends on our ability to engage and suspend our identities. Learning from our interactions with other practices is not just an intellectual matter of translation. It is also a matter of opening up our identities to other ways of being in the world. Third, our identities are the living vessels in which communities and boundaries become realized as an experience of the world. Whenever we belong to multiple communities, we experience the boundary in a personal way. In the process, we create bridges across communities because, in developing our own identities, we deal with these boundaries in ourselves.

Which way is up?

Our identities are not necessarily strong or healthy. Sometimes, they are even self-defeating. In fact, a whole self-help industry has flourished by offering advice for building healthy identities (Giddens, 1991). Navigating the social landscape defined by communities and their boundaries requires a strong identity. Progress can be described in terms of a few crucial qualities that must coexist to constitute a healthy social identity.

- *Connectedness.* Where are enduring social relationships through which an identity gains social depth? An identity is not an abstract idea or a label, such as a title, an ethnic category, or a personality trait. It is a lived experience of belonging (or not belonging). A strong identity involves deep connections with others through shared histories and experiences, reciprocity, affection, and mutual commitments.

- *Expansiveness.* What are the breadth and scope of an identity? A healthy identity will not be exclusively locally defined. It will involve multimembership and cross multiple boundaries. It will seek a wide range of experiences and be open to new possibilities. It will identify with broad communities that lie beyond direct participation.

- *Effectiveness.* Does an identity enable action and participation? Identity is a vehicle for participating in the social world, but it can also lead to non-participation. A healthy identity is socially empowering rather than marginalizing.

There are potential tensions and conflicts between these qualities. How "big" can your identity be and still be engaged as well as effective (not merely an abstract kind of identification)? Can you really think globally and act locally, feel like a citizen of the earth without losing your ability to connect with specific communities? Can you live on the Internet and still have a good marriage? In other words, it is the combination of these qualities that matters. Table 12.3 explores how each mode of belonging contributes to these three qualities.

Table 12.3 Identity dimensions

	Connectedness	Expansiveness	Effectiveness
Engagement	Is there a community to engage with? How far back do you go? What kinds of interactions do you have? What do you do together? Do you trust and are you trusted?	Is there enough variety of contexts and identity-forming experiences, such as logging on the Internet and chatting with strangers, going on a blind date, or visiting a foreign country?	Do you have opportunities to develop socially recognized competences by participating in well-established practices? Are your communities ready to embrace your experience into their practices?
Imagination	Do you have good conversations? Do you talk about your deepest aspirations? Do you listen well?	Can you see yourself as a member of large communities, for instance, a world citizen, the heir of long-lived traditions, the pioneer of a world to come?	Do you understand the big picture well enough to act effectively?
Alignment	Do you keep your commitments to your communities? Do you uphold their principles? Do you give and receive feedback?	Do you follow guidelines that align your actions with broader purposes, such as saving energy or recycling for the sake of the planet?	Do you know the regimes of accountability by which your ideas, actions, and requests will be judged? Can you convince others of the potential of a new idea?

What is doable?

To help identities achieve simultaneously high degrees of local connectedness, global expansiveness, and social effectiveness, here are some design elements to consider:

Home base

Identity needs a place where a person can experience knowing as a form of social competence. Think of a project-based organization, for instance, where people go from one project to the next, spending a few days in-between on the "available" list. The learning that they do in their projects does not have a social "home", unless they can also belong to a community of practice. In such a community, they are not only recognized as competent for the sake of a project, their need to develop their competence is also part of their belonging. Their professional development and the development of the practice go hand in hand: the identity of the community as it evolves parallels the evolution of their own identity. They can talk with peers who understand the way they look at a problem, who appreciate the potential value of a half-baked idea, and who know where the cutting-edge of the practice lies. With such a "home base," people can engage in a diversity of projects and in interactions with other communities without becoming uprooted.

Trajectories

Identity extends in time. It is a trajectory in progress that includes where you have been and where you are going, your history and your aspirations. It brings the past and the future into the experience of the present. Apprentices in traditional apprenticeship, for instance, are not just learning skills, they are exposed to possible futures. By observing and working with journeymen and masters, they develop a sense of trajectory that expands their identity in time (Lave and Wenger, 1991). Members of a community embody a set of paradigmatic trajectories that provide material for newcomers to construct their own trajectory through a community and beyond. In the generational encounter between newcomers and established members, the identities of both get expanded. Newcomers gain a sense of history. And old-timers gain perspective as they revisit their own ways and open future possibilities for others (Wenger, 1998).

A good way to develop identities is to open a set of trajectories that lead to possible futures. The engagement of one's identity then incorporates imagination and alignment: envisioning these possible futures and doing what it takes to get there. These trajectories can be of various types. Inbound trajectories invite newcomers into full membership in a community. Peripheral trajectories allow a person to interact with the community without making a commitment to becoming a full member. Outbound trajectories, such as the ones offered by schools, point to forms of participation outside the current communities.

Multimembership

Identity extends in space, across boundaries. It is neither unitary nor fragmented. It is an experience of multimembership, an intersection of many relationships that you hold into the experience of being a person, at once one and multiple. It is not something we can turn on and off. When we go to work, we don't cease to be parents, and when we go to the theater, we are still an engineer or a waitress. We bring these aspects of our identity to bear to some extent in everything we do. Even though certain aspects of our identities become more salient in different circumstances, it would be an oversimplification to assume that we merely have a multiplicity of separate identities. Such a view would overlook the extent to which our various forms of membership can and do conflict with, influence, complement, and enrich each other. The work that we do in attempts to combine, confront, or reconcile various aspects of our identities has a double effect. It is a source of personal growth. It is also a source of social cohesion because it builds bridges across practices. As a result, our identities shape the social structures we live in. The work of identity constantly reshapes boundaries and reweaves the social fabric of our learning systems.

Combining concurrent forms of membership in multiple communities into one's experience is a way to expand an identity. Of course, we can only combine core membership in a limited number of communities, but we can also have more peripheral forms of participation, or even transitory one, such as visits, sabbaticals, immersion, or one-time projects. Communities that can include in their forms of participation a large portion of the multimembership of their members are more likely to engage their whole identity. If I do not have to pretend that I am not a parent when I am at work, I am more likely to put my heart into what I do.

Fractals

Identity extends across levels. You are having dinner with your family, ensconced in an intense discussion of international politics with your teenagers, living – in the local context of the dinner table – your sense of identification with the global environmental movement. Similarly, you may belong to a local church, but this belonging is usually an expression of your belonging to a religion that includes many other people in many other churches. Engaging at the local level of your church is a way to belong at the broader level of your religion by combining such engagement with imagination (you can picture many other churches with people very much like you expressing similar beliefs, even though you have never met them) and with alignment (in your church you follow rituals that conform with liturgical formats adhered to by all other churches). Note how the three modes of belonging complement each other. Engagement is enriched by the awareness that others share the same beliefs and follow the same guidelines. Conversely, imagining the whole community and understanding the value of its rituals and norms gains concreteness by the ability to engage in a local group.

Combining modes of belonging this way creates "fractal" layers of belonging. More generally, if a community is large, it is a good idea to structure it in layers, as a "fractal" of embedded subcommunities. If a community is large and does not have a fractal structure with local subcommunities in which people can engage actively, then it can easily happen that beyond a small core group various segments of the community feel disconnected. Subcommunities could be defined regionally as local "chapters" of a global community. Some representatives of these local communities then form a global community among them, whose purpose is to connect the local subcommunities into one large global one. This is how some global communities of well engineers have structured their forms of participation at Shell Oil. Subcommunities could also be defined by subspecialties as engineering communities are at DaimlerChrysler, where engineers can join communities specialized in specific components (e.g. wipers, seats, or dashboards) but clustered into broader communities defined according to systems (e.g. body or powertrain). With such a fractal structure, by belonging to your own subcommunity, you experience in a local and direct way your belonging to a much broader community.

Conclusion: participation in social learning systems

The perspective of a social learning system applies to many of our social institutions: our disciplines, our industries, our economic regions, and our organizations. This view has implications at multiple levels.

- For individuals, this perspective highlights the importance of finding the dynamic set of communities they should belong to – centrally and peripherally – and to fashion a meaningful trajectory through these communities over time.

- For communities of practice, it requires a balance between core and boundary processes, so that the practice is both a strong node in the web of interconnections – an enabler of deep learning in a specific area – and, at the same time, highly linked with other parts of the system – a player in systemwide processes of knowledge production, exchange, and transformation.

- For organizations, this perspective implies a need to learn to foster and participate in social learning systems, both inside and outside organizational boundaries. Social learning systems are not defined by, congruent with, or cleanly encompassed in organizations. Organizations can take part in them; they can foster them; they can leverage them; but they cannot fully own or control them.

This paradox could be bad news because the organizational requirements of social learning systems often run counter to traditional management practices (Wenger and Snyder, 2000). The currency of these systems is collegiality, reciprocity, expertise, contributions to the practice, and negotiating a learning agenda; not affiliation to an institution, assigned authority, or commitment to a predefined deliverable. But there is also good news. The knowledge economy will give more primacy to informal systems. In a traditional industrial setting, the formal design of a production system is the primary source of value creation. Think of an assembly line where value derives from the quality of the design of the formal process. Informal processes still exist, but they produce value to the extent that they conform to and serve the formal design. In the knowledge economy, this relationship is inverted. The primary source of value creation lies in informal processes, such as conversations, brainstorming, and pursuing ideas. Formal organizational designs and processes are still important, but they contribute to value creation to the extent that they are in the service of informal processes.

This framework suggests two directions for organizations. On the one hand, they must learn to manage themselves as social learning systems and develop such systems internally. This means:

- giving primacy to the kind of informal learning processes characteristic of communities of practice and designing organizational structures and processes that are in the service of the informal;

- placing a lot of emphasis on the meaningfulness of participation in the organization, on the possibility of building interesting identities, and on community membership as the primary relationship to the organization (Handy, 1989);

- organizing for complexity, working to link the various communities that constitute the learning systems in which the organization operates; offering channels, shared discourses, processes, and technology platforms by which local forms of knowledgeability can have global connections and effects; and providing coordination among practices to create complex knowledge beyond the purview of any practice.

On the other hand, organizations must learn to participate in broader learning systems in which they are only one of many players. Companies have learned to participate as one of many players in economic markets to sell products and services to customers taken as individual decision-makers. In the knowledge economy, however, they must learn to participate in learning systems as well. Knowledge production is becoming more distributed, complex, and diversi-fied, in disciplines and industries (Gibbons *et al.*, 1994); in regional economies such as Silicon Valley (Saxenian, 1996); and among consumers who have the potential of forming communities (Snyder, 1999).

In these learning systems, organizations find the talents they need, new ideas, technological developments, best practices, and learning partners. The rules of participation in social learning systems are different from those of product markets. You don't simply compete; in fact, your most threatening competitor may be your best partner when it comes to learning together. If you hoard your knowledge in a social learning system, you quickly appear as taking more than you give, and you will progressively be excluded from the most significant exchanges.

In a knowledge economy, sustained success for any organization will depend not only on effective participation in economic markets, but, just as importantly and with many of the same players, on knowing how to participate in broader social learning systems.

References

Anderson, Benedict (1983) *Imagined Communities*, London: Verso.

Brown, John Seely and Duguid, Paul (1999) "Organizing knowledge," *Reflections* 1(2).

Eckert, Penelope (1989) *Jocks and Burnouts: Social Categories and Identity in the High School*, New York: Teachers' College Press.

Gibbons, Michael *et al.* (1994) *The New Production of Knowledge: The Dynamics of Science and Research in Contemporary Societies*, London: Sage.

Giddens, Anthony (1991) *Modernity and Self-identity: Self and Society in the Late Modern Age*, Stanford, CA: Stanford University Press.

Handy, Charles (1989) *The Age of Unreason*, Cambridge, MA: Harvard Business School Press.

Lave, Jean and Wenger, Etienne (1991) *Situated Learning: Legitimate Peripheral Participation*, New York: Cambridge University Press.

McDermott, Richard (1999) "Learning across teams: how to build communities of practice in team-based organizations," *Knowledge Management Review* 8 (May/June): 32–6.

Saxenian, Annalee (1996) *Regional Advantage: Culture and Competition in Silicon Valley and Route 128*, Cambridge, MA: Harvard University Press.

Snyder, William (1999) "Organization and world design: the gala's hypotheses," submitted to the Academy of Management, Division of Organizations and the Natural Environment, John M. Jermier, College of Business, University of South Florida, Tampa, FL.

Star, Susan Leigh and Griesemer, J. (1989) "Institutional ecology, 'Translation,' and boundary objects: amateurs and professionals in Berkeley's Museum of Vertebrate Zoology, 1907–1939," *Social Studies of Science* 19: 387–420.

Wenger, Etienne (1998) *Communities of Practice: Learning, Meaning, and Identity*, New York: Cambridge University Press.

Wenger, Etienne and Snyder, William (2000) "Communities of practice? The organizational frontier," *Harvard Business Review* January–February.

13

Beyond networks and hierarchies: latent organizations in the UK television industry

Ken Starkey, Christopher Barnatt and Sue Tempest

Managers in a wide range of industries are facing the challenges of an increasingly uncertain marketplace. One consequence of this new context of growing uncertainty is a reconsideration of existing forms of organizations and, in particular, a shift away from hierarchy and vertical integration toward more flexible network forms of organization. This entails an increased dependence on outsourcing and external market mechanisms, such as subcontracting and licensing. As Morgan (1989) notes, such network organizations operate in subcontracting mode. A small group of central staff set strategic direction and sustain the network over time. Other individuals and organizations are then bought in on a task-by-task basis.

Networks represent an alternative to hierarchies and markets. Hierarchies impose high staffing costs, directly through the need to retain personnel, and indirectly through the needs for administration and supervision. Markets are more efficient in reducing costs but are more risky when it comes to ensuring quality. Networks represent an alternative to both hierarchies and markets with some of the advantages of each, but without some of their disadvantages. Networks reduce costs by externalizing in-house activities, and they guarantee minimum quality by holding out the promise of repeat contracting upon satisfactory performance. However, for networks to be viable over the longer term it is necessary that the volume of transactions is sufficient to sustain relationships more or less continuously, an assumption that is problematic in industries organized around intermittent contracting.

In this chapter we argue that in industries where transactions focus upon intermittent projects, networks can best sustain their effectiveness if they are sustained between projects by what we call latent organizations. Latent organizations are forms of organization that bind together configurations of key actors in ongoing relationships that become active/manifest as and when new projects demand. Because latent organizations offer the means of reuniting key actors for specific projects, they constitute an important source of continuity and of guaranteed quality of output in industries ostensibly characterized by impermanence and change.

We begin the chapter with an elaboration of latent organizations as a viable and necessary organizational form. We then examine latent organizations in the UK television industry. Our research is based upon field and archival research, which is described in the Methodology section on page 269. This is followed by a consideration of the factors that explain the survival and durability of latent organizations. In conclusion, we argue that effective cultural industry production benefits from the long-term relationships that underpin the success of latent organizations in coping with a highly uncertain and risky environment.

Defining the latent organization

Miles and Snow (1986) identified the emergence of network structures in a number of contexts, including cultural industries. A dynamic network comprises a central core which, through the efforts of individual 'brokers', draws upon the services of different specialist agents as and when productive demands dictate. Miles and Snow further argue that such networks are the most effective organizational arrangement to cope with an increasingly turbulent competitive environment. In this chapter, we identify a form of network – the 'latent organization' – which, we argue, is of particular relevance to the changing structures and processes that constitute cultural industries.

In contrast to other forms of network, the latent organization persists through time as a form of organization that is periodically made manifest in particular projects. Latent organizations remain dormant until market demand presents an opportunity for them to reanimate themselves as active production systems. Latent organization provides an alternative to hierarchy, market, and other network forms of organization in contexts where relationships are ongoing but projects are episodic and spread unpredictably over time. Latent organizations offer a unique way of managing the key strategic challenges of controlling costs and ensuring quality in this context, as they guarantee that key players who know and trust each other can be brought together for critical projects on a recurring basis.

It is our contention, therefore, that a useful way of thinking about emerging forms of organization in a culture industry such as television is as forms of 'latent organization' – 'latent' in the sense of 'existing but not developed or manifest' (Oxford English Dictionary). In photography a 'latent image' is not yet made visible as it awaits developing. In the same manner, in cultural industries such as television, particular groupings of individuals and teams of individuals exist as latent configurations of individuals and groups of individuals in the minds of brokers who pull the constituent agents together on a recurring project basis.

Latent organizations, therefore, come to exist when a central broker reconstitutes the same creatively unique set of agent partners on a recurring basis. Latent organizations may therefore be conceptualized as snapshots of particular agent-broker relationships that persist through time. The brokers act as catalysts reactivating the latent coalition into existence, and within such organizational configurations, quality is maintained via a specific broker working with a specific set of agents in order to achieve not just cost and flexibility optimization but in addition some competitive output differentiation. The latter is derived by leveraging value from a shared knowledge of recurring working arrangements between talented individuals who have established a track record of working together.

In terms of relationships, latent organizations are clearly distinguished from other forms of dynamic networks due to the enduring nature of the connections that exist between their broker and agents over time. External parties purchasing the services of such a productive structure hence gain the certainty of drawing upon the services of known individuals who have already climbed a combined learning curve. In other words, latent organizations make it possible to maintain a constant configuration of the same members that can be used intermittently over time. Latent organizations can therefore draw from a shared and evolving knowledge base rooted at the level of the organization and not just its component individuals, thus offering the possibility of leveraging learning and talent synergies.

Crucially, what latent organizations offer is the possibility of creating ongoing relationships, if only to reduce the costs and uncertainties of constant network coupling and decoupling. They offer the opportunity to generate competitive advantage from a specific resource mix in an increasingly networked, competitive, and uncertain production environment. They do this because they constitute a permanent structure that offers ongoing benefits – primarily, an assured level of quality at predictable cost – from what are perceived by their customers as optimal production configurations. They are able to do this because they build upon an accumulation of knowledge and trust that develops as a result of ongoing if episodic relationships. This knowledge and trust are specific to the members of this form of organization. Table 13.1 distinguishes the latent organization from other forms of network.

Latent organizations in the UK television division industry

In UK television, historically, the traditional organizational context for this form of production project has been within large, vertically integrated organizations with their own technical, creative, and facilities experts (Tunstall, 1993; Curran, 1979). Up until the early 1980s, the UK television environment was dominated by a few large, bureaucratic organizations which produced programmes in-house for their own captive, terrestrial broadcast channels. The majority of the production flexibility within the above organizations was achieved with internal reconfigurations of personnel in fixed departments, although some external parties, mainly in the form of creative staff such as actors and writers, were introduced on an ad hoc basis. More recently, there has been a shift towards programmes that are made by independent producers working outside of the confines of the traditionally dominant organizations.

Since the 1980s, the United Kingdom has witnessed marked changes in the structure of its television industry. The UK television industry of the late 1990s contains a complex and diverse array of both independent production

Table 13.1 Distinguishing latent organizations from other network forms

Characteristic	Network	Latent organization
Relationships	Constantly redefined by dictates of market transactions	Enduring
Resource Base	Fluctuating web of agents facilitated by broker on a project-by-project basis	Constant configuration and reconfiguration of same members
Knowledge Base	Individual and transitory for duration of the project	Shared between specific members and developed over time
Differential Offering	Cost effectiveness delivered through functional and numeric flexibility	Trustworthy track record of working together as guarantee of quality

companies and an expanded number of suppliers who amalgamate programmes into channels and distribute them to the viewing public. Millions of viewers have access to cable and satellite channels, whilst the traditional BBC and ITV have also been joined by two new publisher-broadcasters, Channel 4 and Channel 5. These two new entrants have become extremely successful at championing independent programme makers as a major new source of innovation, flexibility, efficiency, and competition. In recent years, the BBC and ITV franchise holder companies have also increasingly moved away from a total reliance on in-house production.

In no small part this has been due to the 1990 Broadcasting Act, which imposed quotas upon the BBC and ITV companies to source at least 25% of their programming from independent producers by 1993. Local political agendas (Home Office, 1988) and increasingly global forces impacting upon the industry have led to the emergence of the 'publisher-broadcaster' model, wherein those who provide programmes to viewers increasingly buy in such product from external suppliers. Twenty years ago, integration of a wide range of staff and production facilities under a single monolithic corporate umbrella was the norm. In the late 1990s, such organizations were increasingly becoming publisher-broadcasters at the centre of organizational networks. This new model has become so pervasive that new entrants to the broadcast television supply marketplace in the UK boast no internal production capacity at all.

As a result of the above changes, we are witnessing a significant shift in the architecture of the TV industry in the UK BBC and ITV franchise holders, along with the other new entrants, may now all be pictured as the brokers of 'primary' programme *amalgamation and supply* networks, with some or all of their production outsourced to independent programme makers who play an increasingly important role in the new architecture. The number of listed independent producers in the UK has grown from a handful of firms in the late 1970s to around 1000 companies commercially active in the production of all genres of first-run television programming (PACT, 1996).

The primary network of amalgamation and supply is supported by a secondary programme production network. This consists of independent producers who typically pull in their resources on a project basis, with performing artists, technical services, writers, directors, and other freelancers coupled to the productive centre as and when required. In turn, these independent programme makers buy in freelance labour resources and production facilities from the marketplace within 'secondary' networks at the production level. The emergent, multinetwork value chain of programme production, amalgamation and distribution in the television industry can be represented as in Figure 13.1.

For many years, the leveraging of established teams in the creation of new programme materials has been common within vertically integrated producer broadcaster organizations. For example, the BBC had few reservations commissioning the successive and successful situation comedies *You Rang M'Lord* and *Oh, Doctor Beeching!* from Jimmy Perry and David Croft, as they were not only delivered from the same writer/producer team, but in addition featured the same cast, and were even set in an identical 1950s setting, as was their previous success *Hi Di Hi!*. However, with the shift towards more external sourcing of programmes from the external marketplace, many feared that the ability of large organizations to constantly draw and redraw from the same successful and specific production teams would be lost. It is therefore within the above context that our concept of latent organization, as detailed in Table 13.1, becomes both identifiable and of critical value.

For example, the commission of any new situation comedy is a risky business. However, a publisher-broadcaster will perceive a far lesser risk in commissioning a new situation comedy if it comes from the pen of the same writer, features the same cast, and is under the same direction as a previous smash hit. Whilst success can never be guaranteed in such a programming genre, the existence of a latent organization that has successfully worked in this genre will allow the leveraging of an existing knowledge base and network of interpersonal relationships.

In particular, the learning curve climbed by all members of the production team of the new show will be less steep. Writers, artists, directors, and other production staff, like most individuals, prefer to work in the same productive and social groupings over time, particularly when these prove successful. Similarly, those looking to source new programmes – especially from the external programme marketplace – feel more comfortable when commissioning them from known organizations, characterized by knowledge and trust, rather than new webs of unknown individuals. A sense of partnership is crucial. As explained by one programme seller:

> Some people don't appreciate that when they get a commission for television it is a partnership. They are not simply going to be funding your idea – we want

Figure 13.1 Multilevel networks across the television value chain

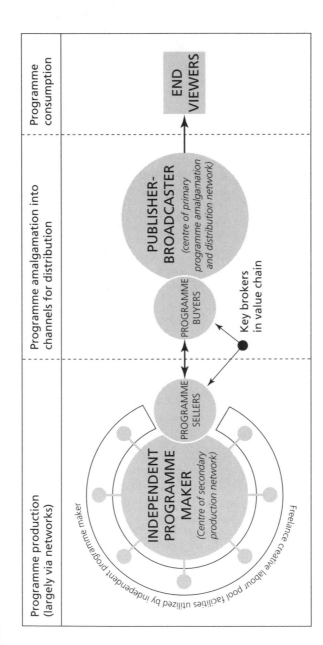

to make a programme with you, not we want to pay you to make a programme – and that therefore they have got to coordinate, they have got to cultivate, to actually have a dialogue, and know where they are strong, and then to listen. It is really those [independent programme makers] that can do that get commissions again.

Individuals and companies develop a reputation for their ability to satisfy these criteria. For example, Hat Trick Productions has become an established source of comedy chat and quiz television programmes, some of which – such as *Clive Anderson Talks Back*, *Clive Anderson All Talk*, and *Whose Line is it Anyway?* – bring together the same production staff, writers, and regular guests/panellists, and, of course, the same host (Clive Anderson). Thus, companies build up a reputation in particular market segments. Another example, Bazal Productions, has an ongoing relationship with the BBC to produce new home improvement and lifestyle shows following its early successes in this recent mass genre and, in particular, its ability to guarantee output from an established group of collaborators which persists, between commissions, as a latent form of organization awaiting remanifestation.

Sustainability of latent organizations

Latent organizations within the television industry are highly dependent on 'brokers' that connect the 'programme buyers' to the 'programme sellers' within the context of an amalgamation and supply network. These two key sets of actors are primarily responsible for maintaining the latent organization upon which the TV networks depend. Firstly, there are the 'programme buyers' (commissioning editors and other managers) who work for the publisher-broadcaster, and who have the ultimate responsibility for buying in programme product. Secondly, there are the 'programme sellers' who work for the independent programme maker, and whose role is to promote their company's ideas, to respond to broadcast tenders, and to engage in commission negotiations related to the same.

For the 'programme sellers', who represent the production talent base, fostering and managing a knowledge of and relationships with the relatively few programme buyers (and their organizations) therefore proves critical. In the words of one independent television producer, 'We don't think up ideas and then try to flog them to broadcasters. We start from finding out what broadcasters want. So we are not really in the business of selling programmes, we are in the business of selling scheduling solutions'. They then have to convince buyers that they can deliver the quality of programme that is required through access to the best mix of knowledge and skills for particular projects through the medium of latent organization.

Successful programme buyers need to foster a strong knowledge of any programme seller's ability to consistently develop and access talent in a given latent organization. Partnership and knowledge develop in tandem. In terms of the skills necessary to develop a latent organization, this means that both programme buyers and sellers will become most successful by obtaining and maintaining the best knowledge of each other. The ability to realize differential advantage from a programme idea relies to a large extent upon pulling together key creative specialists, often at relatively short notice, to meet the demands for cost and quality of the programme buyers. By having particular knowledge combined with relational affiliations, programme sellers with mental maps of latent organizations derive powerful competitive advantage over other programme makers in a talent-driven industry like television. Mental maps of possible organizational configurations are not enough, however, on their own, to realize the value of a latent organization. It is only through effective ongoing relationships that programme buyers can fulfil their broker role to reconvene freelance talent and, thus, make a latent organization manifest for the duration of a particular project.

In situations where buyers expect innovative, quality programming, the creative and financial risks are often high for both programme buyer and seller. Firms seeking differentiation advantage aim to build upon the benefits accruing from repeat contracting with key freelance workers and the ability to reconvene proven production teams. Programme sellers who can transform their knowledge of latent organizations into manifest production teams have competitive advantage over production firms that combine production workers on a more piecemeal basis when pitching for commissions. Programme buyers are more willing to work with production firms that can offer good programming ideas if this is combined with the knowledge and relationships to broker a creative team with a proven track record.

The broker within the production firm, therefore, derives differentiation advantage from the ability to make a latent organization manifest. This is particularly important in high budget cultural work such as drama production. As one manager expressed it, 'Each time we have got the same crew back, the same production manager, the same producer, the same two writers etc., and that is really of the essence'. The ability to reconvene a successful production team in a fluid environment where the majority of workers are essentially 'nomadic' is key to firms seeking advantage from innovative programming. Issues of continuity of the production team seem particularly relevant where mutual understanding of a complex programme concept is the key to realizing the creative potential of the programme idea.

All of the above processes depend on the development of networks of relationships in which the main currencies are knowledge and trust. Such relationship qualities are key defining characteristics in our segmentation of latent organizations from more generic brokerage productive structures. The persistence of latent organizations is not possible without the interaction and coevolution of knowledge, trust, and organization. It is the accumulation of knowledge and trust that determines the enduring nature of latent organizations. For managers of production firms, building up trust relationships with potential programme buyers is crucial for the survival of latent organizations:

... really I think that our best asset is the ideas; the creative bit really and the fact that people now know that we can do it and trust us to do it. I mean the fact that we have got three in the eight [proposals submitted], that are still in the hat. I mean I am really pleased with that, but it is partly to do with the fact that when they were sent in, the person that was reading them knew us and that we could do it, and we targeted them very, very specifically.

There is a specificity of competence which is aligned with a specificity of knowledge and relationship. What is created in such an ongoing relationship is a sense of mutual commitment. This is how the manager of a production firm describes the evolving relationship between a programme buyer and its core suppliers:

... what [name of channel] are doing is choosing to work with only five to ten companies. So basically, they are honing it down so that they serve ten production companies well, rather than serving 60 to 70 badly ... which means that again those ten companies will have the knowledge that they have; they will have a constant supply of work; [the channel] will be confident that they will be able to deliver the work because they will know the work that they do and the standards that they work to. So there is the kind of mutual trust on both sides.

The catalysts of latent organization therefore trade upon the back of a detailed knowledge of the capabilities of practitioners who have worked within a community of shared norms knowing not just what to do, but how, and to what standard. In the past, such communities were nurtured internally within by vertically integrated production giants. However, more often than not, today they have to survive as latent organizations reliant upon key brokers to once again make their talents and achievements manifest in the marketplace.

Conclusions

In UK television, we have witnessed major changes in organizational form, due partly to a fragmentation in programme supply due to new channels, and – in the early 1990s at least – as a result of direct political interventions in the programme supply marketplace forcing the BBC and ITV companies to source 25% of output externally. What traditional, vertically integrated producer-broadcasters like the BBC did provide were environments within which production teams with strong knowledge bases, embedded in relationships established and maintained in durable organizational contexts, could be sustained. We contend that the role of such relationships and the durability of these knowledge bases has been largely ignored by those who have advocated networks as the most suitable form of organization for future television production.

What networked production arrangements across the TV industry have created has been an environment of high uncertainty and high creative risk.

Dynamic networks certainly can provide an efficient (cost-effective) form of network production structure and they are, therefore, suitable for some production genres. But there is a danger that the perpetual reconfiguration of such networks might compromise production effectiveness due to the continual learning curves that new production teams constantly have to renegotiate. We, propose, therefore, that it is only when network structures sacrifice some degree of functional and numeric flexibility by becoming latent organizations that they become capable of delivering the lower-risk and higher-certainty production output that programme buyers increasingly demand to 'guarantee' customer viewing choice.

Effective cultural industry production usually benefits from a combination of those talent synergies, shared knowledge development activities, and production continuity that can best be sustained within a set of relationships that persists and develops over time. This suggests that cultural industry organizational catalysts will prove most successful in trading their wares in the long term if they identify a specific and potentially optimal mix of productive agents whom they seek to hold together as a latent organization over time. This will enable them to offer not just programmes to purchasers thereof but, and in addition, programmes to be produced by known teams with proven track records of quantifiable success.

Within this chapter, the existence and importance of 'latent organization' as an emerging production structure has been surfaced in our analysis of the UK television industry. The trend to sustain and continually reanimate successful latent forms of production network is likely to proliferate for at least three distinct reasons. Firstly, as the commercialization of the cultural industries continues, the risks of costly projects will have to be managed in disaggregated industry structures. Secondly, from the perspective of content sellers, the need to recapitalize on past successes, if only in order to survive in increasingly harsh market conditions, cannot be ignored. Indeed, it might be creatively foolhardy not to reanimate a network from a latent to a manifest state and to start again with a new and untried configuration. Finally, in an industry characterized by great uncertainty and mass unemployment, the desire for on-and off-screen talent to belong to a durable community as a psychological home beyond the death of the vertically integrated company should not be underestimated. Latent forms of organization, therefore, seem likely to persist as points of stability in a dynamic industry, illustrating the value of a shared, sustained, and sustaining social network in achieving cultural industry success.

Acknowledgements

With thanks to those individuals with television companies across the UK whose time and insights have proved invaluable in gathering the empirical data upon which the conclusions of this chapter are founded. The authors would also like to thank Joseph Lampel, Jamal Shamsie, and two anonymous referees for their very helpful comments on previous versions of the chapter.

Methodology

The research presented in this chapter is based upon three sources of qualitative data: a series of 32 interviews with managers and relevant third parties concerned with television production or its performance outcomes; the experience of one of the authors as a freelance programme maker in the television industry; and site visits to observe television workers in action and the functioning and atmosphere of different television firms. Conceptually driven sequential sampling was used whereby those interviewed and events observed unfolded with the emerging concepts and ideas (Miles and Huberman, 1994: 27). Informants were drawn from firms that were regional, national and global in scope. The aim of the study was to maximize the range in order to explore the variation of issues across the sample (Weiss, 1994). Informants were sought from firms recognized for their innovative programme production and commercial success in attracting buyers and viewers for their programmes. To locate these firms and the informants within them various television industry directories were consulted (for example BFI, 1995; PACT, 1996). As the fieldwork progressed, a snowball technique of asking informants who else in the industry was particularly worth talking to was selectively employed (Goodman, 1961).

Informants were sought from the independent production companies that supply the publisher-broadcasters, the larger television companies that both supply and buy programming to fill their schedules, and relevant third parties that have a regulatory or human resource development role within the industry. At the independent production companies informants were sought at the level of managing director, director, or senior partner. Such individuals played a key strategic role in the establishment and/or development of the firm. These individuals frequently retained key hands-on executive producer or director roles on productions, enabling them to offer both strategic and operational insights on the issues surrounding network production in practice. In the larger television companies, informants were drawn from various levels and functions, including senior executive, director of programmes, executive producer, commissioning editor, or human resource manager. Because of the rapid and recurring reorganization occurring in the industry, interviewees were able to draw on a range of experience in different organizational contexts. For example, the majority of those working in now independent production firms had worked previously in large producer-broadcasters, enabling them to draw on that prior experience in discussing the changes occurring in the industry. The formal interviews were conducted during site visits in 1996 and 1997 and supplemented with informal and ongoing discussion with a range of industry contacts. Informants were drawn from two of the three large independent television companies, publisher-broadcasters, 17 independent production firms, and various third-party organizations central to the development and regulation of the industry. Unless otherwise attributed, the quotations in the chapter are drawn from these interviews.

References

Barnatt, C. (1995) *Cyber Business: Mindsets for a Wired Age*, Chichester, UK: John Wiley.

British Film Institute [BFI] (1995) *BFI Film and Television Handbook: 1996*, London, UK: British Film Institute.

Brown, J.S. and Duguid, P. (1991) *Organizational learning and communities-of-practice: Toward a unified view of working, learning and innovation*. Organization Science 2(1): 40–57.

Curran, C. (1979) *A Seamless Robe: Broadcasting Philosophy and Practice*, London, UK: William Collins.

Davidow, W.H. and Malone, M.S. (1992) *The Virtual Corporation*, New York: Harper Business.

Goodman, L.A. (1961) 'Snowball sampling', *Annals of Mathematical Statistics* 32: 148–70.

Home Office (1988) *Broadcasting in the 1990s: Competition, Choice, and Quality – the Government's Plans for Broadcasting Legislation*, London, UK: HMSO.

Kramer, R.M. and Tyler, T.R. (eds) (1996) *Trust in Organizations. Frontiers of Theory and Research*, Thousand Oaks, CA: Sage Publications.

Miles, M.B. and Huberman, A.M. (1994) *Qualitative Data Analysis*, 2nd edn Beverly Hills, CA: Sage.

Miles, R.E. and Snow, C.C. (1986) 'Organizations: New Concepts for New Forms', California Management Rev 28 (Spring) 62–73.

Morgan, G. (1989) *Creative Organization Theory*, Beverly Hills, CA: Sage.

PACT [Producers Alliance for Cinema and Television] (1996) *The PACT Directory of Independent Producers*, London, UK: PACT Ltd.

Piore, M. and Sabel, C. (1984) *The Second Industrial Divide*, New York: Basic Books.

Storper, M. (1989) 'The transition to flexible specialisation in the U.S. film industry: External economies, the division of labour, and the crossing of industrial divides'. Cambridge Journal Economics 13(3): 273–305.

Storper, M. (1993) 'Flexible specialisation in Hollywood: a response to Aksoy and Robin. Cambridge Journal Economics 17: 479–84.

Tunstall, J. (1993) *Television Producers*, London, UK: Routledge.

Weiss, R.S. (1994) *Learning from Strangers: The Art and Method of Qualitative Interview Studies*, New York: The Free Press.

Communities of creation:
managing distributed innovation in turbulent markets
Mohanbir Sawhney and Emanuela Prandelli

In the network economy, no firm is an island. On the one hand, the knowledge required to compete in technology markets is becoming more diverse as markets converge and industries collide. On the other hand, firms are narrowing their knowledge base in an effort to specialize and focus. In this business environment, firms can no longer produce and manage knowledge autonomously. They need to co-operate with their trading partners and customers to create knowledge. While distributed innovation offers exciting possibilities for a firm to capitalize on the creativity of its partners and customers, the management of distributed innovation requires firms to re-examine the mechanisms they use to govern innovation.

An important issue in managing distributed innovation is to find a governance mechanism that strikes a balance between order and chaos. When the locus of innovation is internal to the boundaries of the firm, innovation is managed through a *hierarchical* governance mechanism. Traditional R&D departments epitomize this mechanism. The hierarchical governance mechanism is a closed model, because intellectual property is proprietary to the firm, and the firm retains full control over the development process. The closed model is efficient, because it reduces transaction costs that arise from coordination. However, it does not allow the firm to benefit from the creativity, diversity, and agility of its partners. In a world where innovation, change, and uncertainty are the rules, knowledge socialization is needed for increasing flexibility and reducing the risk of autonomous knowledge production. Firms that function as closed systems have no way to renew themselves. Their main goal is to minimize disturbances, perturbations, and change.[1] Over time, these "machine-like" firms tend to wind down and find it difficult to innovate.[2]

In recent years, a dramatically different model called the "open source movement" has gained currency as a *market-based* mechanism for coordinating distributed innovation. The open source movement, exemplified by products such as the Linux operating system and the Apache web server software, benefit from the creativity and collaborative efforts of a large number of developers. This governance mechanism is completely "open" in that intellectual property rights are not controlled by any single entity. However, the lack of strong governance and the absence of coordination mechanisms tend to make such open systems unstable and susceptible to chaos. Therefore, innovation systems that are either too closed or too open tend to be ineffective in turbulent environments.[3]

We propose a new governance mechanism for managing distributed innovation called a *"community of creation."* The community of creation is a permeable system, with ever-changing boundaries. It lies between the closed hierarchical model of innovation and the open market-based model. Intellectual property rights are owned by the entire community. The community is governed by a central firm that acts as the sponsor and defines the ground rules for participation.

The community of creation model blends the benefits of hierarchies and markets by offering a compromise between too much structure and complete chaos. Firms have traditionally tended to favor centralization and mechanisms to control and protect the knowledge they accumulate over time. On the other extreme, knowledge can be freely traded on the free market, but the free market tends to lack the coordination mechanisms for creating new knowledge. The community of creation is a governance mechanism that reconciles these antithetic tendencies. This mechanism is particularly relevant at a time when knowledge is the main source of economic rents and new knowledge is being created at a furious pace. Today's turbulent markets demand speed and flexibility, variety and cohesiveness. They also demand collaborative knowledge creation with players that are outside the direct control of the firm.

The community of creation model relies on extended participation and distributed production. It overcomes the lack of coordination typical of markets, while emphasizing the contribution to a shared project of all contributors, including peripheral contributors who are usually neglected by firms. Within the community, explicit knowledge as well as tacit knowledge can be shared because participants build up a common context of experience, allowing them to socialize knowledge developed in specific contexts.

The community of creation model is grounded in the concept of *"ba"* suggested by Nonaka and Konno.[4] A *ba* is a shared space for emerging relationships that serves as a foundation for knowledge creation. Participating in a *ba* means transcending one's own limited perspective or boundary and contributing to a dynamic process of knowledge development and sharing. Similarly, participating in a community of creation involves socializing one's individual knowledge and contributing to the creation of a joint output that is superior to the sum of the individual outputs, because new knowledge is created through the emerging relationships. The community functions as a complex adaptive system, changing its configuration as a fractal entity on the basis of the specific contributions it is able to attract and select. It is neither closed nor completely open. Like the *ba*, the community can be physical as well as virtual or mental. Such an emergent system has the ability to self-organize and evolve into higher levels of order that are both more complex and more stable.[5]

The literature on complexity theory and chaos has gained popularity in the areas of organizational design[6] and strategy.[7] However, these ideas can also be fruitfully applied to the management of innovation in turbulent environments. The community of creation allows firms to innovate in a complex environment by maintaining high internal variety and flexibility without degenerating into chaos. The locus of innovation is no longer within the firm; it is within a *community* of members in an opportunity arena. Every member of the community of creation can access and contribute to the community. However, the community has specific rules for membership, and it needs a sponsor as well as a system for managing intellectual property rights that allows members to extract rents from the intellectual property they help to create.

The sociological perspective on knowledge creation and sharing

In recent years, several theorists have considered knowledge as the main source of competitive advantage.[8] These theorists argue that post-industrial society – and indeed the entire economy – is increasingly based on knowledge production. Therefore, the expression "Knowledge Society" is an apt description of the contemporary world. The emergence of the knowledge society can be conceptualized on a *relative* or on an *absolute* basis in relation to industrial society. From the relative perspective, the knowledge society is an evolutionary development, where the production of knowledge becomes *relatively* more important than the production of tangible goods in the economy. From the absolute perspective, the knowledge society represents a more radical change, because it enables new forms of knowledge socialization and new possibilities to store the output of learning across time and space. In the absolute approach, knowledge society is *contrasted* with industrial society as post-industrial society, with capitalism as post-capitalist society, and with modern society as postmodern society.[9]

We favor the absolute or radical point of view, based on the observation that two key factors are changing business in irreversible ways. First, advances in information technology are allowing more effective information and knowledge management. Interactive technologies reduce distances both in time and space, catalyzing knowledge sharing and transfer.[10] Physical distances are often becoming less relevant than cognitive distances. Indeed, the digital revolution can be seen as a "cognitive revolution," a revolutionary way to organize and share knowledge.[11] As Burrus argues, "The great opportunity and challenge ... is to move beyond information access to knowledge-sharing networks, because knowledge increases in value when it is shared."[12] Second, the increasing complexity of the business environment implies a stronger need for knowledge to reduce uncertainty. To overcome individual cognitive limits, knowledge must be shared through a process of socialization.

The importance of sharing in knowledge creation requires a sociological evolution of the traditional *epistemology* of knowledge that is concerned with understanding the origin, nature, and validity of knowledge.[13] In the information age, social, cultural, and technological changes present new challenges to ways of knowing and understanding. These changes require going beyond the traditional focus on solitary knowers, towards a social epistemology.[14]

In the sociological concept, relationships between several kinds of knowledge are social relationships between the individuals and the groups who develop and possess them.[15] As a consequence, creating new knowledge means creating new relationships or new ways to combine and manage existing relationships. Social learning processes based on interaction are increasingly important to transform information (data collected with a specific purpose) into knowledge (information with a specific meaning, integrating past and present information)[16] that is shared at a social level (see Figure 14.1). Several theoretical contributions support this thesis,[17] including the sociology of knowledge,[18] organizational behavior,[19] studies of the social impact of advanced technologies,[20] theories of learning,[21] social systems theories,[22] and international comparative analysis.[23]

From the sociological perspective, knowledge can be defined as:[24]

- socially spread and influenced by social settings;[25]
- a social construction, embedded in a system of individual, lasting relationships;[26]
- based on the interaction of several meanings;[27]
- shared by "agents who process data" through cultural processes;[28]
- shared among organizational members, both demanding and allowing for languages;[29]
- material, but also mental and social;[30]
- developed through participation in "communities of practice";[31]
- catalyzed by the development of network organizational structures;[32] and
- continuously changing: from individual to social, and from tacit so explicit.[33]

Figure 14.1   The sociological view of knowledge co-creation and sharing

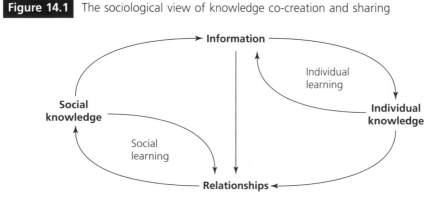

The common denominator of all these approaches is their opposition to the traditional rational-cognitive assumptions about management and organization. The sociological approach views knowledge creation as an emerging, dynamic, and diffuse process.[34] New knowledge is the output of a synergistic interplay between individual contributions and social interactions.[35] These interactions foster the development of a common meaning that transcends individual contributions, as in Nonaka and Konno's concept of *ba*, where knowledge creation is achieved by self-transcendence through a spiraling process of interactions between explicit and tacit knowledge, involving individuals as well as organizations.[36] This process of deep and recurrent knowledge sharing explains the origins of every community – social or political, cultural or scientific – defining riot only its shape, but also its goals.[37]

The sociological perspective on knowledge creation is consistent with the notion that the meaning of reality is the output of an enactment process.[38] It is also consistent with a view of individual and organizational behavior continually striving for innovation, instead of viewing innovation as an outcome of a rigid planning process. Finally, it supports the notion that knowledge is not necessarily owned by individuals, but that it can be distributed across a community of individuals.

Managing distributed innovation: contributing literatures

The sociological perspective on knowledge creation suggests a model for managing the knowledge creation process that is very different from traditional models for managing innovation. Specifically, it demands the recognition of the relevance of social interactions and communities in knowledge creation. Four research streams provide insight into this community-centric model for managing distributed innovation (see Figure 14.2).

First, mechanisms are needed to understand governing organizations that are "partially open." Transaction cost analysis explains why the evolution from markets to hierarchies can be reconciled with an opposite shift from hierarchies to markets or communities. Next, understanding is needed about the nature of communities, different types of communities, and the techniques to manage them. Third, complexity theory provides insights into how such communities can be designed to operate in a complex environment without degenerating into chaos. Specifically, community-based organizations behave like complex adaptive systems, creatively evolving and self-organizing to renew themselves to maintain internal coherence. Finally, it is difficult to sustain the collaborative approach to innovation without appropriate incentives. The important implication of community-based knowledge creation is that intellectual property rights should also be distributed across the community.

Figure 14.2 Communities of creation: contributing literatures

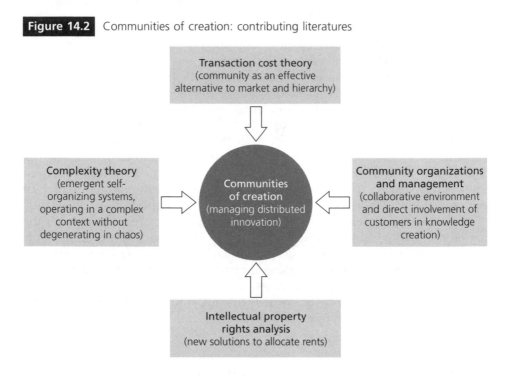

Governance of distributed innovation

The transaction cost analysis (TCA) literature argues that a shift from markets to hierarchies will reduce transaction costs in situations characterized by uncertainty, bounded rationality, and opportunism.[39] TCA is "a perspective that examines the efficiency of alternative mechanisms for minimizing the risk of being exploited by one's exchange partner."[40] This perspective is limited because it focuses on the benefits to the individual firm. Within an economy where processes of knowledge socialization are needed to overcome individual cognitive limits, this firm-centric approach is inadequate. It emphasizes a single-party cost minimization and neglects the interdependence among exchange partners in the pursuit of joint value. Further, it emphasizes the structural features of interorganizational exchange but neglects the processual and behavioral aspects of interorganizational exchange.[41]

At a time when the value chain concept is giving way to value constellations[42] or value networks,[43] the emphasis needs to shift from *minimizing transaction costs* incurred by *individual firms* to *maximizing transactional value* created by *networks of firms*. The transactional value perspective argues that minimizing the transaction costs associated with pre-empting opportunistic behavior is less meaningful than maximizing "net present value of exchange relationships."[44] Thus, interorganizational strategies that have greater joint value may be more *effective*, even though they may involve the use of less *efficient* governance mechanisms from a transaction cost perspective. Consequently, to increase the variety of organizational knowledge and its potential for innovation, a shift may be needed from hierarchies to markets. This is the reverse of what classic TCA would predict.

Within the software industry, this shift has been called the evolution of "agoric systems," where "agora" is the Greek term for a meeting and market place.[45] An agoric system is a software system using market mechanisms, allowing for software to be distributed across and to serve different owners pursuing different goals. The proponents of agoric systems argue that decentralized planning is potentially more rational, since it involves more minds taking into account more information. However, the agoric system is more complex than classic decentralization, because decentralization has to be combined with a central direction of resource allocation. Therefore, a hierarchical structure remains the basic governance mechanism for coordinating knowledge socialization processes, but these processes are fed and catalyzed with the contribution of the market for transaction types that are not effectively supported within hierarchical organizations. For instance, computers have become too complex for central planning, and managing computer networks requires harnessing more knowledge than contained in any one mind. Thus, instead of designing rules that embody fixed decisions, the firm needs to act as a coordinator, designing rules that enable flexible decision making.[46] This idea of combining market and hierarchical models is a central insight in our conception of the community of creation.

Knowledge exchange and co-creation also have important implications for the cost of innovation. Unlike the sharing of physical assets, knowledge sharing does not imply a simple re-distribution of the initial stock of resources. On the contrary, knowledge increases in value when it is shared, thanks to a process of incremental development and diffusion.[47] Therefore, the value of knowledge that is shared can increase more than compensating transaction costs associated with sharing the intellectual capital. The increasing returns to sharing knowledge present new opportunities for developing knowledge assets beyond hierarchies, but within a community of creation that facilitates the shared creation of knowledge.

Shifting the locus of innovation to the community

The network economy requires firms to re-think their boundaries. The distinction between the firm and its customers, suppliers, and competitors is getting blurred. Each of these "interlocutors" of the firm possesses specific and specialized knowledge.[48] Creating barriers to "protect" a company from its suppliers and its clients may be counter-productive, and could even be dangerous, because it reduces the potential variety of knowledge firms need to increase their innovation potential.[49] The firm's problem becomes not how to "defend" itself from the members of its value network, but how to involve them in its processes of knowledge creation.

This perspective of blending production and consumption is reminiscent of the notion of *prosumption* suggested by Alvin Toffler. However, our perspective is different in important ways. Alvin Toffler argues that production and consumption activities are becoming more and more close, often tending to collapse. Toffler suggests that this trend favors the consumption of goods that are self-produced by their final user, within an autarchic regime. In contrast, we argue that the most significant effect of the overlap between production and consumption activities is in a new open and democratic regime of knowledge creation and idea sharing. This model favors socialization of individual contributions and participation in a common final output, to which consumers as well as producers actively contribute.[50]

Any process of knowledge socialization and collective learning is based on relationships of meaning building and sharing. Such relationships cannot be enacted in the absence of a context of co-participation. It is important to create a "cognitive minimum common denominator" for all the individuals and the groups participating in knowledge creation. This context promotes the development of shared values, reciprocity, and mutual trust.[51]

These pre-requisites allow for the emergence of various kinds of communities[52] – "communities of practice"[53] and "communities of knowing,"[54] to name a few.

However, the emergence of the Internet is changing the scale of the community phenomenon.[55] As millions of computer users get connected to the Internet, a number of communities[56] have sprung up to serve consumer needs for communication, information, and entertainment.[57]

In the context of knowledge creation, a key challenge is to create incentives for participation and co-operation within the community by recognizing the contribution of any actor who shares his knowledge assets. In particular, firms need to involve customers who lead their user communities.[58] The concept of direct involvement of customers to create knowledge assets is not new.[59] However, what is new is to shift from a perspective of "exploiting customer knowledge" by the firm to a perspective of "knowledge co-creation" with customers by allowing customers to interact among themselves and involving them as partners in innovation. This is the essence of community-centric innovation development, where co-learning and new knowledge co-development activities are the basis of community formation and operation. To preserve a semblance of order, such a community requires a coordinator, as well as screening mechanisms to avoid misleading contributions. It functions like a "gated community," where residents move about freely inside the community, but only if they satisfy some pre-specified access rules.

The governance structures for a community of creation are informal, but this does not mean that they are necessarily weak. In some cases, control can be based on restricting access to the best information assets. Therefore, the problem becomes how to define the required contribution, as well as the "business card" that allows participation to its holder. Further, the community needs a sponsor who defines the architecture and the standards around which the community is organized. The sponsor facilitates the interaction, and assures that the emergent organization is both efficient and effective. However, facilitator roles typically represent a small component of the community. Most of the community members are "adapters," contributing distinct pieces of the overall value offering. This is the revolutionary aspect of the community – there is a new relevance to the "periphery" relative to the "center" of the network.[60] This is crucial for creating an effective environment for new knowledge creation in a world where knowledge is increasingly distributed and embedded in specific contexts of experience, making it tacit and difficult to communicate. The community-centric innovation model is more democratic than the traditional hierarchical innovation model, because it empowers peripheral players, giving them the right to contribute their own experience and individual knowledge to the final output.[61]

Maintaining balance between order and chaos

Distributed innovation is by nature more chaotic than innovation within a firm's boundaries. Complexity theory is useful for understanding the role of chaos and order in the behavior of systems. Complexity theory argues that organizations that mirror the functioning of natural (organic) systems are better suited for turbulent business environments because of their ability to create and adapt. Firms that structure themselves as complex adaptive systems are able to operate in complex contexts with high degree of flexibility, without degenerating into chaos. They are organic systems open to their environment, creatively evolving and self-organizing to renew themselves maintaining internal coherence.[62]

Such firms focus not only on "how to be a good competitor," but also on "how to be a good evolver," i.e., an adaptive innovator. Their strategies are more robust than focused, calling for the ability to pursue a set of potentially conflicting paths at the same time. Long-term superior performance is achieved by continuously developing and adapting new sources of temporary advantage. These firms continually search for a balance, standardizing designs that work but seeding the population with enough variation to provide a basis for future innovation.[63] The proponents of agoric systems, for instance, argue that the shaping force of consumer choices can result in "computational market ecosystems" that serve human purposes better than anything programmers could plan. This increase in the ability to exploit knowledge may be essential to harness the power of large computational systems.[64]

Complex adaptive systems also call for a very different role of leadership within a firm, and within a firm's ecosystem of partners. Instead of "command-and-control" planning towards well-known goals, leadership needs to promote the richest possible environment for self-organization to occur. This involves three main tasks for the leader,[65] First, the leader needs to promote a clear organizational identity through purpose, principles, strategy, and culture, all of which cumulate into a "shared vision." Second, the leader needs to work to sufficiently de-stabilize the organization: "perturbations" are needed from the equilibrium state of the system[66] to allow the development of a "creative chaos," that in turn favors new knowledge creation in a continuously changing context.[67] Finally, the leader needs to nurture the relationships in an organization, just as a gardener cultivates his garden. This involves promoting the sense of ownership of participants in the success of the joint enterprise; actively favoring collaboration and mutual enrichment within a web-like structure. It also involves promotion of mechanisms for diffused learning that not only favor trial-and-error and risk-taking, but also a tolerance for failures and mistakes.

In summary, the healthy functioning of "living organizations" requires the transfer of both authority and accountability to all the individuals, groups, or institutions who accept responsibility for producing results.[68] This distributed authority favors emergent learning and innovation. The nature of this learning is collective and diffused, and it allows for the enactment of differentiated knowledge contributions within a "map of distributed knowledge."

At the same time, the co-operative nature of such a process favors a strong identification within the group of collaborating partners, who share a common purpose and a specific culture, either professional or social, economic or political. The gradual strengthening of relationships among the members of the group transforms it into a community. This community has a stable structure and basis for existence, but simultaneously evolves and self-organizes to face the challenges of a complex and uncertain environment. Sustaining such a self-organizing community, however, requires that the management of intellectual property rights be addressed.

Allocating economic rents from distributed innovation

If knowledge increases in value when it is shared, and it can be easily reproduced and distributed, how can knowledge be protected and how can its creators capture economic rents? In other words, what incentives can assure the continuous creation and distribution of knowledge needed to fuel innovation?

These questions require reconsideration of existing frameworks for intellectual property rights management. Knowledge socialization and digitization of information progressively detach information from tangible objects, by allowing information to be transported freely and instantaneously. Traditional intellectual property law, with its history of copyrights and patents, was created to protect expression – the "physical transformation" of ideas. In a world where expression and physical transformation are no longer synonymous, and no relevant knowledge can be produced within an autarchic regime, a new approach is needed to assure reliable payment for knowledge creation and sharing. Otherwise, the risk of piracy may stifle innovation, because the only way to protect ideas is not to communicate them, which in turn dramatically reduces their intrinsic value.

Co-operation in knowledge creation requires recognition of the property rights of *ideas*, and not only of their *expressions*. At the same time, intellectual property ownership associated with the product can be separated from the brand. This is what Red Hat Inc. has done by creating Red Hat Linux, a branded version of the Linux operating system. Red Hat owns no intellectual property in Linux, because Linux was developed within a community of creation that owns and maintains the intellectual property upon the product. However, Red Hat adds its brand, services, and support and uses its trademarks as a coordination tool.

Such a model of innovation seems particularly important at a time when most knowledge is being created collaboratively in cyberspace, when networks are what build value and when networks are often created by "giving things away," as both Netscape and Microsoft did.[69] In fact, new technologies seem to have made old rights unenforceable and, at the same time, to have created new potential forms of intellectual property rights. As Thurow argues, "pieces of a human being can not be patented."[70] So the best *way* to protect intellectual property is to act on it. It is not enough to invent and patent. It is important to apply and innovate. This is the basis of competition in the new "Economy of Participation," where value is based more on relationships than on possession, and more on partnership than on ownership.[71] This shift calls into question much of what is known about managing intellectual property.

While traditional intellectual property management frameworks are inadequate to manage the allocation of rents in the community-centric innovation model, it is unclear what mechanisms can take their place. The only certainty is the need for new approaches that recognize that the most innovative ideas are often the output of a joint process, within which it is difficult to discern the specific contributions of single actors. As such, intellectual property rights should vest in the community that creates innovation, rather than belonging to individuals within the community who participate in the process. Further, the new approaches should recognize the trade-off between two inherently conflicting objectives: more production of ideas versus faster distribution. More production can be encouraged by rewarding individual inventors within the community to bring new ideas into existence. However, once a piece of knowledge exists, the social incentives are completely reversed. The wider the use and the faster the distribution of the new knowledge (ideally, by giving the ideas away), the greater the benefit to the community to society.[72] As monopoly power wanes and social interest in encouraging the development of new intellectual property grows, the balance should shift toward favoring the production of new knowledge, and away from being concerned about the distribution of existing knowledge.

Agoric systems offer some interesting clues on how to manage this paradox. To motivate decentralized planning and division of labor, computer scientists have proposed the notion of "encapsulation of information" to manage intellectual property rights. Encapsulation relies on a separation of the internal state and implementation from external behavior, preventing one object from examining or tampering with the contents of another. Combined with communication of access, encapsulation ensures that communication rights are controlled and transferable only by mutual consent. In this way the encapsulation mechanism provides a sphere within which an object may act with complete control and predictability, deeply investing in the production of new knowledge without fearing that the rewards for the creation of valuable code and information would be reduced or destroyed.[73]

Comparing innovation management mechanisms: case studies from the computer industry

The computer industry is an excellent setting to understand the evolution (and revolution) in learning and innovation processes because the technologies that make distributed innovation possible originated in this industry. Within the computer industry, "exemplar" firms have adopted very different governance mechanisms for managing innovation. These extremes highlight the different approaches to knowledge creation and innovation (see Figure 14.3). There are three different models of innovation management in the computer industry.

The first model is exemplified by Xerox, which conducts all its Research and Development "in-house." This is a case of a closed, ordered, and structured approach to innovation, where the control of activities is strictly centralized. Next, we consider are two examples of a completely open market-based approach to innovation: the AlphaWorks unit of IBM, whose role is to serve as IBM's "trading post" for technologies in Silicon Valley, and Linux, the well-known free operating system. Both function as unstructured systems, where new contributions to knowledge creation are "traded" on the market and the innovation process is not controlled by any single entity. Finally, the experience of the Jini group at Sun Microsystems provides an emerging example of

Figure 14.3 Three models of organizing for innovation

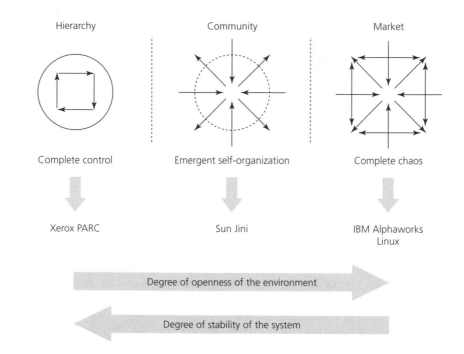

Hierarchy	Community	Market
Complete control	Emergent self-organization	Complete chaos
Xerox PARC	Sun Jini	IBM Alphaworks Linux

Degree of openness of the environment

Degree of stability of the system

community-centric development. The *Sun Community Source License* (SCSL) blends aspects of the proprietary licensing and the "Open Source" licensing models.

Xerox PARC: the closed "hierarchy" model

Ever since its beginnings as the Haloid Company, Xerox has invested a significant portion of its revenues in fundamental and applied research. Many of the technologies that form the basis of computing originated by Xerox. However, such innovations have always been developed directly inside its research laboratories and technology centers in the United States, Canada, Europe, and Japan. The most famous of such labs is the Xerox Palo Alto Research Center (PARC),[74] but it includes several others, like the Digital Imaging Technology Center and the Xrce. Together, they constitute the Xerox Corporate Research and Technology. The locus of innovation is distributed across these entities, but it always stays within the boundaries of the firm. As a consequence, even if this system is decentralized, it is still a closed system; control mechanisms still follow the hierarchical model of organization.

For instance, through the Eureka Knowledge Sharing Process, Xerox favors the growing of community knowledge within its organization. The basic idea is that technical reps around the world have relevant insights. Entering such insights into a database creates documents and peers are able to review, validate, and warrant their content. Thus, the best insights can be used as new knowledge in the field. For example, at XFrance, Eureka deployment allowed for cost savings around 5–10% in parts, time savings around 5–10% on time spent at customer sites, and higher customer satisfaction and employee morale. After three years of using Eureka, Xerox France, historically one of the worst service organizations in Europe, is now considered a benchmark. However, it still does not include external partners and customers in its process of community knowledge creation.

When new partners are needed to develop new product opportunities, they rarely operate as autonomous agents. Most often, they are absorbed into the organization. In fact, to leverage emerging opportunities that do not align with any particular division's near-term strategy or even do not fit into the corporate structure, Xerox has established the "Xerox New Enterprise" (XNE) system. XNE operates much like a venture capital firm: organizations function like small start-ups, while maintaining the benefits of being part of a big company. They are set up for a specified period of time, during which Xerox explores the market to understand how the technology can best be exploited. At the end of this period, a decision is made whether to fold the company into Xerox as a part of a business division, to fold it in as a new unit, to find a strategic partner, or to sell off the company. Thus, the dominant tendency is to limit the autonomy of the participants in Xerox research activities in an effort to maintain centralized control.

This hierarchical system maximizes efficiency, minimizing "perturbations" and focusing innovation efforts toward a common purpose. The goal alignment is facilitated by processes for training and knowledge sharing across the Xerox field service organization and between service technicians and sales representatives. In addition, researchers frequently migrate between research and product operations, facilitating cross-pollination of knowledge within the company. Research teams also engage other divisions early in project development. This helps Xerox people to share their individual competencies and promotes the development of a common language and a strong culture. In fact, one of the most important aspects of Xerox Research is the tight coupling between Research and Corporate Strategy, which improves the alignment between what the Research Centers create and what Xerox is positioned to act on. However, this reduces the variety of potential contributions, as well as the ability of the system to self-organize to face uncertainty. In the long run, the absence of cooperation with external sources of knowledge and innovation could lead to partial stasis. Xerox also maintains a traditional, albeit very effective, approach toward its lead user clients. It studies them through innovative research methods, but it does not involve them in its new knowledge creation processes directly. PARC's pioneering ethnographic research on work practice is well known, as are the firm's competencies in community-based computing, natural languages, physics, psychology, systems, and user interfaces. In all these cases, however, the customers' role tends to remain rather passive.

Finally, Xerox takes an aggressive stand on defending intellectual property, to protect technological capabilities that represent strategic advantages, it uses intellectual property as a form of currency to "barter" with other companies holding interesting patents. Beyond that, licensing of intellectual property to other organizations is considered a revenue stream. Thus, a proprietary-licensing model is the norm at Xerox, as well as in Bell Laboratories (now part of Lucent Technologies), in the Core Research Group of Microsoft Research, and in Hewlett-Packard Laboratories.

This hierarchical model has three main advantages: it provides protection for intellectual property; it guarantees structured innovation (innovation planned within a single responsible organization); and it allows a clear understanding of who owns what. However, it also has important drawbacks. It puts "innovation on a schedule," making its quality dependent solely on the owner organization. If the schedule is ill timed or if the owner organization does not correctly interpret user needs, frustration and lost opportunities can result. It also limits the creativity and the genetic diversity of the ideas, as well as the richness of the dialoguing process that is so important in creating knowledge.

IBM AlphaWorks and Linux: the open "market" model

Both IBM, through its "AlphaWorks" team, and Linux, under the GNU General Public License, have developed an open approach to innovation, cooperating and trading with potential partners in an open "knowledge market." Technologies are promoted through online Web marketing initiatives including banner advertisements, newsgroup postings, and newsletters. In particular, AlphaWorks is chartered with the task of accelerating the transfer of technology out of IBM Research and into new product development, using the Web. The team works to bring IBM researchers amid developers, product groups, and decision-makers together to learn more about the opportunities for commercial use of IBM's emerging technologies. When it makes business sense, AlphaWorks has been a vehicle for IBM support of the "Open Source" movement. The basic idea is simple: a piece of software will evolve more rapidly if programmers on the Internet can co-operate and freely modify its sources, adapting it and fixing possible bugs.

This logic also informs Linux, the best expression of the Open Source Movement since 1991. Its General Public License is designed to make sure that everyone has the opportunity to distribute copies of free software, to receive source code, and to change the same software or to use pieces of it in new free programs. The recipients automatically receive a license from the original licensor to copy, distribute, or modify the Program, subject to the same terms of the original distributor. In this way individual developers have no warranties, but assure themselves a unique opportunity to favor the greatest possible use of their software to the public. In particular, as a benefit to the source code for the Linux kernel being freely distributed, a number of companies have developed their own "distribution" of Linux.

As Linux's mission is to "evangelize the world," disseminating the most recent programs, AlphaWorks' mission is to provide early adopter developers direct access to IBM's emerging "alpha-code" technologies: IBM surfaces the latest software technologies, allowing its lead user clients to download and evaluate them. In this way, AlphaWorks has redefined the way IBM conducts new product development by offering to any innovative developer a chance to work directly with its researchers through discussion forums and to influence the earliest phases of new product development. The feedback generated by AlphaWorks' users is incorporated into IBM's technologies.[75] reducing development time.

AlphaWorks also provides a "venture capital" function for emerging technologies from IBM Research, attracting promising projects, and aiding IBM researchers by building a business case – the so-called AlphaBrief – around emerging technologies. Instead of actual funding, AlphaWorks invests information capital in an IBM Research project, using real-time application developer feedback to discover what the market thinks about the new technologies. This is a lean, flat organization, with low overhead and little infrastructure, It enables IBM to preserve its reputation for providing solid commercial code, while making available "alpha-level" technologies for evaluation and scrutiny by early adopters. This improves the flexibility and increases opportunities to experiment and co-develop innovations.

Both in AlphaWorks and Linux, lead-user clients (leading professional developers) can self-select and self-signal themselves as knowledge co-creators. Participation in the process is voluntary, and the process provides a means for researchers to gain visibility for new technology projects. In AlphaWorks, some product managers have even begun submitting "wish lists" of new technology features that would enhance their products.

Such an approach has a deep impact on intellectual property management: AlphaWorks and Linux place valuable intellectual property in the hands of early adopters at a point in time that can help shape subsequent product development. The major problem in this model is to create the incentives for developers to share their knowledge with the company. One approach IBM has adopted is to offer free commercial licenses to developers for products such as its XML Parser and the source code of its Jikes compiler for Java. In addition to content and commercial opportunity, AlphaWorks also provides Web developers with a community environment. Moderated bulletin boards offer a mechanism for sharing tips, debugging and identifying new uses for emerging technologies. In this way, AlphaWorks has made IBM more responsive to the marketplace. Similarly, Linux allows that if identifiable sections of the modified work are not derived from the original Program and can be reasonably considered independent works in themselves, then the license does not apply to such sections when they are distributed as separate works. However, in both cases, the problem of motivating lead customers still represents a challenge for sustaining this co-operative process.

The second major problem arises in screening mechanisms for single contributions. IBM states a sort of "honor code," forbidding the transmission of material that is unlawful, vulgar, or defamatory. However, IBM does not take responsibility for the content of this Community Exchange. Similarly, Linux asks all the developers to clearly specify every change made in a file and the data of such changes, but it does not take direct responsibility for the quality of the output. If the program should prove defective, the user has to support all the costs for the necessary correction. The absence of a clear form of control and responsibility can potentially lead to fragmentation and chaos, introducing excessive perturbations into the system.

The main benefits of this open market-based approach are rapid innovation, flexibility in schedules and priorities, and self-organization. This approach recognizes that the primary value of a piece of software is the expertise represented by the people who developed it. This is the reason why Microsoft is now trying to determine which portions of its source code to release and whether the code should be licensed or available to everyone via the Internet.[76] This is also the reason that has pushed Sun Microsystems to move away from a closed system, to embrace the new, partially open model of innovation of the community of creation.

On the other hand, the drawbacks of the open system are the absence of clear control over compatibility and quality issues. This can provoke fragmentation and make progress chaotic and undirected. In addition, weak screening mechanisms can dilute the quality of the community and "vitiate" the atmosphere. Finally, this model does not adequately address the issue of incentives to assure the lasting participation of the best knowledge sources in the market. This is the reason why companies like Red Hat are trying to evolve the open system into a community model that can combine the best characteristics of the completely closed and the completely open innovation systems.

Sun's Jini project: the emergent, dynamic and self-organizing "community" model

Sun Microsystems is attempting to combine the advantages of the closed hierarchy-based model and the open market-based model in commercializing its Jini technology. It has created a community of widely available software source code – the so-called "Community Source." The Community Source functions like the Open Source model, but with two significant differences:

- Compatibility among deployed versions of the software is required and enforced through testing, so that internal coherence and cohesion are assured.
- Proprietary modifications and extensions including performance improvements are allowed, granting for variations that catalyze innovation.

These differences make the Community Source a hybrid of the hierarchical proprietary-licensing model favored by Xerox and the open source technology-licensing model implemented by IBM and Linux. According to Sun, the Sun Community Source License (SCSL) is designed to balance the organizations' needs to innovate rapidly in order to grow, with their needs to leverage a community's expertise while maintaining proprietary advantages. Sun recognizes that it is difficult for a single company to house all the expertise it needs to succeed, especially when it wishes to build infrastructure on which other businesses depend. At the same time, it is aware that a completely open system, working like a pure free market, lacks the coordination mechanisms needed to make the process effective as well as efficient.

As complexity theory suggests, systems that are too static and too chaotic are both likely to adapt poorly to a turbulent business context. The SCSL addresses this problem by creating a new way to distribute and share cognitive work involved in innovation. The main attractor is a common interest. The community is architected around this common interest. Such a community is neither a market nor a network. A market consists of spot transactions; its players are not obligated to participate in long-term relationships. Only if there are adequate incentives will such a mechanism sustain itself. As soon as payoffs are considered unfair, trading will tend to grind to a halt. A network, in contrast, consists of strategic alliances that persist over time, but its internal cohesion is generally weak: individuals and institutions are participants, not members. Networks tend to lack a deep common interest, a shared culture, and a legitimized identity.[77] The community model strikes a balance by creating a distributed system of innovation within a group of individuals and/or organizations centered on an infrastructure provided by the so-called "developing organization," like Sun for Jini. Sun invented and built the initial Jini technology infrastructure. Jini is a network-based technology that allows computers and devices like televisions and printers to federate into a single distributed system.[78] Such a network, however, can work only if the underlying protocols and infrastructure become pervasive through a strong community of participants and partners. The SCSL is the mechanism to build such a community around Jini technology. Within this community, Sun is opening the source code for Jini software to the Jini technology licensees, who are free to use, extend, improve, and repair it.

It is important to note that this is a "gated community." It is not open to the general public. On the contrary, it consists only of those who have agreed to the license and have signed the SCSL contract. This contract clearly defines the ground rules for the co-operation, as well as the members' rights and responsibilities. As a consequence, there is no need to create strong screening mechanisms for filtering misleading contributions, as in the case of IBM and Linux.

The Sun CSL envisages an emergent structure, which is neither closed nor open. It is closed outside the gated community, and open inside it. This structure grants SCSL high flexibility without excessive disorder. Sun can screen for the best partners on the market, at the same time allowing for enough variations to favor innovation. Several benefits can derive from such an innovation model. First, outside developers are likely to evolve the technology for their products and markets more rapidly than the original developers would ordinarily be able to do using a proprietary licensing approach. Thus, a new marketplace based on such an infrastructure is created more rapidly than would otherwise be the case. Second, a "short loop" for learning by errors can develop, allowing the firm to internalize mistakes before registering a negative performance on the broader market.[79]

Such a balance between being closed and open – i.e., structured and unstructured organizational forms – has important implications for intellectual property management as well. In particular, because the members of the community are bound by a common license, intellectual property is maintained and there is no requirement to share openly everything developed for the infrastructure. Thus, while error corrections to the licensed technology must be given back to the community, other modifications can remain proprietary at the discretion of the participating organizations that created them; the only requirement is that interfaces must be published for other community members in order to preserve the community openness. As a consequence, in such a cooperative environment, there is a place for both incremental improvements and rewards for invention.

By combining benefits of the proprietary licensing model and the open source model, the community model allows the co-participation of community members to self-maintain over time. The developing organization is responsible for the original code base and the community for the contributed portions, so that intellectual property is protected and structured innovation is granted. Therefore, even if the platform is open, and has published and specified interfaces, it is clear "who knows what" and control over compatibility is ensured, as would be the case in a hierarchical proprietary model. Further, more developers working on the common source code make for higher quality and more rapid innovation: each participant can determine appropriate quality levels and work toward them by himself or with other participants. In other words, the community pulls organizations and developers into a circle of shared concerns, allowing them to self-organize, with only a little assistance from the developing organization.

While there is a schedule for the developing organization's structured innovation, the SCSL provides each participant with freedom and the authority to move forward independently. This helps the company to avoid "alignment gaps"[80] that arise when priorities the owner company assigns to technology development are not aligned with customer priorities. With SCSL, the community members share common source code and can set their own priorities, working on the code as, when, and how much they wish. There is a force that tends to keep the infrastructure stable because all the participants depend on it, but innovation can take place anywhere in the technology base. This is the main idea at the basis of knowledge co-creation and diffuse innovation processes: the *locus* of innovation is no longer in the firm; the locus of innovation is the *community*. To paraphrase Sun, the network is the innovator.

Table 14.1 provides a summary of the main features of the different innovation models. The Proprietary Licensing model by Xerox is a hierarchical model that is closed and structured. This allows for order, but it might lead to a partial stasis. At the opposite end of the continuum, IBM AlphaWorks and Linux Open Source model resemble a free "knowledge market," completely open and unstructured. This model tends to lack coordination and screening mechanisms and could easily degenerate into disorder and chaos. In the middle of the continuum, the Sun Community Source Licensing offers an early example of an "emergent self-organization," where it is closed outside of the community combined with being open inside of it. Within this community of creation, the diversity of the peripheral sources' contributions can enact a creative tension, favoring continuous and diffused innovation while at the

Table 14.1 Key features of models for technology development and licensing

	Proprietary licensing	Community source licensing	Open source licensing
Governance	Hierarchy	Community	Market
Closed/open	Closed system	Emergent system	Open system
Degree of structure	Basically structured	Self-organizing	Basically unstructured
Degree of order	Order	Creative tension	Disorder
Degree of change	Stasis	Emergent self-organization	Chaos
Example	Xerox	Sun	IBM Linux

same time preserving internal cohesion and intellectual property rights Although it is too early to comment on the eventual success of Sun's community-centric model – and several implementation hurdles still remain – there are still important insights to be gleaned from this experiment.

Lessons for managers

A key challenge for managers in the network economy is to set up the rules of the new competitive game, where organizations have continuously to evolve into higher levels of order, both more complex and more stable, to increase innovation without losing internal cohesion. Using the computer industry as the canvas, we have painted a picture of a new approach to innovation, where the *locus* of innovation shifts from the firm to a community. This community is open on the inside, but closed on the outside. It has specific rules for membership. It also needs a sponsor and property rights to prevent it from lapsing into chaos. However, there are several open questions that managers need to consider before they can implement the community of creation model. Table 14.2 summarizes the questions and their answers.

The first important question is: What level of control should the sponsor company maintain? The community of creation requires a sponsor that plays the role of the developing organization. This organization offers a body of intellectual property rights to a community of developers. Ideally, the sponsor should provide the rhythm, but then leave the singers free to play their song. The sponsor also needs to establish rules for ensuring compatibility: everybody can improvise, but nobody can be out of tune. Finally the sponsor needs to provide a business model that rewards innovation and invention by allowing licensees to create proprietary enhancements.

There are rules for membership as well as rules for protecting and recognizing intellectual property rights. The community functions like a democracy – rights are granted, but responsibilities also have to be stated. First, by getting access to intellectual property, members can help each other to refine and improve knowledge far more efficiently than in a closed system. Second, by sharing responsibilities, members are assured their efforts will align with others in the community. Finally, by providing a means to appropriate some specific modifications and establishing a business model tailored for specific needs, the community model encourages and rewards invention.

With respect to the question of how such a community of creation can evolve, the secret is to achieve and preserve a balance between intellectual property rights and responsibilities. If this balance is maintained, the system can combine continuous innovation with internal cohesion, disorder with structure. Such a community can become self-organizing and continue to evolve even in the face of a turbulent environment. For example, Sun's CSL may function like a complex adaptive system by spawning emergent and self-organizing communities that coalesce into interest groups supporting different services. Sub-communities may arise within the SCSL, favoring

Table 14.2   Managing a community of creation: key questions and lessons

Key questions	Lessons for managers
What level of control should the sponsor company maintain?	• It has to "give the rhythm" to the developers' community: it pulls individual organizations and developers into a circle of shared concerns, then allows them to self-organize. • It coordinates individual schedules and priorities, at the same time allowing for emergent modifications. • It helps establish responsibilities to ensure compatibility.
How can property rights be managed?	• Intellectual property has to be maintained and there is no requirement to share openly everything developed for the infrastructure. • Rights have to be directly proportional to responsibilities.
What incentives favor a direct involvement in the long run?	• The sponsor has to provide a business model that encourages and rewards individual invention. • By creating a gated community that is not completely public, quality of innovation within the community is protected.
How can the community evolve?	• Preserving and renewing the balance between continuous innovation and internal cohesion, between openness and closeness • The community has to be conceived as self-referential: tolerance for diversity has to co-exist with redundancy to favor innovation. • The sponsor firm has to fund support for the entire community of licensees as well as for further development
Should the sponsor firm also provide physical support? Can the community remain only virtual?	• A community can not self-maintain during time if physical support is not granted. • The sponsor has to offer different services, depending on the intensity of the individual members' involvement. • At the most advanced level, the company has to make available capital for personalized assistance and co-marketing activities.

rapid and effective innovation. These sub-communities can function as resilient organizations, adapting quickly to changes. Individual users can enter and exit, but the communities keep on living. Thus, they are open structures that maintain self-referentiality, preserving their internal cohesion and carefully balancing tolerance for diversity and redundancy to favor innovation.

For such a mechanism to work effectively, the experience of Sun suggests that the sponsor may need to provide physical support as well. For example,

Sun offers a full spectrum of developer support, sustaining different levels of co-operation, depending on the levels of partners' involvement. "Level A Services" are available for anyone in the community. They include technical and advisory support programs, from white papers to a listing in Sun's online catalog. "Level B Services" can be chosen *a la carte*. They include education and training services, as well as custom-tailored professional services, concerning design, development, and implementation of pilot projects employing Jini technology. Finally, for the community members who want maximum support, Sun offers "Level C Services," granting personalized assistance with co-operative advertising and participation in the Jini technology marketing advisory program. With this layered approach to physical support, Sun eliminates any barriers related to support from affecting the community's potential for distributed innovation.

Theoretical and managerial issues

The different models of innovation pursued within the computer industry represent new ways to distribute not only physical, but also cognitive work. Social relationship extension is needed to reduce knowledge generation costs and risks and to increase the intrinsic value of knowledge, To survive in an increasingly uncertain and complex environment, the firm has to transform its "organizational intelligence" into a new "relational intelligence," enacting an open communication process with its stakeholders.[81] The implications for knowledge creation are evident: the hierarchical structure is no longer the best organizational architecture because it is designed to centralize the organizational intelligence, not to maximize it. Social and cumulative learning processes require new ways of organizing for innovation, even if this means greater chaos and uncertainty. In the network economy, it is much more valuable to play in an orchestra than to be an outstanding soloist. Value creation is the output of a process that encourages creativity and diversity, yet does not allow the players to go out of tune completely.

While these processes are not completely new, the ubiquity of the Internet allows the scale of these processes to be greatly enlarged. The Internet explodes the cognitive capabilities of society. New knowledge and competencies develop, and the intensive deployment of these capabilities catalyzes value generation. Such an increased value can in turn be reinvested in new knowledge creation, leading to a virtuous circle of knowledge creation (see Figure 14.4). This virtuous mechanism has important consequences in finding new ways of managing the tradeoff between leveraging existing knowledge and creating new knowledge. Thanks to knowledge socialization within the "networked digital environment,"[82] tradeoffs such as "isolated-connected," "concentrated-distributed," "de-contextualized-re-contextualized," which characterized the diffusion of knowledge in the industrial economic society, will be mitigated in post-industrial society.

Figure 14.4 The virtuous cycle of knowledge creation in the network economy

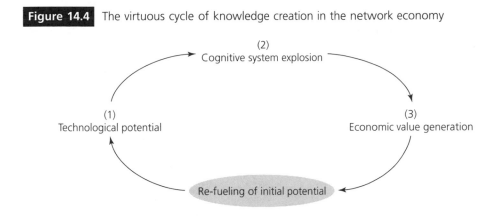

As the potential for organizational connectivity increases, so do the possibilities for developing knowledge socialization and communities of creation.[83] These communities benefit all participants. On the supply side technical solutions to problems in product development or customer service can be socialized; on the demand side, word-of-mouth can increase, modifying product evaluation processes and customer satisfaction.[84] However, the greatest benefits accrue to the developing organization to the extent that it is able to transform itself into a "relational intelligence," evolving from the "physical transformation of products" to the "cognitive transformation of ideas." The community paradigm promotes learning *with* suppliers, instead than *from* them, as well as creating value *with* customers instead than *for* them. This is a radical shift in perspective, from the Learning Company to a new Learning Society, where the boundaries of the firm, its suppliers, and its customers begin to overlap. This overlapping creates more effective, concurrent learning that shortens innovation cycle time, lessens risk, and cuts costs.[85]

Within this society, the firm can evolve into a community where knowledge co-creation is the mechanism through which it self-reproduces over time, coordinating co-operative efforts and redistributing benefits among all the participants. The boundaries of the firm broaden and change over time, becoming highly permeable to differentiated external knowledge contributions (see Figure 14.5). Firms conceived as "communities of creation" can function as complex organic systems whose "extension" and "shape" are defined by the co-operative and co-evolving relationships they enact with their partners.

As a consequence, strategic compatibility between single economic actors is no longer enough. "Cognitive compatibility" is needed as well. This has implications for organizational and knowledge management theories. While knowledge production within the company emphasizes internal assets or the purchase of know-how from the market, the knowledge co-creation process eliminates the dichotomy between "make" and "buy," and what is "inside" and "outside" the firm.

Figure 14.5 The community of creation as an overlap between a community of production and a community of consumption

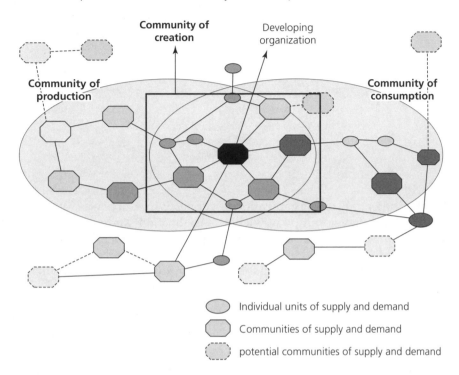

On the supply side, these ideas are finding use in firms like Caterpillar Inc., where an Extranet[86] network has been implemented to favor joint experimentation of new product solutions, promoting co-operation between the company technicians and experts from other organizations. The objective is to reduce turnaround time on product design by inviting experts to collaborate within exclusive "virtual spaces" where they can exchange files and CAD/CAM applications in real-time. Similarly, the Italian car producer Fiat has since 1990 been working on projects to integrate knowledge held by several institutions and firms outside Fiat. In addition, individual business units co-operate in co-design activities with suppliers of components, progressively increasing the autonomy of such partners in suggesting innovation.[87]

Co-operation in knowledge creation is increasing on the demand side, as well. Fashion Box, the Italian producer of the label "Replay," allowed its customers to design T-shirts online in a project called E-Play. The Internet Underground Music Archive (IUMA) invites customers to take part in virtual auditions, interact among themselves, and jointly decide which artistes to promote.[88] Similarly, Adobe, one of the world's largest software companies considers the buying experience as part of a direct and ongoing dialogue with the company and other customers via the Web.

The community of creation model overcomes the rigid and centralized control mechanisms that are typical of hierarchical structures and emphasizes the role of peripheral knowledge contributors. At the same time, however, it preserves the coordination mechanisms that promote "encounters" between strategic assets that are often too dispersed to "meet" on the free market. Self-organization is the hallmark of communities where participants tend to self-signal and self-segment, like in an ideal *ba* that acts as a platform to concentrate distributed knowledge assets and intellectualizing capabilities within a common knowledge creation process. At the same time, implicit and explicit sanction mechanisms and the assignment of individual responsibilities assure that community participation is limited to those who are really interested in knowledge sharing. This regulation of access assures the quality of the joint innovation process.

However, this is still a definition of the community of creation model in terms of, and in relation to, alternative models for managing innovation. There are conditions that are necessary albeit not sufficient, to define the Community of Creation as a new, distinct organizational architecture. Specifically, the development of a Community of Creation requires:

- a common interest,
- a sense of belonging,
- an explicit economic purpose,
- a sponsor,
- a shared language,
- ground rules for participation,
- mechanisms to manage intellectual property rights,
- physical support of the sponsor, and
- co-operation as a key success factor.

The community of creation begins with a reconfiguration of cognitive labor through information technology. It results in the transformation of the firm into a "res cogitans,"[89] a relational intelligence that leverages existing knowledge and builds new knowledge through processes of socialization.

The managerial challenge in developing communities of creation is to balance order and disorder, stasis and chaos, intellectual property rights and individual responsibilities, common priorities and flexibility, and tolerance for diversity and redundancy. Only if firms can continuously feed and renew this creative tension will they be able to catalyze innovation in a complex environment, maintaining high variety and variability, without degenerating into chaos.

Notes

1. See S. Vicari. *L'Impresa Vivente* (Milano: Etaslibri, 1991); S. Vicari, *La creatività d'impresa. Tra caso e necessità* (Milano: Etaslibri, 1998): S. Vicari and G. Troilo, "Errors and learning in organizations," in G. von Krogh, J. Roos. and D. Klein, eds., *Knowing in the Firm: Understanding, Managing and Measuring Knowledge* (London: Sage, 1998); S. Vicari and G. Troilo, "Organizational creativity: a new perspective from cognitive systems theory," in *Proceedings of the Second Conference on Comparative Studies of Knowledge Creation* St. Gallen, Switzerland, 1998.

2. E.D. Beinhocker, "Strategy at the edge of chaos," *McKinsey Quarterly*, 1(1997): 24–39.

3. M.D. Youngblood, "Leadership at the edge of chaos: from control to creativity," *Planning Review*, 5 (1997): 8–14.

4. I. Nonaka and N. Konno, "The concept of 'ba': building a foundation for knowledge creation," *California Management Review*, 40/3 (Spring 1998): 40–54.

5. For more on theory of chaos, see A. Van de Vliet, "Order from chaos," *Management Today* (November 1994), pp. 62–5; S. Kauffman, *At Home in the Universe: The Search for Laws of Self Organization and Complexity* (New York, NY: Oxford University Press. 1995); Beinhocker, op. cit., pp. 46–53; Youngblood, op. cit.; P. Cilliers, *Complexity and Postmodernism: Understanding Complex System* (London: Routledge. 1998).

6. Kauffman, op. cit.

7. K. Eisenhardt and S.L. Brown, "Competing on the edge: strategy as structured chaos," *Long Range Planning*, 5 (1998): 786–9.

8. For a fuller description of knowledge creation, see: I. Nonaka, "Toward middle-up-down management: accelerating information creation," *Sloan Management Review*, 29/33 (Spring 1988): 9–18; I. Nonaka, "The knowledge-creating company," *Harvard Business Review*, 69/6 (November/December 1991): 96–104; J.L. Badaracco, *The Knowledge Link: How Firms Compete Through Strategic Alliances* (Boston, MA: Harvard Business School Press. 1991); Vicari (1991), op. cit.; B. Kogut and U. Zander, "Knowledge of the firm, combinative capabilities, and the replication of technology," *Organization Science*, 3 (1992): 383–96; J.B. Quinn, *Intelligent Enterprise: A Knowledge and Service Based Paradigm for Industry* (New York. NY: The Free Press. 1992); P.F. Drucker, *Post-Capitalist Society* (Oxford: Butterworth Heinemann, 1993); A.D. Garvin, "Building a learning organization," *Harvard Business Review*, 71/4 (July/August 1993): 78–91; D. Leonard, *Wellspring of Knowledge: Building and Sustaining the Sources of Innovation* (Boston, MA: Harvard Business School Press, 1995): I. Nonaka and H. Takeuchi, *The Knowledge-Creating Company* (New York, NY: Oxford University Press, 1995); G. von Krogh and J. Roos. *Managing Knowledge: Perspectives on Cooperation and Competition* (Thousand Oaks, CA: Sage Publications, 1996).

9. G. Böhme, "The structures and prospects of knowledge society," *Social Science. Information sur les sciences sociales*, 3 (1997): 447–68.

10. L. Applegate, *Managing in the Information Age* (Boston. MA: Harvard Business School Press, 1996); F. Cairncross, *The Death of Distance: How the Communication Revolution Will Change Our Lives* (Boston, MA: Harvard Business School Press, 1997).

11. E. Rullani, "Tecnologie che generano valore: divisione del lavoro cognitivo e rivoluzione digitale," *Economia e Politica industriale*. 93 (1997).

12. From an interview to Daniel Burrus, available at www.asaenet.org/publications/Amjun97/6norris.htm, p. 2.

13. See F.F. Schmitt, ed., *Socializing Epistemology – The Social Dimensions of Knowledge* (Boston. MA: Rowman & Littlefield, 1994); G. von Krogh and J. Roos, *Organizational Epistemology* (New York, NY: St. Martin's Press, 1995).

14. A.I. Goldman, *Knowledge in a Social World* (Oxford: Oxford University Press, 1999).

15. Böhme argues, "As a concept in a critical analysis of contemporary society, it makes it possible to examine the relations between the knowledge forms themselves as social relations between the bearers of knowledge and their groups. Grasped as cultural capital, knowledge is comprehended as a power factor, a social development potential and a source of opportunities." Böhme, op. cit., p. 458.

16. There is a rich literature on the differences between data, information, and knowledge. See Vicari (1991), op. cit.; D.M. Rogers Amildon, "The challenge of fifth generation R&D," *Research Technology Management* (July/August 1996); Rullani, op. cit.

17. The origins of knowledge as a social construction can be ascribed to Durkheim. He was the first to note that, by sharing knowledge, groups can develop and stock knowledge in ways that go beyond every individual's cognitive capacities.

18. M. Boisot, *Information Space: A Framework for Analyzing Learning in Organizations, Institutions and Cultures* (New York, NY: Routledge, 1995a); Böhme, op. cit.

19. Nonaka and Takeuchi, op. cit.

20. T. Durand, "The dynamics of cognitive technological maps," in Lorange *et al.*, eds., *Implementing Strategic Processes: Change, Learning, and Co-operation* (Oxford: Blackwell, 1993).

21. B. Levitt and J. March, "Organizational learning," *Annual Review of Sociology*, 14 (1988): 3 19–340; R. Stata, "Organizational learning: the key to management innovation." *Sloan Management Review*, 30/3 (Spring 1989): 63–74; G. Huber, "Organizational learning: the contributing processes and the literatures," *Organization Science*, 1 (1991): 88–115.

22. S. Vicari (1991), op. cit.; G. von Krogh and S. Vicari, "An autopoiesis approach to experimental strategic learning," in Lorange, Chakravarthy, Roos, and Van de Ven, eds., *Strategic Processes: Designing for the 1990s* (London: Basil Blackwell, 1993); von Krogh and Roos (1996), op. cit.

23. G. Hedlund and I. Nonaka, "Models of knowledge management in the West and Japan." in Lorange *et al.*, eds., op. cit.

24. See also F. Blackler, "Knowledge and the theory of organizations: organizations as activity systems and the reframing of management," *Journal of Management Studies*, 6 (1993): 863–84.

25. A. Schutz, *On Phenomenology and Social Relations* (Chicago, IL: University of Chicago Press, 1970); E. Hutchins, "Understanding micronesian navigation." in D. Genter and A. Stevens, eds., *Mental Models* (Hillsdale, N.J: Erlbaum, 1983).

26. P. Berger and T. Luckmann, *The Social Construction of Reality* (New York. NY: Penguin, 1966); K.E. Weick. *The Social Psychology of Organization* (New York. NY: Random House, 1979); Kogut and Zander, op. cit.

27. J. Derrida, *Writing and Difference* (Chicago, IL: Chicago University Press, 1978).

28. M. Boisot (1995a), op. cit.; M. Boisot, "Is your firm a creative destroyer? Competitive learning and knowledge flows in the technological strategies of firms," *Research Policy*, 24 (1995b): 589–606; M. Boisot, D. Griffiths, and V. Moles, "The dilemma of competence: differentiation versus integration in the pursuit of learning," in R. Sanchez and A. Heene, eds., *Strategic Learning and Knowledge Management*, (Chichester: John Wiley & Sons, 1997).

29. G. von Krogh, J. Roos, and K. Slocum, "An Essay on Corporate Epistemology," in G. Von Krogh and J. Roos, eds., op. cit.

30. B. Latour, *Science in Action* (Cambridge, MA: Harvard University Press, 1987).

31. By the expression "community of practice" we mean "a sustained, cohesive group of people with a common purpose, identity for members, and a common environment using shared knowledge, language, interactions, protocols, beliefs, and other factors not found in job descriptions, project documentation or business processes." W.L. Miller, "A Broader Mission for R&D," *Research Technology Management*, 38/6 (November/December 1995): 24–36. For more information about communities of practice, see also J. Lave and E. Wenger, *Peripheral Legitimated Learning* (Cambridge: Cambridge University Press. 1991); E. Wenger, *Communities of Practice: Learning, Meaning, and Identity* (Cambridge: Cambridge University Press, 1998).

32. B. Di Bernardo and E. Rullani, *Il management e le macchine* (Bologna: Il Mulino, 1990); E. Rullani, "Divisione del lavoro e reti di impresa: il governo della complessita," in F. Belussi, ed., *Nuovi Modelli d'Impresa – Gerarchie Organizzative e imprese a rete* (Milano: Franco Angeli, 1992).

33. Nonaka (1991), op. cit.; G. von Krogh and J. Roos, "From knowledge to competitive advantage," in Nordhaug, ed., *Strategic Human Resource Management* (Oslo: Norwegian University Press. 1993); Nonaka and Takeuchi, op. cit.; A.C. Inkpen, "Creating knowledge through collaboration." *California Management Review*, 39/1 (Fall 1996): 123–40.

34. Youngblood, op. cit.; S. Micelli, "Il consumo post-fordista: dalla cultura della delega alla cultura della interazione," in Rullani and Romano, eds., *Il postfordismo* (Milano: Etaslibri. 1998);

S. Micelli, "Comunità virtuali: apprendimento e valore nell'economia delle reti," *Economia e Politica Industriale*, 1 (1999); Vicari and Troilo, op. cit.

35. M. Kenney, "The role of information. Knowledge and value in the late 20th century," *Futures*, 8 (1996): 695–707.
36. Nonaka and Konno, op. cit.; H. Schimizu, "Ba-principle: new logic for the real-time emergence of information," *Holonics*, 5/1 (1995): 67–79.
37. J. Caraca and M.M. Carrilho, "The role of sharing in circulation of knowledge," *Futures*, 8 (1996).
38. Weick, op. cit.; Vicari (1991), op. cit.
39. O.E. Williamson, *The Economic Institutions of Capitalism* (New York, NY: The Free Press, 1985).
40. B. Zajac [p. 581] in N. Nicholson, ed., *The Blackwell Encyclopedic Dictionary of Organizational Behaviour [Blackwell Encyclopedias of Management]* (Oxford: Blackwell, 1998).
41. B. Zajac and C. Olsen, "From transaction costs to transactional value analysis: implications for the study of interorganizational strategies." *Journal of Management Studies*, 30 (1993): 131–45.
42. R. Normann and R. Ramirez, "From value chain to value constellation: designing interactive strategy," *Harvard Business Review*, 71/4 (July/August 1993): 65–77.
43. For an overview, see S. Balasubramanian, V.V. Krishnan, and M. Sawhney, "New offering realization in the networked digital environment," Working Paper, Northwestern University, Chicago, 1998; M. Sawhney and P. Kotler, "Marketing in the age of information democracy," Working Paper, Northwestern University Chicago, 1999; D. Tapscott, *Creating Value in the Network Economy* (Boston, MA: Harvard Business School Press, 1999).
44. Zajac and Olsen, op. cit., p. 137.
45. M.S. Miller and K.E. Drexler, "Markets and computation: agoric open systems," in B. Huberma, ed., *The Ecology of Computation* (New York, NY: North-Holland, Elsevier Science Publisher, 1988).
46. Miller and Drexler, op. cit.
47. J.B. Quinn, P. Anderson, and S. Finkelstein "Leveraging intellect." *Academy of Management Executive*, 10 (1996): 7–27.
48. Micelli (1999), op. cit.; Micelli and Prandelli, "Net marketing: gestire le relazioni di mercato in un mondo senza consumatori," *Economia & Management* (2000).
49. Leonard, op. cit.; R. Fiocca and E. Prandelli, "La reingegnerizzazione dei processi di marketing orientatata alla time-based competition," in E. Valdani and F. Ancarani, eds., *La reingegnerizzazione dei processi di marketing* (Milano: Egea, 1997); F.E. Webster, Jr., "Interactivity and marketing paradigm shift," *Journal of Interactive Marketing*, 1 (1998): 54–5.
50. For a review of the literature on the development of a community, see B. Cova, "Community and consumption: towards a definition of the 'linking value' of product and services," *European Journal of Marketing* (1997), pp. 297–316.
51. M. Taylor, *The Possibility of Cooperation* (Cambridge: Cambridge University Press, 1987).
52. I. Nonaka, "Come un'organizzazione crea conoscenza." *Economia & Managerment*, 2 (1994); K.E. Sveiby, "Transfer of knowledge and the information processing professions." *European Management Journal* 4 (1996): 379–88: J. Hagel and A.G. Armstrong, *Net Gain: Expanding Markets Through Virtual Communities* (Boston, MA: Harvard Business School Press, 1997).
53. Lave and Wenger, op. cit.; Wenger, op. cit.
54. R.J. Boland, Jr., and R. Tenkasi, "Perspective making and perspective taking in communities of knowing." *Organization Science*, 4 (1995): 350–72.
55. See also H. Rheingold, *The Virtual Community: Homesteading on the Electronic Frontier* (Reading, MA: Addison-Wesley, 1993); L. Komito, "The net as a foraging society: flexible communities,' *Information Society* (1998), pp. 97–106; V. Kozinets, "E-Tribalized Marketing?: the strategic implications of virtual communities of consumption," *European Management Journal*, 3 (1999): 252–64: Micelli and Prandelli, op. cit.
56. By the year 2000, it is estimated that over 40 million people worldwide will participate in "virtual communities." Kozinets, op. cit., p. 253.
57. A. Armstrong and J. Hagel, "The real value of online communities," *Harvard Business Review*, 74/3 (May/June 1996): 134–41.
58. Kozinets, op. cit., p. 256.

59. E. von Hippel, "Sticky information and the locus of problem solving: implications for innovation," *Management Science*, 4 (1994): 429–39; E. von Hippel, "Economics of product development by users: the impact of 'sticky' local information," *Management Science*, 5 (1998): 629–44.
60. Micelli and Prandelli, op. cit.
61. Sawhney and Kotler, op. cit.
62. Vicari (1991), op. cit.; Kauffman, op. cit.; Beinhocker, op. cit.; Youngblood, op. cit.
63. Beinhocker, op. cit.
64. Miller and Drexler, op. cit.
65. Youngblood, op. cit.
66. Vicari (1991, 1998), op. cit.; Vicari and Troilo, op. cit.
67. Nonaka and Takeuchi, op. cit.
68. Youngblood, op. cit.
69. M. Iansiti and A. MacCormack, "Developing product on internet time," *Harvard Business Review*, 75/5 (September/October 1997): 108–17.
70. L.C. Thurow, "Needed: a new system of intellectual property rights," *Harvard Business Review*, 75/5 (September/October 1997): 94–103.
71. Drucker, op. cit.
72. Thurow, op. cit., p. 98.
73. Miller and Drexler, op. cit.
74. Xerox PARC is a research center divided into five major laboratories, several smaller research groups, and an operational support department. These include Eletronic Materials Laboratories, Computer Science Laboratory, Document Hardware Laboratory, Information Science and Technologies Laboratory, Systems and Practices Laboratory; an Office of the Chief Technologist and the RED, Research in Experimental Documents.
75. During the past two years, thirty percent of the technologies posted to AlphaWorks have been incorporated into IBM products or licensed to third party developers. By comparison, typical venture capital firms boast a ten percent success rate for new technologies.
76. Microsoft President Steve Ballmer argues: "We do have a team out thinking through what kind of strategy is appropriate to make our source code, or parts of it, more available to customers so they can be more effective in what they do … I don't call that a full embrace of the open source model … On the other hand, we're trying to understand what it is that really brings the benefit." Diederich, 1999 [Note to author: Need full reference for Diederich].
77. For a discussion on the relevance of a recognized identity as the basis for the emergence of strong communities, see Lave and Wenger, op. cit.; Wenger, op. cit.
78. For instance, connecting home appliances allows for controlling them centrally, connecting office equipment allows for people to share resources, and so on.
79. Vicari (1991), op. cit.; S. Vicari, "Verso il resource-based management," in S. Vicari, ed., *Brand Equity: Il potenziale generativo della fiducia*, (Milano: Egea, 1995): Vicari and Troilo, op. cit.; Balasubramanian, Krishnan, and Sawhney, op. cit.
80. For the notion of the "alignment gap," see E. Valdani. B. Busacca and M. Costabile, *La soddisfazione del cliente. Un'indagine empirica sulle imprese italiane* (Milano: Egea, 1994); M. Sawhney and E. Prandelli, "Beyond customer knowledge management: customers as knowledge co-creators," in J. Malhotra, ed., *Knowledge Management and Virtual Organization*, (2000).
81. E. Rullani, "Prefazione," in *Reti di marketing. Dal marketing della merci al marketing delle relazioni*, (Milano: Etaslibri, 1993).
82. Balasubramanian, Krishnan and Sawhney, op. cit.
83. Boland and Tensaki, op. cit.
84. Adobe states that its online customer community, known as user-to-user forums, provides a virtual place where customers with common personal and professional interests can congregate, trade industry gossip and practical product tips, share ideas, and create a buzz around Adobe products. As this online community solidifies and expands, Adobe believes customers will become better spokespeople for Adobe than Adobe itself. From Gartner Group's Business Technology Journal: http://btj.gartner.com

85. Miller, op. cit., p. 24.
86. The Extranet represents the bridge between the public Internet and the private corporate Intranet, connecting multiple organizations on-line behind virtual fire-walls, where those who share in trusted circles can network and co-ordinate their value-activities in order to achieve common business objectives. This definition is from "The extranet solution: the business software application for the 21st century" published within the Web site by OneSoft Corporation.
87. B. Auteri, "Nuove basi organizzative per l'impresa eccellente," *L'Impresa*, 1(1994); L. Falduto and M. Palitto, "Un modello manageriale per l'organizzazione che apprende." *L'impresa*, 7 (1996).
88. J.F. Rayport and J.J. Sviokla, "Exploiting the virtual value chain," *Harvard Business Review*, 73/6 (November/December 1995): 75–85.
89. Rullani (1997), op. cit.

Knowledge management

Introduction

Knowledge management is a recent term with a long history. The novelty of the contemporary concern for 'knowledge management' lies in its emergence as a key part of managerial discourse rather than merely an abstract, academic concept. The flood of management interest in 'knowledge' reflects not just an awareness of the value of intangible assets but also that *organizational* innovation – perhaps more than product or process innovation – is vital to sustainable competitiveness. Knowledge management acknowledges – even celebrates – the innovative potential of the prosaic. In an important sense, knowledge management represents a continuation of management's turn to new organizational forms, empowerment and teamworking in search of incremental innovations in working practices. Dating from the early 1980s, many of these initiatives were categorized as part of the 'Japanization' movement. Knowledge management represents an extension of these concerns from manufacturing to the service sector, and to professional and clerical work. 'Japanization' represented a managerial awareness that Taylorized work routines were contrary to the competitive necessity of flexibility. Coupled with successive waves of downsizing, delayering, and corporate restructuring, this awareness of the importance of the tacit knowledge held by local workgroups, has proved fertile ground for the introduction of knowledge management initiatives. If tacit knowledge is an asset then it is all but impossible to value or trade and intensely difficult to 'manage'. In Chapter 15 Paul Adler explores the complex interaction between organizational structures and the changing nature of the social 'glue' that binds organizations together. Above all, in the most dynamic sectors of advanced capitalism Adler provocatively suggests that 'reflective trust' is eroding not just hierarchy but the legitimacy of capitalism itself.

In the broadest sense, *all* work is 'knowledge work'. That is, even the most routinized work processes require the development of individual and collective capabilities that make us all 'architects' rather than 'bees', able to envisage the labour process and alternatives to it. All work requires the mobilization of 'tacit' knowledge to be efficient, safe, or to offer the possibilities of unmanaged social space at work. 'Tacit' knowledge represents the hidden, latent pools of expertise and innovation that knowledge management seeks to drain. By its very nature, tacit knowledge is endlessly replenished and ceaselessly imaginative. The very existence of tacit knowledge, its covert – and sometimes oppositional – nature is an affront to the very idea of management. The complexities of the concept of knowledge and knowledge work are considered in Chapter 16. Again, knowledge management signifies a supreme managerial self-confidence, an assurance that organizational systems need no longer be geared towards nullifying employees' practical expertise but to convert it into a public good willingly shared by all. Taylorism is no longer required to prise tacit knowledge from recalcitrant workforces: if only appropriate knowledge management mechanisms can be embedded in everyday routines to convert local, tacit knowledge into codified practices. For this is the paradox of tacit knowledge. Unlike codified knowledge that is not tied to a specific time, place or workgroup, tacit knowledge is dynamic and inescapably embedded in the collective experience of a particular workgroup. The few longitudinal empirical studies of the introduction of knowledge management systems are chastening tales of vaulting managerial ambitions and patchy outcomes. Chapter 17 suggests a much more modest managerial agenda whose key objective is to allow space for the expansion of 'practical mastery'. Management, in this view, has to understand the limits of knowledge management and the inevitably elusive nature of tacit knowledge.

Yet for all its imprecision the term knowledge work undoubtedly captures something of the contemporary experience. Certainly, much of today's 'knowledge work' is nothing more than yesterday's expert or professional labour. To this group we can add those involved in the production of professional services such as consultancy or work that overlaps with the creative industries, graphic designers and advertising executives. This is the context for Mats Alvesson's investigation of knowledge work in the advertising industry in Chapter 18. Above all, Alvesson contends that the products and services produced by knowledge work are difficult to specify in advance and that the knowledge labour process is equally difficult to monitor. Similarly, Chapter 19 looks at knowledge work and knowledge management in the context of a global pharmaceutical company. Here, McKinlay invokes the figure of the 'flaneur' to capture the marginal and ephemeral nature of groups seeking to open up unmanaged spaces for radical innovation. But this is not the whole story. For if we were to adopt a highly restrictive definition of 'knowledge work' our rigour might be at the expense of registering vital changes in the nature of labour. The readiness with which survey respondents affirm that they see themselves as 'knowledge workers' suggests not just the wide currency of the term but also that it resonates with their experience. Unlike professionals, knowledge workers have not mastered a body of knowledge and practices subject to external verification and guided by an ethical and legal framework. Yet knowledge workers perform complex tasks, often without clear parameters or instructions and also rely on highly developed networks as repositories of shared technical and social expertise. Such networks may or may not be confined to a specific organization, geographic, or digital location. In a path-breaking study of Silicon Valley, English-Lueck *et al.* report on an anthropological study tracing the digitization of work, domestic and community life. Chapter 20 considers the relationship between the 'immaterial labour' of home and employment. Similar themes are reviewed in Chapter 21 which looks at the transfer of knowledge in social networks outside of the workplace and the importance of trust and reputation in such settings. We know something of the labour process and identity formation of knowledge workers in these different environments but little about career strategies or the dynamics of internal/external labour markets. Similarly, as 'stocks' of professional knowledge become 'flows' of changing discourses and practices so – perhaps – more and more professions have to adapt to a continual process of renewal or *emergence* that renders their experience ever closer to that of knowledge workers. Equally, it is plausible to suggest that knowledge work will become increasingly important as the organizations become more complex admixtures of hierarchy, market and network. Knowledge work is that which fills in the cracks in labour processes opened up inside delayered, structurally restless organizations. Again, this begs a series of questions that must look beyond specific knowledge management projects and to their structural, processual and ideological contexts. We have little sense of how knowledge is organized and managed across different sectors, firms and nations. Only by adopting a historical and comparative perspective can we gain a broader understanding of the role of knowledge in sustaining innovation and competitive advantage.

15

Market, hierarchy and trust:
the knowledge economy and the future of capitalism
Paul S. Adler

Introduction

Considerable attention has been focused recently on data suggesting that the secular trend toward larger firms and establishments has stalled and may be reversing (Brynjolfsson *et al.*, 1994). Some observers argue that the underlying new trend is toward the disintegration of large hierarchical firms and their replacement by small entrepreneurial firms coordinated by markets (Birch, 1987). This argument, however, understates the persistence of large firms, ignores transformations underway within these firms, and masks the growth of network relations among firms. How, then, should one interpret the current wave of changes in organizational forms?

Zenger and Hesterly (1997) propose that the underlying trend is a progressive swelling of the zone between hierarchy and market. They point to a proliferation of hybrid organizational forms that introduce high-powered marketlike incentives into firms and hierarchical controls into markets (Holland and Lockett, 1997), make a similar argument. This proposition is more valid empirically than a one-sided characterization of current trends as a shift from hierarchy to market. The "Swelling-middle" thesis is also a step beyond Williamson's (1991) unjustified assertion that such hybrid forms are infeasible or inefficient. However, this chapter argues that Zenger and Hesterly's thesis, too, is fundamentally flawed in that it ignores a third increasingly significant coordination mechanism: trust.

In highlighting the importance of trust, this chapter adds to a burgeoning literature (e.g. *Academy of Management Review 1998*: further references below): my goal is to pull together several strands of this literature to advance a line of reflection that positions trust as a central construct in a broader argument. In outline, the argument is, first, that alongside the *market* ideal-typical form or organization which relies on the price mechanism, and the *hierarchy* form which relies on authority, there is a third form, the *community* form which relies on trust. Empirically observed arrangements typically embody a mix of the three ideal-typical organization forms and rely on a corresponding mix of price, hierarchy, and trust mechanisms. Second, based on a well-established body of economic and sociological theory, I argue that trust has uniquely effective properties for the coordination of knowledge-intensive activities within and between organizations. Third, given a broad consensus that modern economies are becoming increasingly knowledge intensive, the first two premises imply that trust is likely to become increasingly important in the mechanism mix. I present indices of such a knowledge-driven trend to trust within and between firms, specifically in the employment relationship, in interdivisional relations, and in interfirm relations. Fourth, I discuss the difficulties encountered by the trust mechanism in a capitalist society and the resulting mutation of trust itself. Finally, the concluding section discusses the broader effects of this intra- and interfirm trend to trust, and argues that this trend progressively undermines the legitimacy of the capitalist form of society, and simultaneously lays the foundations for a new form.

Both the theory and the data underlying these conclusions are subject to debate: I will summarize the key points of contention, and it will become obvious that we are far from theoretical or empirical consensus. In the form of an essay rather than a scientific paper, my argument will be speculative and buttressed by only suggestive rather than compelling evidence. My goal, however, is to enrich organizational research by enhancing its engagement with debates in the broader field of social theory.

The limits of market and hierarchy

Knowledge is a remarkable substance. Unlike other resources, most forms of knowledge grow rather than diminish with use. Knowledge tends, therefore, to play an increasingly central role in economic development over time. Increasing knowledge-intensity takes two forms: the rising education level of the workforce (living or subjective knowledge) and the growing scientific and technical knowledge materialized in new equipment and new products (embodied or objectified knowledge).

Recapitulating a long tradition of scholarship in economics and organization theory, this section argues that neither market nor hierarchy, nor any combination of the two, is particularly well suited to the challenges of the knowledge economy. To draw out the implications of this argument, I will assume that real institutions, notably empirically observed markets and firms, embody varying mixes of three ideal-typical organizational forms and their corresponding coordination mechanisms: (a) the hierarchy form relies on the authority mechanism, (b) the market form relies on price, and (c) the community form relies on trust. For brevity's sake, an organizational form and its corresponding mechanism will be referred to as an organizing "mode." Modes typically appear in varying proportions in different institutions. For example, interfirm relations in real markets embody and rely on varying degrees of trust and hierarchical authority, even if their primary mechanism is price. Similarly, real firms' internal operations typically rely to some extent on both trust and price signals, even if their primary coordination mechanisms is authority.

Hierarchy uses authority (legitimate power) to create and coordinate a horizontal and vertical division of labor. Under hierarchy, knowledge is treated as a scarce resource and is therefore concentrated, along with the corresponding decision rights, in specialized functional units and at higher levels of the organization. A large body of organizational research has shown that an institution structured by this mechanism may be efficient in the performance of routine partitioned tasks but encounters enormous difficulty in the performance of innovation tasks requiring the generation of new knowledge (e.g. Burns and Stalker, 1961; Bennis and Slater, 1964; Mintzbert, 1979; Scott, 1992; Daft, 1998). When specialized units are told to cooperate in tasks that typically encounter unanticipated problems requiring novel solutions, tasks such as the development of a new product, the hierarchical form gives higher-level managers few levers with which to ensure that the participating units will collaborate. By their nonroutine nature, such tasks cannot be preprogrammed, and the creative collaboration they require cannot be simply commanded. Similarly, the vertical differentiation of hierarchy is effective for routine tasks, facilitating downward communication of explicit knowledge and commands, but less effective when tasks are nonroutine, because lower levels lack both the knowledge needed to create new knowledge and the incentives to transmit new ideas upward. Firms thus invariably supplement their primary organizational model, hierarchy/authority, with other modes that can mitigate the hierarchy/authority mode's weaknesses.

The market form, as distinct from the actual functioning of most real markets, relies on the price mechanism to coordinate completing supplies and anonymous buyers. With standard goods and strong property rights, marginal pricing promises to optimize production and allocation jointly. The dynamics of competition, supply, and demand lead to a price at which social welfare is Paretooptimal (that is, no one's welfare can be increased without reducing someone else's). A substantial body of modern economic theory has shown, however, that the price mechanism fails to optimize the production and allocation of knowledge (Arrow, 1962; Stiglitz, 1994). Knowledge is a "public good;" that is, like radio transmission, its availability to one consumer is not diminished by its use by another. With knowledge, as with other public goods, reliance on the market/price mode forces a trade-off between production and allocation. On the one hand, production of new knowledge would be optimized by establishing strong intellectual property rights that create incentives to generate knowledge. On the other hand, not only are such rights difficult to enforce, but more fundamentally, they block socially optimal allocation. Allocation of knowledge would be optimized by allowing free access because the marginal cost of supplying another consumer with the same knowledge is close to zero.

Over several decades, discussion of this trade-off between production and allocation was framed as a debate at a macroeconomic level over the relative merits of market, hierarchy in the form of central planning, and intermediate forms such as regulated markets and market socialism (Arrow and Hurwicz, 1977; Stiglitz, 1994). This "mechanism design" literature has more recently been applied to the analysis of individual firms (Miller, 1992) – with the same results. On the one hand, hierarchy could simply mandate the free availability of knowledge and thus outperform market as far as allocation is concerned. On the other hand, hierarchy would have far greater difficulty than market in creating the incentives needed to optimize the production of new knowledge. Formal modeling has shown that neither market nor hierarchy nor any intermediate form can resolve the dilemma, leaving us stuck in a "second best" equilibrium (Miller, 1992).

Recent research on knowledge and coordination mechanisms has highlighted the importance of tacit knowledge. The recognition of the importance of tacit knowledge does little, however, to restore confidence in the ability of the market form to assure optimal outcomes. First, tacit knowledge brings with it all the challenges of hidden knowledge in principal/agent relations. Second, notwithstanding the current scholarly interest in tacit knowledge codified forms of knowledge continue to be an important factor in economic growth. The reasons are straightforward: The transfer of knowledge is much more costly when the knowledge is of a tacit kind, and the generation of new knowledge is usually much faster when it builds on a base of explicit rather than tacit knowledge.

As knowledge becomes increasingly important in the economic development of firms and nations, the question of whether we can improve on the second-best allowed by market and hierarchy is posed with increasing urgency. Much recent economic scholarship has, however, argued for resignation: The second best achievable in pure or mixed markets and hierarchies is redefined as the best feasible and "relatively efficient" (Alchian and Demsetz, 1972; Williamson, 1975). This resignation is not warranted. Hierarchy and market are not the only possible organizational forms. Community is an alternative (Ouchi, 1980; Dore, 1983; Bradach and Eccles, 1989; Powell 1990).

The power of community and trust

Community

Community is a term with many interpretations (Kirkpatrick, 1986). However, the salience of some such notion is demonstrated by what we know of both intra and interfirm relations.

Analysis of action within real firms reveals the ubiquity and importance of "informal" organization – this is one of the founding insights of organization theory (see Scott, 1992: Chapter 3). Views differ as to how best to conceptualize the informal organization and its differentiation from the formal structures of hierarchy. Without preempting this ongoing debate, we can posit that the informal organization constitutes its members as a community.

Analysis of real market relations between firms reveals a similar dependence on informal ties (Macaulay, 1963). Pure-spot market-relations between anonymous buyers and sellers is in reality rather unusual. Firms transact primarily with long-standing partners, and in the continuity of their relations, shared norms and understanding emerge that have their own efficacy in shaping interactions.

Trust

Trust is the key coordinating mechanism in the community form. Following Gambetta (1988), one could define trust as the subjective probability with which an actor assesses that another actor or group of actors will perform a particular action, both before she or he can monitor such action (or independently of his or her capacity ever to be able to monitor it) and in a context in which it affects his or her own action. This broad definition captures many uses of the word, including the possibility of feared as well as welcomed actions. Another narrower and more benign definition is confidence in another's goodwill (Ring and Van de Ven, 1992).

The difference between these definitions obliges us to make a short digression on the notion of trust. Both the generation of trust – i.e., its sources and mechanisms – and its targets – i.e., the objects and the features of those objects in which we invest our trust – are manifold.

First, we can distinguish three *sources* of trust. Familiarity through repeated interaction can lead to trust (or distrust). Interests can lead to a calculative form of trust via a sober assessment of the costs and benefits to the other party of exploiting my vulnerability. Values and norms can engender trustworthy behavior that leads to confidence (Liebeskind and Oliver 1998). (We should note that there is some confusion in the literature about precisely what it is about values and norms that creates trust. We might reasonably distinguish a spectrum running from weaker forms of trust based on the predictability

| Figure 15.1 | Dimensions and components of trust |

Dimensions	Components
sources	• familiarity through repeated interaction • calculation based on interests • norms that create predictability and trustworthiness
mechanisms	• direct interpersonal contact • reputation • institutional context
objects	• individuals • systems • collectivities
bases	• consistency, contractual trust • competence • benevolence, loyalty, concern, goodwill, fiduciary trust • honesty, integrity • openness

imparted to other actors' behavior by their adherence to any stable norm, to stronger forms of trust based on the predicted benevolence of actors with whom we share norms that privilege trustworthiness; see Ring 1996.) Empirically, all three sources of trust are important in the real world of business (cf. Williamson, 1993) and in practice, although excessive focus on the calculative form can undermine the normative form, all three tend to be intertwined complements.

Second, we can distinguish three *mechanisms* by which trust is generated. As Coleman (1990) points out, trust can be engendered by direct interpersonal contact, by reputation through a network of other trusted parties, or by our understanding of the way institutions shape the other actor's values and behavior. Like the three sources, the three mechanisms are primarily complements rather than substitutes: They tend to build on each other.

Third, we can distinguish three generic *objects* of trust: Our trust can be in a person, an impersonal system, or a collectivity. Social psychologists have focused most of their efforts on the first (Bigley and Pearce, 1998), and indeed some social theorists would reserve the concept of trust for interpersonal relations and use the term "confidence" to refer to related assessments of abstract systems (Luhmann, 1979; Seligman, 1997). Notwithstanding the terminological issue, sociologists such as Barber (1983) Zucker (1986), Giddens (1990), and Shapiro (1987) highlight the importance to the functioning of contemporary society of confidence/trust in anonymous systems such as money and law. The concept of procedural justice (e.g., Brockner and Siegel 1996) is one form of system trust familiar to organizational researchers. The importance to comparative economic performance of trust in a collectivity – that is, generalized trust in others who are part of that collectivity – is foregrounded by Fukuyama (1995).

Finally, we can distinguish the features of those objects in which we feel trust, often referred to in the literature as the *bases* of trust. The list of bases invoked by various authors is long and partially overlapping, and none of the typologies has a strong theoretical foundation. They include the other party's consistency (Sako, 1992, "contractual trust"), competence, benevolence, (or loyalty, concern, or Sako's "goodwill trust"), honesty (or integrity), and openness. While much of the discussion of bases has taken interpersonal trust as its context, it is clear that system and collectivity trust also have diverse bases (see e.g. Barber, 1983, on fiduciary trust – i.e., benevolence – and competence trust in government). Like sources and mechanisms, both objects and bases are primarily complements: Community, system, and interpersonal trust typically buttress each other, as do the various bases (e.g., Kurland, 1996).

Community/trust as a third mode

While trust is a complex, multifaceted phenomenon, the complementarities between the components of each of its four key dimensions enable trust to function as a highly effective coordinating mechanism. Groups whose cohesion is based primarily on mutual trust are capable of extraordinary feats. Trust is therefore usefully seen as a third coordination mechanism that can be combined in varying degrees with price and authority.

The thesis that trust constitutes a third coordination mechanism contrasts with three other views. Williamson (1991) suggests we see market and hierarchy as two discrete alternatives, and declares trust to be irrelevant to business transactions. The "swelling middle" thesis invites us to see a continuum between these points, but implicitly assumes a trade-off between mechanisms, and still ignores trust. Ouchi's (1980) discussion includes trust but still implies a three-way trade-off.

It is more fruitful, I submit, to map institutions in three dimensions according to the salience of community/trust, market/price, and hierarchy/authority modes (Figure 15.2). This three-dimensional representation has the advantage of allowing us to think of the way the various modes combine in different settings. In the absence of trust, market coordination takes the form of spot markets. However, trust can be combined with the price mechanism in the form of "relational contracts" (Macneil, 1980), as found in long-term partnership-type supplier relations (Bradach and Eccles, 1989; Sako, 1992; Uzzi, 1997).

Figure 15.2 Alternative conceptualizations of organizational modes and hybrids

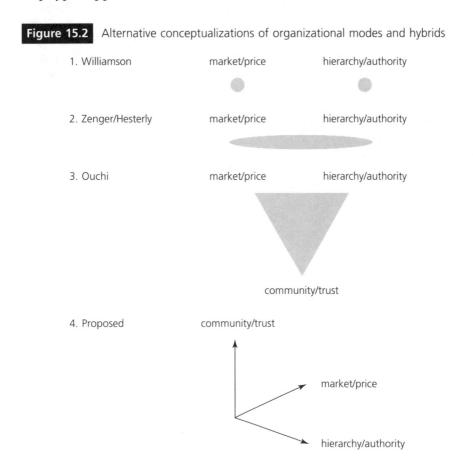

Hierarchy often appears in a low-trust form, as reflected in the colloquial, pejorative use of the term "bureaucracy," and in cases such as those presented by Crozier (1964). However, hierarchy can be combined with trust, as in the "representative," "dynamic," and "enabling" types of bureaucracy described respectively by Gouldner (1954), Blau (1955), and Adler and Borys (1996).

Market and hierarchy too are often combined, as reflected in the mix of incentives and authority typically found in employment relations, in relations between divisions and headquarters within large multidivisional firms, and in relations between firms and their suppliers. Sometimes this market/hierarchy mix takes a low-trust form, but sometimes trust is an important third ingredient. Within firms, high-trust hybrids can be found in "collaborative" multidivisional corporations characterized by high levels of interdivisional and interlevel trust (Eccles, 1985). Between firms, high-trust hybrids can be found in keiretsu-type configurations characterized by high-trust, hierarchically structured, market relations (Gerlach, 1992; Dyer, 1996). Figure 15.3 summarizes these alternatives, building on the framework suggested by Figure 15.2.

I should note that under this view, the growing importance of "network" forms of organization within and between firms does not so much answer the question motivating this chapter as it poses a further question: Figure 15.2 suggests that we ask of these networks whether the content of their constituent ties is market exchange, hierarchical authority, or community trust. Korczynski (1996) and Carney (1998) contrast high-trust and low-trust network forms, and show that the low-trust form can help lower costs but performs relatively poorly in generating or sharing new knowledge.

Figure 15.3 A typology of institutional forms (low trust forms in lower left triangles, high trust forms in upper right triangles)

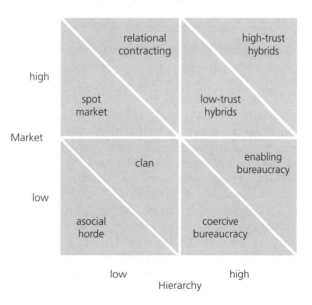

A hypothesis: the trend of trust

Using these three-dimensional schemas, we can map the vector of change in the mix of organization modes associated with the increasing knowledge-intensity of the economy. Compared to pure authority and price, trust makes possible an enlarged scope of knowledge generation and sharing. Trust can dramatically reduce both transactions costs – replacing contracts with handshakes – and agency risks – replacing the fear of shirking and misrepresentation with mutual confidence. Trust can thus greatly mitigate the coordination difficulties created by knowledge's public good character. Also, insofar as knowledge takes a tacit form, trust is an essential precondition for effective knowledge transfer. Therefore, as knowledge management becomes an increasingly important performance determinant, I hypothesize that trust becomes an increasingly attractive mechanism to economic agents.

In the following sections, I will adduce some evidence – suggestive, but certainly not compelling – that firms are indeed being drawn to increasing reliance on trust. A constellation of somewhat contradictory trends is developing as firms attempt to deal more effectively with the knowledge management challenge. First, firms are sharpening marketlike processes. Second, they are developing more effective hierarchical processes. And third, in apparently growing numbers, they are adopting approaches to knowledge management that rely on community and trust between employees and managers, between divisions within the corporation, and between firms and their suppliers. The evidence I present for a trend to trust is not compelling, but given the stakes, it is sufficient to warrant a preliminary assessment and an exploration of its implications.

Employment relations

Viewed over the longer period, the economy's growing knowledge-intensity is pushing the employment relationship in several somewhat contradictory directions. A trend to trust may nevertheless be emerging.

First, one can identify a range of efforts to strengthen the authority mechanism in the employment relations. In response to competitive pressures, firms are fine-tuning their management structures and planning processes, demanding greater accountability at every level, and enforcing more discipline in the planning and execution of operations. The most common motivation for these efforts appears to be greater efficiency and control, but firms sometimes see this refinement of hierarchy as a path to more effective knowledge management too. It is under this latter rationale that many firms are introducing more formalized procedures such as TQM and highly structured product and software development processes. Many firms are also developing more elaborate project planning and human resource planning techniques to ensure that the right mix of skills is available to support the development and launch of innovative products. They are developing more complex metrics, the "balance scorecard" for example (Kaplan, 1996), that go beyond market performance criteria for the assessment of these projects. Firms are attempting to identify their "core competencies" and nurture development of these competencies over the longer term, even when purely market-based financial assessments do not support such risky investments.

Second, alongside these refinements of hierarchy, one sees efforts designed to strengthen the market form of the employment relation. Downsizing and contingent employment are sometimes seen as ways not only to reduce labor costs and increase "numerical" (head-count) flexibility, but also as paths to greater flexibility in the mix of knowledge and skills available to the firm (head content). Reliance on market-type mechanisms is also visible in the shift, albeit modest, toward contingent compensation at lower levels in the organizational hierarchy, creating higher-powered incentives for performance in general and for risky innovation and knowledge creation in particular (Lawler *et al.*, 1998). These efforts are most often motivated by efficiency and flexibility concerns, but here again, improvements in knowledge management capability are sometimes seen as another benefit. Firms like Microsoft invoke both motives when they use market relations in the form of large pools of contingent contract employees and high-powered stock incentives for regular employees.

Third, firms are trying to improve their knowledge management capabilities by strengthening employee trust. The rationale is explicit. Effective *development* of knowledge – whether new concepts in the research lab, new products in the development department, or process refinement suggestions on the shop floor – depends on employee commitment and on collaborative teamwork for which mutual trust is a critical precondition (Bromiley and Cummings, 1995). Effective *sharing* of knowledge depends equally critically on a sense of shared destiny, which in turn both depends on and engenders a sense of mutual trust (e.g., Nahapiet and Ghoshal, 1998). Firms like 3M and Hewlett Packard thus attempt to create high levels of community and trust by providing material and nonmaterial expressions of commitment to their employees (Collins and Porras, 1994).

Trust is a crucial ingredient both in high-commitment vertical relations between employees and management and in collaborative horizontal relations between specialist groups. Building on many decades of research on the critical role of informal organization in innovation, community – particularly in the form of "communities of practice" (Wenger, 1998) – is increasingly recognized as the organizational principle most effective in generating and sharing new knowledge.

In the language of transaction cost economics, we would say that when the firm needs high levels of firm-specific knowledge and when metering individual output is difficult – conditions that are arguably typical in knowledge – intensive firms – the most efficient form of the employment relation is that of a "relational team" (Williamson, 1981). Notwithstanding Williamson's own reservations regarding the use of the notion of trust in sociological research (1993), relational teams seem in practice to rely on high levels of trust. As illustration, consider a recent book on knowledge management by two particularly thoughtful observers of its practice, Thomas Davenport and Laurence Prusak (1998). They appear at first to advance a thesis contrary to mine, arguing for the need for improved "knowledge markets" within and between firms. But this, it turns out, is merely a metaphor, since the "currencies" of these markets are reciprocity, repute, and altruism, and "mutual trust is at the heart of knowledge exchange" (p.35).

Note the complex three-way tensions between market/price, hierarchy/authority, and community/trust. On the one hand, in some cases the three modes function as mutually exclusive substitutes. Efforts to sharpen market forms can undercut efforts to strengthen trust. Downsizing, for example, is rarely a propitious time for a shift toward teamwork. Efforts to improve hierarchical planning processes often require that market forms be moderated, and changes in the structure of hierarchy can be hampered by the long-term stability implied by strong trust. On the other hand, these three modes can be mutually supportive if they are designed and implemented appropriately. Employee participation, for example, is one way to link community and hierarchy so that the two are complements rather than substitutes (Adler *et al.*, 1999). While Figure 15.2 represents the three mechanisms as three orthogonal dimensions, it is not intended to preempt questions of substantive interdependencies. Unfortunately, these interdependencies have so far eluded compelling theorization. See e.g. Hirschman (1970) on the variable relationship between exit (read: market) and voice (read: community). For now, all we can say is that hierarchy, market and community are sometimes complements and sometimes substitutes.

Some counterarguments

The hypothesis that as the knowledge-intensity of the economy increases, firms will be drawn in increasing numbers to higher-trust forms of the employment relation runs counter to a long tradition in sociology. This tradition draws on several theoretical perspectives: Here I review some that pertain directly to the employment relationship. In a subsequent section, I return to others of more general import.

A venerable line of sociological scholarship has argued that the capitalist employment relation is an essentially low-trust one. The hallmarks of the capitalist firm – scientific management and mass production – are engines of war against community: fragmenting workers' roles, separating conception and execution, and centralizing control. From this vantage point, writings in the human relations tradition and, more recently, on empowerment are seen as ideological inflation of a thin veneer of trust that managers try to overlay on the underlying reality of domination. Indeed, the concept of trust was rarely invoked in industrial sociology until Alan Fox's 1974 study – which argued that trust was systematically undermined in capitalist firms. His argument seemed so convincing that the topic essentially disappeared for another decade (Heisig and Littek, 1995).

Some contributors to this sociological tradition work from the Marxist theoretical premise that the core or the employment relation is an inescapable struggle between workers and managers over work intensity (e.g., Braverman, 1974; Burawoy, 1979). Researchers working in this perspective highlight the deceptive nature of management efforts to inculcate a sense of trust in workers and the "false consciousness" of workers who take the bait.

Other contributors are grounded in Weber rather than Marx, and for these the hypothesis of a trend to trust in the employment relationship arouses skepticism rather than radical hostility. Weberians, like Marxists, remind us that a trend to trust would be likely to encounter enormous impediments in the rivalry of competing social groups. These scholars can point to a substantial body of research accumulated over many decades that documents the frequency and potency of both management and worker opposition to "progressive" management ideas. Enlightened self-interest does not diffuse easily in a society where so many personal, organizational, and contextual factors encourage managers, and sometimes workers, to choose hierarchy and market over community/trust.

As a result of these impediments to trust, scholars in these traditions expect to find a trendless pattern of fluctuation in the employment relation's mechanism mix. Consistent with this interpretation, Ramsay (1977) argues that trust in the employment relation has fluctuated over the century as a function of the balance of power between labor and management. Barley and Kunda (1992) and Abrahamson (1997) document cyclical swings between the rhetorics of rational control and normative commitment in management discourse over the last century.

The hypothesis reaffirmed

These Marxist and Weberian objections are, however, not convincing. The radical scepticism of trust in the traditional Marxist view is justified only if one accepts that the interest of workers and managers are never even partly congruent. This assumption appears empirically implausible. Moreover, it is based on an unfortunately narrow reading of Marx (Adler 1990). It ignores Marx's insights into the role of community within the firm, expressed in his analysis of "co-operation" and the "collective worker" – a collective that includes managers in their "productive," as distinct from "exploitative" roles (Carchedi, 1977).

Once this facet of Marx's analysis is retrieved, it is no longer difficult to conceive of a progressive expansion of trust under capitalist relations of production. Trust, under this view, becomes a feature of work organization, and as such it is at the intersection of the forces of production (society's accumulated productive resources) and the relations of production (the structure of ownership and control of these resources) – embodying both structures simultaneously and subject to the dynamics of both (Adler, 1997). Insofar as its trajectory is shaped by fundamentally antagonistic capitalist relations of production, the growth of trust is necessarily limited: but insofar as it is shaped by the forces of production, trust grows cumulatively with the progressive expansion of those forces. In sum, this alternative reading of Marx suggests the possibility of a trend to trust, albeit a trend that is limited in its form and extent by the persistence of capitalist relations.

The version of Weber invoked by those skeptical of a trend to trust is a somewhat truncated one too. In its insistence on the enduring conflict between competing social groups, this reading downplays the importance Weber attached to rationalization in the development of modern society. As traditional bases of domination are displaced by rational-legal ones, the authority of managers within the firm is increasingly a function of the perceived legitimacy of their claim to expertise and to functional necessity. The brute assertion of positional prerogative loses legitimacy, and some kind of trust becomes increasingly critical to the exercise of authority. (Below, I take up the question of which kind of trust.)

Nor is an expansion of trust contradicted by evidence of fluctuations in the mix of mechanisms constituting employment relations. A closer look at the data cited by Barley *et al.*, suggests that a secular trend line underlies these cycles. In both the sequence of rational control phases – from scientific management (whose dominance Abrahamson dates from 1894 to 1921) to systems rationalism (1944–1971) and to reengineering (1990–) – and the sequence of normative commitment phases – from welfare and personnel management (1921–1944) to culture-quality (1971–1990) – we observe the growing importance of themes of employee consent and trust. In the normative approaches, for example, there is a clear shift from the earlier emphasis on paternalism, to relatively impersonal bureaucratic norms of procedural justice, to the recent emphasis on empowerment and mutual commitment.

Perhaps more striking is the trend to trust found in the sequence of control rhetorics. Within two or three years of publishing a text popularizing a rather brutally coercive method of business process reengineering (Hammer and Champy, 1993), both James Champy and Michael Hammer published new volumes (Champy, 1995; Hammer, 1996) stressing the importance of the human factor and the need for job redesigns that afford employees greater autonomy. The undeniably autocratic character of much early reengineering rhetoric and its rapid "softening" compares favorably with unilateral and enduring forms of domination expressed in post-War systems rationalism. It compares even more favorably with the even more unilateral and rigid rhetoric in turn-of-the-century scientific management: scientific management only softened its relations with organized labor after nearly two decades of confrontation (Nyland, 1998).

Clearly there is a gap – often a huge one, as Marxist and Weberian commentators have pointed out – between these trends in rhetoric and the reality of the employment relation. However, this long-term evolution of rhetoric both reflects and reinforces a real trend to trust. It reflects the evolving expectations of an increasingly educated (read: knowledge-intensive) work-force and the evolving needs of an increasingly advanced (ditto) economy. And it reinforces that trend because the rhetoric of trust legitimizes the idea that management authority depends on employee consent.

Interdivisional relations

Large multibusiness corporations are under increasing pressure to show real benefits for asserted synergies. A first result of this pressure is the trend to divest unrelated businesses in the interest of "focus." Therefore, the increasingly common configuration is that of related-diversified firms, that is, firms in which divisions are neither integrated vertically as suppliers and users nor totally independent of each other. However, in related-diversified firms, if divisions seek only to meet their own divisional objectives, they will behave in ways that are detrimental to the firm's global objectives. A second result of the performance pressure on large corporations is, therefore, a cluster of innovations that appear to be pushing beyond the limits of market and hierarchy and towards greater collaboration.

The multidivisional corporation is in effect a miniature economy in which business units function as miniature firms. Such a corporation must struggle with precisely the dilemma of knowledge management articulated in the market/plan debate. Headquarters' hierarchical control over divisions might help assure the dissemination across divisions of existing knowledge, but such control undermines incentives for the divisions to create new knowledge. The more common approach gives divisions profit and loss responsibility and engenders the corresponding problems of the market form. When divisions function as autonomous profit centers and charge a market-based price for sales of intellectual assets to sister divisions, the effectiveness of the corporation as a whole suffers because the optimal allocation of knowledge assets is blocked (Kaplan, 1984; for an example at TRW, see *Business Week* 1982). Because one division's use of these knowledge assets does not preclude their use by another, the corporation would benefit from a regime of free sharing among divisions.

Eccles (1985) finds that in the microeconomy of the firm there is no mix of transfer prices and hierarchical procedures that simultaneously can optimize incentives to invest in the development of new knowledge and to share the results of those development efforts. Not surprisingly, this finding supports at a micro level the prediction of Arrow's and Hurwicz's (1997) analysis of whole economies. The multidivisional form of the corporation was constructed to counterbalance the merits and limits of hierarchy, as embodied in the functional form, with those of market, as embodied in the holding-company form. In this, the M-form resembles the intermediate cases of regulated market or market socialism mentioned above. However, even this hybrid model becomes increasingly inefficient when the corporation must encourage simultaneously the creation of new knowledge within divisions and the sharing of existing knowledge across divisions (Miller, 1992).

In response to these problems and to their growing urgency in an increasingly knowledge-intensive economy, multidivisional firms are actively experimenting with new ways to stimulate collaboration between profit centers within the firm. The notion of core competencies, as articulated by Prahalad and Hamel (1990), is premised on the insight that corporate competitiveness depends on bodies of expertise that are typically distributed across divisions rather than contained within them. Collaboration across divisions, therefore, is a critical, not a secondary issue (see also Porter, 1985: Part III on "horizontal strategy"). Collins and Porras (1994) document a whole panoply of mechanisms designed to encourage a bond of common identity and a norm of sharing. Davenport and Prusak (1998) describe a range of methods used in large firms to enhance the trust and shared identity needed for the easy flow of ideas across divisional boundaries.

These shifts in interdivisional relations are reflected in changes in corporate control systems. Eccles' (1985) research shows that the most effective transfer pricing scheme in such cases is based neither on market prices nor on internal costs but on what he calls "rational trust." Under rational trust, division managers' confidence in top management's ability to evaluate and reward performance fairly is based on two measures: first, the judicious use of quantitative measures of subunit performance, and second, the enlightened use of subjective measures of the subunit managers' contributions to total company performance, even when these contributions hurt their subunits' own performance (1985: 279).

Consistent with Eccles' argument, empirical research finds that in firms with relatively high levels of knowledge-intensity, where collaboration between divisions is therefore at a premium, headquarters commonly use subjective judgments of how well division managers help their peers. These subjective judgments both assess and require trust, in contrast with the more traditional approaches that rely exclusively on quantitative, market performance-based formulae or hierarchical-bureaucratic criteria to determine division managers' bonuses (Gupta and Govindarajan, 1986; Lorsch and Allen, 1973; Salter, 1973; Hill *et al.*, 1992).

The shift to trust is not, however, unproblematic. The ethos of common destiny that underpins trust blurs the allocation of accountability and decision rights at the heart of both hierarchy and market forms. Powerful actors resist this blurring. Within hierarchies, superiors resist giving up the case of control afforded by the principle of accountability (see e.g., Ashkenas *et al.*, 1993: 125). Unilateral control is a far simpler organizational process to manage than shared control. More fundamentally, as agents of owners, senior managers are themselves held accountable to brutally simple norms imposed by the product and financial markets. The implacable, anonymous irrationality of the market often makes a mockery of efforts to create and sustain trust. Senior executives, whose fortunes are tied to the firm's market performance, cannot, therefore, commit more than half-heartedly to trust (Hyman, 1987).

Notwithstanding this resistance, increasing knowledge-intensity appears to encourage a trend to trust in interdivisional relations. This trend might help explain the proliferation of titles such as chief technology officer and chief knowledge officer. These positions have broad responsibility for building cross-division knowledge and sharing, but typically they have no formal authority – they rely on trust in their attempts to build more trust (Adler and Ferdows, 1992; Earl and Scott, 1999). As firms learn how to infuse trust into the immensely complex task of coordinating action in multidivisional firms, and in particular as they learn how to combine trust with the necessary elements of hierarchy and market, Eccles' "rational trust" model appears to be gaining legitimacy.

Interfirm relations

In parallel with these trends toward trust in employment and interdivisional relations, firms are increasingly infusing trust into their relations with other firms. Alliances and other forms of interfirm networks are proliferating, and the consensus in the field is that this proliferation is driven in large measure by the challenge of growing knowledge-intensity. Here, too, firms are juggling market/price, hierarchy/authority, and community/trust modes and scholars are debating their relative importance (e.g., *Organization Science* 1998). While some argue that trust is increasingly important in interfirm relations, others argue that firms are unlikely to suspend self-interest in alliances and that trust may often be a result rather than a cause (Koza and Lewin, 1998). Whether trust plays an independent causal role is an open question: in this section, I present the case for the affirmative.

First, we should note the countertendencies. On the one hand, we see some firms imposing ever sharper market discipline on their suppliers by aggressively demanding lower prices and moving rapidly to cut off suppliers who cannot deliver (e.g., Ashkenas *et al.*, 1993: 240). On the other hand, we see firms trying to force improvements in their supplier base by introducing more complex "hierarchical contracts" (Stinchcombe, 1985) into their market relations. Such hierarchical elements control not only product specifications but also the supplier's internal processes. Korczynski (1996), for example, documents a trend toward a low-trust combination of market and hierarchical relations between management contractors and building contractors in the U.K. engineering construction industry in the 1980s and 1990s. Hancké (1997) makes a similar diagnosis of the evolution of subcontracting relations in the French automobile industry.

We also see, however, a growing number of firms building long-term, trust-based partnerships with their suppliers. A burgeoning body of research shows that when firms need innovation and knowledge inputs from suppliers rather than just standardized commodities, no combination of strong hierarchical control and market discipline can assure as high a level of performance as trust-based community (Dyer, 1996; Sako, 1992; Helper, 1991; Bensaou and Venkatraman, 1995; Ring, 1996, 1997). By contrast, Korczynski's (1996) study shows how low-trust relations in the U.K. construction industry enabled schedule and cost improvements but were unable to stimulate the creation of new knowledge.

The hierarchy/authority mode of interfirm relations clearly risks impeding innovation by stifling the upward flow of new ideas from subordinate suppliers. Their narrow specialization leaves them without the technological know-how needed for innovation, and their subordination leaves them few incentives to contribute innovative ideas to customers.

The market/price mode facilitates innovation by creating incentives to generate new ideas, but this mode, too impedes innovation because suppliers and customers of innovations have difficulty agreeing on a price for these innovative ideas. The suppliers are not sure what price would cover their costs, for two reasons. First, the main source of a firm's innovative ideas is society's total stock of knowledge rather than assets held privately by the innovating firm. Given the public-good character of much of that knowledge stock, identifying or justifying a "raw materials" cost for new ideas generated from this knowledge stock is difficult. Second, an innovative idea is just as likely to arise during free time as on the job, so identifying a "transformation" cost is difficult. Whereas competition between suppliers of most other types of goods drives prices toward their marginal costs, no comparably grounded "supply schedule" guides the price of knowledge.

The customer side is no easier. The potential customer for an innovation typically cannot judge the worth of the idea without having its secret revealed, and intellectual property protection is cumbersome and expensive. Moreover, intellectual property rights, compared to property rights in other kinds of assets, lack a legitimating material substratum. We have already pointed out the difficulty of determining the price of knowledge based on its production cost; the alternative basis would be rent, but rent is only a viable price-form when the asset in question is not reproducible and is rivalrous in use, whereas knowledge (at least in its codified forms) is reproducible at close to zero cost and nonrivalrous in use. Its price is therefore less grounded in any material considerations: it is purely a function of convention and relative power. Lacking a legitimating material basis, intellectual property is amongst the most contentious of forms of property. Perhaps that is why patent rights are so often bundled and bartered in dyadic trade rather than sold on open markets.

These implications of growing knowledge-intensity for the market form were identified by Marx more than a century ago (1973: 700). The forces of production of modern industry are progressively socialized – increasingly, they take the form of society's total knowledge stock. As a result, labor inputs and production costs become increasingly irrelevant to the formation of prices, and the price mechanism becomes an increasingly unreliable basis for economic calculation. The difficulties encountered by efforts to create "metrics" for knowledge management are perhaps more fundamental than commonly recognized.

Hierarchy and market are relatively more effective for the governance of low-knowledge-intensity transactions where efficiency, rather than innovation, is critical. Where knowledge management is the critical task, the more effective approaches rely on long-term partnership-style relationships based on "good-will" trust, as well as competence-and contract-trust (Sako, 1992; Bensaou and Venkatraman, 1995; Ring, 1997). Thus, trust is at the heart of effective knowledge-intensive interfirm networks (Powell, 1990).

As with the employment relation, the most effective approaches to knowledge management in interfirm relations deploy a complementary mix of price, authority, and trust mechanisms. Toyota, for example, rarely allows itself to become dependent on a single supplier, and tries to maintain two sources for any noncommodity inputs. Toyota always makes these suppliers aware of the ultimate power of the market test. However, the relationships between Toyota and these suppliers are hardly composed of anonymous, arm's-length, spot-market transactions. First, these contracts embody a comprehensive set of documents specifying in detail product requirements and management processes. Second, these hierarchical documents are embedded within a long-term, high-trust, mutual-commitment relationship.

While some observers might argue that Japanese firms like Toyota put so much emphasis on trust because of the importance of this norm in the broader Japanese culture, the evidence appears strong that such a trust-heavy mix of mechanisms is productively superior in a broad range of cultures. Two indicators come from the U.S. auto industry. First, Dyer and Chu (1998) find that, compared to their U.S. counterparts, Japanese auto firms established recently in the United States were able rapidly to create higher-trust relations with their U.S. owned suppliers. Second, in response to this Japanese challenge, U.S. auto manufacturers have shifted toward higher trust relations with their suppliers. The percentage of U.S. auto parts producers who provide sensitive, detailed information about their production process to their customers grew from 38% to 80% during the 1980s (Helper and Sako, 1995). However, in the case of supplier relations, unlike that of employment relations, research has not yet assessed whether such a shift is more than a swing of the pendulum back to what may have been relatively high-trust relations in interfirm relations in earlier periods of capitalism (see, e.g., Sabel and Zeitlin, 1997).

Evidence for a trend to interfirm trust is stronger in the proliferation of multilateral network forms of organization for the most knowledge-intensive tasks and industries (Nelson, 1998; Powell, 1990; Liebeskind et al., 1996). The multiplication of such tasks and industries over time warrants the hypothesis that the proliferation of high-trust multilateral interfirm networks is not just a pendulum swing. Patent pooling and cooperative R&D consortia have multiplied in recent decades. Formal professional and technical societies and informal community ties among scientists constitute other, less direct forms of interfirm networking whose importance appears to be growing.

One should not ignore the countervailing forces. These high-trust network forms may be more productive, but because the market principle is also present, they suffer the risk of opportunistic defection. Self-interested behavior can sometimes encourage trustworthiness, particularly when the "shadow of the future" is long. However, self-interest does not reliably ensure the diffusion and persistence of trust-based networks, and whole regions can find themselves stuck at low-trust and poor-performing equilibrium. However, when these regions are subject to competition from regions that have attained a higher-trust, higher-performing equilibrium, one sometimes observes serious, sustained, self-conscious efforts to create trust (Sabel, 1992). Some of these efforts succeed. One might hypothesize that if efforts to create trust as a response to competition do not succeed, economic activity will tend to shift to higher-trust regions. In either case, the trend towards trust seems likely to emerge, if only at a more global level.

The difficulties of trust

The preceding overview of changes within and between firms suggests that all three coordination mechanisms – price, authority, and trust – have a role to play in the knowledge economy, but that trust is becoming increasingly important in this mix. Relative to their respective low-trust forms, the high-trust forms of intraorganizational, interdivisional, and interfirm relations encourage more effective knowledge generation and dissemination. The objective need for trust is, to be sure, counterbalanced by the resistance of those whose prerogatives would be threatened by it, but the defense of these prerogatives is increasingly inconsistent with the interests of economic performance. I leave empirical testing of this argument to another occasion, and focus here on the theoretical obstacles. The section above on employment relations discussed several such obstacles. We must now broaden that discussion.

A first obstacle is posed by some economists and sociologists who argue that trust can never, even in principle, become a stable and dominant mechanism. Theoretical economists such as Arrow do not deny that trust would greatly improve the effectiveness of markets; and organizational economists such as Williamson add that trust would also no doubt improve the effectiveness of hierarchy. However, economic theory argues that trust, like knowledge itself, is a public good, and that the spontaneous working of the price mechanism (assumed to be the dominant one) will generate too large a free-rider problem, and consequently will fail to produce the optimal quantity of trust. In repeated games, tit-for-tat co-operation – a minimal form of community – may emerge, but the emergence of co-operation is neither necessary nor predictable. Economists therefore doubt that trust can ever become a stable, dominant mechanism.

The flaw in such reasoning is in the assumption that individuals' preferences are essentially egotistical and exogenous. If people have propensity for altruism that coexists and competes with the propensity for egoism, and if the relative importance of these two propensities varies with the circumstances, then there is no reason to believe that trust cannot become an important, even dominant, mechanism of coordination in the right circumstances (Ring and Van de Ven, 1992).

Some sociologists, too, have expressed skepticism of trust, based on the intuition that trust is far easier to destroy than to create and that its most powerful forms are those that accumulate over long periods (e.g. Putnam, 1993; Hardin, 1992) Evans (1996) contrasts this "endowment" view with a "constructibility" view of trust and social capital. While future empirical research might perhaps cast light on the relative merits of these views, common experience tells us that trust can be created, at least under some conditions. Sabel (1992) describes the processes by which previously distrustful actors can overcome the temptation to free-ride and deliberately create the trust they recognize as being in their common interest (see also Ring, 1997).

Assuming that trust can emerge, a second obstacle arises: Trust has its own dark side. Trust can fail us because it makes betrayal more profitable (Granovetter, 1985). More fundamentally, it can fail us because its success can prove dysfunctional. Trust-based institutions are often exclusivistic and elitist, particularly when the source of trust is shared norms or familiarity. These institutions are poorly equipped to deal with the knowledge management challenge. Social psychologists have shown that trust within teams can lead to complacency and poor performance in innovative tasks (Kim, 1997). When trust based on familiarity or norms becomes the dominant mechanism, firms can come to look like premodern "clans" with the associated traditionalistic domination, and whether this domination takes an autocratic or a paternalistic form, such organizations are clearly handicapped in their knowledge management. When suppliers become trusted partners, the risk of discrimination against potential new suppliers grows correspondingly, reducing innovative potential (Uzzi, 1997; Kern, 1998). In the language of sociology, one would say that in settings governed by norm – or familiarity – based trust, ascribed status often replaces achieved status – which is surely not a promising move in a dynamic knowledge economy.

The most appropriate theoretical response to this challenge is to invoke the potential complementarities between price authority and trust. The downsides of trust and closed communities can be mitigated by the presence of market and hierarchy. Compared to traditional normative trust, the pure, low-trust market is a powerful lever for creating opportunities, especially opportunities for knowledge development. Uzzi's (1997) study of the New York women's apparel industry, for example, shows how firms combine arm's-length market relations with trust-based social relations in their supplier and customer networks. Uzzi argues that firms that balance trust and market can maintain trust's benefits while avoiding the rigidity associated with exclusive reliance on trust relations. Communitarians sensitive to the risks of closed communities make a parallel argument for the importance of hierarchy: at the level of specific organizations, the pure, low-trust bureaucratic hierarchy is a powerful lever for assuring equity and stability, and at a more macrosocietal level, a healthy society needs a mutually supportive combination of community and hierarchy in the form of government and law (Walzer, 1999).

A third and potentially greater obstacle is identified by several currents of social theory that argue that the overall dominance of the price mechanism in capitalist society tends over time to corrode the foundations of trust. Hirschman (1982) reviews these arguments in his discussion of "self-destructive" views of market-based society. Scholars inspired by both Marxist and reactionary thought and by writers such as Weber, Simmel, and Durkheim have argued that the "cash nexus" characteristic of the market-based capitalist form of society progressively undermines the social conditions of capitalism's effectiveness. First, the market undermines the familiarity source of trust by corroding the traditional bonds of community and extended family, leading to the anonymity of urban life. And second, the market undermines the normative source of trust by corroding traditional shared beliefs, leading to "the dissolution of pre-capitalist bonds of loyalty and obedience" (Schumpeter, 1976).Without the buttressing effect of familiarity and traditional shared norms, self-interested calculative trust alone provides only an unreliable foundation for capitalism: "(self-) interest is what is least constant in the world" (Durkheim, 1984) (orig. 1893); see also Ring 1996 on "fragile trust." And Barney and Hansen 1994, on "weak form" (trust).

Hirschman (1982) points out, however, that this self-destructive view has competed with another, more benign view of the effect of the market of society. He labels this benign view the "doux commerce" (Fr: gentle commerce) thesis. Thomas Paine in *The Rights of Man* (1951) (1792), (p. 215) expressed it in the prepositional "(Commerce) is a pacific system, operating to cordialise mankind, by rendering Nations, as well as individuals, useful to each other." Markets may undermine the strong ties of closed community, but they weave an ever-broader web of weaker ties that draws us into "universal interdependence" (Marx and Engels, 1959). A host of observers (but few social theorists) argue that capitalism encourages the emergence of "modern" norms such as industriousness, frugality, punctuality, probity, (Rosenberg, 1964). Some of these modern virtues are arguably propitious for the propagation of at least some forms of trust.

In the contest of these two views, the self-destruction thesis has fared better than the *doux commerce* view. Durkheim's celebration of organic versus mechanical solidarity, for example, echoes Paine's view of the importance of functional interdependence in modern society, but Durkheim was notably pessimistic concerning the possibility of the spontaneous emergence of the requisite normative foundations. Marx's celebration of capitalism's civilizing effects were eclipsed by his denunciation of its inhumanity. Indeed, Hirschman shows that the *doux commerce* thesis all but disappeared after the eighteenth century.

Toward reflective trust

My summary of the corrosive effects of the market distinguished its effects on the three sources of trust: market society seems inimical to strong forms of familiarity trust; market society encourages calculative trust, but such trust alone is unreliable; and market society dissolves the traditional foundations of normative trust. Given the ineluctable quality of the first and second of these effects, the burden of a hypothesized trend to trust must fall on normative trust. Is there any reason to believe that normative trust can be sufficiently renewed to meet the challenge of the knowledge economy?

Further research is needed to test the proposition, but the available evidence suggests that alongside the apparently irresistible decline of traditional trust, we might be observing the gradual emergence of a distinctively modern form of trust.

Leadership is one domain in which some of the tensions between the old and new forms of trust seem to manifest themselves. While some leaders at both the corporate and national levels still seek to legitimize their authority by reference to tradition, a growing number appear to have accepted that if leadership is going to support effective knowledge management, then leadership's legitimacy must be based on more rational norms. The trust that leaders build must be an inclusive, open, democratic kind, or knowledge creation and sharing will falter (Bennis and Slater, 1964; Bennis and Nanus, 1997). Charismatic bases of leadership, as Weber predicted, still wax and wane in popularity, continually finding new pertinence, but the balance between traditional and rational bases seems to be shifting progressive in favor of rationality. Within firms, leadership seems to have shifted toward a form of trust consonant with the ethos of "fact-based management" independent injury, and collaborative problem-solving rather than traditionalist deference to established authority.

A modern form of normative trust can be distinguished from its premodern form. The modern form is less blind and tradition bound. It is more "studied" (Sabel, 1992), "rational" (Eccles, 1985), and "tentative" (Barnes, 1981). Its rationality is not of the purely calculative kind assumed by economics. Norms play a central role in modern trust, but these norms do not derive their legitimacy from affective sources such as tradition or charisma, nor from their own calculative, purposive-rational utility. Rather, the legitimacy of modern trust is derived from grounding in open dialogue among peers. Habermas (1990) has attempted to characterize this form of legitimization in terms of the "ideal speech situation," and Apel (1987) in the "ideal community of communication."

The modern form of trust might be labeled "reflective." The values at work in modern trust are those of the scientific community: "universalism, communism, disinterestedness, organized skepticism" (Merton, 1973: 270). Modern trust is inclusive and open. Referring to the discussion above of the bases of trust, one could hypothesize that whereas traditional trust elevates loyalty over the other bases (Schumpeter's "precapitalist bonds of loyalty and obedience"), modern rust ranks integrity and competence more highly (Butler and Cantrell, 1984; Schindler and Thomas, 1993: see Gates, 1998 for a case study of the shift from loyalty to competence in the basis of trust among President's staff in the White House).

From these considerations, I tentatively conclude that the efficacy of trust for knowledge management and the likelihood of its growth over time are maximized if: (a) trust is balanced by hierarchical rules to ensure stability and equity, (b) trust is balanced by market competition to ensure flexibility and opportunity, and (c) trust is modern and reflective rather than traditionalistic and blind. Space does not permit, but a parallel argument

contrast was between market (externally coordinating entrepreneurial firms) and hierarchy (internally coordinating oligopolistic firms, and eventually coordinating activity across entire economies). This contrast and Schumpeter's analysis of it have continuing pertinence: Both the persistent crisis tendencies of capitalism and the incapacity of markets to cope effectively enough with the growing knowledge-intensity of modern society reinforce Schumpeter's concerns about the efficacy of market coordination. Also, the long-term trend toward larger firms and bigger government confirms his prognosis of the growing importance of hierarchy.

A critic might argue that this prediction is at variance with the real trends observed in the United States and elsewhere in the advanced industrial economies over the last couple of decades, where an intensification of global and domestic competition and a wave of deregulation have reasserted the dominance of the market. The Schumpeterian view, however, invites us to enlarge our temporal horizon: If one considers the changes witnessed over the last 50 to 100 years. Schumpeter's prediction of the replacement of market by hierarchy becomes more plausible. The last couple of decades have made little progress in "turning back the clock." Even if the average size of establishments has stabilized, the weight of large firms relative to small in the economy has grown, and the weight of (federal and state) government relative to private industry has grown too.

Schumpeter's thesis, however, also needs revision. Both the continued vitality of small entrepreneurial firms in the capitalist knowledge-creation process and the demise of state socialism give us reasons to doubt the efficacy of hierarchy alone as a form capable of effectively structuring firms and societies. Schumpeter's implicit market-hierarchy model must be extended to include trust: We must add a dialect of trust to Schumpeter's market-hierarchy dialectic. On the one hand, over the longer run, the economy's increasing knowledge-intensity undermines the efficacy and therefore legitmacy of (low-trust) market and hierarchy. Market's costly fluctuations and manifest failures and hierarchy's coercive domination and alienating specialization reveal the inadequacies of these two forms relative to the knowledge-management challenge. Low-trust market thus loses legitimacy as a model of governance of interfirm and interdivisional relations, and (low-trust) hierarchy loses legitimacy as a model of governance of employment relations. On the other hand, the gradual infusion of trust into hierarchies and markets popularizes and legitimates a range of more participative and democratic notions of how firms should be run (Levine, 1995; Lawler, *et al.*, 1998) and of how society and the economy as a whole should be governed (Lodge, 1975; Unger, 1975; Etzioni, 1988).

Do these trends, however, spell the demise of capitalism? Hirschman (1982) criticizes Schumpeter and other proponents of the self-destruction thesis for ignoring capitalism's ability to adapt to pressures such as these. Hirschman argues that through a series of innovations from factory legislation to social security to countercyclical macroeconomic management, demands to socialize the economy have been accommodated within a basically capitalist framework.

At a micro level of intra- and interfirm relations, one could follow Hirschman and point to the evidence that trust can indeed infuse hierarchy and market relations without provoking crisis: As argued above, the three forms are often complementary.

These complementarities should, nevertheless, not obscure the fact that in a capitalist society the varying combinations of market, hierarchy, and community operate under the overall predominance of the market. If, as I argued above, the three basic coordination modes are sometimes substitutes and only sometimes complements, then it follows that all three modes cannot peacefully co-exist in any proportions. There is little doubt which of the three dominates in advanced economies today. While the functioning of a market-based economy is greatly enhanced by modest doses of hierarchy and community, the dominance of the market form places limits on the growth of hierarchy and community. Whatever hierarchy and community are created within and between firms, market pressures that are beyond any actor's control – in the form of unpredictable market fluctuations and crises – can force management to renege on its commitments (laying off employees or breaking supply relationships) or can simply force the firm out of business. In an era of globalization, intensified competitive rivalry, and international financial crisis tendencies, the dominant role of the market has been brutally brought back into focus.

It is against this backdrop that Schumpeter's thesis acquires its force. The development of greater knowledge–management capability will necessitate the displacement of the market as the dominant form. However, whereas Schumpeter saw the progressive displacement of market by hierarchy, first in large corporations, then at the societal level in the form of socialism, this essay suggests a "friendly amendment" to Schumpeter's thesis: The institutional framework likely to emerge from capitalism's development is not any form of socialism but a form characterized by high levels of trust. If socialism can be construed as a form of society in which hierarchy dominates market at both the firm level and the economywide level, then the form of socialism that can successfully confront the challenges of modern, knowledge-intensive industry will have to be one in which hierarchy is combined with high levels of trust.

Opinions are divided as to whether the most viable form of postcapitalist society will prove to be one based on comprehensive centralized but democratic planning or a form of market socialism in which markets supplement democratic planning (Nove, 1982). What seems indubitable, however, is that the planning process must be one in which citizens feel a high degree of trust. Evidence for this assertion comes first from the demise of (decidedly low-trust) state socialism. While external pressures clearly played a role in this demise, low-trust central planning was also a key factor. Evidence also comes from research on the vitality of industrial districts in regions such as Northern Italy. Whereas Putnam (1993) argues that long-standing community ties in those regions created a fabric of horizontal trust, which in turn led to high levels of civic engagement and economic prosperity, critics have shown the economic vitality of these regions stems not only from horizontal trust but also from the vertical trust earned and enjoyed by active local governments (e.g. Tarrow, 1996). This is also the lesson of Evans' (1995) analysis of the importance for economic development of governments with high levels of "embedded autonomy."

The various configurations of capitalist and postcapitalist societal forms can be located in a typology that reflects at the macrosocietal level the typology presented earlier of institutional forms at the firm level (see Figure 15.4). Indeed, substitution of the three terms of Figure 15.3 – market, hierarchy, and community – with corresponding dimensions already well established in sociological analysis – market, state, and civil society – is conceptually straightforward. (Concerns voiced by critics of this market/state/civil society trichotomy focus on the way much prior research fell prey to "classificatory angst" (Edwards and Foley, 1988: 128) and degenerated into arguments over whether a given institution falls into this or that type. The approach suggested by this chapter avoids that dead end by using these ideal-types to understand the hybrids in which they are typically presented.)

For trust to become the dominant mechanism for co-ordination within organizations, broadly participative governance and multistakeholder control would need to replace autocratic governance and owner control – even if hierarchy, in a high-trust form, continued to characterize large-scale enterprise. And, for trust to become the dominant mechanism for co-ordinating between organizations, comprehensive but democratic planning would need to replace market competition as the dominant form of resource allocation – even if market retained an important subsidiary role. If capitalism can be defined as a

Figure 15.4　A typology of societal forms　(low trust forms in lower left triangles, high trust forms in upper right triangles)

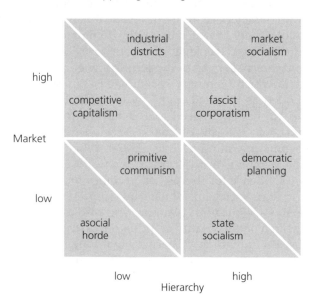

form of society characterized by (hierarchically controlled) wage labor and (market coordinated) competing firms, then such a trust-based form of society would surely qualify as postcapitalist. A host of institutional components of capitalism, notably property rights, corporate law, labor law, and even the form of government, would need to change accordingly. "Vertical trust" – trust in government – would have to be radically increased.

This extension of Schumpeter's thesis must immediately acknowledge that we know little about what any postcapitalist form of society might look like. The demise of state socialism has highlighted the importance of combining hierarchy with high levels of trust and the possible value of market as a subordinate mode, but whether and how such combinations can be attained and sustained is still an open question. Indeed, the central thesis of this chapter is that the trends at work today in the fabric of intra- and interfirm relations might give us valuable clues to the answer.

Acknowledgments

This chapter is based on a presentation at the University of California Berkeley Forum on "Knowledge and the Firm," September 1997. Contributors were asked to err on the side of interesting provocation, thus the speculative nature of this article. It has benefited from the comments of several colleagues who bear no responsibility for the author's reluctance to accept their advice: Eileen Appelbaum, Nick Argyris, Reinhardt Bachmann, Rose Batt, Warren Bennis, David Finegold, Susan Helper, Peter Kim, Marek Korcynski, Nancy Kurland, David Levine, Arie Lewin, Julia Liebeskind, Larry Prusak, Peter Ring and Carroll Stephens. *Organization Science* referees offered valuable suggestions and challenges.

References

Abrahamson, E. (1997) "The emergence and prevalence of employee management rhetorics: the effects of long waves, labor unions, and turnover, 1875–1992," *Academy of Management Journal* 40(3): 491–533.

Academy of Management Review (1998) Special topic forum on trust in and between organizations 23(3).

Adler, P.S. (1990) "Marx, machines and skill," *Technology and Culture* 31(4): 780–812.

Adler, P.S. (1997) "Work organization: from Taylorism to teamwork," *Perspectives on Work* (June) 61–5.

Adler, P.S. and Borys, B. (1996) "Two types of bureaucracy: coercive versus enabling," *Administrative Science Quarterly* 41(1): 61–89.

Adler, P.S. and Ferdows, K. (1992) "The chief technology officer: a new role for new challenges," Gomez-Mejia, L.R. and Lawless, M.W. (eds) *Advances in Global High-Technology Management: Top Management and Executive Leadership in High Technology*, vol. 2, Greenwich CT: JAI Press, 49–66.

Adler, P.S., Goldoftas, B. and Levine, D.I. (1999) "Flexibility versus efficiency? A case study of model changeovers in the Toyota production system," *Organization Science* 10(1): 43–68.

Alchian, A. and Demsetz, A.H. (1972) "Production, information costs, and economic organization," *American Economic Review* 62(5): 777–95.

Apel, K.O. (1987) "The problem of philosophical foundations in light of a transcendental pragmatics of language," in Barnes, K., Bohnmann, J. and McCarthy, T. (eds) *After Philosophy: End or Transformation?* Cambridge, MA: MIT Press, 250–90.

Arrow, K. (1962) "Economic welfare and the allocation of resources for invention. Universities – National Bureau Committee for Economic Research," *The Rate and Direction of Inventive Activity,* Princeton, NJ: Princeton University Press 609–25.

Arrow, K. and Hurwicz, I. (eds) (1977) *Studies in Resource Allocation Processes,* Cambridge, MA: Cambridge University Press.

Askenas, R., Ulrich, D., Jick, T. and Kerr, S. (1993) *The Boundaryless Organization,* San Francisco, CA: Jossey-Bass.

Barber, B. (1983) *The Logic and Limits of Trust,* New Brunswick, NJ: Rutgers University Press.

Barker, J.R. (1993) "Tightening the iron cage: concertive control in self-managing teams," *Administrative Science Quarterly* 38: 408–37.

Barley, S.R. and Kunda, G. (1992) "Design and devotion: surges of rational and normative ideologies of control in managerial discourse," *Administrative Science Quarterly* 37: 363–99.

Barnes, L.B. (1981) "Managing the paradox of organizational trust," *Harvard Business Review* (March–April) 59(2): 107–16.

Barney, J.B. and Hansen, M.H. (1994) "Trustworthiness as a source of competitive advantage," *Strategic Management Journal* 15 (Special Issue) 175–216.

Bell, D. (1993) *Communitarianism and Its Critics,* Oxford, U.K: Clarendon Press.

Bennis, W.G. and Nanus, B. (1997) *Leaders: Strategies for Taking Charge,* 2nd edn New York: Harper Business.

Bennis, W.G. and Slater, P.E. (1964) "Democracy is inevitable," *Harvard Business Review* (March–April).

Bensaou, M. and Venkatraman, N. (1995) "Configurations of interorganizational relationships: a comparison between US and Japanese automarkers," *Management Science* 41(9): 1471–92.

Bigley, G.A. and Pearce, J.L. (1998) "Straining for shared meaning in organization science: Problems of trust and distrust," *Academy of Management Review* 23(3): 405–21.

Birch, D.L. (1987) *Job Creation in America,* New York: Free Press.

Blackburn, P., Coombs, R. and Green, K. (1985) *Technology, Economic Growth and the Labor Process,* New York: St Martin's Press.

Blau, P.M. (1955) *The Dynamics of Bureaucracy,* Chicago IL: University of Chicago Press.

Bradach, J. and Eccles, R. (1989) "Markets versus hierarchies: From ideal types to plural forms," in Scott, W.R. (ed.) *Annual Review of Sociology,* 15: 97–118.

Braverman, H. (1974) *Labor and Monopoly Capital,* New York: Monthly Review Books.

Brockner, J. and Siegel, P. (1996) "Understanding the interaction between procedural and distributive justice: the role of trust," in Kramer, R.M. and Tyler, T.R. (eds) *Trust in Organizations,* Thousand Oaks, CA: Sage 390–413.

Bromiley, Philip and Cummings, Larry L. (1995) "Transaction costs in organizations with trust," in Bies, R.J., Lewicki, R.J. and Sheppard, B.L. (eds) *Research on Negotiations in Organizations,* Greenwich, CT: JAI.

Brynjolfsson, E., Malone, T.W., Gurbazani, V. and Kambil, A. (1994) "Does information technology lead to smaller firms?" *Management Science* 40(12): 1628–44.

Burawoy, M. (1979) *Manufacturing Consent,* Chicago, IL: University of Chicago Press.

Burns, T. and Stalker, G. (1961) *The Management of Innovation,* London, UK: Tavistock.

Business Week (1982) "TRW leads a revolution in managing technology," (November 15).

Butler, J.K. and Cantrell, R.S. (1984) "A behavioral decision theory approach to modeling dyadic trust in superiors and subordinates," *Psychological Reports* 55: 19–28.

Carchedi, G. (1977) *The Economic Identification of Social Classes,* London, UK: Routledge & Kegan Paul.

Carney, M. (1988) "The competitiveness of networked production: the role of trust and asset specificity," *Journal Management Studies* 35(4): 457–79.

Champy, J. (1995) *Reengineering Management,* New York: Harper Business.

Coleman, R. (1990) *Foundations of Social Theory,* Cambridge, MA: Belknap Press.

Collins, J.C. and Porras, J.I. (1994) *Built to Last,* New York: HarperCollins.

Crozier, M. (1964) *The Bureaucratic Phenomenon*, Chicago, IL: University of Chicago Press.

Daft, R.L. (1998) *Essentials of Organization Theory and Design*, Cincinnati, OH: South-Western College Publishing.

Davenport, T.H. and Prusak, L. (1998) *Working Knowledge*, Boston, MA: Harvard Business School Press.

Dore, R. (1983) "Goodwill and the spirit of market capitalism," *British Journal of Sociology* 34: 459–82.

Downs, A. (1967) *Inside Bureaucracy*, Boston, MA: Little, Brown.

Durkheim, É. (1984) *The Division of Labor in Society*, trans W.D. Halls, New York: Free Press.

Dyer, J.H. (1996) "Does governance matter? Keiretsu alliances and asset specificity as sources of Japanese competitive advantage," *Organisation Science* 7(6): 649–66.

Dyer, J.H. and Chu, W. (1998) "The determinants of interfirm trust in supplier-automaker relationships in the US, Japan and Korea," Unpublished, Wharton.

Earl, M.J. and Scott, I.A. (1999) "What is a chief knowledge officer?" *Sloan Management Review* (Winter) 40(2): 29–38.

Eccles, R. (1985) *The Transfer Pricing Problem*, Lexington, MA: Lexington.

Edwards, B. and Foley, M.W. (1998) "Civil society and social capital beyond Putnam," *American Behavioral Scientist* 42(1): 124–39.

Etzioni, A. (1988) *The Moral Dimension*, New York: Free Press.

Evans, P. (1995) *Embedded Autonomy: States and Industrial Transformation*, Princeton, NJ: Princeton University Press.

Evans, P. (1996) "Government action, social capital and development: reviewing the evidence on synergy," *World Development* 24(6): 1119–32.

Fox, A. (1974) *Beyond Contract: Work, Power and Trust Relations*, London, UK: Faber and Faber.

Fukuyama, F. (1995) *Trust: The Social Virtues and the Creation of Prosperity*, New York: Free Press.

Gambetta, D. (ed.) (1988) *Trust: Making and Breaking Cooperative Relations*, Oxford, UK: Basil Blackwell.

Gates, H.L., Jr (1998) "The end of loyalty," *The New Yorker* (March 9) 34–44.

Gerlach, M.I. (1992) *Alliance Capitalism: The Social Organization of Japanese Capitalism* Berkeley, CA: University of California Press.

Giddens, A. (1990) *The Consequences of Modernity*, Stanford, CA: Stanford University Press.

Gouldner, A.W. (1954) *Patterns of Industrial Bureaucracy*, New York: Free Press.

Granovetter, M. (1985) "Economic action and social structure: the problem of embeddedness," *American Journal Sociology* 91 481–510.

Gupta, A.K. and Govindarajan, V. (1986) "Resourcing sharing among SBUs: strategic antecedents and administrative implications," *Academic Management Review* 29(4): 695–714.

Habermas, J. (1990) *Moral Consciousness and Communicative Action*, Cambridge, MA: MIT Press.

Habermas, J. (1993) *The Philosophical Discourse of Modernity*, Cambridge, MA: MIT Press.

Hammer, M. (1996) *Beyond Reengineering*, New York: HarperBusiness.

Hammer, M. and Champy, J. (1993) *Reengineering the Corporation*, New York: HarperBusiness.

Hanck, B. (1997) "Trust or hierarchy? Changing relationships between large and small firms in France," *Small Business Economics* 11(3): 237–52.

Hardin, R. (1992) "The street-level epistemology of trust," *Politics and Society* 21: 505–29.

Harvey, D. (1990) *The Condition of Modernity*, Cambridge, MA: Blackwell.

Heimer, C. (1992) "Doing your job and helping your friends: Universalistic norms about obligations to help particular others in a networks," in Noria, N. and Eccles, R.G. (eds) *Networks and Organizations: Structure, Form and Action*, Boston, MA: Harvard Business School Press, 143–64.

Heisig, U. and Littek, W. (1995) "Trust as a basis of work organization," in Littek, W. and Charles, T. (eds) *The New Division of Labour: Emerging Forms of Work Organization in International Perspective*, Berlin/New York: de Gruyter, 17–56.

Helper, S. (1991) "Strategy and irreversibility in supplier relations: the case of the US automobile industry," *Business History Review* 65(4): 781–824.

Helper, S. and Sako, M. (1995) "Supplier relations in the auto industry in Japan and the USA: are they converging?" *Sloan Management Review* (Spring) 36(3): 77–84.

Hill, C.M. and Hoskisson, H.R. (1992) "Cooperative vs competitive structures in related and unrelated diversified firms," *Organisation Science* 3(4) 501–21.

Hirschman, A.O. (1970) *Exit, Voice and Loyalty,* Cambridge, MA: Harvard University Press.

Hirschman, A.O. (1982) "Rival intrerpretations of market society: civilizing, destructive or feeble?" *Journal of Economic Literature* 20: 1463–84.

Holland, C.P. and Lockett, A.G. (1997) "Mixed mode network structures: the strategic use of electronic communication by organizations," *Organization Science* 8(5): 475–88.

Hyman, R. (1987) "Strategy or structure? Capital, labor and control," *Work, Employment and Society* 1(1): 25–55.

Kaplan, R.S. (1984) "The evolution of management accounting," *The Accounting Review,* (July).

Kaplan, R.S. (1996) *The Balanced Scorecard: Translating Strategy into Action,* Boston, MA: Harvard Business School Press.

Kern, H. (1998) "Lack of trust, surfeit of trust: some causes of the innovation crisis in German industry," in Lane, C. and Bachmann, R. (eds) *Trust Within and Between Organizations,* New York: Oxford University Press, 203–13.

Kim, P.H. (1997) "Working under the shadow of suspicion: the implications of trust and mistrust for information sharing in groups," unpublished, University of Southern California, Los Angeles, CA.

Kirkpatrick, F.G. (1986) *Community: A Trinity of Models,* Washington, DC: Georgetown University Press.

Korczynski, M. (1996) "The low trust route to economic development Interfirm relations in the UK engineering construction industry in the 1980s and 1990s," *Journal of Management Studies* 33(6): 787–808.

Koza, M.P. and Lewin, A.Y. (1998) "The co-evolution of strategic alliances," *Organizational Science* 9(3): 255–64.

Kurland, N.B. (1966) "Trust, accountability, and sales agents' dueling loyalties," *Business Ethics Quarterly* 6(3): 289–310.

Lakoff, G. (1996) *Moral Politics: What Conservatives Know That Liberals Don't,* Chicago, IL: University of Chicago Press.

Lawler, E.E. III, Mohrman, S.A. and Ledford, G.E. Jr. (1998) *Strategies for High Performance Organizations,* San Francisco, CA: Jossey-Bass.

Levine, D. (1995) *Reinventing the Workplace: How Business and Employees Can Both Win,* Washington, DC: Brookings Institution.

Lewicki, R.J. and Benedict Bunker, B. (1996) "Developing and maintaining trust in work relationships," in Kramer, R.M. and Tyler, T.R. (eds) *Trust in Organizations,* Thousand Oaks, CA: Sage, 114–9.

Liebeskind, J.L., Oliver, A.L., Zucker, L. and Brewer, M. (1996) "Social networks, learning and flexibility: sourcing scientific knowledge in the new biotechnology firms," *Organizational Science* 7(4): 428–43.

Liebeskind, J.L., Oliver, A.L., Zucker, L. and Brewer, M. (1998) "From handshake to contract: trust, intellectual property, and the social structure of academic research," in Lane, C. and Bachmann, R. (eds) *Trust Within and Between Organizations,* New York: Oxford University Press 118–45.

Lodge, G.C. (1975) *The New American Ideology,* New York: Knop.

Lorsch, J.W. and Allen, S.A. III (1973) "Managing diversity and inter-dependence," Division of Research, Graduate School of Business Administration, Harvard University, Boston, MA.

Luhmann, N. (1979) *Trust and Power,* Chichester, UK: Wiley.

Macaulay, S. (1963) "Non-contractual relations in business," *American Sociology Review* 28: 55–70.

Macneil, I.R. (1980) *The New Social Contract,* New Haven, CT: Yale University Press.

Marx, K. (1973) *Grundrisse: Foundations of Political Economy,* Harmondsworth: Penguin.

Marx, K. and Engels, F. (1959) "Manifesto of the Communist Party," in Feuer, L.S. (ed.) *Marx and Engels Basic Writings on Politics and Philosophy,* Garden City: Doubleday.

Mashaw, J.L. (1983) *Bureaucratic Justine: Managing Social Security Disability Claims,* New Haven, CT: Yale University Press.

Merton, R.K. (1973) *The Sociology of Science,* Chicago, IL: University of Chicago Press.

Miller, G.J. (1992) *Managerial Dilemmas: The Political Economy of Hierarchy,* New York: Cambridge University Press.

Mintzberg, H. (1979) *The Structuring of Organizations,* Englewood Cliffs, NJ: Prentice-Hall.

Nahapiet, J. and Ghoshal, S. (1998) "Social capital, intellectual capital and the organizational advantage," *Academic Management Review* 23(2): 242–66.

Nelson, R.R. (1988) "Institutions supporting technical change in the United States," in Dosi, G., Freeman, C., Nelson, R., Silverberg, G. and Soete, L. (eds) *Technical Change and Economic Theory,* London, UK: Pinter 312–29.

Nove, A. (1982) *The Economics of Feasible Socialism,* London, UK: Allen & Unwin.

Nyland, C. (1998) "Taylorism and the mutual-gains strategy," *Industrial Relations* 37(4): 519–42.

OECD (1996) *Employment and Growth in the Knowledge-Based Economy,* Organization for Economic Co-operation and Development, Paris, France.

Organization Science, (1998) Special issue on managing partnerships and strategic alliances 9(3).

Ouchi, W. (1980) "Markets, bureaucracies and clans," *Administrative Science Quarterly* 25 (March) 125–41.

Paine, T. (1951 (1792)) *The Rights of Man,* New York: E. P. Dutton.

Porter, M.E. (1985) *Competitive Advantage,* New York: Free Press.

Powell, W. (1990) "Neither markets nor hierarchy: network forms of organization," *Research in Organizational Behavior* 12: 295–336.

Prahalad, C.K. and Hamel, G. (1990) "The core competencies of the corporation," *Harvard Business Review* 86: 79–91.

Putnam, R. (1993) *Making Democracy Work: Civic Traditions in Modern Italy,* Princeton, NJ: Princeton University Press.

Ramsay, H. (1977) "Cycles of control: worker participation in sociological and historical perspective," *Sociology* 11(3): 481–506.

Ring, P.S. (1996) "Fragile and resilient trust and their roles in economic exchange," *Business Society* 35(2): 148–75.

Ring, P.S. (1997) "Transacting in the state of union: a case study of exchange governed by convergent interests," *Journal of Management Studies* 34(1): 1–25.

Ring, P.S. and Van de Ven, A.H. (1992) "Structuring cooperative relationships between organizations," *Strategic Management Journal* 13: 483–98.

Ring, P.S. and Nathan, R. (1964) "Neglected dimensions in the analysis of economic change," *Oxford Bulletin of Economic Statistics* 26(1): 59–77.

Rothschild-Witt, J. (1979) "The collectivist organization: an alternative to rational-bureaucratic models," *American Sociological Review* 44: 509–27.

Sabel, C.F. (1992) "Studied trust: building new forms of co-operation in a volatile economy," Pyke, F. and Sengenberges, W. (eds) *Industrial Districts and Local Economic Regeneration,* Geneva, Switzerland: International Institute for Labour Studies.

Sabel, C.F. and Zeitlin, J. (eds) (1997) *World of Possibilities: Flexibility and Mass Production in Western Industrialization,* Cambridge, UK: Cambridge University Press.

Sako, M. (1992) *Prices, Quality and Trust: Interfirm Relations in Britain and Japan,* Cambridge, UK: Cambridge University Press.

Salter, M.S. (1983) "Tailor incentive compensation to strategy," *Harvard Business Review* (March–April) 51(2): 94–102.

Satow, R.L. (1975) "Value-rational authority and professional organizations: Weber's missing type," *Administrative Science Quarterly* 20 (Dec) 526–31.

Schindler, P.L. and Thomas, C.C. (1993) "The structure of interpersonal trust in the workplace," *Psychological Reports* 73: 563–73.

Schumpeter, J. (1976 (1942)) *Capitalism, Socialism and Democracy,* New York: Harper.

Scott, W.R. (1992) *Organizations: Rational, Natural and Open Systems,* Englewood Cliffs, NJ: Prentice Hall.

Seligman, A.B. (1997) *The Problem of Trust,* Princeton, NJ: Princeton University Press.

Shapiro, S.P. (1987) "The social control of impersonal trust," *American Journal of Sociology* 93(3): 623–58.

Sparrow, M.K. (1994) "Imposing duties: government's changing approach to compliance," Westport, CT: Praeger.

Spencer, M.E. (1970) "Weber on legitimate norms and authority," *British Journal of Sociology* 21(2): 123–34.

Stiglitz, J.E. (1994) *Whither Socialism?* Cambridge, MA: MIT Press.

Stinchcombe, A.L. (1985) "Contracts as hierarchical documents," in Stinchcombe, A.L. and Heimer, C. (eds) *Organization Theory and Project Management*, Bergen, Norway: Universitetsforslaget.

Tarrow, S. (1996) "Making social science work across space and time: a critical reflection on Robert Putnam's Making Democracy Work," *American Political Science Review* 90(2): 389–401.

Unger, R.M. (1975) *Knowledge and Politics*, New York: Free Press.

Uzzi, B. (1997) "Social structure and competition in interfirm networks: the paradox of embeddedness," *Administrative Science Quarterly* 42(1): 35–67.

Walton, R.E. (1985) "Toward a strategy for eliciting employee commitment based on policies of mutuality," in Walton, R.E. and Lawrence, P.R. (eds) *HRM Trends and Challenges*, Boston, MA: Harvard Business School.

Walzer, M. (1999) "Rescuing civil society," *Dissent* 46(1): 62–7.

Weber, M. (1947) *The Theory of Social and Economic Organization*, New York: Free Press.

Wenger, É. (1998) *Communities of Practice*, New York: Oxford University Press.

Wicks, A.C., Berman, S.L. and Jones, T.M. (1999) "The structure of optimal trust: moral and strategic implications," *Academic Management Review* 24(1): 99–116.

Williamson, O.E. (1975) *Markets and Hierarchies*, New York: Free Press.

Williamson, O.E. (1981) "The economics of organization: the transaction cost approach," *American Journal of Sociology* 87: 548–77.

Williamson, O.E. (1991) "Economic institutions: spontaneous and intentional governance," *Journal of Law Economics and Organization* 7: 159–87.

Williamson, O.E. (1993) "Calculativeness, trust, and economic organization," *Journal of Law Economics and Organization* 36: 453–502.

Zelizer, V.A. (1996) "Payments and social ties," *Sociological Forum* 11(3): 481–96.

Zenger, T.R. and Hesterly, W.S. (1997) "The disaggregation of corporations: selective intervention, high-powered incentives, and molecular units," *Organizational Science* 8(3): 209–22.

Zucker, L.G. (1986) "Production of trust: Institutional sources of economic structure, 1840–1920," *Research on Organizational Behavior* 8: 53–111.

16 Knowledge, knowledge work and organizations:
an overview and interpretation[1]
Frank Blackler

Introduction

Ever since Galbraith (1967) suggested that a powerful new class of technical-scientific experts was emerging, and Bell (1973) proposed that knowledge is a central feature of post-industrial societies, the significance of experts in contemporary society has attracted much comment (see Reed, 1991 for a discussion of contemporary trends). Indeed, in recent years, the importance of expertise for competitive advantage has been emphasized again by economists and business strategists who have suggested that wealth creation is less dependent on the bureaucratic control of resources than it once was, and more dependent on the exercise of specialist knowledge and competencies, or the management of organizational competencies (e.g. Prahaled and Hamel, 1990; Hague, 1991; Reich, 1991; Drucker, 1993; Florida and Kenny, 1993). This debate has found echoes in discussion about 'knowledge-intensive firms', that is, organizations staffed by a high proportion of highly qualified staff who trade in knowledge itself (Starbuck 1992, 1993; Alvesson, 1993a), in the suggestion that organizational competencies can be nurtured by the development of inter-organizational links (Kanter, 1989; Badaracco, 1991; Wikstrom and Normann, 1994), and in the proposal that, because of technological changes, team organization is becoming of crucial importance and employees generally should be managed as 'knowledge workers' (Zuboff, 1988).

Within the literature on the established professions the privilege suggested by the term 'knowledge' and the opportunities it offers occupational groups to protect their positions and 'black box' their skills (for example, by claiming the authority of medicine, law, or other complex bodies of knowledge) have been well documented (e.g. Baer, 1987; Abbott, 1988). Writing in a special edition of the *Journal of Management Studies* on knowledge work Alvesson (1993a) notes how specialists in the new generation of knowledge firms are, in exactly the same way, attracted to the mystique associated with the terms such as knowledge and knowledge worker; knowledge-intensive firms are, above all else he suggests, systems of persuasion. Developing a similar point Knights, Murray and Willmott (1993) suggest that the growing use of such terms may be regarded as normalizing discourse which, as it legitimates a particular division of labour, distracts attention from the knowledge that is an essential characteristic of all forms of activity.

This chapter explores the relevance of the terms knowledge, knowledge work and knowledge-intensive firms for organization studies, by developing an approach which seeks neither to perpetuate the mystique often associated with abstract, codified knowledge nor to present claims to knowledge merely as normalizing discourse. Conventional images of knowledge within the literature on organizational learning are first identified and are distinguished by the assumptions they make about the location of knowledge, i.e. in bodies, routines, brains, dialogue or symbols. Recent commentary on the emerging significance of knowledge work amounts to the suggestion that, in place of a strong reliance on knowledge located in bodies and routines (in the terminology of this chapter, in place of knowledge which is 'embodied' and 'embedded'), emphasis is increasingly falling on the knowledge that is located in brains, dialogue and symbols (i.e. knowledge which is 'embrained', 'encultured' and 'encoded'). Conventional assumptions about the nature of knowledge are not without their difficulties, however; a point which has emerged strongly from studies of the impact of new information and communication technologies. Inspired by such studies, and drawing from recent debates in philosophy, linguistics, social theory and cognitive science, an alternative approach is outlined. Rather than regarding knowledge as something that people have, it is suggested that knowing is better regarded as something that they do. Such an approach draws attention to the need to research ways in which the systems which mediate knowledge and action are changing and might be managed. The conclusion of the chapter is that debate about the growing importance of esoteric experts and flexible organizations should be located within a broader debate about the nature of expertise and of the changing systems through which activities are enacted.

Images of knowledge within organization studies

Within the organization studies literature a variety of approaches to knowledge can be identified. One obvious place to begin exploring these is the literature on organizational learning. The metaphor or organizational learning is not new, it has attracted attention at least since Chandler (1962). Interest in the United States has been consistently high (see, e.g., Argyris and Schon, 1978; Duncan and Weiss, 1979; Nelson and Winter, 1982; Daft and Weick, 1984; Fiol and Lyles, 1985; Nonaka and Johansson, 1985; Levitt and March, 1988; Zuboff, 1988; Henderson and Clark, 1990; Senge, 1990; Brown, 1991; Kochan and Useem, 1992; Dixon, 1994; and special editions of *Organization Science* 1991 and of *Organization Dynamics* 1993) although, especially in recent years, a strong interest has been developing in the United Kingdom and Europe also (Hedberg, 1981; Garratt, 1987; Pedler *et al.* 1991; Swieringa and Wierdsma, 1992; Dodgson, 1993, and see also Douglas, 1987). At least five images of knowledge can be identified in this literature. Adapting and extending a categorization of knowledge types suggested by Collins (1993) these are knowledge that is *embrained*, *embodied*, *encultured*, *embedded* and *encoded*.

Embrained knowledge: is knowledge that is dependent on conceptual skills and cognitive abilities (what Ryle 1949, called 'knowledge that' and James 1950, termed 'knowledge about'). As discussed further below, within Western culture abstract knowledge has enjoyed a privileged status, and in the organizational learning literature a number of commentators have emphasized its importance. Fiol and Lyles (1985), for example, reflect the predominant view of the distinctive status of abstract knowledge when they contrast 'routine' behavioural adjustments with what they term 'higher level' abilities to develop complex rules and to understand complex causations. Perhaps the best known theorist of organization learning who has featured embrained knowledge is Argyris, whose theory of 'double-loop' learning (e.g. Argyris and Schon, 1978) encourages an explicit recognition and reworking of taken-for-granted objectives. A recent account in this tradition is Senge (1990) who synthesizes personal insights, models, systems thinking and shared visions in a general account of organization learning.

Embodied knowledge: is action oriented and is likely to be only partly explicit (what Ryle 1949, called 'knowledge how', and James 1950, 'knowledge of acquaintance'). A contemporary account of embodied knowledge is included in Zuboff (1988): such knowledge, she says, depends on peoples' physical presence, on sentient and sensory information, physical cues and face-to-face discussions, is acquired by doing, and is rooted in specific contexts. Other accounts include Scribner's (1986) description of 'practical thinking', i.e. problem-solving techniques which depend on an intimate knowledge of a situation rather than abstract rules, Hirschhorn's (1984) analysis of mechanization and his conclusion that operators' tacit understandings of machine systems are more important than their general knowledge, and Suchman's (1987) studies of how people spontaneously construct interpretations of technologies as they interact with them.

Encultured knowledge: refers to the process of achieving shared understandings. Cultural meaning systems are intimately related to the processes of socialization and acculturation; such understandings are likely to depend heavily on language, and hence to be socially constructed and open to negotiation. As Swidler (1986) indicated, in periods of social transformation explicitly formulated ideologies become the main vehicle for promoting new recipes for action. Following Pettigrew (1979) and Ouchi's (1980) discussions of organizational culture there has, of course, been considerable interest in the relevance to organizations of such processes. Within the literature on organizational learning, Srivastva and Barrett (1988) demonstrated how the imagery in the language of a group can change over time: as people grasp for new insights, they experiment with new metaphors into their talk which others may take up and develop; and Czarniawska-Joerges (1990) illustrated how consultants explicitly endeavour to manage this process. Other important contributions include Orr's (1990) account of stories shared by maintenance technicians about complex mechanical problems, and Nonaka's (1991, 1994) discussions of 'knowledge-creating' organizations (these are discussed further below).

Embedded knowledge: is knowledge which resides in systemic routines. The notion of 'embeddedness' was introduced by Granovetter (1985), who proposed a theory of economic action that, he intended, would neither be heavily dependent on the notion of culture (i.e. be 'oversocialized') nor heavily dependent on theories of the market (i.e. be 'under-socialized'): his idea was that economic behaviour is intimately related to social and institutional arrangements. Following Badaracco (1991), the notion of embedded knowledge explores the significance of relationships and material resources. Embedded knowledge is analysable in systems terms, in the relationships between, for example, technologies, roles, formal procedures, and emergent routines. This is how, for example, Nelson and Winter (1982) analysed an organization's capabilities. They noted that an individual's skills are composed of subelements which become co-ordinated in a smooth execution of the overall performance, impressive in its speed and accuracy with conscious deliberation being confined to matters of overall importance; thus, they maintained, may an organization's skills be analysed. In addition to the physical and mental factors that comprise individual skills however, organizational skills are made up of a complex mix of interpersonal, technological and socio-structural factors. Similar approaches include Levitt and March's (1988) development of the notion of organizational routines (which, they suggest, make the lessons of history accessible to subsequent organizational members) while other writers refer to 'organizational competencies' (Prahaled and Hamel, 1990). A related orientation has been proposed by Henderson and Clark (1990) who distinguish between the knowledge of specialist elements in an organization ('component knowledge') and knowledge about how such elements interact ('architectural knowledge'); architectural knowledge is often submerged within an organization's taken-for-granted routines and interactions, yet is central to an understanding of its strengths and weaknesses.

Encoded knowledge: is information conveyed by signs and symbols. To the traditional forms of encoded knowledge, such as books, manuals and codes of practice, has been added information encoded and transmitted electronically. Zuboff's (1988) analysis of the 'informating' power of information technologies explores the significance of this point for organizations: information encoded by decontextualized, abstract symbols is inevitably highly selective in the representations it can convey. Poster's (1990) thesis on how the new information technologies may be 'culturally alien' and Cooper's (1992) analysis of the significance of technologies of representation for the theory of organization are amongst the writings which have complemented such lines of analysis.

Brown's (1991) account of efforts to develop Xerox as a learning organization provides an example of how the development of each of these different forms of knowledge may contribute to organizational learning. Brown pointed to the advantages for a company like Xerox of undertaking new product development in close association with potential customers (i.e. in the terminology of this chapter, he identified the relevance of the embedded knowledge of Xerox's customers for an understanding of their reactions to new office machinery).

He illustrated how design engineers at Xerox learned from ethnographic studies of how people interact with machines (i.e. from studies of the ways in which encoded knowledge interacts with, and may disrupt, embodied knowledge) and he emphasized too how studies of communications between engineers in Xerox have revealed how essential dialogue is between them (i.e. encultured knowledge) to increase their effectiveness in solving problems. Finally, Brown emphasized the importance of encouraging senior managers to develop new appreciations of their company's established practices (i.e. he pointed to the importance of developing embrained and encultured knowledge at senior management levels).

Derived as it is from the literature on organizational learning, the five types of knowledge identified here do not focus on the commodification of knowledge into products, systems, or services. (Thus, economists' interests in the immediate competitive potential of industrial secrets, patents, etc. – see e.g. Winter 1988 – or with the cumulative advantages that such knowledge may provide, Arthur 1990, are not included within this typology). What the variety of images of knowledge identified here serves to emphasize is the complexity of issues that any discussion of knowledge within organizations must address. For example, it indicates that all individuals and all organizations, not just so-called 'knowledge workers' or 'knowledge organizations', are knowledgeable. As is discussed in the following sections, the typology can also be used to review claims that significant changes are presently taking place in the relationship between knowledge and economic success, and to introduce a critique of conventional approaches to analysing such developments.

Organizations and different types of knowledge

Drucker (1993) has offered an historical interpretation of the suggestion that, within the demands of contemporary capitalism, a shift is occurring in the relationship between knowledge and wealth creation. In the eighteenth century, he suggests, the basis for an economic system based on machines and factories was laid with the development of 'technologies'. These he describes as 'knowledge applied to tools, processes and products' (in the terminology introduced above, this involved the development of new approaches to the study of embodied knowledge, i.e. craft skills, supported by the granting of patents to inventors and entrepreneurs). Later, in the early years of the last century, F. W. Taylor's development of a technology of work analysis provided the basis for a further impetus to productivity. Drucker describes this as 'knowledge applied to human work' (in the terminology used above this involved the systematic development of systems of embedded knowledge). Now, Drucker maintains, a society is emerging that is dependent upon the development and application of new knowledges. 'Knowledge is being applied to knowledge itself.' In the terminology of this chapter, Drucker's thesis can be taken to imply that embrained and encultured knowledge are beginning to assume predominant importance.

Both the practical and the theoretical implications of Drucker's thesis are significant. Just as the nature of organization and management changed dramatically at the time of industrial revolution and later as a result of Taylorism, Drucker maintains that new approaches are now becoming necessary. Productivity is becoming dependent on the application and development of new knowledges, and on the contributions of specialist knowledge workers. Drucker's thesis is that knowledge workers are unlike previous generations of workers, not only in the high levels of education they have obtained, but principally because, in knowledge-based organizations, they own the organization's means of production (i.e. knowledge). Drucker suggests that, in these circumstances, familiar images of organizations as hierarchical, decentralized or as a matrix should be discarded. Alternative models can be developed from examples of organizations based on key specialist experts, such as hospitals, symphony orchestras or the British Colonial administration in India.

In recent years, other American commentators have presented related ideas. Shortly before his appointment as US Secretary of State for Labour the political economist Reich (1991) suggested that the globalization of the world's economy is creating a split between the production of standardized products in low-wage economies, and high value-added problem solving which may be undertaken wherever useful insights can be found. Accordingly, the maxim that a nation's chief economic asset are the skills and insights of its citizens assumes new significance. From his discussions with a range of senior executives in major American corporations, Reich believes that the strategies of big businesses no longer focus on products as such, rather, they are endeavouring explicitly to exploit the competitive advantage that specialized knowledge can provide. High value-added depends on problem solving; in the international economy, value-added accrues anywhere around the world where useful insights can be channelled to respond to the particular needs of individual customers. The tendency for manufacturing and service companies to concentrate on the provision of speciality services has become so advanced, Reich believes, that the traditional distinction in economics between goods and services has broken down. Moreover, he emphasizes the undesirable social consequences that are likely to result from the dependency of low pay, low status workers in service industries or routine production, on highly paid, high status 'knowledge workers'.

The skills of what Reich calls 'symbolic analytic' workers are varied. They command high rewards, he believes, because they are difficult to duplicate. Such skills include problem solving (research, product design, fabrication), problem identification (marketing, advertising, customer consulting), and brokerage (financing, searching, contracting). When combined, Reich observes, these skills allow technical insights to be linked both to marketing know-how and to strategic and financial acumen. In the terminology suggested in this chapter, Reich is highlighting the contemporary significance of embrained knowledge. Such knowledge can be used to support new forms of organization based on networks, partnerships or contractual arrangements.

Both Drucker and Reich attribute particular significance to knowledge workers. While Drucker's thesis is clearly influenced by Bell's theory of post-industrialism, Reich's analysis is strongly influenced by the current difficulties of the American economy, especially the reduced international dominance of American conglomerates, changes in American manufacturing industry, an influx of foreign capital, and acute social inequalities. Yet both claim their approaches reach beyond the American experience, and locate their interpretations in a world perspective, suggesting that as national economies are integrated into the global economy, similar developments are occurring in other countries as well.

A less sophisticated account than either Drucker's or Reich's, but one which anticipated a number of their points had been presented by a Swedish businessman and a British journalist in the mid-1980s. Sveiby and Lloyd (1987) developed an account for general managers not of knowledge workers but of knowledge organizations. Defining know-how as 'value added information' they suggested that 'know-how companies' provide a non-standard, creative, problem-solving service. To be successful, know-how companies must, Sveiby and Lloyd suggested, be high on what they called professional skills, yet in itself this would be insufficient. The new breed of know-how organizations also need a high level of 'managerial skills' (defined as 'the ability to preserve added value'). Examples of professional know-how organizations that they provided included highly entrepreneurial (and very profitable) merchant banks, advertising agencies, software firms, and management, architectural and engineering consultancies.

Sveiby and Lloyd's account is not without its problems but their analysis of knowledge-intensive organizations (rather than capital, technology, or labour intensive) was unusual. Anticipating some of Drucker's observations they noted how such firms present particular problems of organization and management (for example, power in know-how companies stems primarily from ability and reputation; new forms of employment relationship may be demanded by know-how workers; high short-term profit is likely to be a mistaken goal for know-how companies, what matters is the company's ability to convince clients of the value of a long-term relationship). Rather than the specifics of their observations, it was the powerful image of the 'professional know-how organization' that attracted the attention of academics. Starbuck in the United States and Alvesson in Sweden both preferred a different terminology, 'knowledge-intensive firm', but their interests covered similar ground to Svieby's. Thus, in presenting his comments on knowledge-intensive firms Starbuck (1992) emphasized the economic significance of esoteric knowledge over common knowledge and pointed to the potential distinctions between specialist expertise and the skills of the established professions. He emphasized the importance of social skills and client relationships to the activities of knowledge workers and the success of their companies, and explored the difficulties that knowledge-intensive firms may have in developing their own learning (for example, experts may not be receptive to new ideas). In a subsequent paper (Starbuck 1993) he further explores the distinctive identities of knowledge-intensive firms, and the need to analyse them within their particular market situations.

Alvesson (1993b), on the other hand, has reported how the managers of knowledge-intensive firms may cope with their dependency on their specialist workers. In an analysis of a computer consultancy, he identifies the ideological controls that management used, striving to create a 'strong' culture, by manufacturing a sense of community, using performance related rewards, cultivating a positively buoyant outlook, and systematically intervening in an attempt to influence the ways in which employees thought of themselves and the company.

Recent commentaries on knowledge-intensive firms in the popular management literature have concentrated less on knowledge workers as the recipients of cultural manipulation and more on their active participation within their organization's dialogue. Daft and Weick's (1984) notion of organizations as systems of interpretation anticipated many of the issues that are now being raised: to survive, they argued, organizations must find ways to interpret events. Indeed, the processes of 'sensemaking' that Daft and Weick highlighted are likely to be especially important for firms that concentrate on the solution of unfamiliar problems; thus, Petes's (1992) discussion of the consultancy firm McKinsey's points to the central role that communication plays in that organization where energetic efforts are made to share key reports, a data bank of project lessons is maintained to create 'an internal marketplace of readily accessible ideas', and experienced consultants routinely make themselves available to other staff for comments or guidance. The conclusion that Webber (1993) takes from Peter's description is that, in a sense, conversations are McKinsey's.

Drawing from four of the knowledge types identified at the start of this chapter, an overview of the knowledge work literature reviewed in this section is offered in Figure 16.1. Organizations which depend differentially on knowledge that is embodied, embedded, embrained, and encultured are distinguished in a two-by-two matrix. This is developed by distinguishing between organizations which first, focus on problems of a routine kind versus those that are preoccupied with unfamiliar issues and second, depend heavily upon the contributions of key individuals versus those who are more obviously dependent upon collective effort. Four kinds of organization are thus differentiated in Figure 16.1: (i) expert-dependent organizations, which depend heavily on embodied knowledge; (ii) knowledge-routinized organizations, which depend heavily on embedded knowledge; (iii) symbolic-analyst dependent, which depend heavily on embrained knowledge; and (iv) communication-intensive organizations, which depend heavily on encultured knowledge. This classification provides a way of summarizing key suggestions in the knowledge work literature. The arrows depicted in Figure 16.1 highlight the trends many of the commentators reviewed in this section purport to have identified: that a shift is occurring away from dependence on the embodied and embedded knowledge towards embrained and encultured knowledge.

| **Figure 16.1** | Organizations and knowledge types (arrows summarize trends suggested in the knowledge work literature) |

	(ii) Knowledge-routinized organizations:	**(iv) Communication-intensive organizations:**
Emphasis on collective endeavour	*Emphasis on knowledge embedded in technologies, rules and procedures.* Typically capital, technology, or labour intensive. ⟶ Hierarchical division of labour and control. Low skill requirements. *Example:* 'Machine bureaucracy' such as a traditional factory. *Current issues:* Organizational competencies and corporate strategies. Also, the development of computer integrated work systems.	*Emphasis on encultured knowledge and collective understanding.* Communication and collaboration the key processes. Empowerment through integration. Expertise is pervasive. *Example:* 'Ad hocracy', 'innovation mediated production'. *Current issues:* 'Knowledge-creation', dialogue, sense-making processes. Also, the development of computer supported cooperative work (CSCW) systems.
Emphasis on contributions of key individuals	**(i) Expert-dependent organizations:** *Emphasis on the embodied competencies of key members.* Performance of specialist ⟶ experts is crucial. Status and power from professional reputation. Heavy emphasis on training and qualifications. *Example:* 'Professional bureaucracy' such as a hospital. *Current issues:* Nature and development of individual competency. Also, computer displacement of action skills.	**(iii) Symbolic-analyst-dependent organizations:** *Emphasis on the embrained skills of key members.* Entrepreneurial problem solving. Status and power from creative achievements. Symbolic manipulation is a key skill. *Example:* 'Knowledge-intensive-firm' (KIF) such as a software consultancy. *Current issues:* Developing symbolic analysts, the organization of KIFs. Also, information support and expert systems design.
	Focus on familiar problems	Focus on novel problems

Encoded knowledge, and criticisms of conventional approaches to knowledge

The accuracy of these very general claims can only, of course, be established by empirical investigation and it may be that current developments are not all one way (for example there would appear to be a trend in the United Kingdom to organize certain professional bureaucracies in the public sector, not as symbolic-analyst-dependent or communication-intensive organizations, but as machine bureaucracies). However there remains a more basic problem. In recent years, taken-for-granted assumptions about the nature of knowledge, which underpin the distinctions presented on Figure 16.1, have been exposed as problematic. Studies of the ways in which new forms of encoded knowledge have affected organizations have played a major part in this reassessment.

It would be a mistake to regard the new generation of information and communication technologies as neutral tools that can merely be grafted onto existing work systems. Of particular interest to the present discussion is the way such technologies have been found to disrupt conventional practices, as Hirschhorn (1984) has noted of automated work systems, Zuboff (1988) of informated work systems, and Pava (1986) of how such technologies demand new approaches to socio-technical systems design. The way the technologies intimately interlace with the minutiae of everyday practices is exposing processes which, previously, were taken for granted, ignored or misunderstood.

Zuboff's studies, for example, document in detail how action oriented skills (in the terms used here, embodied knowledge) are being displaced by computer technologies (encoded knowledge). The new technologies bypass the use of immediate, physical responses to situated cues; instead they require operators to interpret the selective, decontextualized and abstract symbols that machines present to them. Computers require sophisticated cognitive abilities; the skills of deduction and a knowledge of systems and procedures are essential for their satisfactory operation. Zuboff (1988) and Weick (1985) have suggested that it is foolish to believe that high-technology work systems can be managed as if conventional processes of sense making are outmoded. Talk about computer-mediated information and the transformation of isolated problem-solving attempts into a shared activity are crucial to the effective operation of the 'informated' organization. It is only through such processes that the process of collective interpretation can be recreated. The point may be summarized in the suggestion that managers in informated organizations must contrive to develop the skills which are referred to here as encultured knowledge.

It is not only through their 'informating' effects, however, that technologies based on micro-electronics are transforming organizations. Such technologies are also associated with the changes precipitated by economic globalization. This is not to say that the transformations associated with contemporary capitalism are technologically determined. As Castells (1989) documents in his account of changes occurring in contemporary capitalism, governmental enactment of post-Keynesian policies in, for example, weakening trade unions, developing fiscally austere policies, retreating from policies of wealth redistribution, and reducing the size of the public sector are fundamental to an understanding of developments. By the operations they support, the new technologies are playing a vital role in facilitating the internationalization of capital, production and labour processes. Castells summarizes how modern information technologies have transformed money markets and eroded the distinctions between mass- and customized-markets, and at the same time they make it possible for organizations to develop flexible methods of production, to disperse their operations, and to compete in alliances. The communication and control operations they support within organizations are also facilitating the demise of bureaucratic approaches of organization, promising vigorous internal networks, collaborative work relations and significantly reduced hierarchical structures of control (developments explored in detail by Malone and Rochart, 1991, and Sproull and Kiesler, 1991).

Thus, just as familiar working patterns are being transformed by the encodification of knowledge, at the same time, the new technologies are making it possible for organizations to operate relatively independently from geographical location, thereby blurring the boundaries between one organization and another, and freeing internal communications within organizations. During the 1980s, much social science commentary on the relationship between information technologies and organizations emphasized how technologies are not deterministic in their effects (Buchanan and Boddy, 1983). Instead, it was maintained, they open a range of options from centralization to decentralization, from automation to work enrichment. Current developments suggest, however, that rather than thinking of the new technologies as flexible tools for organizations to use as they believe is appropriate, it may be better to consider the technologies as the medium for organizing itself. Organizations that are heavily dependent on the new technologies are, simultaneously, being imploded into electronic codes and exploded into (global) information networks.

Some of the tensions involved in these processes are not new. The uneasy relationship that encoded knowledge may have to other forms of knowledge has been documented before. For example, Zuboff quotes the mediaeval historian Clanchy, (1979) who recorded the slow and largely reluctant acceptance in eleventh and twelfth century England of written documentation: 'both to ignorant illiterates and to sophisticated Platonists, a written record was a dubious gift, because it seemed to kill living eloquence and trust and substitute for them a mummified semblance in the form of a piece of parchment'. Yet the extent of the disruption to knowledge bases associated with electronically encoded information is new. As summarized in Figure 16.1, the new media of encoded knowledge not only affect embodied knowledge, but may also affect the nature and significance of embrained knowledge (as information becomes ever more accessible and expert computer systems are developed), encultured knowledge (as new communication systems are introduced to support group working between individuals who are separated in time and space), and embedded knowledge (through, for example, the development of integrated manufacturing systems).

The close relationship between encoded knowledge and the other images of knowledge highlighted in this discussion illustrate the point that it is a mistake to assume that embodied, embedded, embrained, encultured and encoded knowledge can sensibly be conceived as separate one from the other. Knowledge is multi-faceted and complex, being both situated and abstract, implicit and explicit, distributed and individual, physical and mental, developing and static, verbal and encoded. Analysis of the relationships between different manifestations of knowledge identified in this chapter is at least as important as any delineation of their differences.

From theories of knowledge to theories of knowing

Nonaka's (1991, 1994) descriptions of the 'knowledge-creating' organization provides a useful starting point for theorizing about the links between the different forms of knowledge identified in this chapter. Nonaka is concerned with the management of innovation. This he regards as an ongoing process in which organizations create problems, define them, then develop new knowledge for their solution. He develops the idea that knowledge is created out of a dialogue between peoples' tacit and explicit knowledge. Knowledge may move from tacit to tacit (e.g. in a craft apprenticeship), from explicit to explicit (e.g. when hitherto distinct but related bodies of information are brought together), from tacit to explicit (e.g. the study of craft skills), and from explicit to tacit (e.g. the internalization of new knowledge). Nonaka maintains that all four of these patterns exist in dynamic interaction in 'knowledge-creating' companies. He does not wish to suggest, however, that the processes involved here are merely a recycling of knowledge. Knowledge creation, he believes, is closely associated with language and communications, requiring the creative use of metaphors, analogies and models, and a resolution of the conflicts and disagreements that new approaches may provoke. In the terminology of this chapter, Nonaka is suggesting that encultured knowledge is intimately related to the development of embodied, embrained and embedded knowledge. His approach traces the link between different forms of knowledge to the processes through which they are created.

In other respects, however, Nonaka's approach is rather traditional. He insists that knowledge is a specific entity, formed in the minds of individuals (albeit generated in interactions with others), and conceptually distinct from the material technologies around which organizations are structured (see Nonaka, 1994). Similarly, while his concept of 'knowledge-creation' pushes the distinction between knowledge and learning to its limits, he wishes to maintain a distinction between them.

To develop the analysis of the interrelations between different types of knowledge further, it is necessary to address the basic question: what is knowledge? (or perhaps as Pear 1972, asks, what is not knowledge?). In recent years there has been considerable debate about this issue. Postmodernists, for example, have challenged the idea of fundamental truth by suggesting that truth is a story (see, e.g., Lawson, 1989): cognitive anthropologists, ethnomethodologists and symbolic interactionists have queried the value of abstract plans and the notion of social structure and have demonstrated the significance of situated skills and pragmatic knowledge (e.g. Suchman, 1987); and sociologists of science have challenged deep-rooted assumptions about the privileged status of explicit abstract knowledge by studying knowledge creation as a cultural process and by de-emphasizing conventional distinctions between people and technology (e.g. Latour, 1987; Law, 1992).

The various implications of such approaches remain to be fully described. Yet it is becoming clear that traditional conceptions of knowledge as abstract, disembodied, individual, and formal are unrealistic. Polkinghorne (1992), for example, reviews the implications of postmodernism for the theory of practice. Practical knowledge, he suggests, is foundationless, partial, constructed and pragmatic. A similar outlook is presented by Lave (1993), who reviews points of agreement between cognitive anthropologists, ethnomethodologists and activity theorists. Such theorists agree, she says, that major difficulties occur when educationalists assume that knowledge can be divorced from context and transmitted either as abstract data or as universally applicable approaches to problem solving; learning is not a passive process, she argues, but an active one. Defining learning as a creative (and collective) interpretation of past experiences she summarizes the emerging consensus between educational researchers as agreement that:

1. Knowledge always undergoes construction and transformation in use.
2. Learning is an integral aspect of activity in and with the world at all times. That learning occurs is not problematic.
3. What is learning is always complexly problematic.
4. Acquisition of knowledge is not a simple matter of taking in knowledge; rather, things assumed to be natural categories, such as 'bodies of knowledge', 'learners', and 'cultural transmission', require reconceptualization as cultural, social products. (Lave 1993: 8)

Star (1992) has also presented a summary of patterns of agreement between contemporary social theorists, drawing on a similar literature to Lave's although placing a heavier emphasis on research studies in the actor-network tradition. The emerging consensus that conventional views of knowledge are unacceptable is so widespread, Star believes, that she refers to it as 'an invisible college' and 'an intellectual movement that as yet has no name'. Reviewing detailed studies of technology and work, she echoes Lave's points in her observation that the boundaries of knowledge in complex organizations are fluid and overlapping. Star explains this by reviewing studies which suggest that cognitions are situated (as the circumstances of action shape even the most abstractly represented tasks); cognitions are collective (as practices are distributed socially and technologically); and that, rather than being a mere internal manipulation of ideas, cognitions are also forms of material practice (i.e. cognitions not only involve an internal manipulation of ideas but they involve physical, manual and interactional actions as well).

Accounts such as these (see also Brown and Rogers 1991, for a similar approach developed for the theory of communication) provide a useful starting point for the development of a unifying theory of organizational knowledge. First, rather than talking of knowledge, with its connotations of abstraction, progress, permanency and mentalism, it is more helpful to talk about the process of knowing. Second, to avoid segregating the forms of knowing identified in this chapter, old concepts (such as the split between the abstract and the specific, individuals and communities, and the social and the technical) need to be abandoned and new approaches to conceptualizing the multi-dimensional processes of knowing and doing need to be created. One approach to this task could be to develop from the insights that knowing is situated, distributed and material.

Activity theory, knowing and doing

Out of the range of theoretical approaches that both Lave (1993) and Star (1992) include in their reviews which might be of value in this project, activity theory offers particular promise. Activity theory has its origins in the ideas of the Russian psychologist Vygotsky who, working in the 1920s, endeavoured to develop an understanding of mind and society which did not depend upon the dichotomies (e.g. mind versus body, thought versus action, individual versus society, etc.) that have characterized mainstream Western thought (and which lend credence to the clear distinctions assumed between embodied, embedded, embrained and encultured knowledge). Basic to the Vygotsky approach is the Marxist idea that it is not the consciousness of humans that determines their social being, but social experiences which shape their consciousness: psychological processes can only be understood by an appreciation of the, culturally provided, factors that mediate them. (Vygotsky thought, for example, that it would be a mistake to think that children pass through a stage of egocentric speech before they use language socially, his view was the opposite, i.e. that children learn to internalize speech which is, from the start, oriented to their external social environment, see Kozulin, 1990).

Contemporary versions of activity theory take a variety of forms. However, all are explicit in their attempts to develop a unified account of knowing and doing, and all emphasize the collective, situated and tentative nature of knowing. Some (e.g. Brown, Collins and Duguid, 1989; and Lave and Wenger, 1991) concentrate on the processes through which people develop shared conceptions of their activities. Others, (Hutchins, 1983; Engestrom, 1987, 1993) model the relationships that exist between a community's conceptions of its activities and the material, mental and social resources through which it enacts them. While the former approach develops a model of learning as socialization, the latter explores the circumstance in which communities may enact new conceptions of their activities.

Orr's (1990) analysis of Xerox maintenance technicians is in the Brown/Lave tradition of activity theory. He describes how the stories shared by maintenance personnel about complex technical problems is an essential part of their activities. In the first place the stories they tell each other serve a key informational function, preserving and circulating essential news about particular problems. Second, the storytelling has an educational function: not only do the technicians learn about particular faults on the machines, they also help the participants develop their diagnostic and trouble-shooting skills. Finally, the stories provide an opportunity for the technicians to establish their identity within the community of technicians itself; as newcomers contribute to the storytelling process they begin both to demonstrate their identity as professionals and to contribute to the collective wisdom of their group. In their discussion of the wider implications of this study Brown and Duguid (1989) emphasize the general significance for organizations of such processes. Learning is a socially constructed understanding, they argue, that emerges from practical collaboration. Collective wisdom depends upon communal narratives. Note that this analysis suggests that it is not just esoteric consultancies like McKinsey's (see Peters 1993; and Webber 1993, discussed earlier) which benefit from lively internal communications; collective dialogue is also an essential aspect of life in other, less glamorous, organizations, developing skills and abilities which are distributed (often unnoticed) amongst the employees within them.

Engestrom's (1989, 1991) study of a medical practice in Finland illustrates a second version of activity theory. Partly through discourse analysis, partly from observation, and partly from accounts of the history of medicine he was able to distinguish the variety of conceptions that doctors may have of their activity. Doctors may conceive of their work in biomedical, administrative-economic, psychiatric, socio-medical, or in system-interactive terms. Doctors in the same medical practice may, perhaps unknowingly, be enacting different conceptions of health care, yet attempts to refocus priorities may not be easy to achieve. In Engestrom's study, attempts to reorientate priorities towards psycho-somatic and socio-medical priorities were hampered by the resource system within which the doctors operated: (i) the division of labour between doctors and other health-care professionals proved inflexible; (ii) the way patients are randomly allocated to doctors in the Finnish health-care system created problems of continuity of care; and (iii) the biomedical concepts and techniques that the doctors had become accustomed to using encouraged them to continue treating health-care problems as biomedical problems.

The analysis Engestrom offers of this, and other, work settings is explicitly intended to avoid separating the individual from the collective, or the social from the technical. Fundamental to his approach is the unit of analysis he adopts, namely, the socially-distributed activity system. The general model he offers of such systems is shown in Figure 16.2. Essential to such systems are the relations between agents, the community of which they are members, and the conception(s) people have of their activities (the inner triangle of relations in Figure 16.2). Such relations are mediated by a further series of factors, including the language and technologies used by participants within the system, the implicit and explicit social rules that link them to their broader communities, and the role system and division of labour adopted by the community.

A summary model of Engestrom's analysis of the dynamics of the medical practice he studied is shown on Figure 16.3. Note that the relations depicted in this figure are neither static nor are they necessarily harmonious. The three points of tension noted in Engestrom's fieldwork, detailed above, are featured on the model (see points (i), (ii) and (iii)).

Indeed Engestrom's approach suggests that, far from being unusual, tensions such as these are commonplace within distributed work systems. His analysis of the dynamics of activity systems is reminiscent of Perrow's

Figure 16.2 A general model of socially-distributed activity systems

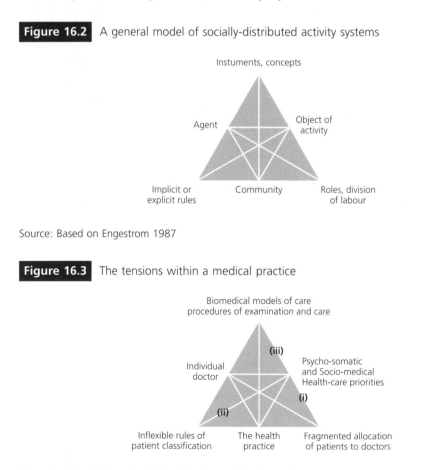

Instuments, concepts

Agent

Object of activity

Implicit or explicit rules

Community

Roles, division of labour

Source: Based on Engestrom 1987

Figure 16.3 The tensions within a medical practice

Biomedical models of care
procedures of examination and care

(iii)

Individual doctor

Psycho-somatic and Socio-medical Health-care priorities

(i)

(ii)

Inflexible rules of patient classification

The health practice

Fragmented allocation of patients to doctors

Points (i), (ii) and (iii) mark points of tension within the activity system
Source: Adapted from Engestrom 1991.

(1984) suggestion that accidents are a normal feature of life in complex industrial work systems. Likewise, for the most part, everyday interruptions and breakdowns in the workings of activity systems are skilfully, regularly and normally repaired (although system breakdown may sometimes occur). It is through their collective determination and skill, both in their actions and their language, that participants enact particular frames (i.e. impose conceptions of their activities on situations they believe appropriate) and maintain a (seemingly) smooth flow of events.

Note that the incoherencies, paradoxes and conflicts that feature within activity systems provide a potential driving force for change. Engestrom's analysis suggests that organizations and institutions are a lot less stable and rational than is usually recognized. The incoherencies and contradictions that feature within them are obscured, however, partly no doubt by conventional imagery of the organization as a rational machine, but also by the skills of participants who learn to work within the situation in which they find themselves. New ways of knowing and doing can emerge if communities begin to rethink what, in a different context, Unger (1987) has called the 'false necessity' of everyday life, and to engage with the tensions in their activity systems. The complexities of socially distributed activity systems suggest that incoherencies and tensions are inevitable; the issue is not how can they be eradicated but how they should be treated.

Rethinking knowledge and organizations

As the review presented in the first part of this chapter indicated, current interest in knowledge and knowledge work marks a change of emphasis within contemporary capitalism away from knowledge that is embodied and embedded, to knowledge that is embrained, encultured and encoded. The approach presented in the second part of this chapter offers a different orientation. To summarize:

1. Lave suggests that knowledge should not be conceived as a timeless body of truth that experts have internalized and which organizations may harness. She suggests that the notion of 'bodies of knowledge' (with its connotations of universal truth) is a problem in its own right. General abstractions are no more than resources to be used in specific circumstances where (in actions, improvisation and dialogue) creativity is ubiquitous. By focusing on knowing rather than knowledge, the distinction that is conventionally assumed between knowledge and learning is avoided.

2. Engestrom's interpretation of the dynamic relationships between individuals, their communities and the objects of their activities provides a clear alternative to approaches which attempt to study such entities, or the factors which mediate the relationships between them, in isolation one from the other. His suggestion is that the appropriate unit of analysis

is neither individuals nor organizations, but socially-distributed activity systems. People act on the world, with others, utilizing (and contributing to the development of) the linguistic, material and social resources currently available. Knowledge does not appear as a separate category in Engestrom's model, rather, it permeates the relations he depicts. His approach models the dynamics of knowing: each moment is a compromise, the balance within an activity system changes constantly. Participants employ their situated knowledge in a situation which is itself constantly developing. In response to this changing situation participants' knowledge and behaviour will also inevitably develop.

3. Activity theories in general argue that knowledge is constantly evolving. Analysis of the tensions that inevitably develop within socially-distributed activity systems points to the opportunities for system development that (routinely) arise. Orr, Brown and Duguid demonstrate how essential language is to this process. Talk enables collective interpretations, negotiates behavioural priorities, signals group membership, and helps to create a community. Language is an archetypal communal activity, integral to the enactment of practical actions.

Thus, helpful though it can be to characterize knowledge as embodied, embedded, embrained, encultured and encoded, the concept of knowledge is problematic. Rather than studying knowledge as something individuals or organizations supposedly have, activity theory studies knowing as something that they do and analyses the dynamics of the systems through which knowing is accomplished. Recast in this way, knowing in all its forms is analysed as a phenomenon which is: (a) manifest in systems of language, technology, collaboration and control (i.e. it is mediated); (b) located in time and space and specific to particular contexts (i.e. it is situated); (c) constructed and constantly developing (i.e. it is provisional); and (d) purposive and object-oriented (i.e. it is pragmatic).

Before considering how these conclusions can be used to inform debate about knowledge and knowledge work, however, it should be noted that, in at least one respect, an extension of activity theory is required. Activity theory is not alone in its attempts to draw attention to the need to rethink supposed distinctions between events and contexts, language and action, the social and the technical, etc.; as noted above, similar suggestions have also been made by anthropologists, social theorists, and linguists and others. Of the comparisons that might be made between these various approaches, one point stands out: activity theory is weak in the analysis it offers of the relationship between knowledge and power. This is not to say that power as an issue does not occur at all in the writings of activity theorists. (For example, in her criticism of the term 'bodies of knowledge', highlighted above, Lave 1993, adopts Latour and Woolgar's 1979, terminology to suggest that claims to the possession of decontextualized knowledge are frequently no more than examples of erasure, collusion or domination.) However, analysis of power in everyday life has featured far less in the writings of activity theorists than it has in the work of others who are theorizing practice from different traditions. This is well illustrated by the issues that preoccupied Ortner (1984) in her discussion of the relevance to anthropology of theories of practice (such as Bourdieu, 1978; and Giddens, 1979) that were emerging in the early 1980s. Ortner supported the attempts being made in these writings to treat societies and cultures as integrated wholes and to avoid segregating social, economic and political factors from values, ideals and emotions, but she emphasized how it would be a mistake to treat all the elements of a social system as if they are of equal analytical significance. Social systems are fundamentally unequal. Gramsci's (1957) notion of hegemony and Foucault's (1980) notion of a 'discourse of perversions' serve as reminders that any theory of knowing as a cultural activity must acknowledge the, often self-reproducing, dynamics of domination and subordination that are a feature of everyday life.

To the suggestion just made that knowing is *mediated*, *situated*, *provisional* and *pragmatic* must therefore be added the point that it is also *contested*. As noted at the start of this chapter, this point has not passed unnoticed within the literature on knowledge work and knowledge-intensive firms (see Alvesson, 1993a; and Knights, Murray and Willmott, 1993).

Applied to the study of knowledge work, the approach developed here suggests that, as an alternative to focusing on the kinds of knowledge that capitalism currently demands, attention should focus on the systems through which knowing and doing are achieved. Because of the changes that are occurring in capitalism touched on earlier (such as moves towards the globalization of markets and finance, new information and communication technologies, post-Keynesian governmental policies, and new approaches to strategy, management and organization, etc.) activity systems are changing significantly. Rather than asking 'what sorts of knowledge are needed in contemporary capitalism and how may organizations harness them?' the question thus becomes 'how are systems of knowing and doing changing, and what responses would be appropriate?'

This revised formulation promises to establish links between the knowledge work literature and broader studies of economic and organizational changes. The analysis of knowing as mediated, situated, provisional, pragmatic and contested, provides a basis for identifying research priorities. Taking each of these in turn:

Knowing as mediated: Research is needed into the dynamics of activity systems and how they are currently changing. As discussed earlier, changes associated with the new information and communication technologies are combining with other developments, such as new economic and organizational structures and new approaches to management to transform the contexts of action. Further work is needed into such changes. One key consequence of these developments is that activity systems which were previously segregated are becoming interlinked and, therefore, are growing larger and becoming more complex. Research is needed to document such developments. Detailed ethnographic studies are needed to illuminate the ways in which people improvise, communicate and negotiate within expanded activity systems.

Knowing as situated: Work is needed to develop the relevance of the notion of situated knowledge to the knowledge work debate. As already noted, the concept of situated knowledge avoids the problems associated with abstract, decontextualized knowledge; it emphasizes the significance of peoples' interpretations of the contexts within which they act and the key role that 'communities of practitioners' play in the acquisition and development of skill. The knowledge work debate draws attention to the differences in approach that may develop between employees whose work involves them in action skills or in the execution of procedural routines, and those who are involved in creative problem solving. Little is known about the ways in which peoples' understanding of their activities are changing as a consequence of the developing complexity of the contexts within which they are working.

Knowing as provisional: Research is needed into the idea that knowing is, essentially, provisional and developing. Activity theory suggests that developments in systems of knowing and doing will occur constantly as tensions (inevitably) emerge within them. However, changes in activity systems may or may not be planned (for example, the unanticipated impacts of advanced information and communication technologies), and may or may not be fully understood or articulated by participants (for example, computer mediated interactions may erode traditional practices in bureaucracies but people may continue to describe their organizations through a terminology that is familiar to them). Activity theory points to the opportunities that might be created to help participants become more proactive in the development of their activity systems. At a general level, research is needed into Engestrom's proposal that, by alerting people to the tensions in activity systems that would otherwise be ignored or tolerated, a process of dialogue, experimentation and collective learning can be triggered that may transform participants' understandings of their activities and the systems through which they are enacted. Issues specific to the knowledge work debate include the study of the tensions within expert-dependent and knowledge-routinized organizations at the present time, and the ease with which they may transform themselves into symbolic-analyst dependent and communication-intensive organizations.

Knowing as pragmatic: Central to activity theory is the idea that collective action is driven by the conceptions people have of the object of their activities. Further research is needed into the influence that 'informed' and 'communication-intensive' environments have on the approaches people take to their work. It seems likely that, as activity systems become interrelated and complex, traditional approaches to organizing are likely to be ineffective. Research is needed into the possibilities for developing communal narratives within expanded activity systems. Study is also needed of the anxiety that individuals and communities may experience in the face of significant, ongoing, and perhaps conflicting demands for changes in their work methods and priorities.

Knowing as contested: Finally, as noted before, the concepts of knowledge and power are interrelated. Conflicts are to be expected within and between the new generation of symbolic analysts and problem solvers, and established professionals and managers. Beyond this, the far-reaching social, technological, and economic changes that are at the heart of the knowledge work debate indicate that issues of domination and subordination are fundamental to the development of a general theory of knowing as praxis.

Enquiry along the lines sketched out here is unlikely to contradict the suggestion that symbolic-analytical work and communication-intensive organizations are of growing significance at the present time. Rather, it promises to explain why this is so and, by reframing the problem, to illuminate some of the difficulties associated with such developments. In summary, the approach introduced here extends the debate about the importance of creative experts and flexible organizations to the (more general) discussion of the nature of expertise and of the systems through which people enact their activities. The study of knowledge work and organizations is, in other words, best located within a broader analysis of knowing as a cultural phenomenon.

Note

1. Prepared for the EU Human Capital and Mobility Project 'European Competitiveness in a Knowledge Society'. I am most grateful to Colin Brown, David Courpasson, Bente Elkjaer, Manuel Graca, Henrik Holt Larson, Karen Legge, Yves-Frederic Livian, Mike Reed and Alan Whitaker for their comments on an earlier version, and also to Arndt Sorge, Mats Alvesson and anonymous reviewers for OS.

References

Abbott, A. (1988) *The system of professions: an essay on the division of expert labour*, Chicago: University of Chicago Press.

Alvesson, M. (1993a) 'Organization as rhetoric: knowledge-intensive firms and the struggle with ambiguity', *Journal of Management Studies* 90: 997–1016.

Alvesson, M. (1993b) 'Cultural-ideological modes of management control: a theory and a case study of a professional service company' in Communication yearbook 16, Deetz, S. (ed.) London: Sage. 342.

Argyris, C. and Schon, D. (1978) *Organizational learning: a theory of action approach*, Reading, MA: Addison Wesley.

Arthur, W. B. (1990) 'Positive feedbacks in the economy', *Scientific American* (February): 885.

Badaracco, J. (1991) *The knowledge link: how firms compete through strategy alliances*, Boston, MA: Harvard University Press.

Baer, W. (1987) 'Expertise and professional standards', *Work and Occupations* 13: 532–52.

Bell, D. (1973) *The coming of post-industrial society: a venture in social forecasting*, New York: Basic Books.

Bourdieu, P. (1978) *Outline of a theory of practice*, Cambridge: Cambridge University Press.

Brown, J. S. C (1991) 'Research that invents the corporation', *Harvard Business Review* (Jan.–Feb.): 102–11.

Brown, J. S., Collins, A. and Duguid, P. 1989a 'Situated cognition and the culture of learning', *Educational Researcher* 18: 32–42.

Brown, J. S. and Duguid, P. (1989) 'Innovation at the workplace, a perspective on organizational learning', paper presented at the CMU Conference on 'Organizational Learning', May.

Brown, J. and Rogers, E. (1991) 'Openness, uncertainty, and intimacy: an epistemological reformulation', in Coupland, N., Giles, H. and Wiemann, J. (eds) *Miscommunication' and Problematic Talk*, London: Sage, I 146–65.

Buchanan, D. and Boddy, D. (1983) *Organizations in the Computer Age*, Aldershot: Gower.

Castells, M. (1989) *The Informational City: Information Technology, Economic Restructuring and the Urban-Regional Process*, Oxford: Basil Blackwell.

Chandler, A. (1962) *Strategy and Structure*, Boston: MIT Press.

Clanchy, M. (1979) *From Memory to Written Record: England 1066–1307*, Cambridge, MA: Harvard University Press.

Collins, H. (1993) 'The structure of knowledge', *Social Research* 60: 95–116.

Cooper, R. (1992) 'Formal organization as representation: remote control, displacement and abbreviation', in *Rethinking Organization: New Directions in Organization Theory and Analysis*, Reed, M. and Hughes, M. (eds), London: Sage, 254–72.

Czarniawska-Joerges, B. (1990) 'Merchants of meaning: management consultants in the Swedish public sector' Turner, B. (ed.) in *Organizational Symbolism*, Berlin: Walter de Gruyter 139–50.

Daft, R. and Weick, K. (1984) 'Toward a model of organizations as interpretation systems', *Academy of Management Review* 9: 284–95.

Dixon, N. (1994) *The Organization Learning Cycle: How We Can Learn Collectively*, London: McGraw Hill.

Dodgson, M. (1993) 'Organizational learning: a review of some literatures', Organization *Studies* 14(3): 375–94.

Douglas, M. (1987) *How Institutions Think*, London: Routledge and Kegan Paul.

Drucker, P. (1993) *Post-Capitalist Society*, Oxford: Butterworth-Heinemann.

Duncan, R. and Weiss, A. (1979) 'Organizational learning: implications for organizational design', in Staw, B. (ed.), *Research in Organizational Behaviour*, vol. 1. Greenwich, CN: Jai Press 75–123.

Engestrom, Y. (1987) *Learning by Expanding: An Activity Theoretical Approach to Developmental Research*, Helsinki: Orienta-Konsultit.

Engestrom, Y. (1989) 'Developing expertise at the changing workplace; towards a redefinition of expertise', Technical Report 130, La Jolla, California. Centre for Information Processing, University of San Diego.

Engestrom, Y. (1991) 'Developmental work research: reconstructing expertise through expansive learning', in Nurminen, M. and Weir, G. (eds) *Human Jobs and Computer Interfaces*, Amsterdam: North Holland 265–90.

Engestrom, Y. (1993) 'Work as a testbed of activity theory' in Chaiklin, S. and Lave, L. (eds) *Understanding Practice: Perspectives on Activity and Context*, Cambridge: Cambridge University Press, 65–103.

Foucault, M. (1980) *The History of Sexuality*, New York: Vintage.

Fiol, C. and Lyles, M. (1985) 'Organizational learning', *Academy of Management Review* 10: 803–13.

Florida, R. and Kenney, M. (1993) 'The new age of capitalism: innovation mediated production', *Futures* (July–August): 637–51.

Galbraith, J. (1967) *The New Industrial State* Boston: Houghton Mifflin.

Garratt, B. (1987) *The Learning Organization and the Need for Directors Who Think*, London: Fontana.

Giddens, A. (1979) *Central Problems in Social Theory: Action, Structure and Contradiction in Social Analysis*, Cambridge: Cambridge University Press.

Gramsci, A. (1957) *The Modern Prince and Other Writings*, New York: International Publishers.

Granovetter, M. (1985) 'Economic action and social structure: the problem of embeddedness', *American Journal of Sociology* 91: 481–510.

Hague, D. (1991) 'Knowledge society, university challenge', *Marxism Today* (September): 12–17.

Hedberg, B. 1981 'How organizations learn and unlearn', in Nystrom, P. and Starbuck, W. (eds), *Handbook of Organizational Design*. Vol. 1: *Adapting Organizations to their Environment*, Oxford: Oxford University Press, 3–27.

Henderson, R. and Clark, K. (1990) 'Architectural innovation: the reconstruction of existing product technologies and the failure of established firms', *Administrative Science Quarterly* 35: 9–30.

Hirschhorn, L. (1984) *Beyond Mechanization: Work and Technology in a Post-industrial Age*, Cambridge, MA: MIT Press.

Hutchins, E. (1983) 'Understanding Micronesian navigation', in Gentner, D. *Mental Models* and Stevens, A. (eds) Hillsdale, NJ: Erlbaum, 191–225.

James, W. (1950) *The Principles of Psychology*, New York: Dover.

Kanter, R. (1989) *When Giants Learn Dance*, New York: Simon and Schuster.

Knights, D., Murray, F. and Willmott, H. (1993) 'Networking as knowledge work: a study of interorganizational development in the financial services sector'. *Journal of Management Studies* 30: 975–96.

Kochan. T. and Useem, M. (eds) (1992) *Transforming Organizations*, Oxford: Oxford University Press.

Kozulin, A. (1990) *Vygotsky's Psychology: A Biography of Ideas*, Hemel Hempstead: Harvester Wheatsheaf.

Latour, B. (1987) *Science in Action: How to Follow Scientists and Engineers through Society*, Milton Keynes: Open University Press.

Latour, B. and Woolgar, S. (1979) *Laboratory Life: The Social Construction of Scientific Facts*, London: Sage.

Lave, J. (1993) 'The practice of learning', Chaiklin, S. and Lave, J. (eds) in *Understanding Practice: Perspectives on Activity and Context*, Cambridge: Cambridge University Press, 3–32.

Lave, J. and Wenger, E. (1991) *Situated Learning: Legitimate Peripheral Participation*, Cambridge: Cambridge University Press.

Law, J. (1992) 'Notes on the theory of the actor-network ordering, strategy and homogeneity', *Systems Practice* 5: 375–94.

Lawson, H. (1989) 'Stories about stories', Lawson, H. and Appignanesi, L. (eds) in *Dismantling Truth: Reality in the Postmodern World*, London: Weidenfeld and Nicolson, ix–xxviii.

Levitt, B. and March, J. (1988), 'Organizational learning'. *American Review of Sociology* 14: 319–40.

Malone, T. and Rockart, J. (1991) 'Computers, networks and the corporation', *Scientific American* (September): 92–9.

Nelson, R. and Winter, S. (1982) *An Evolutionary Theory of Organizational Change*, Cambridge, MA: Harvard University Press.

Nonaka, I. (1991) 'The knowledge creating company',. *Harvard Business Review* (November–December): 96–104.

Nonaka, I. (1994) 'A dynamic theory of organizational knowledge creation', *Organization Science* 5: 14–37.

Nonanka, I. and Johansson, J. (1985) 'Japanese management: what about the "hard" skills?', *Academy of Management Review* 2: 181–91.

Orr, J. (1990) 'Sharing knowledge, celebrating identity: community memory in a service culture', in Middleton, D. and Edwards, D. (eds) *Collective Remembering*, London: Sage, 169–89.

Ortner, S. (1984) 'Theory in anthropology since the sixties', *Comparative Studies in Society and History* 26: 126–66.

Ouchi, W. (1980) 'Markets, bureaucracies and clans', *Administrative Science Quarterly* 25: 129–41.

Pava, C. (1986) 'Redesigning sociotechnical systems design: concepts and methods for the 1990s', *Journal of Applied Behavioural Science* 22: 201–21.

Pear, D. (1972) *What is Knowledge?* Oxford: Basil Blackwell.

Pedler, M. Burgoyne, J. and Boydell, T. (1991). *The Learning Company: A Strategy for Sustainable Development*, London: McGraw-Hill.

Perrow, C. (1984) *Normal Accidents: Living With High-Risk Technologies*, New York: Basic Books.

Peters, T. (1992) *Liberation Management: Necessary Disorganization for the Nanosecond Nineties*, New York: Alfred Knopf.

Pettigrew, A. (1979) 'On studying organizational cultures', *Administrative Science Quarterly* 24: 570–81.

Polkinghorne, D. (1992) 'Postmodern epistemology of practice' in Kvale, S. (ed.), *Psychology and Postmodernism*, London: Sage, 146–65.

Poster, M. (1990) *The Mode of Information: Post-Structuralism and Social Context*, Cambridge: Polity Press.

Prahaled, C. and Hamel, G. (1990) 'The core competence of the corporation', *Harvard Business Review* (May–June): 79–91.

Reed, M. (1991) 'Experts, professions and organizations in late modernity: the dynamics of institutional, occupational and organizational change in advanced industrial societies', Lancaster, Lancaster University, Department of Behaviour in Organizations.

Reich, R. (1991) *The Work of Nations: Preparing ourselves for 21st-Century Capitalism*, London: Simon and Schuster.

Ryle, G. (1949) *The Concept of Mind*, London: Hutchinson.

Scribner, S. (1986) 'Thinking in action: some characteristics of practical thought', in Sternberg, R. and Wagner, R. (eds) *Practical Intelligence: Nature and Origins of Competence in the Everyday World*. Cambridge: Cambridge University Press, 13–30.

Senge, P. (1990) *The Fifth Discipline. The Art and Practice of the Learning Organization*, London: Century Business.

Sproull, L. and Kiesler, S. (1991) *Connections: New Ways of Working in the Networked Organization*, Cambridge, MA: MIT Press.

Srivastva, S. and Barratt, F. (1988) 'The transforming nature of metaphors in group development: a study in group theory', *Human Relations* 41: 31–64.

Star, S. (1992) 'The Trojan door: organizations, work, and the "open black box",' *Systems Practice* 5: 395–410.

Starbuck, W. (1992) 'Learning by knowledge intensive firms', *Journal of Management Studies* 29: 713–40.

Starbuck, W. (1993) 'Keeping a butterfly and an elephant in a house of cards: the elements of exceptional success', *Journal of Management Studies* 30: 885–922.

Suchman, L. (1987) *Plans and Situated Actions*, Cambridge: Cambridge University Press.

Sveiby, K. and Lloyd, T. (1987) *Managing Know-How: Add Value by Valuing Creativity*, London: Bloomsbury.

Swidler, A. (1986) 'Culture in action: symbols and strategies', *American Sociological Review* 51: 273–86.

Swieringa, J. and Wierdsma, A. (1992) *Becoming a Learning Organization: Beyond the learning curve*, Reading, MA: Addison Wesley.

Unger, R. (1987) *False Necessity: Anti-Necessitarian Social Theory in the Service of Radical Democracy*, Cambridge: Cambridge University Press.

Webber, A. (1993) 'What's so new about the new economy?', *Harvard Business Review* (January–February): 24–42.

Weick, K. (1985) 'Cosmos versus chaos: sense and nonsense in electronic contexts', *Organizational Dynamics* (Autumn): 50–64.

Wikstrom, S. and Normann, R. (1994) *Knowledge and Value: A New Perspective on Corporate Transformation*, London: Routledge.

Winter, S. (1988) 'Knowledge and competence as strategic assets', in Teece, D. (ed.) *The Competitive Challenge*, Cambridge, MA: Ballinger, 159–184.

Zuboff, S. (1988) *In the Age of the Smart Machine: The Future of Work and Power*, New York: Basic Books.

17 What is organizational knowledge?[1]

Haridimos Tsoukas and Efi Vladimirou

Introduction

The aim of this chapter is to explore the links between individual knowledge, organizational knowledge, and human action undertaken in organized contexts. Those links have remained relatively unexplored in the relevant literature, a large part of which, captive within a narrowly Cartesian understanding of knowledge and cognition, has tended to privilege 'pure' knowledge and thinking at the expense of outlining the forms of social life which sustain particular types of knowledge (Tsoukas, 1996, 1997, 1998; Varela *et al.*, 1991; Winogrand and Flores, 1987).

Moreover, although most people intuitively identify knowledge with *individual* knowledge, it is not quite evident how knowledge becomes an individual possession and how it is related to individual action, nor is it clear in what sense knowledge merits the adjective *organizational*. Despite the insights gained by the research of leading experts on organizational knowledge, there are still crucial questions unresolved. For example, Nonaka and Takeuchi (1995: 58–9) argue that:

> Information is a flow of messages, while knowledge is created by that very flow of information, anchored in the beliefs and commitment of its holder. This understanding emphasizes that *knowledge is essentially related to human action.* (Emphasis in the original)

Other researchers have similarly stressed the close connection between knowledge and action: whatever knowledge is, it is thought to make a difference to individuals' actions (Choo, 1998; Devenport and Prusak, 1998; Leonard and Sensiper, 1998; Suchman, 1987; Wigg, 1997). However, while this is a useful insight, it is not clear *how* knowledge is connected to action, nor, more fundamentally, what knowledge is. True, knowledge makes a difference, but how? How is knowledge brought to bear on what an individual does? What are the prerequisites for using knowledge effectively in action?

Davenport and Prusak (1998: 5) have provided the following definition of knowledge:

> Knowledge is a flux mix of framed experiences, values, contextual information, and expert insight that provides a framework for evaluating and incorporating new experiences and information. It originates and is applied in the minds of knowers. In organizations, it often becomes embedded not only in documents or repositories but also in organizational routines, processes, practices, and norms.

While this definition correctly highlights the dynamic character of knowledge (i.e. knowledge is both an outcome – 'a framework' – and a process for 'incorporating new experiences and information'), it is not clear in what sense knowledge is different from information, nor how it is possible for values and contextual information to originate and apply in the minds of individuals alone. Moreover, Davenport and Prusak pack into knowledge too many things, such as 'values', 'experiences' and 'contexts', without specifying their relationships, thus risking making 'knowledge' an all-encompassing and, therefore, little-revealing, concept. Also, while it is acknowledged that knowledge becomes embedded in organizations, it is not mentioned in what form, nor how individuals draw on it.

For some researchers and practitioners (see Gates, 1999; Lehner, 1990; Terrett, 1998) organizational knowledge tends to be viewed as synonymous with information, especially digital information, in which case the interesting issue is thought to be how knowledge-as-information is best stored, retrieved, transmitted and shared (cf. Brown and Duguid, 2000; Hendriks and Vriens, 1999). In contrast, for some researchers, such as Kay (1993), organizational knowledge becomes the essence of the firm. For example, as Kay (p. 73) remarks, '[organizational knowledge] is distinctive to the firm, is more than the sum of the expertise of those who work in the firm, and is not available to other firms'. Here knowledge is thought to be profoundly collective, above and beyond discrete pieces of information individuals may possess; it is a pattern formed within and drawn upon a firm, over time. While few would take issue with this definition, it does not quite reveal what are the characteristic features of organizational knowledge, and does not even hint at the relationship between individual and organizational knowledge.

From the above admittedly cursory review, it follows that it is still not clear what knowledge is, nor what makes it organizational. Realizing that knowledge is indeed a tricky concept, some researchers have gone as far as to suggest (mostly in the context of academic conferences) that, perhaps, we do not need more formal definitions of knowledge, since they, very likely, end up complicating things further. We do not agree with this view. Our understanding of organizational knowledge (or any other topic of interest) will not advance if we resign ourselves to merely recycling commonsensical notions of knowledge for, if we were to do so, we would risk being prisoners of our own unchallenged assumptions, incapable of advancing our learning. On the contrary, what we need is ever more sophisticated theoretical explorations of our topic of interest, aiming at gaining a deeper insight into it. Those who think such an attempt is futile need to ponder the great extent to which Polanyi's notion of 'personal knowledge' has advanced our understanding of what knowledge is about and, accordingly, how much impoverished our understanding would have been without that notion. If theoretical confusion is in evidence the answer cannot be 'drop theory' but 'more and better theory'.

In this chapter we will argue that our difficulties in getting to grips with organizational knowledge stem from a double failure: to understand the generation and utilization of knowledge we need a theory of knowledge, *and* to understand organizational knowledge we need a theory of organization. Moreover, it needs to be pointed out that, although no self-respecting researchers have so far failed to acknowledge their debt to Polanyi for the distinction he drew between tacit and explicit knowledge, Polanyi's work, for the most part, has not been really engaged with. If it had been it would have been noticed that, since all knowledge has its tacit presuppositions, tacit knowledge is not something that can be converted into explicit knowledge, as Nonaka and Takeuchi (1995) have claimed (cf. Cook and Brown, 1999; Tsoukas, 1996). Moreover, and perhaps more crucially, it would have been acknowledged that Polanyi (1962), more than anything else, insisted on the *personal* character of knowledge – hence the title of his magnum opus, *Personal Knowledge*. In his own words: '*All* knowing is personal knowing – participation through indwelling' (Polanyi, 1975: 44; emphasis in the original).

In this chapter, we will take on board Polanyi's profound insight concerning the personal character of knowledge and fuse it with Wittgenstein's claim that all knowledge is, in a fundamental way, collective, in order to show on the one hand how individuals appropriate knowledge and expand their knowledge repertoires, and, on the other hand, how knowledge, in organized contexts becomes organizational, with what implications for its management. We will ground our theoretical claims on a case study undertaken at a call centre in Panafon, the leading mobile telecommunications company in Greece.

The structure of the chapter is as follows. In the next section we describe what personal knowledge is and develop further the notion of organizational knowledge. In a nutshell, our claim is that knowledge is the individual capability to draw distinctions, within a domain of action, based on an appreciation of context or theory, or both. Similarly, organizational knowledge is the capability members of an organization have developed to draw distinctions in the process of carrying out their work, in particular concrete contexts, by enacting sets of generalizations whose application depends on historically evolved collective understandings. Following our theoretical exploration of organizational knowledge, we report the findings of a case study carried out at a call centre in Panafon, in Greece. In line with our argument that all organizations can be seen as collections of knowledge assets (cf. Wenger, 1998: 46), we investigate how call operators at a call centre – a unit which, conventionally, would not be called knowledge-intensive – answer customer calls by drawing on and modifying organizational knowledge to suit their particular circumstances. Finally, we explore the implications of our argument by focusing on the links between knowledge and action on the one hand, and the management of organizational knowledge on the other.

On personal and organizational knowledge

The distinction between data, information, and knowledge has often been made in the literature (Boisot, 1995; Choo, 1998; Davenport and Prusak, 1998; Nonaka and Takeuchi, 1995). What differentiates knowledge from information, it has been argued, is that knowledge presupposes values and beliefs, and is closely connected with action. Similarly, Bell (1999: lxi–lxiv) has provided a neat definition of these terms, which is particularly useful for our purpose here. For Bell *data* is an ordered sequence of given items or events (e.g. the name index of a book). *Information* is a context-based arrangement of items whereby relations between them are shown (e.g. the subject index of a book). And *knowledge* is the judgement of the significance of events and items, which comes from a particular context and/or theory (e.g. the construction of a thematic index by a reader of a book).

What underlies Bell's definition of knowledge is his view that data, information, and knowledge are three concepts that can be arranged on a single continuum, depending on the extent to which they reflect human involvement with, and processing of, the reality at hand. For example, the name index of a book is merely data, since it involves minimal effort on the part of an individual to make such an index – the names are there, it is just a matter of arranging them alphabetically. The subject index of a book, however requires more processing on the part of the individual, since it depends on his/her judgement to construct the appropriate headings for such an index. Finally, when a reader relates the content of a book to his/her own interests, he/she may construct his/her own analytical index – in other words, the reader in this case has a far greater degree of involvement and exercises far greater judgement in organizing the material at hand. Put simply, data require minimal human judgement, whereas knowledge requires maximum judgement. Knowledge is the capacity to exercise judgement on the part of an individual, which is either based on an appreciation of context or is derived from theory or both (Bell, 1999: lxiv).

Drawing on Dewey's (1934) conception of aesthetic experience, Bell (1999: lxiv) goes on to argue that 'judgement arises from the self-conscious use of the prefix *re:* the desire to re-order, to re-arrange, to re-design what one knows and thus create new angles of vision or new knowledge for scientific or aesthetic purposes'. The self-conscious desire to re-arrange what one knows implies that the individual wishes to see things differently, to disclose aspects of a phenomenon that were hitherto invisible, or simply to see more clearly than before. But this is not all: the individual will re-arrange his/her knowledge while being located somewhere – a certain standpoint or tradition. Thus the capacity to exercise judgement involves two things. First the ability of an individual to draw distinctions (Reyes and Zarama, 1998; Vickers, 1983) and, secondly, the location of an individual within a collectively generated and sustained domain of action – a 'form of life' (Wittgenstein, 1958), a 'practice' (MacIntyre, 1985), a 'horizon of meaning' (Gadamer, 1989) or a 'consensual domain' (Maturana and Varela, 1988) – in which particular criteria of evaluation hold.

Why does the capacity to exercise judgement imply the capability of drawing distinctions? Because when we draw a distinction we split the world into 'this' and 'that', we bring into consciousness the constituent parts of the phenomenon we are interested in (Dewey, 1934: 310). Through language we name, and constantly bring forth and ascribe significance to, certain aspects of the world (including, of course, our own behaviour) (Schutz, 1970; Taylor, 1985; Winogrand and Flores, 1987). When our language is crude and unsophisticated, so are our distinctions and the consequent judgements. The more refined our language, the finer our distinctions. Our attempt to understand and act on reality is simultaneously enabled and limited by the cultural tools we employ – with language being one of the most important (Vygotsky, 1978: 23–30; Wertsch, 1998: 40). Just like someone with a rudimentary knowledge of English cannot easily tell the different kinds of accent of English speakers (that is, he/ she cannot draw fine distinctions related to accent), so a person untrained into a particular activity has only a rule-based, undifferentiated outline of it in mind, rather than a set of refined distinctions (Dreyfus and Dreyfus, 1986). Polanyi (1962: 101) has perceptively captured this point in the following illustration:

> Think of a medical student attending a course in the X-ray diagnosis of pulmonary diseases. He watches in a darkened room shadowy traces on a fluorescent screen placed against a patient's chest, and hears the radiologist commenting to his assistants, in technical language, on the significant features of these shadows. At first the student is completely puzzled. For he can see in the X-ray picture of a chest only the shadows of the heart and the ribs, with a few spidery blotches between them. The experts seem to be romancing about figments of their imagination; he can see nothing that they are talking about. Then as he goes on listening for a few weeks, looking carefully at ever new pictures of different cases, a tentative understanding will dawn on him; he will gradually forget about the ribs and begin to see the lungs. And eventually, if he perseveres intelligently, a rich panorama of significant details will be revealed to him: of physiological variations and pathological changes, of scars, of chronic infections and signs of acute disease. He has entered a new world. He still sees only a fraction of what the experts can see, but the pictures are definitely making sense now and so do most of the comments made on them.

The medical student refines her ability to read an X-ray picture through her exposure to the relevant material (what Lakoff (1987: 297) calls 'the basic-level interactions with the environment') *and* the specialized language she is taught to apply to that material (Schon, 1983). How does this happen? Having a body, the medical student is capable of obtaining preconceptual experience, that is experience that is tied to gestalt perception, mental imagery and motor movement (Lakoff, 1987: 267–8, 302–3). At the same time, being a language user, the medical student operates in the cognitive domain, namely a domain within which she recursively interacts with his/her own descriptions (i.e. thoughts). What initially appears only as a shadow of the heart and the ribs (i.e. a description), is further processed, through language and with the help of an instructor or with peers, until a much more refined picture emerges. As Mercer (1995: 13) remarks, 'practical, hands-on activity can gain new depths of meaning if it is *talked about*' (emphasis added). Relating her hitherto knowledge to the X-ray picture and talking about it with her instructor, the medical student is forced to revise and refine her understanding about the matter at hand (Hunter, 1991). In Von Foerster's (1984: 48) second-order cybernetics language, cognitive processes are never-ending processes of computation. Cognition consists in computing descriptions of descriptions, namely in recursively operating on – modifying, transforming – representations. In doing so, cognizing subjects re-arrange and re-order what they know, thus creating new distinctions and, therefore, new knowledge (Bell, 1999: lxiv; Dewey, 1934).

Individuals draw distinctions within a collective domain of action, namely within a language-mediated domain of sustained interactions. For the medical student to be able to discern the medically significant pattern of an X-ray picture, she necessarily draws on medical knowledge, namely on a collectively produced and sustained body of knowledge (Hunter, 1991). Likewise, for an individual copier technician to be able to diagnose a faulty photocopier, he needs to draw on a specific body of expertise, which is produced and sustained by the company making photocopiers and by the community of technicians as a whole (Orr, 1996; cf. Wenger, 1998). Why is this so? The reason is that the key categories implicated in human action, for example, 'physiological variation', 'pathological change' (Polanyi, 1962: 101), 'faulty photocopier' (Orr, 1996), or 'clunky flute' (Cook and Brown, 1999: 396; Cook and Yanow, 1996), derive their meanings from the way they have been used within particular forms of life (the medical community or the community of photocopier technicians or the community of flutemakers). One learns how to recognize a pathology on the lungs or a 'clunky flute', only because one has been taught to use the category 'pathological lung' or 'clunky flute' within a domain of action (Toulmin, 1999).

In other words, knowing how to act within a domain of action is learning to make competent use of the categories and the distinctions constituting that domain (Wenger, 1998). As Spender (1989) has shown, upon entering a particular industry, managers learn a particular 'industry recipe', that is a set of distinctions tied to a particular field of experience. The distinctions pertain to a number of issues ranging from how markets are segmented to the kind of employees suited to an industry or to the technology used. To put it broadly, to engage in collective work is to engage in a discursive practice, namely in the normative use of a sign system which is directed at influencing aspects of the world and whose key categories and distinctions are defined through their use in discourse (Harré and Gillett, 1994: 28–9; Taylor, 1993; Tsoukas, 1996, 1998).

On the basis of the preceding analysis, the definition of knowledge mentioned earlier may be re-formulated as follows: *knowledge is the individual ability to draw distinctions within a collective domain of action, based on an appreciation of context or theory, or both.* Notice that such a definition of knowledge preserves a significant role for human agency, since individuals are seen as being inherently capable of making (and refining) distinctions, while also taking into account collective understandings and standards of appropriateness, on which individuals necessarily draw in the process of making distinctions, in their work.

The individual capacity to exercise judgement is based on an appreciation of *context* in the ethnomethodological sense that a social being is (or, to be more precise, becomes) knowledgeable in accomplishing routine and taken-for-granted tasks within particular contexts (e.g. taking measurements, driving, holding a conversation, filling in a medical insurance form, etc), as a result of having been through processes of socialization (Berger and Luckmann, 1966; Garfinkel, 1984; Schutz, 1970). We do not need a PhD in linguistics to carry out a conversation, nor do we need specialized training in economics or agricultural science to buy cheese at the grocers. We know how to deal with the practical things in life because we have picked up through interaction (with the world and with others) what is expected of us, or what works (Heritage, 1984; Wenger, 1998). 'We bring to situations of interaction', notes McCarthy (1994: 65), a 'tacit awareness of the normative expectations relevant to them and an intuitive appreciation of the consequences that might follow from breaking them'.

The individual capacity to exercise judgement is based on an appreciation of *theory* in the epistemic sense that, as Bell (1999: lxiii) has noted, 'theory allows one to take a finding and generalize from any one context to another context. From verified theory – Newton's laws of motion – we can accept the finding in a new context as knowledge'. Choosing a theory and applying it in a new context involves judgement, and the capacity to make such judgements is knowledge. The notion of 'theory' here is a broad one to include any framework, set of generalizing principles, or abstract instructions. Just as a judge brings a set of legal principles to bear on a particular situation, so a copier technician draws upon, among other things, a set of abstract instructions in order to repair a faulty photocopier. Whatever abstract principle enables an individual to generalize across contexts counts as theory and forms an additional basis for exercising judgement.

If the above is accepted then it becomes possible for us to see the sense in which knowledge becomes organizational. In a weak sense, knowledge is organizational simply by its being generated, developed and transmitted by individuals within organizations. That is obvious but unrevealing. In a strong sense, however, knowledge becomes organizational when, as well as drawing distinctions in the course of their work by taking into account the contextuality of their actions, *individuals draw and act upon a corpus of generalizations in the form of generic rules produced by the organization.*

Why is this the case? A distinguishing feature of organization is the generation of recurring behaviours by means of institutionalized roles that are explicitly defined. For an activity to be said to be organized it implies that *types* of behaviour in *types* of situations are connected to *types* of actors (Berger and Luckmann, 1966: 22; Scott, 1995). An organized activity provides actors with a given set of cognitive categories and a typology of action options (Scott, 1995; Weick, 1979). Such a typology consists of rules of action – typified responses to typified expectations (Berger and Luckmann, 1966: 70–3). Rules are prescriptive statements guiding behaviour in organizations and take the form of propositional statements, namely 'If X, then Y, in circumstances Z'. As Twining and Miers (1991, p. 131) remark, 'a rule prescribes that in circumstances X, behaviour of type Y ought, or ought not to be, or may be indulged in by persons of class Z'.

On this view, therefore, *organizing implies generalizing* the subsumption of heterogeneous particulars under generic categories. In that sense, formal organization necessarily involves abstraction. Since in an organization the behaviour of its members is formally guided by a set of propositional statements, it follows that an organization may be seen as a *theory* – a particular set of concepts (or cognitive categories) and the propositions expressing the relationship between concepts. Organization-as-theory enables organizational members to generalize across contexts. For example, the operators of the call centre we researched had been instructed to issue standardized responses to standardized queries: if this type of problem appears, then this type of solution is appropriate. From a strictly organizational point of view, the contextual specificity surrounding every particular call (a specificity that callers tend to expand upon in their calls) is removed through the application of generic organizational rules.

Rules, however, exist for the sake of achieving specific goals. The generalizations selected and enforced are selected from among numerous other possibilities. To have as a rule, for example, that 'no caller should wait for more than one minute before his/her call is answered' is not self-evident. It has been selected by the company, in order to increase its customer responsiveness, hoping that, ultimately, it will contribute to attracting more customers, thus leading to higher market share, and so on. In other words, a rule's factual predicate ('If X …') is a generalization selected because it is thought to be causally relevant to a *justification* – some goal to be achieved or some evil to be avoided (Schauer, 1991: 27). A justification (or to be more precise, a set of logically ordered justifications) determines which generalization will constitute a rule's factual predicate. This is an important point for it highlights the fact that rules exist for the sake of some higher-order goals.

Moreover, rules do not apply themselves; members of a community-of-practice, situated in specific contexts, apply them (Gadamer, 1980; Tsoukas, 1996; Wittgenstein, 1958). Members of a community must share an interpretation as to what a rule means before they apply it. As Barnes (1995: 202) remarks, 'nothing in the rule itself fixes its application in a given case, … there is no "fact of the matter" concerning the proper application of a rule, … what a rule is actually taken to imply is a matter to be decided, when it is decided, by contingent social processes'. Since rules codify particular previous examples, an individual following a rule needs to learn to act in proper analogy with those examples. To follow a rule is, therefore, to extend an analogy. Barnes (1995: 55) has put it so felicitously that we cannot resist the temptation to quote him in full:

To understand rule-following or norm-guided behavior in this way immediately highlights the normally open-ended character of norms, the fact that they cannot themselves fix and determine what actions are in true conformity with them, that there is no logical compulsion to follow them in a particular way. Every instance of a norm may be analogous to every other, but analogy is not identity: analogy exists between things that are similar yet different. And this means that, although it is always possible to assimilate the next instance to a norm by analogy with existing examples of the norm, it is equally always possible to resist such assimilation, to hold the analogy insufficiently strong, to stress the differences between the instance and existing examples. If norms apply by analogy then it is up to *us* to decide where they apply, where the analogy is sufficiently strong and where not. (Emphasis added)

Notice that, on this essentially Wittgensteinian view, the proper application of a rule is not an individual accomplishment but is fundamentally predicated on collectively shared meanings. If formal organization is seen as a set of propositional statements, then those statements must be put into action by organizational members, who 'must be constituted as a *collective* able to sustain a shared sense of what rules imply and hence an agreement in their practice when they follow rules' (Barnes, 1995: 204; emphasis added). The justification (purpose) underlying a rule needs to be elaborated upon and its meaning agreed by the organizational collective. Organizational tasks are thus accomplished by individuals being able to secure a shared sense of what rules mean (or by agreeing upon, reinforcing, and sustaining a set of justifications) in the course of their work. This suggests an organization as a densely connected network of communication through which shared understandings are achieved.

A collectivist understanding of organizational knowledge has been evident in Penrose's (1959) work on the theory of the firm. The key to understanding firms' growth, wrote Penrose, is to focus not on the given resources a firm possesses but on the *services* rendered by those resources. This means that, according to Penrose, firms have discretion over how they use their resources and, therefore, over the services derived from them. Such discretion stems from the fact that firms view, and thus utilize, their resources differently. On this view, organizational knowledge is the set of collective understandings embedded in a firm, which enable it to put its resources to particular uses. Penrose's view of organizational knowledge identifies the latter with cultural or collective knowledge (Blackler, 1995; cf. Collins, 1990) – *it is a distinctive way of thinking and acting in the world*.

There is an interesting parallel between the preceding Wittgensteinian view of rule following and Polanyi's conception of personal knowledge. Both philosophers showed that even the most abstract formalisms we use ultimately depend, for their effective deployment, on social definitions. Abstract systems cannot be self-sustained; they are necessarily grounded on collective definitions, hence they depend on human judgement (Toulmin, 1999). Polanyi extended this argument further. For him, human judgement is manifested not only at the level of collective significations that happen to have historically evolved; it is equally manifested at the individual level. All knowledge is personal knowledge.

Seeking to highlight the nature of science as a skilful practice, Polanyi described, time and again, the exact sciences as 'a set of formulae which have a bearing on experience' (Polanyi, 1962: 49). It is precisely the establishment of this 'bearing on experience' that renders all scientific knowing, ultimately, *personal* knowing. In so far as even the most abstract mathematical formalisms need to be empirically checked, that is predictions to be made, measurements to be taken, and predictions to be compared with measurements, there will bound to be discrepancies between theory and observations, no matter how minor, which will need to be assessed by personal judgement on the part of the scientist (Polanyi, 1975: 30). In his several illustrations, from map reading, through piano playing and bicycle riding, to scientific work, Polanyi consistently pointed out that all abstract systems, from the shortest set of instructions right to the most abstract and comprehensive set of formalisms, ultimately encounter experience – the real world with all its messiness, imperfection, and complexity – and that encounter is inevitably mediated through human judgement. In Polanyi's (1975: 31) words,

> Even the most exact sciences must therefore rely on our personal confidence that we possess some degree of personal skill and personal judgement for establishing a valid correspondence with – or a real deviation from – the facts of experience.

Acknowledging that all knowledge contains a personal element or, to put it differently, '[recognizing] personal participation as the universal principle of knowing' (Polanyi, 1975: 44), implies that knowing always is, to a greater or lesser extent, a skilful accomplishment, an art.

What is the structure of such a skill? What does it consist of? Either we refer to everyday or expert knowledge or, to use Bell's terminology, to knowledge based on an appreciation of context or theory, the structure of knowing-as-a-skill is identical. In order to know something, the individual acts to integrate a set of particulars of which he/she is subsidiarily aware. To make sense of our experience, we necessarily rely on some parts of it subsidiarily in order to attend to our main objective focally. We comprehend something as a whole (focally) by tacitly integrating certain particulars, which are known by the actor subsidiarily. Knowing has a *from – to* structure: the particulars bear on the focus *to* which I attend *from* them. Subsidiary awareness and focal awareness are mutually exclusive. Action is confused if the individual shifts his/her focal attention to the particulars, of which he/she had been previously aware in a subsidiary manner.

Thus, knowing consists of three elements: subsidiary particulars, a focal target, and, crucially, a person who links the two. Polanyi's (1975: 36) classic example is the blind man probing a cavity with his stick. The focus of his attention is at the far end of the stick, while attending subsidiarily to the feeling of holding the stick in his hand. The difference between a seeing man blindfolded and a blind man is that, for the former, probing feels like a series of jerks in his palm, whereas for the latter probing indicates the presence of certain obstacles of a certain hardness and shape. In the first case, the stick has not yet been assimilated (and, as a result, it receives focal awareness), while in the latter case the stick is being subsidiarily aware of and, as a result, it is used as a tool to a certain end.

On Polanyi's view, practical knowledge has two features. First, it is inevitably and irreducibly *personal* since it involves personal participation in its generation. In his words, 'the relation of a subsidiary to a focus is formed by the *act of a person* who integrates one to another' (Polanyi, 1975: 38). And secondly, for knowledge to be effectively applied, it needs to be *instumentalized* – to be used as a tool. On this point, Polanyi was very clear, echoing the Heideggerian line of thinking (Winogrand and Flores, 1987). 'Hammers and probes', he wrote, 'can be replaced by intellectual tools' (Polanyi, 1962: 59). As we learn to use a tool, any tool, we gradually become unaware of how we use it to achieve results. Polanyi called this 'indwelling' – dwelling in the tool, making it feel as if it is an extension of our own body (Polanyi, 1962, 1975). We make sense of experience by assimilating the tool through which we make sense. The lapse into unawareness of the manner in which we use a tool is accompanied by an expansion of awareness of the experiences at hand, on the operational plane. We refine our ability to get things done by dwelling in the tools (both physical and intellectual) through which we get things done. The increasing instrumentalization of certain actions in the service of some purpose (or what we earlier called 'justification') enables the individual to expand his/her awareness of the situation he/she encounters and thus to refine his/her skills (Dreyfus and Dreyfus, 1986). The ongoing process of transforming experience into subsidiary awareness or, in Polanyi's (1962: 64) words, 'the pouring of ourselves into the subsidiary awareness of particulars', allows one to reach ever higher levels of skilful achievement (e.g. the improvement of the medical student's ability to read the X-ray picture).

To sum up, knowledge is the individual capability to draw distinctions, within a domain of action, based on an appreciation of context or theory, or both. Organizations are three things at once: concrete settings within which individual action takes place; sets of abstract rules in the form of propositional statements; and historical communities. Organizational knowledge is the capability members of an organization have developed to *draw distinctions* in the process of carrying out their work, in particular *concrete contexts,* by enacting sets of generalizations *(propositional statements)* whose application depends on historically evolved *collective understandings* and experiences. The more propositional statements and collective understandings become instrumentalized (in Polanyi's sense of the term); and the more new experiences are reflectively processed (both individually and collectively) and then gradually driven into subsidiary awareness, the more organizational members dwell in all of them, and the more able they become to concentrate on new experiences, on the operational plane.

Having developed the notion of organizational knowledge and shown its links with personal knowledge and human action, we will proceed below to empirically investigate these claims through a case study.

Organizational knowledge in action: a case study

Research setting

A case study on organizational knowledge was undertaken at the Customer Care Department at Panafon, Greece's leading mobile phone operator. The company was formed in 1992, employs 900 people, and is controlled by the UK-based Vodafone group. With more than 2 million subscribers, Panafon holds a 38 per cent share of the mobile phone market in Greece, one of the fastest growing markets in Europe *(Financial Times,* 28 December 2000). The company is listed on the Athens stock exchange and provides a wide range of standard and enhanced GSM services as well as services such as voice mail, short message services, personal numbering and data, fax transmission services, and internet-related services (Panafon, 1998).

The quality of customer care is, along with price, network coverage, and range of services, a determining factor for customers to choose to subscribe to one of the three providers of mobile telecommunications services in Greece. Considering the great importance of Customer Care for Panafon's ability to maintain and attract customers, the empirical part of this study is focusing on organizational knowledge within the Customer Care Department (CCD), although the latter is not what might be called a knowledge-intensive department. This however, is immaterial for us, since, as was hopefully made clear in the preceding section, knowledge is *de facto* implicated in all types of organizational work (Wenger, 1998). Indeed, one of our claims in the preceding section has been that human action in organizations (all kinds of organizations) *necessarily* draws on organizational knowledge, namely on sets of generalizations underlain by collective understandings, activated in particular contexts. Of course, this is not to deny that there are, indeed, important differences between organizational forms concerning the dominant types of knowledge to be found in each one of them (Lam, 2000). But, such differences are not analytically relevant in the context of the present argument, just like differences between societies are not analytically relevant in the context of an inquiry that sets out to investigate the structuring and enactment of social relations (Garfinkel, 1984).

The Customer Care Department (CCD) has been in operation since the commencement of Panafon's commercial operation, and it was the first customer care centre in Greece to operate 24 hours a day. Today the CCD has a total of 250 employees and consists of four call centres. The volume of calls to CCD has increased significantly in recent years, due to both the growth in the customer base and new services introductions. Currently, the department receives an average of 60,000 calls a day, although volumes fluctuate by month of the year day of the week, time of the day, and maturity of service. Operators, working in eight-hour shifts, are responsible for answering calls about specific Panafon services according to their experience and training on the corresponding services.

The aim of CCD is to provide information support to Panafon subscribers, including directory inquiries, connection through directory assistance, secretarial messaging services, general information on the company's services (e.g. tariffs, network coverage), voice mail inquiries, as well as general information and assistance, including information about mobile phones, to both contract and pre-paid customers. Customer care is provided by Customer Care Operators (hereafter referred to as operators), all of whom have been formally trained in Panafon's products and services and in the techniques of providing customer support. In addition, operators have received on the job training before taking on their duties.

Data collection and analysis

Data collection was conducted in two phases. In Phase I, we participated in a two-day induction programme, designed for new employees. Our aim was to familiarize ourselves with the company, and get an overall picture about its operation, products and services, departments, etc. In Phase II data about the CCD were collected using unstructured and semi-structured interviewing and document review. In addition, Phase H involved extensive on the job observation, and review of relevant work-related material.

Observation took the form of sitting with operators when they were on and off the phones as well as attending their coffee breaks, and taking notes on their work practices. Operators were encouraged to give explanations about what they were doing, and these descriptions were supplemented with questions probing particular issues, especially for explanations and clarifications both for the use of the available technology and work manuals, and for operators' initiatives and tacit understandings in dealing with customer calls. Materials reviewed included the work manuals provided by Panafon to employees and operators' personal notes. Detailed interviews in Phase II were taken from three Customer Care Operators, the fault coordinator, the shift supervisor, and supervisor of one of the four call centres, as well as three employees at Engineering and one at Operations and Support departments who work in contact with Customer Care. Qualitative techniques were used to analyse the data collected, in line with the recommendations by Miles and Huberman (1984).

Knowledge practices within Panafon's customer care department

To answer most customer queries, operators draw upon electronically provided and printed information. Concerning electronically provided information, operators use computerized databases containing pertinent information for each of the services provided by CCD. For example, for general inquiries concerning contract customers, the computerized database contains, among other things, information about which services the customer has subscribed to and who is his/her service provider. This information enables operators to help customers identify whether, for example, a customer has indeed subscribed to a particular service the customer has inquired about (e.g. whether the customer has subscribed to having voice mail). The system can also help operators to activate the connection of pre-paid customers or even to activate call recognition for these customers if they wish.

The system is also used in the case of directory inquiries. Everyday operators are required to check their computer screens for new information that may have become available (concerning, for example, network coverage problems, tariff changes, etc), which operators need to know about in order to answer customer queries accurately and efficiently. As for the printed material operators draw upon, it consists of company manuals containing information about a range of issues, such as details about all services provided by Panafon, countries in which roaming may be activated, information on different types of mobile phones, etc.

Drawing on both printed and electronically available information, operators are, in principle, in a position to handle customer queries. As an experienced operator put it

Answers to 95 per cent of the questions we are asked exist somewhere in the computer system, or in the manuals, or somewhere. Most likely the subscriber will be given the information he wants. The only question is how fast this will be done.

Indeed, the question of speed is an important indicator of high-quality service since, if a particular customer is served quickly, he/she will very probably be a satisfied customer. Prompted to explain what she meant by 'somewhere', the above mentioned operator carried on exalting the significance of 'work experience' in that it provides operators with a repository of instances upon which they may regularly draw in their work.

Viewed this way, the information systems used by the operators include not only the organizationally provided technical means for accessing relevant information, but also the informal memory system (both individual and collective) which has gradually been built over time, consisting of the individual stocks of experience held by each operator, and by the stories shared in their community. As the operators often pointed out in their interviews with us, accessing that informal collective stock of knowledge is a valuable source of information for them. This is quite important because it highlights the significance of the web of social relations at work, since it is within those relations that such informal knowledge is preserved and drawn upon (Davenport and Prusak, 1998).

Indeed all operators interviewed emphatically mentioned how important it is for them to be able to draw upon the accumulated experience and knowledge of one another at work. We noticed that operators, while carrying out their tasks, often consulted one another about matters unknown to them. Communication about work-related issues occurs also during their breaks. It is noteworthy that such communication occurs naturally; it is part of the informal story telling that goes on among operators. Narrating work-related episodes to one another about, for example, awkward customers and uncommon questions tackled creates an environment in which the ties of community are reinforced, collective memory is enriched, and individual knowledge is enhanced. Researchers such as Orr (1996), Weick (1995), Brown and Duguid (1991), and Wenger (1998) have also mentioned the strong links between community ties, individual learning, and story telling.

Providing customer support is not as easy a job as it might first appear Operators must be able to continuously provide efficient, courteous and helpful customer support services to subscribers – at least that is the official company policy. Moreover, customers are rarely 'sophisticated' mobile phone users, which often makes communication between operators and customers difficult: customers do not always express themselves in a clear and articulate manner, whereas sometimes they are not even sure what exactly they want. For example, we noticed that when asking for information, several customers tended to provide plenty of contextual details while describing their query. Often such contextual information was, strictly speaking, redundant and actually tended to blur, to some extent, the point of their query.

Customer queries, thus contain some ambiguity. Such ambiguity requires that operators be adept in helping customers articulate their problems, probe them further in order to get customers to clarify what they want, and locate the appropriate information that will answer customers' queries. As well as doing all this, operators must be courteous towards customers and efficient in carrying out their tasks. Given that, as stated earlier, information about customers' calls normally exists 'somewhere' in the call centre, the primary task for the operator is to dispel the ambiguity surrounding customer calls and understand what the problem really is, and how, consequently, it ought to be solved. Even seemingly simple problems require diagnostic skills on the part of operators.

For example, a particular customer complained that he did not have the identification call service, whereby a caller's phone number appears on the receiver's mobile phone display, although he had paid for it. This could have been a technical problem (i.e. something wrong with his mobile phone), it could have been an error on the part of the company in having failed to activate that service, or it could have been the fact that certain callers did not wish that their phone numbers appear on other people's mobile phone displays. An inexperienced operator would probably have investigated all preceding possibilities. An experienced operator, however, would know that the first two possibilities were not very common and would, therefore, focus on the third. Indeed, through appropriate questioning, the particular operator observed first asked the customer about the extent to which the problem appeared and, when told that it tended to occur only in relation with a certain caller, the operator was immediately able to reach the conclusion that the caller, in all probability, did not wish for his/her number to be identified. The operator's ability to see through a customer's query, that is to make ever-finer distinctions, is an important skill, which is developed and constantly refined on the job.

Through experience and their participation in a 'community of practice' (Brown and Duguid, 1991; Wenger, 1998), operators develop a set of diagnostic skills which over time become instrumentalized, that is to say, tacit. This enables them to think quickly, 'on their feet', and serve customers speedily. Over time, operators learn to dwell in these skills, feel them as extensions of their own body and thus gradually become subsidiarily aware of them, which enables operators to focus on the task at hand.

For example, for operators to become effective in their job, they need to develop sophisticated perceptual skills in the context of mediated interaction (Thompson, 1995). Hearing only a voice deprives an operator of the multiple clues associated with face to face communication. The message a customer conveys to the operator is communicated not only through words but also through the tone of voice and other associated verbal clues. An operator realizes that she is dealing with an unhappy customer, a confused customer, or a puzzled customer not only by what they say to her but also by *how* they say it. High quality service means that the operator has instrumentalized her ability to discern such nuances in customer behaviour (i.e. to draw fine distinctions) and act accordingly.

An operator's perceptual skills, therefore, in understanding what is going on at the other end of the line is very important. It may be perhaps interesting to note that operators had refined their perceptual skills to the extent that they could tell straight away whether the caller at the other end was an electrical appliances retailer acting on behalf of a customer or whether it was the customer himself/herself. Recognizing nuances in callers' voices and acting accordingly (for example, to pacify an angry customer, to reassure a panic-stricken customer, or to instruct an utterly ignorant customer) was an important part of an effective operator's skill.

The tacitness of operators' knowledge was manifested when they were asked to describe how and why they tackled a particular problem in a particular way. To such questions, operators were at a loss for words; 'you feel it', 'you know so', 'I just knew it', were some of the most often repeated expressions they used (cf. Cook and Yanow, 1996). Such knowledge was difficult to verbalize, let alone codify. Although operators did make use of the information systems provided by the company, they did so in a manner whose distinguishing features were, on the one hand, the exercise of operators' judgement in diagnosing problems, while, on the other hand, the way in which operators' judgement was exercised had been crucially shaped by the overall company culture. Given that the latter placed heavy emphasis on high quality service, which was constantly reinforced through corporate announcements, induction programmes, training, and performance appraisal systems, the operators had internalized a set of values which helped them orient their actions accordingly.

Operators were drawing on a plethora of data and information (in Bell's sense of these terms), provided to them by the company in an electronic and printed form. Such data consisted of discrete items (e.g. addresses and phone numbers), while information consisted of generic propositional statements in the form of 'if this problem appears, then look at this or that' (Devlin, 1999). What was interesting to notice was the transformation of such information to knowledge by the operators themselves. To enact abstract 'if then' statements, operators had to take into account the particular context of their conversation with a caller and quickly make a judgement as to what is required. To do so, the operators did not simply (and mindlessly) put the organizational rules into action, but they adapted those rules to the circumstances at hand.

As argued earlier, the encounter of a formalism with experience necessitates the exercise of human judgement, out of which new experience emerges, which is drawn upon on subsequent occasions. If Polanyi's claim that all knowledge is personal knowledge is accepted, it follows that, at least as far as organizational knowledge is concerned, there always is an improvisational element in putting knowledge into action. Indeed, this is the sense in which Bell differentiates knowledge from information: the former involves an active re-arrangement of the latter; it 'involves judgements, and judgements are derived from the knowledge of the "that it is so", or from a theory of the subject' (Bell, 1999: lxiv).

For example, through her experience, one operator knew that a particular type of mobile phone presented certain problems. The same operator also came to know that the set of instructions to customers to activate another type of cardbased mobile phone were perceived as somewhat confusing by several customers. Having such knowledge, and faced with a particular problem, an operator might first ask what type of mobile phone a particular customer had been using and, depending on his/her answer, the operator would then proceed accordingly. Notice that such knowledge was not to be found in the official information system: it rather developed as a result of operators repeatedly facing (and learning from) particular types of problems to which they developed (i.e. they improvised) particular solutions.

As Orlikowski (1996) has persuasively shown, operators improvise in order to meet the demands of their tasks more effectively. Several operators observed were constructing their own personal information systems, which contained photocopies of the relevant corporate manuals plus personal notes. The latter consisted of notes they had taken during their training, and notes on which they had scribbled answers to customer queries they had faced in the past without, at the time, being able to locate the requisite information through the use of the formal information system. This is an important point that has not been given adequate coverage in the literature on knowledge management, although the phenomenon of 'improvisation' per se has received attention (Orlikowski, 1996; Weick, 1998): alongside formal organizational knowledge there exists informal knowledge that is generated in action. This type of knowledge (what Collins (1990) calls 'heuristic knowledge') is gained only through the improvisation employees undertake while carrying out their tasks. Heuristic knowledge resides both in individuals' minds and in stories shared in communities of practice. Such knowledge may be formally captured and, through its casting into propositional statements, may be turned into organizational knowledge. While this is feasible and desirable, the case still remains that, at any point in time, abstract generalizations are in themselves incomplete to capture the totality of organizational knowledge. In action, an improvisational element always follows it like shadow follows an object.

Discussion and implications

From the preceding analysis it follows that what makes knowledge distinctly organizational is its codification in the form of propositional statements underlain by a set of collective understandings. Given, however, that individuals put organizational knowledge into action by acting inescapably within particular contexts, there is always room for individual judgement and for the emergence of novelty. It is the open-endedness of the world that gives rise to new experience and learning and gives knowledge its not-as-yet-formed character. As Gadamer (1989: 38) has perceptively noted, at issue is more than the correct application of general principles. Our knowledge of the latter is 'always supplemented by the individual case, even productively determined by it'. What Gadamer points out is that 'application is neither a subsequent nor merely an occasional part of the phenomenon of understanding, but codetermines it as a whole from the beginning' (p. 324). In other words, individuals are not given generalizations which must be first understood before being put into application afterwards. Rather, individuals understand generalizations only *through* connecting the latter to particular circumstances facing them; they comprehend the general by relating it to the particular they are confronted with. In so far as this process takes place, every act of interpretation is necessarily creative and, in that sense, heuristic knowledge is not accidental but a necessary outcome of the interpretative act.

A condition for organizational members to undertake action is to be placed within a conceptual matrix woven by the organization. Such a conceptual matrix contains generic categories (e.g. 'service quality', 'happy customer', 'efficient service') and their interrelations (e.g. 'high quality service makes customers happy'). By categorizing and naming the situation at hand, organizational members begin to search for appropriate responses. Commenting on Joas's (1996) *The Creativity of Action,* McGowan (1998: 294) aptly remarks: 'My judgement takes the raw data and raw feels of the present and names them. I decide to take this action because I deem this situation to be of this kind. The novelty of situations, the newness of the present, is tempered by this judgement'. Of course my judgement may be wrong. After all, it is only a guide to action, a tentative hypothesis, which may prove erroneous. The expected results may not occur; I need to reflect on this fact and revise my judgement. In other words, categorization and abstraction are conditions of possibility for human action (Lakoff, 1987). But categories *qua* categories may fail to match the particularities of the situation at hand. However, the abstract indeterminacy of categories is not a problem in practice, for it is situationally dealt with by the practical reasoning of competent language users. What gives organizational knowledge its dynamism is the dialectic between the general and the particular. Without the general no action is possible. And without the particular no action may be effective (McCarthy, 1994: 68).

If all organizational work necessarily involves drawing on knowledge, then the management of organizational knowledge must have been a time-old managerial activity. In a sense this is as true as the realization that marketing has been around since the dawn of the market economy. But, in another sense, this is not quite the case, if by management we mean the distinctly modern activity of purposeful coordination of socio-technical processes. For organizational knowledge to be managed, an unreflective practice needs to be turned into a reflective practice or, to put it differently, practical mastery needs to be supplemented by a quasi-theoretical understanding of what individuals are doing when they exercise that mastery.

An unreflective practice involves us acting, doing things, effortlessly observing the rules of our practice, but finding it difficult to state what they are. In that sense we are all unreflective practitioners: in so far as we carry out the tasks involved in our practice, we do so having instrumentalized, appropriated, the tools (i.e. abstract rules and collective understandings) through which we get things done. As Strawson (1992: 5) elegantly notes:

> When the first Spanish or, strictly, Castilian grammar was presented to Queen Isabella of Castile, her response was to ask what use it was. [Her response was quite understandable since] the grammar was in a sense of no use at all to fluent speakers of Castilian. In a sense they knew it already. They spoke grammatically correct Castilian because grammatically correct Castilian simply *was* what they spoke. The grammar did not set the standards of correctness for the sentences they spoke; on the contrary, it was the sentences they spoke that set the standard of correctness for the grammar. However, though in a sense they knew the grammar of their language, there was another sense in which they did not know it.

What was that? If Queen Isabella had been asked to judge whether a particular sequence of Castilian words was grammatically correct, she would have to state the rules of the language in terms of which she would need to make her judgement. The speaking of Castilian sentences by the Queen and her subjects showed that they, indeed, observed such rules, but they could not easily state what they were, unless there was a grammar available.

The point of this example is that we may have (unreflectively) mastered a practice but this is not enough. If we need to teach efficiently new members to be effective members of the practice, or if we need to reflect on ways of improving our practice, or if we want to rid ourselves of likely confusions, then we need to elucidate our practice by articulating or making explicit its rules and principles. Knowledge management then is primarily the dynamic process of turning an unreflective practice into a reflective one by elucidating the rules guiding the activities of the practice, by helping give a particular shape to collective understandings, and by facilitating the emergence of heuristic knowledge.

Without any doubt the management of organizational knowledge today certainly implies the ever more sophisticated development of electronic corporate information systems, which enable a firm to abstract its activities and codify them in the form of generic rules (Gates, 1999). In this way, a firm provides its members with the requisite propositional statements for acting efficiently and consistently. Ideally, on this view, an organizational member should have all the information that he/she needs, instantly. To a considerable extent that was the case in the call centre under study, although the relative simplicity of operators' tasks does not make it look like an impressive achievement.

However, the above is only one aspect of organizational knowledge management. Another less appreciated aspect, one that has hopefully been made more evident in this chapter, is the significance of heuristic knowledge developed by employees while doing their job. This type of knowledge cannot be 'managed' in the way formally available information can, because it crucially depends on employees' experiences and perceptual skills, their social relations, and their motivation. Managing this aspect of organizational knowledge means that a company must strive to sustain a spirit of community at work, to encourage employees to improvise and undertake initiatives of their own, as well as actively maintain a sense of corporate mission. To put it differently, and somewhat paradoxically, the management of the heuristic aspect of organizational knowledge implies more the sensitive management of social relations and less the management of corporate digital information (Tsoukas, 1998). In addition, the effective management of organizational knowledge requires that the relationship between propositional and heuristic knowledge be a two-way street: while propositional knowledge is fed into organizational members and is instrumentalized through application (thus becoming tacit), heuristic knowledge needs to be formalized (to the extent this is possible) and made organizationally available. Managing organizational knowledge does not narrowly imply efficiently managing hard bits of information but, more subtly, sustaining and strengthening social practices (Kreiner, 1999). In knowledge management digitalization cannot be a substitute for socialization.

Note

1. An earlier draft of this chapter was presented at the conference, Knowledge Management: Concepts and Controversies, 10–11 February 2000, Warwick University, UK. We would like to thank Guest Co-editor Jacky Swan and two anonymous reviewers for their valuable comments.

References

Barnes, B. (1995) *The Elements of Social Theory*, London: UCL Press.
Bell, D. (1999) 'The axial age of technology foreword: 1999', in *The Coming of the Post-Industrial Society*, New York: Basic Books, Special Anniversary Edition, ix–lxxxv.

Berger, P. and Luckmann, T. (1966) *The Social Construction of Reality*, London: Penguin.

Blacker, F. (1995) 'Knowledge, knowledge work and organizations: an overview and interpretation', *Organization Studies* 16(6): 1021–46.

Boisot, M. H. (1995). *Information Space: A Framework for Learning in Organizations, Institutions and Culture*, London: Routledge.

Brown, J. S. and Duguid, P. (1991) 'Organizational learning and communities of practice: toward a unified view of working, learning and innovation', *Organization Science* 2(1): 40–57.

Brown, J. S. and Duguid, P. (2000) *The Social Life of Information*, Boston: Harvard Business School Press.

Choo, C. W. (1998) *The Knowing Organization: How Organizations Use Information to Construct Meaning, Create Knowledge, and Make Decisions*, New York, NY: Oxford University Press.

Collins, M. H. (1990) *Artificial Experts: Social Knowledge and Intelligent Machines*, Cambridge, MA: MIT Press.

Cook, S. D. and Brown, J. S. (1999). 'Bridging epistemologies: the generative dance between organizational knowledge and organizational knowing', *Organization Science* 10: 381–400.

Cook, S. D. and Yanow, D. (1996). 'Culture and organizational learning', in Cohen, M. D. and Sproull, L. S. (eds) *Organizational Learning*, Thousand Oaks, CA: Sage, 430–59.

Davenport, T. H. and Prusak, L. (1998) *Working Knowledge*, Cambridge, MA: Harvard University Press.

Devlin, K. (1999) *Infosense: Turning Information into Knowledge*, New York: W.H. Freeman.

Dewey, J. (1934) *Art as Experience*, New York: Perigee Books.

Dreyfus, H. L. and Dreyfus, S. E. (1986) *Mind over Machine*, New York: Free Press.

Gadamer, H.-G. (1980) 'Practical philosophy as a model of the human sciences', *Research in Phenomenology* 9: 74–85.

Gadamer, H. G. (1989) *Truth and Method*, 2nd edition. London: Sheed & Ward.

Garfinkel, H. (1984) *Studies in Ethnomethodology*, Cambridge: Polity Press.

Gates, B. (1999) *Business @ the Speed of Thought*, London: Penguin Books.

Harré, R. and Gillett, G. (1994) *The Discursive Mind*, Thousand Oaks, CA: Sage.

Hendriks, P. H. J. and Vriens, D. J. (1999) 'Knowledge-based systems and knowledge management: friends or foes?', *Information and Management* 35: 113–25.

Heritage, J. (1984) *Garfinkel and Ethnomethodology*, Cambridge: Polity Press.

Hunter, K. M. (1991) *Doctors' Stories*, Princeton: Princeton University Press.

Joas, H. (1996) *The Creativity of Action*, Cambridge: Polity Press.

Kay, J. (1993) *Foundations of Corporate Success*, New York: Oxford University Press.

Kreiner K. (1999) 'Knowledge and mind', *Advances in Management Cognition and Organizational Information Processing* 6: 1–29.

Lakoff, G. (1987) *Women, Fire, and Dangerous Things*, Chicago: The University of Chicago Press.

Lam, A. (2000) 'Tacit knowledge, organizational learning and societal institutions: an integrated framework', *Organization Studies* 21(3): 487–514.

Lehner, F (1990) 'Expert systems for organizational and managerial tasks', *Information and Management* 23(1): 31–41.

Leonard, D. and Sensiper, S. (1998) 'The role of tacit knowledge in group innovation', *California Management Review* 40(3): 112–32.

MacIntyre, A. (1985) *After Virtue*, 2nd edition, London: Duckworth.

Maturana, H. and Varela, F. (1988) *The Tree of Knowledge*, Boston: New Science.

Mercer, N. (1995) *The Guided Construction of Knowledge*, Clevedon: Multilingual Matters.

McCarthy, T (1994) 'Philosophy and critical theory', in McCarthy, T. and Hoy, D. C., *Critical Theory*, Oxford: Blackwell, 5–100.

McGowan, J. (1998) 'Toward a pragmatist theory of action', *Sociological Theory* 16: 292–7.

Miles, M. B. and Huberman, A. M. (1984) *Qualitative Data Analysis: A Sourcebook of New Methods*, Newbury Park, CA: Sage Publications.

Nonaka, I. and Takeuchi, H. (1995) *The Knowledge-Creating Company: How Japanese Companies Create the Dynamics of Innovation*, New York, NY: Oxford University Press.

Orlikowski, W. J. (1996) 'Improvising organizational transformation over time: a situated change perspective'. *Information Systems Research* 7(1): 63–92.

Orr, J. E. (1996) *Talking about Machines*, ILR Press/Cornell University Press.

Panafon, November (1998). Initial Public Offering.

Penrose, E. (1959) *The Theory of the Growth of the Firm*, New York: Wiley.

Polanyi, M. (1962) *Personal Knowledge*, Chicago, IL: University of Chicago Press.

Polanyi, M. (1975) 'Personal knowledge', in Polanyi, M. and Prosch H. (eds) *Meaning*, Chicago, IL: University of Chicago Press, 22–45.

Reyes, A. and Zarama, R. (1998) 'The process of embodying distinctions – a reconstruction of the process of learning', *Cybernetics and Human Knowing*, 5: 19–33.

Schauer, F. (1991) *Playing by the Rules*, Oxford: Clarendon Press.

Schon, D. (1983) *The Reflective Practitioner*, New York: Basic Books.

Schutz, A. (1970) in Wagner (ed.) *On Phenomenology and Social Relations*, Chicago: The University of Chicago Press.

Scott, W. R. (1995) *Institutions and Organizations*, Thousand Oaks, CA: Sage.

Spender, J.-C. (1989) *Industry Recipes*, Oxford: Blackwell.

Strawson, P. F. (1992) *Analysis and Metaphysics*, Oxford: Oxford University Press.

Suchman, L. A. (1987) *Plans and Situated Actions: The Problems of Human-Machine Communication*, Cambridge: Cambridge University Press.

Taylor, C. (1985) *Philosophy and the Human Sciences*, Vol. 2, Cambridge: Cambridge University Press.

Taylor, C. (1993) 'To follow a rule . . .', in Calhoun, C., LiPuma, E. and Postone, M. (eds) *Bourdieu: Critical Perspectives*, Cambridge: Polity Press, 45–59.

Terrett, A. (1998) 'Knowledge management and the law firm', *Journal of Knowledge Management* 2(1): 67–76.

Thompson, J. B. (1995) *The Media and Modernity*, Cambridge: Polity Press.

Toulmin, S. (1999) 'Knowledge as shared procedures', in Engestrom, Y., Miettinen, R. and Punamaki, R.-L. (eds) *Perspectives on Activity Theory*, Cambridge: Cambridge University Press, 53–64.

Tsoukas, H. (1996) 'The firm as a distributed knowledge system: a constructionist approach', *Strategic Management Journal* 17: Winter Special Issue, 11–25.

Tsoukas, H. (1997) 'The tyranny of light: the temptations and the paradoxes of the information society', *Futures* 29(9): 827–44.

Tsoukas, H. (1998) 'Forms of knowledge and forms of life in organized contexts', in Chia, C. H. R. (ed.) *In the Realm of Organization*, London: Routledge, 43–66.

Twining, W. and Miers, D. (1991) *How to Do Things with Rules*, 3rd edition, London: Weidenfeld and Nicolson.

Varela, F. J., Thompson, E. and Rosch, E. (1991) *The Embodied Mind*, Cambridge, MA: MIT Press.

Vickers, G. (1983) *The Art of Judgement*, London: Harper & Row.

Von Foerster, H. (1984) 'On constructing a reality', in Watzlawick, P. (ed.) *The Invented Reality*, New York: W.W. Norton & Co., 41–61.

Vygotsky, L. S. (1978) *Mind in Society*, Cambridge, MA: Harvard University Press.

Weick, K. E. (1979) *The Social Psychology of Organizing*, 2nd edition, Reading, MA: Addison-Wesley.

Weick, K. (1995) *Sensemaking in Organizations*, Thousand Oaks, CA: Sage.

Weick, K. E. (1998) 'Improvisation as a mindset of organizational analysis', *Organization Science* 9(5): 543–55.

Wenger, E. (1998) *Communities of Practice*, Cambridge: Cambridge University Press.

Wertsch, J. V. (1998) *Mind as Action*, New York: Oxford University Press.

Wigg, K. M. (1997) 'Integrating intellectual capital and knowledge management', *Long Range Planning* 30(3): 399–405.

Winogrand, T and Flores, F. (1987) *Understanding Computers and Cognition*, Reading, MA: Addison-Wesley.

Wittgenstein, L. (1958) *Philosophical Investigations*, Oxford: Blackwell.

18 Knowledge work: ambiguity, image and identity

Mats Alvesson

On knowledge-intensive companies

The category of knowledge-intensive companies (Alvesson, 1995; *Journal of Management Studies*, 1993; Robertson and Swan, 1998; Starbuck, 1992) refers to firms where most work is said to be of an intellectual nature and where well-educated, qualified employees form the major part of the work force. The company claims to produce qualified products and/or services.

Typical examples of companies in this category are law and accounting firms, management, engineering and computer consultancy companies, advertising agencies, R&D units and high-tech companies. The category of knowledge- intensive organization overlaps with, and includes, the notion of a professional organization. It is broader and does not emphasize the features ascribed to a typical profession, such as a code of ethics, standardized education and criteria for certification, a strong professional association, monopolization of a particular labour market through the regulation of entry, etc. Professional organizations tend to be characterized by the relative homogeneity of the profession; its (claimed) common knowledge base and its significance for the identities of professionals typically reduce variation between organizations, while other knowledge-intensive organizations may have a more organizationally specific knowledge base and be more idiosyncratic (Morris and Empson, 1998; Robertson *et al.*, 1999).

The idea of knowledge-intensive companies and related concepts such as knowledge work is problematic. It is difficult to substantiate knowledge-intensive companies and knowledge workers as distinct, uniform categories. The distinction between these and non- (or less) knowledge-intensive organization/non-knowledge workers is not self-evident, as all organizations and work involve 'knowledge' and any evaluation of 'intensiveness' is likely to be contestable. Nevertheless, in many crucial respects, there are differences between many professional service and high-tech companies on the one hand, and more routinized service and industry companies on the other, e.g. in terms of broadly socially shared ideas about the significance of a long theoretical education and intellectual capacities for the work. It makes sense to refer to knowledge-intensive companies as a vague but meaningful category, with sufficient heuristic value to be useful. The category does not lend itself to precise definition or delimitation and it includes organizations which are neither unitary nor unique. Perhaps *the claim to knowledge-intensiveness* is one of the most distinguishing features. The emphasis of knowledge can be seen as a matter of legitimation as much as mirroring what knowledge-intensive organizations and workers actually do. De-emphasizing knowledge work as the skilful application of cognitive rationality based on superior knowledge provides a point of departure radically different from mainstream thinking.

This chapter critically addresses the significance of knowledge and suggests other candidates for capturing what is really crucial in knowledge intensive companies. This means a new theoretical framework for thinking about knowledge and knowledge work. Central to this framework are three kinds of ambiguity: (a) of knowledge; (b) of the significance of knowledge; and (c) of results claimed to be contingent upon knowledge work. The chapter explores the consequences of ambiguity for management, client relations, organization and identity. It is argued that the regulation of identity is crucial to cope with the strains of – and exploit the possibilities associated with – the indeterminacies in this kind of work and organization.[1]

Problematizing knowledge: questioning functionalism

Knowledge – at least in the context of the business world and of management studies – is normally treated as a functional resource, representing a 'truth' or at least something instrumentally useful on a subject matter and/or a set of principles or techniques for dealing with material or social phenomena.

In the literature, distinctions between different forms of knowledge are proposed (e.g. Blackler, 1995; Nonaka, 1994; Scarborough, 1995; Spender, 1996), typically based on a combination of two dimensions producing a four-fielder. It is common to distinguish between tacit and explicit knowledge, individual and social, ideational and materialized, etc. These distinctions are seldom unproblematic:

> Knowledge is a slippery and elusive concept, and every discipline has its own secret realization of it. Problems of interpretation haunt every attempt to use the concept effectively, such as that even basic typologies that talk about, say, formal versus tacit knowledge (Polanyi, 1967) actually can be quite meaningless in certain contexts. (Scarborough and Burrell, 1996: 178)

Many authors acknowledge that knowledge is very difficult to define but treat it nevertheless as a valuable capacity which can bring about good results. A key characteristic for knowledge-intensive organizations is said to be the capacity to solve complex problems through creative and innovative solutions (e.g. Hedberg, 1990; Sveiby and Risling, 1986). Thus, a knowledge-intensive organization is a firm that can produce exceptionally good results with the help of outstanding expertise. Starbuck (1992) suggests, for example, that 'to make the kif [knowledge-intensive firm] a useful category, one has to require that exceptional expertise makes important contributions' (p. 716). But these contributions are a matter of interpretation and beliefs; expectations and symbolism are also important. Expertise is not just valuable for its technical functions and 'objective results', it also symbolizes rationality, wisdom, intelligence etc. Through symbolizing these virtues, the impression is communicated that something rational, sensible and valuable is being accomplished. However, knowledge often creates problems through imprinting a norm of how things should be and indicating a gap between current imperfections and the ideal. This is frequently the situation exploited by, for example, management consultants (Clark, 1995; Sturdy, 1997) and other people merchandizing new panaceas for business practice.

Against objectivistic and reified understandings of knowledge, one can point to the uncertainties and controversies characterizing much of science (Brante, 1988) as well as the limitations of the rationality of people working with science and science-like forms of knowledge (Fores *et al.*, 1991). Few knowledge-workers in business operate according to a handbook of scientific methodology, making knowledge work or esoteric expertise in practice different from the application of superior cognitive rationality.

In addition to such counterpoints to the robust, functionalist view of knowledge, one can argue (a) that it is extremely difficult to isolate and point to knowledge as a particular factor that is in itself important, and (b) that the success of knowledge-intensive work is more contingent upon rather loose *beliefs* about them being able to offer something specific to clients and customers. Against an objectivistic and functionalist understanding of knowledge and knowledge-intensity, social constructivism (Knorr-Cetina, 1994; Steier, 1991) and institutionalism (Meyer and Rowan, 1977; Scott, 1987) offer valuable insights.

Knowledge as a limited element in the work of 'knowledge-workers'

Besides emphasizing the ambiguity of knowledge and its development and application, one may also question its centrality in much work on organizations and professions addressed in this chapter. In a study of the work of psychologists and architects, Svensson (1990) found a discrepancy between the rational model of knowledge and the uncertainty, complexity, instability and uniqueness that characterize their day-to-day work. Theoretical knowledge plays a marginal part in their work.

In a case study of a computer consultancy firm it was found that managers and employees often downplayed the role of technical expertise in their work (Alvesson, 1995). The work tasks varied considerably and often people were assigned to jobs for which they had very little formal education or relevant experience. Of course, this capacity to adapt to various contexts and tasks is an important part of consultants' skills, but it is a bit different from the application of a specialized set of knowledge. To say that the work of professionals and other knowledge-intensive organizations and workers is only – or even mainly – the direct or 'creative' application of a systematic, institutionalized body of formal knowledge or esoteric expertise may be misleading. Knowledge – in the sense of a body of information, theories, methodologies broadly considered to have passed some tests of validity, being institutionally backed up, calling for a high level of cognitive ability and being broadly shared by members of a profession or organization claimed to be based on a specific type of knowledge – is thus *not* necessarily that significant in work.

Also, from a slightly different angle, the claimed significance of the knowledge and talents of the employees in at least some large-scale knowledge-intensive companies can be questioned in organizations offering relatively standardized services. In some professional service companies, for example, the quality of service is mainly contingent upon the company's ability to organize and run large, long-term projects, implying the coordination of a great number of personnel trained in the company's method of being able to put people to work quickly (Maister, 1993). Individuals are placed in work groups and allocated well-delimited and specified tasks. The possibilities for making use of special talents or esoteric forms of expertise are thus restricted (Bergström, 1998). Of course, this would be contingent upon management ability (including knowledge), but the significance of sophisticated knowledge seems to be limited in most of the activities involved.

To conclude, the extent to which knowledge is a particularly significant element in the functions of knowledge-intensive companies remains an open question. It is frequently impossible to separate knowledge and 'pure' intellectual skills (symbolist–analytical work) from flexibility, organizing capacity, a high level of motivation, social skills, less esoteric technical skills, the ability to follow company methods, standardized ways of operating and other elements in knowledge-intensive companies.

The ambiguities of work evaluation

A third form of ambiguity concerns the results produced. Persistent uncertainty is by definition a part of the area in which most professionals and other knowledge workers are operating. Fields of action with low uncertainty, or where the knowledge required to evaluate problems and solutions is easily accessible, do not provide the space necessary for the development of socially recognized expertise (Beckman, 1989). This means that professional work is also very difficult to evaluate, at least for those outside the sphere of the experts concerned. In practice, such expert evaluations rarely take place.

In much professional work, the criteria for evaluating work are unreliable or entirely absent. Comparisons of the decisions of expert and novice auditors indicate no relationship between the degree of expertise (as indicated by experience) and consensus; in high-risk and less standard situations, the experts' consensus level was lower than that of novices (Bédard and Chi, 1993). Mozier (1992) remarks that 'judging the quality of an audit is an extremely problematic exercise' and says that consumers of the audit service 'have only a very limited insight into the quality of work undertaken by an audit firm' (p. 2). It is also claimed that in these firms there is a high premium on the idiosyncratic knowledge of the client, and great difficulty in monitoring performance and developing clear performance contracts (Fichman and Leventhal, 1991). In the advertising profession, representatives of clients and the advertising agency very often have different evaluations of a particular proposal for an advertisement (Alvesson and Köping, 1993). Evaluation of the work of computer consultants is often the object of uncertainty and 'agreement on problem definitions and solutions requires active communication and negotiation' (Deetz, 1997: 156). A study of the construction of the Channel Tunnel, found that the perceived role and significance of engineering consultants diverged considerably between the consultants themselves and the permanent staff (Henriksson, 1999). While the consultants 'frequently put across the notion of being the committed rescuers who salvaged the project from complete failure' (p. 145), many of the people they said they were helping frequently blamed them for 'having done more harm than good' (p. 146).

Some knowledge-intensive companies standardize their products; for example, in management consultancy it is increasingly common for companies to develop methodologies for systematic work (Werr et al., 1997). However, the idiosyncrasies of clients and the considerable amount of interaction between consultants and their clients in the production process, adds to task uncertainty and to the difficulties of evaluating quality of results and the performance of knowledge-intensive companies.

Due to the difficulties of evaluating the performances of many knowledge-intensive forms of work and the close interaction between consultant and client, market control can often be expected to be relatively ineffective:

> Because of the esoteric body of knowledge, as well as the intrinsic opacity of agent behavior and indeterminacy of outcome, however, analogous market control mechanisms are either ineffective or not at all present in the principal–professional context. (Sharma, 1997: 780)

This implies that the rationality of the market is not sufficient to counteract ambiguity.

In many cases, the idea that there is a very strong and causal relation between knowledge and problem-solving appears simplistic as results are often almost impossible for the non-expert to evaluate – something that is equally difficult for the expert. How can anyone tell whether a headhunting firm has found and recruited the most suitable candidates, or if an audit has been carried out to the highest standards? Of course, sometimes one may observe whether something works or not (e.g. after the intervention of a plumber), but normally the issues concerned are not that simple in the context in which the concept of knowledge-intensiveness is frequently used. Here we are mainly dealing with complex and intangible phenomena. Even if something seems to work, it might have worked even better or the cost of the intervention might have been much lower if another professional or organization had carried out the task.

It thus can be argued that the distinctiveness of knowledge-intensive firms lies in the ambiguities characterizing (a) their claimed core product/service (knowledge); (b) what they are doing (working with 'knowledge' compared to behaving in ways that are loosely connected to this quality); and (c) the results of their work. A deep and persistent interest in ambiguity uncertainty that cannot be solved through information or expertise offers a strong counterpoint to a conventional approach proceeding from an idea of cognitive rationality as the 'essence' of knowledge-intensive work and organizations. Saying this is not contradictory to acknowledging that ambiguity exists – or is a possible theme for interpretation – in all organizational life (Feldman and March, 1981; Jackall, 1988; Martin and Meyerson, 1988). Focusing on ambiguity may, however, be particularly fruitful in the study of knowledge-intensive organizations.

Emphasizing ambiguity as a general feature of not only knowledge but also what characterizes contemporary societies and organizations in general, encourages an alternative understanding of why experts are frequently used, compared to what functionalists claim. Rather than being employed for their problem-solving capacity, they may be used because institutionalized 'truths' (myths) say that one should do so (see Meyer and Rowan, 1977). Experts imply legitimacy. In the context of uncertainty, the enrolment of consultants may also make the avoidance of responsibility easier if and when 'blametime' occurs. As Jackall (1988) points out, managers want to avoid making (difficult) decisions and are inclined to involve many people in the decision-making process in order to distribute the blame if the decision appears to be wrong in retrospect. Having consultants and other experts involved is one possibility here.

There are thus good reasons to explore other dimensions than those assuming that knowledge and organizations based on esoteric expertise (symbolic–analytical skills, expert knowledge) express cognitive rationality and accomplish valuable results. Ways of dealing with ambiguity provide themes for understanding the nature and management of knowledge-intensive organizations.

Image intensity

The ambiguity of knowledge and the work of knowledge-intensive companies means that 'knowledge', 'expertise' and 'solving problems' to a large degree become matters of beliefs, impressions and negotiations of meaning. Institutionalized assumptions, expectations, reputation, images, etc. feature strongly in the perception of the products of knowledge-intensive organizations and workers. In the absence of the existence of tangible qualities available for inspection, it is extremely important for those claiming to be knowledge-intensive to nurture an image of being so. Image becomes vital as a substitute for the ambiguities of the content of the skills and knowledge of the personnel, for the difficulties in finding out what knowledge people actually do and for evaluating the results (Alvesson, 1990). This image must be managed on different levels: professional–industrial, corporate and individual. Image may be targeted in specific acts and arrangements, in visible symbols for public consumption but also in everyday behaviour, within the organization and in interaction with others. Thus image is not just of importance in marketing and for attracting personnel but also during and after production. Size and a big name are therefore important for many knowledge-intensive companies – and here we perhaps have a major explanation for all the mergers and acquisitions in accounting, management consultancy and other professional service companies. A large size is reassuring. A well-known brand name substitutes for difficulties in establishing quality.

The significance of image also affects the discipline of the workforce at the individual level. In a study of a Big Six accounting firm Covaleski *et al.* (1998) found that the appearance of being 'professional' was highly significant for the career prospects of the accountants. One person, identified by his superiors as a 'revenue stream', reported that his success was closely associated with mimicking the behaviour of his mentor and his mentor's mentor, both of whom were partners. There was a strong focus on physical appearance – to give a strong impression of being tightly disciplined and accountant-like. Virtues such as appearing clean, proper, impersonal, objective, standardized, predictable and reliable are, presumably, communicated. A study of Swedish advertising workers indicated much effort in presenting the right appearance, of fashion-conscious, casual but elegant clothes, frequent changes of dress, etc. (Alvesson and Köping, 1993).

Rhetoric intensity

In view of the notoriously ambiguous character of (a significant part of) knowledge-intensive workers and organizations, the demands on the agents involved in terms of providing convincing accounts of what they do, and what sort of people they are, become central. This means that rhetorical skills and rhetorical acts become highly significant for the constitution of the company, its workers, activities and external relations.

There are good reasons to resist a clear-cut objectivist or realist dualism between rhetoric, ideology, symbols and other 'non-real' elements, on the one hand, and the real, the true, substance and other 'non-invented' elements on the other hand. However, a strong rhetorical, relativist, symbolist, postmodernist or subjectivist thesis in which all distinctions between reality and appearance are viewed as fiction is unsatisfying. I am certainly not denying that we sometimes can sort out the real from the fabricated (the Holocaust was not a fiction, the knowledge behind and invested in the use of penicillin by authorized medicine seems to have been strongly validated). Most interesting research questions for social science do not, however, fit into such a pattern of thinking. The 'constructedness' of reality and the reality of construction, the realness of symbols and the symbolic character of reality should be borne in mind (Peters and Rothenbuhler, 1989). Especially, perhaps, when the knowledge-intensive is studied.

Rhetoric, then, is not just external to the core of knowledge-intensive, but is in a way its core. Rhetoric does not simply mean persuasive talk being in some kind of opposition to 'reality' or 'truth', but refers to elements of argument and persuasion which may, or may not, be backed up by 'facts'. Seldom can these be separated from a rhetoric aiming to convince sceptics that a particular claim simply is based on, or reports, 'facts'. Even scientific reports are rhetorical products (Watson, 1995). An aspect that differentiates many knowledge-intensive companies from other kinds of companies is thus the degree of elaboration of the language through which one describes oneself and one's organization, regulates client orientations and engages in identity work (Alvesson, 1993, 1994). Comparatively 'non-ambiguous' organizations (relating to elements of products and a great deal of operations and many employees' work content), such as fast food, railways and nail manufacturers, and occupations such as typists and machine operators, can be managed without highly developed rhetorical skills. Organizations and jobs that score high on ambiguity – such as the ones we are addressing here – cannot be managed without skills in, and attention to, rhetoric. This is perhaps most salient for management consultants described by Czarniawska-Joerges (1988) as merchants of meaning trading in words.

A strict separation between having knowledge and marketing it is misleading. Knowledge does not exist in a vacuum as something fixed and packaged, ready to be sold and distributed. This implies a change of focus from an emphasis on formal knowledge to persuasive strategies of convincing all concerned about the expertise and superior rationality one is governed by, and which can benefit the clients.

Social connections and interaction-intensity

As a socially constructed phenomenon, knowledge does not exist on its own, but is dependent on social recognition; without being perceived and recognized by others, for all practical matters, knowledge does not appear as such – except for Robinson Crusoe and people in similar situations. A company that claims to be in the knowledge business – and to offer services or products with a sophisticated knowledge content – calls for the specific or institutionalized confirmation and support of significant others.

The rather heterogeneous aspect of the dependence on significant others for validation – the relational character of knowledge-intensiveness – involves (a) (being perceived as) having links with bodies that confirm one's knowledge-intensiveness; (b) forming and maintaining specific ties with clients and customers; and (c) orchestrating the interactions around carrying out the work in socially and politically fine-tuned ways.

Social links with others known for knowledge-intensiveness

The relational–interactional issues are relevant on different levels. Professionals get their recognition from professional bodies and authorization. As a layman, one 'knows' that a person is knowledgeable because credible institutions have declared that such is the case. An expert belongs to a community of experts: authorization and membership of associations are often the criteria for expertise. For members of so-called professions this is, of course, necessary and is formally regulated. Within the professions, the criteria and rules for evaluations are determined by the professionals themselves (Jamous and Peloille, 1970). Even though other knowledge-intensive occupations, weaker on formal professionalization, have developed less of an aura of mystique and more vulnerability to critical evaluations and opinions of outsiders, they are still strongly dependent on other insiders' recognition. Outsiders rely on the insiders to determine what is rational and valuable. For most knowledge-intensive companies other kinds of relationships and indications of inclusion than professional associations become more vital. For companies claiming to be knowledge-intensive it is very important to have (be broadly perceived as having) the right – advanced and demanding – clients, joint partners and other organizations in the network. This is sometimes seen as important because it facilitates the development of new or better knowledge (Wikström *et al.*, 1993). My point is that it is important also because it is typically read as confirming the claim of the focal company's knowledge-intensiveness. As Håkansson and Snehota (1989) suggest, the invisible assets of companies 'consisting largely of knowledge and abilities, fame and reputation, are mainly created in external relationships. Furthermore they cannot be separated from these relationships' (p.193). Knowledge – as a social construction – is maintained, developed and communicated through such interactions and the best way of indicating that a knowledge-intensive company deserves this label is to point at prestigious customers or partners, well-known for *their* knowledge. A consultancy firm refers to having the 'right' client, and the client refers to using the 'right' consultants. Through such mutual confirmations, internal and external audiences 'know' that advanced knowledge is there. The symbolic function of networks is thus significant.

Developing and maintaining social relationships

Partly for this reason, but also of course in order to capture and keep customers, managing social relationships is important. It is just as crucial for knowledge-intensive service firms. Auditing firms typically make investments in relationships with clients and make efforts to generate social attachment (Fichman and Leventhal, 1991). In the absence of the availability of competition parameters such as price (which tends to be less significant for knowledge-intensive business) and quality (which is hard to evaluate), personal relationships and ambiguity reduction through personal contact take on extra significance. In knowledge-intensive contexts, the high level of uncertainty makes actors inclined to stick with the actors they know well.

For knowledge-intensive organizations, especially in the service sector, relations and 'relations knowledge' become very significant. Covaleski *et al.* (1998) refer to one employee in an accounting firm who observed that his 'emerging identity of being "chargeable" was less associated with possessing expertise and wielding knowledge than with managing business relations with clients' (p. 317). In another study of a Big Six accounting firm, Grey (1994) reports pressure for those aspiring to be partners to exploit their private life in order to develop and maintain business contacts.

Familarity and personal experience do not guarantee the capacity to clearly evaluate the competence and contributions of a knowledge-intensive company, but knowing the company and its personnel is one way of reducing the uncertainty experienced by the client. Clients of knowledge-intensive companies are often inclined to stay with the companies of which they have experience; dealing with unknown companies would only aggravate their feelings of uncertainty and anxiety. Consequently, investment in, and maintenance of, an established relationship become crucial.

Orchestrating interaction process

Partly, but perhaps loosely, connected to the forming of social bonds is the significance of the management of interaction processes as a cornerstone of carrying out knowledge-intensive work. Here marketing becomes central. In the absence of something very specific to offer or tangible results that can be inspected, the way the social process runs comes to represent how the work is done. According to Clark (1995) 'a key objective for consultants is to manage and manipulate the interaction process in such a way that they convince clients of their value' (p. 53).

According to the computer consultants that I studied, technical aspects were less crucial for the success of projects than the social relations within project groups and in relationship to clients: getting along, clarifying expectations and obtaining acceptance for solutions were critical (Alvesson, 1995). According to a group of advertising professionals, relationships with clients were also difficult to handle. To develop a good proposal was sometimes easier than getting the client to accept it, they said (Alvesson and Köping, 1993). Often knowledge-intensive service work is carried out in a political context and the service provider is expected to be prepared to provide political support, including letting the client take the credit for any perceived good result and accepting that any blame is ascribed to the service provider (Fincham, 1999; Jackall, 1988).

Of course, managing the client relationship is to some extent a part of a professional–functional concept of knowledge, including the development of a shared understanding of what the problem is, as well as gaining acceptance for the proposed solution; working with implementation issues calls for good social interaction and knowledge involving social skills. The interaction aspects pointed to here, however, go beyond this kind of professional–functional knowledge and include keeping the client on the hook, keeping him or her happy (more than serving the client organization as a whole), acting in a politically sensitive way, preserving an image of knowledge-intensive work being carried out and of using all kinds of methods to secure a personal relationship, where the demonstration of strongly justified superior excellence seldom can be accomplished.

Consequently, the management and manipulation of social relations and belonging to the right association or informal network of knowledge-intensive players are vital elements in demonstrating one's capacity in the absence of clear-cut and solid proof. The orchestration of social processes in an image-sensitive and politically sensitive way is important to compensate for the intangible, ambiguous character of the service being offered. Social relations and personal knowledge sometimes matter as much as or more than market transactions and quality/price-based competition.

Knowledge work and the matter of substance: The contingency of ambiguity, impressions and image?

It is reasonable to ask whether there is any variation in the centrality of ambiguity within the overall category of knowledge-intensive companies and occupations. Perhaps some of these companies may bother less about the environment's perceptions of their knowledge-intensiveness and choose instead to rely on their results to speak more or less for themselves. Social scientists typically disagree with the latter and emphasize the socially constructed nature of even the most sophisticated experiment-based science (Knorr-Cetina, 1994). Even here, the negotiation of meaning and social construction of the truth characterize knowledge.

Nevertheless, one may consider the possibility that there is strong variation among knowledge-intensive sectors in terms of possibilities of demonstrating knowledge and/or accomplishing a high level of consensus amongst stakeholders about problem-solving capacity. Perhaps professional service work, then, is more ambiguous and dependent on rhetoric than high-tech work, which results in a product that lends itself better to inspection. Those engaged in 'internal activities' (i.e. who do not regularly face clients/customers) may not directly bother about appearances, etc. as affecting how the environment perceives the product. Market/environment-oriented rhetorical and image work may to some extent be centralized and much activity carried out 'internally', protected from the gaze of the customers in high-tech companies offering a physical product. On the other hand, the knowledge-intensive work of professionals, groups and units within such companies are not easy to detect through inspecting the qualities of an end-product, which may take several years to develop and produce and where specific strengths and weaknesses – themselves an outcome of social judgement processes – may be difficult to ascribe to particular workers or units. More or less relevant or reliable indicators of – surrogates for – knowledge qualities become central to the constructions of the knowledge-intensiveness at stake. Rhetoric, image manipulation and coping with social relations thus also become significant in an internal organizational context. In addition, tangible products do not speak for themselves: the value of pharmaceutical products, IT systems and other material outcomes is also dependent on persuasive tactics and the fabrication of a favourable social context.

It is thus not self-evident whether some knowledge work or organizations may be much less well understood through emphasizing ambiguity, rhetoric, image and interaction than others. The question 'Does it work (well) or not?' may, however, cause disagreement amongst experts to varying degrees and the demonstration of technical competence may be more or less important. Also within a specific professional service organization there may be considerable variation in this respect. Based on a study of a large accounting firm, Grey (1998) talks of a 'technical–behavioural' spectrum. In some areas, such as tax work, considerable command of technical issues was required, while in other areas, like insolvency, behavioural–symbolic issues were much more central.

Arguably, knowledge-intensive companies and their work, while typically dealing with complex, mainly intangible phenomena, are generally well conceptualized through the key concepts and framework linking these examples presented here. This should, however, be balanced against the insight that the category of the knowledge-intensive company is neither unitary nor unique. A sensitivity to variation within this rather broad category is important, and an openness for the productivity of other vocabularies and dimensions must be borne in mind. Where technical skills are significant and the companies take great pains to standardize their products, attention to ambiguity, image, rhetoric and the symbolism of social and business relations may have a somewhat less prominent interpretive capacity. However, in such cases, the concept of knowledge-intensive work/organization also becomes less relevant – knowledge-intensity to some extent runs against technical skills and product standardization. Consequently, where knowledge-intensity is central, so is ambiguity and, contingent upon this ambiguity, issues of image, rhetoric, orchestrating social relations and processes.

Identity

Identity constructions are of great significance for management and subordinates in knowledge-intensive companies due to problems of control as well as the consequences of ambiguity on self-esteem. The difficulties of employing good performance measures and the ad hoc nature of much work lead many authors to emphasize cultural–ideological or clan control (Alvesson, 1995; Kunda, 1992; Wilkins and Ouchi, 1983), although, of course, typically a variety of control measures are employed. Cultural–ideological control means the targeting of values, ideas, beliefs, emotions and identification of employees. A considerable amount of self-organization is necessary. Even in those companies trying to standardize their products, 'client involvement adds to task uncertainty, requiring professionals to create their roles to some extent in the course of a client assignment' (Morris and Empson, 1998: 619).

Identity is central in forms of control associated with corporate culture, but also in other contexts where senior management tries to form or discipline the professionals through other means than pushing for (what is claimed to be) a company-specific set of ideas, virtues and ways of doing things. In addition, hierarchy and the prospect of making a career involve regulating identity through the creation and maintenance of a particular career mentality. Identity thus becomes significant as an object of management control and regulation to accomplish a 'subjectivity base' for the right kind of action, including whatever is in line with the image, rhetoric and orchestration of social interaction deemed to be appropriate.

Given the high level of ambiguity and the fluidity of organizational life and interactions with external actors, involving a strong dependence on somewhat arbitrary evaluations and opinions of others, many knowledge-intensive workers must struggle more for the accomplishment, maintenance and gradual change of self-identity, compared to workers whose competence and results are more materially grounded.

Contemporary social life in many ways destabilizes a coherent sense of self-identity. Compared to other groups, knowledge-intensive workers have some strong advantages in developing and maintaining a positive work identity. Education, status, high pay and interesting work tasks facilitate positive identity constructions. At the same time, the traditional mystique and exclusiveness of the professions and other knowledge-intensive workers have been weakened. The centrality of work and thus work-related identities to these workers, means that much is at stake and there is a strong sensitivity to lack of confirmation of the valued identity. Compared with people who invest less self-esteem in their work and who have lower expectations, people in knowledge-intensive companies are thus vulnerable to frustrations contingent upon ambiguity of performance and confirmation. My main point, however, is that despite the comparatively high status of knowledge workers, their self-esteem cannot be taken for granted and must be secured in an ambiguous and fluid world. In a study of a public relations company, a vice president spoke very favourably about a young man in the company but when asked about his promotion prospects, the interviewee said: 'Well, just because he is great today does not mean he will be great tomorrow. Anything can happen. He has to keep his clients happy if he wants us to stay happy with him' (Jackall, 1988: 172).

The unpredictable, relationship-dependent and fluctuating character of this kind of work thus makes it difficult to accomplish and sustain a stable, steady growing feeling of competence and respect. As Deetz (1997) writes, 'the largely fluid nature of anything external to interactional accomplishments, provides for very active symbolic labour' (p. 157). A computer consultant interviewed by the author said that in the worst case, you can get an assignment where you do not know what it is supposed to lead to, you do not know the machine, the people you are supposed to work with do not want you there because the project has been sold on the wrong level, etc. Even though we should be careful not to overstress the fragility of people's self-esteem and identity (Newton, 1998) there are some indications that we should take this aspect seriously in much knowledge-intensive work, in particular the high demands on the 'level' of identity constructions that corporate and individual success and well-being call for.

Corporate identity – constructions of what the company stands for and in what respects it is more or less unique – is important here, as a bastion against perceptions of ambiguity and as a resource for employees. I will, however, concentrate on the identities of the employees, i.e. personal and social identity rather than organizational identity. In the rather extreme 'people-intensive' organizations that many knowledge-intensive companies may be said to be, systems, structures, technologies and products matter much less than what the personnel do and, in particular, how they impress clients, partners and others. Marketing and production are heavily sensitive to the identities of the personnel.

Identity regulation in knowledge-intensive companies

Management, in general, but perhaps even more strongly so in many knowledge-intensive companies, is partly about regulating people's identities – establishing standards for how employees should define themselves (Alvesson and Willmott, 2000). When complexity rules out, or reduces the efficiency of, direct control of employee behaviour or results, making an impression on how people see themselves is one way of safeguarding what are deemed to be suitable priorities and efforts. I will here analyse four kinds of identity-focusing control in many knowledge-intensive companies: identification with the company as an institution, cultural control, normalization and subjectification.

Corporate identity and the institutionalization of the company

While most executives want to promote their employees' identification with, and love for, the organization, in some companies the opportunities for, and/or the value of, success in this respect will be better than in others. Many large knowledge-intensive firms are prestigious and membership of them brings status and identity-support.

The identification then works via a combination of internal corporate pride and status of being affiliated through the prestige of the organization. For the employee, there is a strong value attached to being a successful member of this specific institution, perceived as representing a value in itself (Selznick, 1957). The more distinctive, well-known and respected the organization, the more likely employees are to define themselves as belonging to it (Ashforth and Mael, 1989; Dutton *et al.*, 1994). For less fortunate companies, managers may engage in great efforts to construct an appealing corporate identity. Efforts include elaborated rhetoric and image management regarding the claimed unique characteristics and excellence of the company (Alvesson, 1995).

To some extent, the very notion of being (constructed as) a knowledge-intensive company increases the chance of people letting their identities be formed and constrained through organizational membership. Issues around knowledge-intensiveness offer valuable raw material for identity constructions.

Cultural control

As mentioned earlier, most knowledge-intensive companies rely on a corporate ideology – a set of guiding ideas, beliefs, emotions and values, often being more influential than formal structures in controlling people. The specific control accomplished – reminders, (symbolic) rewards and reprimands – is typically decentred and exercised by a myriad of sources. Kunda (1992), for example, observed in his study of a large high tech company:

> ... a decentralization of power ... agents of control are everywhere; one is surrounded and constantly observed by members (including oneself) who, in order to further their own interests, act as spokespersons and enforcers of the organizational ideology. (p. 155)

Normalization

Normalization means disciplining people through a standard of behaviour and performance, where any perceived or experienced discrepancy between the norm and the actual triggers efforts to reduce the discrepancy (Foucault, 1980). Normalization works through a mixture of self-perception and signals from others (superiors, colleagues, subordinates) systematically or sporadically engaging in surveillance and (informal or formal) examination.

The notion of 'being a professional' frequently serves as a control in this sense. Grey (1998) illustrates the normalizing capacity of this notion in an accounting firm through discussions with managers about rumours of sexual harassment. Neither the human resource problem – talented female workers may leave – nor the ethical issue seemed to bother the interviewees, but Grey's suggestion that such behaviour may appear 'unprofessional' seems to make a stronger impression (even though professionalism may be seen as unrelated to the issue of harassment). Sometimes professional and organizational defini-tions of optimal ways of behaving may be at odds with each other but in this case the definition of 'professional' was what senior partners and other people in the company meant by the term: 'being a professional meant being a BSF [name of the firm] type, implies that identification with the profession and the organization were coterminous' (p. 581). Sometimes the norms to be followed are internalized to the point where people fully adopt the orientations deemed to be best for the company. As one partner in an accounting firm expressed it:

> I do what I want, but the things I want are likely to help the firm because that is the way I have been trained. At one level we are completely independent, but we all march to the same tune without even thinking about it. (Morris and Empson, 1998: 618)

Subjectification

This concept, also drawing upon Foucault, refers to a process tying individuals to a particular model of self-knowledge, i.e. individuals create themselves as distinct kinds of subjects. The subjects then mould themselves around a specific self-definition.

One example of this phenomenon, orchestrated by the company, is cultural matching, i.e. how the company encourages a fit between candidates and their job through a 'realistic' job description and by giving candidates the chance to choose whether they fully match the job and the organization. This means a change of focus from surveillance of individual abilities, knowledge and traits to surveillance of candidates' own self-understanding and subjectification. Cultural matching exemplifies a kind of control in which individuals experience their work as a result of their autonomous and well-informed choice (Bergström, 1998: 200). Employees are encouraged to define themselves as the kind of people who would have chosen this kind of work; this definition then produces a standard to which subjects become committed.

Deetz (1995) observed the consequences of relabelling a computer professional service unit as an 'internal consultant group' and 'a profit centre'. This affected the identity of employees and meant new control processes:

> Conceptions of self-value changed from pleasing a client and doing a good job as goods in themselves to the instrumentalization of these in the service of making money. Most worked harder for the same pay. Employees defined themselves as being of value based on feeling more important if someone was paying the company for their services, rather than based on work quality or the level of their own pay. (p. 149)

These four forms of identity regulation 'from above' work partly through the receptiveness of people to developing and stabilizing work identities in the context of the investments in frequently prestigious and well-paid work, as well as the uncertainties and fluctuations of the confirmation of the self in work interactions.

Conclusions

This chapter does not, of course, suggest that knowledge is unimportant or that knowledge-intensive companies lack 'substance'. Technical skills, theoretical knowledge, practical experience, etc. are often vital and can be reduced neither to mere social opinions and ill-founded myths, nor to objective capacities existing beyond social meaning, doubt, judgement and negotiations. But we need to be more sceptical about the popular view that knowledge is increasingly significant and is the key feature for many organizations and workers.

We can thus take seriously not only that knowledge 'in itself' is frequently ambiguous but also that it is highly ambiguous as to what role this 'factor' plays in most knowledge-intensive – but presumably also in many other – work and organizations. This perspective is quite different from traditional views of professions and contemporary functionalist writings about knowledge-intensive organizations. Abbott (referred to by Sharma, 1997) for example, claims that abstract knowledge is the key distinguishing characteristic of professions.

This article offers a counterpoint to the prevalent position. It inspires a more suspicious understanding of knowledge-intensive organizations and workers. This is in line with some recent work on the sociology of professions (e.g. Brante, 1988; Fores *et al.*, 1991; Jamous and Peloille, 1970) rather than the 'mainstream' on knowledge-intensive organizations. Without denying that, as a key resource behind cognitive rationality in action, knowledge may sometimes be a functional resource that is directly applied in work, other functions and aspects of knowledge and knowledge talk may be as, or even more, central. Knowledge, i.e. claims of knowledge in social contexts, plays various roles, such as being: (a) a means for creating community and social identity through offering organizational members a shared language and a common way of relating to themselves and their world; (b) a resource for persuasion in marketing and interactions with customers; (c) a means of creating legitimacy and good faith with regard to actions and outcomes; and (d) obscuring uncertainty and counteracting doubt and reflection. This last point indicates that 'knowledge' and 'knowledge work' may lead to the opposite of what they claim – to ignorance and uncritical attitudes. In all these roles, knowledge may be seen as helpful in the construction of the identity of knowledge workers. Knowledge claims can thus also be seen as identity work.

The ambiguities involved in the notion of knowledge, what knowledge workers do and the difficulties in evaluating their work, mean that a potential (experienced) shakiness, arbitrariness and vulnerability characterize many knowledge-intensive workers and organizations. Difficulties in 'grounding' lead easily to problems securing organizational identity as well as worker identities. However, the options for imaginatively constructing the organization, work and workers in various ways are considerable as interpretations of material circumstances are less likely to provide an argument against the proposed constructions. In 'ambiguity-intensive' organizations, rhetoric, image management and ongoing negotiations become necessary and are offered a large arena (Alvesson, 1990). As clients and customers often have problems estimating the value of the product/service offered, establishing close social links between the knowledge-intensive company and the customer/client becomes vital. Interactions must be carefully orchestrated and efforts to strengthen ties given priority. Rhetoric, image production and the fine-tuning of social bonds rely upon supportive work identities. Successful talk, appearance and interaction call for the right kind of subjectivity. There is a close and complex relationship between these qualities; identity constructions are being backed up by rhetoric and images, at the same time as the fluid and fluctuating nature of persuasive talk, appearance and adapting to the whims and wants of clients undermine the prospect of, as well as the usefulness of, fixed identity constructions. This is illustrated in Figure 18.1. All this implies that a vital part of management includes developing, controlling and securing work and organizational identities.

In sum: knowledge-intensive work tends to be ambiguity-intensive, which makes abilities to deal with rhetoric, regulate images and manage relationships and interactions with clients central. All these circumstances put some strain on, as well as lead to the centrality of, the securing and regulating of identity. Ambiguity leads to space for innovative constructions of identity at both organizational and personal levels, but also puts pressure on activities to develop and obtain validation of these constructions. Ambiguity, in other words, provides an open arena for positive action, but also represents a tendency calling for defensive measures. Consequently, intensiveness not only includes knowledge, but also those other issues central to any claim for knowledge to become successful. Knowledge-intensive signifies an intensity of rhetoric, image, interaction and identity-regulation.

Figure 18.1 Some connections between ambiguity, image, rhetoric and identity in knowledge work and organizations

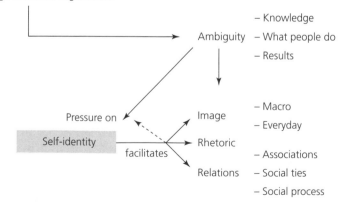

Note

1. Parts of this chapter draws upon Alvesson (1993). Ambiguity, rhetoric and image are themes treated in the present chapter that were also covered in the earlier work. In order to expand and develop the approach, some overlap is necessary. In those few paragraphs where I draw upon the earlier work, most of the literature referred to was published after 1993 and novel comments and arguments have been added. The major points regarding social connections and interaction, identity and identity regulations are entirely new.

References

Alvesson, M. (1990) 'Organization: from substance to image?', *Organization Studies* 11: 373–94.

Alvesson, M. (1993) 'Organization as rhetoric: knowledge-intensive companies and the struggle with ambiguity', *Journal of Management Studies* 30(6): 997–1015.

Alvesson, M. (1994) 'Talking in organizations: managing identity and image in an advertising agency', *Organization Studies* 15: 535–63.

Alvesson, M. (1995) *Management of Knowledge-Intensive Companies*, Berlin/New York: de Gruyter.

Alvesson, M. and Köping, A.S. (1993) *Med känslan som ledstjärna* [Guided by the feeling], Lund: Studentlitteratur.

Alvesson, M. and Willmott, H. (2000) 'Producing the appropriate individual: identity regulation as organizational control', Working paper, Department of Business Administration, Lund University.

Ashforth, B. and Mael, F. (1989) 'Social identity theory and the organization', *Academy of Management Review* 14: 20–39.

Ashforth, B. and Mael, F. (1996) 'Organizational identity and strategy as a context for the individual', *Advances in Strategic Management* 13: 19–64.

Beckman, S. (1989) 'Professionerna och kampen om auktoritet', in Selander, S. (ed.) *Kampen om yrkesutövning, status och kunskap*. Lund: Studentlitteratur.

Bédard, J. and Chi, M. (1993) 'Expertise in auditing', *Auditing: A Journal of Practice and Theory*, 12: Suppl., 12–45.

Bergström, O. (1998) *Att passa in* [To fit], Gothenburg: BAS.

Blackler, F. (1995) 'Knowledge, knowledge work and organizations', *Organization Studies* 16(6): 1021–46.

Brante, T. (1988) 'Sociological approaches to the professions', *Acta Sociologica* 31: 119–42.

Clark, T. (1995) *Managing consultants*, Milton Keynes: Open University Press.

Covaleski, M. *et al.* (1998) 'The calculated and the avowed: techniques of discipline and struggles over identity in Big Six public accounting firms', *Administrative Science Quarterly* 43: 293–327.

Czarniawska-Joerges, B. (1988) *Att handla med ord* [To trade with words]. Stockholm: Carlsson.

Deetz, S. (1995) *Transforming Communication Transforming Business: Building Responsive and Responsible Workplaces*, Cresskill, NJ: Hampton Press.

Deetz, S. (1997) 'Discursive formations, strategized subordination, and self-surveillance', in McKinley, A. and Starkey, K. (eds) *Foucault, Management and Organization Theory*, London: Sage.

Dutton, J., Dukerich, J. and Harquail, C. (1994) 'Organizational images and member identification', *Administrative Science Quarterly* 39: 239–63.

Feldman, M. and March, J. (1981) 'Information in organizations as signal and symbol', *Administrative Science Quarterly*, 26: 171–86.

Fichman, M. and Leventhal, D. (1991) 'History dependence in professional relationships: ties that bind', in Bacharach, S. *et al.* (eds) *Research in the Sociology of Organizations*, Greenwich, CT: JAI Press.

Fincham, R. (1999) 'Extruded management: contradictions and ambivalences in the consultancy process', paper presented at the 1st Critical Management Studies Conference, Manchester, July.

Fores, M., Glover, I. and Lawrence, P. (1991) 'Professionalism and rationality: a study in misapprehension', *Sociology* 25: 79–100.

Foucault, M. (1980) *Power/Knowledge*, New York: Pantheon.

Grey, C. (1994) 'Career as a project of the self and labour process discipline', *Sociology* 28: 479–97.

Grey, C. (1998) 'Homogeneity to heterogeneity: being a professional in a "big six" firm', *Accounting, Organization and Society* 5/6: 479–97.

Håkansson, H. and Snehota, I. (1989) 'No business is an island: the network concept of business strategy', *Scandinavian Journal of Management* 5: 187–200.

Hedberg, B. (1990) 'Exit, voice, and loyalty in knowledge-intensive firms', paper presented at the 10th Annual International Conference of the Strategic Management Society, Stockholm, September.

Henriksson, K. (1999) *The Collective Dynamics of Organizational Learning: On Plurality and Multisocial Structuring*. Lund: Lund University Press.

Jackall, R. (1988) *Moral Mazes*, New York: Oxford University Press.

Jamous, H. and Peloille, B. (1970) 'Professions or self-perpetuating systems? Changes in the French university-hospital system', in Jackson, J. (ed.) *Professions and professionals*, Cambridge: Cambridge University Press.

Journal of Management Studies (1993) 30(6).

Knorr-Cetina, K. (1994) 'Primitive classification and postmodernity: towards a notion of fiction', *Theory, Culture and Society* 11: 1–22.

Kunda, G. (1992) *Engineering Culture: Control and Commitment in a High-Tech Corporation*, Philadelphia, PA: Temple University Press.

Maister, D. (1993) *Managing the Professional Service Firm*, New York: Free Press.

Martin, J. and Meyerson, D. (1988) 'Organizational cultures and the denial, channeling and acknowledgement of ambiguity', in Pondy, L. *et al.* (eds) *Managing Ambiguity and Change*, New York: Wiley.

Meyer, J.W. and Rowan, B. (1977) 'Institutionalized organizations: formal structure as myth and ceremony', in Zey-Ferrell, M. and Aiken, M. (eds) *Complex Organizations: Critical Perspectives*, Glenview, IL: Scott Foresman.

Morris, T. and Empson, L. (1998) 'Organisation and expertise: an exploration of knowledge bases and the management of accounting and consulting firms', *Accounting, Organizations and Society* 23(5/6): 609–24.

Mozier, P. (1992) 'The response of UK auditing firms to a changing environment', paper presented at Workshop on the Organization and Management of Professional Service Firms, University of Alberta, Edmonton, May.

Newton, T. (1998) 'Theorizing subjectivity in organizations: the failure of Foucauldian studies?', *Organization Studies* 19: 415–48.

Nonaka, I. (1994) 'A dynamic theory of organizational knowledge creation', *Organization Science* 5: 14–37.

Peters, J.D. and Rothenbuhler, E. (1989) 'The reality of construction', in Simons, H. (ed.) *Rhetoric in the human sciences*, London: Sage.

Robertson, M. and Swan, J. (1998) 'Modes of organizing in an expert consultancy: a case study of knowledge', *Organization* 5(4): 543–64.

Robertson, M., Scarborough, H. and Swan, J. (1999) 'Creating knowledge within expert consultancy firms: the role of organizational and institutional arrangements', paper presented at Warwick Business School.

Scarborough, H. (1995) 'Blackboxes, hostages and prisoners', *Organization Studies* 16: 991–1020.

Scarborough, H. and Burrell, G. (1996) 'The axeman cometh: The changing roles and knowledges of middle managers', in Clegg, S. and Palmer, G. (eds) *The Politics of Management Knowledge'*, London: Sage.

Scott, W.R. (1987) 'The adolescence of institutional theory', *Administrative Science Quarterly* 32: 493–511.

Selznick, P. (1957) *Leadership in Administration – A Sociological Interpretation*, New York: Harper & Row.

Sharma, A. (1997) 'Professional as agent: knowledge asymmetry in agency exchange', *Academy of Management Review*, 22: 758–98.

Spender, J.-C. (1996) 'Workplace knowledge as a competitive target'. in Malm, A. (ed.) *Does Management Matter?* Lund: Lund University Press.

Starbuck, W. (1992) 'Learning by knowledge-intensive firms', *Journal of Management Studies* 29(6): 713–40.

Steier, F. (ed.) (1991) *Research and Reflexivity,* London: Sage.

Sturdy, A. (1997) 'The consultancy process – an insecure business', *Journal of Management Studies* 34(3): 389–414.

Sveiby, K.-E. and Risling, A. (1986) *Kunskapsföretaget* [The knowledge company]. Malmö: Liber.

Svensson, L. (1990) 'Knowledge as a professional resource: case studies of architects and psychologists at work', in Torstendahl, R. and Burrage, M. (eds) *The Formation of Professions',* London: Sage.

Watson, T. (1995) 'Rhetoric, discourse and argument in organizational sense making: a reflexive tale', *Organization Studies* 16: 805–21.

Werr, A., Stjernberg, T. and Docherty, P. (1997) 'The functions of methods of change in management consulting', *Journal of Organizational Change Management* 10(4): 288–307.

Wikström, S., Normann, R., *et al.* (1993) *Knowledge and value,* London: Routledge.

Wilkins, A. and Ouchi, W. (1998) 'Efficient cultures: exploring the relationship between culture and organizational performance', *Administrative Science Quarterly* 28: 468–81.

Smart workers, dumb organizations?

Alan McKinlay

Introduction

The debate on knowledge management has been long on technological promise and managerial prescription but short on analyses of knowledge *work*. Our objective is to examine the experience of knowledge workers in a global pharmaceutical company, WorldDrug. From the mid-1990s, WorldDrug launched a series of knowledge management initiatives all geared to opening up local, incremental innovations in working practices to wider corporate audiences. The nature of these initiatives ranged from inter-personal learning to a technology-led corporate-wide attempt to archive, classify and compare formal and informal working practices. We begin by outlining the main features of recent research on 'communities of practice', essentially anthropological research on the nature of tacit, collective knowledge in the contemporary workplace. We then turn to the experience of knowledge workers in the central research function of WorldDrug. The majority of employees in this area understand and categorize themselves as 'knowledge workers', largely irrespective of their professional qualifications. For these WorldDrug employees, the most important form of 'knowledge' is of the unofficial processes and networks that *enable* formal structures and procedures to function effectively. Importantly, the most important form of 'knowledge' is that which allows them not just to cope with formal procedures but to blur, sidestep or temporarily ignore the boundaries between 'functional' hierarchies and project teams. For the individual knowledge worker, mobilizing social networks and drawing on their collective knowledge was vital to effectiveness in a company experiencing near continuous restructuring. Finally, we examine waves of knowledge management interventions inside WorldDrug. Despite major investment and strong corporate support, no knowledge management initiative delivered the anticipated leveraging of the tacit knowledge housed in the organization. Here we draw on the metaphor of the 'flaneur', a doomed, romantic figure to capture the marginal and ultimately ephemeral experience of the most innovative form of knowledge management, 'Café'.

Communities of practice?

Perhaps the most important new developments in understanding knowledge work has come from the growing research on 'communities of practice'. The 'community of practice' literature has uncovered, or, more accurately, rediscovered, the significant collective and hidden knowledge that underpins, even the most mundane forms of work. Etienne Wenger, for instance, examines the way that workers cope with tightly managed clerical routines by short-circuiting official procedures or make their targets by juggling workflows. The medical insurance claims processors' work is strictly choreographed by procedures and tightly monitored for quality and efficiency. In such settings, tacit knowledge is the precondition of effective coping strategies: knowing what work to prioritise in order to make performance management tolerable, the ability to identify anomalies, and to derive satisfaction through their participation in a 'community of practice'.

> What claims processors learn cannot easily be categorized into discrete skills and pieces of information that are useful or harmful, functional or dysfunctional. Learning their jobs, they also learn how much they are to make sense of what they do or encounter. They learn how not to learn and how to live with the ignorance they deem appropriate. They learn to keep their shoulders bent and their fingers busy, to follow the rules and to ignore the rules. They learn how to engage and disengage, accept and resist, as well as how to keep a sense of themselves in spite of the status of their occupation. They learn how to weave together their work and their private lives. They learn how to find little joys and how to deal with being depressed. What they learn and don't learn makes sense only as part of an identity, which is as big as the world and as small as their computer screens, and which subsumes the skills they acquire and gives them meaning. They *become* claims processors. (Wenger, 1998: 40–1)

In one sense, Wenger is rediscovering socialization processes, the maintenance of informal workgroup behavioural codes familiar from previous generations of industrial sociologists (see, *inter alia*, Gouldner, 1954). Or, more broadly, the subterranean world of work – the unruly, unmanaged, barely perceptible dimension that parallels the official, managed and contested organizational processes and discourses (Gabriel, 1995). Equally important, Wenger points to the deep affiliation individuals develop to their occupation. The term 'community of practice' does, however, denote significant differences between the hidden, communal life of the contemporary knowledge worker and her manufacturing counterpart or, more aptly, predecessor. Apprentices in manufacturing or construction experienced highly ritualized learning processes that stretched over three to seven years. Crucially, the content and pace of the novice's learning was determined by an experienced craft worker, with little or no managerial control. The gradual socialization of the apprentice culminated with his entry into the craft community. Membership of the craft community entailed profound responsibilities that spanned time and space, responsibilities that found institutional presence in powerful, exclusive craft unions. That is, the expectations of the craft were not tied to specific organizational settings and were binding on the individual for his entire working life. Membership of a craft community inescapably entailed obligations to others that the individual would never meet. Membership of a community of practice, by contrast, is pragmatic and involves no comparable obligations to a shared tradition or to strangers. Significant managerial prerogatives were qualified by agreements with trade unions or negotiated informally with craft groups. For example, individual workloads were not assigned unilaterally by management but negotiated with craft workgroups. Most commonly, tasks were allocated by the craft group according to norms of equity with little regard to efficiency: carpenters would ensure that older workers were not exposed to the heaviest tasks but be left to concentrate on less physically demanding finishing work. Such small exchanges between generations of craft workers signified their continued adherence to an ethic that was no less binding for being informal and oral in nature. Craft workers claimed the right to monopolize specific tools, tasks or processes in return for developing and sustaining highly developed manual and conceptual skills with, at most, marginal management regulation. The corollary was a jealously guarded tradition of craft autonomy that resisted managerial incursions. Resistance to managerialism was essential to the craft tradition. Symbolism was vital to the craft tradition. One early twentieth century Scottish engineer drew a chalk circle around his machine and refused entry to all supervisors: any negotiations with management took place outside the craftsman's private work domain. Secrecy was not simply an inherent part of work but in itself constituted a form of resistance. Indeed, the defining objective of Taylor's scientific management was to counter the ruses of the craft worker. The contrast with contemporary 'communities of practice' is profound. Membership of Wenger's 'community of practice' entails neither the lengthy socialization nor the exclusiveness of the craft community. Equally, the tacit knowledge that is the cornerstone of the 'community of practice' is derived *entirely* from managerially prescribed routines as opposed to the autonomous judgement and skill essential to craft. Where the craft ethic bound the individual throughout their working life, the 'community of practice' is tied to a particular time, place and organizational process. Where skills were developed and protected by the craft community, the tacit knowledge of the 'community of practice' is ephemeral and finds no institutional expression comparable to the craft union. In many respects, then, we should be wary of the term 'community' when applied to the mobilization of tacit knowledge in the contemporary, rationalized workplace. This is not to say that Wenger's 'communities of practice' do not exist or that the concept is fatally flawed. Rather, the comparison reminds us of the essentially transitory nature of skill and knowledge – codified or tacit – in the contemporary workplace. Knowledge workers may inhabit communities of practice but this does not signify the development of an occupational ethic comparable to that of their craft predecessors.

The developing literature on 'communities of practice' is not dispassionate research but tied to a managerialist project. That is, its explicit purpose is to alert managers to the *necessary* existence and social organization of tacit knowledge in the workplace. In effect, beneath Wenger's insightful anthropology is a corporate project to capture knowledge that is no different in intention from classical Taylorism. In contrast to Taylorism, the 'communities of practice' research adopts a more modest approach that accepts that there is a certain inherent unknowability about social learning that requires managerial guile. Seely Brown and Duguid (1998), central figures in this debate, express this managerialist purpose most clearly. Astute managers must think 'dialectically', forget command, control and empowerment and instead develop new skills of brokerage and translation if they are to successfully capture knowledge from the hidden 'communities of practice' that undergird the formal world of work and organization.

Knowledge work is awkward to monitor and even its products or services are difficult to evaluate by clients or peers (Alvesson, 2001). Self-regulation is the key mode of control in knowledge-intensive firms. Corporate culture is both a means of control *and* a resource for employees. Cultural conformity is read through an individual's demonstrations of commitment. The workplace becomes a theatre of commitment. Most obviously, commitment to one's self, colleagues and the project is demonstrated through long hours, particularly at milestone moments in product development. But commitment is also displayed by participation in office gossip or debates about local and corporate strategies. Gossip and strategic conversations allow individuals to develop a sense of their own identity that is interwoven with that of the confidantes and the corporation. Equally important, trust and knowledge are signalled by relaying information about organizational politics. Trust, in that the individual passing on an interpretation of what a strategic or structural change may mean for a project or workgroup, signals not only that the person is being trusted with information but also that the originator is making himself vulnerable. Such exchanges also signal the knowledgeability or 'connectedness'of the originator. English-Lueck's (2002) path-breaking anthropology of knowledge work in California's Silicon Valley takes this still further. English-Lueck points to the interpenetration of work and home, of employment and family identities and notes the overlap between 'high-tech' and knowledge work. Knowledge work is information arbitrage, of mobilizing work and social networks to receive, decode, manipulate, and disseminate information. This is an inherently creative process based on a combination of technical expertise and a deep awareness of the practical value of one's social networks.

Managing knowledge in WorldDrug

Much of what we do is not factual, is not objective. It's transcendental management. It's about creating a theology, a credo. (Interview, WorldDrug Vice President, USA)

The production process in knowledge-intensive firms is highly variable, ranging from the few weeks to design, develop and market a multimedia object through to the decade plus long 'molecule to market' process in pharmaceuticals. Equally, there is a huge contrast in the nature of the production process. In multimedia production the constant interactions between producer and client blur, or even temporarily obliterate, organizational boundaries and fuse design and production phases (Wittel *et al.*, 2002: 194). In pharmaceuticals, by contrast, outsourcing of drug trials is carefully controlled both technically and legally. Reducing development time is vital to profitability and competitiveness in pharmaceuticals. Compressing distinct functional phases and globalizing clinical testing are the main routes to shorter lead times. Automated screening has radically altered the nature and pace of the discovery process, but the development phase remains reliant upon lengthy clinical trials and the compilation and testing of the enormous documentation required by regulators (Chiesa and Manzini, 1997; Pisano, 1998). For WorldDrug executives, corporate restructuring and technological innovation merely established the grounds for competition in the sector: sustainable competitive advantage could only be derived from organizational innovation and knowledge management.

In a multinational organization such as WorldDrug, the intranet was critical to the business, the source of the latest version of a document or database. Given that tasks were performed on a common data source sequentially by international workgroups, the intranet was also an essential element of work organization in Europe and the USA. The centrality and ubiquity of the intranet increased the demands on a system originally designed to be marginal to the core business process. The intranet, in other words, had to be managed as a critical piece of business infrastructure. Managing access to and transactions within key areas of the intranet was both essential to ensuring the integrity of data and the security of the system. Nor was the management of information flows simply a technical issue, however complex. Rather, the intranet was also a key social domain in which corporate strategies and local management practices were discussed. Maintaining a balance between increased formal control and supporting the informal user groups that generated useful operational innovations was a novel dilemma that WorldDrug addressed by slowly enhancing system security. WorldDrug rejected any sudden or radical extension of control over intranet traffic, except in those areas that directly impinged on submissions to regulatory bodies. Callaghan (2002) provides a telling contrast to the WorldDrug experience. In 'CoreTech' management deliberately shifted the company towards a much more controlled intranet environment in which all web documents and links to electronic newsgroups had to comply with centrally authorized design protocols and be subject to central review. The firm's tightened information management policy conflicted with sections of the workforce's expectations of unlimited and uncontrolled access to the intranet, an autonomy that was an essential aspect of their identity as knowledge workers. For management, the newsgroups were not just informal, but unregulated. Indeed, newsgroups were open fora whose very existence blurred the line between work and non-work. It was impossible for management to know whether an individual was working or not, far less to inspect the value of participation in a newsgroup. This difficulty was particularly acute with software developers who would flit in and out of newsgroups, eavesdropping on the conversations, while waiting on their machine to complete a parallel task: 'work' and 'non-work' co-existed simultaneously and unknowably. By contrast, WorldDrug not only tolerated but, as we shall see, stimulated the formation of informal user groups.

We share Warhurst and Thompson's (1998) misgivings that the descriptive and analytic value of the term 'knowledge worker' is threatened by over-generalization. However, more than two-thirds of survey respondents in WorldDrug's European R&D function defined themselves as a 'knowledge worker'. Two-thirds of respondents were team members with generic responsibilities and skills: 'team member' or 'data analyst'. The remainder had a management responsibility or dedicated, singular roles. Individuals' tenure was relatively stable. 59% of respondents had been with their primary team for more than one year; 30% for more than three years; and only 11% for less than six months. The teams were stable. Just under half (47%) of respondents had been employed with WorldDrug for more than five years; 37% had between three and five years' tenure; while only 16% had less than two years' employment with the organization. For some two-thirds of respondents, their primary occupational identification was as a 'knowledge worker' and only secondarily to their professional, scientific or educational status or, indeed, their formal job title. Nor was this a temporary affiliation. All of those who regarded themselves as knowledge workers saw this as a permanent condition rather than a temporary expedient caused by their current task or involvement in a specific project. For those with higher degrees or professional qualifications, to designate oneself as a 'knowledge worker' was tinged with regret, a sense that the individual's expertise had been eroded or compromised through the development of organization-specific skills, including networking. When asked to reflect on their own particular task, such respondents emphasized the importance of tacit knowledge. For 44%, their job comprised both explicit and tacit knowledge; a third regarded tacit as more important than explicit; and 5% saw their job as based predominantly or exclusively upon tacit knowledge. New skills were most commonly (57%) developed by the individual's immersion in a task or through dialogue with others (24%). 'Our skills are nebulous. People can talk about what they *used* to be experts in, but nobody can really say that they are an expert *in* anything (laughs) – except surviving in here'. For those with a first degree or with no higher education, however, the term 'knowledge worker' was almost entirely positive, an acknowledgement of their organization-specific skills. All knowledge workers recognized that this designation was linked to their career in an internal labour market. For those with a higher education or a professional qualification, this entailed a recognition that they had developed skills that were non-transferable that may limit their mobility outside WorldDrug. A majority of respondents defined most of their colleagues as 'knowledge workers'. Just 7% of respondents defined fewer than 20% of the Central Research population as 'knowledge workers'. 58%, on the other hand, indicated that they believed that over 60% of the workforce was 'knowledge workers'. There was no significant variation by gender, age, education, location, or tenure. For all but 4% of respondents, 'knowledge' was defined as 'important' or 'very important' to organizational effectiveness. Importantly, interviewees distinguished between product and process knowledge. Process knowledge was assessed over technical skills. That is, 'localized' knowledge, highly specific to a particular drug development project was rated as 'much more important' than 'abstract' or 'technical' knowledge.

Here we have to distinguish between codified and tacit knowledge. In WorldDrug, codified knowledge was equated with the basic technical competence that an individual brought to a task. However, technical competence was understood as an *abstract* capability that had limited value without an appreciation of how the organization necessarily melded formal procedures and informal practices. One project manager explained,

> You can hire technical skills from anywhere . . . . it's the contextual, organisational knowledge and the understanding of the business processes and the people that sets some people apart. . . . So we tend to start with the raw technical skills and try to fill them with knowledge of WorldDrug – we put the organisation around them so that they become *comfortable* with the organisation. ('Eric', Project Manager)

Technical or professional expertise and experience may have little impact on the allocation of tasks and roles to individuals in knowledge-intensive firms (Alvesson, 1995). For 70% of respondents their job was defined in terms of broad goals rather than detailed objectives and defined procedures. Some 16% had jobs without broad objectives and had little or no job description but felt that their job 'changed with circumstances'. Only a small minority (6%) had their work defined by line management without their participation. 59% reported that they had some flexibility to modify their work processes and 30% that they were encouraged to find new ways to work. Organizational structures – reporting schemes, role definitions, team formations – were perceived as flexible or, more accurately, as malleable.

> The New York skyscrapers were built by Apache Indians. The Apaches erected the girders, the steel frames. They worked without safety harnesses. We erect the frameworks, then move around them as a background, or ignore them. People like me operate like that: we're nomads who move on as soon as structures start to get too close. We build the skyscrapers but we wouldn't want to live in them. ('Chris', US Team Leader)

This striking, romantic image captures four essential features of the identity of WorldDrug knowledge workers. The knowledge worker is essential to the construction – and reconstruction – of administrative procedures while their identity is, at least, ambiguous or, at most, antithetical to routine. The cityscape viewed from the skyscraper eyrie and the dangerous spaces between the building's skeleton, speak of a weightlessness that is a world away from the grounded, mundane existence of routine office work. Equally important is the knowledge worker's sense of rootlessness, of belonging to neither function, nor project, far less to a particular organization. This is ironic given that the embeddedness of the individual in a specific workgroup was – and was understood to be – the taproot of tacit knowledge. The knowledge worker – the 'Apache Indian' – belongs to a nomad group with only a ghostly presence in the organization. Finally, this image speaks of the knowledge worker's sense of themselves as a risk-taker, as a group that works at the edge of the known and the predictable.

The formal organizational structure was widely perceived as a practical irrelevance to individuals' day-to-day tasks. Corporate HR schemes were also of limited importance in skills development. Informal communication was rated (82%) as the most important means of transferring knowledge inside *and* between teams.

> We're realistic; we're not monks. We're not meditative – never will be. Meditation is for the individual's enlightenment. We're after reflection, and reflection is a collective endeavour. (CKS Director)

Even more paradoxical, however, was the limited value ascribed to knowledge transfer between teams. For 77% of respondents, the knowledge generated by one team was 'seldom' or only 'occasionally' used by other teams. Tacit knowledge was understood as intensely local, specific to a particular team's collective experience. Yet tacit knowledge was rated as more important to *organizational* functioning than explicit, codified knowledge. Broadly, tacit knowledge was perceived (38%) as twice as important as explicit (19%). This perception does not necessarily indicate that working knowledge was tacit by nature, and not by practice. Rather, tacit knowledge must be distinguished from knowledge that *could* be codified. There was some resistance to codifying working practices, but this was limited and reflected respondents' perception that knowledge capture would not receive the necessary investment in time and resource. More importantly, teams – especially those with the greatest exposure to the industry regulator – were reluctant to commit experience and opinions to recordable media as all documentation was subject to recall and investigation that may delay the product's entry to the market. In turn, this fosters the sense that all knowledge was tacit by nature rather than solely by practice. The importance of tacit knowledge was underscored by the long learning curve identified by respondents. 82% of respondents indicated that more than one year's experience was required to become proficient in *any* job in their team; 30% suggested that more than three years' experience was necessary for proficiency. There was a strong correlation between length of tenure and user perceptions regarding training and experience. 96% of new team members – those with less than six months membership of a team – indicated that it would take no more than six months for others to learn 'their job'. Conversely, 33% of team members with over five years' experience, replied that it would take more than three years for others to master 'their job'. The paradox was that those who stressed the lengthy period necessary to master their role also perceived their knowledge as dynamic, ephemeral, and crucially, cumulative.

> We're trying to build a new culture of interpretation. The ability of our people to *interpret* corporate initiatives, not to follow slavishly or to reject. But always, *always*, to engage. We're not after corporate clones, we don't want to win hearts and minds – we want to challenge their minds. ('Bill', Knowledge Consultant)

Process knowledge, the procedures for generating the tables and analyses required by the regulator, was much more complex. On the one hand, there were the formal procedures for information flows and data management, for project management and budgetary control. The *formal* procedures were thorough but not comprehensive and were obstinately linear, despite work processes that *informally* were increasingly concurrent. Formally, in biometrics, for instance, drug tables were compiled only after the data was completely 'clean' and a range of statistical tests completed. Informally, however, technicians would make judgements about when a batch of data was sufficiently clean to be handed to other teams so that testing and tabulation could begin. Meantime, 'cleansing' the original data would continue. This allowed the formal process to remain on its designated timeline, the most important criteria for evaluating individual and team effectiveness in drug development work. For the originating team, this was an important judgement: a mistaken early release would result in a significant amount of rework, and incur additional time penalties in the imposition of additional statistical scrutiny of the data. To make such a mistake was both highly visible and left the team leader and team members open to sanction for contravening formal procedures. This tacit knowledge was vital for individual careers and for the viability of the project.

> There has to be complete trust inside the team. We must share our experience. Your experience is what allows you to make risk assessment of when to release data and who to. That's why team leaders are so important. The team leader sets the culture for the team. If he wants everything buttoned down completely then you simply can't make the timeline. A *good* team leader is smart enough to give everyone a bit of space. A *great* team leader keeps the culture open even when he's under pressure to deliver. ('Kirsti', DevOps Team Leader)

Similarly, Tsoukas and Vladimirou (2001: 987), describe the tacit knowledge that allows call centre operators to understand enquiries from unsophisticated customers by contextualized prompts and to eliminate less likely causes without recourse to the standardized, automated responses authorized by the firm. 'Through experience and their participation in a "community of practice", operators develop a set of diagnostic skills which over time become instrumentalized, that is to say tacit. This enables them to think quickly, "on their feet", and serve customers speedily. Over time, operators learn to dwell in these skills, feel them as extensions of their own body and thus gradually become subsidiarily aware of them, which enables operators to focus on the task at hand.' This ability to interpret and to use soft or oblique information in order to focus on possible solutions is knowledge that is 'difficult to verbalise, let alone codify'. The mutual recognition of individuals' ability to develop, share, use and police tacit knowledge was an essential dimension of the identity and daily experience of the contemporary 'knowledge worker'.

Knowledge, work and organizational innovation

The worlds of memory replace themselves more quickly, the mythic in them surfaces more quickly and crassly, (and) a totally different world of memory must be set up even faster against them. (Walter Benjamin, cited in Buck-Morss 1989: 278).

The earliest and most enduring form of knowledge management in WorldDrug is 'Lessons Learned'. The 'Lessons' exercise was conducted just after the completion of a major phase of the development process. 'Lessons' was a compulsory element of every significant project and was often completed as part of wrap-up celebrations. Typically, 'Lessons' simply reported administrative gaps to be filled on 'standard operating procedures' or minor adjustments to contracts with outsourced drug testing companies. At best, 'Lessons' was a postscript to a project rather than an organic element of a corporate learning process. Importantly, there were no formal or informal mechanisms to diffuse 'Lessons' to other project teams. Despite the obvious inadequacies of this approach, 'Lessons' became the main element of the second form of knowledge management in WorldDrug: 'Warehouse'. The 'Warehouse' project had the backing of WorldDrug's corporate executive and was supported by a global consultancy (McKinlay 2000). 'Warehouse' signified two significant innovations. First, it attempted to capture both the technical and social dimensions of work organization in order to disseminate tacit knowledge. Second, 'Warehouse' used groupware technology to open up the possibility of new horizontal conversations between originators and potential users of *process* knowledge (McKinlay 2002). For corporate executives, the appeal of 'Warehouse' was the promise that a single system would capture and codify tacit knowledge. More than this, the growth, utility, cost, and benefit of 'Warehouse' were all calculable and predictable. In practice, 'Warehouse', like 'Lessons' before it, failed to engage widespread support of employees. With little incentive to participate and no sanction for abstention, 'Warehouse' was left to wither on the vine.

In Europe, one group – Central Knowledge Support (CKS) – developed a radical alternative vision of knowledge management. CKS was a European group that provided information technology support to the drug development teams. CKS' hybrid role provided it with access to corporate management. CKS provided operational support to the consultants' development of 'Warehouse', but were not complicit with its failings. For CKS, 'Warehouse' was deeply flawed:

> All we're doing is producing a reservoir of information – the swimmer is *not* the knowledge, it's the *act* of swimming – maybe synchronised swimming would be a better way of putting it. Yes (pause), synchronised swimming as a form of collective knowledge. ('Anthony', CKS)

The final form of knowledge management was the 'Electronic Café'. The 'Café' was a set of linked web sites based on the stories of individuals linked to drug development programmes. Essentially, CKS siphoned resources from the 'Warehouse' project to initiate highly interactive digital spaces where otherwise isolated individual innovators could meet and share their experiences. The aim was to construct a digital community of practice. 'Warehouse' was based upon a strictly linear and hierarchical logic, of compiling, sorting, and normalizing to construct a transparent archive of best practice. 'Café', by contrast, pursued a more fluid logic, based upon the construction of montages of administrative alternatives. The objective was to open up more – and unexpected – spaces for reflexivity, spaces that were dialogic in nature and shorn of short-term deadlines. Participation in the 'Café' process was entirely voluntary and regarded as at least as important as the production of 'useful' outcomes. Participation in 'Warehouse', on the other hand, was mandatory and only the outcomes of the process were evaluated, not the process itself. The objective of the narratives was to convey the experience of individuals and groups, to relay something of the texture of the social relationships inside the project team: 'things are changing too quickly for SOPs to work the day after tomorrow. What we offer is a way to create and capture knowledge – an organic process rather than an administrative machine' (Consultant, 'Café' Design Team). 'Café' was not burdened by corporate expectations of utility; participation in 'Café' was regarded as important in itself. At its heart, 'Café' comprised a series of interviews or dialogues about their experience of development work that attempted to convey something of the texture of the social relationships inside different project teams. Each narrative was linked thematically to similar or contrasting sites, to offer the visitor the opportunity to compare and contrast experiences, not to effect the artificial closure of an improved administrative standard. The underlying premise was that insight and innovation are not derived from the rigid discursive structures of 'benchmarking' and 'best practice'. Aphorisms, anecdotes, and warnings were easily reconfigured by individuals. 'Café' was also the site where individuals could discuss imaginary forms of work organization. The aim was to dissolve the certainties of WorldDrug structures into a set of infinitely malleable possibilities. Short-life discussion groups were formed around specific, pressing organizational issues. Other, more durable discussion groups of anonymous participants formed to consider generic organizational issues, such as the management of international development projects. Contributions were archived and hypertext linked to team repositories, the shared digital space where development teams compile the protocols and results required by regulatory bodies. There was, then, a link between the radical space of 'Café' and daily administrative routine. That link, however, remained fragile and under-developed.

If 'Lessons Learned' saw participants as instrumental administrators then, for the 'Café' designers, patrons were conceived of as drawn by the sites' different pace and expectations. In 'Café' mode the image was that of the organizational flaneur, rather than the diligent bureaucrat. The flaneur was one of the archetypical figures used by Walter Benjamin to engage with the labyrinthian urban form of modernity. For Benjamin, Paris, 'the capital of the nineteenth century', was the archetype of the modern city. The deep visual fields of Haussman's boulevards, designed to maximize the visibility of the citizen and to deter insurrection, were a central part of the rationalization of the urban form. The shopping arcades that ran between the boulevards were small-scale, almost intimate spaces that constituted a realm of play, production and of consumption. For Benjamin, the Arcades permitted – encouraged – the collision of bourgeois and bohemian lifestyles, of the dissolute and the respectable. And it was in the Arcades that both archaic and prefigurative social types co-existed, just as 'Café' was designed to develop an inconclusive, perhaps contradictory, montage of narratives. If Paris epitomized the rational form of the modern city, then the Arcades were both a refuge and a stage for marginal life-styles. The emblematic figure of the Arcades was the flaneur, the urban dandy who embodied a rejection of rationality but who also depended upon the crowd to define his uniqueness. The flaneur's idle promenade through the Parisian shoppers was a futile gesture, a gesture whose power lay precisely in his awareness of his futility and the ultimately ephemeral nature of flanerie itself. His was a 'demonstration against the division of labour', a symbolic confrontation with 'the obsession of Taylor, of his collaborators and successors'. The flaneur both embodied the solipsism of consumer society and the aestheticization of social space, the transformation of the public arena into a theatre of private pleasures. But, here again, Benjamin stressed the deeply ambiguous nature of the flaneur, at once a flagrant rebuke to dull routine but also deeply complicit in hedonist consumption: 'The flaneur is the observer of the marketplace. His knowledge is akin to the occult science of industrial fluctuations. He is a spy for the capitalists, on assignment in the realm of consumers' (Benjamin, 1999: 427). But flanerie could be more than the ostentatious display of mere idleness. Rather, Benjamin insists on the creative – *productive* – possibilities of flanerie: that the observant flaneur will be attentive to the neglected details of city life. The flaneur's oblique glance at the social world can reveal more and is infinitely more creative than the disciplinary gaze (Benjamin, 1999: 453–4). Or, as Bauman (1994: 141) put it, 'the art the flaneur masters is that of seeing without being caught looking'. Scandalously, one flaneur dawdled through the Arcades with a tortoise on a lead, at once contrasting his studied leisure with the hurly burly of the labour market, his contrived marginality at odds with the immersion of the individual in bureaucratic routine. But, for Benjamin, there was much more to the flaneur than historical curiosity. The flaneur was also an acute observer of the Parisian crowd, its 'chronicler and philosopher' (Benjamin, 1973: 37). This ambiguous figure, this knowing idler had, in Frisby's (1985: 229; Weigel, 1996: 96) memorable phrase, a highly developed 'knowledge of living'.

> Preformed in the figure of the flaneur is that of the detective. The flaneur required a social legitimation of his habitus. It suited him very well to see his indolence presented as a plausible front, behind which, in reality, hides the riveted attention of an observer who will not let the unsuspecting malefactor out of his sight. (Benjamin, 1999: 439)

The image of Benjamin's flaneur resonates with the image CKS designers had of 'Café' patrons who were both expert in and sceptical of the formal procedures and informal mores of WorldDrug. As one sympathetic manager put it, 'we have to *live* the logic of the future while living in the present' (*Pfizer Director*). There are parallels between the self-consciously transformative role of CKS and the group's difficulty in developing a clear business raison d'etre and the difficulties of incorporating the flaneur's insights into a 'scientific' discourse. For, in the case of Walter Benjamin,

> the 'theorist' is the gifted meditative walker, purposefully lost in the city's daily rhythms and material juxtapositions. The walker possesses both a poetic sensibility and a poetic science that is almost impossible to distil as a methodology ... Benjamin, for example, was doing much more than opening himself to the transitivity of Naples, Moscow and Marseilles. He was not the naïve and impressionable dilettante. He was armed instead with a transcendental speculative philosophy that allowed him to select, order and interpret his sensory experiences of the city. These were reflexive wanderings underpinned by a particular theorization of urban life, with the demand from theory to reveal the processes at work through the eye of a needle. (Amin and Thrift 2002: 11)

Again, we hear echoes of Benjamin's tragic hero, the flaneur's walks through the Parisian Arcades. Like the flaneur, 'Café' patrons understood the desire for ever-more perfect administrative procedures but remained distant from it. Reflexivity was critical to the identity of the 'Café' participant and to the flaneur (Missac, 1995: 190).

> ... he hardly ever buys anything, and his interest remains abstract or distracted, like his movements. While strolling ... he looks at the marble walls, which become transparent and reflect back to him an image in which he recognises himself. ... The conflict between the two functions of the arcade, pedestrian traffic and commerce, is succeeded by the conflict between pedestrian traffic and profit, on the one hand, and usefulness, on the other.

There are also parallels between WorldDrug's 'Café' and Lefebvre's notion of 'spaces of representation', lived forms of spatiality produced in the process of human creativity, feeding off and into the rhythms of everyday urban – or organizational – life and possessing symbolic value (Lefebvre, 1996: 101). 'Spaces of representation' are products of the imagination that try to envisage new meanings or possibilities for urban or organizational life: any practice that introduces an element of drama, spontaneity and play into the mundane routines of organization would constitute the formation of a 'space of representation', however ephemeral. At such times the city – or the organization – ceases to be the stencilled object of bureaucrats and instead becomes the site of struggle, fluidity and festival. 'Spaces of representation' contain a degree of spontaneity which disrupts the usual conventions of order. 'Café' and CKS aspired to become spaces of representation. But the CKS team members' *self-*understanding hinged upon their perception of themselves as the 'other', always at odds with and defined against corporate conventions. To maintain this narrative of difference required the maintenance of CKS as a marginal, and always relatively powerless function. Indeed, for CKS' members their notable and significant influence in corporate decision-making signified their individual and collective guile in surpassing their official impotence. Similarly, the 'Café' patron and the flaneur are figures on the cusp of several different modes of being: between consumption and production; immersed in and distinct from the crowd. But the reflexivity, the knowingness, of both patron and flaneur are undercut by a brittle narcisissism that is accentuated by electronic media.

> ... the office-oriented design of the GUI interface and the workstation complete the illusion that the centre of the network is always a sovereign individual, cross-dressing and touring the playworld in which s/he can achieve mastery over both environment and self. The net is effectively organised around this socially engineered hyperindividual, for whom all variety can be resolved into self and other, with the self in imperial mode, click by click assimilating the alien into the longed for stability of the same. (Cubitt, 1998: 140)

Cafés' designers were aware of the contradictions of their position at the edge of a major corporate initiative such as 'Warehouse'.

> One of our problems is we have gate-keepers who restrict access to information. This is a constant frustration. But if we get ride of them then everyone had access to everything and we have opened up a Pandora's Box because we've surrendered control over knowledge – there is *no* management of knowledge. (CKS, PA, Interview, 2001)

Inevitably, 'Café' slowly disappeared as successive waves of corporate restructuring and increased financial scrutiny limited CKS's autonomy. Paradoxically, as executive support was gradually withdrawn from 'Warehouse' this made it impossible for CKS to disguise the resources required to maintain, far less to extend 'Café'.

The Flaneur's epitaph

> We used to be about innovation. Now we are about sucking value out of *established* processes, *established* kit, *established* applications. (Team Member, 'Right Shaping' Project)

> We've go to change *our* playground into *their* factory. (CKS Team Leader)

CKS's role as the consecrated heretics of WorldDrug was developed against a stable corporate strategy that prioritized organic growth over acquisition. Relentless product and organizational innovation were the twin imperatives of operational management. An abrupt shift in corporate strategy occurred in 2000. Growth was now to be achieved through aggressive acquisition. At the operational level the priority was no longer innovation but efficiency. For the knowledge workers of CKS, coping with a near constant round of organizational restructuring and budget cuts proved a novel and alarming prospect: 'we don't know how to rationalise: we've never had to do it before. Now it's pure terror. And that is the only weapon they've got' (CKS Team Member, 2003). A critical part of the success of CKS was the ability to sustain a narrative of successful innovation. The triumph of 'efficiency' was understood not just as final and definitive but also as the beginning of an onslaught on the very possibility of sustained innovation. The key corporate executive responsible for reducing CKS's role to a prosaic service role was dubbed the 'evil doughboy', a loaded term that referred both to his girth and to the tight fiscal regime he installed. The loose budgets that had accommodated innovations such as 'Café' were now broken down into restrictive categories and time-lines. The ability of CKS members to work from the margins and interstices of the organization was crucial to its success. From 2001 CKS members were no longer seconded onto drug development teams. Drug development teams now purchased specific services from CKS, a structural change that seriously compromised the 'thick' ties that CKS cultivated and then used to introduce significant software and operational innovations. The 'communities of practice' that CKS formed across functional areas and between drug development teams were fatally disrupted. CKS's oral tradition was quickly effaced or, far worse, became a cautionary tale of excess and self-indulgence.

An essential part of the CKS identity lay in their aestheticization of work. The subtle pleasures of the flaneur lies in their appropriation of the city as a place of pleasure. There is a danger of using the metaphor of the flaneur too far. The nobility of the flaneur is in his recognition of his vulnerability as he promenades through the crowd. The flaneur *knows* that either assimilation or annihilation is his inevitable fate. This self-knowledge is the necessary concomitant of his appraisal of the crowd and of his distance from it. CKS, similarly, was acutely aware of the precariousness of its role as the creator and disseminator of novel organizational practices but regarded this as a *weakness* that could be addressed through forging political alliances. Marginality and precariousness were *regretted*, rather than understood as *essential* characteristics of CKS' ability to understand and innovate. The failure to comprehend the *necessarily* ephemeral nature of their role condemned CKS not just to corporate oblivion but also all but obliterated all but the faintest traces of its existence. In this the knowledge workers of CKS shared the paradoxical, transitory existence of the flaneur.

References

Alvesson, M. (1995) *Management of Knowledge-Intensive Companies*, Berlin: de Gruyter.

Alvesson, M. (2001) 'Knowledge work: ambiguity, image and identity', *Human Relations* 54(7): 863–86.

Amin, A. and Thrift, N. (2002) *Cities: Reimagining the Urban*, Cambridge: Polity.

Bauman, Z. (1994) 'Desert Spectacular', in Tester, K. (ed.) *The Flaneur*, London: Routledge.

Benjamin, W. (1973) *Charles Baudelaire: A Lyric Poet in the Era of High Capitalism*, London: New Left Books.

Benjamin, W. (1999) *The Arcades Project*, Cambridge, MA: Belknap Press.

Buck-Morss, S. (1989) *The Dialectics of Seeing: Walter Benjamin and the Arcades Project*, Cambridge, MA: MIT Press.

Callaghan, J. (2002) *Inside Intranets and Extranets: Knowledge Management and the Struggle for Power*, London: Palgrave.

Chiesa, V. and Manzini, R. (1997) 'Managing virtual R&D organizations: lessons from the pharmaceutical industry', *International Journal of Technology Management* 13(5): 471–85.

Cubitt, S. (1998) *Digital Aesthetics*, London: Sage.

English-Lueck, J.A. (2002) *cultures@siliconvalley*, Stanford, CA: Stanford University Press.

Frisby, D. (1985) *Fragments of Modernity: Theories of Modernity in the Work of Simmel, Kracauer and Benjamin*, Cambridge: Cambridge University Press.

Gabriel, Y. (1995) 'The unmanaged organization: stories, fantasies and subjectivity', *Organization Studies* 16(3): 477–501.

Gilloch, G. (1996) *Myth and Metropolis: Walter Benjamin and the City*, Cambridge: Polity Press.

Gouldner, A. (1954) *Patterns of Industrial Bureaucracy*, New York: Free Press.

Grey, C. (1994) 'Career as a Project of the Self and Labour Process Discipline', *Sociology* 28: 479–97.

Lefebvre, H. (1996) *The Production of Space*, Oxford: Blackwell.

McKinlay, A. (2002) 'The limits of knowledge management', *New Technology, Work and Employment* 17(2): 19–31.

McKinlay, A. (2000) 'The bearable lightness of control: organisational reflexivity and the politics of knowledge management', in Pritchard, C., Hull, R., Chumer, M. and Willmott, H. (eds.) *Managing Knowledge: Critical Investigations of Work and Learning*, Macmillan, Basingstoke.

Marschall, D. (2002) 'Internet technologists as an occupational community: ethnographic evidence', *Information, Communication and Society* 5(1): 51–69.

Missac, P. (1995) *Walter Benjamin's Passages*, Boston, MA: MIT Press.

Morris, T. (2001) 'Asserting property rights: knowledge codification in the professional service firm', *Human Relations* 54(7): 819–38.

Pisano, G. (1998) *The Development Factory*, Cambridge, MA: Harvard Business School Press.

Quinn, S. (2002) *Knowledge Management in the Digital Newsroom*, Oxford: Focal Press.

Seely Brown, J. and Duguid, P. (1998) 'Organizing knowledge', *California Management Review* 40(3): 90–111.

Tsoukas, H. and Vladimrou, E. (2001) 'What is organizational knowledge', *Journal of Management Studies* 38/7: 973–93.

Warhurst, P. and Thompson, P. (1998) 'Hands, hearts and minds: changing work and workers at the end of the century', in Thompson, P. and Warhurst, C. (eds) *Workplace of the Future*, London: Macmillan.

Weigel, S. (1996) *Body- and Image-Space: Re-Reading Walter Benjamin*, London: Routledge.

Wenger, E. (1998) *Communities of Practice: Learning, Meaning and Identity*, Cambridge: Cambridge University Press.

Wittel, A., Lury, C. and Lash, S. 'Real and virtual connectivity: new media in London', in Woolgar, S. (ed), *Virtual Society? Technology, Cyberbole, Reality*, Oxford: Oxford University Press.

Trusting strangers:
20 work relationships in four high-tech communities[1]

J.A. English-Lueck, Charles N. Darrah and Andrea Saveri

New media industries, a concept embracing such business entities as dot.coms, incubators, and other multimedia start-up companies, is part of a "new business ecology" which is the result of the penetration of information technologies into work and the globalization of commerce (Institute for the Future, 1999: 4–7). The result is a global high-tech work ecosystem of organizations linked through technologically saturated work processes. That ecosystem can be parsed using several structural criteria. It can be dissected by industry type and artificially divided into such categories as computer hardware-related production, software, telecom, wireless telecom, biotechnology, and so forth. Within industries, some work organizations design a mobile phone, others write the appropriate software, while others fund and market. The ecosystem can be classified by business strategy, such as separating organizations related to the industrial "old" or "new" media economies. However, the merger of internet-based strategies into "brick and mortar" companies problematizes this approach. Urban planners can examine the impact of the twin forces of technofication – the specialization of the local economy around high technology – and globalization, and determine if the region is a "Silicon place" and how it fits into a larger web of Silicon places. Those concerned with economic development may be more concerned with whether a high-tech company is part of a multinational organization based elsewhere or part of an indigenous effort.

What is obscured in these structural perspectives is the work that is entailed in being participants in the global high-tech ecosystem. What matters to them on a day-to-day basis is that work routinely involves substantial technological use, often related to technological production, across international boundaries. These workers merge technical skills, largely centered around communication and information technologies, and knowledge of their social environment to solve managerial and technical problems, create new markets, and find alternative partners in their global enterprises. They work in a web of shifting interdependencies in which building trust among strangers becomes an important set of skills. How they accomplish this is the subject of this chapter.

Knowledge workers in high-tech industries, ranging from prototype machinists to CEOs (Chief Executive Officers), describe working within a web of connections. Some of these connections are face-to-face and reflect near daily interaction. Others are physically and socially distant and mediated by communications technologies, particularly the complex ecosystem of telephony and computer-based devices. The communication patterns have much in common. The interactions are intermittent and reciprocal. Flows of information, people, talent, money and material are necessary to get tasks done, whether those tasks are in the creation of technology or its distribution. Favours are asked that require extra effort, competence and reliability. These requests are often made under trying political and cultural circumstances. Internal competition and cultural differences make interdependent work more problematic. High-tech knowledge work is done by networks of interdependent global workers that must share information, act under severe time constraints, and establish effective relationships at a distance. In short, this work requires trust that is not simply an affective or cognitive state of being, but an active tool used to manage and negotiate expectations between co-workers.

The study

A comparative, cross-cultural approach is necessary in order to understand the construction and use of trust. Cross-site analysis allows us to see that differing social and technical infrastructures shape the way trust is built and maintained. Locating research sites in different countries also emphasizes the problematic nature of technologically-mediated relationships, since networks built at a distance and maintained virtually have risks that locally-constructed networks do not. The management of interpersonal and organizational expectations that is embodied in the concept "trust" is an example of how locally-constructed cultural realities are enacted on a global stage.

This chapter is drawn from ten years of ethnographic effort that has been, in part, directed toward understanding "Silicon places." We define these as globally interacting regions with dominant economic foci on high technology industries that play out in social organization and cultural texture of the daily lives of people living in them. Our primary site has been Silicon Valley, in Northern California, home to at least 8,000 officially constituted work organizations within several high-tech industries. Thirty-seven per cent of Silicon Valley's gross regional product is from high-tech (DeVol, 1999: 55). This core of high-tech workplaces has a halo of institutions subtly transformed by the presence of high-tech, and technological metaphors and technologically-informed problem-solving strategies dominate public discourse. Although Silicon Valley is the most robust and visible such community, other "Silicon places" reflect the marriage of high-tech work and globalization. Dublin, Ireland has experienced an economic renaissance based on software production. As an English-speaking member of the European community with connections to educated ethnic Irish around the world, Ireland has positioned itself to be a key player in the world of knowledge work. Bangalore, India also harnesses the potential of software production. Its rich pool of elite technical workers, again English-speaking, initially made it ideal as a source of software production for multinational organizations. Expatriate Indians who are socially and electronically linked to those who have gained experience in the corporate sector form the basis of a new indigenous Indian technological domain (Saxenian, 1999). The Taipei-Hsinchu corridor of Taiwan, while increasingly involved in software localization for the Chinese market, is primarily identified with information technology (IT) production. Taiwan's unique historic connection with Japan, as a former colony, and with the US, adds to the cultural capital that can be used in developing its own economic infrastructure. Workers in each Silicon place use its distinctive local cultural history and demographic profile to create potentially useful connections to those who can serve as suppliers, capitalists, or markets. The relationships and interactions of the knowledge workers in each of these places are shaped by and shape local identity and work practice.

Traditional anthropological tools such as in-depth ethnographic interviews and participant-observation were used to investigate how extensive use of communication technologies (technological saturation) and global interaction are enacted in daily life. In one of the projects that informs this chapter, we conducted a series of ethnographic interviews and observations of workspaces with 175 people in Silicon Valley, each informant situated in a different kind of work, socio-economic sector or cultured background. We sampled workers in a variety of workplaces, including @Home Networks, Detente Technologies, Advanced Technical Staffing, Adobe Systems, Apple Computers, Cisco Systems, Daimler-Benz, Ericcson, Hewlett-Packard, Phoenix Computers, Peoplesoft and Xilinx, Knight Ridder's Mercury News as well as government and non-profit organizations. Only the first few of those organizations can be strictly classified as new media, but each one partakes of some aspect of the new economy. Some people we interviewed within large, established companies use those organizations as safe havens between risky ventures. The purpose of this project was to explore the social realities experienced by high-tech workers, examine their material world, probe their social connections, and elicit beliefs and values to get an overview of work practices and their impact on daily family and community life (English-Lueck, 2000; English-Lueck et al., 2000).

This approach not only yielded descriptive information, but told us what various practices and artifacts meant to the people themselves. We used physical settings and projective techniques such as mapping "work spaces" and "networks" to elicit stories about relationships and daily work life. These stories not only provide rich descriptions, but also gave informants a chance to elaborate on the meaning of their daily practices. For example, when Irene,[2] a diversity consultant in a major personal computer firm, drew a map of her work day, placing a giant telephone at the center of her world, she was making a symbolic statement about the supreme significance of technologically-mediated communication, as well as elaborating on the way she spent her time at work. We augmented this research with detailed examinations of fourteen dual-career middle-class families in Silicon Valley, each family enduring hundreds of hours of participant and structured observations at work and at home. Several of those families contained new media knowledge workers. Interestingly, the workers in such organizations were very much like high-tech workers from more traditional venues in their daily practices, and in fact they were connected to more traditional high-tech organizations as clients, and former or future employers. In another project, under the auspices of the Institute for the Future we did fieldwork, primarily through in situ open-ended and semi-structured interviews, on work practices, social networks and global interconnections with fifty-nine workers in four different silicon places, Bangalore, India; Taipei-Hsinchu, Taiwan; Dublin, Ireland; and Silicon Valley in the USA. The cross-cultural component allows us to elicit commonalities in global high-technology work and explore distinctive cultural and social differences. Participants in the project included organizations such as Arthur Andersen, a well-established consultant for the new economy, and Internet and start-up organizations such as Baltimore Technologies, Iona, Inforian, Zcom, and Magic Media. Other more traditional technology corporations – Gateway, IBM, Motorola, Novell, Irish Express Cargo, ISSI, Polaris, Arvin Mills Limited and Wipro – were still sites of a distinctive work style that merged technologically-mediated work and global interconnections. The boundaries around new media eroded when we looked at the connections that organizations had with new media companies, and particularly with the relationships that workers had outside of their immediate employer: Polaris finances new media ventures in Taiwan; Irish Express Cargo develops innovative software to handle cargo shipping for new media products in Ireland as well as more antiquated material that must be moved from place-to-place.

Interdependency and trust

Among the knowledge workers represented in our sample, informants described a world in which they gather and pass intellectual and material resources in order to do their work. Issues of trust emerge when successful work depends on the kindness of strangers. Research on the importance of trust at work is, of course, not original to us (Barber, 1983; Douglas, 1986, 1992; Baba, 1999). Douglas points out that interdependent work itself is an insufficient reason for developing trust within an institution (Douglas, 1986: 55). Trust evolves as people engage in a complex symbolic dance, assessing and developing cultural constructions of risk, delineating accountability, and negotiating trust (Douglas, 1992). More recently, anthropologist Marietta Baba has synthesized the literature on workplace trust to better understand how it is constructed from different organizational positions within a high-tech work-place – managers, engineers, security and sales staff. She views trust as a function of the reciprocity that is part of interdependent work practice, and calls for an anthropological discussion of reciprocity in "transactions in which *information itself* is the object of exchange" (Baba, 1999: 343). By focusing on the daily experience and social relations of knowledge workers in a comparative framework we can see the range of reciprocity-related processes that define trust – its inception, development, maintenance and failure.

Trust is a psychosocial construction, defined as "the subjective expression of one actor's *expectations* regarding the behavior of another actor (or actors)" (Baba, 1999: 333). We found it not only to be a manifestation of expectation, but a tactical management tool for manipulating expectations. Trust may be a demonstrated requirement of interdependent work, an intrinsic feature of high-technology practice, but it is constituted differently in diverse contexts. The canon on workplace trust in the psychological literature, although culturally embedded in an American context, parses trust into five components that mirror how our informants described the elements of trust: competence, consistency, integrity, interpersonal loyalty and openness, the latter being more important in peer work relationships than in hierarchical ones (Schindler and Thomas, 1993: 563). The components of trust become especially problematic when enacted and communicated across cultural boundaries. An obvious example emerges when examining the schema for the component "competence." In Silicon Valley, at least in discourse if not in daily practice, there is a stated tolerance for failure. Failure, operationalized as a canceled product or a bankrupt company, is not as grave in Silicon Valley as it would be in Taipei, where success and failure is bound up with *mianzi*, or "face," a concept that is culturally specific. In Silicon Valley the number of options for retreat, that is, getting another job, are more secure. If one company fails, there are literally thousands more to which one could apply. Moreover, the local culture of Silicon Valley invokes the concept of personal "reinvention," allowing people to build personal narratives in which they "learn from their mistakes," and thus "add value" to their individual competencies. However, there are fewer such practical options in Taipei and the Confucian legacy of "face" is derived from a personal narrative in which individuals can deliver a continuous pattern of hard work and success. How then would "competence" be differentially negotiated across those cultures? This plays out in multicultural teams in Silicon Valley where the free admission of possible prototyping errors or design flaws to quality assurance engineers is viewed with alarm by Taiwanese engineers, but as necessary non-threatening procedure by others. Beyond the differences in cultural construction, trust across cultures must reflect the social, economic and political realities of late capitalism. Silicon Valley can tolerate failure because its hegemonic position as the leading technological region has become relatively unquestioned. Bangalore faces different political legacies as a former colonial site. Power differences that exist between organizations, regions and nations can make trust impractical. There are also inherent contradictions in trust relationships. Honest disclosure to a fellow engineer may build trust, whilst the same disclosure to a customer measures failure. Trust is thus context dependent – redefined in various interactions, with peers, customers, supervisors, and larger organizations.

The problems of common cultural constructions of trust are compounded when direct social information is limited – for example, when interactions are international and primarily mediated by information technologies. Establishing trust at a distance, in a vast virtual community requires social effort. If trust, as Baba persuasively indicates, is a function of balanced reciprocity – wherein favors are exchanged in an asynchronous, asymmetrical transaction with the expectation that future exchanges should be equivalent – then good intelligence about the trust partners is essential (Baba, 1999: 335). Such intelligence gathering for establishing, building and maintaining trust is made both more convenient and more problematic by the use of technological-mediated communications. An infrastructure rich in media alternatives – exemplified by Silicon Valley – functions differently than one, in which company-sponsored e-mail is the only reliable method of communicating, an observation made in Bangalore.

As a tool for managing work-related expectations, trust is also intimately intertwined with time. Knowledge works in high-tech industry proceeds at different rhythms. Work is governed by the timing of activities, patterns that reflect "rhythms, cycles, beginnings, endings and transitions" (Barley, 1988: 125). Rhythms vary from the early stages of project work, to the compressed moments around milestones and deadlines. Relying on co-workers to deliver information "on time," particularly when time is compressed, intensifies and defines "competence-based" trust – a kind of trust that is dependent on "affective" delivery of service (Barber, 1983: 160–1; Baba, 1999: 333). As the interpersonal connections must be invoked for information exchange at various, and sometimes unpredictable, moments, knowledge about the complex rhythms of other people's work becomes valuable.

Each informational interconnection must be anticipated and managed. In order to lay the groundwork for that exchange, a substantial amount of social work – initiating and nurturing relationships – must already be in place. The goal of this work is to move other people incrementally along a continuum from the domain of stranger toward that of friend, at least in some contexts. Jeff, a software engineer tries to explain how his work gets done, drawing a verbal picture of a network of colleagues, some in his current company, others from past connections. Jeff says:

> [The corporation's] products are large and complex enough – most products are, these days – that it's more than one person can do. A team is going to consist of marketing people who decide what features the product has to have or the new upgrade has to have, managers who try to schedule the time and decide what's feasible to do, engineers who do the coding, international people who do the translations into other languages, test people who do the testing, and tech writers do the manuals. There's a ton of people involved ... Most of my time I spend on my own in my office working on my chunks of code, but there are two or three other people that I have to talk with and coordinate with on the code, including my manager. And the number of people I have to work with varies. Every so often I find I need someone's expertise that I haven't worked with before. I'll be talking to the QA [quality assurance] people more. I've been talking to the installer person a bit. Occasionally I have to talk to a marketing person. So – it's kind of fuzzy ... There's a once-a-week staff

meeting for the product I'm working on that nearly everybody shows up at, and common issues are raised and discussed there. And then you use e-mail and voice mail and drop into the office for some of the other stuff. Voice mail and e-mail are really good because you don't have to find somebody in their office and free ... And there are others that I chat with when something of mutual interest comes up, but I don't keep them up to date on, you know, how the kids are doing in school, or anything. There aren't a whole lot of them, but a couple of them are very good friends, so they're worthy of mention ... one of them is in upstate New York, another is on a farm in Minnesota, and one of them is a software developer in Perth, Australia.

Jeff goes on to elaborate that each year he throws a party at his house for his developer friends during an international software developer conference especially those from other countries – thirteen hours of playful shop talk that sets up a year of virtual interactions. Far from being a trivial entertainment, Jeff's party sets up his subsequent work interactions.

Mark, an MIS (management of information systems) specialist in a computer company, reinforces the need to build his interpersonal relationship across the global connections. In response to a question on where he works and what he does in those places, Mark elaborates:

I go to Taiwan and Tokyo every three, four months ... Usually three or four days at each location ... In Taiwan and Tokyo in the office itself it's usually around eight hours ... usually there is two to three hours at each end for meetings ... going to dinner with people there ... the work, and socializing with people at work, talking about work, depending if you want to classify that as work ... Am I sitting here with a paper and pencil doing a spreadsheet for work?

"No." Am I talking and planning and establishing relationships with my workers? "Yes." ... You have to. It's not an option. It's not an option if you're going to be successful.

This sensitivity to interdependence and relationship-building takes place among elite knowledge workers as well as their support staff. Andie, an "admin" [administrative assistant] in high-tech, relates a story about the payoff that occurs when trust relationships are in place. She is responsible for scheduling and implementing meetings and trips. She consciously creates an aura of cordiality, learning names and asking about personal details. She tells how she once needed to get a piece of equipment to an airport, but could not find the right people. She says, "all the sudden, somebody came around and it's like 'God sent them to me' ... This is my idea of synergy. The people that I was trying to call, they just happened to come around with the type of equipment that I needed ... when they saw, that it was me, they said, 'Oh, I'd be happy to help'."

One result of relationship-building is, hopefully, the creation of robust and useful networks. Gurjinder, a Bangalore project manager in an international IT firm, discusses the scope of his network. He notes:

I connect to the other project managers and the customer, [the company's] project managers. I connect to the people, technical people. I connect to my own guys sitting there, international there ... Plus sometimes I connect to some vendors, for example, tool vendors. I have to purchase tools, so I need to talk to those people. And then, I need to deal with my own people, my own managers. I deal with the business partner people they supply people to me ... I need more skills I don't have, so I don't need them on my head count, I buy them, buy the people, the sources ... I deal with a lot of people from in [the corporation] internally [in Bangalore], who support me, like HR [human resources], finance, IS [information systems], business partner management people, the sourcing people, besides my team ... And they're very important because, they don't report to me, but if they don't support me, I'm doomed ... And then, many times, we use the customer's equipment, too, so we need to connect to their people to make sure that it works. And then, I deal with external customers here in India ... I'm part of the CII, the Council of Indian Industries ... that's a body of industry there, discussing the problems in India, Y2K problems, how can we help and suggest, comment, etc.

Gurjinder's comments point to the correlation between social networks and trust relationships. The networks act as a source for reciprocal relationships and provide a structure for converting strangers into friends. However, the ambiguity of working within "weak" networks is problematic to building and nurturing trust relationships. Trusting someone to have the necessary "competence, consistency, integrity," as well as "loyalty" and "openness" is harder at a cultural and geographic distance. Global knowledge work necessitates working interdependently at a distance, a less than reassuring situation. Accurate prediction of needs, an important feature of managing expectations, is made trickier and the worker's ability to do so is limited. Anna, a multimedia division manager in Taipei noted:

You're information driven. Since you're co-working with other people, it's not just the Taiwan experience that will count. If I want to work with a designer in the US, I need to know how they work. It makes me, in terms of working – I feel constantly a lack of information. Because I need to work with people, not just in Taiwan but other areas. Those people are virtual ... But my work partly relies on them. So it makes me feel a little less secure because you can't really see things. You can't control it.

Predictability is valued and behaving as expected is a reassuring aspect of organizational life. It is part of the trust building. Listening and responding to the needs of others, be they colleagues or customers, builds trust. Neal, a Dublin based CEO of an indigenous Irish company, echoed this sentiment noting, "we appear to be listening to what they're saying ... [and the customers] like the assurance that if anything were to go wrong they can always pick up the phone and know that we would react." The limits to predictability are thus met with careful listening, although this presumes the ability to recognize the relevant messages. A premium is thus placed on producing performances that both elicit necessary information from an audience and that can be interpreted as evidence of trustworthiness by it.

Trust at a distance

Global knowledge workers confront a vast world of potential interactions and they must establish an organizational presence from which to be heard. Inter-organizational trust, not just interpersonal reciprocity, is thus essential (Dodgson, 1993: 78). Key to establishing that presence is developing a pattern of trustworthiness and reliability at the level of the organization. Mayfair, the co-founder of an IT company in Taipei, reflects:

> At first, we had the idea to be a global company but we didn't know how to do that. Because we didn't have any reputation. We didn't have any connections. We didn't have money at first. We only had technology. That's the only thing we had. So we tried to prove that we had very good technology. We cooperated with Microsoft, with IBM Taiwan ... in the first year. After we proved that people can trust us, we had a very good reputation in Taiwan. Lots of very big companies looked at us and wanted to cooperate with us. So that was the beginning.

Mayfair goes on to reflect that global communications have shifted significantly with the advent of e-mail and Internet access. While telephone communications are still significant, e-mail makes multiple communications convenient. However, it also poses problems. She notes, "If I send a file to you, you can send this file to others, forward it to others or 'cc' (copy) it to others, so there are no secrets. You only can trust people that they won't do that ... I should trust you, or I can not send anything to you. We could not share anything." Inherent in group production practices is the need to share information, be it source code or budget restrictions. Prem, a project manager in Bangalore, notes: "We are the same engineering group. In an ideal situation, we should have a very high level of trust. We should be able to share everything." The act of openly sharing work-related information is one way trust is constructed, precisely because of its acknowledged risks.

In the trust literature, there is a moral and affective component to trust that goes beyond predictability and demonstrated competence. In both Taipei and Silicon Valley there was a strong emotional component in the way trust was described. The Taiwanese talked of *ganqing*, cordiality, and creating a level of "comfort" in interpersonal relationships. It is established by creating a network of known players that can be accessible to co-workers and customers. A known relationship can be the platform for trust while interacting with anonymous workers' causes. This need to have a personal relationship, even if shallowly constructed, is magnified in the Silicon Valley interviews.

In Silicon Valley we asked workers to describe "a trustworthy person" and to give examples of how that trust was enacted, as well as how it could be violated. Trust occurs when people "care" about each other and act out of motives other than self-advancement. This is the classic definition of a "fiduciary form of trust" in which there are expectations that "another will behave in a way that preserves and advances our interests while abstaining from opportunism" (Baba, 1999: 333). The reasoning behind trust in Silicon Valley is remarkably coherent. Trust is designed to protect valuables both "physical and emotional." Building personal relationships is important beyond merely creating a history of professional reliability. Establishing confidentiality breeds trust. If a person divulges personal information, including opinions and perhaps even expressions of doubt about personnel and acknowledgement of organizational foibles, then trust is established when those confidences are not divulged throughout the organization. Trustworthy colleagues do not hide direct criticisms, but do not air those criticisms publicly. Instead, they put a positive "spin" on possible mistakes.

To create that effective common ground, effort is made to personalize culturally and technologically distant relationships. In Bangalore, Prem discussed what he did when he had to transfer his people to another distant team. Instead of merely communicating job specification, Prem tried to communicate more personal information to the new supervisor. He worked at conveying the social context – the engineers' "intra personal relationships" and working styles. This sensitive information is "locally confidential," and he hopes that the supervisors will rise to the occasion and understand the burden of trust placed on them. While he admits this strategy is not always successful, his objective in sharing this information to fellow managers is to achieve the necessary trust to complete the work.

In addition to the psychological components of trustworthiness, the moral reasoning behind trust embodies a series of work virtues. Technical competence is an obvious requirement. In many work practices punctuality and time consciousness are also noteworthy, particularly when finishing one's work is necessary for others to complete their tasks, especially across time zones. Waiting half a day in Dublin might delay an Australian counterpart's work for days. An ethic of accountability is cited. "Ownership" of work is lauded. People lay the groundwork for trust by taking responsibility for seeing a task through beyond the narrowly defined scope of work. This may mean crossing internal organizational boundaries or even going beyond the company to get information or to make sure a task is completed. Paramount in building a trust relationship in Silicon Valley is having "clean motives." It is assumed that politics exists and that people have agendas, but those agendas must not derail the working relationship.

Jaime, a Silicon Valley engineer, lists three components to trustworthiness, echoing the psychological literature – "honesty and integrity and commitment." He goes on to elaborate that he has observed these features in co-workers, by "seeing how they handle customers." He adds:

Commitment is pretty straight forward. I mean they finish what they do. Honesty – when you work with them, they tell you straight up how things are. They are ... given the politics factor, they are pretty much honest about achieving a task. And they are honest about helping to achieve that task. Integrity means that they only go so far to get the job done and if it means going outside the rules or demeaning someone else, they don't do it ... They are committed to accomplishing a task within defined boundaries and do in an open way.

Ironically, informants often found it difficult to recite a single episode of trust, for it was the product of an incremental process. In contrast, there was no difficulty in retelling stories of specific incidents in which trust was broken. While many small events shaped the profile of a trustworthy soul, one episode defined an untrustworthy person. As Mary Douglas puts it, "Public memory is the storage system for the social order" (1986: 70). In this case, memories of success build into an amorphous whole, providing the basis for trust. In contrast, a single episode of trust betrayed is remembered vividly and embodied in the organizational memory. As Rupal, an Indian materials manager opines, "Trust is ... built by [making] a commitment and meeting the commitment." Jeff, a software engineer in Silicon Valley, puts it this way:

Specific instances might be hard to come by, but I feel that I trust them because I know them well, I've worked with them before, smoothly and without friction, and productively. So it's less a particular occasion where someone has come through for me, than just years of, "Yeah, this person's been there a long time, and I've never had any trouble. When things happen this guy gets things done right." A popular phrase is, "This guy gets it."

Initializing trust is a tenuous and delicate process. The social context for creating trust was clearly different than the one for maintaining or building it. Technological mediation was one factor. We were told that jump-starting relationships through virtual media was viewed as a difficult, if not an impossible proposition. Reilly, a web designer in Dublin, notes:

You can't do that if the only communication you've had with them is an electronic one. Technology, I think, is brilliant for once relationships are in place. You can actually maintain those relationships. With initiating and getting to know someone there's no substitute for face to face contact ... A lot of the signals are picked up from body language and the way a person looks at you and what not. You're never going to get that with technology. So you can't build up a true picture of their personality. Hence you won't be able to trust them until you sit in the same room with them.

Perm's voice adds, "In fact, e-mail actually complicates matters for these things. Sometimes when you're talking straight issues, people read (in) a lot of other things. For building trust and all these things, we have to meet or it doesn't happen ... The trust never really gets built to a higher level." People think they have communicated effectively but lack the context to know if they have made disastrous assumptions. Even limited social context, developed over a dinner conversation or a pint of Guinness at the pub, can create a social contract for the suspension of distrust.

Learning personal context beyond the tasks of the moment is essential for maintaining the relationship once it is established. This is done in various ways. Face-to-face contact several times a year, "lunch" and "a real talk" affirm the relationship. Once the relationship is in place a quick task-oriented note, that does not have to include the context or motive, "will," as Rajarshi notes, "cut short the communication." Even indirect intelligence can smooth the communication. Prem talks about accessing the Internet to understand the prevailing jokes made by his American counterparts. Otherwise, their references and social context are unintelligible and "I just miss it completely." The knowledge manipulated by these workers is thus, itself, differentiated by purpose and context. Recognizing the tacit categories of salient knowledge becomes a valued, if largely hidden, skill.

Verifying, manipulating and derailing trust

Social identity plays a role in the verification of trust. In one Taiwanese IT company, Van, the CEO, noted that as a young Taiwanese person he did not symbolically convey confidence to potential customers and investors. Seniority is deeply valued in Chinese social organization, so as a result they were planning to hire a middle-aged American figure-head CEO who would inspire the necessary trust.

Personal networks play a part in verifying trust interactions as well. In Taiwan, Anna, an IT worker, discusses how she gives her home phone number to "trusted clients." She also trusted her family members to screen the calls for her – knowing which ones to pass on to her and which ones to delay. In the observations of dual-career workers in Silicon Valley, spouses were repeatedly consulted to verify the credibility of individuals in work networks and their information. Rennie, an immigrant engineer in Silicon Valley, points out the artifacts of various projects he has worked on, highlighting the photos of the engineering team that seemed "like family" during a particularly grueling project. Family, and even co-workers turned fictive-kin, define, filter and test potential trust relationships. Establishing trust also contains an element of cultural manipulation. Ryan, a quality assurance manager in an international organization, discussed how his Irishness created a link with his American counterparts. He capitalizes on the "memory" of Ireland possessed in popular culture writ large and Irish-Americans in particular, noting:

> If you look at this little island that we have here, we call it the Island of Saints and Scholars, years and years ago, our culture lends itself to matching very, very well we're almost chameleon like the American culture, and we can understand

the American culture ... and we can develop those relationships. And if you look at Ireland, for example, there's not that many Japanese companies here, but there's a hell of a lot of American companies here. And you [have to] ask yourself why is that? (Hewlett) Packard is here, Xerox is here, Intel, IBM, Motorola. (Dublin 12).

Tim, another Irish executive, speculates that the very powerlessness of Ireland makes it an ideal purveyor of trust in global business. He ruminates:

But this whole business, technology, information, security, the information age, has methods that you can do business in all of these arenas virtually shall we say, or using telecommunication technology. So, it provides great opportunities. And one of the things that we got to see going forward ... is authenticating information. To authenticate anything, you always want to have it authenticated by a trusted method I mean, we supply a problem which issues digital certificates to individuals or people who want to trust each other. Networks of trust. ... somebody in Argentina ... if they want to do business with somebody in New Zealand, how do they actually verify their network of trust? How do they know? The guy in New Zealand may want to meet all of your family. It's a bit like the difference before you get married when you're meeting different potential partners. Some of them will want you to meet the parents early. Some of them won't want you to meet the parents at all. And who makes the call? ... I trust a third party can do it ... You could have a trusted third party in a small country which is traditionally independent and neutral and no major allegiances at the cutting edge of technology, say, like Ireland, to act as that kind of hub for almost all global (e-commerce).

The flow of information that simultaneously necessitates and builds trust is not without disruptions and conflicts. Poor infrastructure may sabotage reliability, no matter how worthy the intentions. One manager in Bangalore discussed the need to establish trust and reliability in a climate where the post, the telephone system and transportation were unpredictable. Building trust included being able to predict or at least manage the failures of the system and find ways to communicate glitches to customers and co-workers. Building a network helps, but is not sufficient to make the post run on time.

People move within and between organizations for a variety of reasons, including corporate reorganization, expansion and demise. Individual workers also may be promoted or simply change jobs. This is particularly prevalent in Silicon Valley with its thousands of high-tech organizations. International relocation poses particular problems in maintaining trust relationships. People disappear from the social network, only to later reappear electronically and once gain grant access to information, although that cannot be assumed.

Building social relationships to distant customers can be a tricky proposition. Tunjen, a manager in Hsinchu, Taiwan reflected on the inherent difficulty in information disclosure. He notes:

> Because high speed networks develop very fast, we need to know the status of our company. I will collect the competitors' product information, test their product and generate our benchmark report. We will provide [two] benchmark reports. One is our inside reference and the other is [for] our customer. I will show [the customers] our advantage and then I will hide the report. [He laughs] I will hide the drawbacks and tell them "it's good, good, good, good, always it's good." But inside I will always [think] "drawback, drawback, draw back."

Open communications with customers also poses practical political and cultural difficulties. Realpolitik dictates diplomatic communications. When a customer from the People's Republic of China makes jokes to Taiwanese Tunjen about his "need to learn to swim," tacitly boasting about the naval superiority of the PRC, he keeps his peace. Tunjen notes, "The customer is 'first', so we can say nothing." Trust must be constructed knowing the inequalities which create barriers to be negotiated. For example, simply examining Silicon Valley "trust," as inherently multicultural as that community might be, would have obscured the role of national identity in forming trust – using Irishness or Chineseness to create an image of trustworthiness. Global economic and political power is a key factor in how trust is enacted and defined. Viewed only from Silicon Valley, currently the premier technological producer-community, the effect of power would have been invisible, for it is taken for granted. The role of power is more easily seen from those who labor below.

Even if international politics do not interfere, corporate politics potentially sabotage trust relationships. Repeatedly, our Silicon Valley informants warn us of the dangers of the "hidden agenda." Peter, a marketing program manager at a major Silicon Valley corporation, notes the inherent contradiction. People are constantly, "in an environment where, myself included, we ARE selling [ourselves] all the time ... We do have our agendas. We have our own goals. We all have our own things that we're working on." Yet those agendas must not undermine the network of reciprocal favors that support the trust-building relationships.

In complex organizations with international components, hidden agendas force a reaction of self-protection that sabotages trust. Ryan in Dublin notes, "(The other divisions) may have hidden agendas that may not suit what you're doing. Like if they were out for themselves, I'd be looking to do what's right for (the corporation in) Europe, here. If they were out for their own personal achievements and goals, then that's somebody else, you couldn't build the same level of relationship." Leah, a Silicon Valley administrator, describes her relationship with her supervisor, a master of hidden agendas, "like one of those little slinky spiral things" that just keeps looping around preventing action. Sabotaging competent and effective production is a grave violation of work ethic embodied in trust. Even corporate politics can overshadow the trust relationship of worker to organization. Downsized several times, Jeff notes that, "As much as a company likes to feel it's a big happy family – it's not a family, it's a business." That is a reality he has learned to accept. He cannot trust the organization to employ him, but he can hope they will act openly and responsibly in the inevitable betrayal.

Not all workers can maintain the complex dance of network building and trust maintenance. If enough violations occur, there is no public memory of the many mutual efforts to sustain trust. In Silicon Valley, Chris notes matter-of-factly that he trusts no one except his cat and his computer. "It's not a concept that I have ... My cat's about the only thing, my computer – they're trustworthy because if they break I know why. I can usually figure out they're going to break just on their own randomness. No, people ... I don't see [trust] as a value in people. I don't hold that in esteem and at the same time I don't think I even look for it." Yet, despite his skepticism Chris necessarily looks to others for evidence of competency, consistency, integrity, loyalty and openness – the ingredients of trust.

Conclusion

The very nature of work in new media industries thrusts some workers into global interdependencies that constrain their abilities to work effectively. These interdependencies are difficult to manage when face-to-face interactions are rare. They are exacerbated when differences in culture and power are present, often unbeknownst to the workers. It is in this context that trusting strangers is especially important and simultaneously difficult to accomplish. A comparative, ethnographically-informed approach reveals the complex strategies people use to become effective workers. They try to convert strangers into friends of a specific sort. They build networks that can be used to provide service or to intercede on their behalf at a distance. They analyze local cultural resources in order to understand their position in a wider web of relationships and to support performances that are satisfying to people far removed.

In summary, they explicitly work on the people and organizations in their environment. They simultaneously work on themselves to become people who can be read by strangers as trustworthy. They do so not through a broad skill of trustworthiness, but through countless small acts with specific people for various purposes. How they do this builds on their idiosyncratic abilities and situations, their local knowledge, and their position in a global web of exchanges. In effect, workers who perform such global trust-based work are participating in the early stages of a large-scale social experiment. Particularly striking is that the experiment is largely backdrop to the more recognizable "real work" of design, manufacture, distribution, and support. Ironically, building trust with strangers at a remove may be as challenging as accomplishing the tasks of that "real work."

Notes

1. This chapter is based on a presentation at the Society for Philosophy and Technology, Eleventh Biennial International Conference, 16 July 1999, San Jose, CA, USA.
2. All informant names used in this chapter are pseudonyms.

References

Baba, M. (1999) "Dangerous liaisons: trust, distrust, and information technology in American work organizations," *Human Organization* 58: 331–46.

Barber, B. (1983) *The Logic and Limits of Trust,* New Brunswick, NJ: Rutgers University Press.

Barley, S. (1988) "On technology, time and social order: technically induced change in the temporal organization of radiological work," in Dubinskas, F. (ed.) *Making Time: Ethnographies of High-Technology Organizations,* Philadelphia, PA: Temple University Press, pp. 123–69.

DeVol, R. (1999) *America's High-Tech Economy: Growth, Development, and Risks for Metropolitan Areas,* Santa Monica, CA: Milken Institute.

Dodgson, M. (1993) "Learning, trust, and technological collaboration," *Human Relations* 46: 77–95.

Douglas, M. (1986) *How Institutions Think,* Syracuse, NY: Syracuse University Press.

Douglas, M. (1992) *Risk and Blame: Essays in Cultural Theory,* New York: Routledge.

English-Lueck, J.A. (2000) "Work, identity and community in Silicon Valley," Final report for award 9810593. Washington, DC, National Science Foundation.

English-Lueck, J.A., Darrah, C.N. and Freeman, J.M. (2000) Silicon Valley Cultures Project. Online. Available: http://www.sjsu.edu/depts/anthropology/svcp/ (January 1, 2002).

Institute for the Future (1999) "Organizing for innovation: self-generating Webs," proprietary document SR-672a, Menlo Park, CA.

Saxenian, A. (1999) *Silicon Valley's New Immigrant Entrepreneurs,* San Francisco: Public Policy Institute of California.

Schindler, R. and Thomas, C. (1993) "The structure of interpersonal trust in the workplace," *Psychological Reports* 73: 563–73.

Cool projects, boring institutions: temporary collaboration in social context

Gernot Grabher

Practice gives words their meaning. (Ludwig Wittgenstein, *Remarks on Colour* § 317)

Economic geography during the last two decades made its mark, with some success, in transforming simplistic models of economic governance from solid analytical foundations into conceptual construction sites. From the 1980s onwards, investigations into the social and spatial logics of an increasingly broad and complex spectrum of inter-firm relations turned conceptions of 'firms as islands of hierarchical co-ordination in a sea of market relations' into mere caricatures (Richardson, 1972: 883). Joint ventures, strategic alliances and collaborative supplier relations in industrial districts increasingly blurred the lucidity of the market vs. hierarchy dichotomy *à la* Williamson, 1985. During the 1990s, such hybrid organizational arrangements in the 'swollen middle' between markets and hierarchies (Hennart, 1993) became more and more theoretically anchored in the notion of networks (see Powell, 1990; Nohria and Eccles, 1992; Grabher, 1993). Inter-firm networks were seen as an increasingly relevant unit of economic action and, consequently, an appropriate unit of analysis. Although firm boundaries no longer were taken for granted but conceived as a strategic parameter, firms were still regarded as key actors in making (and breaking) network agreements.

More recently, the search for ever more fluid and market-responsive organizational forms has directed attention towards projects (see Lundin and Söderholm, 1995; Midler, 1995; Lundin and Midler, 1998; Lindkvist *et al.*, 1998; Ekstedt *et al.*, 1999; Hobday, 1998, 2000; Gann and Salter, 2000). The debate on projects as 'temporary systems' with 'institutionalized termination' (Lundin and Söderholm, 1995) seems to suggest a further shift (or widening) of focus from the inter-firm to the inter-personal level. In fact, some authors (Boltanski and Chiapello, 1999) see project teams, whose success is measured in part precisely in their transience, as *the* new unit of economic action.

The short-cyclical nature of projects, however, challenges some of the key assumptions of organizing that inform much current reasoning in economic geography. The limited duration of project-based organizing appears hardly reconcilable, at first glance at least, in particular with basic causalities that underpin current debates on learning (see, for example, Asheim and Cooke, 1999; Maskell and Malmberg, 1999; for a critical review, see Oinas, 2000: 60–6).

These accounts stress the importance of *long term* relationships for the generation of trust which is regarded as a normative precondition for successful learning and innovation, particularly when complex tasks are involved.

Projects, however, often entail high-risk and high-stake outcomes, yet they seem to lack institutional safeguards like 'conventions' (Storper, 1997) and normative structures that minimize the likelihood of failure. They depend on an elaborate body of collective knowledge and diverse skills, yet there is mostly not sufficient time to clarify abilities and competencies of members in order to plan for a detailed division of labour in advance. Most importantly, there seems to be not enough time to engage in the usual forms of confidence-building activities that could compensate for the absence of a stable institutional context through the development of personal relations of mutual trust (Meyerson *et al.*, 1996: 167).

Aims and approach

The aim of this chapter in conceptual terms, is to provide analytical keys for resolving these apparent paradoxes of project-based organizing. We start from the assumption that a solution to these paradoxes has to be found in the interrelation between 'temporary' projects, on the one hand, and the 'permanent' organizations,[1] ties and networks around which they are built, on the other (see Ekstedt *et al.*, 1999; Sydow and Windeler, 1999; Gann and Salter, 2000; Grabher, 2001b). Phrased differently, the intention is not to lend empirical support to arguments of an increasing and, eventually, complete replacement of more traditional permanent forms of organization by (allegedly) new temporary systems. Rather than relations of substitution, we seek to explore interdependencies between projects and the, firms, networks, localities and institutions that feed vital sources of information, legitimization, reputation and trust that provide the very preconditions for the 'projectification' (Midler, 1995) of production.

By delving into the interdependencies between temporary and permanent organizations, we are venturing into a conceptual gap that is reproduced in current academic debates. On the one hand, the new 'learning' orthodoxy stresses, as mentioned, the importance of long term relations for learning and innovation processes within and between firms and regions. To the same extent that this orthodoxy celebrates long-termism and 'systemness' of inter-organizational relations, it seems to ignore learning in and across temporary or episodic projects (see Söderlund and Andersson, 1998: 181).

The literature on project management, on the other hand, is largely moulded by engineering approaches towards 'optimization' that focus on critical factors for 'successful' design, management and execution of projects (see, for example, Morris, 1994; Kerzner, 1995). This literature is based on a perception of the project 'as a distinct, manageable activity system that, once having been designed using the proper scheduling techniques, can be isolated from the environment' (Blomquist and Packendorff, 1998: 38). In other words, this focus is restricted to projects only, leaving out the permanent ties and organizations in and through which projects operate (Gann and Salter, 2000: 958).

This chapter is positioned between these two strands of literature. By investigating into the interdependencies between projects and their environments, we aim to provide conceptual co-ordinates for further investigations into the relations between temporary and permanent organizational forms. By opening up a discussion on projects, we do not propose to introduce yet another organizational master design to an economic geographic readership. Nevertheless, we are convinced that projects under the current conditions of increasing demands for customized 'packages' of products and services, and a deepening division of labour between firms due to outsourcing and concentration on 'core competencies', have become an increasingly influential organizational practice (see Ekstedt et al., 1999; Ekstedt, 2001; Hobday, 2000: 875)

Project organization no longer seems to be confined to industries which traditionally have been characterized by the 'one-off' nature of the production process like construction,[2] ship-building, engineering (for example, Winch, 1986) or film (see Faulkner and Anderson, 1987; Defillippi and Arthur, 1998). More recently, project organization seems to have taken hold in industries like automobiles, chemicals, or textiles in which projects have not previously been part of the canonical repertoire of organizational routines and practices (see Lundin and Midler, 1998; Ekstedt et al., 1999; Tödtling et al., 2001; see also Boltanski and Chiaparello, 1999).

The spectrum of industrial settings analysed corresponds with the degree of diversity of conceptual approaches of individual contributions to this Special Issue. Whereas some studies are written from a predominantly economic geographic perspective, others view projects through the perspective of economic sociology, management and organization science. Admittedly, such diversity of approaches risks conceptual coherence, a most notoriously lamented weakness of edited collections. However, without detracting from the editorial responsibility to limit such bias, it might be worthwhile to bear such risk – if heuristic surplus in a comparatively new field of (geographic) inquiry is yielded.

Here, the aim is to provide a synoptic reading of the 'received wisdom' of project management accounts. First, the chapter briefly sketches the emergence, spread, professionalization and institutionalization of projects as a distinct organizational 'form'. Second, it proposes a classification of defining features of project organizing which is robust and broad enough to cover the variety of industrial and regional contexts explored, and yet is specific enough to denote the particular characteristics of projects vis-à-vis other organizational forms and processes. Third, the introduction investigates into the societal context in which projects typically operate; it demonstrates that networks, localities and institutions are feeding essential sources of project-based organizing. Theorizing on functions of the societal context is, in a sense, theorizing about structural limitations of project based organizing or, phrased differently yet again, thinking about the realm of permanent organizations. Fourth, the introduction aims at locating this particular realm of permanent systems by analysing the role of firms as 'incubators' and 'sponsors' of projects and in providing organizational arenas for cross-project learning.

Projects as form: professionalization, certification, institutionalization

'There always have been projects, even if they were not called that way' (Lundin and Midler, 1998: 1). Until the late 1950s, the term project was mainly associated with 'draft' or 'proposal'. This connotation still prevails today when, for example, an architect proposes a 'project' for a new building or an investment banker presents 'projects' for new investment opportunities to clients. In this more traditional sense, the notion of the project denotes a *proposed idea* or *object* (Engwall, 1998: 32). The current understanding of projects evolved in the middle of the twentieth century and is associated with a new development and procurement philosophy of the US Department of Defense.

Instead of fragmenting and pre-specifying the development of military technologies along traditional functional disciplines (for example, mechanical or electrical engineering), these technologies were described in relation to their objectives, i.e. military parameters of weapons. The pacing of these concentrated efforts was crucial: parameters had to be met, goals had to be accomplished according to a grand scheme designed to win the armaments 'race'. Development processes that earlier were conceived as separate activities were now conceptualized as an integrated entity, called a 'program', 'system' or 'project'. The overwhelming scale of these projects in terms of financial and scientific resources as well as their ambitious timing created formidable problems of co-ordination and control. Experiments with various forms of organizational control ultimately led to the professionalization of the role of the 'project manager' (Lundin and Söderholm, 1998: 19).

From the 1960s onwards, the conception of projects and project management developed by the US military-industrial complex (Gaddis, 1959) diffused widely into the business world and, increasingly, beyond. 'Research projects', 'theatre projects' or projects in social work became standard organizational practices which emphasize the *process of realizing an idea* or *objective*. Admittedly, the differences in connotation between the traditional and the current connotation of projects are small, but significant (see Engwall, 1998).

The diffusion of the notion of projects into a broad spectrum of economic and societal spheres is fuelled by mimetic processes of organizational imitation. Moreover, the last decades witnessed increasing efforts of standardization and certification or, in the sense of Thévenot, 1984, growing societal 'investment in the form' of the project. Such investment manifests itself, for example, in the foundation of professional associations like the US-based Project Management Institute (PMI) and the younger European-dominated International Project Management Association (IPMA). Both contribute to the legitimization of the form through conferences and trade journals like the *Project Management Journal (PMJ)* and the *International Journal of Project Management (IJPM)*. Through these infrastructural investments, the project as a distinctive form increasingly gets codified in forms, formulae, manuals and text books (see, for example, PMI, 1987, 1996).

Whereas journals like the *IJPM* and the *PMJ* mainly cover issues of technical optimization of project organization and propagate current latest 'best practice' (see Themistocleous and Wearne, 2000), first systematic analytical accounts are related to the conception of projects as 'temporary systems' (Goodman and Goodman, 1976; Goodman, 1981). The very notion of *temporary* systems denotes *the* essential feature of projects around which common definitions, despite semantic variations, are built. Phrased in more explicit terms, projects are defined by their temporal *limitation* and not, as implicitly suggested in rather loose applications of the term, by their *duration*.

Based mainly on their research on theatre production, Goodman and Goodman, 1976: 494, define such temporary systems as 'a set of diversely skilled people working together on a complex task over a limited period of time'. The breadth of subsequent efforts to conceptualize projects, to some extent, reflects the spectrum of industrial and organizational contexts in which they are performed. In most common classificatory exercises, projects are located within three main contexts (see Lundin and Söderholm, 1998: 15).

First, projects are standard organizational practice in industries which are virtually exclusively populated by 'one-off' activities. The example *par excellence* is the construction and engineering business; consulting services represent a more recently most dynamic expanding field in which projects are dominating practice. Second, projects populate other industrial fields only partially but crucially when projects are restricted, in the typical case, to research and development activities. Third, rather than standard practice, projects are used as an organizational vehicle for exceptional efforts like, for example, organizational restructuring or computerization.

Projects as process: tasks, interdependence, power, deadlines

A robust classification of defining properties of projects with heuristic validity across different contexts and settings might be built around the following five features. First, the legitimization of a project is based on a particular *task* that either might be complex and non-routine or rather standardized. The particular task of a temporary system, in Lundin and Söderholm's, 1995: 440, conception is equivalent with a permanent organization's devotion to goals. While goals primarily provide foci for decision making, a task focuses on action. Such an action-oriented perspective directs attention from the more traditional 'project as idea' to the 'project as process' view.

Second, *interdependence* characterizes the definition as well as the accomplishment of the task. Particularly in cases where the task is complex and cannot be decomposed in detail autonomously *ex ante* 'members must keep interrelating with one another in trying to arrive at viable solutions' (Goodman and Goodman, 1976: 495). The strength of these interdependencies is elucidated in the observation that projects are not only *for* a particular client but also, to some extent, a project *with* a client (Girard and Stark, 2002, forthcoming). By stressing that the course of a project is not programmable, the 'complexity and ambiguity... is not defined away but it is emphasised' (Sahlin Andersson, 1992: 144).

Third, the project is assembled by a *contractor* or, corresponding with the particular semantics of the respective business context, by a project leader, integrator, broker, producer, impresario, etc. (see, for example, Briner *et al.*, 1996). Beyond the obvious role in managing projects, the contractor might be seen as the 'link pin' on which trust is focused. This is the more crucial the less time project members have to develop personalized trust to all other project members (Meyerson *et al.*, 1996: 171). Particularly in the case of more complex projects, the role of the contractor has crystallized into a distinct professional profile. In the more traditional construction sector (Gann and Salter, 2000: 967) and in a new media context alike (Girard and Stark, 2002), independent contractors are increasingly populating the professional ecology of project-based business. Fourth, the role of the contractor is also a most visible manifestation of the general phenomenon that projects are embedded in, and reflect the *power* relations between and within, participating organizations (Lovell, 1993; Zeller, 2002). Power, on the one hand, moulds the asymmetry of framing key coordinates of projects such as deadlines, divisions of labour and revenues. In particular large-scale projects might develop finely tuned and strict internal hierarchies, resembling military analogies and, in fact, even might echo its terminology (Blair, 2001). On the other hand, power in projects is also unmasked when neophytes are barred from access either explicitly or, more subtly, through such barriers as informal codes of conduct (Ekinsmyth, 2002).

Fifth, meeting *deadlines* is a main criterion for evaluating project performance (see Wenger and Snyder, 2000). Deadlines are *the* constituent feature of projects as 'temporary systems' with 'institutionalized termination' (Lundin and Söderholm, 1995: 449). Deadlines and, during the course of a project, milestones 'appear to have the potential to function as "globalizing" mechanisms preventing participant people and organizations from being guided by overly localistic and atomistic orientations' (Lindkvist *et al.*, 1998: 948). In this sense, project schedules preserve the diversity of, and tensions between, professional and organizational cultures from turning into collaborative paralysis. Milestones in financing and 'staging' of venture capital funding, for example, are also instrumentalized to focus attention in research-driven project contexts which, as Powell *et al.*, p. 294, demonstrate for life-sciences ventures, 'is no small feat'.

Deadlines and milestones might be no less important in the symbolic sense of a *'carte blanche'* (Sapolsky, 1972), legitimating execution without interference from outside: 'As long as the show was on time, it was not important ... how it was achieved' (Hartmann *et al.*, 1998: 272). Moreover, institutionalized termination cannot simply be reduced to a discrete point in time but, in fact, has to be seen as a procedure that spans a considerable period of time. Termination, in other words, constitutes a 'trading zone' in a temporal sense (Galison, 1998) in which experience is summarized, evaluated and transferred to the organizational home base and subsequent projects.

The reference to 'home base' and 'subsequent projects' is indicative here. It elucidates that the practice of project-based organizing, obviously, is only captured insufficiently in the notion of the *temporary* system since 'individuals have other "homes" before, during and after being involved in a temporary organization' (Lundin and Söderholm, 1995: 442). In the perspective developed in this Special Issue, projects are embedded in layers of networks, localities and institutions (Grabher, 2001b). These multiple layers, on the one hand, contribute key resources for the performance of projects. On the other hand, however, they also imply multiple perceptions and loyalties of the project members. The embeddedness of projects in personal ties and social structure, put briefly, is as much a source of vital ingredients as it is a persisting cause of tension and conflict. In this view, projects appear as 'political issues on the organizational agenda rather than as closed activity systems' (Blomquist and Packendorff, 1998: 38).

Networks: reputation, pools, latency

Projects apparently operate in a milieu of recurrent collaboration that, after several project cycles, fills a pool of resources and 'gels' into latent networks. Project organizing is mostly directed towards the actual realization of a potential that is generated and reproduced by the practice of drawing on core members of (successful) prior projects to serve on derivative successor projects. Such chains of repeated co-operation are held together (or cut off) by the reputation members gain (or lose) in previous collaborations (Defillippi and Arthur, 1998: 126; Jones, 1996; Blair, 2001; Pratt, 2002, forthcoming). Project business, essentially, is reputation business: 'Who you know matters almost as much as what you know' (Christopherson, 2002, forthcoming). In general, it is rather this particular 'know who' and, to a lesser extent, the 'know how' that tends to become tacit knowledge (Gann and Salter, 2000: 969).

Reputation in project organization refers, first and foremost, to the techniques of the trade, particularly in industrial settings like media, in which crucial skills are hardly codified in certificates. Second, the success of projects, more generally, depends on co-operative attitude, reliability and other inter-personal skills that, rather than objectivized in formal degrees, are bound to personal experience. An indication of the strong orientation towards these skill sets is the typical *curriculum vitae* in new media which 'has become a presentation of skills and projects rather than a chronology of positions' (Christopherson, 2002).

Human capital and social capital appear thus inextricably interwoven and determine if an actor either occupies a central or peripheral position in the pool of potential co-operation partners – or is excluded altogether from getting access to these networks of reputation (Ekinsmyth, 2002, this issue). The smaller this pool and the thinner talent, the quicker information on performance diffuses and, hence, the more vulnerable reputation becomes (Meyerson *et al.*, 1996: 171). Although vulnerable indeed, reputation tends to be 'sticky'. In other words, you are probably not *just* as good (bad) as your last project.

The practice of project organizing is thus shaped both by past experience and affected by the shadow of potential future collaboration. This recursive interrelation between activities and relations in the current project and those that are enduring the actual project might transform latent networks either into 'project networks' of legally independent organizations (Sydow and Staber, 2002), or else latent networks in settings which are virtually exclusively populated by projects might crystallize into 'serial project-based enterprises' (Pratt, 2002, forthcoming).

Localities: noise, enculturation

Repeated project collaboration quite often, though by no means necessarily, takes place in densely-knit clusters. At first glance, the logic of co-location is driven by the more or less obvious benefits of spatial proximity around which much of current economic geographical reasoning revolves. First, as unremittingly stressed in particular by the 'new' economic geography (Krugman, 1991, 1995; see also Martin, 1999; Feldman, 2000), co-location of project partners allows for significant savings of different variants of transaction costs like search costs, costs of transacting, and supervising and enforcing contractual agreements. Second, co-location provides for favourable preconditions for rapid face-to-face interaction (see Sassen, 1995; Scott, 1997, 1999) which accelerates localized learning processes (see Maskell and Malmberg, 1999). The tighter the project schedule and the less a clear separation of specific tasks can be programmed, the stronger are the imperatives for face-to-face exchange. And finally, spatial proximity facilitates the continuous 'monitoring' of the relevant pool of resources and potential collaborators. Performance of potential partners in other projects, their reliability and availability are key parameters of such monitoring.

While these standard arguments are hardly controversial, they seem to capture the logic of co-location of project partners only partially. Whereas the notions of 'monitoring', 'scanning' or 'supervising' suggest intentional and strategic activity, I rather would like to propose the view that actors who are located – literally – *in* the pool are exposed to 'noise' (Grabher, 2002). That is, actors are not deliberately 'scanning' their environment in search of a specific piece of information but rather are surrounded by a concoction of rumours, impressions, recommendations, trade folklore and strategic misinformation (Pratt, 2002, forthcoming). The point, in fact, is not the richness and diversity of the noise as such. Rather, co-location facilitates the emergence of 'interpretive communities' (Brown and Duguid, 1996: 68) which filter and process noise into patterns of signals. Phrased differently, rather than the mere availability of information, processes of 'negotiating meaning' tie project clusters together (see Grabher, 2002).

Moreover, agglomeration of potential project collaborators provides for favourable preconditions for 'hanging out' (Barrett, 1998: 616) in local communities of practice. These communities of practice serve as a sort of informal training ground for disseminating knowledge that goes far beyond technical competencies of the trade but also includes language and dress codes and, more generally, the codes of conduct and '*habitus*' (Bourdieu, 1977) of the particular community of practice (Wenger, 1998). From this viewpoint, learning is not about acquiring knowledge; it is much more about becoming an *insider* (Brown and Duguid, 1996: 69).

In this view, peripheral participants rather than explicit 'expert knowledge' are acquiring the embodied ability to behave as community members. In short, they are *enculturated*. For example, participants learn to tell and appreciate community-appropriate stories, discovering in doing so the narrative-based resources. To acquire a repertoire of appropriate stories and, even more importantly, to know what are appropriate occasions for telling them, is then part of what it means to become a member of a community of practice (*ibid.*, 1996: 69). In research-driven project contexts like the life sciences, for example, imperatives of co-location of project members imply far more than the mere spatial dimension: 'to understand science, one has to participate in its development' (Powell *et al.*, 2002: 293).

Hanging out is facilitated in project settings in particular in which participants alternate between 'frenetic activity and enforced idleness' (Defillippi and Arthur, 1998). Such periods of idleness are used by senior members, in media industries for example, to demonstrate specific craft routines to neophyte members. Viewed through the narrow perspective of productive efficiency, idleness appears an indulgent squandering of resources that, consequently, has to be minimized. In the perspective proposed here, the tolerance of this idleness is a basic precondition for 'learning-by-watching' (Defillippi and Arthur, 1998: 132) and, more generally, reflexivity.

While peripheral participation in projects seems strongly tied to particular geographically fixed places, core members increasingly appear to operate in and through 'project spaces' (Zeller, 2002, see also Bengtsson and Söderholm). Such project spaces, on the one hand, might be entirely confined to virtual localities when, for example, communication is channelled through project-specific mailing lists or password-protected websites. On the other hand, core members who are managing an entire portfolio of projects increasingly rely on communications technology. More traditional forms of using communications technologies are thereby, in a sense, reversed. Instead of controlling various projects from the organizational homebase, communications technology provides a means for multiplying face-to-face interaction with participants in a whole range of projects while keeping in touch with the organizational homebase. In short, 'homebase comes visiting' (Thrift, 2000a: 686).

The physical infrastructure for this managerial practice consists of geographically extended networks of 'touch down' areas (in hotels or at branch offices abroad, for example) located at or close to the different off-site projects. The importance and reach of these networks also reflect the non-substitutability of face-to-face interactions at critical stages before or during a project when 'it is important to gesticulate' (chief knowledge officer of PriceWaterhouseCoopers, Ellen Knapp, quoted in Thrift, 2000a: 686; see also Leonard and Swap, 1999). Imperatives of face-to-face interaction thus do not necessarily imply co-location at a particular geographical place for the entire project duration. At least some aspects of project management seem to become increasingly disembedded from specific project places. Face-to-face interactions hence are not substituted by communications technology, but technology is used by project managers as a means for compressing cycles of periodic face-to-face interactions at geographically dispersed project sites – while keeping in touch with the organizational homebase.

Institutions: swift trust, systemness, learning by switching

In addition to these multiple layers of personal networks, virtual and physical localities, project organizing draws, deliberately or unconsciously, on a range of institutional sources. On a rather general level of conventions, norms and regulations, institutions provide the critical ingredients for the emergence of 'swift trust' (Meyerson et al., 1996). Swift trust, most importantly, is category-driven trust, that is actors can deal with one another more as roles than as individuals. Expectations, consequently, are more standardized and stable and defined more in terms of tasks than personalities: 'We trust engineers because we trust engineering and believe that engineers are trained to apply valid principles of engineering' (Dawes, 1994: 24).

A similar function as by roles might be played by organizational forms (i.e. trusting the form of the project as such), by organizational cultures and by industries which shape expectations on the basis of a more or less stable body of principles and practices. Moreover, conventions, norms and regulations accelerate and stabilize the formation of inter-personal as well as inter-organizational expectations (Meyerson et al., 1996; Sydow and Staber, 2002: 217–19).

The stabilizing functions of category-driven trust, however, unfold only in project contexts in which these categories – like professions, for example – have clear boundaries (see Girard and Stark, 2002). That is a context in which specialists in one field can 'black box' the inputs from specialists in another. In a field like new media where these categories are fluid and where boundaries constitute overlapping areas rather than clear demarcations, sources of this sort of category-driven 'swift trust' might be rather difficult to mobilize.

Moreover, the role of institutions in project organizing is not confined to the provision of a basic societal infrastructure upon which to act in a rather passive fashion. The formation and stabilization of inter-organizational perceptions in a more specific and active manner also appears on the agenda of initiatives of institution building in regions as diverse as old industrial areas (Tödtling *et al.*, 2001) and media clusters (Sydow and Staber, 2002). Organizationally crystallized in local 'development agencies' in the broadest sense of the term, institution building might aim at mobilizing *latent* networks and *potential* pools of resources which, by their very definition, lack transparency. By targeting this trivial yet effective obstacle to the formation of local linkages, agencies thus provide cognitive preconditions for converting latent pools into productive resources for collaboration by uncovering complementarities.

Local agencies might also be devoted to facilitate a transformation of episodic project collaboration into more enduring project networks. In this capacity, they increase the 'systemness' of collaborative patterns or, in other words, they contribute to a transformation of a merely spatial agglomeration into a systemic cluster (Tödtling *et al.*, 2001: 23–4). In the absence of any traditions or individual experience of inter-organizational collaboration, agencies, to a limited extent at least, are able to take on the role of the 'linchpin' on which trust can be focused and 'delegated'. In this way, they substitute for the lack of any personalized trust. While these two targets might require local agencies to modify their repertoire of instruments, they hardly would imply a more fundamental change in the traditional understanding of their mission.

Against the background of post-socialist transformation, Dornisch, 2002, however, elaborates a further function of institution building that interferes with collaborative practices in a way that implies an outright reversal of more established notions of promoting local development. More specifically, local learning processes do not necessarily occur through sustained interaction but through 'switching' in which minimal connectivity between projects is present. Diffuse 'learning by switching' evinces itself through decoupling occurring within particular projects and through the competition motivating movements from project to project. Learning by switching, potentially at least, breaks up collaborative dead-ends and interrupts positive feedback loops of spiralling downward (*ibid*: 317–18). Studying project-based organizing, more generally speaking, thus might yield insights into organizational antidotes against lock-in dynamics inherent in networks.

Firms: incubation, cross-project learning, brands

Initiatives of local institution building to govern project-based organizing aim at substituting the particular role that, in other contexts, is fulfilled by firms which are building project networks around them. The role of firms, however, is more complex than that of a permanent organization which provides infrastructure for an *external* ecology of projects between firms. Rather, the *intra*-organizational ecology of firms in project-based fields is populated by both temporary and permanent systems. In other words, firms *are* both project and project infrastructure. On the one hand, their resources are temporarily and partially allocated to temporary and unique project tasks. On the other hand, they have to sustain a range of ongoing and repetitive business processes which are instrumental in organizing individual projects as well as in managing portfolios of projects (Gann and Salter, 2000: 955–8). These permanent processes are instrumental for project-based organizing in several ways.

Although the project is *the* prototypical form of conducting research, more complex research projects involving a diverse range of collaborators, roles and skills can be performed only after a certain 'incubation' and lead-up period. In other words, projects are leveraged off from a platform of deliberation, preparation and pre-selection that is not provided for by the project in itself. This is, expressed in the graphic language of business practice, 'very hard for a[n] ... independent company to handle ... which is hustling from job to job and needs immediate cash return' (manager of a media firm, quoted by Lash and Urry, 1994: 124).

Despite various opportunities for 'learning-by-watching' and participation in communities of practice, project-based organizing notoriously lacks *formal* structures and incentives for cross-project learning (Ekstedt *et al.*, 1999: 60). Since the 'learning silos', typically built around functional departments are mostly absent, project-based organizations are exposed to the risk of 'learning closure' (Hobday, 2000: 885). Irrespective of good individual project performance, the high pressured work environment may leave little organizational space for systematic formal training and stay development. Formal activities associated with organizational learning and improvement – like skills networks, post-project reviews or technical mentoring – might simply not be performed. These emblematic deficits of structures, as well as incentives with regard to both incubation and training, mirror the absence of organizational redundancies in project-based organizing: 'there is no fat at all in [this] system' (Lash and Urry, 1994: 124; see Hobday, 2000: 888).

Finally, the proliferation of project-based organizing is mostly attributed to its ability to provide efficient solutions to the problem of flexible allocation of *productive* resources. Their inherent flexible and episodic character constitutes a systemic limitation when reach and persistence of market presence is called for. Indeed, it is not by coincidence that project-based organizing has been pioneered in markets for capital and investment goods, that is, in markets with highly individualized user-producer interactions. Markets in which economic success increasingly is related to brands rather than to performance-related attributes of products afford considerable financial muscle for building brands and controlling channels of distribution (see Lash and Urry, 1994: 137–8). Taken together, the practice of project-based organizing does not repeal 'classical' textbook assumptions of economies of scale and size. All too easily, the appearance of projects as focused, organizationally and temporarily clearly limited ventures obscures the view on 'big' corporate structures that are nourishing, linking, sponsoring, suspending and preventing projects.

Conclusions

The formation and operation of projects essentially relies on a societal infrastructure which is built on and around networks, localities, institutions and firms. Relations between temporary and permanent systems, to recapitulate the basic assumption of this Special Issue, are not a matter of straightforward substitution but have to be regarded in terms of interdependence. 'Cool' projects, indeed, rely on 'boring' institutions.

By delving into the mutual conditioning of temporarily limited, often short-cyclical project organization on the one hand, and permanent ties and organizational affiliations on the other, the presented analysis challenges predominant views in economic geography. The new 'learning' orthodoxy stresses, above all, the vital importance of long term relations for successful innovation and interactive learning processes, particularly when complex tasks are involved (see Asheim and Cooke, 1999; Maskell and Malmberg, 1999). The canonical regional success story is a success story of stable ties (see also Christopherson, 2002; Dornisch, 2002: 308). The perspective developed in this Special Issue, of course, is not aimed at denying the beneficial aspects of such systemic patterns of inter-organizational linkages altogether. Instead, it intends to probe into the particular preconditions, forms and impacts of learning and innovation that accrue in the interrelation between transient collaborative arrangements and more enduring organizational and institutional arrangements.

Economic geography made its mark in the analysis of network relations and it can contribute as well to the debate on project-based organizing. In contrast to the concerns for organizational optimization that echo through the respective management and engineering literatures (see, for example, Jones and Decro, 1993), such an approach would conceive the relation between temporary and permanent systems not simply in terms of a neat complementarity. Rather than celebrating projects as a 'best-of-best' configuration that meets the all-pervasive imperatives of flexibility, economic geographic analysis could extend the view to the inherent limitations of 'hyper-efficient' project-based organizing; the dynamics of tensions between different professional and organizational cultures involved in projects; conflicting loyalties of participants *vis-à-vis* the project and their homebase; the geographies of physical as well as virtual 'project spaces'; and so on.

In focusing on such issues, economic geographic analysis would shift the perspective beyond the perception of organizational practices as being passively 'embedded' in social structure. By exploring the interdependencies between projects, personal ties, local relations and organizational affiliations it, in fact, could play a part in elucidating the mutual constitution of economic behaviour and social structure (see Yeung, 2001: 298). Venturing further into the terrain of the dialectical relationships between temporary and permanent systems, between projects and networks, localities and institutions would also mark a further step away from an economic geography that confines itself to mapping the 'wheres' while it leaves the 'whys' to other disciplines (Thrift, 2000b: 698).

Acknowledgements

I would like to thank Robert Hassink, Ray Hudson, Woody Powell, David Stark, Jörg Sydow and Henry Wai-chung Yeung for comments and suggestions. I am also grateful to all referees of the Special Issue and contributors to the workshop 'Beyond the Firm? Social and Spatial Dynamics of Project Organization', organized by the Research Area Socio-economics of Space, Bonn, 27–28 April 2001. Generous financial support of this workshop by the Federal Ministry for Education and Science is gratefully acknowledged. The success of 'temporary' projects crucially depends on a 'permanent' infrastructure providing organizational support. For the reliable assistance in managing this project infrastructure, I would particularly like to thank Thorsten Hülsmann and Bodo Kubartz. Finally, I would like to express my thanks to E.R. for patiently sharing her expertise during the entire course of the project.

Notes

1. The term 'permanent' organization in this context, of course, is not applied in the literal meaning of the word. Rather it is intended to depict organizational structures which are built on the assumption 'as if ' time were eternal. 'Permanent' organizations are 'planned to exist, if not forever, then for the foreseeable future' (Ekstedt et al., 1999: 41).
2. The quintessential role of project organization in the construction industry is also reflected in the fact that 46% of all papers in the leading trade journal, the *International Journal of Project Management* between 1984 and 1998 were devoted to this industry (Themistocleous and Wearne, 2000: 11).

References

Asheim, B. and Cooke, P. (1999) 'Local learning and interactive innovation networks in a global economy', in Malecki, E. and Oinas, P. (eds) (1999) *Making Connections: Technological Learning and Regional Economic Change*, Aldershot: Ashgate.

Barrett, F.J. (1998) 'Creativity and improvisation in jazz and organization: implications for organizational learning', *Organization Science* 9: 605–22.

Bengtsson, M. and Söderholm, A. (2002) 'Bridging distances: organizing boundary-spanning technology development projects', *Regional Studies* 36: 263–74.

Blair, H. (2001) 'Interpersonal networks in conditions of uncertainty: the case of film production in Britain', paper presented to the workshop 'Beyond the firm? Social and spatial logics of project-organisation', Bonn, April.

Blomquist, T. and Packendorff, J. (1998) 'Learning from renewal projects: content, context and embeddedness', in Lundin, R.A. and Midler, C. (eds) *Projects as Arenas for Renewal and Learning Processes*, Boston/Dordrecht/London: Kluwer Academic.

Boltanski, L. and Chiaparello, E. (1999) *Le nouvel esprit du capitalisme*, Gallimard, Paris.

Bourdieu, P. (1977) *Outline of a Theory of Practice*, Cambridge: Cambridge University Press.

Briner, W., Hastings, C. and Geddes, M. (1996) *Project Leadership*, Aldershot: Gower.

Brown, J.S. and Duguid, P. (1996) 'Organizational learning and communities of practice: towards a unified view of working, learning, and innovation', in Cohen, M.D. and Sproull, L.S. (eds) *Organizational Learning*, Thousand Oaks, CA: Sage.

Chandler, A.D. (1990) *Scale and Scope: The Dynamics of Industrial Capitalism*, Cambridge, MA: Harvard University Press.

Christopherson, S. (2002) 'Does innovation require trust? Risk and workforce strategies in media work', *Environmental Planning A*.

Dawes, R.M. (1994) *House of Cards: Psychology Built on Myth*, New York: Free Press.

Defillippi, R.J. and Arthur, M.B. (1998) 'Paradox in project-based enterprise: the case of film making', *California Management. Review* 40(2): 125–38.

Dornisch, D. (2002) 'The evolution of post-socialist projects: trajectory shift and transitional capacity in a Polish region', *Regional Studies* 36: 307–21.

Ekinsmyth, C. (2002) 'Projects, embeddedness and risk in magazine publishing', *Regional Studies* 36: 229–43.

Ekstedt, E. (2001) 'Contracts of work in a project-based economy', unpublished manuscript, National Institute of Working Life, Stockholm.

Ekstedt, E., Lundin, R.A., Söderholm, A. and Wirdenius, H. (1999) *Neo-industrial Organising: Renewal by Action and Knowledge in a Project-intensive Economy*, London: Routledge.

Engwall, M. (1998) 'The project concept(s): on the unit of analysis in the study of project management', in Lundin, R.A. and Midler, C. (eds) *Projects as Arenas for Renewal and Learning Processes*, Boston/Dordrecht/London: Kluwer Academic.

Faulkner, R.R. and Anderson, A.B. (1987) 'Short-term projects and emergent careers, evidence from Hollywood', *American Journal of Sociology* 4: 879–909.

Feldman, M.P. (2000) 'Location and innovation: the new economic geography of innovation, spillovers, and agglomeration', in Clark, G.L., Feldman, M.P. and Gertler, M.S. (eds) *The Oxford Handbook of Economic Geography*, Oxford: Oxford University Press.

Gaddis, P.O. (1959) 'The project manager', *Harvard Business Review* 39(3): 89–97.

Galison, P. (1998) *Image and Logic*, Chicago: University of Chicago Press.

Gann, D.M. and Salter, A.J. (2000) 'Innovation in project-based, service enhanced firms: the construction of complex products and systems', *Research Policy* 29: 955–72.

Girard, M. and Stark, D. (2002) 'Distributing intelligence and organizing diversity in new media projects', *Environmental Planning A*.

Goodman, R.A. (1981) *Temporary Systems*, New York: Praeger.

Goodman, R.A. and Goodman, L.P. (1976) 'Some management issues in temporary systems: a study of professional development and manpower – the theatre case', *Administration Science Quarterly* 21: 494–501.

Grabher, G. (1993) *The Embedded Firm: On the Socio-economics of Industrial Networks*, London: Routledge.

Grabher, G. (2001a) 'Ecologies of creativity: the village, the group, and the heterarchic organization of the British advertising industry', *Environmental Planning A* 33: 351–74.

Grabher, G. (2001b) 'Locating economic action: projects, networks, localities and institutions', *Environmental Planning A* 31: 1329–31.

Grabher, G. (2002) 'The project ecology of advertising: tasks, talents and teams', *Regional Studies* 36: 245–62.

Hartmann, F., Ashrafi, R. and Jergaes, G. (1998) 'Project management in the live entertainment industry: what is different?', *International Journal of Project Management* 16(5): 269–81.

Hennart, J.F. (1993) 'Explaining the swollen middle: why most transactions are a mix of "market" and "hierarchy"', *Organization Science* 4: 529–47.

Hobday, M. (1998) 'Product-complexity, innovation and industrial organisation', *Research Policy* 26: 689–710.

Hobday, M. (2000) 'The project-based organisation: an ideal for managing complex products and systems?', *Research Policy* 29: 871–93.

Jones, C. (1996) 'Careers in project networks: the case of the film industry', in Arthur, M.B. and Rousseau, D.M. (eds) *The Boundaryless Career*, New York: Oxford University Press pp. 58–75.

Jones, R.E. and Decro, R.F. (1993) 'The social psychology of project management conflict', *European J Operational Research* 64: 216–28.

Kerzner, H. (1995) *Project Management: A Systems Approach to Planning, Scheduling, and Controlling.* New York: Van Nostrand-Reinhold.

Krugman, P. (1991) *Trade and Geography,* Cambridge, MA: MIT Press.

Krugman, P. (1995) *Development, Geography and Economic Theory,* Cambridge, MA: MIT Press.

Lash, S. and Urry, J. (1994) *Economies of Signs and Spaces,* London: Sage.

Leonard, D. and Swap, J. (1999) *When Sparks Fly: Igniting Creativity in Groups.* Boston: Harvard Business School Press.

Lindkvist, L., Söderlund, J. and Tell, F. (1998) Managing product development projects: on the significance of fountains and deadlines', *Organization Studies* 19(6): 931–51.

Lovell, R.J. (1993) 'Power and the project manager', *International Journal of Project Management* 11(2): 73–8.

Lundin, R.A. and Midler, C. (1998) *Projects as Arenas for Renewal and Learning Processes.* Boston/Dordrecht/London: Kluwer Academic.

Lundin, R.A. and Söderholm, A. (1995) 'A theory of the temporary organization', *Scandinavian Journal of Management* 11(4): 437–55.

Lundin, R.A. and Söderholm, A. (1998) 'Evolution of projects as empirical trend and theoretical focus', in Lundin, R.A. and Midler, C. (eds) *Projects as Arenas for Renewal and Learning Processes,* Boston/Dordrecht/London: Kluwer Academic pp. 1–11.

Martin, R. (1999) 'The new "geographical turn" in economics: some critical reflections', *Cambridge Journal of Economics* 23: 65–91.

Maskell, A. and Malmberg, A. (1999) 'The competitiveness of firms and regions: "ubiquitification" and the importance of localized learning', *European Urban & Regional Studies* 6(1): 9–25.

Meyerson, D., Weick, K.E. and Kramer, R.M. (1996) 'Swift trust and temporary groups', in Kramer, R.M. and Tyler, T.R. (eds) *Trust in Organizations: Frontiers of Theory and Research*, Thousand Oaks, CA: Sage pp. 166–95.

Midler, C. (1995) '"Projectification" of the firm: the Renault case', *Scandinavian Journal of Management* 11(4): 363–75.

Morris, P.W.G. (1994) *The Management of Projects,* London: Thomas Telford.

Nohria, N. and Eccles, R.G. (1992) *Networks and Organizations: Structure, Form, and Action*, Boston: Harvard Business School Press.

Oinas, P. (2000) Distance and learning: does proximity matter?, in Boekema, F., Morgan, K., Bakkers, S. and Rutten, R. (eds), *Knowledge, Innovation and Economic Growth: The Theory and Practice of Learning Regions*, Cheltenham: Edward Elgar pp. 57–73.

Penrose, E.T. (1995) *The Theory of the Growth of the Firm*, Oxford: Basil Blackwell (originally published in 1959).

Project Management Institute (PMI) (1987) *Project Management Body of Knowledge*, Drexel Hill, PA: PMI.

Project Management Institute (PMI) (1996) *A Guide to the Project Management Body of Knowledge*, PA: Upper Darby, PMI.

Powell, W.W. (1990) 'Neither market nor hierarchy: network forms of organization', *Res. Organizational Behavior* 12: 295–336.

Powell, W.W., Koput, K.W., Bowie, J.F. and Smith-Doerr, L. (2002) 'The spatial clustering of science and capital: accounting for biotech firmventure capital relationships', *Regional Studies* 36: 291–305.

Pratt, A. (2002) 'Firm boundaries? The organization of new media production in San Francisco 1996–98', *Environmental Planning A* (forthcoming).

Richardson, G.B. (1972) 'The organization of industry', *Economic Journal*, 82: 883–96.

Sahlin-Andersson, K. (1992) 'The use of ambiguity – the organizing of an extraordinary project', in Hägg, I. and Segelod, E. (eds) *Issues in Empirical Investment Research*, Amsterdam: Elsevier pp. 143–58.

Sapolsky, H.M. (1972) *The Polaris Systems Development: Bureaucratic and Programmatic Success in Government*, Cambridge, MA: Harvard University Press.

Sassen, S. (1995) 'On concentration and centrality in the global city', in Knox, P.L. and Taylor, P.J. (eds) *World Cities in a World System*, Cambridge, MA: Cambridge University Press.

Scott, A. J. (1997) 'The cultural economy of cities', *International Journal of Urban and Regional Research*, 2: 323–39.

Scott, A.J. (1999) 'From Silicon Valley to Hollywood: growth and development of the multimedia industry in California', in Braczyk H.J., Cooke, P. and Heidenreich, M. (eds) *Regional Innovation Systems: The Role of Governances in a Globalized World*, London: UCL Press.

Söderlund, J. and Andersson, N. (1998) 'A framework for analysing project dyads – the case of discontinuity, uncertainty and trust', in Lundin, R.A. and Midler, C. *Projects as Arenas for Renewal and Learning Processes*, Boston/Dordrecht/London: Kluwer Academic.

Storper, M. (1997) *The Regional World: Territorial Development in a Global Economy*, New York/ London: Guilford Press.

Sydow, J. and Staber, U. (2002) 'The institutional embeddedness of project networks: the case of content production in German television', *Regional Studies* 36: 215–27.

Sydow, J. and Windeler, A. (1999) 'Projektnetzwerke: Management von (mehr als) temporären Systemen' (Project networks: management of (more than) temporary systems), in Engelhardt, J. and Sinz, E. (eds) *Kooperation im Wettbewerb* (Co-operation in Competition), Wiesbaden: Gabler pp. 213–35.

Themistocleous, G. and Wearne, S.H. (2000) 'Project management topic coverage in journals', *International Journal Project Management* 23(1): 1–45.

Thévenot, L. (1984) 'Rules and implements: investment in form', *Social Science Information* 23(1): 1–45.

Thrift, N. (2000a) 'Performing cultures in the new economy', *Annals of the Association of American Geographers* 90(4): 674–92.

Thrift, N. (2000b) 'Pandora's box? Cultural geographies of economies', in Clark, G.L., Feldman, M.P. and Gertler, M.S. (eds) *The Oxford Handbook of Economic Geography*, Oxford: Oxford University Press pp. 690–704.

Tödtling, F., Bratl, H. and Trippl, M. (2001) 'Networking and project organisation in the automotive industry: the case of Styria', paper presented to the workshop 'Beyond the Firm? Social and Spatial Logics of Project Organisation', Bonn, April.

Wenger, E. (1998) *Communities of Practice: Learning, Meaning, and Identity*, Cambridge, MA: Cambridge University Press.

Wenger, E. and Snyder, W.M. (2000) 'Communities of practice: the organizational frontier', *Harvard Business Review* 1: January/February, 139–45.

Williamson, O.E. (1985) *The Economic Institutions of Capitalism: Firms, Markets and Relational Contracting*, New York: Free Press.

Winch, G.M. (1986) 'The labour process and labour market in construction', *International Journal Sociology and Social Policy* 6: 103–16.

Yeung, H.W.C. (2001) 'Regulating the "firm" and sociocultural practices in industrial geography II', *Progressive Human Geography* 25(2): 293–302.

Zeller, C. (2002) 'Project-teams as means for restructuring research and development in the pharmaceutical industry', *Regional Studies* 36: 275–89.

Introduction

Part IV focuses upon the link between strategy, leadership and learning. Chapter 22 explores the critical link between learning and leadership, arguing that truly learning organizations will remain only a distant vision until the leadership skills they require are more readily available. First of all, we have to overcome our obsession with control and the notion that people are to be rewarded only for conforming to the rules of others rather than for developing better rules themselves. Competitive advantage increasingly depends upon 'experimentation', the continuous exploration of opportunity. This experimentation requires generative rather than adaptive learning. Adaptive learning accepts the world as it is. It is reactive to external events. Generative learning involves recreating the world. It gets below the surface of events to look for underlying patterns and below those the underlying structures (systems) that condition events. The new leaders will be teachers and stewards with a range of new skills that recreate 'followers' as active participants in their own destiny. Such leaders will be designers of the 'social architecture' of organization, responsible for fostering the governing ideas of purpose, vision and values and then translating these governing ideas into business decisions via policies, strategies and structures. This means surfacing, challenging and changing, where necessary, managers' mental models of their business. In this process the leader acts as teacher, coach, guide or facilitator, focusing attention upon the generative systemic structures upon which organizations depend.

The next chapter, Chapter 23, addresses the vexed question of teambuilding in the top management context. It starts with a searching analysis of when teamwork is necessary. Teamwork is at a premium in strategic decisions when the future fate of the whole organization is at issue. Strategic work is characterized by high levels of choice and conditions of great uncertainty. There is a temptation to approach these issues in an operational manner, by forcing them to fit into existing strategy frameworks for example, but this is usually dysfunctional because it tends to oversimplify the problems the organization has to face. It is crucial in the strategic dialogue between top managers that they expose and share their uncertainties and their own subjective views of the world. Out of such frank dialogues teams can build common perceptions and a new sense of possibility. In conditions of shared uncertainty new management processes are needed, new skills and a new mode of leadership. In working with uncertainty people's feelings – anxiety, excitement and trust – are as important as the 'objective' facts and the leader has to work with the group to contain high levels of feeling that can threaten the integrity of the task at hand, the decisions about the future. The leader has to cultivate the interpersonal skills that are necessary to fulfil the process – for example empathy, cooperation, communication, listening, hearing, sharing.

Chapter 24 offers a critical examination of the effects the composition of top management teams has upon strategic renewal. It also proposes a new model of management (creative management) as an alternative to conventional thinking about strategic management. The creative management model – grounded in a psychodynamic analysis of top team relations and cognitive styles – starts with the assumption that reality is actually a social construction. The environment is 'enacted' by the interaction of actions, events and cognitions. Innovation involves 'creating' a new reality and convincing people that they need to reconfigure their expectations about existing and future products and services. Radical innovation involves a clear break with past thinking and creative learning about future possibilities. Intuition taps into our tacit, hidden knowledge. Creative management espouses and validates new ways of seeing things (new visioning), in particular in early stages of organizational and strategic renewal when managers have to respond creatively to ambiguity and uncertainty. It gives rise to new metaphors that liberate our thinking and new organizational myths that inspire people to come up with new ideas by promoting collaborative efforts in conditions of uncertainty. Having stimulated a range of new ideas/possibilities the intuitive stage of strategy cedes centre stage to a feeling stage during which the work of management is to work with people's emotions to align motivation with the choice of a new strategic direction that is acceptable to a range of actors who might start this stage with differing views of which option to choose.

One criticism levelled against theories of organizational learning is that they ignore organizational politics and the exercise of power by individuals or interest groups to advance their own interests at the expense of others. This issue is critically examined in Chapter 25, which argues that power is omnipresent, that the learning organization ignores the reality of asymmetries of power and that political activity is likely to impede learning. Power is exercised to secure sectional goals. Theories of the organizational learning assume a unitarist perspective in which goals are shared, levels of trust are high and differences are treated and resolved rationally. According to a political model of organization, top management constructs disciplinary practices to control employee performance and one can construe the new emphasis upon learning as, beneath the veneer of responsible autonomy, a more subtle way of exercising control. The rewards of improved performance remain uneven and even inequitable. Much learning is about learning new modes of defensive behaviour. The emphasis upon organizational learning might disguise the underlying structure of relationships but it does not fundamentally change them.

Chapter 26 explores the complications and the politics affecting the diffusion of learning in the context of the multinational corporation in a perspective that emphasizes the important role of the top management team dynamic in enabling or in inhibiting learning. Ford, like other US firms, tends to use foreign subsidiaries as staging posts in the career development of high-fliers who spend relatively short terms of duty on overseas assignments before returning to bigger and better things in the US. It is difficult for these 'executive tourists' to have an impact upon a situation that they experience only briefly and at a distance, both mentally and geographically. Such managers lack local knowledge and it is frequently more sensible from the standpoint of the individual career not to attempt change. They do not spend enough time to learn in depth the factors impacting their situation. As a result, without high-level integrated championship of new agendas, the status quo tends to prevail, to the detriment of performance.

Chapter 27 focuses on a newly emerging topic in the organizational learning debate, wisdom, which is sometimes construed as a stage that is achieved beyond knowledge. The chapter explores the concept of wisdom and its effects on cognition and the behaviour of managers. This chapter, like a number that have preceded it, calls for a philosophical shift in our thinking about the nature of organizations and the nature of learning, based upon the concept of variability. Senior managers have to perform complex information processing and interpretation roles which requires a holistic understanding of complex inter-relationships. Organizational learning involved developing managers sensitive to power, culture, symbolism and meaning. It requires a breadth of and an openness to experience and an advanced level of moral development.

The final chapter, Chapter 28, adopts a psychodynamic perspective to explore a new frontier of learning – organizational identity. It analyses the defensive routines we find in organizations from the perspective of 'ego defence' and the struggle to maintain collective self-esteem. Such defences are pervasive and necessary but can become dysfunctional when they militate against the recognition of the need to change. The chapter argues that to counter the tendency to inertia we need to understand better the psychodynamics of organizational learning and to confront defensive behaviours by promoting critical self-reflexivity and a dialogue about the nature of organizational identity.

The leader's new work:
building learning organizations

Peter M. Senge

Human beings are designed for learning. No one has to teach an infant to walk, or talk, or master the spatial relationships needed to stack eight building blocks that don't topple. Children come fully equipped with an insatiable drive to explore and experiment. Unfortunately, the primary institutions of our society are oriented predominantly toward controlling rather than learning, rewarding individuals for performing for others rather than for cultivating their natural curiosity and impulse to learn. The young child entering school discovers quickly that the name of the game is getting the right answer and avoiding mistakes – a mandate no less compelling to the aspiring manager.

"Our prevailing system of management has destroyed our people," writes W. Edwards Deming, leader in the quality movement.[1] "People are born with intrinsic motivation, self-esteem, dignity, curiosity to learn, joy in learning. The forces of destruction begin with toddlers – a prize for the best Hallowe'en costume, grades in school, gold stars, and on up through the university. On the job, people, teams, divisions are ranked – reward for the one at the top, punishment at the bottom. MBO, quotas, incentive pay, business plans, put together separately, division by division, cause further loss, unknown and unknowable."

Ironically, by focusing on performing for someone else's approval, corporations create the very conditions that predestine them to mediocre performance. Over the long run, superior performance depends on superior learning. A Shell study showed that, according to former planning director Arie de Geus, "a full one-third of the Fortune '500' industrials listed in 1970 had vanished by 1983."[2] Today, the average lifetime of the largest industrial enterprises is probably less than *half* the average lifetime of a person in an industrial society. On the other hand, de Geus and his colleagues at Shell also found a small number of companies that survived for seventy-five years or longer. Interestingly, the key to their survival was the ability to run "experiments in the margin," to continually explore new business and organizational opportunities that create potential new sources of growth.

If anything, the need for understanding how organizations learn and accelerating that learning is greater today than ever before. The old days when Henry Ford, Alfred Sloan, or Tom Watson *learned for the organization* are gone. In an increasingly dynamic, interdependent, and unpredictable world, it is simply no longer possible for anyone to "figure it all out at the top." The old model, "the top thinks and the local acts," must now give way to integrating thinking and acting at all levels. While the challenge is great, so is the potential payoff. "The person who figures out how to harness the collective genius of the people in his or her organization," according to former Citibank CEO Walter Wriston, "is going to blow the competition away."

Adaptive learning and generative learning

The prevailing view of learning organizations emphasizes increased adaptability. Given the accelerating pace of change, or so the standard view goes, "the most successful corporate of the 1990s," according to *Fortune* magazine, "will be something called a learning organization, a consummately adaptive enterprise."[3] As the Shell study shows, examples of traditional authoritarian bureaucracies that responded too slowly to survive in changing business environments are legion.

But increasing adaptiveness is only the first stage in moving toward learning organizations. The impulse to learn in children goes deeper than desires to respond and adapt more effectively to environmental change. The impulse to learn, at its heart, is an impulse to be generative, to expand our capability. This is why leading corporations are focusing on *generative* learning, which is about creating, as well as *adaptive* learning, which is about coping.[4]

The total quality movement in Japan illustrates the evolution from adaptive to generative learning. With its emphasis on continuous experimentation and feedback, the total quality movement has been the first wave in building learning organizations. But Japanese firms' view of serving the customer has evolved. In the early years of total quality, the focus was on "fitness to standard," making a product reliably so that it would do what its designers intended it to do and what the firm told its customers it would do. Then came a focus on "fitness to need," understanding better what the customer wanted and then providing products that reliably met those needs. Today, leading edge firms seek to understand and meet the "latent need" of the customer – what customers might truly value but have never experienced or would never think to ask for. As one Detroit executive commented recently, "You could never produce the Mazda Miata solely from market research. It required a leap of imagination to see what the customer *might* want."[5]

Generative learning, unlike adaptive learning, requires new ways of looking at the world, whether in understanding customers or in understanding how to better manage a business. For years, US manufacturers sought competitive advantage in aggressive controls on inventories, incentives against overproduction, and rigid adherence to production forecasts. Despite these incentives, their performance was eventually eclipsed by Japanese firms who saw the challenges of manufacturing differently. They realized that eliminating delays in the production process was the key to reducing instability and improving cost, productivity, and service. They worked to build networks of relationships with trusted suppliers and to redesign physical production processes so as to reduce delays in materials procurement, production set up, and in-process inventory – a much higher-leverage approach to improving both cost and customer loyalty.

As Boston Consulting Group's George Stalk has observed, the Japanese saw the significance of delays because they saw the process of order entry, production scheduling, materials procurement, production, and distribution *as an integrated system*. "What distorts the system so badly is time," observed Stalk – the multiple delays between events and responses. "These distortions reverberate throughout the system, producing disruptions, waste, and inefficiency."[6] Generative learning requires seeing the systems that control events. When we fail to grasp the systemic source of problems, we are left of "push on" symptoms rather than eliminate underlying causes. The best we can ever do is adaptive learning.

The leader's new work

"I talk with people all over the country about learning organizations, and the response is always very positive," says William O'Brien, CEO of the Hanover Insurance companies. "If this type of organization is so widely preferred why don't people create such organizations? I think the answer is leadership. People have no real comprehension of the type of commitment it requires to build such an organization."[7]

Our traditional view of leaders – as special people who set the direction, make the key decisions, and energize the troops – is deeply rooted in an individualistic and nonsystemic worldview. Especially in the West, leaders are *heroes* – great men (and occasionally women) who rise to the fore in times of crisis. So long as such myths prevail, they reinforce a focus on short-term events and charismatic heroes rather than on systemic forces and collective learning.

Leadership in learning organizations centers on subtler and ultimately more important work. In a learning organization, leaders' roles differ dramatically from that of the charismatic decision maker. Leaders are designers, teachers, and stewards. These roles require new skills: the ability to build shared vision, to bring to the surface and challenge prevailing mental models, and to foster more systemic patterns of thinking. In short, leaders in learning organizations are responsible for *building organizations* where people are continually expanding their capabilities to shape their future – that is, leaders are responsible for learning.

Creative tension: the integrating principle

Leadership in a learning organization starts with the principle of creative tension.[8] Creative tension comes from seeing clearly where we want to be, our "vision," and telling the truth about where we are, our "current reality." The gap between the two generates a natural tension (see Figure 22.1).

Figure 22.1 The principle of creative tension

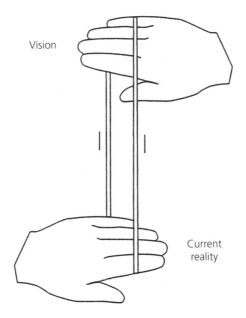

Creative tension can be resolved in two basic ways: by raising current reality toward the vision, or by lowering the vision toward current reality. Individuals, groups, and organizations who learn how to work with creative tension learn how to use the energy it generates to move reality more reliably toward their visions.

The principle of creative tension has long been recognized by leaders. Martin Luther King, Jr., once said, "Just as Socrates felt that it was necessary to create a tension in the mind, so that individuals could rise from the bondage of myths and half truth ... so must we ... create the kind of tension in society that will help men rise from the dark depths of prejudice and racism."[9]

Without vision there is no creative tension. Creative tension cannot be generated from current reality alone. All the analysis in the world will never generate a vision. Many who are otherwise qualified to lead, fail to do so because they try to substitute analysis for vision. They believe that, if only people understood current reality, they would surely feel the motivation to change. They are then disappointed to discover that people "resist" the personal and organizational changes that must be made to alter reality. What they never grasp is that the natural energy for changing reality comes from holding a picture of what might be that is more important to people than what is.

But creative tension cannot be generated from vision alone; it demands an accurate picture of current reality as well. Just as King had a dream, so too did he continually strive to "dramatize the shameful conditions" of racism and prejudice so that they could no longer be ignored. Vision without an understanding of current reality will more likely foster cynicism than creativity.

The principle of creative tension teaches that *an accurate picture of current reality is just as important as a compelling picture of a desired future.*

Leading through creative tension is different from solving problems. In problem solving, the energy for change comes from attempting to get away from an aspect of current reality that is undesirable. With creative tension, the energy for change comes from the vision, from what we want to create, juxtaposed with current reality. While the distinction may seem small, the consequences are not. Many people and organizations find themselves motivated to change only when their problems are bad enough to cause them to change. This works for a while, but the change process runs out of steam as soon as the problems driving the change become less pressing. With problem solving, the motivation for change is extrinsic. With creative tension, the motivation is intrinsic. This distinction mirrors the distinction between adaptive and generative learning.

New roles

The traditional authoritarian image of the leader as "the boss calling the shots" has been recognized as oversimplified and inadequate for some time. According to Edgar Schein, "Leadership is intertwined with culture formation." Building an organization's culture and shaping its evolution is the "unique and essential function" of leadership.[10] In a learning organization, the critical roles of leadership – designer, teacher, and steward – have antecedents in the ways leaders have contributed to building organizations in the past. But each role takes on new meaning in the learning organization and, as will be seen in the following sections, demands new skills and tools.

Leader as designer

Imagine that your organization is an ocean liner and that you are "the leader." What is your role?

I have asked this question of groups of managers many times. The most common answer, not surprisingly, is "the captain." Others say, "the navigator, setting the direction." Still others say, "the helmsman, actually controlling the direction," or, "the engineer down there stoking the fire, providing energy," or, "the social director, making sure everybody's enrolled, involved, and communicating." While these are legitimate leadership roles, there is another which, in many ways, eclipses them all in importance. Yet rarely does anyone mention it.

The neglected leadership role is the *designer* of the ship. No one has a more sweeping influence than the designer. What good does it do for the captain to say, "Turn starboard 30 degrees," when the designer has built a rudder that will only turn to port, or which takes six hours to turn to starboard? It's fruitless to be the leader in an organization that is poorly designed.

The functions of design, or what some have called "social architecture," are rarely visible; they take place behind the scenes. The consequences that appear today are the result of work done long in the past, and work today will show its benefits far in the future. Those who aspire to lead out of a desire to control, or gain fame, or simply to be at the center of the action, will find little to attract them to the quiet design work of leadership.

But what, specifically, is involved in organizational design? "Organization design is widely misconstrued as moving around boxes and lines," says Hanover's O'Brien. "The first task of organization design concerns designing the governing ideas of purpose, vision, and core values by which people will live." Few acts of leadership have a more enduring impact on an organization than building a foundation of purpose and core values.

In 1982 in the USA, Johnson & Johnson found itself facing a corporate nightmare when bottles of its best-selling Tylenol were tampered with, resulting in several deaths. The corporation's immediate response was to pull all Tylenol off the shelves of retail outlets. Thirty-one million capsules were destroyed, even though they were tested and found safe. Although the immediate cost was significant, no other action was possible given that the firm's credo states that permanent success is possible only when modern industry realizes that:

- service to its customers comes first;
- service to its employees and management comes second;
- service to the community comes third; and
- service to its stockholders, last.

Such statements might seem like motherhood and apple pie to those who have not seen the way a clear sense of purpose and values can affect key business decisions. Johnson & Johnson's crisis management in this case was based on that credo. It was simple, it was right, and it worked.

If governing ideas constitute the first design task of leadership, the second design task involves the policies, strategies, and structures that translate guiding ideas into business decisions. Leadership theorist Philip Selznick calls policy and structure the "institutional embodiment of purpose."[11] "Policy making (the rules that guide decisions) ought to be separated from decision making," says Jay Forrester[12] "Otherwise, short-term pressures will usurp time from policy creation."

Traditionally, writers like Selznick and Forrester have tended to see policy making and implementation as the work of a small number of senior managers. But that view is changing. Both the dynamic business environment and the mandate of the learning organization to engage people at all levels now make it clear that this second design task is more subtle. Henry Mintzberg has argued that strategy is less a rational plan arrived at in the abstract and implemented throughout the organization than an "emergent phenomenon." Successful organizations "craft strategy" according to Mintzberg, as they continually learn about shifting business conditions and balance what is desired and what is possible.[13] The key is not getting the right strategy but fostering strategic thinking. "The choice of individual action is only part of ... the policymaker's need," according to Mason and Mitroff.[14] "More important is the need to achieve insight into the nature of the complexity and to formulate concepts and world views for coping with it."

Behind appropriate policies, strategies, and structures are effective learning processes; their creation is the third key design responsibility in learning organizations. This does not absolve senior managers of their strategic responsibilities. Actually, it deepens and extends those responsibilities. Now, they are not only responsible for ensuring that an organization has well-developed strategies and policies, but also for ensuring that processes exist whereby these are continually improved.

In the early 1970s, Shell was the weakest of the big seven oil companies. Today, Shell and Exxon are arguably the strongest, both in size and financial health. Shell's ascendance began with frustration. Around 1971 members of Shell's "Group Planning" in London began to foresee dramatic change and unpredictability in world oil markets. However, it proved impossible to persuade managers that the stable world of steady growth in oil demand and supply they had known for twenty years was about to change. Despite brilliant analysis and artful presentation, Shell's planners realized, in the words of Pierre Wack, that they "had failed to change behavior in much of the Shell organization."[15] Progress would probably have ended there, had the frustration not given way to a radically new view of corporate planning.

As they pondered this failure, the planners' view of their basic task shifted: "We no longer saw our task as producing a documented view of the future business environment five or ten years ahead. Our real target was the microcosm (the 'mental model') of our decision makers." Only when the planners reconceptualized their basic task as fostering learning rather than devising plans did their insights begin to have an impact. The initial tool used was "scenario analysis," through which planners encouraged operating managers to think through how they would manage in the future under different possible scenarios. It mattered not that the managers believed the planners' scenarios absolutely, only that they became engaged in ferreting out the implications. In this way, Shell's planners conditioned managers to be mentally prepared for a shift from low prices to high prices and from stability to instability. The results were significant. When OPEC became a reality, Shell quickly responded to increasing local operating company control (to enhance manoeuvrability in the new political environment), building buffer stocks, and accelerating development of non-OPEC sources – actions that its competitors took much more slowly or not at all.

Somewhat inadvertently, Shell planners had discovered the leverage of designing institutional learning processes, whereby, in the words of former planning director de Geus, "Management teams change their shared mental models of their company, their markets, and their competitors."[16] Since then, "planning as learning" has become a byword at Shell, and Group Planning has continually sought out new learning tools that can be integrated into the planning process. Some of these are described below.

Leader as teacher

"The first responsibility of a leader," writes retired Herman Miller CEO Max de Pree, "is to define reality."[17] Much of the leverage leaders can actually exert lies in helping people achieve more accurate, more insightful, and more *empowering* views of reality.

Leader as teacher does *not* mean leader as authoritarian expert whose job is to teach people the "correct" view of reality. Rather, it is about helping everyone in the organization, oneself included, to gain more insightful views of current reality. This is in line with a popular emerging view of leaders as coaches, guides, or facilitators.[18] In learning organizations, this teaching role is developed further by virtue of explicit attention to people's mental models and by the influence of the systems perspective.

The role of leader as teacher starts with bringing to the surface people's mental model of important issues. No one carries an organization, a market, or a state of technology in his or her head. What we carry in our heads are assumptions. These mental pictures of how the world works have a significant influence on how we perceive problems and opportunities, identify courses of action, and make choices.

One reason that mental models are so deeply entrenched is that they are largely tacit. Ian Mitroff, in his study of General Motors, argues that an assumption that prevailed for years was that, in the United States, "Cars are status symbols. Styling is therefore more important than quality."[19] The Detroit automakers didn't say, "We have a *mental model* that all people care about is styling." Few actual managers would even say publicly that all people care about is styling. So long as the view remained unexpressed, there was little possibility of challenging its validity or forming more accurate assumptions.

But working with mental models goes beyond revealing hidden assumptions. "Reality," as perceived by most people in most organizations, means pressures that must be borne, crises that must be reacted to, and limitations that must be accepted. Leaders as teachers help people *restructure their views of reality* to see beyond the superficial conditions and events into the underlying causes of problems – and therefore to see new possibilities for shaping the future.

Specifically, leaders can influence people to view reality at three distinct levels: events, patterns of behavior, and systemic structure.

Systemic Structure
(Generative)
↓
Patterns of Behavior
(Responsive)
↓
Events
(Reactive)

The key question becomes: *where do leaders predominantly focus their own and their organization's attention?*

Contemporary society focuses predominantly on events. The media reinforces this perspective, with almost exclusive attention to short-term, dramatic events. This focus leads naturally to explaining what happens in terms of those events: "The Dow Jones average went up sixteen points because high fourth-quarter profits were announced yesterday."

Pattern-of-behavior explanations are rarer, in contemporary culture, than event explanations, but they do occur. "Trend analysis" is an example of seeing patterns of behavior. A good editorial that interprets a set of current events in the context of long-term historical changes is another example. Systemic, structural explanations go even further by addressing the question, "What causes the patterns of behavior?"

In some sense, all three levels of explanation are equally true. But their usefulness is quite different. Event explanations – who did what to whom – doom their holders to a reactive stance toward change. Pattern-of-behavior explanations focus on identifying long-term trends and assessing their implications. They at least suggest how, over time, we can respond to shifting conditions. Structural explanations are the most powerful. Only they address the underlying causes of behavior at a level such that patterns of behavior can be changed.

By and large, leaders of our current institutions focus their attention on events and patterns of behavior, and, under their influence, their organizations do likewise. That is why contemporary organizations are predominantly reactive, or at best responsive – rarely generative. On the other hand, leaders in learning organizations pay attention to all three levels, but focus especially on systemic structure; largely by example, they teach people throughout the organization to do likewise.

Leader as steward

This is the subtlest role of leadership. Unlike the roles of designer and teacher, it is almost solely a matter of attitude. It is an attitude critical to learning organizations.

While stewardship has long been recognized as an aspect of leadership, its source is still not widely understood. I believe Robert Greenleaf came closest to explaining real stewardship, in his seminal book *Servant Leadership*.[20] There, Greenleaf argues that "The servant leader *is* servant first ... It begins with the nature feeling that one wants to serve, to serve *first*. This conscious choice brings one to aspire to lead. That person is sharply different from one who is leader first, perhaps because of the need to assuage an unusual power drive or to acquire material possessions."

Leaders' sense of stewardship operates on two levels: stewardship for the people they lead and stewardship for the larger purpose or mission that underlies the enterprise. The first type arises from a keen appreciation of the impact one's leadership can have on others. People can suffer economically, emotionally, and spiritually under inept leadership. If anything, people in a learning organization are more vulnerable because of their commitment and sense of shared ownership. Appreciating this naturally instills a sense of responsibility in leaders. The second type of stewardship arises from a leader's sense of personal purpose and commitment to the organization's larger mission. People's natural impulse to learn is unleashed when they are engaged in an endeavor they consider worthy of their fullest commitment. Or, as Lawrence Miller puts it, "Achieving return on equity does not, as a goal, mobilize the most noble forces of our soul."[21]

Leaders engaged in building learning organizations naturally feel part of a larger purpose that goes beyond their organization. They are part of changing the way businesses operate, not from a vague philanthropic urge, but from a conviction that their efforts will produce more productive organizations, capable of achieving higher levels of organizational success and personal satisfaction than more traditional organizations. Their sense of stewardship was succinctly captured by George Bernard Shaw when he said,

> This is the true joy in life, the being used for a purpose you consider a mighty one, the being a force of nature rather than a feverish, selfish clod of ailments and grievances complaining that the world will not devote itself to making you happy.

New skills

New leadership roles require new leadership skills. These skills can only be developed, in my judgment, through a lifelong commitment. It is not enough for one or two individuals to develop these skills. They must be distributed widely throughout the organization. This is one reason that understanding the *disciplines* of a learning organization is so important. These disciplines embody the principles and practices that can widely foster leadership development.

Three critical areas of skills (disciplines) are building shared visions, surfacing and challenging mental models, and engaging in systems thinking.[22]

Building shared visions

How do individual visions come together to create shared visions? A useful metaphor is the hologram, the three-dimensional image created by interacting light sources.

If you cut a photograph in half, each half shows only part of the whole image. But if you divide a hologram, each part, no matter how small, shows the whole image intact. Likewise, when a group of people come to share a vision for an organization, each person sees an individual picture of the organization at its best. Each shares responsibility for the whole, not just for one piece. But the component pieces of the hologram are not identical. Each represents the whole image from a different point of view. It's something like poking holes in a window shade; each hole offers a unique angle for viewing the whole image. So, too, is each individual's vision unique.

When you add up the pieces of a hologram, something interesting happens. The image becomes more intense, more lifelike. When more people come to share a vision, the vision becomes more real in the sense of a mental reality that people can truly imagine achieving. They now have partners, co-creators; the vision no longer rests on their shoulders alone. Early on, when they are nurturing an individual vision, people may say it is "my vision." But, as the shared vision develops, it becomes both "my vision" and "our vision."

The skills involved in building shared vision include the following:

- **Encouraging personal vision**. Shared visions emerge from personal visions. It is not that people only care about their own self-interest – in fact, people's values usually include dimensions that concern family, organization, community, and even the world. Rather, it is that people's capacity for caring is *personal*.

- **Communicating and asking for support**. Leaders must be willing to continually share their own vision, rather than being the official representative of the corporate vision. They also must be prepared to ask, "Is this vision worthy of your commitment?" This can be difficult for a person used to setting goals and presuming compliance.

- **Visioning as an ongoing process**. Building shared vision is a never-ending process. At any one point there will be a particular image of the future that is predominant, but that image will evolve. Today, too many managers want to dispense with the "vision business" by going off and writing the Official Vision Statement. Such statements almost always lack the vitality, freshness, and excitement of a genuine vision that comes from people asking, "What do we really want to achieve?"

- **Blending** extrinsic and intrinsic visions. Many energizing visions are extrinsic – that is, they focus on achieving something relative to an outsider, such as a competitor. But a goal that is limited to defeating an opponent can, once the vision is achieved, easily become a defensive posture. In contrast, intrinsic goals like creating a new type of product, taking an established product to a new level, or setting a new standard for customer satisfaction, can call forth a new level of creativity and innovation. Intrinsic and extrinsic visions need to coexist; a vision solely predicated on defeating an adversary will eventually weaken an organization.

- **Distinguishing positive and negative visions**. Many organizations only truly pull together when their survival is threatened. Similarly, most social movements aim at eliminating what people don't want: for example anti-drugs, anti-smoking, or anti-nuclear arms movements. Negative visions carry a subtle message of powerlessness: people will only pull together when there is sufficient threat. Negative visions also tend to be short term. Two fundamental sources of energy can motivate organizations: fear and aspiration. Fear, the energy source behind negative visions, can produce extraordinary changes in short periods, but aspiration endures as a continuing source of learning and growth.

Surfacing and testing mental models

Many of the best ideas in organizations never get put into practice. One reason is that new insights and initiatives often conflict with established mental models. The leadership task of challenging assumptions without invoking skills is possessed by few leaders in traditional controlling organizations.[23]

- **Seeing leaps of abstraction**. Our minds literally move at lightning speed. Ironically, this often slows our learning, because we leap to generalizations so quickly that we never think to test them. We then confuse our generalizations with the observable data upon which they are based, treating the generalizations *as if they were data*. The frustrated sales rep reports to the home office that "customers don't really care about quality, price is what matters," when what actually happened was that three consecutive large customers refused to place an order unless a larger discount was offered. The sales rep treats her generalization, "customers care only about price" as if it were absolute fact rather than an assumption (very likely an assumption reflecting her own views of customers and the market). This thwarts future learning because she starts to focus on how to offer attractive discounts rather than probing behind the customers' statements. For example, the customers may have been so disgruntled with the firm's delivery or customer service that they are unwilling to purchase again without larger discounts.

- **Balancing inquiry and advocacy**. Most managers are skilled at articulating their views and presenting them persuasively. While important, advocacy skills can become counterproductive as managers rise in responsibility and confront increasingly complex issues that require collaborative learning among different, equally knowledgeable people. Leaders in learning organizations need to have both inquiry *and* advocacy skills.[24]
  Specifically, when advocating a view, they need to be able to:
  - explain the reasoning and data that led to their view;
  - encourage others to test their view (e.g. Do you see gaps in my reasoning? Do you disagree with the data upon which my view is based?); and
  - encourage others to provide different views (e.g. Do you have either different data, different conclusions, or both?).

  When inquiring into another's views, they need to:
  - actively seek to understand the other's view, rather than simply restating their own view and how it differs from the other's view; and
  - make their attributions about the other and the other's view explicit (e.g. Based on your statement that . . .; I am assuming that you believe . . .; Am I representing your views fairly?).

If they reach an impasse (others no longer appear open to inquiry), they
need to:

- ask what data or logic might unfreeze the impasse, or if an experiment
  (or some other inquiry) might be designed to provide new information.

- **Distinguishing espoused theory from theory in use**. We all like to think
  that we hold certain views, but often our actions reveal deeper views. For
  example, I may proclaim that people are trustworthy, but never lend
  friends money and jealously guard my possessions. Obviously, my deeper
  mental model (my theory in use) differs from my espoused theory.
  Recognizing gaps between espoused views and theories in use (which
  often requires the help of others) can be pivotal to deeper learning.

- **Recognizing and defusing defensive routines**. As one CEO in our research
  program puts it, "Nobody ever talks about an issue at the 8.00 business
  meeting exactly the same way they talk about it at home that evening or
  over drinks at the end of the day." The reason is what Chris Argyris calls
  "defensive routines," entrenched habits used to protect ourselves from the
  embarrassment and threat that come with exposing our thinking. For most of
  us, such defenses began to build early in life in response to pressures to have
  the right answers in school or at home. Organizations add new levels of
  performance anxiety and thereby amplify and exacerbate this defensiveness.
  Ironically, this makes it even more difficult to expose hidden mental models,
  and thereby lessens learning.

  The first challenge is to recognize defensive routines, and then to inquire
  into their operation. Those who are best at revealing and defusing defensive
  routines operate with a high degree of self-disclosure regarding their own
  defensiveness (e.g. I notice that I am feeling uneasy about how this
  conversation is going. Perhaps I don't understand it or it is threatening to me
  in ways I don't yet see. Can you help me see this better?).

Systems thinking

We all know that leaders should help people see the big picture. But the actual
skills whereby leaders are supposed to achieve this are not well understood. In
my experience, successful leaders often *are* "systems thinkers" to a considerable
extent. They focus less on day-to-day events and more on underlying trends
and forces of change. But they do this almost completely intuitively. The
consequence is that they are often unable to explain their intuitions to others
and feel frustrated that others cannot see the world the way they do.

One of the most significant developments in management science today is
the gradual coalescence of managerial systems thinking as a field of study and
practice. This field suggests some key skills for future leaders:

- **Seeing interrelationships, not things, and processes, not snapshots**. Most
  of us have been conditioned throughout our lives to focus on things and
  to see the world in static images. This leads us to linear explanations of

systemic phenomenon. For instance, in an arms race each party is convinced that the other is *the cause* of problems. They react to each new move as an isolated event, not as part of a process. So long as they fail to see the interrelationships of these actions, they are trapped.

- **Moving beyond blame**. We tend to blame each other or outside circumstances for our problems. But it is poorly designed systems, not incompetent or unmotivated individuals, that cause most organizational problems. Systems thinking shows us that there is no outside – that you and the cause of your problems are part of a single system.

- **Distinguishing detail complexity from dynamic complexity**. Some types of complexity are more important strategically than others. Detail complexity arises when there are many variables. Dynamic complexity arises when cause and effect are distant in time and space, and when the consequences over time of interventions are subtle and not obvious to many participants in the system. The leverage in most management situations lies in understanding dynamic complexity, not detail complexity.

- **Focusing on areas of high leverage**. Some have called systems thinking the "new dismal science" because it teaches that most obvious solutions don't work – at best, they improve matters in the short run, only to make things worse in the long run. But there is another side to the story. Systems thinking also shows that small, well-focused actions can produce significant, enduring improvements, if they are in the right place. Systems thinkers refer to this idea as the principle of "leverage." Tackling a difficult problem is often a matter of seeing where the high leverage lies, where a change – with a minimum of effort – would lead to lasting, significant improvement.

- **Avoiding symptomatic solutions**. The pressures to intervene in management systems that are going awry can be overwhelming. Unfortunately, given the linear thinking that predominates in most organizations, interventions usually focus on symptomatic fixes, not underlying causes. This results in only temporary relief, and it tends to create still more pressures later on for further, low-leverage intervention. If leaders acquiesce to these pressures, they can be sucked into an endless spiral of increasing intervention. Sometimes the most difficult leadership acts are to refrain from intervening through popular quick fixes and to keep the pressures on everyone to identify more enduring solutions.

While leaders who can articulate systemic explanations are rare, those who *can* will leave their stamp on an organization. One person who had this gift was Bill Gore, the founder and long-time CEO of W. L. Gore and Associates (makers of Gore-Tex and other synthetic fiber products). Bill Gore was adept at telling stories that showed how the organization's core values of freedom and individual responsibility required particular operating policies. He was proud of his egalitarian organization, in which there were (and still are) no "employees," only "associates," all of whom own shares in the company and participate in its management. At one talk, he explained the company's policy of controlled growth: "Our limitation is not financial resources. Our limitation is the rate at which we can bring in new associates. Our experience has been that if we try to bring in more than a 25 percent per year increase, we begin to bog down. Twenty-five percent per year growth is a real limitation; you can do much better than that with an authoritarian organization." As Gore tells the story, one of the associates, Esther Baum, went home after this talk and reported the limitation to her husband. As it happened, he was an astronomer and mathematician at Lowell Observatory. He said, "That's a very interesting figure." He took out a pencil and paper and calculated and said, "Do you realize that in only fifty-seven and a half years, everyone in the world will be working for Gore?"

Through this story, Gore explains the systemic rationale behind a key policy, limited growth rate – a policy that undoubtedly caused a lot of stress in the organization. He suggests that, at larger rates of growth, the adverse effects of attempting to integrate too many new people too rapidly would begin to dominate. (This is the "limits to growth" systems archetype explained below.) The story also reaffirms the organization's commitment to creating a unique environment for its associates and illustrates the types of sacrifices that the firm is prepared to make in order to remain true to its vision. The last part of the story shows that, despite the self-imposed limit, the company is still very much a growth company.

The consequences of leaders who lack systems thinking skills can be devastating. Many charismatic leaders manage almost exclusively at the level of events. They deal in visions and in crises, and little in between. Under their leadership, an organization hurtles from crisis to crisis. Eventually, the worldview of people in the organization becomes dominated by events and reactiveness. Many, especially those who are deeply committed, become burned out. Eventually, cynicism comes to pervade the organization. People have no control over their time, let alone their destiny.

Similar problems arise with the "visionary strategist," the leader with vision who sees both patterns of change and events. This leader is better prepared to manage change. He or she can explain strategies in terms of emerging trends, and thereby foster a climate that is less reactive. But such leaders still impart a responsive orientation rather than a generative one.

Many talented leaders have rich, highly systemic intuitions but cannot explain those intuitions to others. Ironically, they often end up being authoritarian leaders, even if they don't want to, because only they see the decisions that need to be made. They are unable to conceptualize their strategic insights so that these can become public knowledge, open to challenge and further improvement.

New tools

Developing the skills described above requires new tools – tools that will enhance leaders' conceptual abilities and foster communication and collaborative inquiry. What follows is a sampling of tools starting to find use in learning organizations.

Systems archetypes

One of the insights of the budding, managerial systems-thinking field is that certain types of systemic structures recur again and again. Countless systems grow for a period, then encounter problems and cease to grow (or even collapse) well before they have reached intrinsic limits to growth. Many other systems get locked in runaway vicious spirals where every actor has to run faster and faster to stay in the same place. Still others lure individual actors into doing what seems right locally, yet which eventually causes suffering for all.[25]

Some of the system archetypes that have the broadest relevance include:

- **Balancing process with delay**. In this archetype, decision makers fail to appreciate the time delays involved as they move toward a goal. As a result, they overshoot the goal and may even produce recurring cycles. Classic example: real estate developers who keep starting new projects until the market has gone soft, by which time an eventual glut is guaranteed by the properties still under construction.

- **Limits to growth**. A reinforcing cycle of growth grinds to a halt, and may even reverse itself, as limits are approached. The limits can be resource constraints, or external or internal responses to growth. Classic examples: product life cycles that peak prematurely due to poor quality of service, the growth and decline of communication in a management team, and the spread of a new movement.

- **Shifting the burden**. A short-term "solution" is used to correct a problem, with seemingly happy immediate results. As this correction is used more and more, fundamental long-term corrective measures are used less. Over time, the mechanisms of the fundamental solution may atrophy or become disabled, leading to even greater reliance on the symptomatic solution. Classic example: using corporate human resource staff to solve local personnel problems, thereby keeping managers from developing their own interpersonal skills.

- **Eroding goals**. When all else fails, lower your standards. This is like "shifting the burden," except that the short-term solution involves letting a fundamental goal, such as quality standards or employee morale standards, atrophy. Classic example: a company that responds to delivery problems by continually upping its quoted delivery times.

- **Escalation**. Two people or two organizations, who each see their welfare as depending on a relative advantage over the other, continually react to the other's advances. Whenever one side gets ahead, the other is threatened, leading it to act more aggressively to reestablish its advantage, which threatens the first, and so on. Classic examples: arms race, gang warfare, price wars.

- **Tragedy of the commons**.[26] Individuals keep intensifying their use of a commonly available but limited resource until all individuals start to experience severely diminishing returns. Classic examples: shepherds who keep increasing their flocks until they overgraze the common pasture; divisions in a firm that share a common salesforce and compete for the use of sales reps by upping their sales targets, until the salesforce burns out from overextension.

- **Growth and underinvestment**. Rapid growth approaches a limit that could be eliminated or pushed into the future, but only by aggressive investment in physical and human capacity. Eroding goals or standards cause investment that is too weak, or too slow, and customers get increasingly unhappy, slowing demand growth and thereby making the needed investment (apparently) unnecessary or impossible. Classic example: countless once successful growth firms that allowed product or service quality to erode, and were unable to generate enough revenues to invest in remedies.

The archetype template is a specific tool that is helping managers identify archetypes operating in their own strategic areas (see Figure 22.2).[27] The template shows the basic structural form of the archetype but lets managers fill in the variables of their own situation. For example, the shifting the burden template involves two balancing processes (B) that compete for control of a problem symptom. The upper, symptomatic solution provides a short-term fix that will make the problem symptom go away for a while. The lower, fundamental solution provides a more enduring solution. The side effect feedback (R) around the outside of the figure identifies unintended

| **Figure 22.2** | 'Shifting the burden' archetype template |

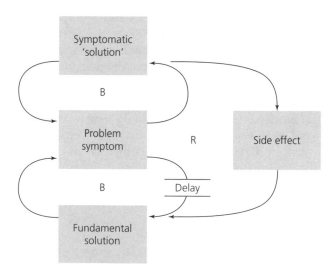

In the 'shifting the burden' template, two balancing processes (B) compete for control of a problem symptom. Both solutions affect the symptom, but only the fundamental solution treats the cause. The symptomatic 'solution' creates the additional side effect (R) of deferring the fundamental solution, making it harder and harder to achieve.

exacerbating effects of the symptomatic solution, which, over time, make it more and more difficult to invoke the fundamental solution.

Several years ago, a team of managers from a leading consumer goods producer used the shifting the burden archetype in a revealing way. The problem they focused on was financial stress, which could be dealt with in two different ways: by running market promotions (the symptomatic solution) or by product innovation (the fundamental solution). Marketing promotions were fast. The company was expert in their design and implementation. The results were highly predictable. Product innovation was slow and much less predictable, and the company had a history over the past ten years of product-innovation mismanagement. Yet only through innovation could they retain a leadership position in their industry, which had slid over the past ten to twenty years. What the managers saw clearly was that the more skillful they became at promotions, the more they shifted the burden away from product innovation. But what really struck home was when one member identified the unintended side effect: the last three CEOs had all come from the advertising function, which had become the politically dominant function in the corporation, thereby institutionalizing the symptomatic solution. Unless the political values shifted back toward product and process innovation, the managers realized, the firm's decline would accelerate – which is just the shift that has happened over the past several years.

Charting strategic dilemmas

Management teams typically come unglued when confronted with core dilemmas. A classic example was the way US manufacturers faced the low cost/high quality choice. For years, most assumed that it was necessary to choose between the two. Not surprisingly, given the short-term pressures perceived by most managements, the prevailing choice was low cost. Firms that chose high quality usually perceived themselves as aiming exclusively for a high quality, high price market niche. The consequences of this perceived either–or choice have been disastrous, even fatal, as US manufacturers have encountered increasing international competition from firms that have chosen to consistently improve quality *and* cost.

In a recent book, Charles Hampden-Turner presented a variety of tools for helping strategic management teams confront strategic dilemmas creatively.[28] He summarizes the process in seven steps:

- **Eliciting the dilemmas**. Identifying the opposed values that form the "horns" of the dilemma, for example, cost as opposed to quality, or local initiative as opposed to central coordination and control. Hampden-Turner suggests that humor can be a distinct asset in this process since "the admission that dilemmas even exist tends to be difficult for some companies."

- **Mapping**. Locating the opposing values as two axes and helping managers identify where they see themselves, or their organization, along the axes.

- **Processing**. Getting rid of nouns to describe the axes of the dilemma. Present participles formed by adding "ing" convert rigid nouns into processes that imply movement. For example, central control versus local control becomes "strengthening national office" and "growing local initiatives." This loosens the bond of implied opposition between the two values. For example, it becomes possible to think of "strengthening national services from which local branches can benefit."

- **Framing/contextualizing**. Further softening the adversarial structure among different values by letting "each side in turn be the frame or context for the other." This shifting of the "figure–ground" relationship undermines any implicit attempts to hold one value as intrinsically superior to the other and thereby to become mentally closed to creative strategies for continuous improvement of both.

- **Sequencing**. Breaking the hold of static thinking. Very often, values like low cost and high quality appear to be in opposition because we think in terms of a point in time, not in terms of an on-going process. For example, a strategy of investing in new process technology and developing a new production-floor culture of worker responsibility may take time and money in the near term, yet reap significant long-term financial rewards.

- **Waving/cycling**. Sometimes the strategic path toward improving both values involves cycles where both values will get "worse" for a time. Yet, at a deeper level, learning is occurring that will cause the next cycle to be at a higher plateau for both values.

- **Synergizing**. Achieving synergy where significant improvement is occurring along all axes of all relevant dilemmas. (This is the ultimate goal, of course.) Synergy, as Hampden-Turner points out, is a uniquely systemic notion, coming from the Greek *syn-ergo* or "work together."

"The left-hand column": surfacing mental models

The idea that mental models can dominate business decisions and that these models are often tacit and even contradictory to what people espouse can be very threatening to managers who pride themselves on rationality and judicious decision making. It is important to have tools to help managers discover for themselves how their mental models operate to undermine their own intentions.

One tool that has worked consistently to help managers see their own mental models in action is the "left-hand column" exercise developed by Chris Argyris and his colleagues.[29] This tool is especially helpful in showing how we leap from data to generalization without testing the validity of our generalizations.

When working with managers, I start this exercise by selecting a specific situation in which I am interacting with other people in a way that is not working, that is not producing the learning that is needed. I write out a sample of the exchange, with the script on the right-hand side of the page. On the left-hand side, I write what I am thinking but not saying at each stage in the exchange (see Figure 22.3).

The left-hand column exercise not only brings hidden assumptions to the surface, it shows how they influence behavior. In the example, I make two key assumptions about Bill: he lacks confidence and he lacks initiative. Neither may be literally true, but both are evident in my internal dialogue, and both influence the way I handle the situation. Believing that he lacks confidence, I skirt the fact that I've heard the presentation was a bomb. I'm afraid that if I say it directly, he will lose what little confidence he has, or he will see me as unsupportive. So I bring up the subject of the presentation obliquely. When I ask Bill what we should do next, he gives no specific course of action. Believing he lacks initiative, I take this as evidence of his laziness; he is content to do nothing when action is definitely required. I conclude that I will have to manufacture some form of pressure to motivate him, or else I will simply have to take matters into my own hands.

The exercise reveals the elaborate webs of assumptions we weave, within which we become our own victims. Rather than dealing directly with my assumptions about Bill and the situation, we talk around the subject. The

Figure 22.3 The left-hand column: an exercise

Imagine my exchange with a colleague, Bill, after he made a big presentation to our boss on a project we are doing together. I had to miss the presentation, but I've heard that it was poorly received.

Me: How did the presentation go?
Bill: Well, I don't know. It's really too early to say. Besides, we're breaking new ground here.
Me: Well, what do you think we should do? I believe that the issues you were raising are important.
Bill: I'm not so sure. Let's just wait and see what happens.
Me: You may be right, but I think we may need to do more than just wait.

Now, here is what the exchange looks like with my "left-hand column":

What I'm thinking	What Is said
Everyone says the presentation was a bomb. Does he really not know how bad it was? Or is he not willing to face up to it?	*Me*: How did the presentation go? *Bill*: Well, I don't know. It's too early to say. Besides, we're breaking new ground here. *Me*: Well, what do you think we should do? I believe that the issues you were raising are important.
He really is afraid to see the truth. If he only had more confidence, he could probably learn from a situation like this. I can't believe he doesn't realize how disastrous that presentation was to our moving ahead. I've got to find some way to light a fire under this guy.	*Bill*: I'm not so sure. Let's just wait and see what happens. *Me*: You may be right, but I think we may need to do more than just wait.

reasons for my avoidance are self-evident: I assume that if I raised my doubts, I would provoke a defensive reaction that would only make matters worse. But the price of avoiding the issue is high. Instead of determining how to move forward to resolve our problems, we end our exchange with no clear course of action. My assumptions about Bill's limitations have been reinforced. I resort to a manipulative strategy to move things forward.

The exercise not only shows the need for skills in surfacing assumptions, but that we are the ones most in need of help. There is no one right way to handle difficult situations like my exchange with Bill, but any productive strategy revolves around a high level of self-disclosure and willingness to have my views challenged. I need to recognize my own leaps of abstraction regarding Bill, share the events and reasoning that are leading to my concern over the project, and be open to Bill's views on both. The skills to carry on such conversations without invoking defensiveness take time to develop. But if both parties in a learning impasse start by doing their own left-hand column exercise and sharing them with each other, it is remarkable how quickly everyone recognizes their contribution to the impasse and progress starts to be made.

Learning laboratories: practice fields for management teams

One of the most promising new tools is the learning laboratory or "micro-world": constructed microcosms of real-life settings in which management teams can learn how to learn together.

The rationale behind learning laboratories can best be explained by analogy. Although most management teams have great difficulty learning (enhancing their collective intelligence and capacity to create), in other domains team learning is the norm rather than the exception – team sports and the performing arts, for example. Great basketball teams do not start off great. They learn. But the process by which these teams learn is, by and large, absent from modern organizations. The process is a continual movement between practice and performance.

The vision guiding current research in management learning laboratories is to design and construct effective practice fields for management teams. Much remains to be done, but the broad outlines are emerging.

First, since team learning in organizations is an individual-to-individual and individual-to-system phenomenon, learning laboratories must combine meaningful business issues with meaningful interpersonal dynamics. Either alone is incomplete.

Second, the factors that thwart learning about complex business issues must be eliminated in the learning lab. Chief among these is the inability to experience the long-term, systemic consequences of key strategic decisions. We all learn best from experience, but we are unable to experience the consequences of many important organizational decisions. Learning laboratories remove this constraint through system dynamics simulation games that compress time and space.

Third, new learning skills must be developed. One constraint on learning is the inability of managers to reflect insightfully on their assumptions, and to inquire effectively into each other's assumptions. Both skills can be enhanced in a learning laboratory, where people can practice surfacing assumptions in a low-risk setting. A note of caution: it is far easier to design an entertaining learning laboratory than it is to have an impact on real management practices and firm traditions outside the learning lab. Research on management simulations has shown that they often have greater entertainment value than educational value. One of the reasons appears to be that many simulations do not offer deep insights into systemic structures causing business problems. Another reason is that they do not foster new learning skills. Also, there is no connection between experiments in the learning lab and real-life experiments. These are significant problems that research on learning laboratory design is now addressing.

Developing leaders and learning organizations

In a recently published retrospective on organization development in the 1980s, Marshall Sashkin and W. Warner Burke observe the return of an emphasis on developing leaders who can develop organizations.[30] They also note Schein's critique that most top executives are not qualified for the task of developing culture.[31] Learning organizations represent a potentially significant evolution of organizational culture. So it should come as no surprise that such organizations will remain a distant vision until the leadership capabilities they demand are developed. "The 1990s may be the period," suggest Sashkin and Burke, "during which organization development and (a new sort of) management development are reconnected."

I believe that this new sort of management development will focus on the roles, skills, and tools for leadership in learning organizations.

Undoubtedly, the ideas offered above are only a rough approximation of this new territory. The sooner we begin seriously exploring the territory, the sooner the initial map can be improved – and the sooner we will realize an age-old vision of leadership:

> The wicked leader is he who the people despise
> The good leader is he who the people revere
> The great leader is he of whom the people say, "We did it ourselves." (Lao-Tzu)

Learning at Hanover Insurance

Hanover Insurance has gone from the bottom of the property and liability industry to a position among the top 25 percent of US insurance companies over the past twenty years, largely through the efforts of CEO William O'Brien and his predecessor, Jack Adam. The following comments are excerpted from a series of interviews Senge conducted with O'Brien as background for his book.

Senge: Why do you think there is so much change occurring in management and organizations today? Is it primarily because of increased competitive pressures?

O'Brien: That's a factor, but not the most significant factor. The ferment in management will continue until we find models that are more congruent with human nature.

One of the great insights of modern psychology is the hierarchy of human needs. As Maslow expressed this idea, the most basic needs are food and shelter. Then comes belonging. Once these three basic needs are satisfied, people begin to aspire toward self-respect and esteem, and toward self-actualization – the fourth- and fifth-order needs.

Our traditional hierarchical organizations are designed to provide for the first three levels, but not the fourth and fifth. These first three levels are now widely available to members of industrial society, but our organizations do not offer people sufficient opportunities for growth.

Senge: How would you assess Hanover's progress to date?

O'Brien: We have been on a long journey away from a traditional hierarchical culture. The journey began with everyone understanding some guiding ideas about purpose, vision, and values as a basis for participative management. This is a better way to begin building a participative culture than by simply "letting people in on decision making." Before there can be meaningful participation, people must share certain values and pictures about where we are trying to go. We discovered that people have a real need to feel that they're part of an ennobling mission. But developing shared visions and values is not the end, only the beginning.

Next we had to get beyond mechanical, linear thinking. The essence of our jobs as managers is to deal with "divergent" problems – problems that have no simple answer. "Convergent" problems – problems that have a "right" answer – should be solved locally. Yet we are deeply conditioned to see the world in terms of convergent problems. Most managers try to force-fit simplistic solutions and undermine the potential for learning when divergent problems arise. Since everyone handles the linear issues fairly well, companies that learn how to handle divergent issues will have a great advantage.

The next basic stage in our progression was coming to understand inquiry and advocacy. We learned that real openness is rooted in people's ability to continually inquire into their own thinking. This requires exposing yourself to being wrong – not something that most managers are rewarded for. But learning is very difficult if you cannot look for errors or incompleteness in your own ideas.

What all this builds to is the capability throughout an organization to manage mental models. In a locally controlled organization, you have the fundamental challenge of learning how to help people make good decisions without coercing them into making *particular* decisions. By managing mental models, we create "self-concluding" decisions – decisions that people come to themselves – which will result in deeper conviction, better implementation, and the ability to make better adjustments when the situation changes.

Senge: What concrete steps can top managers take to begin moving toward learning organizations?

O'Brien: Look at the signals you send through the organization. For example, one critical signal is how you spend your time. It's hard to build a learning organization if people are unable to take the time to think through important matters. I rarely set up an appointment for less than one hour. If the subject is not worth an hour, it shouldn't be on my calendar.

Senge: Why is this so hard for so many managers?

O'Brien: It comes back to what you believe about the nature of your work. The authoritarian manager has a "chain gang" mental model: "The speed of the boss is the speed of the gang. I've got to keep things moving fast, because I've got to keep people working." In a learning organization, the manager shoulders an almost sacred responsibility: to create conditions that enable people to have happy and productive lives. If you understand the effects the ideas we are discussing can have on the lives of people in your organization, you will take the time.

Notes

1. P. Senge, *The Fifth Discipline: The Art and Practice of the Learning Organization* (New York: Doubleday/Currency, 1990).
2. A.P. de Geus, "Planning as Learning," *Harvard Business Review*, March–April, 1988, pp. 70–4.
3. B. Domain in *Fortune*, 3 July 1989, pp. 48–62.
4. The distinction between adaptive and generative learning has its roots in the distinction between what Argyris and Schon have called their "single-loop" learning, in which individuals or groups adjust their behavior relative to fixed goals, norms, and assumptions, and "double-loop" learning, in which goals, norms, and assumptions, as well as behavior, are open to change (e.g. see C. Argyris and D. Schon, *Organizational Learning: A Theory-in-Action Perspective* (Reading, Massachusetts: Addison-Wesley, 1978).
5. All unattributed quotes are from personal communications with the author.
6. C. Stalk, Jr., "Time: The Next Source of Competitive Advantage," *Harvard Business Review*, July–August 1988, pp. 41–51.
7. Senge (1990).
8. The principle of creative tension comes from Robert Fritz's work on creativity. See R. Fritz, *The Path of Least Resistance* (New York: Ballantine, 1989) and *Creating* (New York: Ballantine, 1990).

9. M.L. King, Jr., "Letter from Birmingham Jail," *American Visions*, January–February 1986, pp. 52–9.
10. E. Schein, *Organizational Culture and Leadership* (San Francisco: Jossey-Bass, 1985). Similar views have been expressed by many leadership theorists. For example, see: P. Selznick, *Leadership in Administration* (New York: Harper & Row, 1957); W. Bennis and B. Nanus, *Leaders* (New York: Harper & Row, 1985); and N.M. Tichy and M.A. Devanna, *The Transformational Leader* (New York: John Wiley & Sons, 1986).
11. Selznick (1957).
12. J.W. Forrester, "A New Corporate Design," *Sloan Management Review* (formerly *Industrial Management Review*), Fall 1965, pp. 5–17.
13. See, for example, H. Mintzberg, "Crafting Strategy," *Harvard Business Review*, September–October 1985, pp. 73–89.
14. R. Mason and I. Mitroff, *Challenging Strategic Planning Assumptions* (New York: John Wiley & Sons, 1981), p. 16.
15. P. Wack, "Scenarios, Uncharted Waters Ahead," *Harvard Business Review*, September–October 1985, pp. 73–89.
16. de Geus (1988).
17. M. de Pree, *Leadership is an Art* (New York: Doubleday, 1989), p. 9.
18. For example, see T. Peters and N. Austin, *A Passion for Excellence* (New York: Random House, 1985) and J.M. Kouzes and B.Z. Posner, *The Leadership Challenge* (San Francisco: Jossey-Bass, 1987).
19. I. Mitroff, *Break-Away Thinking* (New York: John Wiley & Sons, 1988), pp. 66–7.
20. R.K. Greenleaf, *Servant Leadership: A Journey into the Nature of Legitimate Power and Greatness* (New York: Paulist Press, 1977).
21. L. Miller, *American Spirit: Visions of a New Corporate Culture* (New York: William Morrow, 1984), p. 15.
22. These points are condensed from the practices of the five disciplines examined in Senge (1990).
23. The ideas below are based to a considerable extent on the work of Chris Argyris, Donald Schon, and their Action Science colleagues: Argyris and Schon (1978); C. Argyris, R. Putnam and D. Smith, *Action Sciences* (San Francisco: Jossey-Bass, 1985); C. Argyris, *Overcoming Organizational Defenses* (Englewood Cliffs, New Jersey: Prentice-Hall, 1990).
24. I am indebted to Diana Smith for the summary points below.
25. The system archetypes are one of several systems' diagramming and communication tools. See D.H. Kim, "Toward Learning Organizations: Integrating Total Quality Control and Systems Thinking" (Cambridge, Massachusetts: MIT Sloan School of Management, Working Paper No. 3037–89–BPS, June 1989).
26. This archetype is closely associated with the work of ecologist Garrett Hardin, who coined its label: G. Hardin, "The Tragedy of the Commons," *Science*, 13 December 1968.
27. These templates were originally developed by Jennifer Kemeny, Charles Kiefer, and Michael Goodman of Innovation Associates, Inc., Framingham, Massachusetts.
28. C. Hampden-Turner, *Charting the Corporate Mind* (New York: The Free Press, 1990).
29. See Note 23.
30. M. Sashicin and W.W. Burke, "Organization Development in the 1980s" and "An End-of-the-Eighties Retrospective," in *Advances in Organization Development*, ed. F. Masarik (Norwood, New Jersey: Ablex, 1990).
31. E. Schein (1985).

23 Second thoughts on teambuilding

Bill Critchley and David Casey

Part 1: teambuilding – at what price and at what cost?

It all started during one of those midnight conversations between consultants in a residential workshop. We were running a teambuilding session with a top management group and something very odd began to appear. Our disturbing (but also exciting) discovery was that for most of their time this group of people had absolutely no need to work as a team; indeed the attempt to do so was causing more puzzlement and scepticism than motivation and commitment. In our midnight reflections we were honest enough to confess to each other that this wasn't the first time our teambuilding efforts had cast doubts on the very validity of teamwork itself, within our client groups.

We admitted that we had both been working from some implicit assumptions that good teamwork is a characteristic of healthy, effectively functioning organizations. Now we started to question those assumptions. First, we flushed out what our assumptions actually were. In essence it came down to something like this:

> We had been assuming that the top group in any organization (be it the board of directors or the local authority management committee or whatever the top group is called) should be a team and ought to work as a team. Teamwork at the top is crucial to organizational success, we assumed.

We further assumed that a properly functioning team is one in which:

- people care for each other;
- people are open and truthful;
- there is a high level of trust;
- decisions are made by consensus;
- there is strong team commitment;
- conflict is faced up to and worked through;
- people really listen to ideas and to feelings;
- feelings are expressed freely;
- process issues (task and feelings) are dealt with.

Finally, it had always seemed logical to us that a teambuilding catalyst could always help any team to function better – and so help any organization perform better as an organization. Better functioning would lead the organization to achieve its purposes more effectively.

The harsh reality we came up against was at odds with this cosy view of teams, teamwork and teambuilding. In truth the Director of Education has little need to work in harness with his fellow chief officers in a county council. He or she might need the support of the Chief Executive and the Chair of the elected members' Education Committee, but the other chief officers in that local authority have neither the expertise nor the interest, nor indeed the time, to contribute to what is essentially very specialized work.

Even in industry, whilst it is clear that the marketing and production directors of a company must work closely together to ensure that the production schedule is synchronized with sales forecasts and the finance director needs to be involved – to look at the cash flow implications of varying stock levels – they don't need to involve the *whole* team. And they certainly do not need to develop high levels of trust and openness to work through those kinds of business issues.

On the other hand, most people would agree that *strategic* decisions, concerned with the future direction of the whole enterprise, should involve all those at the top. Strategy should demand an input from every member of the top group, and for strategic discussion and strategic decision-making, teamwork at the top is essential. But how much time do most top management groups actually spend discussing strategy? Our experiences, in a wide variety of organizations, suggest that 10 per cent is a high figure for most organizations – often 5 per cent would be nearer the mark. This means that 90–95 per cent of decisions in organizations are essentially operational; that is decisions made within departments based usually on a fair amount of information and expertise. In those conditions, high levels of trust and openness may be nice, but are not necessary; consensus is strictly not an issue and in any case would take up far too much time. There is therefore no need for high levels of interpersonal skills.

Why, then, is so much time and money invested in teambuilding, we asked ourselves. At this stage in our discussions we began to face a rather disturbing possibility. Perhaps the spread of teambuilding has more to do with teambuilders and *their* needs and values rather than a careful analysis of what is appropriate and necessary for the organization. To test out this alarming hypothesis we each wrote down an honest and frank list of reasons why we ourselves engaged in teambuilding. We recommend this as an enlightening activity for other teambuilders – perhaps, like us, they will arrive at this kind of conclusion: teambuilders work as catalysts to help management groups function better as open teams for a variety of reasons, including the following:

– They like it – enjoy the risks.
– Because they are good at it.

- It's flattering to be asked.
- They receive rewarding personal feedback.
- Professional kudos – not many people do teambuilding with top teams.
- There's money in it.
- It accords with their values: for instance democracy is preferred to autocracy.
- They gain power. Process interventions are powerful in business settings where the client is on home ground and can bamboozle the consultant in business discussions.

All those reasons are concerned with the needs, skills and values of the *teambuilder* rather than the management group being 'helped'. This could explain why many teambuilding exercises leave the so-called 'management team' excited and stimulated by the experience, only to find they are spending an unnecessary amount of time together discussing other people's departmental issues. Later on, because they cannot see the benefit of working together on such issues, they abandon 'teamwork' altogether. Such a management group has been accidentally led to disillusionment with the whole idea of teamwork and the value of teambuilding.

We began to see, as our discussions went through the small hours, that there is a very *large* proportion of most managers' work where teamwork is not needed (and to attempt to inculcate teamwork is dysfunctional). There is, at the same time, a very *small* proportion of their work where teamwork is absolutely vital (and to ignore teamworking skills is to invite disaster). This latter work, which demands a team approach, is typified by strategic work but not limited to strategic work. It is any work characterized by a high level of choice and by the condition of maximum uncertainty.

Most people find choice and uncertainty uncomfortable. Many senior managers attempt to deny the choice element by the employment of complex models and techniques. We don't think most people's management experience teaches them to make choices about the future for instance; it puts the main emphasis on establishing as many facts as possible and reviewing options in the light of past experience. That's why models like, for example, the Boston portfolio model and the General Electric matrix are so popular. They provide comforting analytic frameworks for looking at strategic options, but they are appealing really to our operational mentality. The hope often is that they will magic up a solution to the strategic question. But of course they can't make choices for people and they don't throw any light on the future.

The top team of an organization, if it is to achieve quality and commitment in its decisions about future directions, will need to pool the full extent of each individual's wisdom and experience. That means something quite different from reacting to a problem in terms of their own functional knowledge and experience. It means *exposing fully* their uncertainties, taking unaccustomed risks by airing their own subjective view of the world and struggling to build some common perceptions and possibilities. This is where that much abused word 'sharing' really comes into its own. In this context it is not merely a value-laden exhortation: it is vital to the future of the organization. Ideas and opinions are all we have to inform our view of the future, but if we are to take a risk with a fragile idea or opinion, unsubstantiated by facts, we will only take it if the climate is right. Conversely, if we take the risk and the sheer airiness and vulnerability of the idea attracts a volley of ridicule and abuse, then it will die on the instant, lost forever, snuffed out like Tinkerbell.

Most functional executives, brought up in the hurly-burly of politics and inter-functional warfare, find the transition from functional to strategic mode very difficult to make. They do not always see the difference, and if they do, they are reluctant to leave their mountain top, the summit of knowledge, experience and hence power, for the equality and shared uncertainty of strategic decision making. And yet this is one area where real teamwork is not only necessary but vital.

We had now got ourselves thoroughly confused. We seemed to be forcing teambuilding on groups which had no need to be a team and missing the one area where teamwork is essential – because choice and uncertainty are at a maximum and for this very reason managers were shying away from the work – work which can *only* be done by a team. We resorted to diagrams to help clear our minds and these new diagrams form the basis of Part 2 of this chapter.

Part 2: theoretical considerations concerning management groups

We found these kinds of discussions taking us farther and farther away from teambuilding and closer and closer to an understanding of why management groups work, or don't work, in the ways they do. In the end, we developed two basic diagrams, showing the relationships between a number of variables which operate in management groups:

- the degree of uncertainty in the management task;
- the need for sharing in the group;
- modes of working;
- different kinds of internal group process;
- different levels of interpersonal skills;
- the role of the leader.

We would now like to present these two framework diagrams as diagnostic tools, which a dozen or so management groups have found very useful in coming to terms with how they work and why. These simple diagrams are helping groups see what kind of groups they are and when and if they want to be a team, rather than jumping to the conclusion that all groups need teambuilding.

Throughout the discussion, we will be talking about the management group – that is the leader plus those immediately responsible to him or her, perhaps five to ten people in all, at the top of their organization or their part of the organization.

The first diagram (Figure 23.1) shows the relationship between the level of uncertainty inherent in any group task and the need for members of that group to share with each other. Expressed simply – 'The more uncertainty – the more need to share.' Everyday examples of this truism are: children holding hands for comfort in the dark or NASA research scientists brainstorming for fresh ideas on the frontiers of human knowledge – any uncertainty, emotional, physical or intellectual, can best be coped with by sharing.

However, the converse is also true – where there is less uncertainty, there is less need to share. The same children will feel no need to hold hands round the breakfast table where all is secure; the NASA scientists during the final launch will each get on with their own well-rehearsed part of the launch programme in relative isolation from each other. Only if something goes wrong (uncertainty

Figure 23.1 The more uncertainty in its task, the more any group has to share

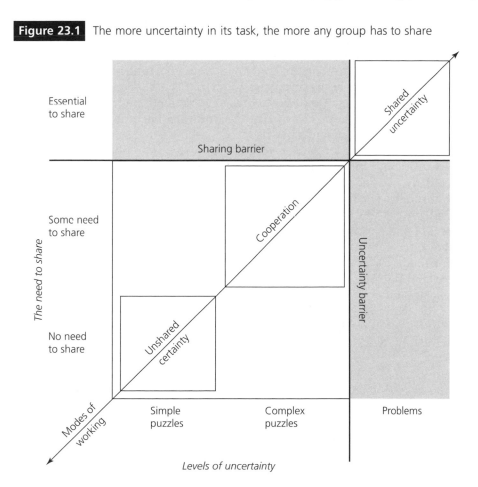

floods back) will they need to share, quickly and fully. It took us a long time to realize the full significance of that in terms of the need to share in a management group.

We are dealing here only with the top group of the organization where task is the dominant imperative. There are other situations in which other objectives demand sharing: for instance if one is dealing with the whole fabric of a complete organization and attempting a global shift in attitudes, then culture-building may become the dominant imperative and sharing at all levels in that organization may become necessary. But that is a different situation – we are focusing here on the top management group where task must be the dominant imperative.

In Figure 23.1 we have used Revans's powerful distinction between problems (no answer is known to exist) and puzzles (the answer exists somewhere – just find it) to describe different levels of uncertainty. To illustrate the difference between a problem and a puzzle – deciding about capital punishment is a problem for society; tracking down a murderer is a puzzle for the police.

Work groups dealing with genuine problems (of which strategy is only one example) would be well advised to share as much as possible with each other. They should share feelings to gain support, as well as ideas to penetrate the unknown. Figure 23.1 shows two shaded areas: *these shaded areas must be avoided.* The shaded area on the right indicates the futility of tackling real problems unless people are prepared to share. The shaded area at the top indicates that there is no point in sharing to solve mere puzzles.

Two 'barriers' appear on our model; they indicate that a positive effort must be made if a breakthrough to a new level of working is to be accomplished. For instance the uncertainty barrier represents a step into the unknown – a deliberate attempt to work in areas of ambiguity, uncertainty and ambivalence. To avoid the shaded areas and arrive in the top righthand corner, the group break through *both* barriers at the *same* time. This is the *only* way to solve genuine problems. Most management groups stay behind both barriers in Figure 23.1 and handle work which is in the nature of a puzzle – and to achieve this they cooperate, rather than share with each other. As long as they continue to limit their work to solving puzzles, they are quite right to stay within the sharing and uncertainty barriers of Figure 23.1.

As teambuilders, we now see that we must spend time identifying which modes of working any management group operates. The three modes of working come out in Figure 23.1 as the diagonal and we would like to describe each mode, by working up the diagonal from left to right:

Mode of unshared certainty. The proper mode for simple puzzles of a technical nature in everyday work where every member of the group is relatively competent within his/her field and speaks from the authority of his/her specialism. Ideal when the work issues are independent of each other – as they often are. A healthy attitude is, 'I will pull my weight and see that my part is done well.' Attitudes can become unhealthy if they move towards 'my interests must come first'.

Mode of cooperation. The appropriate mode for complex puzzles which impinge on the work of several members of the management group. In this mode (very common in local authorities) group members recognize the need for give-and-take, cooperation, negotiation and passing of information on a need-to-know basis. The attitude is, 'I'll cooperate for the good of the whole and because other members of this group have their rights and problems too.' Sharing is restricted to what is necessary and each group member still works from the security (certainty) of his/her own professional base, recognizing the professional bases of colleagues.

Mode of shared uncertainty. A rare mode. Partly because it is appropriate only for genuine problems (such as strategy) where nobody knows what to do, uncertainty is rife and full sharing between members is the only way out; partly because, even when it is the appropriate mode, many management groups never reach these professional heights. The attitude of members has to be 'the good of the whole outweighs any one member's interests – including mine. I carry an equal responsibility with my colleagues for the whole, and for this particular work I am not able to rely on my specialism, because my functional expertise is, for this problem we all face, irrelevant.'

Clearly this top mode of 'shared uncertainty' is extremely demanding and it is not surprising that many management groups try hard to avoid it. We know several boards of directors and even more local authority management 'Teams' who have devised a brilliant trick to avoid handling genuine problems requiring genuine sharing in the top mode. Quite simply – they turn all strategic problems into operational puzzles! How? There are very many variations of this trick available:

- Appoint a working party
- Ask a consultant to recommend
- Recruit a corporate planner
- Set up a think-tank, etc.

To make sure the trick works, the terms of reference are – 'Your recommendation must be short and must ask us to decide between option A or option B.' Choosing between A and B is an operational puzzle they *can* solve and it leaves them with the comfortable illusion that they have actually been engaging in strategic problem resolution work, whereas the truth is they have avoided uncertainty, avoided sharing their fears and ideas, avoided their real work, by converting frightening problems into management puzzles. And who can blame them!

We don't feel we have the right to censure top groups for not working in the top mode of shared uncertainty. We do feel we have the obligation to analyse quite rigorously how top groups actually work, before we plunge in with our teambuilding help.

In Figure 23.1 the size of the box for each mode indicates very roughly how frequently each mode might be needed by most management groups. Sadly, we see many management groups working in modes which are inappropriate to the work being done. It is not just that many top groups fail to push through a lot of the time, when they should be working in the middle mode. On the other hand other groups go through a pantomime of sitting round a table trying to work in the middle mode, but in truth feeling bored and uninterested because the middle mode is inappropriate and each member of the group could carry on separately with his or her own work, without pretending to share it with colleagues, who don't need to know anyway. In other words their appropriate mode is unshared certainty and attempts at sharing are boring or frustrating facades.

Figure 23.1 shows an arrow on both ends of the diagonal to illustrate that all three modes of working are necessary at different times and effective work groups can and should slide up and down the diagonal. We do not see any management group working in one mode all the time – the really effective group is able to move from mode to mode as the *task* requires. Although it may think of itself as a management 'team', a top group will be truly functioning as a team only when it is operating in the top mode.

We use the word team here, in the sense used in the first part of this chapter, which we believe is the sense used by most teambuilders in teambuilding work. Because we now believe that working in the top mode of shared uncertainty is called for infrequently – by the nature of the work – and is actually practised even less frequently, we now doubt the value of teambuilding work with most management groups, when there is so much more urgent work to be done with these groups.

We found in Figure 23.1 that when we plot the level of uncertainty in the work against the need to share we discover three modes of working, on the diagonal of Figure 23.1. These three modes of working are:

Unshared certainty
Cooperation
Shared uncertainty

We now want to go on to answer the questions: How does a management group work in each of these modes? What *processes* are needed, what *skills* are required, and how does the *leader* function?

The format of Figure 23.2 is the same as Figure 23.1, only the variables are different. The vertical axis of Figure 23.2 is the diagonal lifted from Figure 23.1 (modes) and two new variables are introduced – *processes* is on the horizontal axis and *interpersonal skills* becomes the new diagonal.

Processes

To start with the horizontal axis – processes. We distinguish three levels of process in any group. At the most perfunctory there are *polite social processes*, very important to sustain the social lubrication of a healthy group but not focused on the work itself. The work is accomplished largely via *task processes* – the way work is organized, distributed, ideas generated and shared, decisions

Figure 23.2 Different modes of working require different purposes

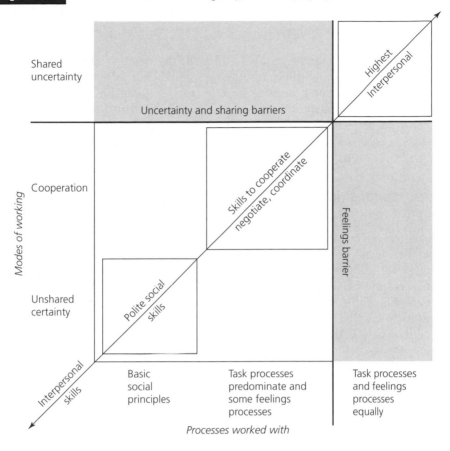

made and so forth. The third level of process concerns people's feelings *(feelings processes)* and how these are handled – by the people themselves and by others.

Reference to Figure 23.2 will make it clear that as the mode of working becomes more difficult, ascending the vertical axis, from unshared certainty towards shared uncertainty, so the processes needed to accomplish this more difficult work also become more difficult, as the group moves along the horizontal axis from simple basic social processes, through task processes, towards the much more difficult processes of working with people's deeper feelings.

Many groups never reach the top mode of shared uncertainty, where people's feelings are actually *part of the work* and all is uncertainty, excitement and trust.

The shaded areas are to be avoided (as in Figure 23.1). The righthand shaded area indicates that it is absurd to indulge in work with people's feelings if the group is working only in the two lower modes of unshared certainty and cooperation – to engage in soul-searching to accomplish this kind of work is ridiculous and brings teambuilding into disrepute. The top shaded area indicates similarly that there is no need to share deeply when only the two lower levels of processes (basic social processes and task processes) are operating.

However, a management group faced with the need to tackle uncertainty can either funk the whole thing, by staying safely behind the barriers (which is what most management groups appear to do), or it can have the courage to break through both barriers simultaneously, arriving (breathlessly) in the top righthand corner where the mode of working is shared uncertainty and the necessary processes are task *and* feelings processes together. Those few management groups which accomplish this become *teams*.

Interpersonal skills

The final variable is the diagonal of Figure 23.2 – 'interpersonal skills' – and clearly there is an ascending order of skill from the lowest (but *not* least important) level of polite social skills to the highest possible level of interpersonal skills required in the rarefied atmosphere of highest uncertainty and real teamwork. But, for the middle mode, a solid raft of straightforward interpersonal skills is needed by all managers – empathy, cooperation, communication, listening, negotiating and many more. We have come to believe that here is the greatest area of need.

The leader's role

The group leader and group leadership have not been mentioned so far, in an attempt to keep things simple. The whole question of leadership is fundamental to the operation of all management groups and we would like to make some observations now.

Leader's role in the mode of unshared certainty

The leader is hardly needed at all in the unshared certainty mode and, indeed, the social lubrication processes of a group working in this mode may well be carried out much better by an informal leader – there is nothing so embarrassing as the formal group leader bravely trying to lead the group through its Christmas lunch in the local pub!

Some local authority chief executives (so called) suffer an even worse fate – they cannot find a role at all, because the members of their management team (so called) steadfastly refuse to move out of the bottom mode of working, tacitly deciding *not* to work together and denying the Chief Executive any place in the organization at all! This is not uncommon.

Leader's role in the mode of cooperation

The leader's role in the central (cooperation) mode is well established in management convention. For example, a clear role at meetings has been universally recognized as that of enabling the leader to manage the *task* processes in particular. This role is of course the chairperson. Coordination of the task is at its core and most group leaders find this role relatively clear.

Leader's role in the mode of shared uncertainty

No such role has yet been universally recognized to deal with the processes in the highest mode, of shared uncertainty. In Britain, we have the added difficulty of our cultural resistance to working with feelings (in action learning language 'No sets please, we're British'). In this sophisticated mode of working, the word 'catalyst' seems more appropriate than the word chairperson and often a teambuilder is invited in to carry out this role. But where does this leave the group leader? All management group leaders have learned to be the chairperson; very few have yet learned to be the catalyst. And in any case, to be the catalyst and the leader at the same time is to attempt the north face of the Eiger of interpersonal skills. It can be done, but not in carpet slippers. If, on the other hand, the role of catalyst is performed by an outsider, the leadership dynamic becomes *immensely* complex and adds a significant overlay of difficulty when working in a mode which we have already shown to be extremely difficult in the first place. No wonder teambuilding often fails.

Conclusions

Many teambuilders are unaware of the shaded no-go areas and dreamily assume that any progress towards open attitudes, free expression of feelings and genuine sharing in any management group is beneficial. This is not so – to be of benefit there needs to be a very delicate and deliberate balance between what *work* the group has decided to pursue (what level of *uncertainty*) and the degree of sharing and expression of feelings the group is prepared for, to accomplish that work. Only if the balance is right will the management group be able to aim accurately at the top righthand corner of Figures 23.1 and 23.2 and succeed in breaking through all the barriers at the same time, to experience real teamwork. Attempts to push through only *one* barrier (trying to handle uncertainty without sharing; sharing for the sake of sharing; being open for the sake of being open) will fail and in failing will probably make things worse for that management group.

Strategic planners are often guilty of pushing management groups towards handling uncertainty *without* the commitment abilities to share and work with feelings. Teambuilders are often guilty of the converse sin – pushing management groups to be open and share their feelings, when the group has no intention whatever of getting into work where the level of uncertainty is high. Neither will succeed. It is no coincidence that both strategic planning and teambuilding can fall quickly into disrepute; it may be too late to save strategic planning from the management scrapheap – it is not too late to save teambuilding.

Summary: putting teambuilding in its place

The problems we described in Part 1 of this chapter centre round the dangers of consultants imposing their own values on a client management group when they engage in teambuilding work, instead of first finding out how that management group actually works, its context within the organization, and hence what it really needs.

In Part 2 we developed a diagnostic tool, in the form of two figures, which in the hands of a management group will enable it to understand how it actually works, and will provide it with a means of articulating the kind of group it wants to become, starting unequivocally from an analysis of its role and purpose and the work it has to do, rather than from some prior assumptions or values about how a management group 'should' work.

Some people will argue that management groups cannot even begin to engage with each other in any kind of serious work, such as for example establishing what the key tasks are, until they have first built a degree of openness and trust. We would disagree on two counts.

In the first place, as our figures illustrate, high levels of openness and trust are only rarely needed, and management groups get most of their work done very well without them, preferring for safety and comfort to remain relatively closed, and, covertly at least, distrustful. To ask such groups to make a major cultural shift, to take such big risks with each other as to be fully open and trusting, requires some mighty cogent justification.

Secondly, we have a theoretical objection to starting with feelings. Most management groups are likely to be task-centred, to be working at an intellectual rather than an emotional level. Approaching such a group suddenly at an emotional level will either generate shock, pain, distrust and confusion, or will produce a warm, cosy, euphoric, one-off experience. In either case it will often be followed by rejection of the approach and its sponsor, the teambuilder.

So we are suggesting to all would-be teambuilders, that if their purpose is to be one of real *value to their clients*, they start by encouraging their clients to clarify the role and purpose of the management group in question, to identify the nature of the tasks which they need to address *as a group* – complex puzzles or real problems – and then to consider the appropriate modes of working, and the skills and processes which go with them. When we have reached this stage, most of us have the skills and technologies to provide what is needed. What is often left out is the diagnostic work that gets us to this stage.

24 Top management teams and organizational renewal

David K. Hurst, James C. Rush and Roderick E. White

Increasingly the makeup of the top management group is believed to affect the development, identification and exploitation of strategic opportunities. This chapter explains a creative management model, which goes beyond conventional strategic management, and identifies the behaviours of top managers needed for the ongoing renewal of their business. It is proposed that these behaviours cluster and can be aligned with different and distinct cognitive styles or types. The implication is that top management groups should be composed of a mix of types. This chapter posits a mix of Jungian types: Intuitives, Feelers, Thinkers and Sensors. This diversity can yield great strength if the differences can be focused and unified. Propositions and suggestions for further empirical research are developed.

The strategic management (SM) framework which has evolved over the past 40 years and has come to dominate North American thinking about the principal functions of senior managers has, more recently, been the subject of a good deal of criticism, both from practitioners (Peters and Waterman, 1983) and theoreticians (Weick, 1979; Pascale, 1984). It seems that while the conventional SM process allows managers to maintain, direct and improve existing activities, it is less able to promote and accommodate the radical ideas and innovative behaviours needed to renew established businesses. Indeed it may be counterproductive in this regard.

With its emphasis on problem-solving, the SM framework implicitly stresses the role of the senior, synoptic, singular executive: one individual, or group with an established understanding of how the business functions. Within this group there exists a shared 'cause map' (Weick, 1979) or 'dominant logic' (Prahalad and Bettis, 1986): a structure of knowledge about their business, which for them defines 'rationality'. Facts which can be plotted onto this map of the business are accepted; data which cannot be assigned coordinates are not perceived, are ignored if they are perceived or are treated as an aberration.

For the top management group, behaviours consistent with rational thought are implied. Individuals predisposed to plan, act and evaluate would fit; others, with different behavioural predispositions, would not. Intuition, insight and feelings are suppressed because they do not fit within the accepted SM process. Individuals openly exhibiting these types of behaviours cannot be accommodated within the conventional SM framework and are often excluded from the process, even though their contributions may be valuable. SM fits the people within its rational-analytic procedures, rather than expanding the process to fit the people, and their different abilities, predispositions and preferences.

For these reasons dissatisfaction with the SM framework has increased, resulting in a renewed focus on the top management group, the dominant coalition (Cyert and March, 1963), as it impacts firm strategy and organizational performance. As Hambrick (1987: 88) explains: 'This view contends that performance of an organization is ultimately a reflection of its top managers.' Implicitly this view holds that when it comes to understanding strategy and performance, the people are equally as important, and perhaps more important, than the process. But neither is this view entirely satisfactory, for it ignores the processes needed by any large organization to make decisions and take concerted action. Even more importantly, it lacks a sense of the role and function of the executive group.

The composition or form of the top management group needs to be related to its function. Barnard (1938: 215) contends: 'Executive work is not that of the organization, but the specialized work of maintaining the organization in operations.' When narrowly interpreted, this view can be construed as supporting the limited plan–act–evaluate functions for the executive implicit in the SM model. However, in any changing, competitive environment, long-term maintenance/existence of the business requires the ongoing (re)creation of the business and the logic by which it is managed. This renewal, too, is a critical executive function.

Large organizations require a process for taking concerted actions. The broad-based adoption of SM technology suggests it has fulfilled a need in this regard. We must be careful not to discard, out of hand, even a partially useful process. The SM model is powerful because it prescribes a process, as well as a function (or functions), for the top management group within that process. However, the process and prescribed functions are limited and do not take advantage of the full range of human cognitive abilities. The SM framework is not so much incorrect as incomplete. A broader perspective on the top management process, an enhanced model, taking more complete advantage of the human potential, could help bridge the gap between the appropriate function of the executive and the makeup of the top management group.

Beyond strategic management

Stepping back and viewing the question from a philosophical perspective, the SM framework's principal shortcoming is its base in a naive realism. It tacitly assumes that reality is given which exists 'out there' and is accessible through our senses. These sensations, these supposed objective perceptions or facts, can then be subjected to rational thought. Although the need for action is recognized, it is regarded largely as the servant of thought. Facts evaluated by a rational analytic thinking process are regarded as more important than insight, feelings and even empirical experience! The classic SM framework emphasizes the use of conscious, analytic thought processes to the exclusion of any other, even though non-rational or, to use Barnard's word, 'non-logical' processes and their importance have long been recognized (Barnard, 1938; McKenny and Keen, 1974; Mintzberg, 1976).

Hurst (1986) suggested that the emphasis of the SM framework on logic and rationality precludes it from being helpful in the innovative, creative processes which allow organizations to enact fundamental change, to renew themselves. Logic and rationality depend upon normative structures based in the past, and methodologies such as SM which appeal to norms of rationality – measurability, efficiency, consistency – perpetuate the past. In short, because SM is based on a logic developed from past experiences, it is an appropriate methodology for defending an established business, but is less able to prospect. It cannot deal well with novelty and ambiguity; it cannot bring into being these new activities which lie outside the structure of the managers' current understanding of their existing business but which may well be required as part of tomorrow's business.

A classic example of a flawed logic based upon past experiences is illustrated by the actions of Sewell Avery, CEO of Montgomery Ward following World War II. Avery convinced himself, based upon a study of economic history and his own experiences after World War I, that economic depressions followed wars. Based on this logic, Montgomery Ward, in the years following 1945, did not expand, and even deferred basic maintenance expenditures in order to preserve cash for the anticipated depression. Meanwhile Robert Wood at Sears correctly perceived the 'tremendous foundation of purchasing power that had been held back by the war'. Sears expanded aggressively to become the dominant US department store chain. Avery was forced to depart Ward in 1955 (Worthy, 1984: 219).

The Avery story provides a simple, yet dramatic, example of a flawed logic retrospectively derived from past experiences. The complex of logics and their relationships underlying a sophisticated SM approach in any large organization are many, subtle and difficult to surface. However, business redefinition requires a shift in the logic that is embedded in any well-developed SM process. Conventional SM incorporates no means to unlearn what has been learnt, although there have been developments in this direction (de Geus, 1988). To deal conceptually with this shortcoming, Hurst (1986) has extended the SM framework to encompass what he calls the creative management model (CMM).

The creative management model

The creative management (CM) model is built on the philosophical assumption that the real world which surrounds the organization is a dynamic construct enacted by the members of the organization over time. This view is shared by Weick (1979: 228). As he explains: 'the environment is viewed as an output rather than an input. On the basis of enactments and interpretations people construct a belated picture of some environment that could have produced these actions.' Organizational realities, like personal realities, consist of complex interactions of the objective, tangible ('out there') and the subjective, cognitive ('in here') elements.

Implicit in the CM model is the assertion that organizations capable of creating tomorrow's businesses while maintaining today's will require a diverse group of senior managers, able to perceive the world differently, yet able to participate in the process that transcends these different views to enact a complex organizational reality. In the CM framework the emphasis is on top management teams which can envision, or recognize and frame, new opportunities, as well as solve or exploit them (Bower, 1982). By embracing recognition, opportunity-framing and problem-solving, the CM model subsumes strategic management and provides additional insights into the composition, leadership and processes of top management teams.

As illustrated in Figure 24.1, the CM process is conceived of as passing though four levels or modes of cognition. When (subjective) time is considered, the model incorporates seven recursive and not necessarily completely sequential stages whereby an original idea is transformed from an intuitive insight, a vision, into action, eventually to become a remembered 'reality'. Tracking the progress of an idea from its original conception to its final realization helps to explain the model. The classic SM model deals explicitly with only Stages 3 through 5, the 'plan–act–evaluate' stages. Because it does not consider the cognitive levels of intuition and feeling, the SM framework is unable to supply insight into the nature of recognition by organizations. How do organizations come to fundamentally new approaches to the way they go about their business? How do they learn? By ignoring the other stages in the

Figure 24.1 The creative management model

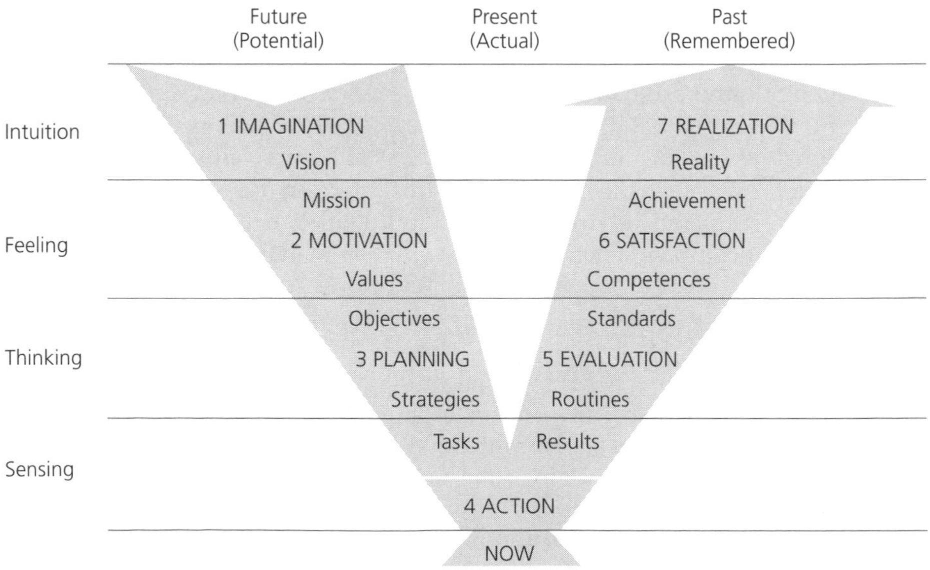

process and overemphasizing the linear, in what is in fact recursive process, the SM paradigm misses key aspects of the creative learning process.

The CM model makes it clear that strategic thinking (Stage 3) does not take place without antecedents. It is based heavily upon earlier expectations and past experiences (Stages 4 through 7), modified by what happens in Stages 1 and 2. In addition, rationality depends on logic structures developed after action. People, and organizations, truly understand (Stage 5) only after they act (Stage 4), not before. Anything else is speculation. The model makes it clear that radical innovation (Stage 1) represents a break with the thought structures, the logic of the past. Initially, an innovation will not be based on rationality and logic because the supporting conceptual structures are not yet in place. Conversely, highly structured thought, as well as tradition, can interfere with, and inhibit, insight and innovation.

Thus, in the CM model a strategy is initially a *post hoc* rationalization of a successful activity. As Weick (1979: 188) explains:

The only thing that can be selected and preserved is something that is already there. This simple reality keeps getting lost amidst the preoccupation of people in organizations with planning, forecasting, anticipating and predicting. . . . Organizations formulate strategy after they implement it, not before. . . . The more common (and misleading) way to look at this sequence in organizations is to say that first comes strategy and then comes implementation. That commonplace recipe ignores the fact that meaning is always imposed after elapsed actions are available for review.

As the activity becomes standardized, feedback from Stage 5 to Stage 3 occurs. Successful behaviours are interpreted into a causal model which drives the organization's routines and corrects deviations from course.

By making explicit the dimension of time the CM model allows the renewal function to be seen as a learning process. The time dimension in Figure 24.1 is not the objective time of physics but subjective time, views of the future and memories of the past as seen from the perpetual 'now' in which all human cognitive systems function (Jacques, 1982). With subjective time the creative process can be seen to be a learning process whereby successful innovations within an organization, new logics for doing business, are institutionalized and made routine. Not all organizations, and more particularly not all top management groups, are necessarily equally adept at, and receptive to, the development of new logics. These biases may be reflected in the organization's pattern of actions: its strategy.

There is more to the CM model than the capacity for prospective or retrospective thought. The model, as shown in Figure 24.1, contends that different modes of cognition are dominant at different levels in the process. These different modes are believed to have an underlying relationship with subjective time orientation; sensing may be associated more with the present, intuition more with the future (Mann *et al.*, 1971) and one might also suspect with the remembered past (in contrast to the experience of the present). But, more fundamentally, these different modes are believed to represent distinct cognitive preferences.

Cognitive modes

The different levels in the CM model are related to and emphasize different modes of cognition corresponding to the four fundamental psychological functions outlined by Jung (1960).

These processes are arranged by CM level and function in Table 24.1. Jung contends that while all individuals have the capacity for, and make use of, all four modes, each has a dominant function. The Myers–Briggs Type Indicator (MBTI) (Myers, 1962) has been used extensively as a measure of an individual's preference on each of these four functions.

The two information gathering modes are Sensation (5) and Intuition (N). Sensation mediates the perception of physical stimuli via the five senses. Through Sensation an individual becomes conscious that something exists physically. Intuition, on the other hand, mediates perception via what is thought to be an unconscious patterning process – the individual goes beyond the differentiations yielded by the Sensation process to see the whole of physical phenomena (Extrovert preference), or the world of ideas (Introvert preference). By allowing the detection of gaps between perceived parts this mode gives individuals the ability to see unrealized potential within the stream of events which surround them. Sensation and Intuition then are opposite but complementary mental processes used to gather information about the world.

The two information evaluation modes are Thinking (T) and Feeling (F). Each mode appeals to a different type of evaluative process. Thinking links ideas impersonally using logic and notions of cause and effect. Feeling, on the other hand, bases evaluation on personal and group values. As Jung makes clear, Thinking and Feeling are complementary functions for the evaluation of information, just as Sensing and Intuition are complementary processes used in the gathering of information. Each process within a pair is in tension with the other, but it can be a creative tension. Subjective time is the dimension which mediates the tension. It is these functions or layers which creative management must transcend.

Table 24.1 Level In the CM and cognitive model

| CM level | Function | |
	Information gathering	Information evaluation
I	INTUITION	
II		FEELING
III		THINKING
IV	SENSATION	

The levels in the CM process are layered to reflect the renewal function of the executive as it relates to Jung's cognitive functions. Sensing deals with physical stimuli, action and reaction, in the here and now. Behaviours based simply on sensation can be thought of as reflexive; a stimulus evokes an instinctive or reflex response. Actions, other than reflex responses, have input from higher levels. For example, the thinking-planning level will, based upon accepted logics, delineate tasks to guide action. The results of actions taken also feed back into the thinking/evaluation activity. Sensing and thinking are adjacent layers in the model because, prescriptively, prospective thinking precedes, and retrospective analysis, or sensemaking, follows action.

At the intuitive level a vision or insight into a new way of doing business does not by itself result in action. Because it is outside the established logic of the business, it cannot be evaluated by the thinking process. Therefore its worth, whether positive or negative, cannot be logically derived and must be based upon personal or group values. A positive feeling must be created for the idea if it is to overcome the established logic, result in action and thus change the understanding of the business. Accordingly, the Feeling mode is positioned between the Intuition and Thinking layers in the model.

The layering in the CM model is based upon Jung's conception of the 'psychological functions' for several reasons. This conception may be related to basic human physiology. As Taggart and Robey (1981: 189) point out, 'Jung's theory of personality identifies two dimensions of human information processing that seem directly related to right and left brain activity.' Typically, Sensing and Thinking are left hemisphere related and Intuition and Feeling right hemisphere related. This duality and Jung's conception may have deep and perhaps related roots in human information processing, psychology and philosophy. Although there are other cognitive typologies (Hampden-Turner, 1981; Gardener, 1985) on which a model of creative management could be built, in our estimation none has as strong a conceptual and philosophical base for this application. However, in the last analysis this model will be judged by its utility; the meaningful implications it has for the practice of management.

Top managers' behaviours and cognitive preference

The conceptual linkages between the creative management process, cognitive mode and behaviours are sketched in Table 24.2. Although the empirical relationships require further validation the table is adapted from existing empirical evidence (Myers, 1962; Keirsey and Bates, 1978; Macdaid et al., 1986). There are other possible arrangements of type (Mitroff and Kilmann, 1975; Keirsey and Bates, 1978). However, they tend to be finer-grained, employing more mixed preferences than the four utilized in Table 24.2, which seem to depict the most natural flow through the stages of the creative management process.

The cognitive preferences, or types, outlined above cover the spectrum of ways in which information is gathered and evaluated by individuals. In Table 24.2 each type has been associated with a particular cluster of behaviours and

Table 24.2 Relationship between cognitive preferences and behaviours

Level in CM process	Cognitive preference	Concerned with	Handle these with	Tends to be	Examples of behaviours
I	Intuition	Possibilities and patterns, ideas	Metaphors and symbols	Ingenious and integrative	Sees what others do not. Espouses new ways of working at things. Proposes new ideas. Disregards practical details. Describes with metaphors and symbols. Creates organizational stories and myths.
II	Feeling	People and values	Force of personality	Enthusiastic and insightful	Inspires peers and subordinates. Responds to a challenge. Sponsors new ideas. Shares information, power and resources. Brings people together. Rewards with recognition and praise. Promulgates organizational stories and myths.
III	Thinking	Cause and effect things	Regulations and language	Reliable and orderly	Matches goals and resources to results (i.e. plans). Organizes people; coordinates. Balances novel with routine. Rewards when outcome exceeds plan.
IV	Sensation	Activities, events	Spontaneity and action	Adaptable and practical	Matches skills to tasks. Attention to practical details. Makes things work. Describes what has occurred in concrete terms. Results are their own reward.

Source: Adapted from Myers (1962) and Keirsey and Bates (1978)

positioned within the layers of the CM model. The implication is that to effectively handle a creative process a management group needs these different behaviours, and accordingly should be composed of individuals with the different cognitive preferences. Although individuals may be able to exhibit a variety of behaviours it is unlikely they will be equally able at each set of behaviours, or indifferent amongst them. They will have a preference.

Of course, cognitive preference is not the only factor to consider in forming a top management team. The model does not indicate the sources of the raw material for cognition, what information is gathered (and evaluated). However, it is reasonable to expect that, within limits, variety in output (actions) is related to variety of input (information). Much of the information available to a top management group will be directly related to the personal background and experience of team members. Simon (1988: 16) contends that 'expertness is the prerequisite to creativity'. He suggests that experts have 50,000 'chunks' of knowledge in their area of expertise which it takes at least 10 years of experience to acquire. But not every expert (with 50,000 chunks of knowledge in a given area) can necessarily use that knowledge creatively.

Indeed, as Koestler (1976) reports, often the insight occurs after the idea generators have dissociated themselves from the specifics of the puzzle they are attempting to solve. James Watson (1969), whose insight uncovered the double-helix structure of DNA, recounts his need to remove himself from data derived from months of chemical and X-ray experiments, while Francis Crick, his co-researcher, felt a need to remain immersed in the data. (Sensation-Thinking Preference versus Intuition-Thinking Preference?)

> The next few days saw Francis becoming increasingly agitated by my failure to stick close to the molecular models. . . . Almost every afternoon, knowing that I was on the tennis court, he would fretfully twist his head away from his work to see the polynucleotide backbone unattended . . . Francis' grumbles did not disturb me, however, because further refining of our latest backbone without a solution to the bases would not represent a real step forward. (Watson, 1969: 114)

None of this is to diminish the importance of expertise acquired through diligence and hard work, but rather to suggest that other factors are also at work. We would argue that individual cognitive preference merits consideration. The involvement of different cognitive preferences at different stages in the process and linking the stages together over time has not received the attention it deserves, either in theory or in practice.

Creative management: a need for integration

The argument has been made above that an effective CM process requires different behaviours, and therefore cognitive styles consistent with the roles implicit in the different layers of the CM model. With such differentiation in cognitive orientations comes a need for integration (Lawrence and Lorsch,

1969) – a way of allowing for, or facilitating, the exchanges necessary to bring about coherent action. The most efficient means of achieving the required integration depends on the type of interdependence (Thompson, 1967; Galbraith, 1973). As illustrated in Table 24.3, the CM process presents different types of interdependences between its different levels.

In explaining the interdependences it is helpful to make the simplifying assumption of a different individual at each level. Even though radically new ideas may be stimulated by certain antecedent conditions, they seem to be the independent creation of a single mind (with intuitive preferences and abilities) (Koestler, 1976). Generating new insights is not thought to be a group activity. Once discerned, the exchange between the intuitive, idea generator, and the feeler would appear to be reciprocal. If the feeler is to inspire and energize the organization, the feeler and idea generator must talk face to face. (They can, of course, be one and the same person.) The feeler must appreciate the idea sufficiently well to move it forward. This requires the feeler to listen to, and question, the idea generator. Also it is likely that articulating the idea causes the idea generator to better define his or her 'vision'.

Because the idea cannot be evaluated logically the feeler must not only communicate it to the thinker, but also create a sense of energy and excitement about the idea. The thinker can then prepare for implementation. This relationship is also a reciprocal type of interdependence, but may tend towards the sequential as the link between idea generator and feeler may need to be richer impersonally than the link between feeler and thinker. Given the nature of the task, and their concern for people, feelers are likely to use task forces to accomplish the necessary integration.

Table 24.3 Integrating cognitive types and levels within the creative management process

Level	Cognitive type	Concern	Integrative mechanism	Type of interdependence
I	Intuitive	Patterns and ←—— possibilities, ideas	Individual's perceptive abilities	Independent
		|←————————	Informal, face-to-face	Reciprocal
II	Feeler	People		
		|←————————	Task forces	Reciprocal/ sequential
III	Thinker	Cause and effect, plans		
		|←————————	Policies, procedures, rules, hierarchy	Sequential
IV	Sensor	Activities, events		

The link between thinkers and sensors can be more sequential. Once the thinker has 'planned' for implementation, the sensor's role (doing) can be communicated by policy, procedures, rules and specification of tasks (hierarchy). However, to the extent that the new idea requires new tasks which are in conflict with established and accepted routines it will be important for the sensor also to have enthusiasm for the initiative.

Such sequencing of interdependent activities may represent a normative ideal; it is not necessarily descriptive of practice. For example, feelers may bypass thinkers, interacting directly with sensors, 'bootlegging' the initial implementation of the creative idea. At the thinking level plans may be developed only after early implementation, not before. Of course, this is more likely to happen when the thinkers in the top management group are wedded to their established plans based upon existing logics and are unwilling to experiment with novel approaches.

This sequence also recognizes that the dominant coalition may not be a group in the social psychological sense, where all members have frequent face-to-face interactions. Rather, it may be a series of interchanges over (objective) time between individuals, each with a predisposition for certain behaviours. These interchanges are the result of complex stimuli, and detailed consideration of them is beyond the scope of this chapter. However, evidence from Belbin's (1981) work with groups of managers in a business simulation suggest that effective groups had members (Belbin called them Chairman and Teamworker) concerned with transcending individual differences and facilitating the process. In our framework such individuals would be oriented towards integrating the levels of the CM process amongst people and organizational units, and over time.

Power and influence in the creative management process

The CM model has significant implications for the study and practice of processes through which power and influence are exercised within organizations. In the SM model the communication channels and relationships considered important in the exercise of power are those of the formal organization hierarchy. This is consonant with the framework's underlying philosophy – if reality exists objectively and is accessible to rational instruments, then where else can the many partial views be integrated except in the synoptic mind of the CEO/strategist? For only he or she has the panoramic view of reality by virtue of a superior position at the apex of the organization. Information flows up, directives down. In contrast the CM model stresses rich and fluid communication channels and relationships making up the 'neural' network, a cognitive framework within which the organization will scan, describe and develop its version of reality.

How then should an organization in search of renewal proceed? The interaction patterns required for renewal assume a broad distribution of influence within the management team, and that all cognitive types are represented. No single cognitive mode dominates the ongoing negotiation process. In support of this view Friedlander (1983: 200) states that sustained 'power imbalances diminish [the benefits of] heterogeneity and contact and thereby diminish system learning'.

This does not necessarily mean power should, or will, be uniformly and statically distributed. Rather, power must shift according to the 'authority of the situation' (Follett, 1941). At the outset, when the issue is highly ambiguous, the intuitive mode is required and those individuals with significant capacity in this area should assume more influence, regardless of their hierarchical level within the formal organization. As the renewal process moves to the feeling dimension the motivation of the team becomes critical. Individuals capable of evoking and expressing shared values should now have more influence. The intuitives, while still involved, would exhibit less influence. Subsequently as the task shifts to planning and action the process requires that thinkers and sensors become predominant. Thus, in an ideal process, each cognitive type assumes influence as determined by the needs of the evolving renewal process. The relationship between the individual in the (temporarily) dominant role and the rest of the team has been described by Greenleaf (1977) as *primus inter pares*, first amongst equals. Like strands in a tapestry, now in the front, now in the back, individuals of the team together weave a cognitive fabric, the pattern of which will express their version of a renewed organizational reality.

What happens when a cognitive type is not available on the team? Theoretically, a cognitive (and therefore behavioural) void exists. There is no one with the cognitive preference needed to influence the renewal process in the desired way at a particular stage. If, however, there exists within the group an awareness of the need for different types of cognition and behaviour, as well as some capacity to perform the role, then it is possible that one or more members of the team may spontaneously assume the 'vacant' role. In this process of self-organization the renewal process proceeds by evoking the needed but less preferred cognitive processes from members of the management team. Organizational adaption and individual learning are combined.

Implications for top management groups

The CM model generates a number of insights into the composition of, and processes within, top management teams. From a prescriptive point of view, the CM model suggests that an 'ideal' top management group would be made up of individuals capable of functioning in each of the four cognitive modes. Since individuals seem to have stable cognitive preferences (Myers and McCaulley, 1985), an 'ideal' team needs several different 'types' of individuals to assume the variety of roles required. The general implication is that in addition to the Sensing and Thinking modes implied by the SM model, Intuition and Feeling modes are required by the CM model. All four modes need to be represented within the effective top management group and utilized in the management process.

From a descriptive point of view, cognitive composition might be expected to evolve as an organization matures. One would expect founders of organizations to be predominantly intuitive in their gathering of information, and to evaluate information using the feeling mode. As organizations mature, intuition and feeling would be expected to give way to sensation and thinking. Although it need not necessarily be the case, the latter style can easily drive out the former. This occurs most dramatically when founders leave (or are forced out) and replaced by 'professional managers', those trained in the SM methodology. More generally, differences in composition within the top management group can be expected to change as an organization develops, and these differences are expected to yield different patterns of behaviour. However, the actions of an organization are not directly impacted by the cognitive preferences of this group and the integration of these behaviours into a pattern of organizational actions which impacts strategy and performance.

Business strategy and the creative management model

The CM model is basically an adaptive process and, as such, relates best to strategy concepts, which share this perspective. For example, Miles and Snow (1978: 21) recognized that 'The strategic-choice approach essentially argues that the effectiveness of organizational adaption hinges on *the dominant coalition's perceptions* of environmental conditions and the decisions it makes concerning how the organization will cope with these conditions' (emphasis added). Based upon their empirical observations, Miles and Snow (1978: 14) identified four patterns of behaviour which they reduced to four strategic archetypes, 'representing alternative ways of moving through the adaptive cycle'. These are defender, prospector, analyser and reactor. Unfortunately, Miles and Snow do not link these types to their underlying concern with the perceptual abilities of the dominant coalition. And while they recognize prospectors as more innovative and willing to experiment with new ideas than their other strategy types, they do not provide much insight into how perceptions impact this process. Furthermore, there is little sense of how established business logics are changed, how unconventional ideas are incorporated into established business strategies. They do not directly address the question of renewal.

In our view, truly prospecting organizations have dominant coalitions which search for new ways of doing business and continually use visions of possible futures, ideas about new and different ways of doing business, to feed forward into present behaviour and actions. By contrast, in preserving organizations past norms and traditions feed back to dominate present behaviour. As shown in Figure 24.2, when viewed in this way, the CM model can be used to distinguish between organizations with a preference for either prospecting or preserving strategies.

The management groups in both prospecting and preserving organizations are oriented towards the intuition and feeling levels of the CM model. Preserving managements are able, with their intuitive ability, to perceive

Figure 24.2 Strategy and the creative management model

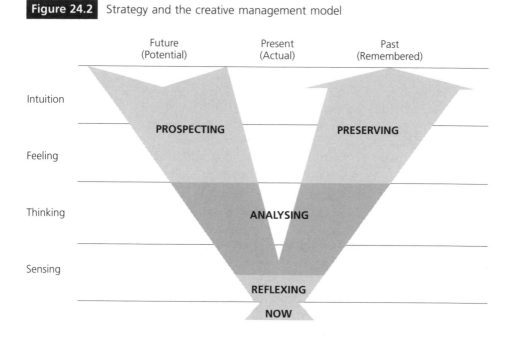

patterns in past decisions, actions and events: and by way of their feeling level they extract and express meaning from their firm's past. They have a strong sense of history and tradition; 'what we have been'. Their orientation is towards the past. Prospective management use the same cognitive abilities (intuition and feeling) but focus them on the future; 'what we might become'. Although both types of organization must function in the perpetual 'now', they do so with different (subjective) time orientations; the managements of prospecting organizations are oriented towards the potential of what might be, the future; in the preserving organization the orientation is towards the remembrance of what has been, the realized vision, the past.

Prospecting organizations can be expected to be radical innovators, willing to experiment with new ideas that do not fit within the accepted logic for business. In preserving organizations realized vision and tradition guide action, resulting in an adherence to past strategies; even incremental adjustments may be difficult because intentions and results are evaluated against values (at the feeling level), not standards derived from a logic (at the thinking level). Both of these strategies, because vision and values drive behaviours, often lack the coherence in their actions that is provided by the thinking-planning level. Furthermore, these organizations are not highly responsive to direct environmental stimuli.

Within the context of the CM model, the dominant coalition of an analysing organization can be seen as more oriented towards the present than either their preserving or prospecting counterparts. It also functions more at the thinking and sensing levels; less so at the intuition and feeling levels. As a consequence the management of an analysing organization is less accepting of radical, unproven ideas than the pure prospecting organization, but also less bound by tradition than a preserving organization. Accordingly, the analysing organization is less likely to be first with a radical innovation, although it may follow an initiative of a prospecting firm once it can be rationalized. It is not just the (subjective) time orientation of the management of an analysing organization that prevents it from pursuing radical innovations. This inability is also bound up in the interrelated issue of their preferred or dominant cognitive function: thinking and sensing. The management of an analysing organization functions more at the thinking and sensing levels, and therefore needs to develop a plausible logic before action. However, the actions they do take are well planned and a coherent extension of the established logic.

The remaining strategy orientation outlined in Figure 24.2 is the reflexing organization. Reflexing organizations (and their managers) exist only in the here and now. They have no view of their firm's future, nor sense of its past. Their behaviours are guided by instinctive or reflex responses to given stimuli. They do not attempt to understand their behaviours and actions, either before or after these actions occur. They function solely at the sensation level. Such organizations are highly responsive to a given set of environmental stimuli, but should the environment and the appropriate response pattern change these organizations are unable to adapt, to learn new behaviours.

Given the strategy types identified within the CM model – prospecting, analysing, reflexing and preserving – what are the corresponding organizational attributes? Consistent with Miles and Snow's original observation about the importance of the dominant coalition's perceptions, the CM model links perception and cognitive preferences, suggesting that the composition of the top management teams and their mix of cognitive and time orientations is the key to understanding this conception of organization strategy.

Prescriptively it would appear that organizations able to renew themselves need some of the attributes of each strategy orientation. The ideal management team needs both prospecting and preserving abilities; these combine a basis in its past with the ability to create its future. This is the problem of renewal: preserving the core of the business while allowing for the ongoing redefinition of that core. Like Janus, the Roman god of the threshold, truly adaptive organizations and their management teams simultaneously look forward, and create their future; and back, and appreciate their past. However, they also strive to understand their actions, and anticipate outcomes while being responsive to environmental stimuli. Even though a balance of all strategy orientations might be desirable, it seems likely that most organizations, like most individuals, will have a distinct preference.

Strategy and the composition of top management

The composition and interactions of the top management group affect behaviours which are ultimately reflected in the decisions and actions of the organization. Therefore, differences in composition of the management group should be manifested in patterns of action, that is, in strategies (Mintzberg, 1978). The behaviours of the dominant coalition derived from the CM model can be related to the different cognitive types. Accordingly, relationships between the makeup of top management group and the strategic types of Preserving, Analysing, Reflexing and Prospecting can be hypothesized (see Table 24.4). The assertions made are largely descriptive. Prescriptive statements require a link to behaviours, patterns of actions and performance.

On causality

To this point the discussion has been largely conceptual, linking cognitive styles, behaviours, team composition and decisions and actions. However, it is recognized that other factors, like personal background and skills, influence managerial behaviours; as do organizational context factors, such as hierarchy, norms, rules, and decision-making style.

Empirical evidence

A complete review of the empirical work related to the CM model and top management team composition is beyond the scope of this chapter. However, this section will examine some of the existing work, much of which indirectly supports aspects of the CM framework.

Much research has focused on the relationship between background characteristics of managers and firm performance. After an extensive review of this literature Hambrick and Mason (1984: 203) observed: 'It is doubtful that this research stream can progress far without greater attention to relevant literature in related fields, especially psychology and social psychology.' This

Table 24.4 Hypothesized relationship between cognitive composition of the dominant coalition and business strategy

	Dominant coalition's	
Cognitive composition	Time orientation	Strategy orientation
Mostly Intuitives with some Feelers	Future	Prospecting
Mostly Thinkers with some Sensors	Near term future and past	Analysing
Mostly Sensors	Now	Reflexing
Mostly Feelers with some Intuitives	Past	Preserving
Mix of Intuitives, Feelers, Thinkers and Sensors	Future ⟷ past	Renewing

chapter attempts to progress from a psychological base while forging the link to decisions and patterns of action (i.e. strategy) for the enterprise. For the sake of simplicity and brevity, the discussion of empirical support for the model will focus on key relationships.

Team composition → decisions/actions/performance

Miles and Snow (1978) observed patterns in action, strategies, consistent with the CM process. Moreover, their strategy typology has been found to be reasonably descriptive of observed strategic attributes (Hambrick, 1983b). However, their observations about the composition of the dominant coalition are limited to functional backgrounds. For Defenders they note that the dominant coalition was typically composed of the general managers, the controller, and the heads of production and sales. They go on to state: 'the Prospector's dominant coalition centres around the marketing and research and development functions. Moreover, the Prospector's dominant coalition is also larger, more diverse and more transitory than the Defender's.' Their rationale is based upon the fit between managerial skills and the technical task requirements of the strategy. Although relationships have been observed between functional background and cognitive preference (McKenny and Keen, 1974; Macdaid *et al.*, 1986) no link was made by Miles and Snow to underlying psychological or cognitive attributes of the top management group.

Individual differences within top management teams such as age (Child, 1974), functional track record, education (Kimberley and Evanisko, 1981) and job tenure (Carlson, 1972) have been studied. These variables are usually recognized as proxy for some underlying psychological dimension (e.g. cognitive style, time orientation, tolerance for ambiguity), and used because they are more easily measured. In reviewing the literature on the relationship between background characteristics of top managers and organizational actions and performance, Hambrick and Mason (1984) developed a list of propositions based on demonstrated associations. However, this approach has several problems. First and foremost, the propositions lack a consistent conceptual view of the top management group and its role in moving the organization forward. Second, the variables are not clearly related to broader theories of personality, or behaviour. Third, despite the observation that the group and group heterogeneity are significant factors, most of the work in this area seems to view the group as uniform. Most work employs either an average measure for attributes of the top management group, or selects one executive, usually the general manager, as singularly important.

A major empirical study associating underlying psychological variables and team performance was done by Belbin (1981). He administered a battery of psychological tests to executives taking part in a management training course. During this course, managers participated in business simulations. Team composition was varied and performance was measured. Evidence from this research suggests that:

1. The effectiveness of a team will be promoted by the extent to which members correctly recognize and adjust themselves to the relative strengths within the team, both in expertise and ability to engage in specific team-roles.
2. Personal qualities fit members for some team-roles while limiting the likelihood that they will succeed in others (Belbin, 1981: 132–3).

Belbin's work, although illuminating and highly descriptive, was not done in managerial settings. Neither was it a test, nor development of a theory of management team effectiveness.

Some work on team composition and effectiveness using Jungian types has been conducted. Blaylock (1983), employing a production simulation with business students, formed 17 groups, four mixed complementary types and 13 compatible or relatively uniform types. Three of the four mixed groups finished in the top five, a significant relationship.

The assertion that heterogeneous groups are more effective than homogeneous groups is not new. Filley *et al.* (1976) surveyed the literature on group dynamics and concluded that novel problems are best handled by a heterogeneous group and routine problems most efficiently dealt with by a homogeneous group. A concurring note was stated by Ziller (1972). Reviewing studies from further afield, he too found that performance is enhanced in groups with heterogeneity in membership. Rather than differentiate on problem types, he suggested that short-term groups ought to have homogeneous membership while long-standing groups have heterogeneous membership. He concluded that heterogeneity on a wide variety of variables including race, age, ability and personality and training in group dynamics, improved productivity.

Indeed, the outstanding question pertains not so much to the situational conditions favouring heterogeneity but rather to the appropriate dimensions for the heterogeneity, given the issues being considered. Addressing this question requires a conceptual perspective. The perspective of the CM model links the executive function of business renewal to cognitive preferences to managerial behaviours and organizational action.

Cognitive modes → behaviours

The empirical link between the group composition based upon differences or similarities in cognitive preferences and outcomes from group activity is sparse. Evidence associating individual behaviours and cognitive preference is more prevalent.

Several studies have indicated a link between MBTI (Myers–Briggs Type Indicator) and behavioural patterns. Mitroff and Kilmann (1975), Mitroff *et al.* (1977), and Hellriegel and Slocum (1980) have researched how different types view ideal organizations and their heroes. Most of these support the relationships posited by Myers (1962). They found that Sensing–Thinking managers concentrated on specific, factual details, preferring situations in which there is certainty, specificity and control. Their heroes used others to get things done; they were problem-solvers. Intuitive–Thinking managers focused on broad, global issues, general concepts and ill-defined macro-level goals. Their heroes were broad conceptualizers and problem-framers. Sensing–Feeling managers were more concerned with specific people issues, not tasks. Their heroes created personal, warm climates and made organizations like 'home'. Finally Intuitive–Feeling managers focused on broad global themes serving mankind. Their heroes were able to envision new goals and create organizations with a personal sense.

Reporting on the validity of MBTI, Carlyn (1977) states that Intuitives are more likely to participate in imagined events and engage in possibilities while Sensors prefer a command of reality. Although validity studies have been done relating MBTI scores to other personality measures, very little evidence is available linking MBTI directly to managerial behaviours. To the extent that profession and position correlate to behaviours, the data presented in Table 24.5 tend to inferentially support the relationships posited in Table 24.3.

As a group, management consultants and high-level executives have a predominant thinking preference for evaluating information; as one would expect, consultants prefer to gather their information more broadly and look for whole relationships (intuition preference). Practising managers, be they high-level executives, supervisors, accountants or small business managers, have a stronger preference for grounding their information gathering in the immediate representations of the world with which they must deal (sensation preference). Moreover, the proportions of cognitive types do appear to differ by level in the hierarchy. Roach (1986) distinguishes between supervisors, managers and executives and reports that 'over half the executives were

Table 24.5 Cognitive style by profession and managerial position

	Information gathering		Information evaluation		
	Intuition	Sensing	Thinking	Feeling	η
Managerial					
Management consultants	58%	42%	92%	8%	71
High-level executives	43%	57%	90%	10%	136
Supervisors and managers	42%	58%	64%	36%	3678
Accountants	38%	62%	59%	41%	427
Small-business managers	14%	86%	81%	19%	150
Other professions					
Artists	91%	9%	30%	70%	114
Architects	82%	18%	56%	44%	124
Steelworkers	14%	86%	74%	26%	105
Teachers (grades 1–12)	26%	74%	31%	69%	281

Intuition–Thinking' while for supervisors Sensation–Thinking was the largest category. Sensation–Feeling declined dramatically in relation to increasing organizational level.

While intuitive preference appears to increase modestly with level in hierarchy, it varies more dramatically among professions. As shown in Table 24.5, professions requiring a high degree of creativity (artists and architects) have a strong intuition preference. Architects, however, deal with a technical subject and tend towards the thinking preference for evaluating the content of their intuitive insights. Artists, unconstrained by many technical requirements, evaluate their insights based upon feelings. Teachers and steelworkers, by way of further example, whose professions require them to deal with and respond to direct stimuli, have a stronger sensation preference. Dealing with children, most teachers (grades 1 to 12) evaluate stimuli using feeling; while steelworkers working with a process technology prefer thinking.

While these data are provocative, they do not directly address the question of whether or not cognitive preferences are associated with the behaviours expected at the different levels of the CM model. These questions need to be addressed by empirical research.

Towards research

Empirical work from other areas tends to support the general relationships implied by the SM model for the composition of top management groups. However, many linkages in the framework need empirical testing. Our global proposition is that the composition of the top management group will affect firm strategy and performance. More specifically, it is proposed that the task variety implied by the CM model requires cognitive style difference within the top management group. However, diversity alone does not ensure effectiveness. The organization must transcend this diversity. We suspect that the patterns of interaction amongst the contributors to strategic actions – who interacts with whom and how they interact – will be a critical aspect of this transcendence.

Although conceptually appealing and with some empirical support, major questions remain to be resolved as the empirical study of top management groups proceeds. These include:

1. What is meant by top management teams? Is the team the management committee? Is membership determined by hierarchical position? Are they the psychometrically determined contributors to major decisions? Does membership vary by decision? Can a parsimonious classification of top management teams be determined?

2. Are effective top management teams composed of individuals exhibiting behaviour required by the CM model? Are these behaviours distributed among team members as would be predicted on the basis of their cognitive style, or are they distributed on some other basis? Are

they integrative/facilitative behaviours exhibited by those with other substantive contributions to the CM process or do they require specific individuals with different cognitive styles or personalities? Do behavioural patterns account for differences in firm performance or is it just sufficient to see the total set exhibited by the group?

Addressing these issues will require a variety of approaches and research methodologies.

Approaches to researching top management teams

There are two broad ways to approach answering the questions raised above. One is to take the theory to practice, the other is to bring practice to theory.

Theory to practice

This approach calls for the explicit statement of testable hypotheses, tight experimental designs and valid measuring tools. Because of the complexity of the phenomenon under study it is advisable first to conduct tests of these hypotheses under highly controlled conditions. We believe that well-developed behavioural simulations[1] provide many of the controls necessary, but recreate real life sufficiently well to be used as vehicles for such tests.

The following propositions could be tested through these simulations:

1. Individuals with certain cognitive styles exhibit specified behaviour, or a cluster of behaviours.
2. Exhibited behaviours cluster to reflect contributions to the levels of the CM process.
3. Certain patterns of interaction are better able to transcend these differences than others.
4. The behaviours and interaction patterns result in the expected patterns in action.

A simple research design would involve assigning individuals to top management teams (TMTs) on the basis of their MBTI types to create both homogeneous and heterogeneous groups. All groups then participate in a behavioural simulation. Following the simulation, participants are asked to complete a behavioural checklist (who did what) and asked to indicate who played what role. Linkages in the logic can be tested. Additional studies can test the effectiveness of different interventions prior to the simulation.

Practice to theory

Generalizability is limited with the designs mentioned above. Simulations, no matter how well developed, cannot completely replicate real life. They may unduly force individuals into roles and behaviours they would not otherwise exhibit, and they may impose norms on group behaviour that do not reflect the real-life behaviour of top management teams. Concurrent with highly controlled theory-to-practice design, real-life top management teams should be observed.

Initially this research should be descriptive. It is hoped that intensive clinical studies of a sample of top management teams would provide the basis for a parsimonious classification of teams. The stability of team membership, who contributes to key decisions and actions, could be examined both over time and over situations. Behaviours exhibited by individuals in different roles can be observed. With a taxonomy of teams and a more detailed behavioural checklist developed, larger-scale research could be conducted to test hypotheses emanating from the theoretical framework. Structured interviews and data collection could be conducted with members of a variety of top management teams. Administered instruments would include measures of cognitive preferences and other behavioural predispositions, checklists of behaviour to be completed of self and other top management team members. Performance of the teams could be measured, and effectiveness accounted for, on the basis of individual background and behavioural difference.

Although little has been said in this chapter about patterns of interaction among team members, it is clear that performance cannot be thought of strictly as a function of team composition. The case studies and survey research could also be useful for observing, documenting and understanding patterns of interaction. For example, do heterogeneous teams which operate with low status and power differentials outperform those that operate on the basis of hierarchical positions? Does job context suppress or extinguish intrinsic cognitive preferences?

Both types of research should proceed concurrently. Much can be learned from one that is useful to the other. Through studies of managers in simulated settings, reliable measures of behaviour could be developed. The validity of these measures could then be assessed in the field. Other intervening variables discovered in the field studies can be manipulated experimentally or statistically in subsequent laboratory studies.

Towards practice

The ideas of teamwork at the top, cognitive style and innovation are not new to practising managers (Rowan, 1979; Sherman, 1984; Moore, 1987). Furthermore, Jungian concepts and MBTI types are to a limited extent already being used to help managers better understand their organizations (Mitroff and Kilmann, 1975; Mason and Mitroff, 1981; Moore, 1987). The CM model synthesizes many of these ideas as they relate to the executive function of business renewal. It infers roles, behaviours and differences in cognitive type for the top management group.

The conceptual insights can still be of use to practitioners even though as yet unsupported by detailed direct evidence. The CM model provides managers with an understanding that can make them more aware of their own behaviours and tolerant of others', especially when they appreciate the individual differences in cognitive preference which underlie those behaviours, and that such behaviours may play an important role in the CM process. In other words, it can be hoped that a conceptual understanding will result in behavioural awareness and modification.

If those responsible for the overall direction of the enterprise were aware of the behavioural requirement of its members as posited by the CM model they could use that understanding in several ways. First, an examination of the members of the TMT may reveal that they are inclined to exhibit the required behaviours, but feel, because of organizational factors, that they cannot do so. A further examination of the cultural norms, power relationships and the reward systems might reveal that those behaviours were discouraged or even punished. It might be a relatively easy step to legitimize those previously suppressed behaviours. Often a change of context can help. The 'outward-bound' experience for managers, by providing a dramatic shift in context and in some respects tasks, presents an opportunity for latent preferences, suppressed in the normal organization context, to surface. It is well accepted that children learn through play. However, playful experiences for managers need not always occur outside the normal organizational context. It is now being suggested that certain organizational activities be conducted in a playful manner in order to facilitate institutional learning (Rutenberg, 1986; de Geus, 1988).

A second, and possibly a more controversial, use would be to employ the CM model for selection to, and development of, the TMT. With an understanding of the model those responsible for these activities might attend to, document and evaluate the behaviours of potential or current members of the TMT in terms of cognitive type. These behaviours, framed within the CM model, could be assessed and used as one criterion for selection. Development activities might also be suggested for some members who could most likely exhibit certain required behaviours. As a cautionary note, we do not believe that use of the MBTI as a cognitive indicator is warranted at this time. The test was not developed, nor has sufficient evidence of reliability and predictive validity been shown, for use in selection or promotion decisions. However, we do feel that Jung's conception of cognitive types does provide a useful way for managers to appreciate observable, individual behaviours and their contribution to the process of organizational renewal.

Throughout these brief suggestions for practice, the emphasis has been on behaviour. Managers attempting to employ the CM model should adopt a similar perspective. It is the insights into the behaviours of the TMT provided by the model that have the greatest utility.

Summary/conclusions

This chapter attempts to build a model of the behavioural requirements for the top management team from two perspectives. First, from the perspective of the individual, it is posited that the behaviours relevant to the renewal function of the executive which need to be exhibited by top managers are at least partly a function of their cognitive preferences. It is argued that the Jungian/Myers–Briggs typology is consistent with the model of renewal based upon the creative management (CM) model and an established framework for understanding and predicting these behaviours. Second, it has been asserted that organizations will evolve a pattern of actions, a strategy reflecting the cognitive composition of the top management team. As the cognitive preferences of the top management group vary so too will strategy.

It is suggested that research follow both a theory-to-practice and practice-to-theory approach, simultaneously developing theory and testing specific hypotheses about team composition and patterns of interaction.

This chapter makes a case for a management process that utilizes the full range of human potential. The need for a CM model to replace the conventional strategic management framework has been argued on the basis of the latter's inability to utilize the full range of cognitive functions and accordingly its failure to promote new and innovative strategies. The CM model, however, has implications for the dominant coalition. Since theory and evidence suggests individuals have superior or dominant functions, a mixture of cognitive types is implied. The CM process suggests that top management groups not only include the Thinkers and Sensors needed by the SM process but also embrace the Intuitives and Feelers needed to generate and infuse unconventional insights and new ideas. But difference without synthesis is anarchy. The organization and its members must also have the ability to achieve unity from diversity, the ability to transcend.

Note

1. Simulations developed by the Center for Creative Leadership, Greensbors, NC, and by the Management Simulations Project Group, New York University, are examples.

References

Barnard, C.I. (1938) *The Functions of the Executive*, Cambridge, MA: Harvard University Press.

Belbin, R.M. (1981) *Management Teams: Why They Succeed or Fail*, London: Heinemann.

Blaylock, B.K. (1983) 'Teamwork in a simulated production environment', *Research in Psychological Type* 6: 58–67.

Bower, J.L. (1982) 'Solving the problems of business planning', *Journal of Business Strategy*, 2(3): Winter, pp. 32–44.

Carlson, R.O. (1972) *School Superintendents: Careers and Performance*, Columbia, OH: Merrill.

Carlyn, M. (1977) 'An assessment of the Myers–Briggs type indicator', *Journal of Personality Assessment* 41: 461–73.

Child, J. (1974) 'Managerial and organizational factors associated with company performance', *Journal of Management Studies* 11: 13–27.

Cyert, R.M. and March, J.G. (1963) *A Behavioral Theory of the Firm*, Englewood Cliffs, NJ: Prentice-Hall.

de Geus, A.P. (1988) 'Planning as learning', *Harvard Business Review*, March–April: 62–9.

Filley, A.C., House, R.J. and Kerr, S. (1976) *Managerial Process and Organizational Behavior*, Glenview, IL: Scott Foresman.

Follett, M.P. (1941) *Dynamic Administration: the Collected Papers of Mary Park Follett*, edited by H. Metcalf and L. Urwick, Harper & Bros, New York.

Friedlander, F. (1983) 'Patterns of individual and organizational learning', in Srivesta, S. and Associates, *The Executive Mind*, San Francisco, CA: Jossey-Bass.

Galbraith, J. (1973) *Designing Complex Organizations*, Reading, MA: Addison-Wesley.

Gardener, H. (1985) *The Mind's New Science: A History of the Cognitive Revolution*, Basic Books, New York.

Greenleaf, R.K. (1977) *Servant Leadership*, New York: Paulist Press.

Hambrick, D.C. (1983a) 'High profit strategies in mature capital goods industries: a contingency approach', *Academy of Management Journal* 26(4): 687–707.

Hambrick, D.C. (1983b) 'Some tests of the effectiveness and functional attributes of Miles and Snow's strategic types', *Academy of Management Journal* 26(1): 5–26.

Hambrick, D.C. (1987) 'The top management team: key to strategic success', *California Management Review*, Fall: 88–108.

Hambrick, D.C. and Mason, P.A. (1984) 'Upper echelons: the organization as a reflection of its top managers', *Academy of Management Review* 9(2): 193–206.

Hampden-Turner, C. (1981) *Maps of the Mind*, New York: Macmillan.

Hellriegel, D. and Slocum, J.W. (1980) 'Preferred organizational designs and problem solving styles: interesting companions', *Human Systems Management* 1: 151–8.

Hurst, D.K. (1986) 'Why strategic management is bankrupt', *Organizational Dynamics* Autumn: 5–27.

Jacques, E. (1982) *The Form of Time*, New York: Crane Russak.

Jung, C.G. (1960) 'The structure and dynamics of the psyche', in *Collected Works*, vol. 8, Princeton, NJ: Princeton University Press.

Keirsey, D.W. and Bates, M. (1978) *Please Understand Me*, Del Mar, CA: Prometheus Nemesis Books.

Kimberley, J.R. and Evanisko, M.J. (1981) 'Organizational innovation: the influence of individual, organizational and contextual factors on hospital adoption of technological and administrative innovations', *Academy of Management Journal* 24: 689–713.

Koestler, A. (1976) *The Act of Creation*, London: Hutchinson.

Lawrence, P.R. and Lorsch, J.W. (1969) *Organization and Environment*, R.D. Homewood, IL: Irwin.

Macdaid, G.P., McCaulley, M.H. and Kainz, R.I. (1986) *Atlas of Type Tables*, Gainesville, FL: Center for Applications of Psychological Types.

McKenny, J.L. and Keen, P.G.W. (1974) 'How managers' minds work', *Harvard Business Review* May–June: 79–90.

Mann, H., Siegler, M. and Osmond, H. (1971) 'The psychotypology of time', in Yaker, H., Osmond, H. and Cheek, F. (eds) *The Future of Time: Man's Temporal Environment*, Garden City, NY: Doubleday, pp. 142–178.

Mason, R.O. and Mitroff, I.I. (1981) *Challenging Strategic Planning Assumptions*, New York: John Wiley & Sons.

Miles, R.E. and Snow, C.C. (1978) *Organizational Strategy, Structure and Process*, New York: McGraw-Hill.

Mintzberg, H. (1976) 'Planning on the left side and managing on the right', *Harvard Business Review* July–August: 49–58.

Mintzberg, H. (1978) 'Patterns in strategy formation', *Management Science*, 24: 934–48.

Mitroff, I.I. and Kilmann, R.H. (1975) 'Stories managers tell: a new tool for organizational problem solving', *Management Review* 64(7): 18–28.

Mitroff, I., Barabba, V. and Kilmarin, R. (1977) 'The application of behavioral and philosophical technologies to strategic planning: a case study of a large federal agency', *Management Science* 24: 44–58.

Moore, T. (1987) 'Personality tests are back', *Fortune*, 30 March: 74–82.

Myers, I.B. (1962) *Introduction to Type*, Palo Alto, CA: Consulting Psychologists Press.

Myers, I.B. and McCaulley, M.H. (1985) *Manual: A Guide to the Development and Use of the Myers–Briggs Type Indicator*, Palo Alto, CA: Consulting Psychologists Press.

Pascale, R.T. (1984) 'Perspectives on strategy: the real story behind Honda's success', *California Management Review*, Spring: 47–72.

Peters, T.J. and Waterman, R.H. (1983) 'Beyond the rational model', *The McKinsey Quarterly*, Spring: 19–30.

Prahalad, C.K. and Bettis, R.A. (1986) 'The dominant logic: a new linkage between diversity and performance', *Strategic Management Journal* 7: 485–501.

Roach, B. (1986) 'Organizational decision-makers: different types for different levels', *Journal of Psychological Type* 12: 16–24.

Rowan, R. (1979) 'Those business hunches are more than blind faith', *Fortune* 23 April: 110–14.

Rutenberg, D. (1986) 'Playful plans', working paper, Queens University, Canada.

Sherman, S.P. (1984) 'Eight big masters of innovation', *Fortune*, 15 October: 66–78.

Simon, H.A. (1988) 'Understanding creativity and creative management', in Kuhn, R.L. (ed.) *Handbook for Creative and Innovative Managers*, New York: McGraw-Hill.

Taggart, W. and Robey, D. (1981) 'Minds and managers: on the dual nature of human information processing and management', *Academy of Management Review* 6(2): 187–95.

Thompson, J.D. (1967) *Organizations in Action*, New York: McGraw-Hill.

Watson, J.D. (1969) *The Double Helix*, New York: Mentor Books.

Weick, K.E. (1979) *The Social Psychology of Organizing*, Reading, MA: Addison-Wesley.

Worthy, J.C. (1984) *Shaping an American Institution: Robert E. Wood and Sears, Roebuck*, Chicago, IL: University of Illinois Press.

Ziller, R.C. (1972) 'Homogeneity and heterogeneity of group membership', in McClintoch, C.G. (ed.) *Experimental Social Psychology*, New York: Holt, Rinehart & Winston.

25 Crucial gaps in 'the learning organization':
power, politics and ideology
John Coopey

Learning is about getting to like what you get. (with apologies to George Bernard Shaw)

Learning has a long history as a concept in organization theory. The essential concern is to enhance processes of learning which can be used within organizations to improve individual and collective actions through better knowledge and understanding (Shrivastava, 1983; Fiol and Lyles, 1985). The notion of the learning organization has emerged more recently, focusing on organizations designed deliberately to facilitate the learning of their members and, hence, much freer collective adaptation (Revans, 1982; Garratt, 1987; Pedler *et al.*, 1988, 1989, 1991). It can be defined as:

> An organization that facilitates the learning of all its members *and* continuously transforms itself. (Pedler *et al.*, 1991: 1; original emphasis)

Three longstanding themes are brought together: how to structure organizations to enhance performance; how to facilitate individual learning and development in a corporate setting; and how to ensure that organizations adapt quickly to changes in their external environment.

Theorizing about learning organizations which emphasizes their potential for transformation fits into a diverse array of recent approaches to achieving greater flexibility, to 'find ways of managing an unprecedented degree of economic uncertainty deriving from a need for continuous rapid adjustment to a market environment that seems to have become permanently more turbulent than in the past' (Streeck, 1987: 295).

In this chapter the most thoroughly worked out model of a learning organization is summarized and placed within a framework of assumptions about power and political activity seemingly lacking in the literature. Arguments are developed regarding the likely incidence of political activity within a learning organization and its implications for employee empowerment deemed important for learning. Finally, we examine the potential use of the language and symbolism of the learning organization to create new ideological representations.

The most detailed exposition of the learning organization, used as the main focus of the chapter, is by Pedler *et al.* (1988, 1989, 1991). Part metaphor, part prescription and called by them a 'learning company', its theoretical framework was sketched in from the organizational learning literature and developed through a Manpower Services Commission project involving managers, consultants and academics. Other sources drawn on are Garratt (1987) and Hawkins (1991). To facilitate the discussion in this chapter the terms Pedler *et al.* use and the relationships between the terms which the authors assert or seem to imply are summarized in a model represented in Figure 25.1. Shown are eleven characteristics of a learning organization, several intervening variables at the level of the individual and the organization, and output variables subsumed under the term 'competitive advantage'. The causal relationships implied in the model are mediated by a control process. Greater detail of the eleven characteristics is provided in Figure 25.2.

Central to the model is the 'control' learning which takes place at three levels, broadly as defined by Argyris and Schon (1978). At level I, or 'operational' learning, performance errors are corrected against norms built into operating plans (Garratt, 1987; Pedler *et al.*, 1991); level II, or 'strategic learning', occurs when existing goals and transformation processes are modified to match perceived changes in the external environment (Garratt, 1987); at level III, learning is related to questions of purpose (Pedler *et al.*, 1991) such that an organization's leaders share the perspective of others in the wider community, tapping new sources of spiritual energy (Hawkins, 1991: 183).

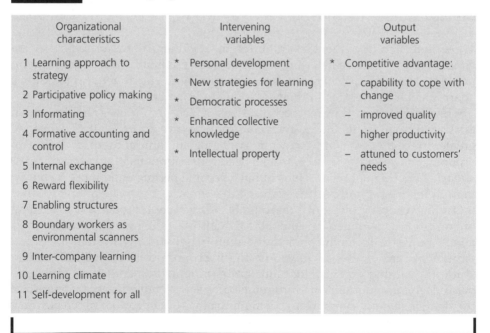

Figure 25.1 The learning organization

Organizational characteristics	Intervening variables	Output variables
1 Learning approach to strategy	* Personal development	* Competitive advantage:
2 Participative policy making	* New strategies for learning	– capability to cope with change
3 Informating	* Democratic processes	– improved quality
4 Formative accounting and control	* Enhanced collective knowledge	– higher productivity
5 Internal exchange	* Intellectual property	– attuned to customers' needs
6 Reward flexibility		
7 Enabling structures		
8 Boundary workers as environmental scanners		
9 Inter-company learning		
10 Learning climate		
11 Self-development for all		

CONTROL PROCESS

Figure 25.2   Learning organization characteristics

* **A learning approach** to strategy requires that the various aspects of forming policy and strategy are structured as a learning process allowing ongoing development and revision of business plans.

* **Participative policy making** ensures that all organizational members can contribute to major policy decisions.

* **Informating** assumes new ways will be found of using information technology not only to provide a model of organizational processes required for control (the cybernetic model) but also to make widely available 'the kind of knowledge [which] will enable competent participation in the processes associated with making things' (Zuboff, 1988: 57).

* **Formative accounting and control** ensures that accounting and budgeting systems meet the information needs of all internal clients of those systems so as to strengthen the 'ethos of self-responsibility' fostering semi-autonomous individuals and groups.

* **Internal exchange** implies that all departments and units relate to each other as potential customers and suppliers within a partly regulated internal market exchanging information on expectations, negotiating, contracting and providing feedback. Collaboration rather than competition is the keynote, yielding positive-sum instead of zero-sum outcomes.

* **Reward flexibility**, within a general framework of Human Resource Management, ensures flexibility in the types of rewards used and in the way in which systems of financial rewards are structured and delivered, requiring that assumptions underlying reward systems are made public and reviewed collectively.

* **Structures** take temporary forms (e.g. Hedberg *et al.*, 1976) which, while catering for current needs, can be shaped through experimentation to respond easily to future changes in the internal and external environments.

* All **boundary workers** are **environmental scanners**, not just those who traditionally have been accorded a scanning role, providing a corpus of information on developments in the external environment for use in strategy formulation.

* **Inter-company learning** carries the learning ethos to suppliers, customers and even competitors through, for example, joint training, shared investment and R&D.

* A **learning climate** is necessary to facilitate individual learning, essentially a cultural template designed around a questioning frame of mind, tolerance of experiments and mistakes, the essential need for differences and the idea of continuous improvement.

* **Self-development opportunities** are available for all, sufficient to allow people to take advantage of the enabling climate.

Power and politics within a learning organization

The assumptions which seem to underlie a learning organization are now reviewed against a framework of power and political behaviour summarized in Figure 25.3. Central is Giddens' (1976, 1979) concept of power, chosen for three reasons: first, its rigour; second, its potential for resolving the duality as between individual agency and the power implicit in the bias built into institutions; and, third, because its use of the notion of 'transformative

Figure 25.3 Transformative capacity and agency

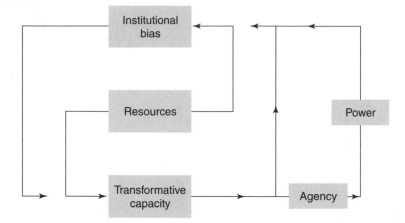

capacity' relates well to key aspects of the learning organization. Later we draw on Clegg (1989) for a more thoroughly developed analysis of the environmental context through which agency and structure are dynamically related. Within the institutional setting are symmetries in the distribution of resources, in actors' access to existing resources and in their scope to create and use new ones. The outcome is a pattern of relative advantage favouring one or more dominant groups. In Figure 25.3 this notion is summed up in the term *institutional bias*.

At the level of individual strategy actors intervene in the course of events, producing certain outcomes through the deployment of their various capabilities denoted by the term *transformative capacity*. Giddens argues that power is expressed in interactions where that capacity is harnessed to actors' attempts to get others to comply with their wants. *Power*, in this relational sense, 'concerns the capability of actors to secure outcomes where the realization of those outcomes depends on the agency of others'. Its use in interaction 'can be understood in terms of the facilities that participants bring to and mobilise as elements in the production of that interaction' (Giddens, 1979: 93).

The structural and action-based levels, of institutional bias and transformative capacity respectively, are mediated through control over *resources* already existing in the institutional setting and created afresh through the application of transformative capacity.

Control and political activity

Central to Giddens' framework are issues of control and political activity on which the learning organization literature seems confused. Pedler *et al.* (1991) focus explicitly on one aspect of control, concerned with ensuring that the learning process develops according to their prescription. They seem not to acknowledge the tension between control and learning, that 'to focus on learning without taking into account legitimate need for control is to embark on a romantic and usually fruitless exercise' (Argyris and Schon, 1983: 4).

Consistent with their egalitarian stance, Pedler *et al.* stress the importance of control of the learning process but do not prescribe who should exercise control; implicit, however, is that 'managers' will play key roles. Garratt (1987) is unashamedly elitist; of the three necessary roles – operational planning and action, external monitoring and integrating and direction-giving – the latter is the directors' 'brain function', that 'monitors what is happening in day-to-day operations, checks what is happening in the wider environment, and then takes decisions on how best to deploy the limited resources it controls to achieve its objectives in the given conditions' (Garratt, 1987: 33). He rates as effective those directors who 'set out to design their world in the way they want it. They act on George Bernard Shaw's maxim: "Get what you like or you get to like what you get"' (ibid.: 54).

To Garratt's 'brain-function' category Hawkins (1991) adds the 'Business Soul': connecting level II and level III learning it incorporates 'the men and women of wisdom an organization needs on its board, among its trustees and facilitating its learning environment' (p. 183).

Giddens's (1979) approach to control is pluralist. Actors are involved in a 'dialectic of control', attempting to maintain some semblance of control over their own work, taking advantage of imbalances in personal access to existing resources and scope to create new ones. Differences of 'wants' as between individuals and of 'interests' between groups are expressed in attempts to exert control over patterns of work through relationships of mutual dependency.

How does Giddens's view square with relationships envisaged within a learning organization? Pedler *et al.* acknowledge plurality but only as regards learning; essential differences are an important element in the framework of a learning organization's internal market, any conflicts which arise are to be settled via constant dialogue. Collaboration based on trust rather than competition in search of advantage is the essence, enabling conflict to be used constructively. So, whilst control is an essential element it is not an overtly political process in the terms used by Giddens. Despite the rhetoric the learning organization seems to be placed within a unitarist framework of relationships, a utopia to be ushered in through the pursuit of shared goals in a climate of collaborative high trust and a rational approach to the resolution of differences.

Such an approach based on principles of fairness, mutual respect and trust might well yield unobtrusive control devices, mitigating the level of political activity. But in circumstances of external turbulence and internal transformation, where greater uncertainty and dissensus might be expected, such devices are not likely 'to be wholly effective in producing a coherent and unified set of goals and definitions of technology'. Instead action will 'result from bargaining and compromise [where] those individuals or groups with access to the greatest power will receive greatest rewards from political interplay' (Pfeffer, 1981: 28). This position is supported by Kanter's (1989) finding that, in new forms of organization designed to deal with external turbulence, political action increases considerably and political skills are at a premium. Such an outcome fits Clegg's (1989) view that political activity is premised on organizations as loci of decisions and action. Decision making and political activity are correlated because of the effect decisions generally have on resource allocation and, consequently, on power relationships.

Pfeffer (1981) suggests ways of moderating the extent of political activity. Slack resources can be created to reduce competition for them; a set of decision makers can be established, homogeneous in respect of attitudes and skill level; and the importance of decisions can be reduced. How far these steps are possible or desirable in a learning organization is questionable. If slack resources existed organizational leaders might perceive a turbulent external environment as less threatening and conceive of more conventional, less risky ways of adapting to it than implied in a learning organization. Second, homogeneity in decision makers would potentially threaten the very interpersonal differences judged so essential to learning and creativity. Finally, it might be possible to reduce the importance of decisions – for example by avoiding them, re-labelling them, breaking them down into less crucial elements – but scope for such tactics would probably be limited in a learning organization where decision making to create new meanings is, presumably, central.

Within the political model managers construct and operate disciplinary practices to ensure that employees perform as expected and to sanction certain forms of creativity (Clegg, 1989). Such creativity-enabling processes are at the heart of a learning organization, as managers seek to construct consent without recourse to cruder forms of control used widely within bureaucracies. But in constructing permissive forms of control they face a tension in the employment relationship, seeking to minimize unit labour costs in the owners' interests as against the employees' interest in maximizing financial rewards. This conflict complicates managerial efforts to ensure employees commit and contribute to the organization while constraining their behaviour in the light of economic realities (Keenoy, 1992).

Employees can draw on two sources of resistance: an ability to regulate the productive use of their capacities and to use their discursive capacity to prevent others' attributing and fixing unacceptable meanings to organizational events (Clegg, 1989). 'Discursive penetration' is a vital element of this process, consisting of knowledge of the structural framework which all actors possess to a degree because 'they draw upon that framework in producing their action at the same time as they reconstitute it through that action' (Giddens, 1979: 144). Within a learning organization employees' discursive penetration would presumably be enhanced through 'informating' – providing an understanding of structures and systems of which the organization is composed – and opportunities to develop 'intellective skills' of abstraction, explicit inference and procedural reasoning (Pedler *et al.*, 1991).

From this reading of a learning organization we can infer that it is a 'form of high discretionary strategic agency ... for which power will be less prohibitive and more productive', the pattern typically of 'the classical conception of the professional discipline as a vocation' (Clegg, 1989: 199). Mutual investment in the process of learning on the part of management and other employees should enable the former to move the frontier of control as noted by Buchanan (1992) in his study of a computer manufacturer, where 'boundaries of what were once considered acceptable work control are being expanded by new environmental pressures' (p. 138).

Despite this, we should note how important it was for those businessmen consulted by Pedler *et al.* (1988), and for those with whom Garratt (1987) regularly works, that any changes proposed within the context of a learning organization should create increased productivity. This implies that, wherever the frontier of control is drawn, time will be a critical term in constructing forms of control. Even given accounting systems which are user oriented, learning organizations will probably not escape the pressures to introduce further time-related techniques in operations, in managing people generally and in strategic evaluation. The likely outcome is more automation or techniques such as 'Just in Time', enabling increased control of operations; the employment of time-related indices to regulate the efficient use of white collar staff; further inroads of 'chronarchy' into managerial autonomy through devices such as 'time management' (Scarborough and Corbett, 1992); and, at the strategic level, techniques such as 'Shareholder Value Analysis' (Coopers and Lybrand *I* MORI, 1991) or the monthly monitoring of 'key control ratios' which Garratt (1987) recommends to his client directors.

These pressures might moderate how far the frontier of control will be displaced within learning organizations in practice, certainly those in the private sector who, Pedler *et al.* claim, have shown considerable interest in the concept. This is consistent with Keenoy's (1990) view that Human Resource Management (placed by Pedler *et al.* at the centre of their model) is neutral as regards the benefits to employees of any particular strategy followed. What makes HRM strategic 'is not how personnel management policies translate into practice but whether or not those policies represent a good *fit* with the prevailing product and labour market constraints' (Keenoy, 1990: 6; original emphasis). The example Keenoy quotes is the withdrawal of recognition from trade unions, an action which supported the overall business strategy. So, the notional moving outwards of boundaries of control implied in a learning organization can be seen as a dependent variable, one of a variety of strategies available to organizations in response to environmental turbulence. Hence the learning organization, like the notion of Organizational Culture (Meyerson, 1991), might well be destined to be transformed from a root metaphor, helping to explain the nature of organizational activities and performance, to a mechanism through which managerial control is improved under dramatically changed external circumstances. If this were so, employees could be expected to resist managerial pressures to conform, using their transformative capacity in defensive ways inimical to the aims of a learning organization.

Power and agency in a learning organization

In this section the institutional setting derived from the work of Giddens and Clegg is used to examine how the members of a learning organization, especially its senior managers, might use their power in order to maintain or enhance their control of the work context. Members will use their discursive capacities and discursive penetration of the organization's structures and systems in attempts to build up agency, alone and in collaboration with others. While Pedler *et al.* do not discriminate between the degree of discursive penetration which different actors or groups enjoy or require, or the level of skills they bring to social relationships, Hawkins (1991) differentiates between the penetration sufficient to handle operations at level I of learning, to enhance organizational effectiveness at level II, and to relate the organization to evolutionary needs at level III. The position assumed by Hawkins is a specific example of the general proposition that discursive penetration is limited in terms of 'the situated character of the action [and] the degree to which tacit knowledge can be articulated in discourse' (Giddens, 1979: 144).

Wherever they are situated participants will attempt to articulate their knowledge, developing explanations for the activities in which they are involved and persuading others to accept their rationalizations. Given that learning organizations are, by design, less structured than more traditional forms, and that structures themselves provide socially accepted rationalizations for specific types of activity, we should probably expect to find a high volume of informal communications as people seek to resolve the uncertainty created by ambiguous situations and the relative dearth of structural cues to behaviour (Pfeffer, 1981). As Kanter (1989) noted, managers engaged in informal networks to achieve influence within 'modern' organizations with less structure and more flexible systems than usual. Within such networks those who have a high level of Giddens' (1979) discursive capacity are more likely to build up a reputation for persuasiveness, for creating new knowledge successfully through their skills in presentation, argumentation and debate (Pfeffer, 1981).

Other personal characteristics which are important in influencing collective meanings include actors' self-efficacy and associated beliefs in the validity of positions they are proposing; through such self-confidence considerable commitment is built up so that conscious self-dealing is rarely necessary. Knowledge of the distribution of interests and power is also an advantage, and of decision processes, as a basis for successful political activity – providing cues to deciding where to invest resources and with whom to collaborate in agency building (Pfeffer, 1981). Such 'cynical knowledge' – though likely to be viewed with suspicion in a high-trust learning organization – is part of Giddens's discursive penetration.

While the personal characteristics referred to are likely to differentiate one actor from another in their potential to build up a reputation as 'influential' – even offsetting to some extent the effect of institutional bias – probably more crucial is the access to penetrative knowledge gained via the position occupied in the organization's structure. But even though learning organizations are likely to be less hierarchical than conventional forms, with fewer managerial levels and positions, the incumbents of such positions will typically occupy quite crucial roles at internal and external boundaries, giving them access to deeper penetrative knowledge than is open to most non-managerial colleagues. This will be in addition to any formal authority they are granted, enabling them to command other people and to allocate conventional, collective resources.

Clegg (1989) would argue that, potentially, such managers are a 'key agency', with scope to further their interests through control of membership and meaning within alliances and coalitions, because they operate at organizational 'nodal points' where two circuits of power intersect:

- circuits of 'dispositional power' out of which organizational forms are created based on membership and shared meanings, and
- circuits of 'facilitative power' through which socially derived forces flow in the external environment, engendering innovation in techniques of production and discipline.

Within the learning organization Pedler *et al.* (1991) argue that all members who operate at the external boundary should act as 'environmental scanners', bringing their interpretations of events in the outside world back into the organization as potentially useful knowledge. But this formulation obscures the degree of penetration which their different roles allow. Boundary roles give varied scope for the accumulation of discursive penetration and for accruing personal influence. It is one thing, for example, to bring back information about the pattern of a competitor's prices in a local market, but insights into that organization's overall market strategy, or the Government's position on competition policy as it affects that market, would constitute much more significant knowledge. This conclusion is most important when focusing on the power of managers at the apex of an organization. At key nodal points in the interlocking circuits of power they can maintain formal and informal social structures which provide essential continuity in the internal organization of people's capacities whilst shaping the collective transformation which takes place under the perceived pressure of competitive trends in the external environment.

The set of institutions which constitute the pathways of the facilitative circuit of power in the wider society and, hence, the external environment of any one organization, has its own structure of rules, resources and systems regulating relationships between the separate institutions. As at the level of the single institution, there are symmetries which favour certain organizations over others in, for example, their dealings with Government or the financial system. In effect, at societal level, networks of agencies control nodal points within an economy's circuits of power so as to establish relatively stable and privileged sets of relationships which enable them to safeguard their access to power and, hence, to build and maintain formal organizational structures. As Scarborough and Corbett (1992) recognize, 'the considerable power which management exercise over technology, for instance, is linked to their relations with external constituencies of owners, technology suppliers and providers of capital' (p.26).

Senior managers are almost certainly at the most salient nodes when considering strategic decisions involved in raising finance, securing new markets, reaching agreements with major suppliers, and influencing Government. This seems to be the reality of Hawkins' (1991) levels II and III of a learning organization, concerned with strategy and evolution. Individuals operating at those levels can use increments of corporate knowledge created through the learning process in their dealings with other agencies in the external environment. It is a conclusion which parallels Kanter's (1989) finding that chief executives of modern forms of organization tend to retain their identity, status and control, occupying positions which still yield considerable power, despite the difficulties they face in creating agency through networks of stakeholders rather than simply controlling subordinates.

Here are reflected Giddens' and Clegg's institutional bias in the distribution of resources and access to them. And since knowledge is such an important resource in a learning organization we might expect much political activity to be associated with how it is acquired and stored and how access to the collective data bank is controlled. Despite Pedler's protestations that information will be widely available in a learning organization, limitations are inevitable. Organizations are, after all, social arrangements in which specialist roles are coordinated to achieve the creation and use of knowledge, overcoming in this way constraints of individuals' bounded rationality and limited cognitive capacities (Simon, 1976). Such specialization is modelled on the development of a corporate information system built up from individual contributions but into which 'the rules expressing hierarchical access to information have come to be incorporated in the provision of levels of access and "security", complete with elaborate passwords and gates' (Scarborough and Corbett, 1992: 14). The 'rationality' embedded in the protocols gives potential power to those experts who devise and incorporate the rules into the system and to their client senior managers who make decisions as to access. They will probably be the only ones able to penetrate in a holistic way the knowledge which can be used to provide meaning for the organization's members in a strategic and evolutionary sense.

Directors' access to the increasing stock of collective knowledge intended to be generated in a learning organization and their control of nodal points of relationships within the broader circuits of facilitative power will enable them to consolidate the membership of existing agencies, to recruit new members to them, and to set up new agencies. In Clegg's (1989) terms their nodal positions, and the internally derived knowledge and control of discourse to which these give access, should enable them to 'translate phenomena into resources, and resources into organization networks of control, of alliance, of coalition, of antagonism, of interest and of structure' (Clegg, 1989: 204).

Kanter (1984) provides an example of this process, describing how the 'integrated' flexible organizational forms which she surveyed facilitated innovation in the body of the organization which could then form part of corporate learning. 'Experiments by middle-level innovators make possible the formulation of a new strategy to meet a sudden external challenge of which even the middle-level innovators might have been unaware. Then the new strategy, in effect, elevates the innovator's experiments to the level of policy' (Kanter, 1984: 290). If a learning organization operates as expected this, presumably, is how powerful people would translate internal phenomena into resources to use in exerting stronger agency in the internal and external environment. By rewarding so tangibly the internal innovators, by bringing their 'brain-children' centre stage, the latter would probably be incorporated into the agency of the top strategists, turning latent opposition into support.

The relatively sparse structure of a learning organization will advantage some and disadvantage others. Those who might lose managerial positions in any structural change would probably attempt to create alternative sources of advantage and power, an assumption supported by Kanter's (1989) insights into managerial behaviour in modern forms of organization. Giddens (1979) argues that 'in modern bureaucracies there are more openings for those in formally subordinate positions to acquire or regain control over organizational tasks than Weber recognized. The more tightly-knit and inflexible the formal relations of authority within an organization, in fact, the more the possible openings for circumventing them' (Giddens, 1979: 147). If this is the case it is not surprising that some members of a learning organization might feel vulnerable within its supposedly more open and facilitative framework. As Kanter (1989) observes, while hierarchy might be a thing of the past in the modern organizations she studied, senior managers wielded power in ways which their subordinates perceived as arbitrary.

The lack of protective structure might also go some way to explaining why those individuals and groups who fear losing their sole rights over a certain body of knowledge – and hence their influence over those dependent on that expertise – might attempt to retain it at the tacit level, or to restrict its use in discourse to oral transmission as in the case of maintenance engineers in Crozier's (1964) classic study of a tobacco plant. Such defensive behaviour is more likely in groups of managers and experts who have the generic knowledge required to make effective choices about technology and structure and who are under pressure from movements in the boundary of control, such as those involving users in decisions about technology (Scarborough and Corbett, 1992), a trend which would probably evolve further in a learning organization. For example, a group of managers with technical expertise were shown not to favour decentralized control of technology by operators (Mueller *et al.*, 1986 quoted by Scarborough and Corbett, 1992) and the introduction of 'quality circles' has to be seen against the background of managers who 'tend to appropriate knowledge to themselves and to disclaim the value of knowledge possessed by other groups' (Scarborough and Corbett, 1992: 132). In such situations of dominant technical rationality, technology is implemented which symbolizes that superiority, signifying meanings which reinforce the domination of systems specialists and associated managers.

In summary, the agency that individuals and groups might be able to build up in a learning organization depends on a variety of factors. Personal characteristics such as learning style and self-efficacy will determine to some extent the influence which can be exerted through relationships. Probably more important will be the level of discursive penetration which individuals, making use of their unique qualities, are able to develop through formal position, boundary spanning activities and expert technical knowledge. Those at the apex, despite the difficulties they might face in exerting control in a learning organization, could be expected to have their power enhanced through occupation of nodal points of power and the holistic nature of the discursive penetration which this makes possible. Their cooptation and patronage of lower-level innovators would also probably enable them to disarm those with expertise critical to the extension of their agency. Others sited less advantageously in a learning organization would probably be active in developing their own agency through similar but less potent tactics. People perceiving themselves to be especially disadvantaged might defend any erosion of their status and influence by restricting the scope for their tacit knowledge to be translated into objective collective knowledge which, potentially, others can use within the dialectic of control. Overall the effect would be, again, to diminish the potential for individual and collective learning as prescribed by proponents of learning organizations.

Ideology and the learning organization

Much new knowledge generated by members of an organization attempting to deal with perceived turbulence in the external environment will probably have a strong normative element, concerned with values and beliefs deemed relevant to solving problems posed by that turbulence (Schein, 1985). In this section we consider how the use made of new knowledge might be constrained by an ideology constructed from the language in which the concepts of a learning organization are couched.

For Geertz (1964), systems of cultural symbols are the stuff of ideology, providing guides for behaviour, thought or feeling – poems and maps for navigating through terrain which is strange, emotionally and topographically. The 'ornate, vivid' style of ideological language, and the psychological pressure of the rituals and settings within which it is employed, helps the construction of situations which encourage commitment and motivate action. In contrast, science seeks intellectual clarity by avoiding semantic devices which construct moral feeling. Like ideology, its focus is a problematic situation, providing information which is lacking. But where science 'is the diagnostic, the critical, dimension of culture, ideology is the justificatory, the apologetic one – it refers to that part of culture which is actively concerned with the establishment and defense of patterns of belief and value' (Geertz, 1964: 71–2).

Geertz construes ideology as a means of reducing social strain and individual tension in times of turbulence when the level of cultural, social and personal dislocation is such that patterns of shared understanding start to break down and newer ideologies can become crucial as sources of revised individual and collective meaning. The concept of a learning organization fits well into this strain theory of ideology. Managements are offered a new formula for dealing with organizational strain produced by turbulence in the external environment, enabling employees to be given some means of reducing the personal tension brought about by that same turbulence. Corporate reassurance is provided by the belief that organizational flexibility and responsiveness will be enhanced by collective learning. Its source in the learning of individual members will enable them to feel more secure about their own identity, especially as it is fixed by their employment, work status and career prospects.

A learning organization can fulfil the four functions of ideology identified by Geertz (1964). There could be a 'cathartic displacement of emotions' onto 'symbolic enemies', in this case those over whom the proposed arrangements should yield competitive advantage. Morale could be sustained by legitimizing the perceived strains in terms of higher values of personal development and spirituality. Solidarity could be engendered in the face of disruptive turbulence, bolstered by the symbols associated with individual and collective learning practices. And, finally, by articulating the relationship between turbulence and learning, those who publicize the learning organization 'state the problems for the larger society, take sides on the issues involved and present themselves in the ideological market place' (Geertz, 1964: 55).

None of the designers of the learning organization seem to claim that it is based on scientific principles. In fact, Pedler *et al.* (1989) note that the learning company can be perceived as scientific hypothesis without empirical evidence. On the other hand, the concept is expressed in language which Geertz might describe as 'ornate, vivid, deliberately suggestive'. Garratt (1987) claims that learning organizations can 'concentrate on their firm's hearts ... people can get enthused, and the dread Kafkaesque stereotype of organizations dispelled' (p. 134). In Pedler *et al.* (1989) 'the learning company is the new frontier and the scouts are busy bringing back reports. In short, we are now standing at the "vision" end of the vision-to-reality sequence in bringing the idea into being' (p. 1). Hawkins's (1991) focus 'is the spiritual learning in worldly organizations, rather than the Ashram' (p. 177) which will require that we 'replace "helicopter thinking" with "satellite thinking"' (p. 179).

Within his strain theory of ideology Geertz (1964) accepts that it is possible to argue that 'interest based' process through which a resolution of the conflicting interests of key actors determines the course of events during a time of rapid change, when political tactics and strategy become paramount. In a turbulent period, competing individuals and groups attempt to enrol others to the values and beliefs which they offer as explanations of collective experience – i.e. to emergent elements of ideology (Giddens, 1979; Clegg, 1989). But the playing field is not level in this competition; instead there are institutional symmetries, created historically through 'economic-based structures and systems of discursive monopoly', which provide the management of organizations with tactical and strategic advantage (Deetz, 1992).

As argued in the previous section, there seems no reason why a learning organization as defined should differ in this respect. Existing symmetries of power are likely to be buttressed by the learning process, giving senior managers access to newly generated corporate knowledge and language, strengthening their hands in internal and external dealings. Through their control of strategic planning activities, senior managers should be able to influence strongly insiders' perceptions of the external environment and outsiders' reciprocal perceptions, moderating any strain and tension by marginalizing representation of interests other than their own, reducing unacceptable alternative courses of action to economic costs (e.g. the time-consuming aspects of worker participation in management), by further socialization of members, and by shifting extra responsibility to the individual (Deetz, 1992).

In this context the language of ideology mediates between individuals and the conditions of their existence. They are positioned as subjects and, as such, assume that they are the authors of the ideology which they speak, as if in control of the meanings which that ideology carries (Deetz, 1992). To this end the management of a learning organization could embark on a process of re-socialization within an overall 'ethos of self responsibility' fulfilled through collaboration rather than competition.

The organization's members would probably be encouraged to see themselves as critical providers of organizational knowledge through their enhanced learning capability; as responsible for experimentation; as wise interpreters of collective knowledge; as honoured participants in decision making; as responsive to the needs of internal and external customers. In imagining themselves as these types of people, individuals would be accepting a revised personal identity, taking on more responsibility for providing solutions to corporate problems and for self-surveillance, enforcing norms which constrain the expression of doubts or disloyalties reflecting differing belief structures. In the process the increased level of organizational commitment induced in employees might place at risk some of their other commitments, e.g. to family and close friends (Randall, 1987). 'To increase organizational commitment involves creating a greater tension and, by implication, places a strain on the other life-worlds in which there is partial inclusion' (Hopfl, 1992).

This perspective takes account of the language used in proposals for a learning organization; but equally important is what is not said, especially about goals and preferences, their origins and the criteria used in decision making to further their achievement (Pfeffer, 1981). Directorial competence in these areas is not questioned by Garratt (1987), Hawkins (1991) or Pedler *et al.* (1991). As for managerial prerogatives, Hawkins's (1991) hierarchical view provides implicit support for the notion, while Garratt (1987) does not question directors' prerogatives, seeing learning organizations as a means of improving directors' performance through better control over organizations made much more productive via individual and collective learning. Pedler *et al.* (1988, 1989, 1991) do not address the issue directly, blurring distinctions between managers and other employees. 'Managerial acts are seen as conscious experiments rather than set solutions', as part of 'the learning approach to strategy' (1991: 18) and all members of the company have a chance to take part, to discuss and contribute to major policy decisions (p. 19). In any but the smallest organizations this would seem to be impracticable and implies only a process of consultation.

Pedler *et al.* provide an example of the constraints managerial prerogative places on employee discretion even within a learning organization. In reviewing the implications of an extensive learning initiative in the Rover Car Group its Chairman, Graham Day, is quoted as saying, 'We realize that by encouraging continuous learning and development among all our employees, they will start to question more and more the way we manage things. We will have to learn to respond appropriately to that, but we are not a democracy – the buck stops with management' (Pedler *et al.*, 1991: 195).

Ideology is expressed not only in language but in artefacts, especially those which constitute an organization's technology. Those who are privileged in the design and implementation of technology are well placed to translate their interests into ideologies, embedded and invisible in the technological process. All those who use the technology are then influenced strongly by the ideology of its controlling logic, made subject to it. There is a circuit of meaning: ideology helps to shape the meanings and perceptions of technology; these influence the development of technological artefacts and language; and in turn, these reflect and reinforce ideology as a natural, taken-for-granted part of the control process (Scarborough and Corbett, 1992).

Whether the ethos of a learning organization takes root or not will depend crucially on its adoption by those who make key decisions at the design and implementation stages in the introduction or modification of technology. If committed to the learning ethos of Pedler *et al.* (1991) they are likely to involve users in the design stage, providing scope for operator discretion, allowing for experimentation and learning, 'informating' as well as automating. But there is a long history of the hegemony of rational, science-based principles, of people's subordination to the ideology of scientific rationality, to the conservative values and rationality of science and its enframement of the technology process (Scarborough and Corbett, 1992: 89).

In summary, ideology is central to questions of choice and especially whether choices are to be made privately by members of dominant coalitions or as the outcome of some more public challenges within an open democratic process. Potentially, the ethos and language of the learning organization provide ideological raw material which people in organizations can use to accommodate to the collective and personal strains of an external environment perceived as turbulent. The language and symbolism, explicitly or by omission, upholds managerial prerogatives in expressing strategic preferences and in pursuing goals. Within the framework of explicit and tacit legitimation which the metaphor of a learning organization provides, those managements who realize its ideological potential will be able to make use of the prescribed language and practices to maintain their hegemony. In the process, employees risk being subjected to further socialization, encouraged to adopt aspects of identity which, as Clegg (1989) anticipates, would ensure their continued obedience, not only in a prohibitive sense, but also creatively.

Conclusions

This chapter has enabled certain problematic aspects of the learning organization to be considered within a theoretical framework related to power, politics and ideology. A confusion in the literature was examined, concerning the extent of political activity within a 'dialectic of control' and where the 'control boundary' between management and other employees might be drawn. Given continuing pressures on organizations operating in turbulent conditions to become ever more productive it was argued that boundaries are unlikely to be moved anything like as far as implied in the more utopian prescriptions, with consequent effects on the scope for individual and collective learning.

This conclusion leads on to a further point about the likely effect of the characteristics of a learning organization on the distribution of power. It seems that the changes in structure and the increments in collective knowledge associated with this and other features will tend to favour those formally appointed as managers, especially at the apex of organizations. In making use of their enhanced discursive penetration at the nodal points where internal and external circuits of power intersect they are likely to build up and safeguard their power. Others who feel that their power is threatened will probably behave defensively, placing restrictions on the possibilities for collectively productive learning.

Finally, it is likely that senior managers within enterprises where the principles of a learning organization are put into practice will be able to bolster and safeguard their prerogatives by articulating aspects of the ideology implicit in the literature of the learning organization. This leads us to conclude that those who propagate the principles of a learning organization risk opening the latest phase of a long history of metaphors which have been used manipulatively (Giddens, 1979) by managers with a long pedigree of instrumental interest in social science as a means of solving industrial problems (Pfeffer, 1981). The force of the metaphors employed stems from the rational, conscious level of explanation and at a deeper level where versions of social science – 'the orthodox consensus' – provide commonsense explanations of lived experience which it serves to justify (Giddens, 1979).

Earlier metaphors proposed by social scientists – most recently 'Organizational Culture' – have served to 'transform compliance into cooperation, consent into commitment, discipline into self-discipline, the goals of the organization into the goals of the employee' (Hollway, 1991: 94). The metaphor of 'learning organization' could well suffer the same fate, translated into an instrument for control so that the ambiguities of organizational life, potentially fruitful for learning and creativity, are suppressed in favour of a dominant and stable set of beliefs and interests (Meyerson, 1991).

References

Argyris, C. and Schon, D.A. (1978) *Organizational Learning: A Theory of Action Perspective*, Reading, MA: Addison-Wesley.

Argyris, C. and Schon, D.A. (1983) Editorial. *Journal of Management Studies*, 20(1): 3–5.

Buchanan, D.A. (1992) 'High performance: new boundaries of acceptability in worker control', in Salaman, C., Cameron, S., Hamblin, H., Iles, P., Mabey, C. and Thompson, K. (eds) *Human Resource Strategies*, London: Sage.

Clegg, S.R. (1989) *Frameworks of Power*, London: Sage.

Committee on the Financial Aspects of Corporate Governance (1992) *Draft Report*, London.

Coopers and Lybrand/MORI (1991) *Shareholder Value Analysis Survey*, Spring, London: Coopers and Lybrand.

Crozier, M. (1964) *The Bureaucratic Phenomenon*, Chicago: University of Chicago Press.

Deetz, S. (1992) 'Disciplinary power in modern corporations', in Alvesson, M. and Willmott, H. (eds) *Critical Management Studies*, London: Sage.

Fiol, C.M. and Lyles, M.A. (1985) 'Organizational Learning', *Academy of Management Review* 10(4): 803–13.

Garratt, B. (1987) *The Learning Organization*, London: Fontana.

Geertz, C. (1964) 'Ideology as cultural system', in Apter, D.E. (ed.) *Ideology and Discontent*, New York: The Free Press.

Giddens, A. (1976) *New Rules of Sociological Method*, London: Hutchinson.

Giddens, A. (1979) *Central Problems in Social Theory*, London: Macmillan.

Hawkins, P. (1991) 'The spiritual dimension of the learning organisation', *Management Education and Development* 22(3): 172–87.

Hedberg, B., Nystrom, P. and Starbuck, W. (1976) 'Camping on seesaws: prescriptions for a self-designing organization', *Administrative Science Quarterly* 21: 41–65.

Hollway, W. (1991) *Work Psychology and Organizational Behaviour*, London: Sage.

Hopfl, H. (1992) 'The making of the corporate acolyte: some thoughts on charismatic leadership and the reality of organizational commitment', *Journal of Management Studies* 29(1): 23–33.

Kanter, R.M. (1984) *The Change Masters: Corporate Entrepreneurs at Work*, London: George Allen & Unwin.

Kanter, R.M. (1989) 'The managerial work', *Harvard Business Review* Nov./Dec.: 85–92.

Keenoy, T. (1990) 'HRM: a case of the wolf in sheep's clothing?' *Personnel Review* 19(2): 3–9.

Keenoy, T. (1992) 'Constructing control', in Hartley, J.F. and Stephenson, G.M. (eds) *Employment Relations*, Oxford: Blackwell.

Meyerson, D.E. (1991) 'Acknowledging and uncovering ambiguities in cultures', in Frost, P.J., Moore, L.F., Louis, M.R., Lundberg, C.C. and Martin, J. (eds) *Reframing Organizational Culture*, Newbury Park, CA: Sage.

Mueller, W.S., Clegg, C.W., Wall, T.D., Kemp, N.J. and Davies, R.T. (1986) 'Pluralist beliefs about new technology within a manufacturing organisation', *New Technology, Work and Employment* 1: 127–39.

Pedler, M., Boydell, T. and Burgoyne, J. (1988) *Learning Company Project Report*, Sheffield: Manpower Services Commission.

Pedler, M., Burgoyne, J. and Boydell, T. (1989) 'Towards the Learning Company', *Management Education and Development* 20(1): 1–8.

Pedler, M., Burgoyne, J. and Boydell, T. (1991) *The Learning Company: A Strategy for Sustainable Development*, Maidenhead: McGraw-Hill.

Pfeffer, J. (1981) *Power in Organizations*, Cambridge, MA: Ballinger.

Randall, D.M. (1987) 'Commitment and the Organization: The Organization Man Revisited', *Academy of Management Review* 12(3): 460–71.

Revans, R.W. (1982) *The Origins and Growth of Action Learning*, Chartwell: Bratt.

Scarborough, H. and Corbett, J. Martin (1992) *Technology and Organization*, London: Routledge.

Schein, E.H. (1985) *Organizational Culture and Leadership*, San Francisco: Jossey Bass.

Shrivastava, P. (1983) 'A typology of organizational learning systems', *Journal of Management Studies* 20(1): 7–28.

Simon, H.A. (1976) *Administrative Behaviour*, 3rd edn, New York: Free Press.

Streeck, W. (1987) 'The uncertainties of management in the management of uncertainty: employers, labour relations and industrial adjustment in the 1980s', *Work, Employment and Society* 1(3): 281–308.

Zuboff, S. (1988) *In the Age of the Smart Machine*, London: Heinemann.

Executive tourism:
26 the dynamics of strategic
leadership in the MNC
Ken Starkey

In the 1980s Ford Motor Company enacted one of the most spectacular turnarounds in corporate history. Ford's US transformation, however, was not replicated in Europe. This chapter analyses Ford's US turnaround and the problems Ford experienced in repeating the experience in Europe, arguing that the roots of these problems lay in leadership and learning.[1]

Ford Motor Company – the US experience

The key strategic question that came to the fore at Ford in the late 1970s was 'How good are we as a world class manufacturer?' The answer, after Japan, was 'Not good enough.' The beginning of the 1980s found the company bereft of attractive product and moving ever more deeply into loss. Don Petersen, who became Ford Chairman and CEO in 1985, describes the company's situation when he became company President and Chief Operating Officer in 1980 in a triumph of understatement: 'Ford was operating in difficult times back then.' Its market share was slipping steadily. Ford was rated lowest among the Big Three US automakers in the quality and styling of its cars. Japanese automakers had gained a substantial edge in the quality of their products and the efficiency of their factories. The growing sense that the company could not continue in the way it had always done, incrementally improving on the way it had done things in the past, led to a fundamental re-examination of the Ford mission and management style. Ford's response was a commitment to radical change.

Pascale (1990: 119–21) concludes his study of a range of American companies – 'Ford stands alone in appearing to have truly transformed itself.' From a loss of $3.3 billion between 1980 and 1982, Ford moved to profits in 1986 that surpassed General Motors for the first time since 1924. In 1987, Ford broke all previous industry records for profitability. In his own analysis of Ford's US turnaround, Don Petersen describes how top management initiated change. 'You have to create a sense of urgency that will dramatize what you're up against and convince everyone that important changes must be made in order to improve' (Petersen, 1991: 18). A top management team set about examining the key concepts they wanted the company to express with a view to putting these on paper in a new mission statement. A Ford task force examined what they considered 'outstanding' American companies and concluded that these companies had ten things in common:

1. Each firm circulated a statement of corporate goals and values, and executives spent a majority of their time outside their offices, trying to communicate those ideas to their employees.
2. All six emphasized the importance of people and respect for the individual.
3. They substituted trust for strict rules and controls.
4. Every firm made a big fuss about being customer-driven.
5. All six used teamwork, particularly multidepartmental teams, to develop cutting edge products and services.
6. They tried to eliminate levels of management and to drive down authority.
7. The companies emphasized free, open, face-to-face communications.
8. Team players were promoted over individualists.
9. All six offered sophisticated training for managers as well as hourly employees.
10. Managers made a habit of asking their people, 'What do you think?'

Ford top management then decided, after much internal dialogue, that Ford's core values could be encapsulated in 'three p's' – people, products and profits. They went on to develop a new statement of Ford's mission, its values and guiding principles of behaviour. The major organizational challenges that top management set itself to support its strategic agenda were employee involvement (EI) and participative management (PM). EI – 'the process by which employees are provided with the opportunities to contribute their minds, as well as their muscles, and hopefully their hearts, to the attaining of individual and Company goals' (Banas and Sauers, 1989) – had as its goal the development of a cooperative employee relations environment. PM had a dual agenda: first, to complement employee involvement by developing the skills that managers need to provide employees and fellow managers with opportunities to participate in the managerial processes (planning, goal setting, problem solving, and decision making); and second, the integration of managerial effort across rigid functional barriers. The latter is the main focus of this chapter.

According to Petersen (1991: 52), PM is 'simply a style of operating in which you give your peers and subordinates an opportunity to say what they think, and you include their ideas in the overall decision-making process'. Former Ford Vice-President of Product Development, Don Frey (1991: 56), describes the managerial legacy of Fordism: 'Watching the company under Mr Ford during the 1970s, I alternated between sorrow and outrage over what was happening. The company grew only more Byzantine, with a chief executive fighting with his president and principal lieutenants who were, at best, inwardly focused;

people who fostered functional isolation among the company's best employees, usually to divide and diffuse power – all antithetical to innovation.' In Ford the propensity of different functional groups to become introverted and self-seeking in their dealings with other units at the expense of the common good is captured in the image of 'organizational chimneys' – an organization structured for vertical relationships *within* functions that work against horizontal linkages *between* functions. Participative management has as one of its main goals the changing of managerial attitudes and the dismantling of what is now perceived as dysfunctional structures. Its aims are to simplify managerial control, devolve authority and break down the barriers between managerial groups which have their basis in hierarchy, functional specialization, organizational culture and managers' cognitions.

Participative management is of crucial strategic significance. The success of Ford's strategic shift towards innovation hinged on the integration of design, manufacture and sales and marketing. Japanese companies, Ford learnt, owe much of their success to the degree to which they are able to manage their inter-management relationships in a way that facilitates responsiveness to increasingly turbulent market conditions. Responsiveness, based on managerial flexibility, is something which a traditionally organized, tightly controlled, bureaucratic, hierarchical company finds extremely difficult (Piore, 1986: 158). President, and later Chairman, Harold 'Red' Poling described the importance of PM as a guiding principle of behaviour: 'there was a time when many found satisfaction in guarding their own turf ... those days are over. Interpersonal skills and team effort are now a key part of the performance review process. All of us – including me – will be judged on success in this area.' PM and product development came together for Ford in a new strategic vision of the company as design leader. Ford's turnaround in the US was design-led with the new Taurus/Sable range. The company hit rock-bottom in 1980 the year it initiated the Taurus and Sable programme in a 'bet the company strategy' (Halberstam, 1987: 647). With participation and involvement came the opportunity to experiment and design innovative products. Creativity was no longer stifled by bureaucracy. Involvement and participation were used to engender a new sense of responsibility for and joint ownership of product development programmes and effective collaboration across organizational divides – employee with employee, employee with manager, manager with manager, function with function. This proved much more difficult to do in Europe.

Strategic leadership – Ford US

Explanations of Ford's transformation in the United States during the 1980s have emphasized the role of top management and the top team dynamic. Pascale (1990) emphasizes the relationship of Don Petersen, President from 1980 to 1985 and Chairman between 1985 and 1990, and Harold 'Red' Poling, Vice-President, Ford North American Automotive Operations, then President from 1984 until he became Petersen's successor as Chairman in 1989. Petersen provided the 'visionary' leadership (Westley and Mintzberg, 1989), Poling kept the company's 'feet on the floor'. One individual alone was not enough. Petersen was responsible for the motivation and excitement of individuals and changing their goals, needs and aspirations through the redefinition of company mission and values. Poling provided the instrumental leadership responsible for making sure that behaviour throughout the organization was consistent with the new goals necessary to transform the company, concentrating on the quantifiable, on getting the quality and the numbers right, ruthlessly benchmarking against key competitors. Petersen dealt with the unquantifiable such as issues of PM and the harnessing of hearts and minds to innovative product development. The complementarity of the top management team is unambiguously regarded as crucial: 'Ford was lucky to have this dynamic of individuals who somehow complemented each other ... . While Red looked after the North American cost structure, Pete became an EI/PM diplomat.' Petersen's own view (1991: 55–6) is that he and Poling became a team whose ability exceeded the sum of the parts.

Having emphasized the complementarity of their roles one does have to stress the importance of Petersen's role in transforming Ford's management process. Petersen was responsible for disrupting conventional thinking in Ford, for getting Ford managers to think the 'unthinkable' and for shifting the focus from the *functional* to the *strategic*. To facilitate this attack upon Ford's conventional, traditional and now outmoded management approach, Petersen's most significant contribution was to set in place the participative approach to top decision-making, thus broadening, deepening and enriching the company's strategic decision-making. He himself became the living proof of PM. 'He lives and breathes participative management, taking to heart suggestions from vice presidents and assembly line workers. Most remarkably, he subordinates his ego to the needs of the company' (Pascale, 1990: 159).

Petersen also stressed the importance of a balanced management team that was comfortable with its own internal differences. Difference was to be encouraged as a virtue rather than excoriated as a threat. Insight into his own personality and that of his peers helped Petersen refine the management process of Ford's top management group. An important part of the development of a new management style was the introduction of the participative management approach to the workings of the top decision-making forums of the company, such as the crucial Policy and Strategy Committee. When Petersen joined this committee in 1975 as head of Diversified Products the approach was non-participative in the sense that committee members spoke only about their own businesses and did not intrude on the views expressed by members from other areas. For example, the rule was that if the manager in charge of cars was discussing product problems, it was inappropriate for Petersen himself to contribute to the discussion, despite his experience in product development. The way the dynamics of the Policy and Strategy Committee were changed to encourage greater participation paralleled the approach used at the plant and operations levels. Poling and Petersen himself held back from expressing their opinions at the beginning of the discussion. Petersen also made a point of telling the committee members that they should feel encouraged to speak up regardless of the subject, something they found very difficult at first, and often polled the members individually for comments and suggestions, in effect serving as the facilitator (Petersen, 1991: 61). To further facilitate the free exchange of ideas committee meetings were sometimes conducted away from traditional committee meeting venues such as the board of directors' room. Breakfast meetings were particularly successful in this respect and top management meetings were conducted off-site with the participants dressed in sweaters and slacks – relaxing the 'dress code' – to generate franker discussion. The shedding of conventional modes of behaviour was symbolic of a shift in thinking about strategy and management style. Petersen feels that these measures led to 'some of the most candid conversations in Ford's history' (Petersen, 1991: 61–2).

American initiatives, European responses

Ford of Europe appeared very successful for much of the 1980s. In 1988 it recorded record profits but since 1989 it has under-performed in a market struggling with the effects of a deepening recession. In 1991 the company achieved record sales in Europe but went into loss. 1992 saw record losses. The company continues to face the twin strategic imperatives of cost reduction and innovation. Its product development record throughout the 1980s was patchy.

Ford of Europe's problems of the late 1980s were exacerbated by its top management's slow awakening to the magnitude of the change agenda it had to address. In the early 1980s there was little generally felt need for fundamental change. The belief persisted that the company only needed to do better what it had always done well. This was, with the benefit of hindsight, shortsighted. In the words of one senior Ford of Europe manufacturing manager: 'When you're making two billion dollars a year it's tough to say our system is inadequate. And suddenly when you're not making two billion dollars profit it's too late.'

In 1979, Ford of Europe initiated its 'After Japan' [AJ] campaign, an internal study of Ford's productivity levels which was the direct response to the company's new awareness of the Japanese competitive edge. The origins of AJ lay in a visit to Japan by Bill Hayden, Ford of Europe Vice-President of Manufacturing, from which he returned, in his own words, in 'a state of shock'. Japan was the crucible of change for Ford. In 1992 Hayden acknowledged how fundamentally Japan had changed the rules of competition.

> The most important change [of the 1980s] is that the company no longer believes today – as it did ten years ago – that its quality was sufficient to match the competition, that customers were loyal to Ford and that our efficiency was more than a match for the rest of the world. It's as basic and fundamental as that. The Japanese have caused us to completely rethink our policies and behaviour patterns and that's what we're desperately trying to do.

This acceptance of the need for radical change was a long time coming. AJ did not go far enough. In the opinion of Lindsey Halstead, Chairman of Ford of Europe from 1988 to 1992, AJ's great limitation was that it 'looked at the world through Ford's eyes'. It was driven by a primary focus on cost differences and a belief that the old Ford system, if intensified, was still capable of matching the Japanese. In this sense, it contributed little to understanding *why* the productivity and quality gap existed between Ford and Japan. The conclusion Ford of Europe's top management derived from AJ was the need for efficiency improvement and lowering the company's breakeven point. The challenge of AJ was to accelerate 'towards greater efficiency *within* our established system: to take the Ford system to its limits'. 'AJ was about cost reduction – it [was] how Ford has always responded to the unknown .... AJ was a typical Ford drive to streamline the organization.' In the words of Lindsey Halstead:

> Because it didn't diagnose that we had a fundamental cultural change problem ... it didn't focus on cultural change ... AJ didn't take us far enough ... it was a hell of a good start. But I don't know that before we did MVGP [the introduction of the new missions, values and guiding principles statement in the US] we knew what a fundamental change [we really needed], how thorough throughout the organization it had to become.

AJ strengthened the managerial emphasis on control. It did nothing to challenge the dysfunctions of Ford's Finance-dominated culture.

> The tradition in Ford has been for functional heads to come to planning meetings with their own plans to defend. It was an adversarial system. And in an organization like Ford where Finance had been top-dog for so long, figures weren't used to improve the quality of decision-making but as weapons to gain a sectional advantage irrespective of what the overall cost was.

The adversarial nature of managerial relations was captured in a joke of the early 1980s: 'the difference between the West and Japan is that they both have boats of eight but in Japan you have seven oarsmen and one cox whereas in the West you have one oarsman and seven coxes!' The joke also captures another crucial issue: the unfavourable ratio of direct to indirect workers in Ford compared to Japanese companies.

AJ was succeeded in Europe by the American change initiative based upon the new company Statement of Mission, Values and Guiding Principles and the new managerial emphasis on teamwork, employee involvement and participative management. In the words of an American human resource manager on secondment to Ford of Europe, 'The idea was to achieve a quick transfusion of the American experience into the European company.' Various barriers to participative management had to be confronted. There were turf battles between functional groups, structural barriers ('chimneys') between functions and an inevitable resistance to change. There was also an important leadership issue. Top management endorsement and leadership in getting the whole organization aligned and working towards the same goal was felt to be lacking.

Pascale (1990) emphasizes the creative tension that existed in the top management team at Ford in the US. What one sees as a result is the complicated working out of a dialectic between old and new, the outcome of which was a synthesis. If Petersen was the champion of the new guard, Poling represented the best of the old with his emphasis on efficiency and discipline. In Europe it was a very different story because there was no comparable balance of champions. Differences in the constitution and dynamics of the top management groups in Ford of Europe and in the US which had a significant effect upon the unfolding of the new management agenda. As a result there are no top-level champions of the new change agenda in Europe with the experience or enough power to make this the centre of Ford of Europe's management agenda.

What we find is a marked difference in top management tenure of position in Ford of Europe compared with the US. European postings are used as career staging-posts by fast-track American executives. In Ford of Europe Europeans refer to American managers as 'executive tourists' – 'This is seen as a place that people need to come for experience to move them up the ladder in the US'. The same contrast of stability in the US and turnover in Europe existed in the positions of Vice-President, *with one crucial exception*. Bill Hayden was Vice-President of Manufacturing in Ford of Europe from 1974 until 1991 when he became the first Ford Chairman of Jaguar after its acquisition. With this steady turnover in Ford's European top management cadre, Hayden, despite the fact that he was never Chairman, exerted a disproportionate influence, not only by sheer force of personality and the iron control he exercised over Manufacturing but also because he had been a source of stability in an otherwise rapidly changing executive team.

Hayden represented the old discipline, the emphasis on efficiency and control as the basis of strategy. He was quite willing to innovate in search of cost-reduction, as with the 'After Japan' initiative, but was more wary of other kinds of innovation. His role in Europe was comparable to that of Poling in the US – incidentally, he declares himself Poling's 'biggest fan' – but in Europe there was no strong countervailing force for change, no Petersen.

> Europe didn't have a Petersen, it didn't have a big name champion of change throughout the 80s in anything like the same way [as the US] so it missed out on that healthy tension, it remained cost-driven. There were change initiatives, there wasn't the same advocacy of change.

Hayden was associated with the urge to centralized control.

> He [ran] Manufacturing in a way which is almost unbelievable that one man could run an organization that large in such a centralized way . . . you would find it difficult to believe how all the decisions have been funnelled into him . . . . Extremely centralized. And of course a man of tremendous ability, not many like him.

One senior manufacturing executive offered the following anecdote as encapsulating the deep-seated tensions of the period in Europe.

> There is conflict between quality and cost. We were having a discussion about our objective of being the lowest-cost vehicle producer in Europe and was that right or should we really be designing the best quality vehicles and sales would come from that rather than cost? Lou Lataif [then President] made a statement that our objective was to be the lowest-cost producer but also the best-quality producer. Bifi Hayden stood up and said, 'Yes, I agree with you Lou, but Manufacturing is totally committed to being the lowest cost vehicle producer in Europe.' And Lou Lataif said, 'Thank you Bill, would anyone in Manufacturing who disagrees with Bill please stand up . . . ' It was a nice blend of Bill saying, 'This is Manufacturing, and this is what we do' and Lou saying, 'Well, perhaps there should be some debate about that.' Everyone laughed because everyone knew damn well that nobody would stand up and contradict Bill. To me it was indicative of some of the conflicts between what we say we're trying to do and what we actually do, especially at the highest level!

One can construe this dialogue in a variety of ways. There are none of the subtleties of 'problem-solving' and 'dilemma management' in the participative management mode. It represents the old politics – the Manufacturing function protecting its power base within the corporation. When Product Development wanted Manufacturing to participate in programme management groups, it was Hayden who said 'No'!

This is not to suggest that Hayden was the 'villain of the piece'. It is far more complex than that. In psychodynamic terms Ford needed and, indeed, had created Hayden as a crucial point of stability but top US management, ultimately responsible for Ford of Europe, had not created the necessary countervailing force for new thinking in Europe. As a result commitment to the implications of Ford's new mission and the values and principles of behaviour necessary to support it, such as PM, was only skin-deep. Lindsey Halstead's description of the topography of the boardroom when he arrived in Europe in 1988 is indicative of the quality of the top management process.

> [How was it possible] to be able to answer any questions in that damn boardroom? . . . There was a horseshoe table and a hierarchy of seating. It's a very cold room. We used to assign seats literally, by tradition, because the damn thing is arranged this way. There would be a name card and the Chairman would sit there, and so it went down in pecking order. We stopped this. We created another conference room. It's got a round table. We don't have any assigned seats, deliberately, we sit wherever there's an empty chair. That's what I would call PM in action, it's living it . . . it makes a statement.

The top management group in Europe was insulated from the reality of European operations both by experience and by its *modus operandi*.

There is a huge gap between the Ford of Europe Executive Committee and most of the rest of the company . . . there's a vacuum. They travel as a cloistered group around Europe and the world and they try to make contact with the rest of management but I don't think it's very successful. They'll never meet plant managers, for example. They're like high-level tourists. Even if we wanted to give them bad news – and we don't – we don't have the opportunity. They receive their information . . . in sound-bites, half-hour briefings. But the budget process, the hard figures are pored over for weeks on end. We're still driven by the numbers at the executive level no matter how hard we try.

The lack of a top management team with a long-term stable membership creates particular problems of institutionalizing change. If the tenure of change agents is transitory then the ownership of the change process becomes difficult if not impossible.

The upshot of the impermanence in the top echelons in Europe was that, in some senses, Hayden was operating in a top management vacuum. He himself says of his experience in the Ford of Europe boardroom:

Ford of Europe is not a very stable organization. By that I mean if you look at the number of chairmen and presidents of the organization over the last twenty-odd years then there's been a change of personnel every two or three years. And it's not like an ordinary organization where the guy tends to come up [through the ranks]. They've come over and gone back. If you come up through the ranks then you're part of the culture and you're less of a shock to the system . . . [they] arrive and you've never met, never worked for or with them . . . It slows down the decision-making process. Because when people arrive they have to buy into the current agenda. Unsettling is a strong word but if you're setting long-term objectives and changing three of the top five players in Europe every other year then it makes it very difficult.

He found the effort of keeping up with the changes in top management personnel an increasing chore.

I had met most of them in Dearborn [Ford's US headquarters], but it wasn't a working relationship. We didn't *know* each other, hadn't worked together. When they arrived I'd usually go and introduce myself. But with time – it would register that a new guy had arrived – but I didn't bother going down the corridor to knock on his door. The business went on as before, new Chairman or not.

The emphasis on cost and efficiency that Hayden represents, the strength of this mind-set and the weakness in political terms of the new change perspective also have to be seen in terms of the relationship between Europe and the parent company. There were pressures from the US that slowed down the European change process.

I think probably that the pressures even from Dearborn caused it to be that way ... Remember Europe was producing profit, it was sort of salvaging North America, the rest of the company was in significantly difficult shape. Part of that you can explain away by the economic conditions and the fact that the Japanese hadn't attacked here. There's a whole bunch of reasons. Therefore I don't think that there was that pressure for change even from Dearborn. The pressure was to keep producing profit and keep doing the job that you're doing. You're doing it well so keep at it, guys. Well what kind of pressure was that? That was a cost-profit pressure, primarily.

Europe was acting as Ford's 'cash cow'.

'We must throw a bridge between Europe and the United States of America' – this was Henry Ford himself as long ago as 1924. In conjunction with its US parent, Ford of Europe still has to negotiate an appropriate governance process at the highest level that will allow it to optimize its development. For the company as a whole 'breaking down the division ... the barriers between countries' remains a strategic imperative. From a strategic leadership perspective the major factor contributing to the weakness of the impetus to diffuse the successful US initiatives (the new mission, values, guiding principles, participative management, employee involvement) to Europe was the dynamic of Ford of Europe's top management group, in itself a reflection of the group's composition and tenure which themselves reflected the way in which Ford's top US management used Ford of Europe as a convenient 'staging-post' in American top management development. In the US there were the top-level champions, 'competing' perspectives had the time to gel, and operating management was brought into the process as were top union representatives. In short, the process was managed. This just did not happen in Europe in the same coherent manner. It was not made to happen.

Conclusion

The Ford experience of the 1980s raises a variety of questions about the dynamics of strategic leadership in the MNC. The 'executive tourist' phenomenon requires further research to chart its prevalence and to assess its effects. More generally, further empirical evidence is needed on how the composition and dynamics of top management teams in MNCs affect strategy and performance. Order is more a matter of beliefs than of structures. Disorder can result when differing top management beliefs and actions prove incompatible or impede necessary change. Of course, one cannot generalize from one case study. A larger sample of cases is needed to uncover patterns of similarity and difference, for example in the balance of locals and 'tourists' at top management level, with a view to developing perhaps a classification of types of career development strategies in the MNC and an explicit statement of testable hypotheses. We need further understanding before the 'experimental' stage is reached and, in this author's opinion, comparative case studies will provide the basis for developing our understanding.

It is perhaps ironic in the Ford case that 'Red' Poling is of the opinion that you have to spend at least four years in a position to get anything out of it and that Don Petersen himself thinks he changed jobs too often – more than fifteen positions in his first twenty years at Ford! But tenure in company alone as a measure needs to be supplemented by the analysis of tenure and movement through positions in the company – for example, functional experience and overseas tours of duty – and with a combined 'measure' of top team experience and outlook. Defining leadership 'periods' and strategic 'eras' solely in terms of the period of office of the CEO is far from ideal (Thomas, 1988: 399). Individual tenure measures on their own are not very helpful in capturing the experience of individuals and its effects or the dynamic nature of the strategy process which is an outcome of team interactions. One also needs to incorporate some measure of individual personality characteristics into the emerging 'equation'. Don Petersen stresses the interaction of personality types in Ford's top team. He used the Myers-Briggs typology to teach Ford managers about the differences between themselves and to illustrate how different types of individuals operate differently. Petersen himself brought to Ford's top team an intuitive and feeling approach to decision-making, something which is rarely found at that level.

Creating the right organizational context for transnational learning depends upon developing managers with broadly-based perspectives and relationships and fostering supportive organizational norms and values that are sensitive to but not submerged by local management dynamics. A firm's ability to develop general managers or programme managers is crucial to its capacity for adapting to changing competitive pressures. Effective teams require a variety of legitimate difference if they are to avoid groupthink manifested in the tendency for a few individuals to dominate discussions and decision-making, insularity, the restricted generation and assessment of alternatives, and, ultimately, inferior decision-making. The strategic mode of decision-making is best managed by a heterogeneous group in which diversity of opinion, knowledge and background allows a thorough voicing of alternatives. In terms of the dynamics of such a process one is talking about what one might term 'constructive dissent' that challenges the status quo in a positive way, not the rather more prevalent 'defending turf'. Such heterogeneity is necessary in a turbulent environment. The crucial strategic leadership skill in the MNC will be the ability to synthesize difference and interdependence.

Postscript

Henry Ford's project of nearly three-quarters of a century ago still remains – the building of a bridge between Ford in the US and Ford in Europe. Ford still has to develop an appropriate management process that will allow it to optimize its development in Europe. In April 1994 the company announced the biggest structural change in its history: its decision to abandon its regional approach to organization with the merging of European and North American operations to create Ford Automotive Operations. The goal is to become a truly global organization based upon five global product lines/vehicle programs, all reporting to a Vice-President of Product Development in the US. The aim is to integrate all automotive processes and eliminate duplication of effort across the company, thus substantially reducing costs by a predicted $2–3 billion a year.

On 1 January 1995, Ford of Europe ceased to exist as a profit centre and as an identity. (Part of the rationale behind the current changes is to 'wipe out the separate profit centre mentality'.) The reorganization is an implicit admission that managing on the basis of senior US staff on temporary secondment to Europe cannot cope with the complexities of this form of regional organization. Indeed, the reorganization is also an admission that the regional approach to organization is itself too complex. Product development across regional divides, as pioneered in the Mondeo/Contour/Mystique development, is too expensive and takes too long. The company is still not competitive in production costs with GM in Europe or with the revitalized Chrysler in the US.

In 1967, with the establishment of Ford of Europe, the European national companies (Ford UK and Ford Germany) were asked to 'think Europe not Britain or Germany'. In 1995 the injunction is to 'think global'. The new senior management for the new Ford Automotive Operations (FAO) has been selected on the basis of its technical and leadership capability. Only one of this new management team is European. The joke doing the rounds during the last days of Ford of Europe was that FAO actually means 'For Americans Only'!

Note

1. Further details of the study upon which this chapter is based can be found in Starkey and McKinlay (1993). Quotes, unless otherwise attributed, are from interviews conducted in the company by the author.

References

Banas, P. and Sauers, R. (1989) 'The relationship between participative management and employee Involvement', Dearborn: Ford Motor Company.

Frey, D. (1991) 'Learning the ropes: my life as a product champion', *Harvard Business Review* September–October: 46–56.

Halberstam, D. (1987) *The Reckoning,* London: Bloomsbury.

Pascale, R. (1990) *Managing on the Edge,* New York: Viking.

Petersen, D.E. (1991) *A Better Idea. Redefining the Way Americans Work,* Boston: Houghton-Mifflin.

Piore, M. (1986) 'Perspectives on labor market flexibility', *Industrial Relations* 25(2): 146–66.

Starkey, K. and McKinlay, A. (1993) *Strategy and the Human Resource. Ford and the Search for Competitive Advantage,* Oxford: Blackwell Business.

Thomas, A.B. (1988) 'Does leadership make a difference to organizational performance?', *Administrative Science Quarterly* 33: 388–400.

Westley, F. and Mintzberg, H. (1989) 'Visionary leadership and strategic management', *Strategic Management Journal* 10 Special Issue: 17–32.

27 Making sense of managerial wisdom

Leon C. Malan and Mark P. Kriger

Our own life is the instrument with which we experiment with truth. (Thich Nhat Hahn)

Practicing managers are faced with thousands of decisions every day. Instead of searching for data from a large pool of comparative organizations, they normally base their decisions on their experience and observations of inputs from their immediate environment. Obviously, some managers are more successful than others, and some are even elevated to some mythical status. When we evaluate some decisions in hindsight, we are often struck by the brilliance and apparent insight of those decisions. How do they do it? Is there something we can call managerial wisdom, and if so, how can we make sense of and develop it? What are the underlying types of variability and their role in the cognition and behavior of managers? These are the questions we try to address in this chapter.

On the nature of variability

Variability plays a crucially important role in much of our scientific research endeavors. As researchers, we try continually to manipulate the variation of variables in our studies. We also often attempt to reduce the unsystematic and error variance and try to increase the systematic variance (Ghiselli, Campbell, and Zedeck, 1981). Similarly, the aim in measurement is to achieve a low level of variability in scales (Nunnally and Bernstein, 1994: 19). In designing research studies, the classic strategy in research design is to avoid threats to internal and external validity by increasing the number of observations (Cook and Campbell, 1979). Prior to data analysis, we remove the outliers to give a more coherent set of data with which to work. This way our results are more representative and are not influenced by one or two errant values. Thus, as organizational scientists, we have a strong obsession to control variables and to reduce so-called unwanted variance. This tends to limit our studies to small, well-defined aspects of organizational life – to attempt to gather data from samples that are large and intended to be representative of the research domain.

Most of the statistical procedures we use (factor analysis, multiple regression, linear models, etc.) call for appropriately large numbers of observations. Yet, despite the preceding cautions of research methodologists, there is an increasing number of organizational researchers who are calling for and conducting small sample studies that are rich in contextual processual data (Dyer and Wilkins, 1991; Eisenhardt, 1989).

When we turn from the writing of organizational researchers to those of consultants and practicing managers, the use of small-sample, context-rich studies to generate practical action rules, relevant knowledge, and wisdom becomes extensive. Works such as Sloan (1963), Rifkin and Harrar (1988), Watson (1990), and Iacocca (1984), covering respectively General Motors, Digital Equipment Corporation, IBM, Ford, and Chrysler, are open to questions of internal validity and generalizability by the standards of normal science. Nonetheless, these in-depth accounts of single organizations have been and continue to be widely read by practicing managers as well as cited by organizational researchers to illustrate their large-sample studies. Some of the so-called classics in the field of management and organizational theory are similarly based on small sample observations. For example, Chester Barnard (1938) based his work mainly on his extensive experience in New Jersey Bell Telephone Company (later AT&T). The work of Alfred Chandler (1962) has been widely cited despite the fact that he did not have the benefit of a large sample size. Scholars such as Pettigrew (1973) and Johnson (1987) used single-site studies to develop and advance our understanding of organizations in significant ways.

We believe that behind the debate between large-sample and in-depth small-sample proponents is a deeper set of issues that cut to some assumptions that most researchers and practitioners make about the nature of organizations. Clues to the wisdom in managerial actions may be found not in the size of the sample but in the ability to distinguish between fine grades of variation in observations. The remainder of this article (a) proposes a theory that managers develop "managerial wisdom" through a process of progressively finer discernment of variability in the range of data they perceive from their environments and (b) presents implications of these propositions for researchers and practicing managers that help us to understand managerial wisdom.

Some core assumptions

This chapter is grounded in a philosophical shift in the conceptualization of organizations – a re-conceptualization in a sense. This shift occurs at both ontological and epistemological levels and has implications for the way in which we understand and research organizations. In trying to make sense of managerial wisdom, we find that certain of our commonly held assumptions about organizational science come into question. Four core assumptions implicit in the current dominant approach to organizations are as follows:

Core Assumption 1: Individuals, groups, and organizations are objects to be studied that are relatively stable over time.

Core Assumption 2: The behavior of individuals, groups, and organizations is best studied through an examination and comparison of means across populations.

Core Assumption 3: The interaction effect between the object of study (e.g., a set of organizations) and the researcher(s) should be minimized, controlled, or eliminated.

Core Assumption 4: "Occam's razor" should be applied so that the largest amount of variation can be explained with the fewest explanatory constructs, variables, or factors.

If we as organizational researchers examine carefully the behavior of practicing managers, we find a different worldview in use. As researchers, we develop theories based on objective measurement – managers act on their perceptions (Starbuck and Mezias, 1996). First, organizations are not really treated as objects of study but rather as complex, continually changing patterns of relationships. Ontologically, the traditional assumption underlying our understanding of individuals and organizations is that they are objective entities. Most studies in the field of organizational and management theory are concerned with measuring the structures, systems, and outcomes of organizations in relation to the objective reality of the environment that lies outside organizations. We suggest, as have others (e.g., Spender, 1996), that organizations are socially constructed networks of relations and patterns of cognitive processes. We hypothesize that it is the nuances of variability in those patterns that interest managers most. Ontologically, this initially requires a shift from an objective reality approach to social construction (Berger and Luckman, 1967; Burrell and Morgan, 1979; Weick, 1979) and beyond social construction to more holistic models of organization (Bohm, 1980, 1990; Bradley, 1987; McKenzie, 1991; Pribram, 1991; Weber, 1986).

Second, managers rarely read, let alone cite the findings of organizational scientists that have complex statistical models at the core of the study. Managers tend to prefer concrete observations over abstract generalizations. Indeed, the degree to which practitioners are influenced by the empirical and scientific studies of academics is questionable (Barley, Meyer, and Gash, 1988). Whereas normal science may want to reduce the effect of outliers, managers can not ignore them. Organizations have learned that homogeneous teams lead to poor decisions and groupthink (Janis, 1982). Instead of decisions based around the means of observations, managers benefit more from looking for the outliers, the unusual, or the extreme points of view (Schwartz, 1996; Starbuck, 1993). Top management teams are encouraged to find ways to increase their interactions, engage in conflict, and use multiple-lens tactics (Eisenhardt, 1997).

Third, practicing managers tend to treat their organizations as learning laboratories. That is, the interaction between the observer and the observed, or the manager participant-observer and the group or organization, is of more interest than the organizational phenomena separate from the observer (Kriger and Malan, 1993). This observation calls for an epistemological position that is "interpretive rather than normative, being concerned with elucidating meaning rather than with determining causality" (Jones, 1983: 150). This position calls for a different way of treating knowledge. Instead of a Cartesian split between an objective (and rational) individual and the object of study (the organization), we accept the arguments of authors such as Nonaka and Takeuchi (1995) and Spender (1996) that call for a different epistemological assumption in management research. We see executives as integrally part of their organizational environments. Executives cannot afford to be passive, objective observers of their organizations. Mintzberg (1989) argues, borrowing from anthropologist Clifford Geertz, that managers ought to be involved in "thick management" (p. 355). Instead of basing decisions on abstract reports, they should allow the "mood of the factory" (p. 355) to inform their intuition. They do not have the luxury of objective distance for which positivist scientists would call. Instead, managers are fully immersed in their firms, and their decisions are based on the knowledge they glean from this strong and constant interaction between them and their context. In fact, the greater that interaction, the greater the variability in sensory observations, the more learning will take place, and hence, we will argue, the greater the development of managerial wisdom.

Fourth, managers' theories in use indicate that they perceive organizations as complex, dynamic, fastpaced patterns of relationships in which the application of simplified assumptions distorts the nature of what they wish to know and understand. How to create more effective organizations may lie more in the ability to identify variability and to manage the construction and destruction of meaning (Gray, Bougon, and Donnellon, 1985; Smircich and Stubbard,1985) of coherent cognitive patterns than in collecting increasingly finer and more accurate data about the atomistic pieces of organizations. Instead of striving to simplify, managers have learned to turn this complexity and uncertainty of multiple interactions into competitive advantage (D'Aveni, 1994).

When combined with practical experience and observation, this philosophical position leads to a different approach in the way organizations are to be described and researched. If one had to accept the set of assumptions that imply that organizations are imbedded in an objective reality, then variability in these objects is to be found primarily via comparisons of the means in a population of organizations. How often have we not heard studies of organizations being questioned in the scientific community because the sample size was not large enough? However, some studies (Barley *et al.*, 1988) indicate that practicing managers do not find a great deal of relevance in our scientific studies with large sample sizes. Instead, managers' bookshelves are lined with books by executives that share their experiences in single organizations (e.g., Iacocca, 1984; Sculley, 1987; Watson, 1990).

If we change the underlying set of assumptions about organizations and variability, then the idea of organization becomes a symbolic and conceptual artifact. Objective measurement is then not the central aim of organizational research; rather, it is the meaning that managers attach to events that becomes most salient (Bolman and Deal, 1984: 150) and how that meaning creates effective learning and action sequences. The attention to meaning aims at a deeper understanding of the organization itself than does the measurement of a supposed objective reality. This emphasis on *verstehen* (understanding) has its roots in the tradition of social thought espoused by German philosophers such as Kant, Husserl, and Weber. One could argue that managers approach the understanding of their organizations from a different social paradigm than do most academics; hence, they have little need for studies that are based on a set of paradigmatic assumptions that attempt to control for variability and to separate the observer from the observed. Practicing managers, on the whole, share an approach that is closer to what Burrell and Morgan (1979) would describe as an interpretive paradigm.

> The interpretive paradigm is informed by a concern to understand the world as it is, to understand the fundamental nature of the social world at the level of subjective experience. It seeks explanation within the realm of individual consciousness and subjectivity, within the frame of reference of the participant as opposed to the observer of action. (Burrell and Morgan, 1979: 28)

But this is not to say that managers are drawn to abstract concepts such as social construction or interpretive paradigm or that they should be.

Some management scholars may ask whether this is an appropriate approach to management science. We are not suggesting that this approach is a scientific revolution replacing any existing theory (Kuhn, 1970). Scientifically, a critical relativist perspective (Anderson, 1986) may be more suitable to our position. For example, in many Eastern cultures there are several different religions that coexist side by side. The classical Chinese and Japanese cultures do not force a choice between often contradictory ways of thinking. Instead, the epistemological approach embraces them all and calls for understanding of different perspectives (Bolman and Deal, 1984).

Organizations exist in multiple environments with several competing values and worldviews. The answer to creating effective organizations lies in understanding the assumptions of these competing views and in finding the appropriate balance (Quinn, 1988). Instead of suggesting a new approach to replace existing assumptions about organizations, we are proposing that there are several complementary ways to understand organizations. The proposed reconceptualization is one where several apparently competing philosophical approaches should not only be accommodated but openly embraced to broaden our ability to understand organizations.

In essence, we argue that executives tend to base their decisions on their observation in organizations and their interpretation of those experiences. Executives strive to discover fine shades of variability within their organizations, their immediate work group, and their perceived competitive environments – which is a continually unfolding world of flux, change, and transformation. Over time, out of this constant discovery process emerges what might be termed managerial wisdom.

Toward a theory of variability in organizations

One way to illustrate variability at work in organizations is by means of an anecdotal story. One of the authors worked some years ago in a large manufacturing operation. The chief executive officer (CEO) and founder of the company had been in the business for many years. On one occasion the author was walking through the plant with the CEO. The plant employed about 600 people, and the manufacturing operation was located in a series of large buildings filled with the noise of machines, forklifts, sirens, and people. Normal conversation was out of the question, and most employees were required to wear protective earplugs. Somewhere on the journey through the factory, the CEO stopped in midstride and started walking to the far end of the building. He went straight to one of the machines and asked the operators what the problem was. They were not aware of any problem. The machine was running, but on closer inspection, there appeared to be a couple of small faults in the finished material. After some adjusting of the machine speed and yarn tension, the problem was corrected, and the CEO continued on his tour of the facilities.

Through the din of the noise in the factory, the CEO was able to pick up the sound of one machine that was not running correctly – something that the operators and managers on the factory floor had missed. To untrained and inexperienced ears, this was all just noise. To the CEO, this was a series of different sounds, all with a different meaning. His ability to distinguish the variability in the sounds enabled him to identify the outliers. If this was possible on the level of the sound of a machine, how much more variability was there in the rest of the organization? What is it that enables a manager to discern such a fine increment of variability? Was it just good hearing? Was it his long experience in the industry? Was it just a hunch or intuition? Was it luck? We argue that this is a due to our search for what we describe as managerial wisdom.

The theory of variability that we are proposing is based on the assumption that managers in organizations act as dynamic interpreters of their environments – intimately connected to those environments and in constant interaction with them. Organizations in this worldview are not objective single entities. Instead, they are complex cognitive networks of socially and personally constructed meaning. Managers in organizations have to make sense of these everchanging phenomena and are charged with the responsibility of managing the meaning.

In this way of viewing organizations, managers (and all other organizational members) are performing complex information processing and interpretation roles that go far beyond the usual machine or computer view of information processing. Managers are both an integral part of information processing and the constructors of the meaning on which they act. However, the information inside organizations is immense, both in its magnitude and in its nature. As the above example illustrates, information can take the form of the sound made by machines, the observation of human behavior, the daily interpretation of sales figures on a computer screen, or a plethora of other information patterns. All of the human senses receive data and experience organizational information on a continuous basis. The point of information overload for any individual is variable, but for all, there is a limit that is eventually reached. Executives experience a near-deafening noise of inputs from their own organizations every day. One of the main challenges to executives is to filter and interpret the noise from within their own organizations and determine the salient points on which to act.

Successful executives are those who have developed the ability to observe a number of varieties of variability, to recognize the outliers of the data they receive, and to construct relevant patterns of meaning. In our story above, the CEO had the ability to recognize the variability in the machine sounds and to attach meaning to a particular sound that differed significantly from the norm.

Often we attribute executives with having a sixth sense or with well-developed intuitive powers.

> Intuitive understanding, sensing the whole in the part and acting accordingly, appeared to our respondents to be a matter of experience. Many claimed that they had been exposed to managerial challenge and responsibility at early stages of their careers and that this experience was invaluable to guiding their subsequent actions. (Mangham and Pye, 1991: 22)

In terms of our description of variability theory, there is nothing magical about those executives who manage to act on seemingly incomprehensible signals. These are the individuals who use a greater range of their senses (hearing, sight, feeling, taste, smell) to recognize the variability in the input and to identify important outliers. The reason why we say that these executives act with gut feeling is because we have not yet developed the same ability or have not developed a language to describe these levels and kinds of variability.

Most normal science studies of organizations isolate a few variables and attempt to measure the degree of so-called correlation and connection between these variables over a large number of organizations. This does not match the predominant sense-making framework used by practicing managers. We argue that managers realize that to identify the crucial variance, they need to take the full spectrum of variation within their own organizations into account. Instead of isolating certain variables, they need to interpret the apparent chaos present in the holistic picture to make sense of the complex signals.

A framework for understanding variability and wisdom

We propose that there are a number of different forms of variation that are salient to the effectiveness of managers and that it is the cognitive, affective, and behavioral variability in these factors that allows managers to make wise decisions. These forms of variability include (a) the range of difference between and within organizational level phenomena; (b) differences over time; (c) cognitive, affective, and skill differences within people in the organization; (d) differences between people in their relationships; and (e) differences in symbolic action and construction of meaning.

Managers need to develop a variety of skills and abilities to detect the degree of variability in the above factors. Effective management depends, in part, on the development of these skills and abilities (see Table 27.1).

In addition to the ability to recognize outliers or perceive fine-grained variability, effective managerial action is also determined by the ability to respond appropriately to the situation. Managerial decisions occur in a contextual framework of time and space. Thus, contextual relevancy of decisions and actions is needed for organizational effectiveness.

Because we argue that managers who are wise perceive greater variety within and between organizations, we will use anecdotes and examples from several sources to behaviorally anchor these forms of variability as used by practicing managers. These practical examples and stories are used to illustrate the skills and abilities of managers as they attempt to detect and interpret different forms of variation in their organizations and industries.

Variation between and within organizational phenomena. What may appear to the untrained ear as just factory noise is in fact a series of sounds, each with specific meanings and meaning constellations. There may be variation between these sounds as well as within these sounds. Effective managers develop over time (a) a fine-grained perception to distinguish between different types of signals and the intensity of signals.

Managers also need to develop (b) the ability to assess the relative salience of events. Very often, when a new manager takes over, one of the first things that he or she does is tour the facilities. It was Peters and Waterman (1982) who introduced the notion of management by walking about (MBWA). When Lou Gerstner joined IBM as CEO in April 1993, he spent his first couple of weeks "moving all over the company, mostly listening to people" (Kirkpatrick, 1993: 57). Managers move around the organization observing and talking to numerous people all the time and for good reason: They use the opportunity to gather data from a large number of sources within the organization to build a cognitive map of the organization (Bougon, 1992; Huff, 1990; Gioia and Poole, 1984).

All events do not have the same degree of importance. What may appear as just a minor blip on the radar could be something with large-scale future consequences. The ability to detect this type of variability often leads to

Table 27.1 Managerial skills and abilities to detect degrees of variation

Form of variation	Managerial skill or ability
Variation between and within organizational phenomena.	(a) Fine-grainedness of perception. (b) Ability to asses the relevant salience of events.
Variation over time.	(c) Ability to perceive changing organizational patterns over time. (d) Ability to perceive rates of change occurring in their internal and external environment of the organization. (e) Ability to judge the importance of short-lived, but significant organizational phenomena.
Variation in the human element in organizations.	(f) Ability to determine the group dynamics of teams. (g) Nonverbal and verbal behavioral exchanges in dyadic and multi-person exchanges. (h) Ability to asses levels of variation in the expertness of individuals.
Variation in power relationships.	(i) Understanding and interpretation of multiple-supplier-buyer relationships. (j) Ability to perceive differential power relationships.
Variation in symbolism, culture, and meaning construction.	(k) Ability to interpret and decode meaning (symbolism, intentional myths, constructed images, culture). (l) The mental maps of organizational members.
Variation in experience and moral development.	(m) Experience base inside and outside the organization. (n) Moral development of managers.

greatness. Steve Jobs' recognition of the potential of a personal computer (Sculley, 1987), Henry Ford's understanding of manufacturing (Womack, Jones, and Roos, 1991), and Lee Iacocca's (1984) insight into the market when he initiated the development of the Mustang at Ford and the minivan at Chrysler are graphic examples of this.

Variation in differences over time. Managers also need to be able to detect the changing patterns in organizations over periods of time not only in terms of single phenomena but also in the way the relations between elements in the organization have changed. Many of the popular biographies and autobiographies of executives (Iacocca, 1984; Sculley, 1987; Watson, 1990) give in-depth historical examples. Managers are attracted to these historical accounts in part because it gives them an indication of change and directions of change from which it is possible to see role models and to deduce future trends. Effective managers need to be able to (c) perceive changing organizational patterns over time, (d) perceive rates of change occurring in the internal and external environments of the organization, and (e) judge the importance of short-lived but significant organizational phenomena. If executives are unable to recognize salient changing patterns and if they spend their time on matters that turn out to be of little relevance, it can have negative or disastrous consequences. Apple Computers in the mid-1990s illustrates this rather poignantly.

In 1988, General Motors reported record profits of $4.9 billion (Taylor, 1989). Four years later, the company had replaced the CEO, appointed a new chairman of the board, and was not showing any signs of recovery from its record-setting $4.5 billion loss of the previous year (Taylor, 1992a). How could this happen? Schwartz (1996) describes how Shell used scenario planning (a way of developing variances on the extreme) to prepare key managers for the shock of the unpredicted oil crises that followed in the 1970s. We suggest that recognizing and making sense of faint signals and slight changes and acting in the right way are elements of managerial wisdom related to the variation of inputs and perceptions over time.

Variation within people in the organization. Southwest Airlines has twice as many passengers and almost half the number of employees per aircraft compared to its rivals (Labich, 1994). Yet, their employee loyalty and performance are almost unheard of in the industry What makes Herb Kelleher such a successful manager? Perhaps it has to do with his habit of being closely in touch with employees and his ability to sense the variability in their perceptions and feelings.

Managers interact with people all the time and continually pick up clues and meaning from these interactions. Sometimes the subtle nod of a head or raise in eyebrows can have more meaning than pages of written material. Some of the skills and abilities needed to use effectively the information from this type of variability are the abilities to (f) interpret the group dynamics of teams (see Bales, 1988; Kriger and Barnes, 1988), (g) detect and interpret nonverbal and verbal behavioral exchanges in dyadic and multiperson exchanges, and (h) assess levels of variation in the expertness of individuals.

> When Frank (Cary) started his new job, I asked him to spend a couple of days alone with me at my ski house in Vermont. I told him there were things I wanted to pass along that I thought he might not know in spite of his MBA. No textbook in the world can tell you how to be the chief executive of IBM, and the most important lessons had been drilled into my head by my Dad ... I had no fixed agenda; I simply gave him every bit of advice that came into my head. I told him a saying of Dad's, about how the head of the business should behave: "Act like a beggar, feel like a king," the idea being that in your dealings with others you should be empathetic and humble, yet utterly self-reliant and confident within. Frank Cary behaved that way instinctively, and this was my way of telling him he was doing the right thing. (Watson, 1990: 400)

When Tom Watson passed the reigns over to Frank Cary, he knew that there were only selected things he could teach him. However, he understood that success often depended on the ability to pick up the often subtle signals from people in the organization. Instead of using a range of different organizational settings, he shared his own in-depth experiences within IBM.

Variation in power relationships. The skills and abilities that effective managers need to detect this type of variation are (i) an understanding and interpretation of multiple supplier-buyer and competitor relationships and (j) the ability to perceive differential power relationships (e.g., in board of directors, task groups, and project teams).

> No, I have not given thought to stepping aside. I believe that the track that the IBM Company is on in transforming our company is the right one. The IBM board supports this management. The board supports me and I do not plan to step aside. (Loomis, 1993: 48).

These were the words of John Akers, CEO of IBM, in January 1993. By the 26th of that month, Akers announced his retirement after the board asked him to leave (Loomis and Kirkpatrick, 1993: 68). This is not an isolated case. Ken Olsen, CEO and founder of Digital Equipment (Steward, 1993), and Donald Petersen of Ford (Taylor,1991) faced similar fates. Robert Stempel from General Motors failed to see the signs of a vote of no confidence when the board made some changes in April 1992 and stayed on until he was replaced in November of that year (Taylor, 1992b). These are cases of executives who failed to see the shift in power relationships and failed to detect the sometimes very obvious signs of changes in these relationships.

Variation in symbolic action and meaning construction. Culture and symbolic action play a very important role in organizations. Managers need (k) the ability to interpret and decode meaning (symbolism, intentional myths, constructed images, culture) and (1) mental maps of organizational members.

Martin (1992) describes organizations as systems of ideas. This is consistent with our argument that organizations are patterns of dynamic relationships. There is almost an infinite degree of variation in the perceptions, symbols, and cultural artifacts within organizations. Books by executives such as Watson and Iacocca are rich accounts of stories, anecdotes, and images. As readers, we can see their organizations by means of the images they present. This rich area of managerial cognition offers a challenge to managers. They have to make sense of the symbolic aspects in their organizations, detect changes, and create their own "mindmaps" so that they can provide leadership for the rest of the organization.

Two additional elements not related to any of the above forms of variability are (m) the experience base of managers and (n) the moral development of managers (Kohlberg, 1981). Part of the success of managers is related to the ability to apply their past experience and moral judgment to analyzing present situations.

For the morality that underlies enduring cooperation is multidimensional. As it expands, it must become more complex, its conflicts must be more numerous and deeper, its call for abilities must be higher, its failures of ideal attainment must be perhaps more tragic; but the quality of leadership, the persistence of its influence, the durability of its related organizations, the power of the coordination it incites, all express the height of moral aspirations, the breadth of moral foundations.

So among those who cooperate the things that are seen are moved by the things unseen. Out of the void comes the spirit that shapes the ends of men. (Barnard, 1938: 284)

Barnard (1938) developed the notion of a "zone of indifference" (p. 169) within which all acceptable behavior will fall. Determining the boundaries of this zone often presents a problem to many managers. The ability to identify where these boundaries are and to determine the outliers that fall outside this zone of indifference is a distinguishing characteristic of managerial wisdom. Courses and case studies in business ethics are replete with examples of managers who clearly understood the narrow and often undefined limits of morality (e.g., Johnson and Johnson in the Tylenol case). We also have many examples of managers who failed because they failed to recognize these boundaries (e.g., Michael Milliken in engaging in insider trading). Managerial wisdom is the ability to detect those fine nuances between what is right and what is not.

It is often not important if the experience base of managers was obtained outside the industry, such as in the cases of John Sculley (Apple) and Lou Gerstner (IBM), or inside the industry, as with Tom Watson (IBM) and Jack Smith (General Motors). What is salient is the ability to use the past experience to construct cognitive maps for the evaluation of present situations. This is another reason why executives are observed to prefer reading books by other executives. They learn from the way John Sculley reorganized Apple computers or from the way Lee Iacocca rescued Chrysler. By experience, we do not mean the length of time in a job. "I learned more about people in three years in Chrysler than in thirty-two years at Ford" (Iacocca, 1984: 230). Wisdom is the ability to capture the meaning of several often contradictory signals and stimuli, to interpret them in a holistic and integrative manner, to learn from them, and to act on them in an appropriate time scale (Jacques, 1989; Jacques and Clement, 1991). Managerial wisdom is to a great extent dependent on experience and the moral development to act in situationally appropriate ways.

Implications

The reconceptualization of organizations as dynamic networks of variability and the proposition of an ability to perceive variability within and between the organization over time and have implications for researchers as well as practicing managers. Managers are faced with the challenge of managing the meaning of an almost overwhelming array of data from both within and around their organizations on a daily and, indeed, moment-to-moment basis. Organizational scientists need to take this into account if they intend for their studies to have real relevance to managers.

For managers, our attempt to portray the range and richness of variability can direct their focus onto the areas inside and outside the organization that provide them with added meaning. Wisdom, we believe, can be learned. By being aware of the forms of variation, managers can develop the necessary skills to detect and interpret the differences in these areas. This chapter argues that there are a number of specific skills and abilities that managers need to be effective. By increasing the awareness that, for instance, there is meaning in factory noise, managers can focus their attention and open a much wider array of informational input to improve their decision making. We believe that practicing managers can improve their decision making by recognizing that they will benefit from taking notice of the fine-grained variability in their surroundings and by exposing themselves to opportunities where they will sense the organizational data not to be found in computer printouts.

For our scientific endeavors to be more relevant and actionable, organizational scientists should address the needs and challenges of those members who work inside organizations. A theory of managerial wisdom based on the ability to perceive variability calls for a different approach to research. Instead of a concern with increasing the number of organizations in samples, it suggests a need to spend more time on ethnographic studies inside single organizations and to examine detailed patterns of unfolding relationships over time. Very simply, the IBM of today is not the same as the IBM of last year or even yesterday. The name and logo of the organization may be the same, but the cast of characters, their roles, and their relationships are continually changing and in flux. We see this chapter as an attempt to sensitize researchers to the importance of measuring variability in managerial skills. The framework that we provide is only a starting point for asking the right questions in our search for managerial wisdom.

The development of a stream of research in managerial and organizational cognition is one very encouraging trend in this direction. Detecting, interpreting, and acting on the variability in organizations is very clearly something that we need to understand better. Reconceptualizing the way in which we look at organizations will hopefully direct our research efforts in ways that are more relevant and meaningful to both managers and teachers of management who wish to take theories and organizational research findings into their classrooms, whether their students are executives, MBAs, or undergraduates.

The complex role of being a manager in today's organizations points toward a simultaneous need for relevance, clarity, action, and reliability in research. Perhaps the most graphic example of variability is the difference between the great writers such as Tolstoy and Shakespeare and the bulk of the writings today in the field of management. Is there a way for organizational researchers to write with the clarity, perception, and quality of purpose of Hemingway or Steinbeck? We may not be capable of achieving such clarity and quality of mind, but we can strive for it and encourage it as part of our role as researchers of managerial cognition and action. Management wisdom, we believe, is not a single construct; however, even the most cursory reading of history and philosophy tells us that managerial wisdom was around at the time of Plato, Aristotle, and even before. It is important for managers and management researchers to explore further how managerial wisdom manifests and can be developed in our organizations of today.

A painting by Van Gogh. A pair of rough peasant shoes, nothing else. Actually the painting represents nothing. But as to what is in that picture, you are immediately alone with it as though you yourself were making your way wearily homeward with your hoe on an evening in late fall after the last potato fires have died down. What is here? The canvas? The brush strokes? The spots of color? (Martin Heidegger)

References

Anderson, P.F. (1986) "On method in consumer research: A critical relativist perspective," *Journal of Consumer Research* 13: 155–73.

Bales, R.E. (1988) "A new overview of the SYMLOG system: measuring and changing behavior in groups," in Polley, R.B., Hare, A.P. and Stone, P.J. (eds), *The SYMLOG Practitioner: Applications of Small Group research*, New York: Praeger, pp. 319–44.

Barley S.R., Meyer, G.W. and Gash, D.C. (1988) "Cultures of culture: academics, practitioners and pragmatics of normative control," *Administrative Science Quarterly* 33: 24–60.

Barnard, C.I. (1938) *The Functions of the Executive*, Cambridge, MA: Harvard University Press.

Berger, P.L. and Luckman, T. (1967) *The Social Construction of Reality*, Garden City, NJ: Anchor.

Bohm, D. (1980) *Wholeness and the Implicate Order*, Boston: Ark.

Bohm, D. (1990) *On Dialogue*, Ojai, CA: David Bohm Seminars.

Bolman, L.G. and Deal, T.E. (1984) *Modern Approaches to Understanding and Managing Organizations*, San Francisco: Jossey-Bass.

Bougon, M.G. (1992) "Congregate cognitive maps: a unified dynamic theory of organizations and strategy," *Journal of Management Studies* 29(3): 369–90.

Bradley, R.T. (1987) *Charisma and Social Structure: a Study of Love and Power, Wholeness and Transformation*, New York: Paragon House.

Burrell, G. and Morgan, G. (1979) *Sociological Paradigms and Organizational Analysis*, Portsmouth, New Hampshire: Heinemann.

Chandler, A.D. (1962) *Strategy and Structure: Chapters in the History of the American Industrial Enterprise*, Cambridge, MA: MIT Press.

Cook, T.D. and Campbell, D.T. (1979) *Quasi-experimentation: Design and Analysis Issues for Field Settings*, Boston: Houghton Mifflin.

D'Aveni, R.A. (1994) *Hypercompetition: Managing the Dynamics of Strategic Maneuvering*, New York: Free Press.

Dyer, W.G. and Wilkins, A.L. (1991) "Better stories, not better constructs, to generate better theory: a rejoiner to Eisenhardt," *Academy of Management Review* 16: 613–19.

Eisenhardt, K.M. (1989) "Building theories from case study research," *Academy of Management Review* 14: 532–50.

Eisenhardt, K.M. (1997) "Conflict and strategic choice: how top management teams disagree," *California Management Review* 39(2): 42–63.

Ghiselli, E.E., Campbell, J.P. and Zedeck, S. (1981) *Measurement Theory for the Behavioral Sciences*, New York: Freeman.

Gioia, D.A. and Poole, P.P. (1984) "Scripts in organizational behavior," *Academy of Management Review* 9: 449–60.

Gray, B., Bougon, M.G. and Donnellon, A. (1985) "Organizations as constructions and destructions of meaning," *Journal of Management* 11(2): 83–98.

Huff, A.S. (1990) *Mapping Strategic Thought*, Chichester, UK: Wiley.

Iacocca, L. (with Novak, W.) (1984) *Iacocca: An autobiography*, New York: Bantam Books.

Janis, I.J. (1982) *Groupthink Psychological Studies of Policy Decisions and Fiascoes*, Boston: Houghton Mifflin.

Jacques, E. (1989) *Requisite Organization*, Arlington, VA: Cason Hall.

Jacques, E. and Clement, S.D. (1991) *Executive leadership*, Arlington, VA: Cason Hall.

Johnson, G. (1987) *Strategic Change and the Managerial Process*, Oxford, UK: Basil Blackwell.

Jones, G.R. (1983) "Life history methodology," in Morgan, G. (ed.) *Beyond Method: Strategies for Social Research* Beverly Hills, CA: Sage pp. 147–59.

Kirkpatrick, D. (1993, May 31) "Lou Gerstner's first 30 days," *Fortune*, pp. 57–62.

Kohlberg, L. (1981) *The Philosophy of Moral Development*, San Francisco: Harper & Row.

Kriger, M.P. and Barnes, L.B. (1988) "Executive leadership networks: Top management group dynamics in a high performance organization," in Polley, R.B., Hare, A.P. and Stone, P.J. (eds) *The SYMLOG Practitioner: Applications of Small Group Research*, New York: Praeger pp. 173–90.

Kriger, M.P. and Malan, L.C. (1993) "Shifting paradigms: the valuing of personal knowledge, wisdom, and other invisible processes in organizations," *Journal of Management Inquiry* 2: 391–98.

Kuhn, T.S. (1970) *The Structure of Scientific Revolutions* (2nd edn), Chicago: University of Chicago Press.

Labich, K. (1994, May 2) "Is Herb Kelleher America's best CEO?," *Fortune*, pp. 45–52.

Loomis, C.J. (1993, January 11) "King John wears an uneasy crown," *Fortune*, pp. 44–8.

Loomis, C.J. and Kirkpatrick, D. (1993, February 22) "The hunt for Mr. X: Who can run IBM?" *Fortune*, pp. 68–72.

Mangham, I. and Pye, A. (1991) *The Doing of Managing*, Oxford, UK: Basil Blackwell.

Martin, J. (1992) *Cultures in Organizations: Three Perspectives*, New York: Oxford University Press.

McKenzie, K.D. (1991) *The Organizational Hologram. The Effective Management of Organizational Change*, Boston: Kluwer Academic.

Mintzberg, H. (1989) *Mintzberg on Management: Inside Our Strange World of Organizations*, New York: Free Press.

Nonaka, I. and Takeuchi, H. (1995) *The Knowledge-Creating Company: How Japanese Companies Create the Dynamics of Innovation*, New York: Oxford University Press.

Nunnally, J.C. and Bernstein, I.H. (1994) *Psychometric Theory* (3rd edn), New York. McGraw-Hill.

Peters, T.J. and Waterman, R.H. (1982) *In Search of Excellence: Lessons From America's Best Run Companies*, London: Harper and Row.

Pettigrew, A.M. (1973) *The Politics of Organizational Decisionmaking*, London: Tavistock.

Pribram, K.H. (1991) *Brain and Perception: Holonomy and Structure in Figural Processing*, Hilldale, NJ: Lawrence Erlbaum.

Quinn, R.E. (1988) *Beyond Rational Management: Mastering the Paradoxes and Competing Demands of High Performance*, San Francisco: Jossey-Bass.

Rifkin, G. and Harrar, G. (1988) *The ultimate entrepreneur: The Story of Ken Olsen and Digital Equipment Corporation*, Chicago: Contemporary Books.

Schwartz, P. (1996) *The Art of the Long View: Paths to Strategic Insight for Your Self and Your Company*, New York: Doubleday.

Sculley, J. (with Byrne, J.A.) (1987) *Odyssey*, New York: Harper & Row.

Senge, P.M. (1989) *The Fifth Discipline: The Art and Practice of Learning Organizations*, New York: Doubleday.

Sloan, A.P. Jr (1963) *My Years with General Motors*, Garden City, NY: Doubleday.

Smircich, L. and Stubbard, C. (1985) "Strategic management in an enacted world," *Academy of Management Review* 10: 724–36.

Spender, J.C. (1996) "Making knowledge the basis of a dynamic theory of the firm," *Strategic Management Journal* 17: 45–62.

Starbuck, W.H. (1993) "Keeping a butterfly and an elephant in a house of cards: The elements of exceptional success," *Journal of Management Studies* 30: 885–921.

Starbuck, W.H. and Mezias, J.M. (1996) "Opening Pandora's box: studying the accuracy of manager's perceptions," *Journal of Organizational Behavior* 17(2): 99–117.

Steward, T.A. (1993, January 11) "The king is dead," *Fortune*, pp. 34–40.

Taylor, A. (1989, March 13) "The tasks facing General Motors" *Fortune*, pp. 52–9.

Taylor, A. (1991, February 11) "The odd eclipse of a star CEO," *Fortune*, pp. 86–96.

Taylor, A. (1992a, May 4) "The road ahead at General Motors," *Fortune*, pp. 94–5.

Taylor, A. (1992b, November 30) "What's ahead for GM's new team?" *Fortune*, pp. 58–61.

Watson, T.J. Jr (1990) *Father Son and Co.: My life at IBM and Beyond*, New York: Bantam Books.

Weber, R. (1986) *Dialogues with Scientists and Sages: The Search for Unity*, New York: Routledge & Kegan Paul.

Weick, K.E. (1979) *The Social Psychology of Organizing* (2nd edn), Reading, MA: Addison-Wesley.

Womack, J.P., Jones, D.T. and Roos, D. (1991) *The Machine that Changed the World*, New York: HarperCollins.

Organizational identity and learning:
a psychodynamic perspective

Andrew D. Brown and Ken Starkey

In this chapter we seek to develop a psychodynamic perspective on the link between organizational identity and organizational learning. That an explicit link between organizational identity and organizational learning has not been made previously is probably due to the perception that organizational identity is a relatively stable and enduring feature of organizations. Gioia and Thomas suggest that we "soften the stricture on the conception of identity as more or less fixed to include a dimension of fluidity" (1996:394). This is in line with the views of others who have depicted organizational identity as incrementally adaptive (Dutton and Dukerich, 1991) or changeable over the long term (Albert and Whetten, 1985). Arguments for the malleability of identity should not, however, be allowed to obscure the fact that learning is frequently restricted by organizations' efforts to preserve their identities (Gagliardi, 1986). If organizations appear to be in continuous states of flux, the types of change being observed are not necessarily those associated with (or constitutive of) organizational learning. That is, they are not necessarily changes that have implications for how participants conceive of their organization's identity (their organizational self-images), but can be superficial and quite possibly transitory.

The psychodynamic perspective we develop here suggests that individuals and organizations are not primarily motivated to learn to the extent that learning entails anxiety-provoking identity change. Rather, they maintain individual and collective self-esteem by not questioning existing self-concepts. In practice, this means that individuals and organizations engage in learning activities and employ information and knowledge conservatively to preserve their existing concepts of self (Baumeister, Tice, and Hutton, 1989; Baumgardner, Kaufman, and Cranford, 1990; Brockner, 1988; Brown, Collins, and Schmidt, 1988; Campbell, 1990; Rhodewalt, Morf, Hazlett, and Fairfield, 1991; Schlenker, Weigold, and Hallam, 1990). The self, we argue, is protected by ego defenses that, in contexts where change is desirable, exert a dysfunctional influence.

There are, of course, complicated issues of levels of analysis here: individual, group, and organizational (Klein, Dansereau, and Hall, 1994; Rousseau, 1985). Individual identity depends upon both one's personal identity and the identity that is shaped from one's relationships with others, although the effect of each of these two factors will differ between individuals and over time (Albert, 1977). Our argument is this: an individual is motivated to preserve/defend his or her personal identity through an individual level need for self-esteem. Like individuals, the psychological group and organization seek to maintain self-esteem, and this generally means acting conservatively to preserve an existing identity. Organizational learning can require that individuals be prepared to challenge the group's or organization's identity. Indeed, learning may become more problematic to the extent that individuals and groups subsume their individual identity in that of the group or organization and see themselves as representative of that social category (Banaji and Prentice, 1994; Brown, 1997). Analysis of the organizational means through which individual and collective self-esteem is regulated in the service of organizational identity thus becomes an important area of inquiry, for an understanding of these dynamics will cast light on the blocks to organizational learning.

In the literature on organizational learning, researchers strive to integrate perspectives drawn from individual and organizational learning, organization and management development, strategic management, and organizational culture (Starkey, 1996). Learning is conceptualized as a virtuous circle in which new information is used to challenge existing ideas and to develop new perspectives on the future and new action routines through "organizational dialogue" – "talk that reveals our meaning structures to each other" (Dixon, 1994: 83). Current accounts of the reasons why organizations fail to learn are incomplete because, although they recognize cognitive limitations (Bettman and Weitz, 1983; Dearborn and Simon, 1958; Einhorn and Hogarth, 1986; Feldman, 1989; Hedberg, 1981; Kahneman, Slovic, and Tversky, 1982; Levitt and March, 1988; Nystrom and Starbuck, 1984; Slovic, Fischhoff, and Lichstenstein, 1977; Starbuck and Milliken, 1988), prior learning (Argyris and Schon, 1978; Miller, 1993; Weick, 1995) political games (Pfeffer, 1981), and certain cultural and structural features of organizations (Dodgson, 1993; Hedberg, 1981; Huber, 1991; Levinthal and March, 1993; Salaman and Butler, 1994) as barriers to learning, they ignore the role of psychodynamic factors in individual and organizational identity maintenance and the negative effects such factors can have on learning.

The reasons most usually given by scholars to account for organizational non-learning are not wrong, but they would benefit from an interpretation of them as individual and collective defenses of self-esteem. Our position is that information that threatens an organization's collective self-concept is ignored, rejected, reinterpreted, hidden, or lost, and the processes by which organizations preserve their identities are, in many ways, analogous to the methods that individuals employ in defense of their own self-concepts. This argument derives from Jacques' suggestion that "institutions are used by individual members to reinforce individual mechanisms of defense against anxiety" (1955: 247), Bion and Rickman's (1943) observation that individual psychology is fundamentally group psychology, and Sofer's contention that administrative problems are the manifestation of individual psychology – that is, the "neurotic problems of persons writ large in organizational terms" (1972: 703). In this chapter we explore the effects on organizational identity of those processes by which organizations seek to insulate themselves from aspects of their internal and external environments and of those mechanisms through which organizational learning is made possible.

Learning to promote critical reflection upon organizational identity is a crucial but undertheorized management task. From a psychodynamic perspective, such learning involves the understanding and the mitigation of those ego defenses that tend toward a regressive retreat from a changing reality. Management's role is to promote mature and adaptive thought and action in pursuit of the collective organizational good – recognizing, of course, that what counts as the collective organizational good is both contestable and identity dependent. This involves critical reflection upon the nature of self-concepts that form the basis of organization as part of an ongoing learning process.

If skillfully managed, the outcome of critical reflection upon the nature of identity is a self-reflexive and wise organization, secure in its ability to negotiate identity change as part of its future strategic development. We conceptualize self-reflexivity from the perspective of the attainment of wisdom – a view that is prefigured in the psychoanalytic literature by Erikson (1965) and, importantly, by Kohut, who defines wisdom as "a stable attitude of the personality toward life and the world, an attitude that is formed through the integration of cognitive function with humor, acceptance of transience, and a firmly cathected system of values" (1978: 458–9). For Kohut, wisdom represents "the ego's ultimate mastery over the narcissistic self, the final control of the rider over the horse" (1978: 459).

In terms of the conceptual framework outlined here, the sort of organizational learning we are primarily interested in is that which constitutes a form of identity change. Our argument is that for an organization to learn, there must be an alteration in its participants' organizationally derived self-images. Organizational learning evolves through modifications, additions, and deletions of existing routines (Albert, 1992). These routines are, at least in part, constitutive of members' collective definitions of the organization's identity (organizational self-images) so that variation in one necessarily implies variation in the other (Dutton and Dukerich, 1991; Gioia and Thomas, 1996; Sproull, 1981).

Two clarifications of this general argument merit close attention before we proceed with its further elaboration. First, it is possible for organizations to engage in routine-based learning in ways that support their existing self-concepts. What we have in mind here are minor alterations to an organization's routines that essentially leave them intact. Here again, we do not wish to argue that organizational self-concept change has occurred. In short, our focus is on what Argyris (1992) has referred to as type II rather than type I learning.

Second, it should be noted that even type II change to an organization's routines does not always constitute a clear-cut change in that organization's self-concept. For example, there may be organizations in which the ability to radically alter, add, or delete core routines is an important part of their concept of self. This opens up the intriguing possibility that, in some instances, although a third party might be inclined to describe an organization as having altered its identity, the participants in that organization might prefer to describe what has occurred as identity preservation.

In this chapter we pursue these arguments in two major sections. First, we elaborate our contention that organizations fail to learn because of the operation of ego defenses that maintain collective self-esteem, focusing specifically on denial, rationalization, idealization, fantasy, and symbolization. Second, we suggest that to mitigate these ego defenses, organizations must embrace an identity as a learning organization. This involves an organization's challenging its assumptions regarding its existing identity and promoting a dialogue focused on desirable future identities – processes promoting attitudes of wisdom. Finally, we sketch five implications for further research and draw brief conclusions.

The dynamics of identity maintenance

Agreement on the meaning of an organization for participants is closely associated with the sharing of assumptions that make routine co-ordinated action possible (Schein, 1985). Expressed another way, "organizational identity concerns those features of the organization that members perceive as ostensibly central, enduring, and distinctive in character that contribute to how they define the organization and their identification with it" (Gioia and Thomas, 1996: 372). Thus, there is a "continuous reciprocal functional interdependence between the psychological processes of individuals" and organizations, for individuals and the social categories they participate in are both "mutual preconditions" and "simultaneously emergent properties" of each other (Turner, 1987: 205–6).

The conservatism of the urge to maintain self-esteem means that the existing self-concept is insulated/defended from self-analysis and challenge. Organizational self-esteem derives from participants' need for self-esteem based on their organizational self-images. Like individuals, the psychological organization seeks to maximize self-esteem and, in so doing, acts conservatively to preserve its identity.

Individual and organizational concepts of self are maintained by a variety of defenses that are engaged in order to avoid psychic pain and discomfort, allay or prevent anxiety, resolve conflicts, and generally support and increase self-esteem. Automatically and unconsciously deployed, the defenses are an attempted means of coping with an otherwise consciously intolerable situation (A. Freud, 1966; S. Freud, 1949; Laughlin, 1970). Such "defensive action may be defined as any invalid addition or subtraction from concrete reality that inhibits detection and correction of error as well as detection of the unawareness that the actions are defensive" (Argyris, 1982: 230).

Up to forty-eight ego defenses have been identified (Laughlin, 1970), but here we focus initially on five: denial, rationalization, idealization, fantasy, and symbolization.[1] It is important to note that a degree of defense is characteristic of psychologically healthy individuals and organizations, who need to regulate their self-esteem in order to function adequately (Cooper, 1986; Frosh, 1991; Kohut, 1971; Shengold, 1995). Taken to one of two extremes, however, ego defenses can make a net negative contribution to psychological health and, thus, be symptoms of pathological disorder (Brown, 1997).

A continuum of organizations, therefore, may be envisaged – one extreme of which is characterized by excessively high self-esteem (overdefended organizations) and the other by extremely low self-esteem (underdefended organizations). In the former, overprotection of self-esteem from powerful ego defenses reduces an organization's ability and desire to search for, interpret, evaluate, and deploy information in ways that influence its dominant routines. In the latter, inadequate protection of collective self-esteem will expose the organization to fears and anxieties that militate against self-confident action and, hence, organizational learning. In healthy organizations, in contrast, the ego defenses operate to reduce doubt and uncertainty and to increase self-confidence in ways that permit complex and ambiguous phenomena to be interpreted and explained.

The role of the ego defenses in individual level learning (Argyris, 1982; Miller, 1993), the idea that groups act to maintain and enhance their shared self-esteem (Brockner, 1988; Swogger, 1993), and the notion that organizations act to preserve their collective identities all have found support (Dutton and Dukerich, 1991; Dutton, Dukerich, and Harquail, 1994). There is also evidence for the view of organizations, their cultures, structures, and work routines, as defense mechanisms against anxiety (Bion, 1968; Bion and Rickman, 1943; Jacques, 1955). For example, Menzies has described how participants in hospital organizations collectively operate psychic defense mechanisms, such as splitting, projection, and regression, in order to avoid "feelings of anxiety, guilt, and uncertainty" (1970: 124). Similarly, Miller and Gwynne have illustrated how the social structures of residential care institutions "equip members with defenses against anxiety" (1972: 124).

The link between group defenses and self-esteem also has been made (Cartwright and Zander, 1968; Janis, 1972). Thus, Cartwright and Zander (1968) have argued that highly cohesive groups provide the sort of security that heightens participants' self-esteem, whereas Janis has suggested that group-think is, in part, a response to threats to "the self-esteem of the members of a cohesive decision-making body" (Janis, 1972: 206). Here, we seek to link and extend these suggestions, arguing that the motivation to conserve and protect organizational identity is self-esteem and that the means for accomplishing this are processes analogous to the ego defenses. These defenses can prove dysfunctional for organizational learning.

Scholars have well attested the idea that organizational identity acts as a perceptual screen that affects individual members' information processing and interpretation of issues (Dutton et al., 1994; Gioia and Thomas, 1996; Whetten, Lewis, and Mischel, 1992). In a sense, we discuss the dynamics of the screening process, which supports organizational identity and how it affects fundamentally organizations' capacity to learn. At an organizational level, defenses inhibit learning through their influence on (1) the external search for information, (2) the interpretation of information, (3) the use of information, (4) the storage of information, and (5) the internal recall of information. To illustrate the process of learning inhibition, we focus on five defenses, which, for reasons of clarity, convenience, and simplicity, we analyze separately, although empirical exploration of the theory outlined here is likely to confirm that they tend to act in concert (synergistically) to reinforce each other. The definitions of the defenses provided here have been derived from a single source (Laughlin's, 1970, exemplary account), in order to minimize the possibility of confusion.

Denial

To deny something is to negate or disown it. Through denial, individuals and organizations seek to disclaim knowledge and responsibility, to reject claims made on them, and to disavow acts and their consequences. Denial is a "primitive" and "magical" process that can lead to increased confidence and that can boost feelings of invulnerability, with profound implications for learning (Laughlin, 1970: 57).

The idea that belief structures can blind decision makers and compromise organizational effectiveness by leading these decision makers to deny the existence of problems has long been recognized (Walsh and Fahey, 1986; Walsh and Ungson, 1991). Employees committed to their organization's strategies and culture may find it so painful to admit that they are obsolete that they collectively "deny that there is a problem" (Miller, 1993: 121). In other organizations participants can seek to protect themselves by denying the validity of feedback data on their activities and then refusing "to test the validity of their denials" (Argyris, 1982: 165), making impossible adequate interpretation and use of available information.

Kets de Vries cites the example of a founder entrepreneur, who "refused to accept reports that sales were dropping rapidly" and "denied responsibility" for mismanagement, until "the banks eventually intervened and declared bank-ruptcy" (1996: 32). Miller and Gwynne have described how denial worked as an organizing principle in a residential care institution, allowing the nursing staff to deny that individual patients had different needs, that emotional bonds between patients and nursing staff were important, and that the primary task of the institution was to assist patients from "social death to physical death" (1972: 126, 179). Other authors have illustrated the tendency of individuals and organizations faced with charges of ethical misconduct to engage in various forms of denial, such as "I am not guilty," and "The event did not occur" (Bradford and Garrett, 1995; Schonbach, 1980; Semin and Manstead, 1983; Szwajkowski, 1992). Nystrom and Starbuck have discussed how "encased learning produces blindness and rigidity that may breed full-blown crises" (1984: 53). Most strikingly, Schwartz has described how "the denial of reality" became "the motivational base of organizational life for committed participants" at NASA (1987: 61), which impeded its ability to effectively recall, interpret, and use information – with disastrous consequences for the Space Shuttle Challenger.

Rationalization

A rationalization is an attempt to justify impulses, needs, feelings, behaviors, and motives that one finds unacceptable so that they become both plausible and consciously tolerable. This process of making what is consciously repugnant seem more acceptable involves a degree of self-deception (Laughlin, 1970), which limits self-knowledge. At an individual level, scholars have often observed that actors offer rationalized statements for their actions (Argyris and Schon, 1978; Morgan, 1986); that executives tend to deal with problems by rationalizing them "away as aberrations, as temporary, or as beyond management's control" (Miller, 1993: 120); and that actors blind to their mental programming often react to failure with rationalized attempts to reduce dissonance, by blaming others or claiming that a certain quota of failed initiatives is inevitable (Argyris, 1982).

Collective rationalizations in the form of "selective principles," which provide categories for thought (Douglas, 1987: 69); "retrospective sensemaking," which ameliorates organizational disappointments (Weick, 1995); and "organizational defensive routines," which negate threats and embarrassments (Argyris, 1992: 286), figure prominently in the organization theory literature (see also Elsbach and Kramer, 1996, and Starbuck, 1983). Janis (1972) has described how those suffering from groupthink develop a set of shared beliefs based on stereotypes and ideology that rationalize their complacency about the soundness of their policy decisions. He suggests that leading up to the Japanese bombing of Pearl Harbor, one rationalization accepted by the U.S. Navy "was that the Japanese would never dare attempt a full-scale surprise assault against Hawaii because they would realize that it would precipitate an all-out war, which the United States would surely win" (Janis, 1972: 87). Some interesting organizational examples include the New York Port Authority's defensive rationalization of its decision not to respond to the issue of homelessness (Dutton and Dukerich, 1991), the Long Island Lighting Company's attempts to rationalize its illicit activities (Ross and Staw, 1993), and General Motors' defense of the unsafe Corvair (Nader and Taylor, 1986; Wright, 1979).

Idealization

Idealization is the process by which some object comes to be "overvalued and emotionally aggrandized" (Laughlin, 1970: 123) and stripped of any negative features. It implies the exercise of an unrealistic judgment, and it results in the creation (in imagination) of a "fantastic" and "impossible" person, standard, or other entity. A classic example of this is Freud's (1949) discussion of how groups idealize their leaders. Bion (1968) builds on Freud's pioneering work to analyze the ways in which groups can idealize a leader, tradition, object, or idea to the extent that learning and work are seriously inhibited. This situation has been described as "a sort of corporate madness in which every member colludes and which stifles any independent thought or co-operative work" (De Board, 1978: 39). Sproull (1981) has commented on how criteria for the evaluation of action can be idealized as providing objective guides regarding the best or most appropriate action. Idealization is directly implicated in Gagliardi's model of organizational culture change, where he argues that idealization leads to the emotional identification of values and that it is only this "idealization of past successes [that] can fully explain why organizations are often unable to unlearn obsolete knowledge in spite of strong disconfirmations" (1986: 123).

In short, idealization processes help explain why organizations can exhibit habitual responses to now-defunct cues (Starbuck and Hedberg, 1977), persevere with failing strategies (Wilensky, 1967), and retain underperforming leaders (Bion, 1968). Idealization-inspired monomaniac fixation has been amply illustrated by Miller (1990) and by Starbuck, Greve, and Hedberg (1978), who have commented on numerous examples of formerly thriving companies that came to focus on just one goal, aspect of strategy, department, or even skill that they credited for their success (see also Colvin, 1982, on ITT; Halberstam, 1986, on Ford; Lyon, 1984, on Dome Petroleum; Starbuck and Hedberg, 1977, on the Facit Company; Wright, 1979, on GM).

Fantasy

A fantasy is a kind of vivid daydream that affords unreal, substitutive satisfactions. Fantasies represent an unconscious endeavor to fulfill or gratify difficult or impossible goals and aspirations (Laughlin, 1970). In organizations, shared fantasies are expressed through linguistic and visual artifacts, such as stories, myths, jokes, gossip, nicknames, graffiti, and cartoons. "Attachment to a fantasy" is a form of collective retreat into imagination, which "converts the ambiguities of history into confirmations of belief and a willingness to persist in a course of action" in ways that are "destructive for the individual organization" (March, 1995: 437).

An illustration of this has been provided by Wastell, who shows how structured methods for improving the quality of software systems can be employed ritualistically to defend against anxiety in a way that encourages withdrawal into a "fantasy world," where "the learning processes that are critical to the success of systems development are jeopardized" (1996: 25). Miller and Gwynne (1972) have argued that in many residential care institutions, fantasies concerned with processes of cure and rehabilitation are common. Bion (1968) has described various group pathologies in which collectivities focus their energies on group fantasies in order to obscure what is actually happening.

Although fantasies are substitutes for effective learning and action, this does not imply that their influence has always been diagnosed negatively. Thus, in the work of Gabriel (1991, 1995), organizations are impersonal and emotionally impoverished locales in which fantasies give vent to such powerful feelings as heroic defiance and the expiation of guilt, humanizing and offering consolation to employees for the harshness and arbitrariness of organizational life.

Symbolization

Symbolization is the process "through which an external object becomes the disguised outward representation for another internal and hidden object, idea, person, or complex" (Laughlin, 1970: 414).[2] The idea that organizations are socially constructed and, thus, essentially symbolic phenomena into which participants read meaning is one prevalent theme in the organization theory literature (Berger and Luckmann, 1966). However, most accounts of symbols in organizations represent them instrumentally, either as mechanisms for comprehension (Daft, 1983; Dandridge, Mitroff, and Joyce, 1980) or as a means by which leaders manipulate and control their organizations (Peters, 1978; Pfeffer, 1981).

What is suggested here is a view of symbols as the unconscious means of allaying anxiety and maintaining self-esteem through the distortion and concealment of unconscious thoughts, impulses, and desires. Symbols, then, place restrictions on our capacity to perceive and process information in ways that facilitate development and learning. Gabriel's (1991, 1995) analyses of myths as shields against reality; Schwartz's (1985) suggestion that "the main activity of organization is the generation of symbols and myths which will serve as vehicles for significance and symbolic immortality" (1985: 38); and the many suggestions that symbols allow individuals to cope with change by concealing, camouflaging, and reconciling differences (Johnson, 1990; Moch and Huff, 1983) are all suggestive of symbolization processes designed to reduce anxiety and raise self-esteem in organizations.

The pervasive importance of symbolization in organizations is suggested by Wilensky's (1967) analysis of leaders' (especially military leaders') tendency to interpret such symbols as uniforms and titles as indicators of both loyalty and ability. This form of symbolization raises these leaders' own self-esteem (because they have the most desirable titles and uniforms) and reduces their anxiety about being deceived or betrayed by others (because by wearing these badges of conformity and commitment, subordinates deserve to be listened to and trusted). In all hierarchical organizations the hierarchy itself may be regarded as evidence of symbolization, which reduces uncertainty regarding reporting relationships and decision-making powers, allocates responsibilities, and provides a sense of coherence and meaning for participants. Symbolization is reassuring but potentially self-deceptive and self-defeating: on the one hand it allows "self-confident action and coherent life," but, on the other, it militates against learning processes that would reveal "the truth about our power-lessness and finitude" (Schwartz, 1985: 35).

To summarize, organizations often engage in defensive information processing in order to maintain individual and collective self-esteem, and, in defending collective self-esteem, organizations are preserving their existing self-concepts. In short, an organization's self-concept is the outcome of the struggle to generate and maintain self-esteem. However, it is clear that there are occasions when organizations do learn and challenge existing self-concepts, Such learning is required when an organization seeks to improve its existing capabilities, either to perform better in a static environment or to adapt to a changing environment. In psychodynamic terms, the task of management in these circumstances is to prevent a regressive retreat from reality (owing to the activation of the defense mechanisms analyzed in this section) and to develop more "mature and reality-adapted sectors and segments of the psyche [by cultivating] a variety of mature and realistic thought and action patterns" (Kohut, 1971: 197). How ego defenses, identity, and learning interact we consider in the next section.

The dynamics of identity change and organizational learning

How identities evolve as organizations learn – that is, how organizations mitigate their ego defenses – is an important conceptual and management issue. Organizations, like individuals, frequently find instituting a fundamental identity change difficult. Crucial to this process is the development of a capacity to deal with the fundamental anxieties that the ego defenses defend against. The idea of the learning organization suggests one way of conceptualizing the identity change process. Once one embraces the identity of a learning organization, the organization accepts that identity formation is never closed and that it will develop a series of identities through time that reflect the organization's and its members' evolving self-concepts. Here, we examine the characteristics of the learning organization, with emphasis upon three features that have particular importance for promoting changes in organizational identity through time: (1) critical self-reflexivity, (2) the promotion of dialogue about future identity as an integral feature of strategic management, and (3) the attainment of an attitude of wisdom.

One feature of the organizational learning literature is that it tends to be overoptimistic regarding the weakness of barriers to learning, so it under-emphasizes the difficulties involved in mitigating them. A psychodynamic perspective suggests that to promote the deeper learning necessary to engender significant identity change, we need to directly engage with the issue of how organizations can deal with the fundamental anxiety that the ego defenses defend against. A psychodynamic perspective also suggests that this is no easy task and one that, with notable exceptions (such as Argyris, 1992), theorists of organizational learning tend to underplay. As Hirschhorn has said,

> In a manner that echoes Freud's pessimism in *Civilization and its Discontents*, we can only be pessimistic about our capacity to live and work in a post-industrial world. The demands on our imagination, our empathic capacities, and our ability to learn seem too great (1988: 204).

A psychodynamic perspective, therefore, does not generate an easy optimism about the magnitude of the task involved in changing identity in a way that mitigates strong, unconscious defense mechanisms. It also recognizes that, in a sense, the self-concepts of individuals and organizations derive from their ego defenses, and that it is an alteration in the relative dominance and combinations of these defenses that is implied by the very idea of identity change.

Organizations, like individuals, defend their existing identities and, in the process, reduce their opportunity to learn. Indeed, group psychodynamic theory would suggest that the process of identity change is more difficult for an organization than for an individual. In his classic study of group psychology, Freud argues that groups promote regressive behaviors that lead to a "collective inhibition of intellectual functioning and the heightening of affectivity in groups" (1949: 23). According to Freud, groups are led almost exclusively by the unconscious, with a consequent tendency for the "disappearance of conscience or of a sense of responsibility" (Freud, 1949: 14, 9–10). Bion (1968) has examined the various mechanisms through which group members defend against the anxiety of group membership, thus disrupting ego functioning and challenging the individual's self-esteem. A core task of the ego is to maintain an individual's self-image. As Eisold has made clear,

> Because the ego's ability to integrate and synthesize is its source of strength and self-confidence, the core element in the identity, group membership thus necessarily disrupts and undermines the member's very sense of a stable and functioning identity. This ... is the greatest source of anxiety [in groups]: a kind of panic arising out of a faltering, disintegrating self that is losing its very capacity to right itself (1985: 45).

In his or her struggle to hold on to the self, the individual clings ever more strongly to his or her particular constellation of individual defense mechanisms. To allay the anxiety of group membership, individuals tend to embrace "extremely narrow identities" (Eisold, 1985: 45). In therapeutic groups the work is to ensure that members confront the regressive pressures of group membership to combat the fragmentation of self and a regressive retreat to more primitive "narrow" identities and so develop the ego's capacity for flexible and integrative behavior. Crucial here is development of a climate of trust in the group so that "members risk change because they come to trust the group as a matrix of corrective emotional experience" (Eisold, 1985: 47).

From a psychodynamic perspective, the underlying task in the management of groups and organizations is the same: to create an emotional climate in which individuals can balance the need to feel they belong to a group without losing their individual identity so that they can work toward organizational goals that enhance their self-esteem. Self-esteem is developed and maintained by finding opportunities to express one's self in organizational work valued by salient others. This is not an easy task, because the achievement of organizational goals depends upon our ability to operate effectively in workgroups, while such groups present regressive experiences that impair the capacity to function.

How are the learning defenses to be mitigated, and how is the learning that can lead to identity change to be promoted? Our understanding of the dynamics of identity change derives from the work of Berzonsky (1988) and Blasi (1988), for whom self-concept development involves the management of three interdependent components: (1) process, the means by which identity is encoded, elaborated, and integrated; (2) structure, the way identity is organized; and (3) content, the information from which identity is constructed (Berzonsky, 1988). If the self-concept is an answer to the question "Who and what am I?" then, in general, the answer consists of achieving a new unity among elements of one's past and expectations about the future, and this creates a deep and fundamental sense of purposeful continuity:

> This is a process of integration and questioning. The answer to these questions leads to integration, a sense of basic loyalty and fidelity as well as deep, preconscious, feelings of rootedness and well-being, self-esteem, and purposefulness (Blasi, 1988: 226–7).

Learning that promotes identity change thus involves a re-synthesis or reintegration of the processual, structural, and content aspects of self in a way that defends against anxiety and satisfies the need for self-esteem.

In work "we are confronted with the regressive pull of anxiety and splitting and the developmental pull of risk taking and reparation" (Hirschhorn, 1988: 10). It is the regressive pull of anxiety that tends to dominate and makes identity change problematic. To promote identity change, therefore, organizations need to confront the psychological boundaries individuals and groups set up to contain anxiety. Hirschhorn (1988) argues that we need a new work culture that helps people contain and transmute their anxieties and in which it is acceptable for people to air their vulnerabilities. This means challenging the modern "masculine" conception of organization, which values the suppression of doubt and ambivalence and which is single minded in the pursuit of its goals and in its unshakable understanding of its unchanging and fully formed identity. The alternative, "postmodern" organization is more "feminine," characterized by "a culture of being open to others," and "uses doubt as a springboard for learning"; its identity "is not fixed but instead unfolds over the adult life course" (Hirschhorn, 1997: 17–18). Hirschhorn describes the transition to this postmodern form of organization as a process of reparation, arguing that work offers the possibility of individual and group reparation to address and heal damaged selves: "The production of valued goods and services for others provides us with a framework for repairing our relationships" (1988: 204).

The heart of the reparation process is to develop an understanding of the individual's own purpose and to align this with the institution's purpose and with the intentions of coworkers. We have to create conditions in which we relate "in depth" to others and recover our own personal authority. In this way we create the conditions necessary for self-fulfillment at work and protect ourselves from isolation and self-estrangement (Hirschhorn, 1997).

Critical self-reflexivity and the evolution of identity through time

While accepting the definition of organizational identity as "central" and "distinctive," those with an organizational learning perspective contest the view that organizational identity should be "enduring" (Albert and Whetten, 1985). Identifying the self's qualities is an integral aspect of self-regulation (Schlenker, 1985). A coherent identity is important in creating a sense of meaning, but as organizational membership and environmental context alter, so the self needs to adapt to these changes. Identity can serve to counter the existential anxiety of a "precariousness of meaning" (Alvesson, 1990: 385), but the absence of a coherent identity can cause insecurity and even a sense of helplessness (Diamond, 1992).

However, although identity provides meaning, premature closure of identity exploration processes, or too tight a closure around an overdefined identity, is inimical to the multiple and alternative meanings that make organization development possible (Lundberg, 1989). Senior management's role in the learning organization is to surface and contest existing mental models and to build shared visions of the future (Bennis, 1993; Senge, 1990). The challenge to existing mental models and the development of new visions need to include organizational identity – a questioning of the mental models that support current views of organizational identity and the development of visions concerning the nature of the new identity the organization is working toward.

We should think about identity from a temporal as well as from a structural perspective, particularly when we confront the issue of change. Organizational learning involves the reflexive consideration of what constitutes self. Learning can be construed as an ongoing search for a time- and context-sensitive identity; it alternates through phases of exploration and commitment (Marcia, 1988). Sometimes exploration of possible identities is to the fore, whereas at other times commitment to one dominant identity for a period of time prevails; even during the commitment phase, however, the limits of identity are being explored. The exploration phase concerns the consideration of alternative future directions and involves a critical, reflexive attitude to the existing identity structure, based upon current commitments. Identity development involves a lifelong process of change, composed of sequences of exploration-commitment-identity. The identity represents the "inner organization of ... needs, abilities, values, personal history, and plans" (Marcia, 1988: 217).

Critical self-reflexivity fosters alternative perspectives of self and institutionalizes the self-questioning of the ongoing viability of existing identity. Pascale (1990) argues that "vectors of contention" are potent forces for change within organizations. Indeed, without contention there is no internal stimulus for change. Unitary cultures with too narrow a definition of their core identities that exclude the possibility of internal dissent run the risk of maladaptation to changing environments. The problems that some of Peters and Waterman's (1982) excellent companies experienced in maintaining excellence can be attributed to this failing (Carroll, 1983; Lundberg, 1989; Pascale, 1990; Ray, 1986; Soeters, 1986). Strong culture organizations with very tightly defined and adhered to configurations of core beliefs and values are destined to become dysfunctional eventually, as their rigidities and closed boundaries reduce learning capacities (Miller, 1993).

Organizational learning that is transformative modifies the cultural core of the organization and its identity (Lundberg, 1989). Organizational transformation requires individuals and groups who have developed alternative scenarios of the future relative to those that characterize the status quo. These alternative perspectives, outcomes of critical self-reflexivity, call into question the viability of existing identity as the environment changes. The process of learning thus depends upon an organization's ability to understand and manage discord.

Identity change requires genuine exploration. When the defensive routines outlined earlier are too strong, "an identity is said to be foreclosed rather than achieved, and that identity is assumed to be less flexible, more brittlely fragile, and in greater need of content-consistent social support" (Marcia, 1988: 219). The goal is not to develop one lasting "core" self. To harmonize a range of contradictory internal desires and external demands, one needs to encourage a more provisional identity – less foreclosed and more enabling of alternative futures – through cultivating empathy among the various manifestations of self (Mitchell, 1993). Satisfaction and the relative richness of life have a great deal to do with the dialectic between multiplicity and integrity in the experience of self – the balance between discontinuity and continuity (Dimen, 1991; Harris, 1991). Where there is too much discontinuity, there is a dread of fragmentation, splitting, dislocation, or dissolution – dread of the "not-me" – and where there is too much continuity, there is dread of paralysis and stagnation (Mitchell, 1993).

Paralysis and stagnation can take a variety of forms. According to Sullivan (1938), the narcissistic illusion, which is clinging to a narcissistic ideal of a perfect self, is "the very mother of illusions" (Mitchell, 1993: 106). At the roots of the narcissistic position is a fear of confronting the inevitable gap between the desire for a perfect self and the profound disappointment of never being able to realize this desire. "Is not Narcissus trying to screen out such fears through his fixation on his own image?" (Epstein, 1995: 50–2).

Another explanation of the demise of excellent companies referred to previously is that they clung to a narcissistic fantasy of an ideal self and, therefore, stagnated because they were unable to realize that there were other possible ways of being – other forms of identity that could serve them more effectively. Theirs was a fantasy of omnipotence founded upon past learning. However, the lessons of the past are not enough to sustain future prosperity. Individuals and organizations need to strike a balance among past, present, and future in the same way that managers need to skillfully manage the tension between continuity and discontinuity (Pettigrew, 1985).

In some companies the dread of discontinuity can reinforce a company's tendency to regress to a past identity with which it is more familiar and comfortable. For example, Xerox developed all the technologies necessary to become a leading player in the personal computer market but was unable to liberate itself from its traditional identity as a copier company, thus failing to capitalize on its technological leadership in computing (Smith and Alexander, 1988). In contrast, Intel was able to re-create itself as a microprocessor company and relinquish, with pain and difficulty, its identity as a memory chip company, even though memory chips had been so central to the company's identity that "Intel stood for memories [and] memories meant ... Intel" (Grove, 1997: 85).

Promotion of dialogue about future identity as an integral feature of strategic management

Strategic management is the facet of management most concerned with the future. Pascale defines the goal of strategic management as maintaining the requisite, most constructive level of debate in organizations – "holding the organization in question" and "posing question[s] [in a] search for a different frame of reference" (1990: 51, 54–5). This enables an organization to adapt, change, or transform itself according to how the future unfolds and the external environment changes (Lundberg, 1989). Creative strategic management involves critical, reflexive analysis of the organization's fundamental premises, which are encapsulated in its identity (Hurst, Rush, and White, 1989). In preparing for an essentially unknowable future, the role of top management is to "generate and institutionalize the constant self -questioning which can facilitate smooth rather than punctuated change" and "create a system-wide learning environment" (Spender and Grinyer, 1995: 913). Identity is most problematic in conditions of high uncertainty. Pascale's (1990) notion of "managing on the edge" and Hamel and Prahalad's (1994) view of strategy as "strategic intent" contest conventional notions of strategy as the search for fit with an environment that is assumed to be stable.

Perhaps the most fully elaborated view of strategic management as an ongoing learning process that embraces the need to rethink organizational identity, in a context where environmental discontinuity is assumed, is scenario planning (Schoemaker, 1993; van der Heijden, 1996). In this approach, managers are urged to relax their conventional modes of thinking and to learn by setting aside their existing frames of reference – both epistemological and ontological. The premise is that our present ways of knowing, and what we already know, form an inadequate basis for learning about an uncertain future. Scenarios essentially are new strategic narratives (Barry and Elmes, 1997) – explorations of, and the media for, exploring new identity possibilities (van der Heijden, 1996). Strategy is conceived of as a reflective, unending search for meaning, the medium for which is akin to the construction of a narrative that makes sense of both past and future and the individual's and the organization's roles in creating this (Schafer, 1992; Spence, 1982). As Weigert has said, "We have only those socially constructed identities that we can construct in our conversations with others. Identities ... are realized in stories" (1988: 268).

What is involved in a successful process of identity development is movement from a stable position into an exploratory phase, experimenting with elements that are, initially, alien to the central core of existing identity. "Challenge" scenarios, for example, call into question the deepest assumptions about an organization and its business, challenging managers to think the unthinkable, such as the overnight obsolescence of their core business. The exploration phase is followed by a phase of resolution and integration, "characterized by an interiorization of elements that were once external" (Marcia, 1988: 222).

Scenario planning involves the assumption that the future is likely to be discontinuous and, therefore, that organizations need to be constantly rethinking their identities. Rutenberg (1985) draws on the work of Winnicott (1974) to develop a psychodynamic perspective on scenario planning, which he describes as "playful planning," the goal of which is to enable managers to develop alternative models of the future. The scenario process is characterized as a complex "game," to distinguish it from strategic planning as a form of scientific forecasting. In the scenario process executives experiment, playfully and "intently" to "envision" different possible scenarios, forcing themselves to challenge existing cognitive assumptions, "while struggling for a language by which they can talk with fellow executives about the uncertainty of a discontinuity" (Rutenberg, 1985: 3).

Play serves to challenge existing belief systems and to restructure cognitions. It facilitates experiments with identity: What kind of person am I, can I be, and do I want to be? What kind of organization? This can best be explained psychodynamically. Play creates what Winnicott (1974) terms a transitional object. As exemplified in the play of children, playing with such objects helps us to resolve the anxiety of coming to terms with a changing reality and an evolving personhood. In play we experiment and role play for different futures, and we learn to cope with the anxieties these futures provoke. Psychologically, this playing takes place in an intermediate area – a "transitional space" between the inner psyche and external reality which is a crucial area in "the perpetual human task of keeping inner and external reality separate yet interrelated" (Winnicott, 1974: 3).

Objects of play serve as important loci for reality testing in an area that lies between primary creativity and objective perception. Play serves an important learning function. Equally important, it provides relief from the strain of relating inner and outer reality.

Play is inherently exciting and precarious. This characteristic derives not from the instinctual arousal but from the precariousness that belongs to the interplay in the child's mind of what is subjective (near-hallucination) and that which is objectively perceived (actual or shared reality) (Winnicott, 1974: 61).

In play, the child establishes her or his identity by satisfactorily reconciling the tension between inner desires and the reality principle.

The wise organization

Critical self-reflexivity and dialogues about future identity, if they are to be successful, need to re-create a more adaptive self-concept by dealing with the psychodynamic layers of experience and the barriers to learning and identity change that we discussed earlier. According to our perspective, ego defenses, exacerbated by the regressive forces of group dynamics, serve to defend a self-concept that hinders change. In this case the strength of the ego defenses constitutes a barrier to learning. Organizational learning leads to positive identity change, if it can promote a new self-concept that mitigates some of the inhibiting effects of the defenses. This process can be viewed as the attainment of an attitude of wisdom. The wise individual or organization is one who accepts that a willingness to explore ego-threatening matters is a prerequisite for developing a more mature individuality and identity. Negotiating such identity change requires a process, of profound self-questioning.

Wise individuals and organizations shape and reshape identity through the ongoing construction/reconstruction of self. This is particularly important in times of discontinuity, when it is important to explore the identity "gap" (Reger, Gustafson, DeMarie, and Mullane, 1994) – the gap between the actual self (what is) and the ideal self (what can be; Ashforth and Mael, 1996) – if the individual and the organization are to learn other ways of being in the world. Some sense of continuity is important. When major change is required, a wise way to proceed in motivating people to accept the necessity of change is to demonstrate how at least some elements of the past are valued and will be preserved (Albert, 1984). As a result, one will develop a sense of one's experience over time. One can measure a new experience in terms of continuity or discontinuity with the past and present; a new experience can represent and express one's history and current state, or "reshape one's history and current state in an enriching way" (Mitchell, 1993: 131). If we "impose" coherence too early (Phillips, 1988), our self-sufficiency is likely to be short lived, precisely because we close ourselves to alternative sources of nurturance and under-standing of ourselves and of our environment.

Too limited a concept of self can lead to unwise behavior that is not consonant with the nature of the environment. Lack of a shared identity creates dissonance and makes collective action and collective sensemaking impossible – groups disintegrate, organizations become less than the sum of their parts. Wisdom, at the individual and organizational levels, is a composite of curiosity, a willingness to learn, and an openness to learn new things about one's environment that challenges the assumption that we know all that we need to know and all that could possibly be relevant to our present situation.

The overconfident attitude assumes environmental stability. The attitude of wisdom assumes complexity and engenders what Weick (1993, 1995) terms complex sensemaking. Collective identity is crucial in making sense of one's environment, particularly in contexts of rapid and unpredictable change. Lacking a shared identity, organizational members have, at best, a limited sense of meaning and connection with the organization and cannot consciously assess the significance of their and others' actions for the organization (Baum, 1987, 1990; Diamond, 1992; Freud, 1949; Hirschhorn, 1988; Kets de Vries and Miller, 1984; Lynch, 1988; Schwartz, 1990).

Wisdom is associated with an ability to perceive the broader picture and "the connectedness of things" (Bigelow, 1992: 147). This involves a shift in self-perception from "self as independent" to "self as part" of a larger whole (Bigelow, 1992: 147), akin to the shift in Kohlberg's (1964) stages of moral development from a perspective of self-interest to one of social cooperation. If we are wise, we learn how to compensate for our weaknesses through facilitating and benefiting from interdependencies (Bigelow, 1992). Wisdom enables people to "transcend personalistic perspectives and embrace collective and universal concerns" (Orwoll and Perlmutter, 1990: 160). From a psychodynamic perspective, wisdom is associated with

> a gradual increase of realistic self-esteem, of realistic enjoyment of success; a moderate use of fantasies of achievement (merging into plans for realistic action); and the establishment of such complex development within the realistic sector of the personality as humor, empathy, wisdom, and creativeness (Kohut, 1971: 199).

Individuals transcend ego defenses to develop empathy – "the ability to ... accommodate to the unique feelings and thoughts expressed by one another" (Kramer, 1990: 296). Empathy permits a more objective view of external reality, a greater receptivity to the views of others, and a more mature view of the self that accommodates previously dissociated parts.

Wisdom also demands the recognition of inevitable limitations, the abandonment of "the narcissistic insistence on the omnipotence of the wish: it expresses the acceptance of realistic values" (Kohut, 1978: 454). For Kohut, wisdom is a characteristic of the mature personality, "created by the ego's capacity to tame narcissistic cathexes and to employ them for its highest aims" (1978: 460). This recalls Erikson's identification of wisdom as a "basic virtue" that is attained in the final, eighth "step" of his psychosocial stages of development: "ego integrity" (1965: 266). The "highest aims" of both Erikson and Kohut are associated with "renunciation" (Erikson) and an acceptance of "transience" (Kohut), which lead to "a shift of the narcissistic cathexes from the self to a concept of participation in a supraindividual existence" (Kohut, 1978: 456).

In summary, in managing learning in order to promote critical reflection upon individual and organizational identity, an organization's key task is to understand and mitigate the ego defenses. These defenses tend toward a regressive retreat from a changing reality. Self-knowledge involves the active contestation of the negative aspects of ego defenses, such as denial, rationalization, idealization, fantasy, and symbolization. Management's role is to promote mature and adaptive wise thought and action in pursuit of the collective organizational good. This involves critical reflection upon the nature of the various self-concepts that form the basis of organization identity as part of an ongoing learning process. Learning depends upon the surfacing of difference and subsequent reintegration of conflicting views of the nature of self in the healing of the divisions that may thus arise. If skillfully managed, the outcome is a self-reflexive and wise organization, secure in its ability to understand and accept its limits and to negotiate identity change as part of its ongoing strategic development.

Implications for research

Here we have suggested that psychological, and especially psychodynamic, approaches to organization studies can yield insights into collective behavior. Our contention that organizations can be understood usefully in terms of the psychology of the participants they are composed of has at least six important implications for research.

First, we should note that in this chapter we have focused on a very limited number of psychodynamically derived concepts – that is, the ego defenses and how these may be overcome through processes of learning. Only a small subset of the ego defenses and learning mechanisms has been examined. The wealth of analytic concepts and frameworks in the psychology and psychodynamics literature represents a latent reservoir of ideas that can assist us in our efforts to theorize about organizations. This chapter illustrates that there is a prima facie case for investigating how we can make use of this material, by direct importation, to add to our stock of metaphors and images of organization (Morgan, 1980, 1983; Tsoukas, 1991, 1993).

Second, although we have argued that the identity of the psychological organization consists of its participants' organizationally relevant self-images, we believe that how participants come to possess and identify with these self-images is an important area for further research. Individuals enter organizations with an existing self-concept that they have learned to defend. From an organizational perspective, the individual might need to learn a new self-concept to align himself or herself with organizational identity.

One influential view of organizations suggests that they are fractured and hierarchical locales in which individuals and groups are implicated in reciprocal but often asymmetric power relationships (Clegg, 1981; Pettigrew, 1992; Pfeffer and Salancik, 1974). This means that some are more able to extend their hegemony (in our terms, able to affect individuals' self-images based on the organization) more than others. In short, how self-images develop is an exercise in power. From a learning organization perspective, learning is less coercive and identity change is based upon the mutual alignment of individual and organization. Our suggestion is that in order for these processes to be surfaced, we need to focus attention on the influence and interplay of the identity narratives that characterize both individuals and organizations (Boje, 1995; Brown, 1998; Bruner, 1990). An important factor for investigation here would be the degree of resistance to change at both the individual and organizational levels. Investigations of this nature would be consonant with the next two implications for research.

Third, we have restrictedly framed this chapter as a contribution to the debate on the relationships between the concepts of organizational identity and learning. However, we believe that our conception of the psychodynamics of organizational identity has far broader implications meriting further scholarly attention. Perhaps the most obvious inquiries to which our arguments are relevant are those concerning organizational change, especially at the strategic level. It seems reasonable to suggest that an organization's strategic discourse is an integral aspect of its identity and that strategic change implies identity change (Gioia and Thomas, 1996). The difficulties inherent in altering an organization's strategic narrative (Barry and Elmes, 1997) illustrate that an understanding of the inertial power of the collective ego defenses might valuably inform research in this area. Similarly, familiarity with processes of identity change may cast some further light on how organizations are, in fact, sometimes able to reshape and reorder the themes that characterize their strategic discourse.

Fourth, our approach has relevance for research into organizational narratives. Identity manifests itself in narrative. Much of effective management depends upon language; indeed, major strategic change depends upon the "art of strategic conversation" (van der Heijden, 1996), yet research into top management conversation is rare (Pettigrew, 1992). Hambrick and Mason's (1984) "upper echelon perspective" was crucial in stressing the strategic importance of top management teams, but the tendency in this line of research has been to focus on demographic data and multivariate analysis. Demographic data can deal with structural but not dynamic phenomena. Hambrick and Mason (1984) argued for greater use of clinical studies in this area, but cross-sectional studies with inconsistent findings still predominate (Priem, 1990). The field requires a concerted effort to penetrate this over-defended space.

Fifth, the perspective we have developed in this chapter also has relevance for research into managerial wisdom. This is an underresearched topic in academic management journals (Bigelow, 1992; Waters, 1980; Weick, 1993), although it has received some attention in practitioner-oriented literature (Hurst, 1984; Lorsch and Mathias, 1987; Mintzberg, 1987). Reliable measures of wisdom have not yet been developed, but there is some agreement about the key phases that characterize its development (Sternberg, 1990). These include the generation of an ability to learn from experience (Bigelow, 1992); a movement to longer-term thinking, which deliberately extends future time horizons (Waters, 1980); and a concern with metaknowledge (Bigelow, 1992) and "epistemic cognition" (Kitchener, 1983), which includes reflection upon the "limits of knowing" created by existing ways of viewing the world. To these we would add "ontological cognition"– a critical reflection upon the status of the categories that we use to describe our current ways of being in the world (Wimsatt, 1970). From a psychodynamic perspective, Kohut suggests that the analysis of wisdom is "our ultimate challenge" (1978: 458).

Sixth and finally, the logic of our argument suggests that we need to think deeply about how we conceptualize meaning in the study of identity and in research into organizations in general. Lundberg (1989) argues that organizations have three levels of meaning: (1) a cognitive, manifest/surface level; (2) strategic beliefs; and (3) basic values and assumptions. We have argued here that there is fourth level – a psychodynamic level – that fundamentally affects the processes and the outcomes of organizational learning and is manifested, but in an indirect fashion, as organizational identity. Analysis of the biographies and autobiographies of organizational leaders and company histories using this perspective offers a rich research potential. Such an analysis will have practical implications for more effective management practice, to the extent that it will demonstrate how increased self-awareness can promote critical reflection upon the limits of self and of an existing identity.

Conclusion

In this chapter we have sought to make a contribution to our field's understanding of individual and collective identities. Although this is primarily a conceptual piece focused on definitional and psychodynamic issues of identity and learning, we believe that the ideas presented herein have important practical implications for how scholars may comprehend and measure these phenomena. Specifically, we suggest that use of our conceptualizations will enable others to more adequately trace identity dynamics, such as how collective identities emerge and change over time. We recognize, of course, that the analytic perspective on identity issues that we offer is partial, and indeed merely one of many possible approaches in this field, but we remain sanguine that it offers opportunities for us to see more clearly and, thus, to explore more deeply the nature of organization and management (Weick, 1987).

Notes

1. Our decision to focus on five ego defenses was made solely because of word-length restrictions.
2. Although symbolization may also refer to the creation of language, with all that follows from that, here we are using the term in the restricted sense of an ego-defensive process.

References

Albert, S. (1977) "Temporal comparison theory," *Psychological Review* 84: 485–503.
Albert, S. (1984) "A delete design model for successful transitions," in Kimberly, J.R. and Quinn, R.E. (eds) *Managing Organizational Transitions*, Homewood, IL: Irwin 169–91.
Albert, S. (1992) "The algebra of change," *Research in Organizational Behavior*, 14: 179–229.
Albert, S. and Whetten, D.A. (1985) "Organizational identity," in Cummings, L.L. and Staw, B.M. (eds) *Research in Organizational Behavior*, vol. 7: Greenwich, CT: JAI Press 263–95.
Alvesson, M. (1990) "Organization: From substance to image?" *Organization Studies* 11: 373–94.
Argyris, C.A. (1982) *Reasoning, Learning, and Action*, San Francisco: Jossey-Bass.

Argyris, C.A. (1992) *On Organizational Learning*, Cambridge, MA: Blackwell.

Argyris, C.A. and Schon, D.A. (1978) *Organizational learning*, Reading, MA: Addison-Wesley.

Ashforth, B.E. and Mael, F.A. (1996) "Organizational identity and strategy as a context for the individual," *Advances in Strategic Management* 13: 19–64.

Banaji, M.R. and Prentice, D.A. (1994) "The self in social contexts," *Annual Review of Psychology* 45: 297–332.

Barry, D. and Elmes, M. (1997) "Strategy retold: toward a narrative view of strategic discourse," *Academy of Management Review* 22: 429–52.

Baum, H.S. (1987) *The Invisible bureaucracy*, New York: Oxford University Press.

Baum, H.S. (1990) *Organizational Membership*, Albany: State University of New York Press.

Baumeister, R.F., Tice, D.M. and Hutton, D.G. (1989) "Self-presentational motivations and personality differences in self-esteem," *Journal of Personality and Social Psychology* 57: 547–79.

Baumgardner, A.H., Kaufman, C.M. and Cranford, J.A. (1990) "To be noticed favorably: links between private self and public self," *Personality and Social Psychology Bulletin* 16: 705–16.

Bennis, W. (1993) *The Invented Life: Reflections on Leadership and Change*, Reading, MA: Addison-Wesley.

Berger, P.L. and Luckmann, T. (1966) *The Social Construction of Reality*, Garden City, NJ: Doubleday.

Berzonsky, M.D. (1988) *Self-Theorists, Identity Status, and Social Cognition*, in Lapsley, D.K. and Clark Power, F. (eds) *Self, Ego, and Identity: Integrative Approaches*, New York: Springer-Verlag, 243–62.

Bettman, J. R. and Weitz, B. A. (1983) "Attributions in the board room: causal reasoning in corporate annual reports," *Administrative Science Quarterly* 28: 165–83.

Bigelow, J. (1992) "Developing managerial wisdom," *Journal of Management Inquiry* 1: 143–53.

Bion, W.R. (1968) *Experiences in Groups*, London: Tavistock.

Bion, W.R. and Rickman, J. (1943) "Intergroup tensions in therapy," *Lancet* 27: 478–81.

Blasi, A. (1988) "To be or not to be: Self and authenticity, identity, and ambivalence," in Lapsley, D.K. and Clark Power, F. (eds) *Self, Ego, and Identity. Integrative Approaches*, New York: Springer-Verlag, 226–42.

Boje, D.M. (1995) "Stories of the storytelling organization: a postmodern analysis of Disney as 'Tamara-Land'," *Academy of Management Journal* 38: 997–1035.

Bradford, J.L. and Garrett, D.E. (1995) "The effectiveness of corporate communicative responses to accusations of unethical behavior," *Journal of Business Ethics* 14: 875–92.

Brockner, J. (1988) *Self-Esteem at Work*, Boston: Lexington Books.

Brown, A.D. (1997) "Narcissism, identity, and legitimacy," *Academy of Management Review* 22: 643–86.

Brown, A.D. (1998) "Narrative, politics and legitimacy in an IT implementation," *Journal of Management Studies* 35: 35–58.

Brown, J.D., Collins, R.L. and Schmidt, G.W. (1988) "Self-esteem and direct versus indirect forms of self-enhancement," *Journal of Personality and Social Psychology* 55: 445–53.

Bruner, J. (1990) *Acts of Meaning*, Cambridge, MA: Harvard University Press.

Campbell, J.D. (1990) "Self-esteem and clarity of the self-concept," *Journal of Personality and Social Psychology* 59: 538–49.

Carroll, D.T. (1983) "A disappointing search for excellence," *Harvard Business Review* 61(6): 78–88.

Cartwright, D. and Zander, A. (1968) *Group Dynamics: Research and Theory*, London: Tavistock.

Clegg, S. (1981) "Organizations and control," *Administrative Science Quarterly* 26: 545–62.

Colvin, G. (1982) "The de-Geneening of ITT," *Fortune* 105(l): 34–9.

Cooper, A.M. (1986) "Narcissism," in Morrison, A. (ed.) *Essential Papers on Narcissism*, New York: New York University Press, 112–43.

Daft, R.L. (1983) "Symbols in organizations: a dual-content framework for analysis," in Frost, P.J. Moore, L.F., Louis, M.R., Lundberg, C.C. and Martin, J. (eds) *Reframing Organizational Culture*, London: Sage, 199–206.

Dandridge, T.C., Mitroff, I. and Joyce, W.F. (1980) "Organizational symbolism: a topic to expand organizational analysis," *Academy of Management Review* 5: 77–82.

Dearborn, D.C. and Simon, H.A. (1958) "Selective perception: a note on the departmental identification of executives," *Sociometry* 21: 140–4.

De Board, R. (1978) *The Psychodynamics of Organizations*, London: Tavistock.

Diamond, M.A. (1992) "Hobbesian and Rousseauian identities: the psychodynamics of organizational leadership and change," *Administration and Society* 24: 267–89.

Dimen, M. (1991) "Deconstructing differences: gender, splitting and transitional space," *Psychoanalytic Dialogues* 1: 335–52.

Dixon, N. (1994) *The Organizational Learning Cycle*, Maidenhead, UK: McGraw-Hill.

Dodgson, M. (1993) Organizational learning: a review of some literatures," *Organization Studies* 14: 375–94.

Douglas, M. (1987) *How institutions think*, London: Routledge and Kegan Paul.

Dutton, J.E. and Dukerich, J.M. (1991) "Keeping an eye on the mirror: image and identity in organizational adaptation," *Academy of Management Journal* 34: 517–54.

Dutton, J.E., Dukerich, J.M. and Harquail, C.V. (1994) "Organizational images and member identification," *Administrative Science Quarterly* 39: 239–63.

Einhorn, E.J. and Hogarth, R.M. (1986) "Judging probable cause," *Psychological Bulletin* 99: 3–19.

Eisold, K. (1985) "Recovering Bion's contributions to group analysis," in Colman, A.D. and Geller, M.H. (eds) *Group Relations Reader*, vol. 2, Washington, DC: Rice Institute, 37–48.

Elsbach, K.D. and Kramer, R.M. (1996) "Members' responses to organizational identity threats: encountering and countering the 'Business Week' rankings," *Administrative Science Quarterly* 41: 442–76.

Epstein, M. (1995) *Thoughts Without a Thinker*, New York: Basic Books.

Erikson, E.H. (1965) *Childhood and Society*, Harmondsworth, UK: Penguin.

Feldman, M.S. (1989) *Order Without Design*, Stanford, CA: Stanford University Press.

Freud, A. (1966) *The Writings of Anna Freud Volume II. The Ego and the Mechanisms of Defense* (revised edn), Madison, CT: International Universities Press.

Freud, S. (1949) (First published in 1922.) *Group Psychology and the Analysis of the Ego*, London: Hogarth Press.

Frosh, S. (1991) *Identity Crisis. Modernity, Psychoanalysis and the Self*, Basingstoke, UK: Macmillan.

Gabriel, Y. (1991) "Turning facts into stories and stories into facts: hermeneutic exploration of organizational folklore," *Human Relations* 44: 857–75.

Gabriel, Y. (1995) "The unmanaged organization – stories, fantasies and subjectivity," *Organization Studies* 16: 477–501.

Gagliardi, P. (1986) "The creation and change of organizational cultures: a conceptual framework," *Organization Studies* 7: 117–34.

Gioia, D.A. and Thomas, J.B. (1996) "Identity, image, and issue interpretation: sensemaking during strategic change in academia," *Administrative Science Quarterly* 41: 370–403.

Grove, A. (1997) *Only the Paranoid Survive. How to Exploit the Crisis Points that Challenge Every Company and Career*, London: HarperCollins.

Halberstam, D. (1986) *The Reckoning*, New York: Avon.

Hambrick, D.C. and Mason, P. (1984) "Upper echelons: The organization as a reflection of its top managers," *Academy of Management Review* 9: 193–206.

Hamel, G. and Prahalad, C.K. (1994) *Competing for the Future*, Boston: Harvard Business School Press.

Harris, A. (1991) "Gender as contradiction," *Psychoanalytic Dialogues* 1: 197–224.

Hedberg, B. (1981) *How Organizations Learn and Unlearn. Handbook of Organizational Design*, vol. 1, Oxford: Oxford University Press, 3–27.

Hirschhorn, L. (1988) *The Workplace Within*, Cambridge, MA: MIT Press.

Hirschhorn, L. (1997) *Reworking Authority*, Cambridge, MA: MIT Press.

Huber, G.P. (1991) "Organizational learning: the contributing processes and the literatures," *Organization Science* 2: 88–115.

Hurst, D.K. (1984) "Of boxes, bubbles, and effective management," *Harvard Business Review* 62(3): 78–88.

Hurst, D.K., Rush, J.C. and White, R.E. (1989) "Top management teams and organizational renewal," *Strategic Management Journal* 10: 87–105.

Jacques, E. (1955) "Social systems as a defence against persecutory and depressive anxiety," in Klein, M., Heimann, P. and Money-Kyrle, R. (eds) *New Directions in Psychoanalysis*," London: Tavistock, 478–98.

Janis, I.L. (1972) *Victims of Groupthink*, Boston: Houghton Mifflin.

Johnson, G. (1990) "Managing strategic change: the role of symbolic action," *British Journal of Management* 1: 183–200.

Kahneman, D., Slovic, P. and Tversky, A. (1982) *Judgment under Uncertainty. Heuristics and Biases*, Cambridge: Cambridge University Press.

Kets de Vries, M.F.R. (1996) *Family Business: Human Dilemmas in the Family Firm*, London: Thompson.

Kets de Vries, M.F.R. and Miller, D. (1984) *The Neurotic Organization*, San Francisco: Jossey-Bass.

Kitchener, K.S. (1983) "Cognition, metacognition, and epistemic cognition: a three-level model of cognitive processing," *Human Development* 26: 222–32.

Klein, K.J., Dansereau, F. and Hall, R.J. (1994) "Level issues in theory development, data collection and analysis," *Academy of Management Review* 19: 195–229.

Kohlberg, L. (1964) "Development of moral character and moral ideology," in Hoffman, M.L. and Hoffman, L.W. (eds) *Review of Child Development Research*, vol. 1, New York: Russell Sage Foundation, 383–427.

Kohut, H. (1971) *The Analysis of the Self*, New York: International Universities Press.

Kohut, H. (1978) "Forms and transformations of narcissism," in Ornstein, P.H. (ed.) *The Search for Self. Selected Writings of Heinz Kohut: 1950–1978*, vol. 1: New York: International Universities Press, 427–60.

Kramer, D.A. (1990) "Conceptualizing wisdom: the primacy of affect-cognition relations," in Sternberg, R.J. (ed) *Wisdom: Its Nature, Origins and Development*, Cambridge: Cambridge University Press, 279–313.

Laughlin, H.P. (1970) *The Ego and its Defenses*, New York: Appleton-Century-Crofts.

Levinthal, D.A. and March, J.G. (1993) "The myopia of learning," *Strategic Management Journal*, 14: 95–112.

Levitt, B. and March, J.G. (1988) "Organizational learning," *Annual Review of Sociology* 14: 319–40.

Lorsch, J.W. and Mathias, P.F. (1987) "When professionals have to manage," *Harvard Business Review* 65(4): 78–83.

Lundberg, C. (1989) "On organizational learning: implications and opportunities for expanding organizational development," in Woodman, R.W. and Pasmore, W.A. (eds) *Research in Organizational Change and Development*, vol. 3, Greenwich, CT: JAI Press, 61–82.

Lynch, I.M. (1988) *Containing Anxiety in Institutions: Selected essays*, vol. 1, London: Free Association Books.

Lyon, J. (1984) *Dome*, New York: Avon.

March, J.G. (1995) "The future, disposable organizations and the rigidities of imagination," *Organization* 2: 427–40.

Marcia, J.E. (1988) "Common processes underlying ego identity, cognitive/moral development, and individuation," in Lapsley, D.K. and Clark Power, F. (eds) *Self, Ego. and Identity: Integrative Approaches*, New York: Springer-Verlag, 211–25.

Menzies, I.E.P. (1970) *The Functioning of Social Systems as a Defence Against Anxiety*, London: Tavistock.

Miller, D. (1990) *The Icarus Paradox*, New York: Harper Business.

Miller, D. (1993) "The Architecture of Simplicity," *Academy of Management Review* 18: 116–38.

Miller, E.J. and Gwynne, G.V. (1972) *A Life Apart*, London: Tavistock.

Mintzberg, H. (1987) "Crafting strategy," *Harvard Business Review* 65(4): 66–75.

Mitchell, S. (1993) *Hope and Dread in Psychoanalysis*, New York: Basic Books.

Moch, M. and Huff, A.S. (1983) "Power enactment through language and symbol," *Journal of Business Research* 11: 293–316.

Morgan, G. (1980) "Paradigms, metaphors, and puzzle solving in organization theory," *Administrative Science Quarterly* 25: 605–22.

Morgan, G. (1983) "More on metaphor: why we cannot control tropes in administrative science," *Administrative Science Quarterly* 28: 601–7.

Morgan, G. (1986) *Images of Organization*, Beverly Hills, CA: Sage.

Nader, R. and Taylor, W. (1986) *The Big Boys: Power and Position in American Business*, New York: Pantheon.

Nystrom, P.C. and Starbuck, W.H. (1984) "To avoid organizational crisis, unlearn," *Organizational Dynamics* 12(l): 53–65.

Orwoll, L. and Perlmutter, M. (1990) "The study of wise persons: Integrating a personality perspective," in Sternberg, R.J. (ed.) *Wisdom: Its nature, Origins and Development*, Cambridge: Cambridge University Press, 160–177.

Pascale, R. (1990) *Managing on the Edge*, New York: Viking.

Peters, T.J. (1978) "Symbols, patterns, and settings: An optimistic case for getting things done," *Organizational Dynamics* 7: 2–23.

Peters, T.J. and Waterman, R.H. Jr (1982) *In Search of Excellence*, New York: Harper & Row.

Pettigrew, A. (1985) *The Awakening Giant: Continuity and Change in ICI*, Oxford: Blackwell.

Pettigrew, A. (1992) "On studying managerial elites," *Strategic Management Journal* 13 (Special Issue): 163–82.

Pfeffer, J. (1981) "Management as symbolic action: the creation and maintenance of organizational paradigms," in Cummings, L.L. and Staw, B.M. (eds) *Research in Organizational Behavior*, vol. 3 Greenwich, CT: JAI Press, 1–52.

Pfeffer, J. and Salancik, G.R. (1974) "Organizational decision making as a political process: the case of a university budget," *Administrative Science Quarterly* 19: 135–51.

Phillips, A. (1988) *Winnicott*, Cambridge, MA: Harvard University Press.

Priem, R.L. (1990) "Top management team group factors, consensus and firm performance," *Strategic Management Journal* 11: 469–78.

Ray, C.A. (1986) "Corporate culture: the last frontier of control," *Journal of Management Studies* 23: 287–97.

Reger, R.K., Gustafson, L.T., DeMarie, S.M. and Mullane, J.V. (1994) "Reframing the organization: Why implementing total quality is easier said than done," *Academy of Management Review* 19: 565–84.

Rhodewalt, F., Morf, C., Hazlett, S. and Fairfield, M. (1991) "Self-handicapping: The role of discounting and augmentation in the preservation of self-esteem," *Journal of Personal and Social Psychology* 61: 122–31.

Ross, J. and Stow, B.M. (1993) "Organizational escalation and exit: lessons from the Shoreham nuclear power plant," *Academy of Management Journal* 36: 701–32.

Rousseau, D. (1985) "Issues of level in organizational research: multi-level and cross-level perspectives," in Cummings, L.L. and Slow, B.M. (eds) *Research in Organizational Behavior*, vol. 7, Greenwich, CT: JAI Press, 1–37.

Rutenberg, D. (1985) "Playful plans," Working paper #85–26, Queens University, Kingston, Ontario, Canada.

Saloman, G. and Butler, J. (1994) "Why managers won't learn," in Mabey, C. and Iles, P. (eds) *Managing Learning*, London: Routledge, 34–42.

Schafer, R. (1992) *Retelling a Life*, New York: Basic Books.

Schein, E.H. (1985) *Organizational Culture and Leadership*, San Francisco: Jossey-Bass.

Schlenker, B.R. (1985) "Self-identification: toward an integration of the private and public self," in Baumeister, R. (ed.) *Public Self and Private Self*, New York: SpringerVerlag, 21–62.

Schlenker, B.R., Weigold, M.F. and Hallam, J.R. (1990) "Self serving attributions in social context: effects of self esteem and social pressure," *Journal of Personality and Social Psychology* 58: 855–63.

Schoemaker, P.J.H. (1993) "Multiple scenario development: its conceptual and behavioral foundation," *Strategic Management Journal* 14: 193–214.

Schonbach, P. (1980) "A category system for account phases," *European Journal of Social Psychology* 10: 195–200.

Schwartz, H.S. (1985) "The usefulness of myth and the myth of usefulness: A dilemma for the applied organizational scientist," *Journal of Management* 11: 31–42.

Schwartz, H.S. (1987) "On the psychodynamics of organizational disaster: the case of the Space Shuttle Challenger," *Columbia Journal of World Business* 22: 59–67.

Schwartz, H.S. (1990) *Narcissistic Process and Corporate Decay. The Theory of the Organizational Ideal*, New York: New York University Press.

Semin, G.R. and Manstead, A.S.R. (1983) *The Accountability of Conduct: A Social psychological analysis*, London: Academic Press.

Senge, P. (1990) *The Fifth Discipline: The Art and Practice of the Learning Organization*, New York: Doubleday.

Shengold, L. (1995) *Delusions of Everyday Life*, New Haven, CT: Yale University Press.

Slovic, P., Fischhoff, B. and Lichtenstein, S. (1977) "Behavioral decision theory," *Annual Review of Psychology* 28: 1–39.

Smith, D.K. and Alexander, R.C. (1988) *Fumbling the Future: How Xerox Invented, then Ignored, the First Personal Computer*, New York: William Morrow.

Soeters, J.L. (1986) "Excellent companies as social movements," *Journal of Management Studies* 23: 299–312.

Sofer, C. (1972) *Organizations in Theory and Practice*, London: Heinemann.

Spence, D. (1982) *Narrative Truth, Historical Truth*, New York: Norton.

Spender, L-C. and Grinyer, P. (1995) "Organizational renewal: top management's role in a loosely coupled system," *Human Relations*, 48: 909–26.

Sproull, L.S. (1981) "Beliefs in organizations," in Nystrom, P.C. and Starbuck, W.H. (eds) *Handbook of Organizational Design*, vol. 2, New York: Oxford University Press, 167–202.

Starbuck, W.H. (1983) "Organizations as action generators," *American Sociological Review* 48: 91–102.

Starbuck, W.H., Greve, A. and Hedberg, B.L.T. (1978) "Responding to crisis," *Journal of Business Administration* 9: 111–37.

Starbuck, W.H. and Hedberg, B.L.T. (1977) "Saving an organization from a stagnating environment," in Thorelli, H.B. (ed.) *Strategy + Structure = Performance*, Bloomington: Indiana University Press, 249–58.

Starbuck, W.H. and Milliken, F.J. (1988) "Executives' perceptual filters: What they notice and how they make sense," in Hambrick, D. (ed.) *Executive Effect: Concepts and Methods for Studying Top Managers*, Greenwich, CT: JAI Press, 35–65.

Starkey, K. (ed.) (1996) *How Organizations Learn*, London: International Thomson Business Press.

Sternberg, R.J. (ed.) (1990) *Wisdom: Its Nature, Origins and Development*, Cambridge: Cambridge University Press.

Sullivan, H.S. (1938) *The Fusion of Psychiatry and the Social Sciences*, New York: Norton.

Swogger, G. (1993) "Group self-esteem and group performance," in Hirschhorn, L. and Barnett, C.K. (eds) *The Psychodynamics of Organizations*, Philadelphia: Temple University Press, 99–117.

Szwajkowski, E. (1992) "Accounting for organizational misconduct," *Journal of Business Ethics* 11: 401–11.

Tsoukas, H. (1991) "The missing link: a transformational view of metaphors in organizational science," *Academy of Management Review* 16: 566–85.

Tsoukas, H. (1993) "Analogical reasoning and knowledge generation in organization theory," *Organization Studies* 14: 323–46.

Turner, J.C. (1987) *Rediscovering the Social Group. A self-categorization Theory*, Oxford: Blackwell.

van der Heijden, K. (1996) *Scenarios: The Art of Strategic Conversation*, Chichester, UK: Wiley.

Walsh, J.P. and Fahey, L. (1986) "The role of negotiated belief structures in strategy making," *Journal of Management* 12: 325–38.

Walsh, J.P. and Ungson, G.R. (1991) "Organizational memory," *Academy of Management Review* 16: 57–91.

Wastell, D.G. (1996) "The fetish of technique-methodology as a social defense," *Information Systems Journal* 6: 25–40.

Waters, J. (1980) "Managerial skill development," *Academy of Management Review* 5: 449–53.

Weick, K.E. (1987) "Organizational culture as a source of high reliability," *California Management Review* 29(2): 112–27.

Weick, K. (1993) "The collapse of sense-making in organizations: the Mann-Gulch disaster," *Administrative Science Quarterly* 38: 628–52.

Weick, K.E. (1995) *Sensemaking in Organizations*, Thousand Oaks, CA: Sage.

Weigert, A.J. (1988) "To be or not: self and authenticity, identity and ambivalence," in Lapsley, D. K. and Clark Power, F. (eds), *Self, ego, and identity. Integrative approaches*, New York: Springer-Verlag, 263–81.

Whetten, D.A., Lewis, D. and Mischel, L. (1992) "Towards an integrated model of organizational identity and member commitment," Paper presented at the annual meeting of Academy of Management, Las Vegas.

Wilensky, R.L. (1967) *Organizational Intelligence, Knowledge and Policy in Government and Industry*, New York: Basic Books.

Wimsatt, W.K. (1970) "Battering the object: the ontological approach," in Bradbury, M. and Palmer, D. (eds) *Contemporary Criticism*: London: Edward Arnold, 61–82.

Winnicott, D.W. (1974) *Playing and Reality*, Harmondsworth, UK: Penguin.

Wright, J.P. (1979) *On a Clear Day You Can See General Motors*, Grosse Pointe, ME Wright Enterprise.

Name index

Subject index